1ST EDITION

MW01659902

Introduction to Investment Planning

Tools & Techniques for Academics

Stephan R. Leimberg, Esq.
Tom Robinson, Ph.D, CFA
Robert R. Johnson, Ph.D., CFA, CAIA
Marvin Keene, Ph.D.

ISBN: 978-1-949506-49-5

This publication is designed to provide accurate and authoritative information in regard to the subject matter covered. It is sold with the understanding that the publisher is not engaged in rendering legal, accounting or other professional service. If legal advice or other expert assistance is required, the services of a competent professional person should be sought. – From a Declaration of Principles jointly adapted by a Committee of The American Bar Association and a Committee of Publishers and Associations.

THE NATIONAL UNDERWRITER COMPANY

The National Underwriter Company
4157 Olympic Blvd. Ste. 225
Erlanger, KY 41018

First Edition

Printed in the United States of America

ABOUT THE NATIONAL UNDERWRITER COMPANY
a division of ALM Media, LLC

For over 120 years, The National Underwriter Company, *a division of ALM Media, LLC* has been the first in line with the targeted tax, insurance, and financial planning information you need to make critical business decisions. Boasting nearly a century of expert experience, our reputable editors are dedicated to putting accurate and relevant information right at your fingertips. With *Tax Facts, FC&S® Expert Coverage Interpretation, Tools & Techniques, Field Guide, Insurance Coverage Law Center, Property & Casualty Coverage Guides* and other resources available in print, eBook, or online, you can be assured that as the industry evolves National Underwriter will be at the forefront with the thorough and easy-to-use resources you rely on for success.

Update Service Notification

This National Underwriter Company publication is regularly updated to include coverage of developments and changes that affect the content. If you did not purchase this publication directly from The National Underwriter Company, *a division of ALM Media, LLC* and you want to receive these important updates sent on a 30-day review basis and billed separately, please contact us at (800) 543-0874. Or you can mail your request with your name, company, address, and the title of the book to:

The National Underwriter Company
a division of ALM Media, LLC
4157 Olympic Boulevard
Suite 225
Erlanger, KY 41018

If you purchased this publication from The National Underwriter Company, *a division of ALM Media, LLC,* directly, you have already been registered for the update service.

Contact Information

To order any National Underwriter Company title, please

- call 1-800-543-0874, 8-6 ET Monday – Thursday and 8 to 5 ET Friday
- online bookstore at www.nationalunderwriter.com, or
- mail to Orders Department, The National Underwriter Company, *a division of ALM Media, LLC,* 4157 Olympic Blvd., Ste. 225, Erlanger, KY 41018

ABOUT THE AUTHORS

Stephan R. Leimberg

Stephan R. Leimberg is CEO of LISI, Leimberg Information Services, Inc., at leimbergservices.com, a provider of e-mail/internet news and commentary for professionals on recent cases, rulings, and legislation; CEO of Leimberg and LeClair, Inc., an estate and financial planning software company; and President of Leimberg Associates, Inc., a publishing and software company in Bryn Mawr, Pennsylvania at leimberg.com.

Leimberg is the author of numerous books on estate, financial, and employee benefit and retirement planning and a nationally known speaker. Leimberg is the creator and/or principal author of the entire nine book *Tools & Techniques* series including *The Tools & Techniques of Estate Planning, The Tools & Techniques of Financial Planning, The Tools & Techniques of Employee Benefit and Retirement Planning, The Tools & Techniques of Life Insurance Planning, The Tools & Techniques of Charitable Planning, The Tools & Techniques of Income Tax Planning, The Tools & Techniques of Investment Planning, The Tools & Techniques of Risk Management, and The Tools & Techniques of Practice Management*. Leimberg is co-author, with noted attorney Howard Zaritsky, of *Tax Planning with Life Insurance, The Book of Trusts* with attorneys Charles K. Plotnick and Daniel Evans, and *How to Settle an Estate* with Charles K. Plotnick, and *The Buy-Sell Handbook.*

Leimberg is creator or co-creator of many software packages for the financial services professional including *NumberCruncher* (estate planning), *IRS Factors Calculator* (actuarial computations), *Financial Analyzer II, Estate Planning Quickview* (Estate Planning Flow Charts), *Toward a Zero Estate Tax* (PowerPoint Estate Planning Client Seminar), *Gifts That Give, Gifts That Give Back* (Powerpoint Client Charitable Planning Seminar), and *Long-Term Care* (Powerpoint Client Seminar).

A nationally known speaker, Leimberg has addressed the Miami (Heckerling) Estate Planning Institute, the NYU Tax Institute, the Notre Dame Law School and Duke University Law School's Estate Planning Conference, The American Bar Association Planning Techniques for Large Estate and Sophisticated Planning Techniques courses of study, the National Association of Estate Planners and Councils, and the AICPA's National Estate Planning Forum. Leimberg has also spoken to the Federal Bureau of Investigation, and the National Aeronautics and Space Administration.

Leimberg, a 2004 recipient of the National Association of Estate Planners and Councils Distinguished Accredited Estate Planner award, was named 1998 Edward N. Polisher Lecturer of the Dickinson School of Law, and was awarded the Excellence in Writing Award of the American Bar Association's Probate and Property Section. He has been honored as Estate Planner of the Year by the Montgomery County Estate Planning Council and as Distinguished Estate Planner by the Philadelphia Estate Planning Council. He is also recipient of the President's Cup of the Philadelphia Life Underwriters, a three time Boris Todorovitch Lecturer, and the first Ben Feldman Lecturer.

Thomas R. Robinson

Tom Robinson, Ph.D, CFA provides leadership to CFA Institute's largest region – the Americas – including Canada, the US, the Caribbean and Latin America. He leads a cross-functional Americas Engagement Team which participates in developing global strategy, implements the global strategy regionally and engages with stakeholders regionally.

Until April 2013, Dr. Robinson served as Managing Director of Education, providing vision and leadership for a one-hundred-member global team producing and delivering educational content for candidates, members, and other investment professionals. Tom joined CFA Institute as Head of Educational Content in 2007. Previously, he was an accounting faculty member at the University of Miami, serving as Director of the Master of Professional Accounting Program and Personal Financial Planning programs. He primarily taught graduate courses in financial statement analysis, personal financial planning, and valuation. Concurrently, he was managing director of a private wealth investment advisory firm and served as a consultant in valuation and financial statement analysis. Prior to working in academia, Tom worked in public accounting, performing tax and financial planning services.

Throughout his academic career, Tom has won several teaching awards and has published regularly in academic and professional journals, such as the *Journal of Accounting, Auditing and Finance* and the *Journal of Financial Planning*. His research includes extensive study of analyst reports for the AICPA Special Committee on Financial Reporting (the "Jenkins" Committee). He was an associate editor of *Research in Accounting Regulation* and has served on the editorial review board of several professional journals.

Dr. Robinson has authored or co-authored many books, including *The Tools and Techniques of Investment Planning* (National Underwriter Co.), *International Financial Statement Analysis* (Wiley and CFA Institute), *Equity Asset Valuation* (Wiley and CFA Institute), *The New Wealth Management: The Financial Advisors Guide to Managing and Investing Client Assets* (Wiley and CFA Institute), and *The Strategic Value Investor* (McGraw Hill).

Dr. Robinson is a CFA charterholder, a Certified Public Accountant (CPA) (Ohio), a Certified Financial Planner (CFP), and a Chartered Alternative Investment Analyst (CAIA). He holds a bachelor's degree in economics from the University of Pennsylvania, and a master's and doctorate from Case Western Reserve University. He was active both locally and nationally as a volunteer for CFA Institute and CFA Miami prior to joining the CFA Institute staff.

Robert R. Johnson

Robert R. Johnson, Ph.D., CFA, CAIA is a Full Professor of Finance in the Heider College of business at Creighton University. He teaches in the Master of Security Analysis and Portfolio Management Program and serves as the editor for the *Quarterly Journal of Finance and Accounting*. Bob also serves on the board of RS Investments, a San Francisco-based investment management firm that is majority-owned by The Guardian Life Insurance Company, and oversees over $27 billion in managed funds. He was formerly Senior Managing Director at CFA Institute, overseeing the Americas region, university relations, and the professional conduct program. He was responsible for all aspects of the CFA Program for the majority of his fifteen-year tenure at CFA Institute. In 2013, he received the Alfred C. "Pete" Morley Distinguished Service Award from CFA Institute in appreciation of his leadership, stewardship and outstanding service.

Prior to joining CFA Institute, Bob was a Professor of Finance at Creighton University from 1984 through 1996. Throughout his academic career, Bob won several teaching awards and in 1994 earned the university-wide Robert F. Kennedy Award for Teaching Excellence. Bob has over sixty refereed articles in leading finance and investment journals. His publications have appeared in the *Journal of Finance, Journal of Financial Economics, Journal of Portfolio Management, Financial Analysts Journal*, and the *Journal of Alternative Investments*. He has extensive media relations experience both in the United States and abroad. He has been quoted in the *Wall Street Journal, Financial Times, Barron's, Forbes, Toronto Globe and Mail, South China Morning Post, Singapore Strait Times, LeTemps*, and *Nikkin Weekly News*paper, among others. He has appeared numerous times on ABC World News, Bloomberg TV (Europe and US), CNN, and China Business News, among others.

Bob received his BSBA in finance (summa cum laude) from the University of Nebraska-Omaha in 1980, MBA (concentration in finance) from Creighton University in 1982, and PhD in finance/investments from the University of Nebraska-Lincoln in 1988. He earned his CFA charter from the Institute of Chartered Financial Analysts in 1991. He earned his CAIA charter from the Chartered Alternative Investment Analyst Association in 2011.

Marvin Keene

Marvin Keene, Ph.D. is a Professor in the Finance and Economics Department at Coastal Carolina University. Professor Keene earned his Ph.D in finance from Florida State University and has taught at Coastal Carolina since 2004. He currently teaches courses in Investments, Corporate Finance, and Financial Statement Analysis.

Professor Keene is the President and Chairman of the Board, Academy of Hope, Inc., a public charter elementary school serving grades K-8 in Conway, South Carolina. He is also on the Coast RTA Board of Directors, and is the Horry County appointee to the Coast RTA Board of Directors Finance Committee and Fund Development Committee.

ABOUT THE EDITOR

Jason Gilbert, J.D., M.A. is the Senior Editor with the Practical Insights Division of The National Underwriter Company, a division of ALM Media, LLC. He edits and develops publications related to tax and insurance products, including titles in the *Advisor's Guide* and the *Tools & Techniques* series of investment and planning products. He also develops content for National Underwriter's other financial services publications and online products. He has worked on insurance and tax publications for more than nine years.

Jason has been a practicing attorney for more than a dozen years in the areas of criminal defense, products liability, and regulatory enforcement actions. Prior to joining National Underwriter, his experience in the insurance and tax fields has included work as a Westlaw contributor for Thomson Reuters and a tax advisor and social media contributor for Intuit. He is an honors graduate from Wright State University and holds a J.D. from the University of Cincinnati College of Law as well as a master's degree in Economics from Miami University in Ohio.

EDITORIAL SERVICES

Connie L. Jump, Senior Manager, Editorial Operations

Patti O'Leary, Senior Editorial Assistant

TABLE OF CONTENTS

APPENDICES

Chapter 1

CAPITAL MARKETS

1.1 REGULATORY ENTITIES, AGENCIES AND MARKET PARTICIPANTS

Section Overview:

1.1.1 The U.S. Securities and Exchange Commission

1.1.2 Self-regulatory Organizations

1.1.3 Other Regulators and Industry Agencies

1.1.4 Market Participants and their Roles

1.1.5 Introduction to Investment Planning

1.1.1 THE U.S. SECURITIES AND EXCHANGE COMMISSION

Overview of the Securities and Exchange Commission

The U.S. Securities and Exchange Commission (SEC) is tasked with the protection of investors in the financial markets as well as the overall regulation of the capital markets. Their mission is to maintain fair, orderly, and efficient capital markets that result in capital formation.

A critical component of the SEC is the continuous oversight of the securities exchanges (e.g. NYSE, NASDAQ, etc.), brokers and dealers, investment advisors, and investment companies. Their oversight is focused on fraud protection, truthful and consistent disclosures, and overall fair dealing with investors.

In addition to the oversight and regulation of the securities markets it also acts as the enforcer. The SEC levies hundreds of civil and criminal claims against individuals and organizations for violations ranging from unfair trading practices to fraud. Most of the claims against individuals stem from uninformed trading that leads to violations of the securities laws. Therefore the SEC has added the education of investors to its list of responsibilities. As such, they offer a number of tools to help support investor education on their website (www.sec.gov).

History of the SEC

Securities and **E**xchange **C**ommission

During the 1920s, or the "roaring 20s", investors were lured to the attractiveness of easy money in the stock market. This attraction and the ease of credit for the purpose of investing led to a dangerously high level of margin investing. In the absence of clear and efficient regulatory oversight the financial markets eventually imploded where more than half of the securities in the reported $50 billion new securities market losing all of its value.

One result of this crash in October 1929 was the loss of confidence in the capital markets. Investors, both professional and household, as well as many financial institutions refused to engage in the securities markets because of the substantial losses they suffered in the crash. During the years following the crash the financial markets suffered from critically low activity which inhibited the capital formation process. In the absence of this process the country's growth was at a standstill. Congress had no alternative but to step in and create the much needed foundation for market efficiency. In 1933 and 1934 Congress passed laws that would change the structure and function of the capital markets, the Securities Act of 1933 and the Securities Exchange Act of 1934. The birth of the SEC and the new regulations for fair dealings, clear disclosures and fiduciary responsibilities began the process of regaining public trust in the financial markets.

SEC Headquarters and Regional Office Locations

Structure of the SEC

The SEC is managed by five Commissioners that are appointed by the President of the United States to serve five-year terms. One of the five Commissioners is designated as the Chairman and Chief Executive of the Commission. The responsibilities of the agency are managed by five Divisions: the Division of Corporation Finance, the Division of Trading and Markets, the Division of Investment Management, the Division of Enforcement, and the Division of Economic and Risk Analysis.

Division of Corporation Finance

The main objective of the Corporation Finance division is to oversee the consistency of corporate disclosures to the investment community. Publically traded companies are required to adhere to disclosure regulations on a periodic or as needed basis. These statutory disclosures include, but are not limited to:

- New offerings registration statements
- Annual (10-K) and Quarterly (10-Q) reports
- Proxy Statements
- Reports of changes (8-K)

Division of Trading and Markets

The Trading and Markets division is primarily tasked with overseeing that the capital markets operate in a fair, orderly and efficient manner. Their oversight is focused on the professional market participants such as the securities exchanges (NYSE, NASDAQ, etc.), brokerage firms and large banks, self-regulatory organizations (SROs), and other influential market participants.

Division of Investment Management

The Investment Management division is responsible for the protection of investors and capital formation in the ever growing investment management sector of the financial markets. The investment management industry includes mutual funds, hedge funds, exchange-traded funds (ETFs), etc. In 2017, this sector of the U.S. capital markets held over $60 trillion of assets under management. Given that most investors in this sector are individual investors the Division of Investment Management has focused the regulatory actions on clear informative disclosures and fair cost structures for investors.

Division of Enforcement

The Enforcement division's role is solely the enforcement of the securities laws through discovery of violations and commencement of civil or administrative actions for any violations. The division also enlist any criminal law enforcement agencies when necessary to handle criminal cases.

Division of Economic and Risk Analysis

The Economic and Risk Analysis division (DERA) serves primarily as support for the other divisions by providing the necessary research they need for the different roles and responsibilities. The main support activities performed by DERA are in the areas of providing analysis for policy development, litigation, and enforcement.

The functions of the Commission are further supported by twenty-two offices that manage the daily operations. The offices are managed by the agency's more than 4,600 employees and are:

- Office of Acquisitions
- Office of Administrative Law Judges

- Office of the Chief Accountant
- Office of the Chief Operating Officer
- Office of Compliance Inspections and Examinations
- Office of Credit Ratings
- Office of Equal Employment Opportunity
- Office of Ethics Counsel
- Office of Financial Management
- Office of the General Counsel
- Office of Human Resources
- Office of Information Technology
- Office of the Inspector General
- Office of International Affairs
- Office of the Investor Advocate
- Office of Investor Education and Advocacy
- Office of Legislative and Intergovernmental Affairs
- Office of Minority and Women Inclusion
- Office of Municipal Securities
- Office of Public Affairs
- Office of the Secretary
- Office of Support Operations

1.1.2 SELF-REGULATORY ORGANIZATIONS

A self-regulatory organization (SRO) is an organization that has the authority to establish and enforce the rules and regulations of an industry. SROs are normally tasked with stakeholder protection and fair dealings. The existence of these organizations allow an industry to govern itself without direct political ties to a particular country. In the financial industry, the National Association of Insurance Commissioners (NAIC) and the Financial Industry Regulatory Authority (FINRA) are two examples of SROs.

FINRA is a non-profit, non-government organization responsible for the oversight of investor protection and market integrity. They monitor an average of 50 billion daily market transactions and supervise over 600,000 brokers.

FINRA serves as the licensing agency for the brokers and broker-dealers in the financial industry. They ensure that financial professionals selling investment products are licensed and qualified. Key objectives of the organization is to ensure that investors receive basic protections, truthful advertisements, suitable products, and adequate disclosures. Overall, they strive to promote transparency and ethical behavior.

SROs often use investor education as a tool for investor protection. Education tools and resources assist investors in making informed decisions and avoiding fraud. For example, FINRA's website offers a number of free resources related to investment knowledge and fraud prevention.

1.1.3 OTHER REGULATORS AND INDUSTRY AGENCIES

U.S. Department of the Treasury and the Internal Revenue Service

The U.S. Department of the Treasury serves as the lead governmental agency in oversight of the U.S. economic and financial systems. The department's mission statement embodies this sentiment and describes their role domestically and globally.

Mission

Maintain a strong economy and create economic and job opportunities by promoting the conditions that enable economic growth and stability at home and abroad, strengthen national security by combating threats and protecting the integrity of the financial system, and manage the U.S. Government's finances and resources effectively.

The Treasury department is a critical component of the U.S. government as the principal agency responsible for stimulating economic prosperity and financial stability in the United States. The department is tasked with:

- Advising the President regarding economic matters
- Stimulating economic growth
- Monitoring of financial institutions
- Oversight of the U.S. financial infrastructure
- Currency production
- Revenue collection
- Other financial duties

The Treasury department has two separate areas of operation: the Departmental Offices and the Operating Bureaus.

The Departmental Offices are responsible for policy creation and daily management of the Treasury Department. The Offices are split into the following thirteen divisions and are managed by Assistant Secretaries and Under Secretaries.

- Domestic Finance – financial institutions, markets, and regulation

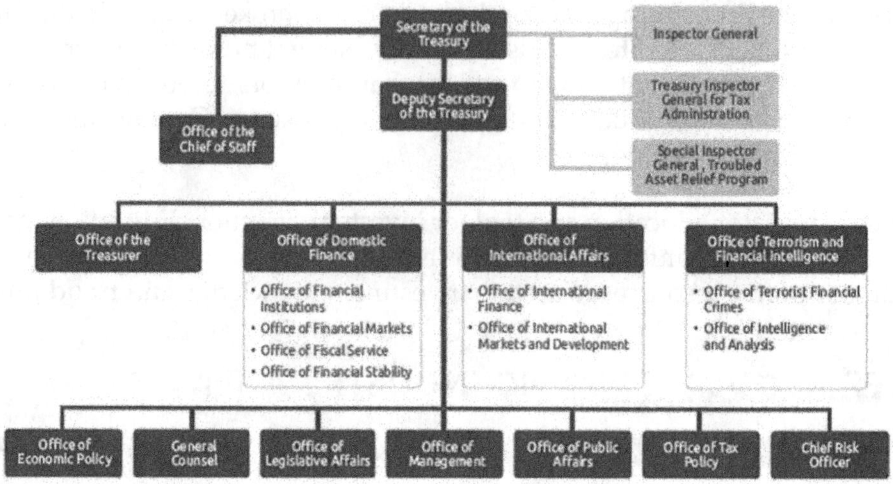

- Economic Policy – review and analysis of economic matters
- Financial Research – provide financial data
- Financial Stability– implement the Troubled Asset Relief Program (TARP)
- General Council – legal and policy advice
- International Affairs – protection and support of U.S. economic prosperity
- Legislative Affairs – congressional relations advice
- Management – internal management (budget, planning, human resources, etc.)
- Public Affairs – create and implement communications strategy
- Risk Management – creation and implementation of an integrated risk management culture
- Tax Policy – develops and implements tax policy and tax programs
- Terrorism and Financial Intelligence – develops and implements techniques to prevent financial terrorism
- U.S. Treasurer – currency management

The Operating Bureaus carry out the daily operations of the Treasury Department and are divided into the following ten bureaus.

- Alcohol and Tobacco Tax and Trade Bureau (TTB)
- Bureau of Engraving & Printing (BEP)
- Bureau of Fiscal Service
- Community Development Financial Institution (CDFI) Fund

- Financial Crimes Enforcement Network (FinCEN)
- Inspector General
- Treasury Inspector General for Tax Administration (TIGTA)
- Internal Revenue Service (IRS)
- Office of the Comptroller of the Currency (OCC)
- U.S. Mint

North American Securities Administrators Association (NASAA)

In addition to the federal regulators (SEC), self-regulatory organizations (FINRA) there are also state organizations that work in conjunction with the others to provide oversight for the brokers, dealer-brokers, and for the protection of investors.

The North American Securities Administrators Association (NASAA) is a SRO that is comprised of state and provincial representatives from the U.S., Canada, and Mexico. For example, the Uniform Securities Agent State law Examination (Series 63) is written by NASAA and administered by FINRA.

NASAA is the oldest existing international SRO, with representatives from the 50 states, Washington D.C., the U.S. Virgin Islands, Puerto Rico, Canada, and Mexico. Similar to the SEC and FINRA, NASAA's primary responsibility is investor protection and market integrity.

The Federal Reserve

The U.S. Federal Reserve serves as the central banking system of the country. The purpose of the Federal Reserve is support the efficient and effective operation of the U.S. economy through the following roles:

- Management of the country's monetary policy
- Stabilization of the financial system

Federal Reserve Banks

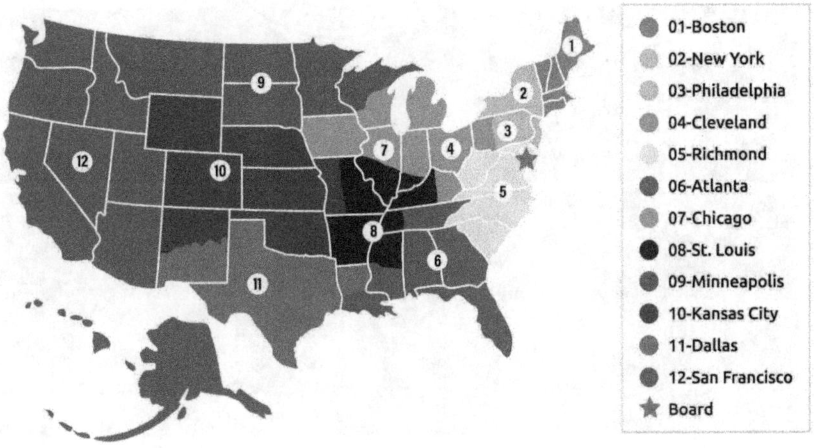

- Safeguard financial institutions
- Promote an efficient payment and settlement system
- Ensure consumer protection and community development

The Federal Reserve System is managed by three distinct bodies: the Board of Governors, 12 Federal Reserve Banks, and the Federal Open Market Committee. These three entities work in conjunction to stimulate a healthy economy and a stable financial system in the United States.

The Board of Governors is set up as a seven member board that is nominated by the President and confirmed by the U.S. Senate. The Board is led by a Chairman and Vice Chairman who are appointed by the President and confirmed by the Senate to a four year term.

The twelve Federal Reserve Banks serve to operate the daily tasks of the system. The Reserve Banks operate as independent entities with their own board of directors, management, and advisory committees. The Federal Reserve Banks are identified by district numbers and location as follows: 1. Boston, 2. New York, 3. Philadelphia, 4. Cleveland, 5. Richmond, 6. Atlanta, 7. Chicago, 8, St. Louis, 9. Minneapolis, 10. Kansas City, 11. Dallas, and 12. San Francisco. The primary functions of the Reserve Banks are to:

- Supervise and examine state member banks
- Serve as lender to depository institutions
- Provide financial services (currency distribution, clearinghouse, etc.)
- Ensure and enforce consumer protection and fair lending laws

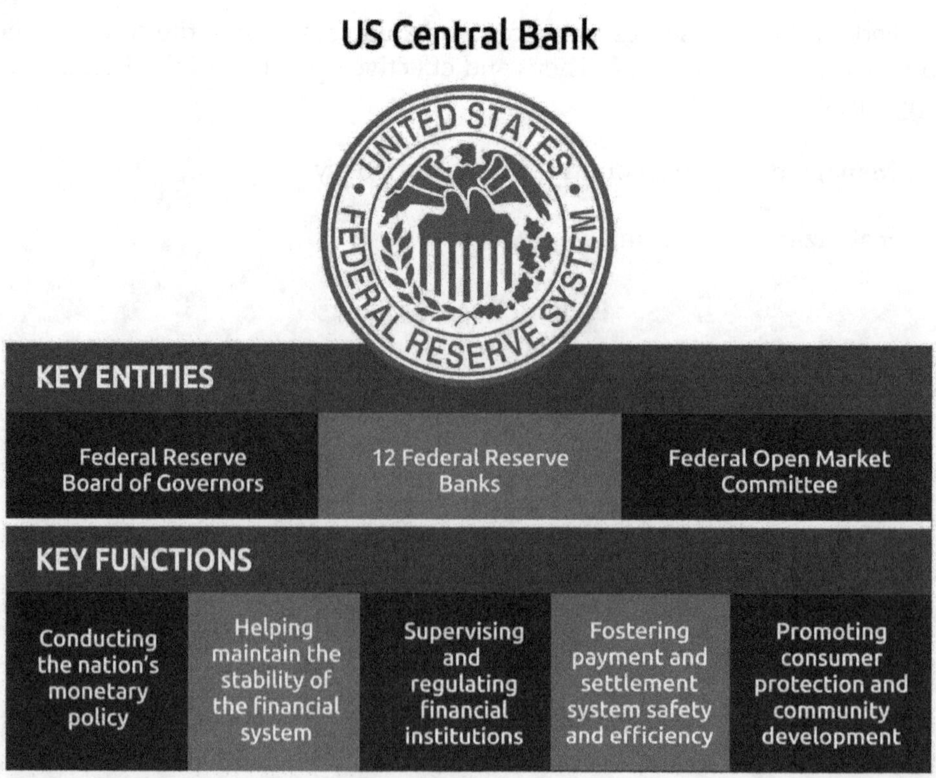

The Federal Open Market Committee (FOMC) is the arm of the system that creates and implements the nation's monetary policy. Led by the Chair of the Board of Governors, the FOMC evaluates the economics conditions and makes decisions about the open market operations. The FOMC consists of twelve voting members, including all seven members of the Board of Governors, the President of the New York Federal Reserve Bank, and four of the remaining Reserve Bank Presidents.

Federal Deposit Insurance Corporation (FDIC)

In the Banking Act of 1933 Congress created the Federal Deposit Insurance Corporation (FDIC) as an independent agency charged with ensuring the stability and integrity of the nation's financial system through three specific programs:

Insurance

- Insure depositors without recourse to taxpayers

Supervision

- Examine financial institutions for safety and soundness
- Maintain adequate consumer protections and community engagement
- Ensure that large and complex financial institutions are resolvable

Receivership Management

- Ensure that resolutions are orderly and receiverships are effectively managed

Securities Investor Protection Corporation

The Securities Investor Protection Corporation (SIPC) was formed under the Securities Investor Protection Act of 1970 with the purpose of protecting customers from certain types of loss as a result of broker-dealer failure. The sole function of the SIPC is the oversight of the liquidation of a member broker-dealer that goes out of business to ensure that customer assets are not mishandled, thereby recovering investor assets from bankrupt or financially troubled brokerage firms. It is important to note that the SIPC does not deal with fraud or the insuring of customer accounts.

1.1.4 MARKET PARTICIPANTS AND THEIR ROLES

Investors

An investor is an individual or entity that gives assets with the goal of receiving financial returns. Investors use various investments in to grow their asset base over a specified investment horizon. These investments instruments include, but are not limited to, stocks, bonds, commodities, mutual funds, exchange-traded funds (ETFs), options, futures, foreign exchange, precious metals, and real estate.

Broker-Dealers

A broker-dealer is an individual or firm that buys and sells financial instruments, who can serve as either a broker or a dealer, depending on the transaction. The term broker-dealer has become the phrase to describe brokers and brokerage firms because they tend to act as both agents and dealers. A broker-dealer acts as a broker (or agent) when it serves to executes orders on behalf of their clients, on the other hand it can act as a dealer when it trades for its in-house accounts.

Investment Advisors

The Investment Advisers Act of 1940 defines an investment advisor as an individual or entity that provides recommendations or performs investment analysis for a fee. Once an investment advisor accumulates a specific amount of assets under management they must register with the Securities and Exchange Commission and become a Registered Investment Advisor (RIA).

Municipal Advisors

The Securities Exchange Act of 1933 defines a municipal advisor as an individual or entity that provides professional advice to, or on the behalf of, a municipal entity regarding municipal securities. This includes advice with respect to the analysis of the structure, timing, terms, and other aspects of the municipal products or issues.

Issuers

An issuer is an entity that directly or indirectly develops, registers and sells securities to fund its operations. An issuer may be a corporation, individual trust, institutional trust, city/local agency, state agency, federal government, or foreign government. Issuers are liable for the claims and commitments of the issue and for all statutory reporting requirements.

Underwriters

An underwriter is an entity that assesses and assumes an issuer's risk for a fee. Underwriters operate in various areas of the financial industry, including the mortgage industry, insurance industry, equity and debt markets.

Traders

A trader is an individual who buys and sells financial securities in various financial markets. The distinction between traders and investors comes from the investment horizon. Traders tend to have a short investment window, while investors tend to have long-term investment strategies.

Market Makers

A market maker is an individual or firm operating under the authority of an exchange that buys and sells securities in two ways: (i) at prices it displays in an exchange's trading system for its own account – principal trades and (ii) for customer accounts – agency trades. In the trading system a market maker will adjust bid and asked quotes, enter and execute orders, and clear any orders.

Custodians

A custodian is an entity that takes physical or electronic possession of a customers' securities for safety to mitigate the risk of loss/theft. Custodian firms tend to be large reputable financial firms and hold large amounts of assets and securities.

Trustees

A trustee is an individual or entity that holds and oversees property or assets for another. Trustees may be court appointed or selected by the beneficiary for a number of reasons, such as bankruptcy, charitable foundations, trust funds, etc. Trustees are entrusted to make decisions that are in the beneficiary's best interests and have a fiduciary responsibility to the well-being of the trust beneficiaries.

Transfer Agents

A transfer agent is an entity, like a trust, bank or other financial institution that has been tasked to maintain records of investors and account balances. The transfer agent should maintain accurate records of transactions, cancels and issues certificates, processes investor mailings and deal with any investor concerns.

Depositories

A depository often refers to an organization, like a bank or other financial institution that holds and supports in the trading of securities. It can also refer to an institution that accepts currency deposits from customers.

Clearing Corporations

An entity that is related to an exchange to manage the verification, settlement and delivery of transactions. The purpose of the entity is to ensure the efficient transfer of assets. They are also often referred to as "clearing firms" or "clearing houses".

1.2 MARKET STRUCTURE

Section Overview:

1.2.1 Types of Markets

1.2.1 TYPES OF MARKETS

The Primary Market

In the primary market new securities are traded for the first time. These new securities are issued by corporations and governments as a means to secure new financing and are referred to as an initial public offering (IPO). New issues can be in the form of debt-financing (notes, bonds, etc.) or equity financing (common or preferred stock). Primary markets transactions are generally managed by investment banks that serve as underwriters of the process. The underwriting process starts with the issuing entity and the investment bank agreeing to the terms of the relationship.

The result of this agreement will determine the level of risk that the investment bank will take on through the process. The investment bank will typically decide to either underwrite the new issue as a "best effort" or "fixed commitment". In the case of a best effort, the investment banker will sell as many of the new issue as they can without a guarantee. On the other hand a fixed commitment arrangement means that the investment bank will guarantee the sale of an agreed upon number of the new issue.

In addition to acting as the underwriter the investment bank will also facilitate the sale and manage the statutory SEC reporting requirements. The process will include the initial SEC registration, road shows, book building, creation of a selling group or underwriting syndicate, and sales of the new securities. After the initial sale of the new securities, future sales between investors occur in the secondary market.

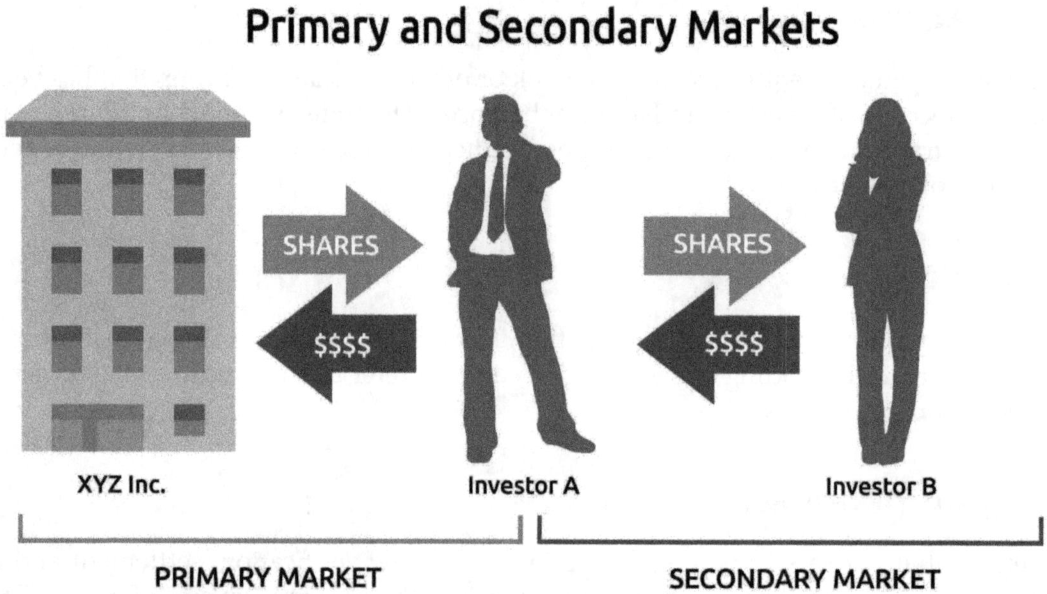

The Secondary Market

The secondary market provides a means of liquidity for investors. This market allows investors to buy and sell (trade) securities that are currently trading with other investors. The secondary market is the market that people intuitively think about when they refer to the stock market. The most popular outlets to trade in the secondary market is by using the New York Stock Exchange (NYSE) or the National Association of Securities Dealers Automated Quotations (NASDAQ).

Investors trade stocks, bonds, mutual funds, among other securities on the secondary market. Other securities can include complex assets like mortgage securities sold by issuing banks. The prices in the secondary market are a function of the demand for the security. As the demand for the security increases the price of the asset will also increase. On the other hand, as more investors sell off the security the price will decrease.

The Third Market

The third market is a relatively unknown sector of the financial markets where brokers or dealers that are not affiliated with a major exchange (NYSE or NASDAQ) trade with large institutional investors (mutual funds or pension funds).

The Fourth Market

The fourth market is a private market where institutional investors can trade large amounts of securities between themselves rather than using the exchanges in the secondary market. The fourth market is sometimes referred to as a dark pool. The term comes from the result of these private transactions having very little transparency and are often completed with little public awareness.

1.3 ECONOMIC FACTORS

Section Overview:

1.3.1 Impact of the Federal Reserve

1.3.2 Business Economic Factors

1.3.3 International Economic Factors

1.3.1 IMPACT OF THE FEDERAL RESERVE

Monetary Policy

Monetary policy refers to a central bank's decisions and actions that are used in order to carry out their policy objectives. These objectives generally include employment stability, economic growth and inflation control. The United States central bank, the Federal Reserve, focuses its attention on employment and inflation.

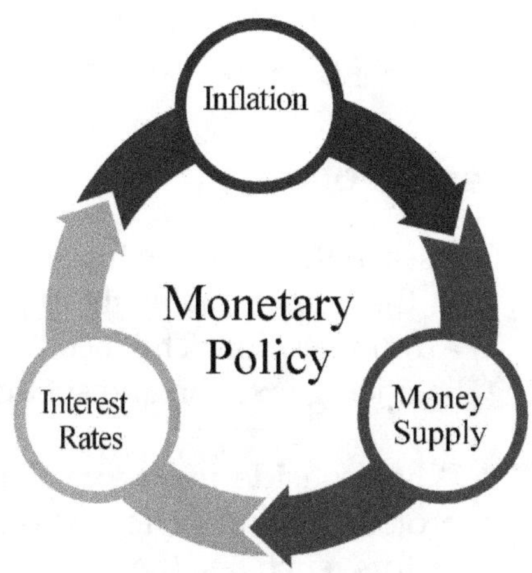

The Federal Reserve uses three primary tools to promote its objectives of maximizing employment and maintaining price stability. These tools include the management of the discount rate, reserve requirements, and their open market operations.

The discount rate is the short-term interest rate that the Federal Reserve charges their member financial institutions for short-term loans. This rate has a direct impact on the Federal Funds rate, the rate that banks charge each other for short-term loans. Subsequently, this will have an effect on the general level of short-term interest rates in the market. This influence over short-term rates allows them to impact long-term interest rates and specific asset prices. These relationships allow the Federal Reserve to influence the decisions of businesses and individuals, given their expectations for the economic and financial conditions of the U.S. economy.

Reserve requirements are mandated funds that must be held by member banks in the form of cash or deposits with a Federal Reserve Bank. These funds represent a percentage of the deposit liabilities that a member bank has outstanding. The minimum requirements are set by the Board of Governors and is determined by using the reserve ratio describe in the Federal Reserve Board's "Regulation D".

Reservable liabilities that are subject to the requirement consist of net transaction accounts, nonpersonal time deposits, and Eurocurrency liabilities. Since the end of 1990 the reserve ratio for both nonpersonal time deposits and Eurocurrency liabilities have been set to 0 percent of liabilities. In January of 2018 the reserve ratio for net transactions was as follows: at or below

$16 million – 0 percent; between $16 million and $122.3 million – 3 percent; more than $122.3 million – 10 percent. The limits are reset each year based on a formula described in the Garn-St. Germain Act of 1982.

The buying and selling of government securities is known as "open market operations". The use of open market operations by the Federal Reserve is usually carried out in order to maintain target rates. Open market operations is often regarded as the most effective and most frequently used monetary policy tool. At the direction of the Federal Open Market Committee (FOMC), the Federal Reserve Bank of New York carries out the purchases and sales of securities issued by the U.S. Treasury, Federal agencies, and government-sponsored agencies.

If the Federal Reserve wants to increase the amount of reserves, they will purchase securities by making a deposit in the primary dealer's Federal bank account. If they want to decrease reserves, they will sell securities by making a withdrawal from the primary dealer's account. Using these open market operations the Federal Reserve can influence the amount of reserves and subsequently the federal funds rate.

The FOMC is the policymaking division of the Federal Reserve System. They meet eight times per year to discuss the current economic and financial conditions and to determine the appropriate monetary policy actions.

Fiscal Policy

Fiscal policy refers to the federal government's policies relating to taxes and government spending. In the United States these policies are created and managed by Congress and the Presidential Administration. The focus in the United States has been to manage the national deficit through balancing taxation and spending.

When considering the economic conditions the FOMC assesses the Administration's current and projected fiscal policy action items to determine the impact they may have on macroeconomic factors such as the gross domestic product (GDP), unemployment, consumer sentiment, inflation, etc.

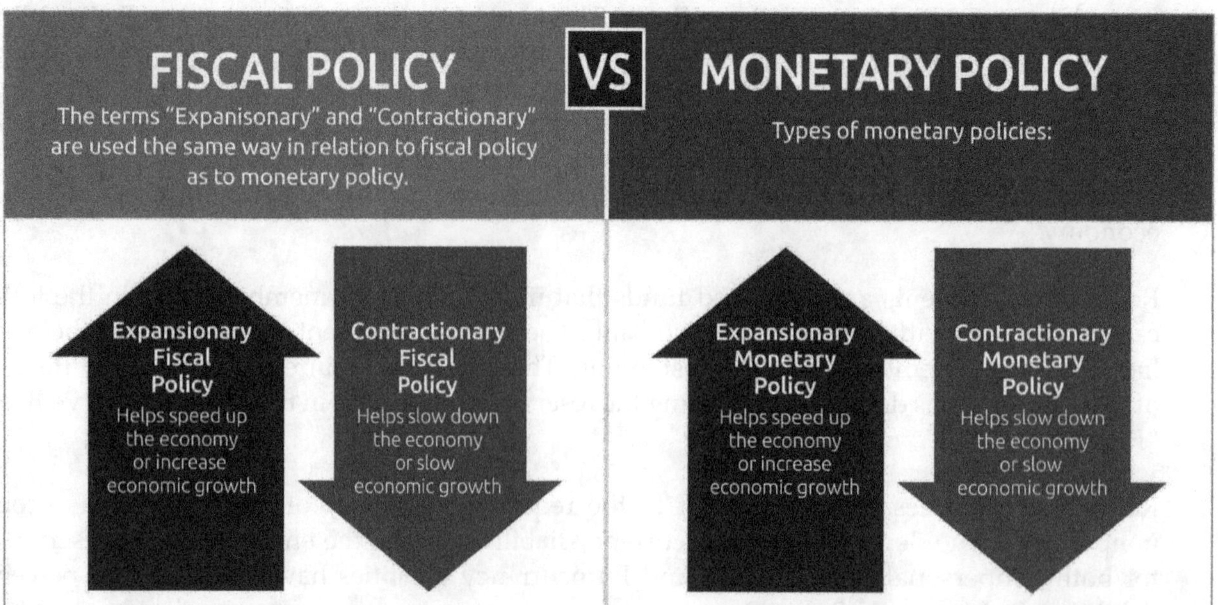

Different Types of Interest Rates

An interest rate in the rate charged, usually expressed as a percentage, by a bank or other lender for borrowed funds. Interest rates are normally quoted in annual terms, referred to as the Annual Percentage Rate (APR).

The Short-rate, or short-term interest rate, is the rate charged for short-term loans in the money markets. These rates are also known as money market rates and are associated with products such as commercial paper, negotiable CDs, and Treasury bills.

Fed Funds Rate

The Federal Funds Rate is the interest rate that U.S. banks charge each other for overnight loans of the funds held in their Federal Reserve accounts. These loans are used to meet the required reserve ratios set by the Federal Reserve.

Prime Rate

The Prime Rate is the interest rate that serves as the benchmark rate for other market loans. Banks or other financial institutions use the prime rate as a base for their variable rate products. In the U.S., the prime rate is the rate that banks charge large corporations for short-terms loans.

LIBOR

The London Interbank Offer Rate (LIBOR) is often considered the most popular global benchmark rate. It is the rate that banks charge each other for Eurodollar loans on the London Interbank market.

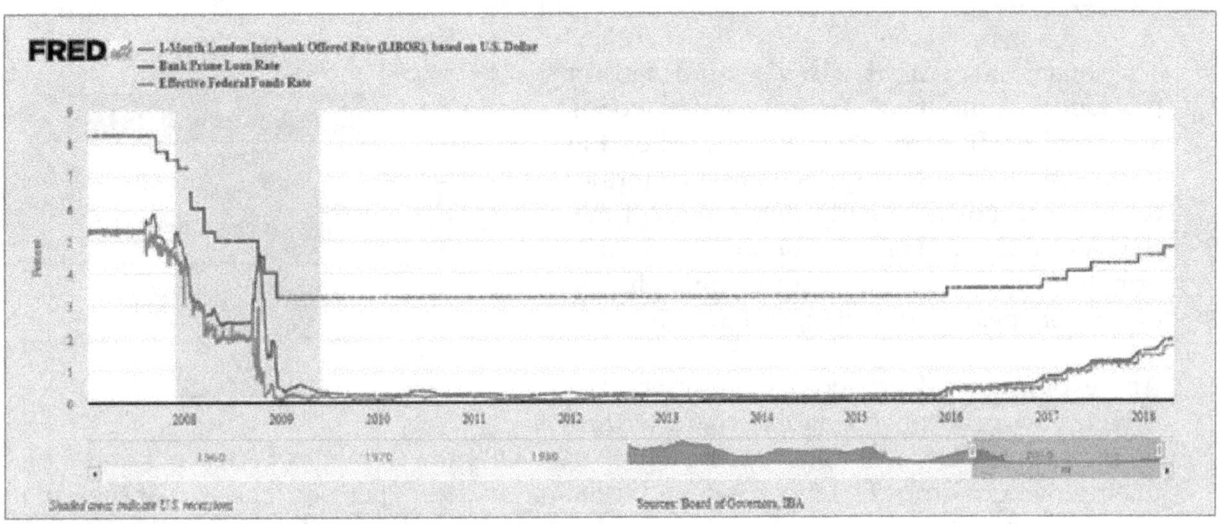

1.3.2 BUSINESS ECONOMIC FACTORS

Purpose of Financial Statements

The purpose of the three main financial statements is to provide useful information regarding the operations of a business or organization. Depending on the user, financial statements can be used to make various business decisions.

Balance Sheet

The balance sheet is often used to provide information about the current state of business assets and funding sources. The information listed can be used to identify the company's position regarding liquidity, asset utilization, and financial leverage.

Income Statement

The income statement is used to provide information about a company's operating efficiency and profitability. The information reported on an income statement will cover a full operating period (usually one year). Often referred to as a profit and loss statement, it documents the revenues, expenses, and profits/losses over the period.

Statement of Cash Flows

The statement of cash flows is used to identify the sources and uses of cash for a company. The information is categorized by business activity into three sections: operating, investing, and financing activities. The statement can also take on one of two formats: an indirect or direct form. The only difference between the two formats is in the operating activities section. The indirect method shows cash after adjustments for accruals while the direct method shows direct cash values for operating inflows and outflows.

Collectively, the financial statements serve to provide valuable information for various business decisions. These decisions include, but are not limited to, credit, financial management, investment, and tax decisions.

Business Cycle

The business cycle is the rise and fall in productive output of an economy's goods and services. It is usually characterized by the change in the country's gross domestic product (GDP). The business cycle therefore captures the natural rise and fall of a country's economic growth over time and has four distinct phases: expansion, peak, contraction, and trough.

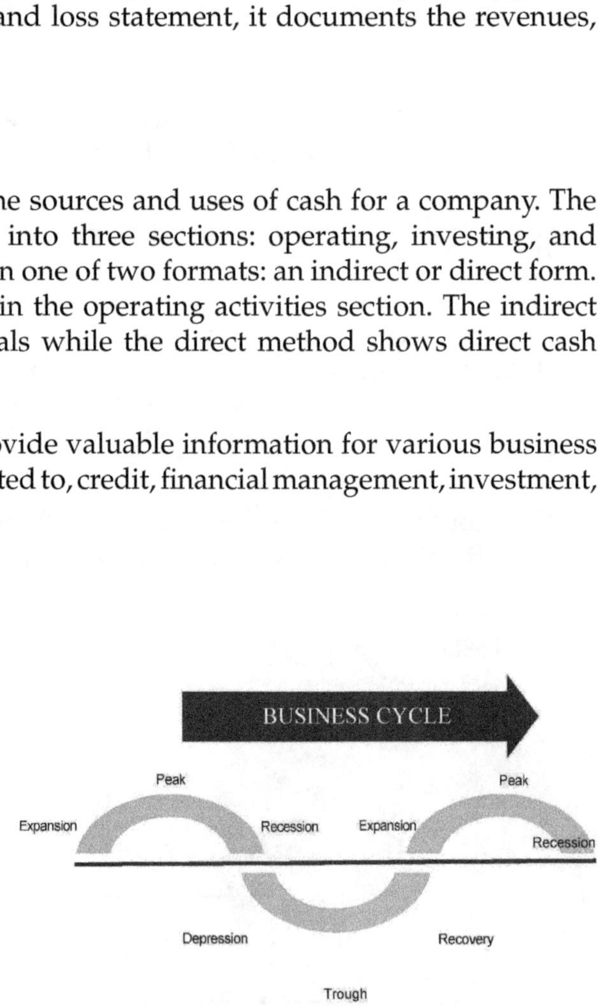

An expansion phase occurs between the trough and peak phases and is characterized by increasing GDP. During an expansion phase GDP growth ranges between 2 and 3 percent, unemployment drops to 4-5 percent, and inflation reaches 2 percent. The end of the expansion phase is typically marked by the "overheating" of the economy. GDP growth increases past 3 percent, inflation increases past targets and markets enter a state of "irrational exuberance" and enters the peak phase.

As the economy passes through the peak phase and enters the contraction phase economic growth slows, unemployment begins to increase, and financials markets show market-wide declines. At the end of contraction phase the economy enters the last phase known as the trough. As the economy bottoms out into the trough phase the economy re-enters the expansion phase.

The National Bureau of Economic Research (NBER) assesses economic conditions to determine the current stage of the business cycle by monitoring GDP growth rates. In addition the NBER uses economic indicators like unemployment rates, growth in industrial production, and changes in retail sales to assess the stage of the business cycle.

Business Cycle Management

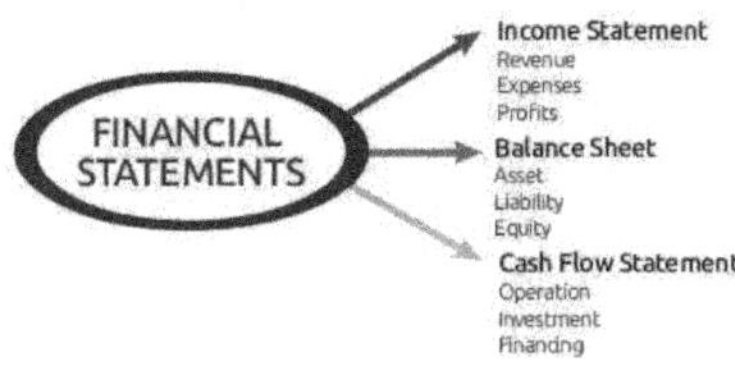

Fiscal policy is the main tool used by the government to manage the business cycle. The administration (the executive branch) and legislators use expansionary or contractionary fiscal policy to influence the business cycle. During an expansionary phase the government can use contractionary policies to prevent the economy from overheating and hitting the peak. They can use expansionary fiscal policies to shorten the length of a contraction phase. In addition, the Fed's monetary policy may also help manage the business cycle.

Economic Indicators

An economic indicator is any statistic that is related to financial or economic trends. There are a number of popular indicators that are often used to identify economic trends. These indicators are classified into three categories based on the relationship they have with the economic cycle. Indexes of these indicators are used as analytical tools. In the U.S., the Conference Board creates composite indexes of leading, coincident, and lagging indicators. The indexes are constructed by averaging a number of statistics that fall into each category and is used to identify peaks and troughs in the business cycle.

Leading Indicators

Leading indicators signal a pending economic downturn and are often used as a predictive tool for economic analysis.

The Conference Board Leading Economic Index (ten leading indicators)

1. Average weekly hours, manufacturing

   The average hours per week worked by production workers in the manufacturing industry. This tends to lead the business cycle because companies usually adjust their employee work schedule before increasing or decreasing their workforce.

2. Average weekly initial claims for unemployment insurance

   The number of new unemployment insurance claims filed. This is typically more sensitive than unemployment measures to overall changes in business conditions. The value has an inverse relationship to an economic downturn, because initial claims increase when employment conditions deteriorate.

3. Manufacturers' new orders, consumer goods and materials

   The value of new orders for consumer goods, after adjusting for inflation, will lead actual production levels because new orders will directly affect the level of both unfilled orders and a firm's inventories.

4. ISM Index of New Orders

The ISM index of new orders is based on a monthly survey conducted by the Institution for Supply Management (ISM). This index reflects the amount of new orders from customers. Specifically it reports increased orders during the previous month compared to the number reporting decreased orders. An index value greater than 50 represents that orders have increased during the past month.

5. Manufacturers' new orders, nondefense capital goods excluding aircraft orders

The value of new orders for capital goods by producers. This index is the producers' counterpart to Manufacturers' new orders, consumer goods and materials.

6. Building permits, new private housing units

As an indicator of construction activity the number of residential building permits issued will typically lead economic production.

7. Stock prices, 500 common stocks

Standard & Poor's (S&P) creates an index of stocks issued by the largest 500 companies in the U.S., with market capitalizations above $6 billion. The index is considered an indicator of the broad equity market movements.

8. Leading Credit Index™

The Leading Credit Index consist of six statistics: two-year swap spread, three-month LIBOR minus three-month Treasury-Bill yield spread, debit balances of margin accounts at broker dealer firms, American Association of Individual Investors (AAII) sentiment survey, senior loan officers commercial and industrial loan survey, and security repurchases from the Federal Reserve.

9. Interest rate spread, ten-year Treasury bonds less federal funds

The interest rate spread is constructed by calculating the difference between the ten-year Treasury bond rate and the federal funds rate. When short rates are higher than long rates and the spread is negative it's a good predictor of a recession.

10. Average consumer expectations for business conditions

This index is an equally weighted average of consumer expectations of business and economic conditions. The information for business conditions come from the Consumer Confidence Survey by the Conference Board. The information for economic conditions come from the Surveys of Consumers conducted by Reuters/University of Michigan.

Coincident Indicators

Coincident indicators have a contemporaneous relationship with economic downturns and are used to confirm that a recession is occurring.

The Conference Board Coincident Economic Index (four coincident indicators)

1. Employees on nonagricultural payrolls

The Bureau of Labor Statistics reports all permanent and temporary employees working full- and part-time.

2. Personal income less transfer payments

   The inflation-adjusted value of the income received from all sources, except government transfers (e.g. Social Security payments).

3. Index of industrial production

   The index represents the added value of physical output of all levels of production in the manufacturing, mining, and utility industries.

4. Manufacturing and trade sales

   The inflation-adjusted value of manufacturing, wholesale, and retail sales which represent real total spending.

Lagging Indicators

Lagging indicators signal the end of an economic downturn and are used to confirm the transition from a contraction to an expansion phase.

The Conference Board Lagging Economic Index (seven lagging indicators)

1. Average duration of unemployment

   The average weekly duration of unemployment that individuals have reported. This value is inversely related to the lagging index where decreases in the value occur after the occurrence of an expansion and increases after the occurrence of a recession.

2. Ratio, manufacturing and trade inventories to sales

   The ratio of inventories to sales is calculated by the Bureau of Economic Analysis (BEA) using inventory and sales data for manufacturing, wholesale, and retail businesses.

3. Change in labor cost per unit of output, manufacturing

   The index is constructed by The Conference Board, including seasonally adjusted information from the BEA for manufacturing employee compensation and manufacturing industrial production values from the Federal Reserve System.

4. Average prime rate charged by banks

   The prime rate is often regarded as the benchmark that banks use as a basis for the interest rate for various loans. The information is collected by the Federal Reserve.

5. Commercial and industrial loans outstanding

   The amount of business loans held by banks and commercial paper issued by nonfinancial companies. The information is compiled by the Federal Reserve.

6. Ratio, consumer installment credit outstanding to personal income

   This ratio represents the relationship between consumer debt and personal income. Consumer installment credit outstanding is compiled by the Federal Reserve and personal income is compiled from the BEA.

7. Change in Consumer Price Index for services

   Compiled by the Bureau of Labor Statistics it measures the rate of change in the services component of the Consumer Price Index.

To summarize, leading indicators predict economic cycles, coincident indicators move along-side economic cycles, and lagging indicators trail economic cycles.

Inflation

Inflation is an increase in the level of prices for goods and services in a specific country, usually measured as an annual percent change. A currency's value is gauged by the purchasing power, which represents the amount of goods and services that can be bought. When inflation increases the purchasing power decreases and less goods and services can be purchased. In the U.S., the Federal Reserve attempts to sustain an inflation rate of 2-3% with the use of monetary policy tools.

Inflation Theories

There are a few competing theories for the cause of inflation.

Demand-Pull Inflation – Inflation caused by increased demand for goods and services, which pushes up market prices. If demand grows faster than supply, then prices will increase. This usually occurs when economies grow too fast.

Cost-Push Inflation – Inflation caused when a businesses' cost of production increase. When their production cost increase they need to increase prices to maintain current margins. Increased costs usually include such items as raw materials, inventory, wages, or even taxes.

Monetary Inflation – Inflation caused by an excess supply of money in the economy. Similar to other commodities, the price of money is determined by its supply and demand. If there is excess supply, then the price or value will drop. The result is that if the value drops then the real cost of things purchased increases.

Deflation occurs when the level of prices falls and is the opposite of inflation. Deflation is far more rare and occurs for shorter periods of time than inflation. Deflation typically happens during times of recession or economic crisis and will generally lead to a deep economic crisis. Researchers often describe this state as a deflationary spiral. The concept is that individuals will rather save their money because they think that money will be more valuable in the future because prices are decreasing. The result is that individuals stop spending and hoard money expecting that prices will fall even further. If this happens business profits will collapse and they will be forced to lay people off. The increased unemployment will lead to even less spending and the spiral will continue.

Disinflation is a situation characterized by positive inflation but at a slower rate than in the previous time period.

Hyperinflation is a condition of rapid inflation, often in excess of 50% in a month. Historically, hyperinflation has led to the dismantling of a country's monetary system and the stability of its economy. In the last century, it has caused major crises in Germany, Zimbabwe, Hungary, and Argentina.

Stagflation is a rare combination of high inflation, high unemployment, and stagnate economy. In the 1970s, a number of industrialized nations experienced this effect as a result of weak economies and the formation of the Organization of Petroleum Exporting Countries (OPEC) and their price hikes for oil.

In summary, inflation takes on many forms – some are good for the economy while some are bad signs for the economy.

Effects on Financial Markets

Investments in cyclical companies are investments that tend to move in the same direction as the overall economy. When the economy is in an expansion phase cyclical investments will generally do well. On the other hand they will suffer during a contraction phase of the business cycle. Typically investments in consumer discretionary companies will exhibit this cyclical behavior.

Defensive companies are generally immune from shifts in the economy. Therefore, they behave relatively independent of the business cycle. During a contraction phase investors will gravitate towards defensive company investments as a safer investment. Companies in the utilities industry are a good example of defensive investments that do not react to changes in the business cycle.

Growth companies offer an investor above average rates of growth for a specific economy. Growth companies tend to have significant growth opportunities and therefore will pay little to no dividends while in its growth phase.

Value companies are those that have prices that are low relative to their internal value. The internal value can be measured using the book value of equity or the net income of the company. In either case the price is not in-line with the internal value of the company and is therefore thought of as "undervalued."

Principal Economic Theories

Keynesian Theory

The General Theory of Employment, Interest, and Money was published by John Maynard Keynes in 1936 as the manuscript for the Keynesian Theory of Economics.

Keynesian Theory generally adheres to the following concepts:

- *Unemployment* – unemployment is often related to high and rigid real wages. Keynes argued that societies are highly resistant to decreasing wages and that decreasing wages would lead to an issue in the economy. Specifically, decreasing wages would reduce spending and result in a downward spiral.
- *Excessive Saving* – Keynes argues that excessive saving is a problem that may lead to economic decline. He believed that excessive saving leads to reduced investment and

reduced spending, which would drive down demand and consumption. The effect would be another spiraling effect as hoarding money will lead to higher unemployment, reduced revenues, and lower future investments.

- *Fiscal Policy* – Keynes was a strong advocate of active fiscal policy where the government could significantly reduce any negative effects of the business cycle. The "counter-cyclical" actions would include deficit spending during recessions and inflation control techniques during prolonged expansion periods. Overall, the government is able to stabilize the economy by using proactive fiscal policy.

- *The Multiplier Effect* – The concept is the opposite of the downward spiral effect caused by unemployment and excessive spending. As the economy exhibits positive signs it may be able to have an upward spiral. Keynes believed this may be possible by putting funds in the hands of individuals that were likely to increase the investments of the economy thereby causing a ripple effect of investments, the multiplier effect.

Monetarist

The focus of the Monetarist theory are the effects of macroeconomic shifts in the money supply and the charge of the central banking system. The ideas of monetarism were first introduced by Clark Warburton in the 1940s and made popular by Milton Friedman in the 1950s.

Monetarist Theory generally adheres to the following concepts:

- An increased money supply will lead to higher spending and vice versa. Subsequently, this relationship would lead to control over aggregate demand.

- Monetarism is correlated to inflation control and increased economic performance.

- The amount of money in circulation should not be determined by the gold standard, instead should be set using monetary policy.

Austrian

The Austrian Theory originated in the 19th century in Vienna, Austria. The early founders of the theory are Carl Menger, Friedrich von Weiser, and Eugen von Bohm-Bawerk. The general perspective of Austrian economic thought is individualism and the recognition that people will act in meaningful ways.

Austrian Theory generally adheres to the following concepts:

- *Opportunity Cost* – The cost of a good must incorporate the value given up of the next best alternative. Each choice a consumer or business makes has the cost of not being able to make an alternative choice, mutually exclusive.

- *Capital and Interest* – Eugen von Bohm-Bawerk identified that the foundation of interest rates and profit are supply and demand considering time preference. Therefore, present consumption is more valuable than future consumption, the time value of money.

- *Inflation* – Prices and wages must rise as a result of increased money supply. Specifically, more money in the system in the absence of a higher demand for money will push down the relative value of a dollar.

- *Business Cycles* – The Austrian Business Cycle Theory (ABCT) is the observation that the issuance of credit creates cyclical economic fluctuations. Essentially, banks will lend money at rates that are lower than the risk in which that money will be used.

- *The Organizing Power of Markets* – No one person knows the true price of a good in the market. Instead, markets naturally shift to an equilibrium value and identify an optimal price point.

Neoclassical

The classical to neoclassical shift in thought began with Adam Smith and David Ricardo. The foundation of the neoclassical theory is that aggregate demand will adjust with supply. The following effect is that consumer goods demonstrate a utility based behavior, which is dependent on each consumer. The most significant tenet of the neoclassical theory is the introduction of marginalism. Marginalism posits that individuals make decisions based on marginal utility and margins.

In considering the Neoclassical theory of economics, it is important to note the following three principles:

- People generally have rational preferences when choosing options or outcomes that can be identified and associated with a given monetary value.

- Individuals maximize their utility while firms maximize corporate profits

- Individuals act independently on full information based on utility.

Neo-Keynesian

Neo-Keynesian theory is sometimes mistaken for the "New Keynesian" theory – theories that apply Keynesian theories to microeconomics. Neo-Keynesian theory is the reevaluation of Keynesian theories by various economist, like John Hicks, Franco Modigliani, and Paul Samuelson.

Keynesian Based Ideas

- *IS-LM Model* – John Hicks modeled the relationship between interest rates and real economic output. This model looks at the investment-saving relationship (IS) compared to the liquidity preference and money supply relationship (LM). The result is an equilibrium where specific interest rates and economic output values are generated.

- *Phillips Curve* – William Phillips considered the relationship between inflation and unemployment and documented the inverse relationship between them.

1.3.3 INTERNATIONAL ECONOMIC FACTORS

U.S. Balance of Payments

Balance of Payments (BOP) is a country's accounting of all international transactions for a specific period of time, usually quarterly of annually. Credits to the BOP are any funds into the country, while debits are funds out of the country. The BOP consists of three accounts that are categorized based on the type of transaction. Transactions involving goods and services are recorded in the current account. Transfers of capital and non-financial assets are recorded in the capital account. All investment flows are recorded in the financial account. For example, if a German manufacturing company purchases bolts from a U.S. steel company, then there would be a debit in Germany's BOP and a credit to the U.S. BOP.

Current Account

The current account has four sub-accounts: income receipts, merchandise trade, services, and unilateral transfers. Income receipts represent any income received from the ownership of certain assets. Merchandise trade includes the purchase or sale of all raw materials, work-in-process, and finished goods. Services consists of funds from transportation, tourism, and professional services (accounting, law, business etc.). Unilateral transfers are one-way transfers of assets or aid, such as direct foreign aid.

Capital Account

The capital account has two sub-accounts: capital transfers and acquisition and disposal on non-produced, non-financial assets. Capital transfers consist of goods and financial assets that are brought in or taken out of a country with migrants. It also includes debt forgiveness, title transfers of fixed assets, and the transfer of funds associated with the sale or acquisition of fixed assets. Acquisition and disposal on non-produced, non-financial assets includes the purchase and sale of natural resources and intangible assets, such as patents and copyrights.

Financial Account

The financial account has two sub-accounts: foreign-owned assets in the U.S. and U.S.-owned assets abroad. Foreign-owned assets in the U.S. include direct investments, financial securities, U.S. currency, and U.S. liabilities. U.S.-owned assets abroad include foreign currency, foreign securities, International Money Fund (IMF) reserves, and direct foreign investments.

Theoretically, the BOP should show that the current account balances with the sum of the capital and financial accounts. Often times the BOP does not perfectly balance because of variations in accounting practices and exchange rate movements. A country typically reports the BOP deficit or surplus based on the current account values, with a focus on the merchandise trade and services sub accounts. For example, if the U.S. sold more goods and services than it purchased it would have a current account surplus.

Gross Domestic Product (GDP)

Gross Domestic Product is a quantitative measure of a country's economic strength. GDP captures the value of the production capacity of the individuals and businesses in a country. All production within the borders of the country is counted in the GDP calculation, regardless of whether it is produced by a domestic or foreign entity. The calculation is comprised of five components of the economy: personal consumption (C), business investments (I), government spending (G), exports (E), and imports (M). A country's GDP is calculated by finding the sum of the personal consumption, business investments, government spending, and net exports (exports minus imports).

$$[GDP = C + I + G + (X - M)]$$

Nominal GDP is the raw value of GDP including inflation. Using a price deflator the real GDP can be calculated without the effects of inflation. The BEA tracks U.S. nominal and real GDP on a quarterly basis using final product values within the United States. They exclude income from individuals and businesses outside of the U.S. as well as input cost for U.S. based production. For example, if a company produces a belt the value of the buckle and the leather strap would not be counted, only the final value of the belt.

The rate of growth in real GDP is an important indicator of the strength of the economy. It shows the speed at which the economy is growing and is used as a gauge for the business cycle. A recession in an economy is marked by two consecutive quarters of negative GDP growth. GDP is often measured on a per capita basis to account for differences in populations across countries and to obtain a more accurate measure of a country's standard of living. The real GDP per capita is calculated by dividing the real GDP by the country's resident population, this measure accounts for inflation, exchange rates and population differences.

Gross National Product (GNP)

Gross National Product is the cumulative value of all goods and services produced by a country's citizens, regardless of where in the world they are. GNP only accounts for the investments and products manufactured by domestic businesses and does not include values from foreign individuals and businesses residing in the country. The measure is calculated similar to GDP using only the domestic values and including the overseas values of the country's residents. GNP is calculated by finding the sum of the personal consumption (C), business investments (I), government spending (G), net exports (X – M), and net income earned overseas by domestic residents minus net income earned domestically by foreign residents (Z).

$$[GNP = C + I + G + (X - M) + Z] \text{ or } [GNP = GDP + Z]$$

Exchange Rates

An exchange rate is the value of a country's currency in relation to another country's currency. The exchange rate is quoted using a domestic currency (DC) and a foreign currency (FC). The quote can either be a direct quote or an indirect quote. For a direct quote, the value of the domestic currency is quoted per unit of the foreign currency (DC/FC). For an indirect quote, the value of the foreign currency is quoted per unit of the domestic currency (FC/DC). Notice that a direct quote and an indirect quote are reciprocals of each other (DQ = 1/IQ and IQ = 1/DQ). Exchange rates have a base currency and a counter currency. For a direct quote, the base currency is the foreign currency and the counter currency is the domestic currency. The opposite is true for an indirect quote where the base currency is the domestic currency and the counter currency is the foreign currency.

Example. In Canada a direct quote to U.S. dollars would be expressed as C$1.2/$1, where the base currency is U.S. dollars and the counter currency is Canadian dollars.

Exchange rates are normally allowed to "float" or change with the natural market forces. Some countries have chosen to fix or peg their currency to more popular currencies, such as the U.S. dollar or the Euro. A country may decide to peg their currency due to volatility concerns.

1.4 NEW ISSUE OFFERINGS

Section Overview:

1.4.1 Offerings

1.4.1 OFFERINGS

Roles of Participants

There are a number of financial firms that act as resources for companies that seek to "go public" and issue new shares of stock to the public, as a way to finance the company. These firms include investment banks and various advisory firms.

Investment Banks

Investment banks serve a number of roles in the financial industry including financial advisory, managing mergers and acquisitions, and underwriting new stock issues. Throughout the new issues process an investment banker's role is to serve as an intermediary between the company and investing public. This process involves the underwriting of new issues of stock and other financial instruments. As an underwriter, the investment bank essentially purchases an agreed upon number of shares from the company and sells them to the public. Investment banks start the underwriting process by meeting with the company and evaluating its financial condition. After this evaluation the investment banker will create a risk assessment, price target, and target number of shares. For larger issuances, the investment bank, the lead underwriter, may seek help from other investment banks in order to mitigate their risk. This risk sharing maneuver can be done using either an underwriting syndicate or a selling group.

Underwriting Syndicate

An underwriting syndicate is a group of investment banks that share the risk and responsibility of marketing and selling the agreed upon number of shares of stock. The syndicate pools its resources in going on road shows and through the book building process.

Selling Group

The underwriting syndicate may look to expand their marketing and selling efforts by enlisting a selling group of additional investment banks. The selling group does not take on underwriting responsibilities, they serve as a salesforce for a selling concession fee.

Underwriting Fees

The underwriters are paid based on the level involvement in the process with the lead underwriter receiving the largest portion of the fees. The lead underwriter earns a management fee for each share that is sold. All members of the underwriting syndicate receive an underwriter's fee based on the number of shares sold and the level of involvement in the process. The selling concession is paid to syndicate and selling group members who sell shares to investors. The combination of the management fee, underwriter fee, and selling concession make up the underwriting spread. The underwriting spread is the difference between the gross proceeds of the new issue and the net proceeds that is paid to the issuing company. For example, a new issue that is sold for $10 may have a selling fee of $1.25, an underwriter fee of $0.50, and a management fee of $0.25. The total underwriting spread would be $2.00 and the net proceeds to the company would be $8.00.

Types of Offerings

- Private placements

  Not all new shares of stock are issued to the general public. Shares may be sold to a select set of accredited investors. The shares sold are considered a private placement sale, usually to large institutional investors like pension funds and mutual funds. Since the sale typically involves professional investment companies the SEC requires only minimal regulatory requirements for private placement sales.

- Initial public offerings (IPO)

  The first time a share of stock is sold to the general public it is known as an initial public offering (IPO). Companies usually start small with funding from owners and private investors. As they grow they will look to increase funding by "going public" and issuing shares to the public through an IPO process.

Seasoned Issue

A company that has already gone through the IPO process may decide to issue an additional block of shares to the markets. Since there are existing shares being traded for the company this set of newly issued shares is considered a seasoned issue, seasoned equity offering, or follow-on offering.

Distribution Agreements

At the beginning of the new issues process (IPO or seasoned issue) the company and the lead underwriter set up an agreement for the sale of the new issues. The lead underwriter will agree to either sell the shares under a firm commitment arrangement or under a best effort arrangement.

Fixed Commitment

In a firm commitment arrangement the underwriting syndicate takes full responsibility for the sale of all of the agreed upon new shares of the company. Effectively the underwriters purchase the shares from the company and resell them to investors.

Best Effort

When a lead underwriter is uncertain about the sale of a new issue because of the market climate or company background they may decide to underwrite the issue under a best effort arrangement. In this arrangement the underwriter only agrees to sell as many shares of the new issue as they can without any guarantee of sales.

SEC Registration

Once all of the agreements between the company and underwriters are complete the underwriters start the process by filing a registration statement with the SEC for the new issue. Under the Securities Act new issues must be approved by the SEC prior to being sold to public investors.

Blue Sky Laws

In addition to the federal laws there are laws at the state level set up to mitigate securities fraud known as Blue Sky Laws. The purpose of these laws is to add an additional layer of protection at the investor level. These laws typically ensure that advisors and brokers have professional licenses and have fiduciary requirements.

Shelf Registrations

A shelf registration allows companies to go through the IPO registration process without immediately issuing any shares. Using a shelf registration companies can delay the initial sale of all or a part of the new issue for up to two years. The benefit of doing so would be to sell shares in a more favorable market.

Official Registration Statement

A SEC registration statement (Form S-1) has two main sections: a prospectus section and a section that includes all statutory SEC filings.

Prospectus

The prospectus includes company information about operations, risks, finances, management, and the past audited financial statements. The prospectus is the official selling statement that must be given to anyone who is offered the new securities.

Red Herring

A preliminary prospectus is known as a red herring and is filed with the SEC as a draft prospectus. It normally includes most of the background information for the company and may only be missing the specifics of the new issue itself, like the initial share price and the number of shares being sold.

Tombstone

A tombstone is an ad placed by the underwriters to announce the sale of the new issue and to direct potential investors to the prospectus.

Chapter 2

ASSET CLASSES AND RISK

2.1 PRODUCTS

Section Overview:

2.1.1 Equity Securities

2.1.2 Debt Securities

2.1.3 Options

2.1.4 Investment Companies

2.1.5 Municipal Fund Securities

2.1.6 Direct Participation Programs (DPPs)

2.1.7 Real Estate Investment Trusts (REITs)

2.1.8 Hedge Funds

2.1.9 Exchange Traded Products (ETPs)

2.1.1 EQUITY SECURITIES

Equity securities represent a shareholders' ownership stake in a company. These securities are usually held in the form of capital stock, common and preferred stock. Equity holders are often considered residual stakeholders because they are not guaranteed income payments, rather they tend to profit from increases in corporate value through capital gains. In addition, in the case of bankruptcy they are typically last in line for any monetary claims.

Common stockholders have an indirect control over the company through their voting rights. They are entitled to vote for the Board of Directors, who in turn hire the top managers of the company.

Common Stock

As a residual stakeholder, common stockholders are forced to fall in line with a hierarchy for income payments and default claims. In the event of a corporate failure and liquidation the creditors of the company are typically first to be repaid, followed by the bondholders and then finally the equity holders. If a company has preferred stockholders they normally have a higher claim than common stockholders and will receive any monetary repayments first. This structure of payment is known as absolute priority. This relationship also covers dividend payments so that preferred dividends have priority over common stock dividends.

In addition to differences in the hierarchy of payments common stockholders typically have different voting rights where they hold the right to vote while preferred stockholders do not.

Overall, there are six rights that common shareholders benefit from: ownership rights, dividend rights, voting rights, transferability, review of company filings, and litigation rights.

Preferred Stock

Preferred stock is sometimes referred to as a hybrid security because it combines features of an equity security and a bond. Similar to a bond it issues a fixed payment paid at a specific rate in the form of a preferred dividend and it carries a defined par value. Like an equity security the dividend is paid at the discretion of the Board of Directors and the security does not have a set maturity date. Other hybrid securities include equity warrants and convertible bonds.

Warrants

Equity warrants are derivative securities that give the holder the right to buy or sell an underlying asset, usually a stock, at a given price called the exercise or strike price. American warrants can be exercised any time prior to the expiration date. European warrants must be exercised on the specific expiration date. A call warrant gives the holder the right to buy the underlying stock and a put warrant gives the holder the right to sell the underlying stock. Warrants are similar to options in the way they are structured but are different in that they are normally issued by the company that issued the stock. In addition, warrants are not generally traded on exchanges and when exercised result in newly issued shares of the company's stock. Historically, warrants were used as sweeteners on new bond and preferred stock issues to entice investors to buy risky securities. They were created as a detachable, wedded, or naked warrants. The detachable warrants act as a security that can be separated and sold as a different security in the markets. The wedded warrants were essentially convertible securities that required the bond or preferred stock be given up in order to exercise the warrant and receive the common stock. Naked warrants are issued without a connection to a bond or preferred stock and trades independently.

Convertible Bonds

A convertible bond is a security that has an embedded option for the holder to exchange the bond for a certain number of shares of the issuing company. The issuing company may use this security as another type of sweetener to entice investors into buying a high risk security.

Rights Offering

In a rights offering existing shareholders are given the right to purchase additional stock based on their percent of ownership. They are generally offered a discounted price per share for the new shares purchased as long as they purchase the shares within a specified period of time, usually within a month. Rights offerings are structured one of two ways: as a direct rights offering or as an insured rights offering. A direct rights offering is generally cheaper for the shareholder because the issuer is dependent on the stockholders to buy enough new shares to fund their needs. On the other hand an insured rights offering is set up with a standby investor, like an investment bank, that is ready to purchase any unexercised rights at an agreed upon price. Since the issuer has this standby investor it is unlikely to offer a lower price for the offering.

A rights offering are rights given to existing shareholders to purchase additional stock shares, known as subscription warrants, in proportion to their existing holdings. In a rights offering, the subscription price at which each share may be purchased is generally discounted relative to the current market price. Rights are often transferable, allowing the holder to sell them in the open market.

American Depositary Receipts (ADR)

American Depositary Receipts (ADR) are negotiable securities issued by U.S. financial institutions that represent a set number of shares of a foreign company's stock. ADRs are sold on U.S. exchanges while the underlying foreign stocks are held by the issuing financial institution.

American Depositary Share

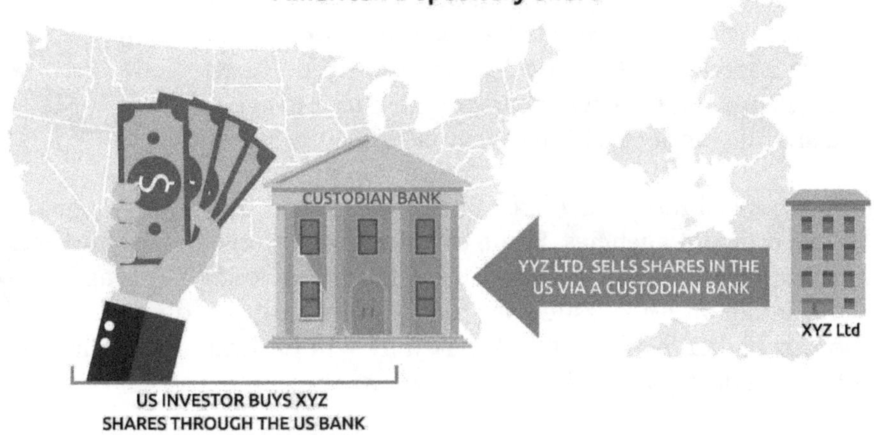

ADRs can be created on a one- for-one basis, on a fractional basis (e.g. 1 ADR for 0.5 shares of the foreign stock), or on a multiple basis (e.g. 1 ADR for 3 shares of the foreign stock). The ratio is set by the issuing institution based on the relative share value compared to the U.S. average market prices as a way to normalize the price for investors.

2.1.2 DEBT SECURITIES

Debt securities represent funds that have been borrowed with an expectation of repayment, normally with interest. Debt securities are often referred to as fixed-income securities because of the fixed payment structure associated with these securities. The fixed payments represent an interest cost, repayment of principal, or a combination of both. Governments as well as corporations issue various types of debt securities.

Treasury Securities

Treasury securities are issued by the federal government and are classified based on the length of the maturity of the security. Treasury Bills (T-Bills) have the shortest durations and mature within one year. Treasury Notes (T-Notes) are intermediate term securities and have maturities that range from two to ten years. Lastly, Treasury Bonds (T-Bonds) have the longest maturities of greater than ten years. T-Notes and T-Bonds act like a typical corporate bond and pays coupon payments, on a semiannual basis, and then a full repayment of the face value at maturity. T-Bills are unique securities that are sold on a bank discount basis. They do not make periodic interest payments, like T-Notes or T-Bonds, instead they are sold at a deep discount from the face value and will repay the full face value at maturity. Investors receive the difference as their return over the life of the security.

Agency Debt

There are two general types of agency debt: Federal Government Agency bonds and Government Sponsored Enterprise (GSE) bonds.

Federal Government Agency bonds are issued by federal agencies and so are backed by the federal government. These bonds are typically issued by the Federal Housing Administration (FHA), the Government National Mortgage Association (GNMA), and the Small Business Administration (SBA). As compared to Treasury securities, agency bonds tend to trade less frequently and often have embedded call provisions. These characteristics lead to agency bonds having a slightly higher yield than its treasury counterpart.

Government Sponsored Enterprise (GSE) bonds are issued by government related institutions rather than by government agencies. Some of these institutions include the Federal Home Loan Mortgage Corporation (Freddie Mac) and the Federal National Mortgage Association (Fannie Mae). Since GSE bonds are not issued by federal agencies that do not have the same federal backing. Given this higher level of default risk they will typically have a higher yield than both Treasury bonds and federal agency bonds.

Corporate Bonds

Corporate bonds are debt securities sold by companies in order to meet their capital requirement needs. Corporate bonds are issued with or without collateral and are repaid based on the future earnings of the company. Since these securities are issued by individual companies and are not backed by the power of the government they carry more default and credit risk than Treasury or government bonds. Corporate bonds are typically issued with a $1,000 face value and are sold at a price that reflects the risk of the bond and the issuing company as compared to the market conditions. Based on the risk level associated with the bond, the market conditions, and the resulting required yield the bond may sell at a premium, discount, or at the par (face) value. If the resulting yield on a bond is higher than the interest rate (coupon rate) set on a bond than the bond will sell at a discount, lower than its $1,000 face value. On the other hand if the yield is lower than the coupon rate, then the bond will sell at a premium, higher than the $1,000 face value. If the yield and the coupon rate happen to be equal then the bond will sell for exactly $1,000.

Corporate bonds that are not backed by some type of collateral are known as debentures or subordinated debentures. They are both unsecured bonds where subordinated debentures, or junior debt, have a lower claim for repayment. Bonds that have an asset pledged as collateral are categorized by the type of collateral that backs the bond issue. A mortgage bond is a secured bond that is backed by real property owned by the issuing company. A collateral trust bond is a secured bond that is backed by a financial asset, such as stock or other bond, owned by the company. Lastly, an equipment trust certificate is a secured bond that is backed by a specific piece of equipment used in the operations of the business.

A mortgage backed security (MBS) is a specific type of asset backed security that has a pool of mortgages as collateral. Those mortgages, in turn, have real property as its collateral. The MBS is a multilayered asset that funds the financing for the pool of mortgages that subsequently funds the financing for the real property that is purchased by the mortgages. The MBS is issued by federal government agencies, a GSE, or a private financial institution and is sold by a broker in the capital markets. The mortgages that underlie the MBS must be issued by an authorized and regulated financial institution. In general, an asset backed security (ABS) is secured by a pool of assets, such as loans, leases, consumer debt, accounts receivables, etc.

Municipal Securities (Munis)

Municipal securities are debt securities that are issued by state and local governments. They are used to finance community projects or institutions, like hospitals, colleges, and transportation services. Munis are normally thought of as an attractive tax advantage investment because it is tax-exempt on interest income. They are usually issued as either general obligation bonds or revenue bonds. The general obligation bonds are backed and repaid by the credit and tax ability of the issuing state or local government. Therefore these bonds are unsecured and issued on the belief that the tax revenue will be sufficient to repay the debt. A revenue bond is backed by specific revenue from the project the bond was used to fund, such as a toll road or sports stadium.

Short-term Debt Securities

The Money Market refers to the market for short-term, highly liquid debt securities. The maturity of the securities that trade in this market range from one day to one year. The most common securities in the money markets are U.S. T-Bills, negotiable certificate of deposit (CD), banker's acceptances, commercial paper, and repurchase agreements (repos).

A negotiable CD is similar to traditional bank CD, except that it carries a minimum face value of $100,000 and can be sold in the secondary markets. Investors are typically larger institutional investors that want a safe, highly liquid, and short-term investment.

Banker's acceptances are funding guarantees by commercial banks for a specific commercial transaction. A banker's acceptance represents the promise of payment at a specified date and is usually sold in the secondary markets at a discount of the face value. Therefore no interest is paid, rather the return for the investor is the difference in price versus face value.

Commercial paper is short-term corporate debt issued with maturities usually less than 270 days. Corporations usually use commercial paper to meet short-term financing needs like inventory purchases and receivable financing. Similar to the other money market securities it is sold at a discount of the face value and pays no interest over the life of the security.

Repurchase agreements (repos) are typically used with short-term government securities like T-Bills. The seller of the repo sells the government security with the intent to repurchase the security from the investor at a higher price the following day. The buyer of the security is engaging in a reverse repo.

Money Market Mutual Funds

Money Market Mutual Funds are portfolios of a collection of money market instruments and are a way of investing in a diverse set of safe and highly liquid securities. In general, these funds maintain a net asset value of $1 per share and invest in high quality short-term debt securities.

Callable Bonds

Callable bonds have an embedded provision for the early retirement of the bond issue at the discretion of the issuer. Typically an issuer will exercise this provision in the event of sharp declines in market yields. A significant drop in market yields will result in a premium bond issue with a coupon rate that is higher than the market required yield for that bond. Therefore the issuer can potentially "call-in" that bond issue and reissue new bonds with a much lower interest rate at par value.

Puttable Bonds

A puttable bond carries a provision that allows the bondholder to choose to have the issuer repurchase the bond at face value prior to the maturity date of the bond. Bondholders will tend to exercise this option when yields rise sharply, resulting in decreased bond values. When market yields increase existing bonds will likely become discount bonds and new bond issues will have higher coupon rates. Therefore bondholders with a put option will sell back the existing bond and repurchase the new higher coupon bonds.

Bond Ratings

Bond rating serve as a qualitative measure of the credit quality of a bond issue and the credit-worthiness of the issuer. There are three main U.S. firms that serve as rating agencies for companies and government agencies: Standard & Poor's, Moody's, and Fitch. These agencies provide independent assessments of an issuer's ability to meet their financial obligations. The rating agencies all use a letter based grading system to show

	Rating Description	Moody's	Standard & Poor's	Fitch
Investment Grade	Highest credit quality; issuer has a strong ability to meet its obligations	Aaa	AAA	AAA
	Very high credit quality/ low risk of default	Aa1 Aa2 Aa3	AA+ AA AA-	AA
	High credit quality, but more vulnerable to changes in the business or economy	A1 A2 A3	A+ A A-	A
	Adequate credit quality for now, but more likely to be impaired if conditions worsen	Baa1 Baa2 Baa3	BBB+ BBB BBB-	BBB
Non-investment Grade	Below investment grade, but a good chance the issuer can meet commitments	Ba1 Ba2 Ba3	BB+ BB BB-	BBB
	Significant credit risk, but issuer is presently able to meet obligations	B1 B2 B3	B+ B B-	BB
	High default risk	Caa1 Caa2	CCC+ CCC	CCC CC
	Issuer failed to meet schedules interests or principal payments	C	D	DDD DD D

their credit ratings with the top rating for all three agencies being a triple-A (AAA or Aaa) rating. Below is a detailed chart of the ratings of each of the rating agencies.

2.1.3 OPTIONS

Options are financial derivative securities that represents the right to either buy or sell an underlying asset. A call option gives the holder the right to buy the underlying asset on or before a specified date (exercise date) for a given price, known as the exercise or strike price. A put option gives the holder the right to sell the underlying asset for the exercise price on or before the exercise date. The cost to the option buyer is the option premium which is function of six factors: time to expiration, market interest rate, underlying asset value, strike price, price volatility of the asset, and income payments of the asset.

Options are typically bought and sold using stocks as the underlying asset. An option buyer can buy options from a seller, or option writer, given their outlook on the stock. For option buyers that are optimistic on the stock and think that the stock will increase they can take a long position by buying call options. For an option buyer that is pessimistic on the stock they can take a short position by buying put options. On the other hand, individuals can also sell or write options given their outlook for the stock. An optimistic option writer that believes the stock will increase can write a put option for a pessimistic option buyer. An option writer that believes that the stock is decreasing can write a call option.

When the underlying asset of an option is an index the security is known as an index option. Therefore the holder has the right, but not obligation, to settle at the value of the index. For example, an investor can buy a call index option on the S&P 500 index if they felt that bullish on the market and that the value would increase. If the investor were correct they would choose to exercise the index option and cash-settle for the difference between the exercise price and index value. Notice that no stocks are bought or sold and that index options are always cash-settled when exercised.

Option Moneyness

In the money options imply that a call option's exercise price is below the value of the underlying asset or that a put option's exercise price is above the value of the underlying asset. An option that is in the money could be exercised at a profit.

Out of the money options imply that a call option's exercise price is above the value of the underlying asset or that a put option's exercise price is below the value of the underlying asset. An option that is out of the money would be exercised at a loss.

At the money options imply that the exercise price and the underlying asset value are equal. In this case both a call and put option with the same exercise price would be at the money.

Option Strategies

An uncovered, or naked, option is when an option writer sells an option without owning the underlying asset. For example, an investor writes a naked call stock option and sells it to another investor without owning the underlying stock. If the call buyer chooses to exercise the option and buy the stock at the exercise price the writer must deliver the stock to the buyer. Uncovered option strategies on either the call or put side are generally considered speculative and somewhat risky.

A covered option strategy is generally used for hedging purposes. A covered call strategy is when an investors has a long position in the underlying stock and writes a call on the underlying stock. The benefit to the strategy is that the investor will gain income from the premium on the option. This strategy is effective when there are only minor fluctuations in the value of the underlying asset.

A protective put strategy is when an investor has a long position in the underlying asset and wants to guard against a significant decline in the asset's value. Therefore to protect against a potential loss the investor also buys a put option contract with an appropriate exercise price. This will give the investor the ability to hedge their downside risk.

A straddle option strategy is used when investors are reasonably sure that a large movement in the underlying asset is pending but is unsure which direction the move will be. In this case the investor will purchase both a call option and a put option to reap a benefit regardless of the direction the price moves. The only caveat is that the movement has to be larger than the combined premiums for the call and put options purchased. For example, if an investor paid $3 per call option and $2 per put option for a straddle option on a stock, then the stock would have to move by more than $5 per share for the strategy to be profitable.

In 1973, the Options Clearing Corporation (OCC) was established to act as an equity derivatives clearing corporation. The purpose of the organization is to maintain stability in the options market, issue and guarantee traded options, and to provide settlement services. The OCC provides guidance for the market through its option disclosure document (ODD) that documents the various types of options, the structure of option contracts, the risks associated with option trading, as well as other option related information.

2.1.4. INVESTMENT COMPANIES

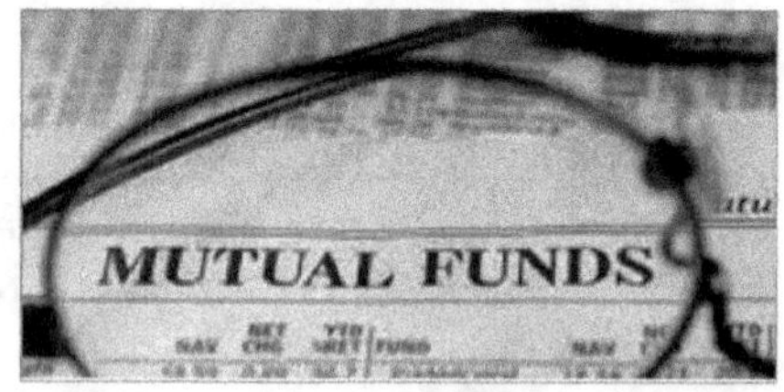

An investment company is a company that pools the funds of investors with the purpose of reinvesting those funds in financial securities. Investment companies are often referred to as mutual funds. Mutual funds are typically structured as a closed-end fund, open-end fund, or unit investment trust. Each mutual fund will have a specific objective that drives the investment philosophy of the fund managers. Investors tend to look to mutual funds as a quick and easy way of investing in a diversified portfolio of securities without the responsibilities of record keeping, legal, accounting, and tax services.

A closed-end fund sells a fixed number of shares of the company. Once all shares of the company are sold trading of the shares is done between investors in the secondary market at a price that is determined by supply and demand. Given this structure the price that the mutual fund sells for tends to be different than the net asset value (NAV) of the company's investments.

An open-end fund allows investors to trade shares with the company at any time. Under this structure the number of shares vary as shares are bought and sold therefore the price of an open-end fund will be the NAV. As investors trade with the fund they are subject to fees for buying and selling their shares, known as loads. A fee to purchase shares of the fund are called front-end loads and fees to sell shares back to the fund are back-end loads.

The shares of a unit investment trust can also be traded with the investment company. While the investment portfolio of a closed-end or open-end will change based on the objective of the company and the strategy of the fund manager the portfolio of a unit investment trust is fixed.

Similar to mutual funds variable annuities give an investor the ability to invest in a diversified portfolio of securities. Variable annuities have a number of subaccounts that cover different asset categories, like stocks, bonds, etc. The main difference between a variable annuity and a mutual fund is the insurance benefits that are offered for a fee. For example, the death benefit feature of the variable annuity protects the invested capital of the asset. While mutual funds have a traditional risk of loss of capital, a variable annuity with a death benefit preserves the capital investment for any beneficiaries of the annuity upon the death of the initial investor.

2.1.5 MUNICIPAL FUND SECURITIES

529 Plan

A 529 plan allows a tax advantaged way for individuals to save and pay for higher education expenses. The plans are offered as either prepaid tuition plans or savings plans. A prepaid tuition plan designates a specific institution and allows individuals to pay for tuition expenses in advance at current tuition rates. Savings plans allow individuals to save for expenses at any institutions.

A 529 plan gives any individual the ability to save money for higher education expenses for any individual they choose, regardless of relation. Given state limits individuals may be able to save for as many individuals they wish. The assets of the plan belong to the holder and can be used for any beneficiary they choose. Qualified distributions for higher education expenses are tax-free on federal tax returns and contributions are tax deductible at the state level.

Local Government Investment Pool (LGIP)

A local government investment pool is managed by a local government for the benefit of that government. Similar to a money market mutual fund a LGIP pools the funds of various jurisdictions and invests the funds in securities allowed under the guidelines of the LGIP. A pool may be set up as a government sponsored pool or as a joint powers agreement between multiple state and local government agencies.

In December 2014, the Achieving a Better Life Experience (ABLE) account provision was signed into law. The provision was created to assist families with disabled children. ABLE accounts are set up to help these families save and pay for expenses related to disability services.

2.1.6 DIRECT PARTICIPATION PROGRAMS (DPPS)

A direct participation program (DPP) is a pool security that allows investors the opportunity to invest in a business and access their cash flow and tax benefits. DPPs are typically investments in real estate or energy companies over a long horizon. A DPP is normally set up as a limited partnership where investors (or limited partners) invest funds that are invested by the general partner. DPPs are not traded assets, which limits the liquidity of the asset and prohibits accurate pricing.

The most common types of DPPs are a non-traded real estate investment trust (REIT), energy exploration companies, non-listed business development companies (BDC), and leasing companies.

2.1.7 REAL ESTATE INVESTMENT TRUSTS (REITS)

A real estate investment trust (REIT) is a company that is created to invest in real estate for income production. REITs are required to meet specific guidelines in order to maintain its active status. In order for a company to be qualified as a REIT is must:

- Be taxable as a corporation
- Have an active board of directors
- Have at least 100 shareholders
- Have no more than half of its shares be held by five or less individuals (entities)
- Invest 75 percent or more of its assets in real estate or cash (or T-Bills)
- Make at least 75 percent of its income from real estate related business
- Payout at least 90 percent of its taxable income to shareholders in the form of dividends

REITs are typically structured as an equity REIT, mortgage REIT, or a hybrid REIT. An equity REIT directly purchases income-producing real estate. A mortgage REIT invests in financial real estate products like mortgages, mortgage backed securities and other real estate loans. A hybrid REIT is a combination of an equity and mortgage REIT and invests in both real property and mortgages.

2.1.8 HEDGE FUNDS

A hedge fund is an investment company that is set up to use various strategies to maximize the return of the fund. Since hedge funds actively seek above average returns their risk profile tends to be higher than normal. Given this atypical management strategy investors are required to be "accredited" and require a substantial initial investment.

Hedge funds often make use of derivatives and international markets in order to earn higher than average returns. Given the variation of the investment strategies and the sophistication of the investors hedge funds have historically had very little SEC regulation.

Hedge funds are normally set up as limited partnerships that restrict the amount of accredited investors. Investors are generally locked into the investment for at least one year with very little expectation of liquidity. Withdrawals from the hedge fund may also be restricted to a quarterly or semiannual basis.

2.1.9 EXCHANGE-TRADED PRODUCTS (ETPS)

An exchange-traded product (ETP) is a security that is valued based on the value of an associated asset, such as indices, currencies or commodities. ETPs can be formed as exchange-traded funds (ETFs) or exchange-traded notes (ETNs) and are generally passively managed since they track a specific index or commodity. The most popular ETF is the SPDR ETF that tracks the S&P 500 index. Since these products are traded on an exchange they require a brokerage account to trade and may incur higher transactions cost, as compared to an open-end mutual fund.

An ETF is a security that is constructed to mimic the movements of an index or commodity. Similar to a closed-end fund an ETF trades similar to a stock as its price changes throughout the day based on the market forces. Given this an ETF price will typically be different than its NAV.

Exchange-traded notes (ETNs) are unsecured unsubordinated debt securities (debentures) with no coupon payments that are traded on secondary exchanges. Financial institutions issue ETNs based on an underlying market index and take its value from the performance of that index, rather than investing in a pool of securities. Upon maturity of the ETN the financial institution makes payments to the investor based on the performance of the underlying index, less any applicable fees.

2.2 INVESTMENT RISKS

Section Overview:

2.2.1 Types of Risk

2.2.2 Risk Reduction Strategies

2.2.1 TYPES OF RISK

Capital Risk

Capital risk is the possible loss of the investment portion of a portfolio. It generally refers to all risky assets that do not have a guarantee of preservation of invested funds. Therefore investors are subject to capital risk when they invest in stocks, corporate bonds, and alternative assets.

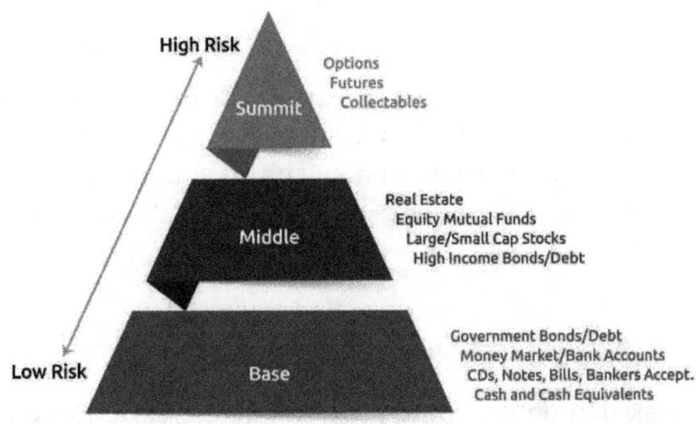

Credit Risk

Credit risk is the possible loss of invested funds due to the failure to pay on the part of a borrower. This risk is typically associated with debt securities like loans and bonds that require an interest and principal payment. The risk reflects the probability that the lender will not receive the scheduled payments. Credit risk also represents the risk that receivables are not paid.

Currency Risk

Currency risk is the risk that a change in the value of a currency will affect the value of another currency. Multinational companies have a higher exposure to currency risk because they operate in a number of countries and use various currencies. Typically translation effects are evident when a company converts operating cash flows from a local currency to the company's main functional currency. In order to mitigate currency risk investors or companies will use hedging techniques to reduce the impact of fluctuations in exchange rates.

Inflationary Risk

Inflationary risk is the risk that the real value of an asset will vary over time. The real value of an asset is usually defined as the nominal value (observed value) minus expected inflation. The inflationary risk is primarily the risk that unexpected inflation will have an unknown impact on the value of an asset.

Interest Rate Risk

Interest rate risk is the risk that the value of an investment, like a stock or a bond, will change as the level of interest rates in the market changes. There is an inverse relationship between an investment's value and interest rates. So that as interest rates rise an investment's value will decrease. Likewise as interest rate fall an investment's value will increase.

Reinvestment Rate Risk

Reinvestment rate risk is the risk that if an investment with fixed payments matures the investor will not be able to reinvest the funds at the same rate. The risk has a higher impact on an investment when the rate on the investment is high and rates in the market are on a decline.

Prepayment Risk

Prepayment risk is the risk that the cash flows of an investment will not occur as planned. For example, if a 30-year bond is called in after ten years the bond holder will not receive the remaining twenty years of coupon payments. The likelihood of that investor reinvesting the principal and getting the same cash flows is usually low and will therefore have negative impact on the investment return.

Liquidity Risk

Liquidity risk is the risk that an investment cannot be converted into cash without a large cost. Investments that are not readily marketable and cannot be bought or sold quickly are considered to be illiquid and will have high liquidity risk. There are a number of ways to determine the amount of liquidity risk an investment carries including the trading volume, trading turnover, and the bid-ask spread. The smaller the volume and turnover the higher the liquidity risk. On the other hand the larger the bid-ask spread the higher the liquidity risk.

Systematic Risk

Systematic risk is the risk of an investment's value changing as a result of market-wide changes. For example, the risk of an economic recession would affect the value of most, if not all, of the securities in that market. Therefore it is often referred to as market, unavoidable or undiversifiable risk.

Unsystematic Risk

Unsystematic risk is the business risk associated with a specific firm or specific industry. For example, the risk of a company losing a major lawsuit and having to make an unexpected substantial payout. This risk is also known as firm-specific, avoidable, or diversifiable risk.

Political Risk

Political risk is the risk that the political landscape could have an adverse effect on the value of an asset. Political risk tends to be more evident during election time when there are changes in the administration or legislative make up.

2.2.2 RISK REDUCTION STRATEGIES

Diversification

Diversification is a tool used to mitigate the risk associated with a single investment. To incorporate the idea of diversification into an investment strategy a portfolio is formed. A portfolio is a combination of two or more negatively correlated securities. The goal of the portfolio is to significantly reduce unsystematic risk by combining securities that will offset losses of other securities in the portfolio. Therefore it is important to find securities that are negatively correlated to maximize the diversification effect. For example, an investor that currently holds Coca Cola stock and wants to create a portfolio to diversify their investment will likely choose to in- vest in Walmart rather than Pepsi stock. Thereby reducing the unsystematic risk associated with Coca Cola and the soft drink industry. While a diversified portfolio, with various domestic securities, may be able to reduce the unsystematic risk it does not have an effect on the systematic risk component of a security. This is because all the securities in the portfolio will be subject to the market factors and market risk. Most research has found that the optimal number of securities in a portfolio to maximize the diversification effect is around twenty-thirty securities, depending on the correlation between the securities.

Portfolio Rebalancing

Portfolio rebalancing is the process of resetting the weights of a portfolio based on the risk and return objectives of the portfolio. The process is guided by the asset allocation structure of the portfolio. Asset allocation is the broad decision of which asset classes the portfolio

will hold. For example, an investor may choose an asset allocation with 60 percent equity investments, 30 percent debt investments, and 10 percent other investments.

Hedging

A hedge is an investment that is used to mitigate the adverse price volatility of an asset. Typically a hedge for an asset buyer consist of entering into a contract that will lock in the current price, given an expectation of rising prices. On the other hand, a hedge for an asset seller consist of entering into a contract that will lock in the current price, given an expectation of falling prices. Derivative contracts like futures, forwards, and options contracts are the main tools for hedging purposes.

Chapter 3

TRADING, CUSTOMER ACCOUNTS AND PROHIBITED ACTIVITIES

3.1 TRADING, SETTLEMENT AND CORPORATE ACTIONS

Section Overview:

3.1.1 Orders and Strategies

3.1.2 Investment Returns

3.1.3 Trade Settlement

3.1.4 Corporate Actions

3.1.1 ORDERS AND STRATEGIES

The major types of orders are market orders, limit orders, and stop orders.

A market order is an immediate order to buy or sell a security at the best price available.

A limit order is a price contingent order that sets a minimum price (sell limit order) or a maximum price (buy limit order) for the order. A sell limit order will only execute at or above the specified price. A buy limit order will only execute at or below the specified price.

A stop order (stop-loss order) is a price contingent order that triggers a market order to buy or sell once a price target is reached. A buy stop order is often used with short selling so that a market will immediately purchase a security once a specified price target is reached. A sell stop order is often used as protection for stocks that are owned so that a market order will immediately sell a security once it hits a specified price.

A stop-limit order is a double price contingent order that triggers a limit order when a specific price target is hit. The limit order will then go into effect and the trade will only execute if the limit order specifications are met.

A day order is an order that has a one day life and expires at the end of the trading day.

A good-till-cancelled (GTC) order (open order) will remain active until it is either executed or cancelled. Long-term GTC orders must be renewed every six months.

A discretionary order is a conditional order that allows for flexibility in the execution and amount of a price contingent trade.

A discretionary account allows a broader level of flexibility for a broker to buy and sell securities for a client without direct consent. Transactions must follow the general objectives of the client's investment goals.

A non-discretionary account does not allow for broker flexibility and is essentially run by the client. Brokers can still make suggestions and will execute the transactions but all decisions will be made by the client.

A solicited transaction is a trade that is made based on the suggestion of a registered agent. An unsolicited transaction occurs when a client makes a trade without the advice of an agent.

A bid price is the price at which a dealer is willing to pay for a security. An ask price is the price a dealer is willing to accept for a security. Therefore the dealer's buy price is the bid price and their sell price is the ask price. The dealer will always set the ask price higher than the bid price so that they "buy low and sell high." The difference between the bid and ask price is known as the bid-ask spread and represents the profit that a dealer makes. It also gives a sense of the liquidity of the security. The lower the liquidity and amount of trading a dealer will make the spread wider to make enough profit. On the other hand, the higher the liquidity and trading volume a dealer will be willing to tighten the spread and make the profit on the volume of transactions.

Depending on market expectations, an investor may choose to either go long or short in their investments. A long (bull) position is one that is based on an expectation of rising values (bullish expectations). An investor would buy a security if they think that the price will increase over time. Thereby they would receive a profit from the increase in value. A short (bear) position would follow an expectation of falling prices (bearish expectations). Given their expectations, an investor would want to sell a security at the current value and buy later when the price drops.

This can be accomplished through a short sale process in which an investor borrows the security from a broker. They sell the borrowed shares today at the higher price and plan to repurchase and return the shares later at the lower price.

Most brokers only allow short sales on certain types of securities and only for customers that have a margin account.

Sales, Stop-Loss Orders, and Short Sales

In many cases, simply closing out or selling a position is the best decision when an investor finds it necessary to diversify as the result of an over weighted security or asset class. Investors can often sell assets that currently have capital losses in their portfolio to offset gains and neutralize the tax effects. But investors overexposed in a security or asset class cannot always be sure that they will recognize the need to rebalance or that they will have sufficient time to "manage" the sale of the position and offsetting loss positions before the appreciated position declines in value. In addition, even after the unprecedented losses experienced during the financial crisis, with the market appreciation of the past few years, some investors may be sitting on substantially appreciated positions where it is often difficult to find offsetting loss positions within their portfolios.

Two relatively simple techniques that investors have to protect themselves from loss in these situations are stop-loss orders and short sales.

Stop-Loss Orders

Stop-loss orders are generally good-till-cancelled or standing orders with brokers to sell (or buy) a security held long (short) if the price moves below (above) a specified value. For instance, if an investor owns (is short) a stock currently worth $100, he could place a stop-loss order with his broker to sell (buy) the stock if it falls (rises) to $90 ($110). In most (but not all) cases, the investor can rest assured that if the price moves adversely, he will lose only about $10.

The problems, however, with stop-loss orders are three-fold. First, (relatively minor, but important nonetheless), the investor has to or should reassess and reset the stop-loss orders as the value of the position changes. For instance, if the investor owns the stock with a market price of $100 and a stop-loss of $90, and the market price moves to $110, he should consider resetting the stop-loss order (e.g., at $100) to protect the increased gain.

Second, (an important consideration in most cases), the broker will actually sell the position if the market price hits the stop-loss price. Therefore, the investor will be liable for tax on any gains realized. In many cases, investors wish to hedge against losses without realizing gains and paying tax—if that is the case, stop-loss orders are generally not a viable choice of strategy.

Third (perhaps, most important) investors have no assurance that trades triggered by their stop-loss orders will take place at a price that is anywhere close to their stop-loss trigger price. For instance, in the market crash of October 1987, many investors who had stop-loss orders in place discovered much to their chagrin, that their trades had taken place at prices 10, 20, or even 30 percent or more below their stop-loss price. In such volatile market situations, the stop-loss orders enter the queue for trades with all the other market orders and might not be executed until the market price has declined far below the stop-loss price. In such markets, large transactions by large institutional investors frequently precipitate or foreshadow the decline in value. If they place their market orders before the security hits an investor's stop-loss price, the market price may move right through (or "gap" through) the stop-loss price before the institutions' and other investors' transactions are cleared, leaving the trades for investors with stop-loss orders to take place after much of the market move (and investment loss) has already occurred.

Short Sales

A short-sale strategy involves selling securities borrowed from a third party. In general, the investor's broker or custodian arranges to borrow the securities from the margin account of one of its other customers. While short-sellers maintain their short position, they must reimburse the lenders for any dividends or interest paid on the borrowed securities. If the securities decline in value, the short-seller may then purchase the securities on the open market at a lower price than the initial sales price. The short-seller returns the purchased stock to the third party and pays tax on the gain (difference between the initial sales price and subsequent purchase price) at long-term or short-term capital gain tax rates, depending on the holding period. If the short-seller closes out the short position by buying the securities after they have appreciated, the loss is treated as long-term or short-term capital loss.

Short Sales against the Box

Investors use short sales for hedging purposes when they sell short "against the box." This means that they sell short securities that they also hold long in their portfolio. This technique offers perfect negative correlation because gains or losses on the long position are perfectly matched by losses or gains on the short position. As long as an investor maintains both the long and short position, the economic value of the investor's position cannot change. The investor is perfectly immunized against loss on the long position, but also foregoes any possibility of further gain while the short against the box is in place.

Originally, investors used this strategy primarily for tax timing purposes. An investor that had an appreciated position that he wanted to sell, but for which he did not want to incur a taxable gain, could enter into a short sale against the box. This allowed the investor to perfectly hedge and thus completely avoid the consequences of any further price changes (equivalent to the situation if the position had been sold outright and the investor simply no longer owned the security) without requiring the investor to declare the taxable gain (because the position was still open). Ultimately, the investor could opt to close out the position at some future point of his choosing. Doing this allowed the investor to defer the tax bill until the position was closed, possibly shift the income to a year that would be more favorable in light of tax laws or other taxable events, but eliminate all risk in the meantime (as though the position had been sold).

Unfortunately, short sales against the box now are treated for income tax purposes as constructive sales, making them much less attractive for hedging purposes. Although investors can still use this technique to prevent economic loss on an appreciated position indefinitely, they generally will have to realize their gain and pay tax on the appreciated long position in the tax year in which they enter into the short sale against the box. Investors step-up the basis of their long position by the amount of the realized gain and start a new holding period for the long position, just as if they had actually sold and then repurchased the securities. If they later close out the short position by delivering the securities they hold long, losses and gains on the long and short positions will cancel out, so they will incur no further taxable consequences. If they later close out the short position by purchasing new securities in the market for delivery, rather than by delivering the securities they hold long, they will recognize long-term or short-term gain or loss on the short position, depending upon the holding period of the short position.

Short Sales of Close Substitutes

In light of the currently unfavorable constructive sale rules for short selling against the box, an investor can, alternatively, select a short sale involving securities of a company in the same industry, which has a close, but not perfect, positive correlation to the securities the investor wants to protect. In general, even if closely correlated, short sales of a different company's securities will not be treated as a constructive sale. For example, an investor who has a very significant holding in Exxon Mobile might sell short a similar amount of Chevron. However, as discussed earlier, the individual business risk generally is greater than the industry or market risk. Therefore, any time correlation is not perfect, a hedging strategy can fail. Chevron's stock could soar while Exxon Mobile's stock plummets, putting the investor in double jeopardy. Simply stated, investors cannot use short-selling strategies to hedge perfectly against company-specific events such as fraud or massive liability, unless they short that specific company's securities.

Short Sale of Exchange-Traded Funds

The strategies just described allow investors to avoid company-specific risk (on at least one side of the position). In recent years, the markets have introduced exchange-traded index funds (ETFs) that permit investors to buy long or sell short certain baskets of stocks (such as the basket of stocks that comprise an index like the S&P 500). This can provide investors with a more broadly diversified correlation (or inverse correlation) for market and industry or asset class risks. For example, the investor mentioned in the previous section could sell short the S&P Energy sector to hedge against his position in Exxon Mobile. This would not protect him from the company-specific risks for Exxon Mobile, but it would perhaps ensure better protection from the sector risks of Exxon Mobile, as compared to when Chevron was used for the short side of the position.

A cash account is a brokerage account that allows an investor to buy securities using the money they deposit in their account.

A margin account is a brokerage account that allows an investor to use their deposited funds as well as to borrow funds from the broker to invest in securities. Trading on margin increases the risk of the investment because the margin loan (plus interest) must be repaid regardless of the profit of the investment.

A naked investment position is a position where an investor is either long or short and does not have any protection from losses. On the other hand, a position can be covered or hedged to limit the potential losses. For example, an investor may decide to mitigate the potential losses of being long on a stock by either purchasing a put contract or going short on a related stock. Either method would offset potential losses of the long position in the original stock.

Investors can also have naked positions in option investments. Option buyers have less risk than option sellers because they are limited to the loss of the premium that they pay for the option contract. On the other hand, an option seller (writer) may be exposed to a much higher level of risk. For example, an option writer sells a naked call option, without owing the underlying asset, on a security that has a sudden drastic increase in value. The call buyer will likely exercise the option at the strike (exercise) price forcing the writer to purchase the security for the extraordinarily high price and suffering a substantial loss.

Naked options can also be covered or hedged using other options, this is often referred to as option combinations.

3.1.2 INVESTMENT RETURNS

An investment's total return is comprised of a cash return and a capital gains yield. The cash return is the return received from payments from interest or dividend distributions. The capital gains yield is the return from the change in the investment's value over time. It represents the actual rate of return on an investment or portfolio for a specific period of time.

Example. The total return of an investment in 100 shares of stock at an initial price of $25 ($2,500 initial investment) and a $1 per share dividend ($100 total dividend payout) can be calculated as follows. Given that after one year the stock value increases to $30 the capital gains portion of the total return would be the $5 per share appreciation in value expressed as a percent of the initial price. Therefore the total change in value of $500 ($5 per share multiplied by 100 shares) divided by the initial $2,500 investment would yield a 20 percent capital gains yield. The cash return, or dividend yield in the case of a stock investment, would be the $100 total dividend payout divided by the initial $2,500 investment or 4 percent. Together the capital gains yield and dividend yield make up the total return of 24 percent.

Dividends

Dividends represent payouts to the shareholders of a corporation. The amount and type of the dividend paid out is at the discretion of the company's board of directors.

Cash Dividend

A cash dividend is the most common type of dividend and is paid based on a schedule, usually on a quarterly basis. Companies normally pay cash dividends using specific dividend dates.

The company first announces a dividend on the declaration date. The declaration will include the amount, type, expected payment date, and the date of record.

The payment date is the actual date that the company will issue payment to the stockholders of record.

The record date (date of record) is the date that an owner must be the registered owner of the stock in order to receive the dividend on the payment date.

The last important dividend date is the ex-dividend date. Since it will likely take a few days to transfer ownership of the stock the ex-dividend date represents the date that a new owner would need to purchase a security to be able to transfer it in time to receive the dividend.

Stock Dividend

A stock dividend is a distribution of additional shares of stock to the stockholders instead of a cash distribution. Current stockholders receive additional shares of stock in proportion to the shares they currently hold.

A scrip dividend is a note that promises to make a cash dividend in the near future. These dividends are issued when a company has too much illiquid assets, like accounts receivable.

A bond dividend is a long-term scrip dividend that also accrues interest over its duration.

A property dividend is a dividend that is made in the form of property instead of cash or stock.

A liquidating dividend is a dividend distribution that pays back the original contributed capital of the business. This is usually associated with the closing of the business.

Yields

A current yield is the cash income return from the interest in a fixed-income security, like a bond. The current yield is the annual income payment expressed as a percentage of the investment's market value.

The yield-to-maturity (YTM) represents the total return of a fixed-income security. It is calculated as the rate of return for receiving interest payments over the life of the security and the rate of appreciation in the value of the security.

The yield-to-call (YTC) is the yield on a fixed-income security with a callable feature. A callable feature allows the issuer to call in or retire a security before its maturity. If a security is retired prior to the end of its life the total return will not equal the anticipated yield-to-maturity, instead it would be a different value known as the yield-to-call.

Cost basis

It is important for investors to keep track of the cost of their investments. Specifically for tax purposes, the cost or cost basis of an investment allows an investor to accurately calculate the taxable gains received from an investment. Brokerage firms and mutual funds are required to disclose the cost basis of all trades annually to their clients.

Benchmarks

A benchmark is a performance standard that allows investors to compare the returns of a security against a related market measure. Broad market indexes and sector indexes serve as ideal benchmarks. For example, the S&P 500 index that tracks the price movements of the 500 largest U.S. stocks is often used as a benchmark for large company stock investments. For small stock investments the NASDAQ composite index may be a more appropriate benchmark than the S&P 500, since it is comprised of smaller stocks.

Identifying an appropriate index is important to measuring the performance of an investment. Benchmark are often chosen based on the risk, size, sector, and other characteristics of the investment.

Investors that want to benefit from broad market increases and do not wish to invest in one specific security may decide to use index investing as an investment strategy. The idea behind index investing is to mimic the performance and return of the market or sector underlying the index. For example, an investor that wants to invest in large stocks may decide to invest in an index that tracks the S&P 500, like the SPDR ETF. The SPDR ETF is an S&P 500 exchange traded fund that closely tracks the actual S&P 500 index.

3.1.3 TRADE SETTLEMENT

A settlement period is the window of time between the settlement date and the actual transaction date. This period gives the related participants time to prepare for the transaction. During this period the buyer gets funds ready while the seller prepares to deliver the asset. Depending on the asset the settlement period ranges from the same day to a few days after the settlement date. The SEC is responsible for setting the settlement period for different assets. For example, commercial paper is often settled on the same day (T), U.S. Treasuries are settled the next day (T+1), most securities like stocks and mutual funds settle within two days (T+2). As technology and trade efficiency has improved the settlement period has shortened from T+5 to T+3 and now down to T+2, as of 2017.

Holding Securities

Investors hold securities in one of three ways: as a physical certificate, as a street name registration, or as a direct registration.

Physical Certificate

A physical certificate registration is where an investor holds a paper certificate for the security as proof of ownership.

Street Name

A street name registration is when the investor's name is not recorded with the issuer instead the broker's name is registered with the issuer. The brokerage firm in turn records the name of the investor on their books. This is also known as book-entry form.

Physical Certificate

A physical certificate registration is where an investor holds a paper certificate for the security as proof of ownership.

Street Name

A street name registration is when the investor's name is not recorded with the issuer instead the broker's name is registered with the issuer. The brokerage firm in turn records the name of the investor on their books. This is also known as book-entry form.

Direct Registration

A direct registration is where the issuer records the investor's name on their books and holds the actual certificate in book-entry form.

Delivery

Physical delivery of an asset has become rare in investments. Most transactions are settled by book-entry. The term physical delivery is often used only in the derivatives markets where the underlying asset is actually delivered. The vast majority of derivative contracts are settled in cash however some are physically delivered by the contract date.

Book-entry of an asset is the come mode of transacting where ownership is transferred electronically without a physical transfer of the asset.

3.1.4 CORPORATE ACTIONS

Stock Split

A stock split is a corporate action that breaks up each share of a company's stock into a specific multiple of shares. For example, a 2-for-1 stock split will break up each share of stock into two shares of stock and a 3-for-1 split will break each share into three shares. The purpose of stock splits is usually to generate more liquidity for investors and to bring the share price in line. The act of a stock split will not change the fundamental value of the company so the total value of the company will be unchanged. This will force the price of the stock to react accordingly.

Therefore, after a 2-for-1 stock split the price of the stock be cut in half and the price after a 3-for-1 split will be a third of the original value.

Reverse Stock Split

A reverse stock split is a corporate action that works in the opposite direction from a stock split. It will decrease the number of shares outstanding and increase the stock price. For example, a 1-for-3 reverse stock split will reduce the number of shares to a third of what they were and triple the stock price.

Spinoff

A spinoff is a corporate action where a division or subsidiary of a parent company is made into an independent company distributing shares of the new company to the parent company's existing shareholders on a pro rata basis.

Share Repurchase

A share repurchase is a corporate action where the company buys back its own shares from the market. There are two methods commonly used to complete a share repurchase, a tender offer or an open market purchase.

Tender Offer

A tender offer is a request to buy back shares from their shareholders. The company will normally request a certain number of shares and the price range that they are willing to pay. After the shareholders respond to the request the company will review the offers and decide if they want to buy back the desired number of shares at the best price. If the company does not get the desired result from the tender offer they will then turn to the open market.

Open Market

An alternative to a tender offer would be to buy back the desired shares in the open market. The concern that companies face in the open markets is that they can't control the price. As soon as they announce the buy back the price of the shares will typically increase, often past their target price.

Mergers and Acquisitions

Mergers and acquisitions (M&A) refers to the action of combining the assets and resources of two or more companies. The process of an M&A can include a number of different types of corporate actions, including but not limited to, mergers, acquisitions, consolidations, tender offers, acquisition of assets, and management acquisitions.

Merger

In a merger the two companies mutually agree to a combination and will get the approval of the board of directors and existing shareholders. After the merger the two companies with usually operate under one name and one executive staff. Mergers are thought of as an agreement between the companies.

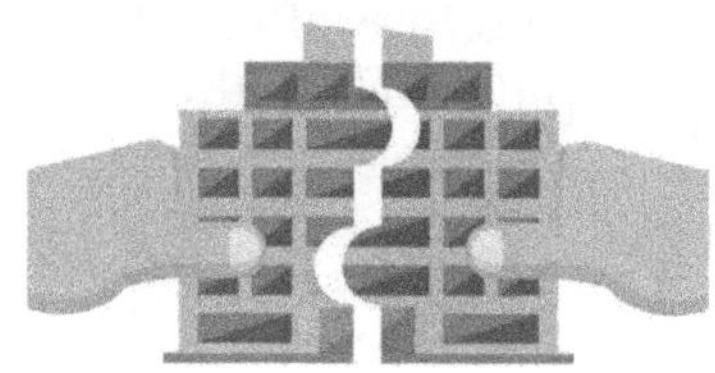

Acquisition

In an acquisition one company acts as the acquirer and takes over the other acquired firm. The process is usually done through the purchase of a majority number of shares of the acquired firm. Once control is established the acquirer will choose to either continue to run the acquired firm independently as a subsidiary or absorb the company in the firm as a division. Acquisitions are often seen in a hostile light especially when there is significant push back from the target company. If there is disagreement then it may be referred to as a "hostile takeover."

Consolidation

A consolidation is a business combination that generally results in the creation of a new company. Similar to a merger there is a discussion and subsequent approval by the board and shareholders. After the discussion and approval the two companies would normally cease to exist and a new company with new shares will emerge.

Tender Offer

In a business combination, one firm may use the tender offer strategy to obtain shares of the other company. The acquiring company will normally put out a communication that it is seeking to purchase a certain number of shares of the target company at a specific price. If they get the desired response from the shareholders they will then make the purchase and decide how to complete the merger or acquisition.

Acquisition of Assets

Under a purchase of assets strategy one company looks to acquire specific assets of another company. The idea is that the acquiring company sees value in a specific part of the target company but not the whole company. If the target company is willing to sell the desired assets then they will seek approval from the shareholders to make the transfer.

Management Acquisition

In a management acquisition the executive staff of the company leads a buyout of the company. In most cases, a management acquisition results in a public company going private through a debt leveraged buyout process. The process is often referred to as a management-led buyout (MBO) since the executives of the company acquire a controlling interest in the company. In the cases where a large amount of debt is used it is known as a levered buyout (LBO).

Proxy

A proxy refers to the authorization for someone to vote in place of another. Since the attendance at most company's annual meetings is low, voting by proxy has become the normal operating procedure. When a shareholder does not attend the annual meeting they have the ability to sign over their right to vote, not ownership, to someone or some group that will attend and can vote on their behalf.

Proxy Statement

A proxy statement is a document that outlines the company's annual report and information regarding topics that likely need to be voted on or discussed during an annual meeting. These topics may include board of director nominations, compensation packages, share decisions (e.g. distribution and repurchase decisions), etc.

3.2 CUSTOMER ACCOUNTS AND COMPLIANCE CONSIDERATIONS

Section Overview:

3.2.1 Account Types and Characteristics

3.2.2 Customer Account Registrations

3.2.3 Anti-Money Laundering (AML)

3.2.4 Books, Records, and Privacy

3.2.5 Communication with the Public and Suitability

3.2.1 ACCOUNT TYPES AND CHARACTERISTICS

Cash

A cash brokerage account is an account that requires investors to buy assets with all cash. This account does not allow the investor to borrow funds to invest on margin.

Margin

A margin brokerage account is an account that gives investors an option to borrow a certain percent of an investment purchase. Investors are charged interest for the borrowed funds and have to follow specific requirements of the account.

Options

An option brokerage account is necessary to trade derivative securities because of the unique characteristics of the securities. Therefore investors that desire to trade options will open a separate account in order to trade options. Most brokerage firms will require additional information regarding investment experience prior to opening an option account.

Discretionary versus Non-discretionary

A discretionary account gives a broker the authority to trade a client's securities without direct authorization from the client. Given a set of general objectives the client gives a blanket approval for transactions that meet their objectives.

A non-discretionary account limits the flexibility of brokers and requires them to get direct approval from the client prior to making a trade. Brokers will still make suggestions based on the client's objectives but are restricted from making trades without prior authorization.

Fee-based versus Commission

A fee-based advisor relationship is when the broker charges a flat fee for their services rather than a commission percentage of the transaction value. A fee-based advisor is subject to certain fiduciary requirements.

The major difference between a fee-based advisor and a commission-based advisor is the compensation arrangement with the client. A fee-based advisor will receive a flat fee for investment advice or for the amount of assets they manage. A commission-based advisor receives a percentage of each transaction value upon opening the account and for all subsequent transactions.

Fee-based advisors are subject to strict fiduciary rules regarding their relationship with their clients. The rules require the advisor to put the client's needs and interest above their firm's or personal needs. They are required to abide by the client's specific objectives and only sell them suitable products.

Commission-based advisors are compensated based only on the products that they sell to the client. They typically sell financial products such as insurance, annuities, and mutual funds. While this type of advisor is not strictly held to certain fiduciary rules they are do have to adhere to the suitability rules.

Educational Accounts

Educational accounts have been created with the specific purpose of saving for college expenses. The popularity of these accounts have grown with the increase in higher education cost. Alongside the popularity, a number of different investment vehicles have been introduced to help save for these expenses, each with their own benefits for different investors.

529 Plans

529 plans are college savings plans that are structured to follow the U.S. tax code which they're named after. There are two types of 529 plans in the market:

a. 529 prepaid tuition plan – investors pay for tuition expenses at the current rate at a specific college or university for future expenses. The money can still be transferred for expenses at another school or for another student.

b. 529 college savings account – investors saves money in this account for any qualified expenses (tuition, books, room and board, etc.) at a qualified college or university.

In either case the investment contributions are taxable but the earnings in the account are tax-free, given that they are used for qualified expenses.

U.S. Savings Bonds

Since the 1930s, savings bonds have been a popular tool for savings for future expenses. Investors have used U.S. EE and I savings bonds as a tool for saving for college related expenses. The benefit to using these bonds are the tax advantages at the local and state levels, as well as the safety of the investment. On the other hand, the return on bonds tends to much lower than other investments like a 529 plan.

Coverdell Education Savings Accounts

A Coverdell account is a tax-advantaged tool that works similar to a 529 plan. Similarly, the earnings in a Coverdell account is tax-free when used for qualified higher education expenses. Some differences between the two include:

a. Annual contribution limits for a Coverdell account

b. Income limits for a Coverdell account

c. Age limits for a Coverdell beneficiary

d. Coverdell accounts can be used for qualified elementary and secondary school expenses, as well as qualified higher education expenses

e. Coverdell investments are not limited to a specific list of products

Custodial Accounts

Custodial accounts do not have the same tax advantages as the alternative college savings tools but do offer other benefits. There are two main types of custodial accounts used for college savings, Uniform Transfers to Minors Act (UTMA) and Uniform Gifts to Minors Act (UGMA) accounts. The main benefits of these accounts is that funds may be invested in any asset and may be used for any purpose, not just qualified higher education expenses.

Brokers Advice and Fee Structure

There are different types of brokerage accounts depending on the level of service that an investor needs. A broker can offer anywhere from zero to extensive investment advice and charge very little to high fees for their services.

Full-service Broker

Investors that want the expertise of professional advisors will likely use a full-service brokerage firm. Financial advisors at a full-service firm will help investors develop an investment plan and frequently help the client update their portfolio of investments.

Discount Broker

Investors that consider themselves do-it-yourself investors will likely find a discount brokerage firm. These firms provide very little advice and simply facilitate transactions at the client's request. Given the hands off approach, discount brokers have much lower fees than full-service brokers.

Online Broker

Investors that do not need any advice have found online brokers to be a good fit for them. Online brokers typically offer free trades without advice. The brokerage firms profit only from interest income and administration fees for margin accounts.

3.2.2. CUSTOMER ACCOUNT REGISTRATIONS

Individual

An individual account is set up with a single owner who makes all the investment decisions and receives all of the distributions.

Joint

A joint account is set up with multiple owners who have the authority to make investment decisions and receive distributions.

Joint Tenant with Rights of Survivorship (JTWROS)

In the event of the death of a joint accountholder, all of the assets will automatically transfer to the surviving owner. The assets in the account are considered equally shared by the joint owners.

Joint Tenants In Common (JTIC)

In the event of the death of a joint accountholder, the assets of the deceased owner will transfer to their estate, not necessarily to the other joint owner. The assets in the account can be split in any way that the owners decide.

Transfer on Death (TOD)

A Transfer on Death account allows the owners to identify exactly who (the beneficiary) they want to assume ownership of their assets in the event of their death. The beneficiary does not have any rights to the account until the death of the owner.

Trust

A trust is a financial tool designed to hold assets for the benefit of its beneficiaries. It is set up with the control of the assets given to a single individual, the trustee, to make decisions regarding the assets with the best interest of the beneficiaries. Trusts are generally created to offer legal protection of the assets from an individual's personal liability.

Living Trust

A living trust is a specific type of trust that allows the original owner of the assets, the trustor, to use the assets during their lifetime. Upon their death the assets in the trust would then go to the beneficiaries under the supervision of the named trustee.

Testamentary Trust

A testamentary trust, or a will trust, is a simple document that specifies the distribution of an individual's assets upon their death.

Revocable versus Irrevocable Trust

A revocable trust can be adjusted or terminated at any time during the life of the trustor. While an irrevocable trust cannot be altered once it is officially established and takes ownership of the assets.

A living trust can either be revocable or irrevocable, while testamentary trusts must be irrevocable. The tax and liability advantages that are associated with trusts are usually reserved for irrevocable trust.

Funded versus Unfunded

A funded trust has taken ownership of the trustor's assets and are being used by them or their beneficiaries. An unfunded trust has been set up but has never received any assets.

UGMA/UTMA Trust Account

A Uniform Gifts to Minors Act (UGMA) or Uniform Transfers to Minors Act (UTMA) trust accounts are established to allow a minor beneficiary to legally own the assets in the trust. They are usually restricted from taking out the principal value until they reach of age.

Corporate/institutional

- Corporate Accounts

    Corporations can buy and sell securities in the same way that individuals can, under the name of the company. A corporation must provide a corporate resolution identifying the individuals authorized to make investment decisions for the company.

- Partnerships

  A partnership account is an account that is established for the benefit of two or more individuals or business entities. The authorizations and restrictions for the account must be listed in the partnership agreement.

- Retirement

  An individual retirement account (IRA) is an account that is established with the primary goal of saving for an individual's retirement needs. Individuals can set up an IRA based on their specific needs through one of the various types of IRAs offered in the market.

  Individuals can choose to establish either a traditional IRA or a Roth IRA depending on their tax preference. A traditional IRA allows investors to make tax-deductible contributions to their account, given certain limits. When withdrawals are made during the individual's retirement they will then be subject to taxes at that point. A Roth IRA allows investors to make after-tax contributions to their account, given certain limits, and then make tax-free withdrawals during retirement.

  Individuals who own small-businesses and who are self-employed can choose to establish either a Simplified Employee Pension (SEP) IRA or a Savings Incentive Match Plan for Employees (SIMPLE) IRA. A SEP IRA is an account set up by the business for the benefit of an employee.

  Contributions to the account are made by the business and are tax-deductible. A SIMPLE IRA is set in the same way as a SEP IRA but both the business and employee make tax-deductible contributions to the account.

  In summary, an individual can set up a traditional or Roth IRA to invest in a range of products like stocks, bonds, and mutual funds in order to save for their retirement needs. Small business owners and self-employed individuals can set up SEP or SIMPLE IRAs for their employees or themselves to save toward retirement goals.

3.2.3 ANTI-MONEY LAUNDERING (AML)

Definition

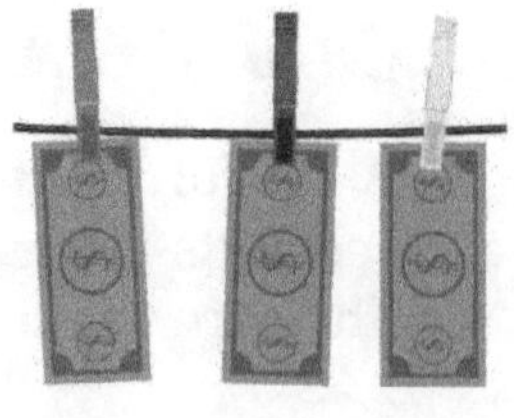

Anti-money laundering (AML) describes the procedures and laws established to thwart illegal financial transactions. AML regulations are present in almost all financial institutions are required to be followed by the institution.

Stages

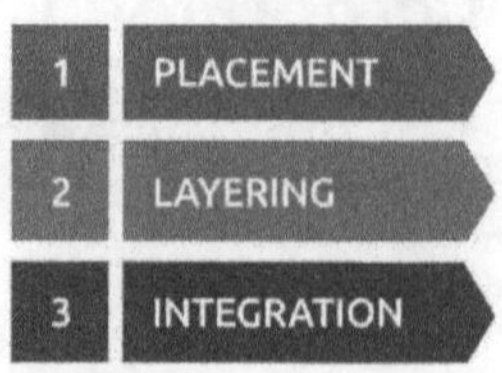

The purpose of money laundering is to convert illegally obtained cash or property into legitimate funds that can be used legally. The process usually goes through three stages: placement, layering, and integration/ extraction.

Placement

The placement stage can take on various forms: adding illegal funds to the legitimate funds of a cash businesses, falsifying invoices, aborted transactions that return legitimate funds, smurfing – adding low amounts of money to bank accounts and credit cards, or using trust and offshore accounts.

Layering

Layering is the second stage of laundering and is simply the repetition of the placement and extraction stages. This is usually done with random amounts per transaction to avoid pattern recognition.

Integration/Extraction

The last stage of the process is actually getting the "clean" money from the placement. To add to the legitimate image, taxes are usually paid on the extraction and "shrinkage" is common. Use of fake employees, loans, and dividends are normally used as extraction tools.

Compliance

Financial institutions are required to adhere to the Bank Secrecy Act and implement AML rules and practices. The goal of the AML rules is to detect and prevent money laundering acts and terrorist funding.

FINRA has established Rule 3310 to require written standards for a firm's AML compliance program. FINRA's Rule 3310 states a program requires the following:

a. Written approval by senior management

b. Able to detect and report suspicious activity

c. Compliance with AML rules

d. A risk-based customer identification program (CIP)

e. Independent testing to ensure AML compliance

f. A registered AML Compliance Officer

g. Continuous AML training for related personnel

Suspicious Activity Report (SAR)

The Suspicious Activity Report (SAR) is a document required by the Bank Secrecy Act of 1970 to monitor activities that are suspected to be fraudulent. The SAR is filed with the Financial Crimes Enforcement Network (FinCEN).

Currency Transaction Report (CTR)

A currency transaction report (CTR) is a document required by the Bank Secrecy Act of 1970 to report cash transactions of more than $10,000. The CTR is filed with the FinCEN to identify and help prevent money laundering.

FinCEN is a division of the U.S. Department of the Treasury with the objective to safeguard the financial system from illegal financial acts, such as money laundering and terror funding.

Office of Foreign Asset Control (OFAC)

The Office of Foreign Asset Control (OFAC) is a division of the U.S. Department of the Treasury with the mission of enforcing economic and trade sanctions against terror or drug related countries.

Specially Designated Nationals and Blocked Persons List (SDN)

OFAC publishes a list of individuals, groups, and companies that are known terror threats or drug affiliates. The individuals and companies on the list are known as Specially Designated Nationals (SDNs) and usually have their assets frozen and are prohibited from U.S. contact.

3.2.4 BOOKS, RECORDS, AND PRIVACY

Books and Record Retention Requirements

Investment Advisors are required to maintain current client records pertaining to financial records, contracts, client reports, inspections, and advertising/sales material sent. The records must be maintained for no less than five years and be easily accessible. The books and record rules are defined by the Securities Exchange Act of 1934, the SEC, and FINRA.

Trade Confirmations and Account Statements

A trade confirmation is a document that an investor receives from their broker outlining the details of their transactions over a specific time period. The details of the confirmation include the total shares traded, transaction price, the order type, the settlement date, etc.

A brokerage account statement provides information regarding your account composition, financial position, asset allocation, and detailed valuation measures.

Customer Mail

Investment advisors may hold a client's mail if they have written instructions from the client, informs the client in writing about other methods of communication, establishes a reasonable timeline for holding the mail, secure the mail from being tampered with, and maintain communication with the client.

Business Continuity Plans (BCP)

FINRA requires all firms to establish and maintain a written business continuity plan (BCP) that outlines the procedures for an emergency or a prolonged business disruption.

FINRA has established RULE 4370 that details the emergency preparedness rule and BCP procedures.

Customer Protection

FINRA requires its member firms to create and maintain policies and procedures that relate to the protection of financial and personal customer information. The SEC has issued Regulation S-P that also requires firms to have policies and procedures that address the protection of customer information and records. In addition, Regulation S-ID requires written policies and procedures relating to identity theft prevention.

Custody of Assets

In order to safeguard investor assets, firms adhere to the custody rule under the Investment Advisers Act of 1940 to prevent the misuse or misappropriation of funds and securities by advisors.

Privacy

Financial institutions are required to provide privacy notices to meet compliance requirements for disclosure of nonpublic personal information. Financial institutions are also required to allow clients to opt out of any disclosure of their information to nonaffiliated third parties.

Gramm-Leach-Bliley Act

The Gramm-Leach-Bliley Act (GLB Act) of 1999 requires the Federal Trade Commission (FTC) to regulate consumer financial privacy in the financial services industry. The GLB Act has three sections dealing with privacy: the financial privacy rule, the safeguards rule, and the pretexting rule. The financial privacy rule relates to the collection and disclosure of information. The safeguards rule relates to the protection of customer information. The pretexting rule that prohibits accessing private information under false pretenses.

Nonpublic Personal Information (NPI)

Nonpublic personal information (NPI) is personally identifiable financial information gathered from clients in relation to purchasing financial products and services.

Confidentiality

FINRA requires registered professionals and firms to take steps to ensure confidentiality of client information. The precautionary measures include training, email encryption, and proper disposal of sensitive information.

3.2.5 COMMUNICATION WITH THE PUBLIC AND SUITABILITY

Communication with the Public

FINRA has established Rule 2210 to regulate communications with the public including content, record retention and filing procedures. The rule defines three categories of firm communication with the public: retail communication, correspondence, and institutional communication.

Telemarketing

FINRA has established rules to regulate the telemarketing practices of registered professionals and firms. These rules restrict calls based on the time of day and the do-not-call lists.

Suitability

FINRA Rule 2111 directly relates to the suitability of customer transactions. Suitability refers to an investment strategy that is appropriate for a client's account given their return and risk objectives. The rule requires financial professionals to have reasonable basis for recommending or carrying out a transaction for a client. Furthermore, the rule requires the advisor to have a clear understanding about the characteristics of the investment product and the customer's profile and financial objectives.

FINRA views the lack of that understanding as a violation of the suitability rule.

3.3 PROHIBITED ACTIVITIES

Section Overview:

3.3.1 Market Manipulation

3.3.2 Insider Trading

3.3.3 Other Prohibited Activities

3.3.1 MARKET MANIPULATION

Market manipulation is the process of intentionally driving securities up or down in order to profit from the artificial change in value. In most situations, the manipulation is an abuse of influence and shown to be illegal. Market manipulation can be done in a number of ways.

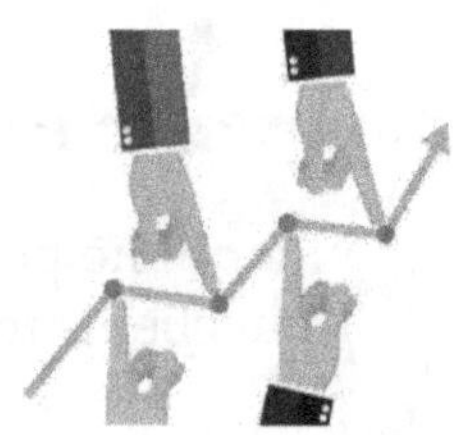

The following five methods are common ways markets can be manipulated:

1. *False News* – use of fake information to move the markets or security price in one direction or another.

2. *Pump and Dump* – the use of positive fake news to drive up the price of a security and then the sale of the stock when others buy into the security. A Poop and Scoop is the opposite use of negative fake news with a short sale tactic.

3. *Spoofing the Tape* – the use of larger fake pending orders to mislead market participants. Painting the tape is a variation of spoofing where a group of investors buy and sell a security between themselves to mislead the market.

4. *Wash Trading* – the simultaneous buying and selling of a security to increase the volume and perceived popularity of the security.

5. *Bear Raiding* – the process of driving down the price of a security by placing large sell orders, in order to profit from short sales.

3.3.2 INSIDER TRADING

Insider Trading

Insider trading is the illegal act of using private information to profit from the financial markets. Specifically the use of material nonpublic information is illegal. While the use of pieces of immaterial nonpublic information may be acceptable. The legality of it is determined by whether the information is considered public versus nonpublic or material versus immaterial.

Insider trading includes the sharing of material nonpublic information with others that use that information for gains. Insider trading can only be legal when company officials buy or sell securities in their personal accounts, given prior public disclosure.

Material Nonpublic Information

Material nonpublic information is any information that has not been released to the general public and that would have a significant impact on the value of the company or security. Material refers to the affect that the information has on the security's value or the influence on an investor's decision about the company or security. Nonpublic information is information that has not been widely disseminated to the general public. The disclosure to a small group is not considered proper dissemination and is still viewed as nonpublic.

Mosaic Theory

The Mosaic Theory is often used by analyst to legally arrive at investment decisions. The theory refers to the process of gathering public and nonpublic immaterial information about a company to establish an investment decision. Since the material is considered immaterial is does not fall into the illegal category.

3.3.3 OTHER PROHIBITED ACTIVITIES

Restrictions on the Purchase and Sale of Initial Public Offerings (IPOs)

FINRA requires that registered professionals and member firms adhere to the following guidelines:

a. Members or their affiliates may not sell any new issue to any account in which a restricted person has a beneficial interest, except where otherwise permitted.

b. Members or their affiliates may not purchase any new issue for any account in which a restricted person has a beneficial interest, except as otherwise permitted.

c. Members or their affiliates may not continue to hold new issues acquired by the member as an underwriter, selling group member or otherwise, except as otherwise permitted.

Use of Manipulative, Deceptive or Other Fraudulent Devices

FINRA restricts any members or their affiliates from influencing any transaction through the use of any manipulative, deceptive or other fraudulent device. The rule covers the use of any device, scheme, ploy to defraud, false statements, intentional omissions, or fraudulent business practices.

Improper Use of Customers' Securities or Funds

FINRA Rule 2330 outlines the use of customer funds, including guarantees of performance. Exceptions to the rule include accounts of family members and prior written authorizations.

FINRA Rule 2370 relates to the borrowing from and lending to customers. The summary of the rule is that borrowing from an unrelated customer account is usually restricted. Exceptions must have prior written authorization and the customer must be an immediate family member of the agent or the loan has to be based on commercial standards.

FINRA Rule 2150 details prohibitions against any guarantees and sharing in accounts. Specifically it states that members or their affiliates are restricted from the improper use of a customer's securities/funds, any guarantee against loss or specific gain, or sharing in the gains or losses of any customer's account, except as otherwise permitted.

Financial Exploitation of Specified Adults

FINRA Rule 2165 restricts the exploitation of individuals that are sixty-five years of age or older and individuals that are eighteen years of age or older and have a mental or physical impairment. The rule defines exploitation as the unauthorized or wrongful use of the person's account, any act or omission to gain control of the person's assets, or any act or omission to trade the person's assets without their knowledge or understanding.

Activities of Unregistered Persons

FINRA Rule 2040 prohibits direct or indirect payments of commissions, fees, concessions, or discounts to unregistered persons. Exceptions are made for retired representatives and foreign affiliates.

Furthermore, FINRA restricts the contact by unregistered persons with clients or potential clients to the following permissible activities.

Unregistered persons may engage in the following activities when contacting the public:

a. Sending invitations to clients or potential clients for a firm-sponsored event

b. Inquiries to potential clients regarding investment discussions with a registered agent

c. Inquiries to potential clients regarding receiving investment literature

Member firms employing any unregistered person should adhere to the following guidelines:

a. Unregistered persons should not discuss investment products or services, pre-qualify customers, or solicit new accounts or orders.

b. Require unregistered persons to undergo training and/or orientation

c. Conduct a comprehensive background check on the unregistered person

d. Compensate the employee on a salary or hourly basis

e. Ensure proper supervisory and behavior procedures are followed

Falsifying or Withholding Documents

FINRA has established guidelines that require registered professional and member firm to restrict the use of signatures of convenience. The guidelines also require that regulatory request for information needs to be addressed immediately and with complete compliance.

Prohibited Activities Related to Books and Records

Registered professionals and member firms are strictly prohibited from falsifying records and must comply with all rules, policies, and procedures regarding the proper maintenance and retention of client records.

Chapter 4

INVESTMENT COMPANIES

4.1 MUTUAL FUNDS

Section Overview:

4.1.1 Closed-End Funds

4.1.2 Taxes

4.1.3 Mutual Fund Investing

4.1.4 Fees

4.1.5 Selection Strategies

A mutual fund is a company (or a trust) that sells shares of its own stock and utilizes the proceeds to make other investments. These investments may include a variety of assets such as the stocks of publicly traded companies, corporate or municipal bonds, real estate, derivatives or short-term money market instruments. By purchasing shares in a mutual fund, the investor obtains a number of benefits that would otherwise be unavailable.

Mutual funds can be an excellent vehicle to carry out a well-conceived investment plan. Once an investor has a disciplined, well thought out strategy, there are many choices available in the mutual fund universe to execute the investment plan with reasonable costs.

Mutual funds can provide a high degree of security of principal and income through diversification of securities. Few individuals could afford to buy as many different types of stocks or other investments as the typical mutual fund holds. This spreading of risk makes it unlikely that poor performance by any one security will result in financial disaster.

The purchase of shares in a mutual fund allows an investor to hire the best investment management expertise, thus freeing the investor from the responsibility of managing the portfolio of securities on a day-to-day basis.

Most mutual funds maintain a market in their own shares. Such funds are referred to as open-end investment companies. This means that the mutual fund company has obligated itself to buy back its shares from investors at the current market value (called Net Asset Value or NAV). An investor can require the fund to redeem its shares at any time. This requirement provides the purchaser of fund shares with a high degree of liquidity.

4.1.1 CLOSED-END FUNDS

A small category of funds, referred to as closed-end funds, do not buy and sell their own shares. Instead, their shares are traded on the open market much like the shares of publicly traded companies. These funds may be listed on the organized stock exchanges or traded on the over-the-counter market. Although closed-end funds technically are not mutual funds, the shareholders of a fund that qualifies and makes the necessary election to be taxed as a regulated investment company will be taxed like mutual fund shareholders.

Several large discount brokerage firms have created fund supermarkets where an investor can have a wide mix of funds, from hundreds of separate fund groups, all in one brokerage account. This makes it easy for an investor to put together a diversified portfolio of funds from different fund families, with top-notch management and low costs. Investors can easily rebalance and make changes within the one brokerage account.

Mutual fund organizations have promoted the concept of a family of funds. A company will sponsor a number of funds with different investment objectives and underlying assets. The investor can decide to switch assets back and forth from one fund to another. The advantage is that the investor can quickly, conveniently (and typically without any additional sales charges) move assets into one or more funds that better meet his investment needs or desires.

From time to time, typically after down periods in the market, mutual funds may have significant realized capital losses that can be used to offset taxable capital gain distributions in the future. Further, the funds may have significant unrealized depreciation in assets. This means that future appreciation, up to the original cost basis of the security, is tax free within the fund itself. These two factors can make some funds more tax efficient, at least in the short run, than if the investor had purchased the same securities themselves.

Purchasing shares from some mutual funds involves payment of a sales charge, commonly called a "load." This charge covers the cost of marketing the fund through brokerage firms and certain other fees. Sales charges can be as high as 8.5 percent of the original investment, but this is very unusual. Market forces have reduced the typical front end load down to an average of about 5 percent. There are now many share classes, and the fees and commission structure can be very confusing (front load, back load, level load, etc.). There are many "no-load" funds that market their products through brokerage firm fund supermarkets or directly to the public by mail and through newspaper advertising. These funds do not charge a sales fee.

Annual management fees and administrative charges can reduce the overall return on the investment. Management fees typically range from 0.10 percent (for some passively managed index funds) to 3 percent (for some actively managed funds). Administrative charges may be imposed in addition to management fees and frequently cost up to $50 annually per account. These small administrative charges are frequently waived for accounts that reach a minimum balance. These fees can eat up a significant portion of the return to an investor. For example, a bond fund earning 3 percent on Treasury notes with a 1 percent expense ratio will only return 2 percent to the investor. The expenses are eating up 33 percent of the returns.

While professional management relieves the investor of certain obligations and responsibilities, it also eliminates his personal involvement in the management of the fund. The purchaser of a mutual fund cannot control the selection of specific assets or the timing of purchases and sales. Unlike the investor who buys stock directly and who can select the time to sell and recognize a gain or loss, the mutual fund shareholder has no choice. He cannot control the amount of any capital gain distribution, or when it must be reported. Capital gain distributions on sales of underlying securities by the mutual fund are paid annually and must be reported each year on the shareholder's tax return.

4.1.2 TAXES

Ordinary income distributions from mutual funds are generally taxed to individual shareholders at ordinary income tax rates. In some recent years, some dividends were classified as qualified dividends and qualified for the preferred tax rate of zero percent or 15 percent. To be a qualified dividend, the investor must have held the stock for more than sixty days during the 121-day period that begins sixty days before the ex-dividend date. The American Taxpayer Relief Act of 2012 (ATRA) extended these low tax rates on qualified dividends for taxpayers with taxable income below $400,000 ($450,000 if married filing jointly). For taxpayers with income above this level, qualified dividends are taxed at 20 percent. Ordinary income dividends paid by mutual funds are eligible for the 15 percent/5 percent tax rates *only if* the income being passed from the fund to shareholders is qualified dividend income in the hands of the fund, and not short-term capital gain or interest from bonds (both of which continue to be taxed at ordinary income tax rates). Mutual funds will report on Form 1099-DIV the nature of the dividend being distributed to shareholders (i.e., whether the dividend is qualified dividend income or a non-qualifying dividend subject to ordinary income tax rates). Unless designated by the mutual fund as net capital gain, all distributions to shareholders are to be treated as ordinary income dividends.

Capital gain distributions are generally treated as long-term capital gain, and are taxable in the year in which the distribution is declared.

The income paid from municipal bond funds is not subject to federal income tax, but is normally taxed at the state level. Capital gains, however, are fully taxable.

Every time a switch is made within a family of funds, shares of one fund are technically sold and shares of another fund are purchased. These sales are taxable events and result in a gain or loss. Of course, if the funds are purchased through an IRA, Keogh, or qualified corporate pension or profit- sharing plan, tax is deferred until an actual or constructive distribution occurs.

The sale or other disposition of less than all of an investor's shares (or of shares acquired on various dates at various prices) can cause difficulty in determining the basis of the shares sold. Several methods are available for establishing the basis of shares and, thus, for determining the amount of taxable gain.

Some funds are set up as limited partnerships in order to allow investors an exemption from state and local taxes on interest from U.S. government securities; however, this exemption does not apply in all states.

When acquiring mutual fund shares, several tax strategies are useful. These include:

- *Timing Purchases Wisely* – For the investor, the purchase of mutual fund shares carries the extra burden of the fund's untaxed dividends and capital gains to date. When distributions are received, the shareholder is taxed on those previously accumulated dividends and gains.

  By timing purchases wisely, the investor can reduce his tax liability. Purchasing shares on, or soon after, the "ex-distribution date" (i.e., the date a shareholder is no longer entitled to the distribution) relieves the investor of this added tax because there is no taxable income to report. This factor is very important if very large capital gains are expected because they carry a large tax burden.

- *Taking Advantage of Tax Deferrals* – Taxes on unrealized gains on stocks are deferred until the shares are sold. Because these gains are compounded on a pre-tax basis, tax deferral on the gains results in a lower effective tax rate. The longer the deferral, the lower the tax rate.

  Likewise, a stock mutual fund investor obtains the same advantages for as long as the fund holds the appreciated shares. Therefore, the lower the portfolio turnover rate, the better the opportunity for tax deferral.

- *Trying to Time the Dispositions of Fund Shares* – so that short-term capital gains can be used to offset long-term capital losses, rather than being treated as ordinary income. A fund's turnover rate is a good indicator of potential short-term gains. A high turnover may mean a greater potential for short-term gains, while a low turnover would indicate a lower proportion of short-term gains.

- *Maximizing Mutual Fund Capital Loss Carryovers* – Because capital losses are not passed on to shareholders, but are offset against capital gains, a carryover loss can be used to reduce capital gains and subsequent taxes.

  The cost method used when calculating gains and/or losses on partial share purchases and redemptions affects the individual's taxable income. Three methods are often used:

- *Average cost method.* An investor whose mutual fund shares are held by a custodian can use this method. The choice of the single-category or double-category method is up to the investor and affects the characterization (i.e., long-term or short-term) of the gain as well as the amount of taxable gain. The double-category method (i.e., where shares are divided based on whether they have been held for more than one year, or for one year or less) gives taxpayers greater control over the amount of gains or losses recognized.

- *Specific identification method.* This is a more flexible method that allows shareholders to choose the specific shares sold in a partial redemption. Identification of shares to be sold must be done at the outset.

- *FIFO method.* This method states that when a sale is made, the shares sold are those purchased earliest. If the price per share has risen since acquisition, then use of this method results in the largest overall gains.

Investors should carefully choose the cost method used in order to reduce their tax liability.

4.1.3 MUTUAL FUND INVESTING

Most load funds are sold through brokerage firms that receive part of the load charge as a fee for selling shares in the fund. Many brokerage firms are affiliated with particular fund groups or have their own set of mutual funds that they market to their clients. These funds will generally include a money market fund, one or more common stock funds, bond funds, and a fund that specializes in tax-exempt securities. Orders to buy and sell fund shares are treated like any other transaction and require that the investor have an account with the brokerage firm. Investors will receive confirming receipts of any trades, and activity will be shown on the monthly statement received from their broker.

Investors should realize that some brokers may be biased toward selling their own funds rather than those of other mutual fund organizations. Also, brokers typically will not sell shares in no-load funds for which they receive no commissions. Investors should be careful to review the recommendations of brokers to see that they are conforming to the investor's particular needs and desires.

As noted, no-load mutual funds are rarely sold through traditional brokerage firms. These funds are bought and sold directly through the funds themselves or are sold through fund supermarkets at the large discount brokers. In the latter case a transaction fee may be charged. No-load funds are widely advertised in the newspapers and most carry on an active campaign of direct mail advertising and solicitation. Investors interested in a specific fund or a particular group of funds can call, write, or visit the fund's website for additional information or the forms needed to open an account.

Once an account has been established with a no-load mutual fund organization or through a fund supermarket, it is relatively easy to purchase additional shares, to switch investments from one fund in the group to another, or to sell shares. Most of these transactions can be done on the telephone, by mail, or via the firm website. After a transaction is made, the firm will send a confirming receipt to the investor within a few days.

4.1.4 FEES

The sales charge for purchasing a load fund generally ranges from 3 to 5.75 percent of the net asset value of the fund. Net asset value is the total value of the fund's assets, minus any liabilities, divided by the number of outstanding shares of the fund. For example, assume that Consolidated Fund, a hypothetical mutual fund, charges a 5 percent load to purchase its shares. If the fund's shares had a net asset value of $10.00 per share, the sales charge would be $0.50, and the purchase price of a share for investors would be $10.50.

The load fee for mutual funds may be as high as 8.5 percent; however, the vast majority of load funds charge less than this amount. Investors should be cautious in purchasing these funds since some also charge a redemption fee that may be as high as 5 percent of the value of any shares sold. This fee is assessed whenever the investor sells shares of the fund and is subtracted from the amount the investor is paid. This redemption fee may be waived if the investor sells shares of the fund but reinvests the money in another fund of the same group.

The entire fee structure of load funds is now quite complex. Over the past ten years, there has been a shift away from front end load funds (commonly called "A" Shares) to back end load funds ("B" shares) and level load funds ("C" shares) and a number of variations. It's imperative that prospective investors understand what they are buying, and what the annual fees are, including 12b-1 fees and surrender charges.

The costs of buying and selling shares of so-called closed-end funds are similar to those of buying and selling any shares of stock. The transaction cost will be determined by the number of shares traded and the total value of the transaction. As the name implies, no-load funds do not charge a fee for the purchase or sale of their shares. These funds may be identified in newspaper listings of mutual funds by the indication of "N.L." in the column of offering prices. These funds may be purchased or sold at the indicated net asset value with no additional sales charges. However, investors should be aware that while these funds do not charge a sales fee, they do assess administrative charges and management fees, and may charge "12b-1 fees" to cover the costs of marketing and advertising (typically on an annual basis). These fees can range from 0.25 to 1 percent. Further, service charges or transaction fees may be charged when shares are purchased.

4.1.5 SELECTION STRATEGIES

Mutual funds have a wide variety of investment objectives and vary considerably in terms of size, fees, management, performance, and services offered to investors. Selecting the right fund for a particular investment situation may not be easy and should be given a great deal of thought. Described below are some of the important factors to consider in making such a decision.

The selection process should begin with an evaluation of the fund's investment objective. This information can be found in the fund's prospectus, which can be obtained from a brokerage firm or from the fund itself. In addition to describing the fund's investment objectives, the prospectus will provide some data on its historical performance. While there are a great many mutual funds, their objectives can be grouped into a few common categories:

- *Growth Funds* – more aggressive than common stock funds, these funds concentrate on long-term capital gains and high future income; generally invest in more speculative issues that provide little or no current income; most of their investments are in common stocks, and possibly a few convertible bonds. The most aggressive funds—with above-average growth potential, high portfolio turnover, high degree of leverage, and high risk—are called performance or "go-go" funds.

- *Income Funds* – specialize in securities that pay higher-than-average current rates of return from either dividends or interest by investing in securities not generally favored by the investment community; frequently invest a high percentage of their assets in bonds rather than common stocks.

- *Balanced Funds* – the most conservative of the funds investing in common stock; these funds have as their primary objective the preservation of capital and moderate growth of income and principal; secondary consideration is capital gains; generally diversify their investments among both stocks and bonds; during bear markets typically offer the best investor protection.

- *Tax-Exempt Funds* – operate principally to provide investors with high after-tax returns on their investments; generally limit their investments to municipal securities or other types of issues that offer tax-sheltered income.

- *Index Funds* – these funds are designed to track a particular market index, such as the S&P 500, with very low annual expenses. The idea is to give an investor a vehicle to achieve market performance in a particular asset class, be it large U.S. stocks, small U.S. stocks, REITs, international stocks, or certain categories of bonds. This is also known as passive investing. The primary advantage of this form of mutual fund investing is the lower costs (both annual expenses and transactional) that give an inherent advantage, and the ability of an investor to eliminate the risk of manager underperformance and be assured of market performance.

- *Sector Funds* – restrict investments to a particular sector of the market, such as energy, electronics, chemicals, or health care; these funds tend to be more volatile than a more widely diversified portfolio.

- *Diversified Common Stock Funds* – concentrate principally on long-term capital growth, with current income being a secondary consideration; a majority of the assets are invested in good quality common stocks with the balance in cash or short-term government notes. These funds follow a more conservative approach.

- *Specialty Funds* – seek to achieve their objectives by concentrating their investments in a single industry, in a group of related industries, in an industry within a specific geographic region, or even in non-security assets such as real estate investment trusts that purchase real property or loans secured by real property.

- *Money Market Funds* – typically no-load funds that invest exclusively in money market instruments such as Treasury bills, CDs, and corporate commercial paper, providing current income and relative safety of principal; offer competitive services such as check writing privileges and free conversion privileges to other types of funds managed by the same investment group.

- *Commodity Funds* – designed to bring the small investor into the commodities market; organized as limited partnerships, these funds offer an inflation-hedge in an inflationary environment and an opportunity for large gains, but with a high degree of risk.

- *Bond Funds* – possess several advantages over direct bond investing, provided expenses are kept low; offer a variety of portfolio types, and proven track records; allow an investor to indirectly participate in the bond market without acquiring the expertise necessary to invest in the market directly.

- *Foreign Stock And Bond Funds* – open-end and closed-end funds that invest in foreign stocks and bonds; some invest exclusively in the securities of one nation while others invest more broadly in foreign regions, or in all foreign markets.

- *Asset Allocation Funds* – in essence, these funds offer one-stop shopping for a complete investment portfolio and offer a substitute for the investor's own allocation of investment dollars among several different traditional funds. These funds offer diversification not only within asset classes but among asset classes, and they may include nontraditional asset classes, such as commodities and real estate.

These categories may be combined or more specifically defined such as growth and income funds and aggressive growth funds. Funds are also classified by subcategories. For example, stocks funds are often classified by the size of the companies they invest in (small capitalization, mid-capitalization or large capitalization) or whether the stocks are considered value or growth stocks. Bond funds are typically classified by the duration of the bonds (short, medium or long term) or their nature (government bonds, municipal bonds or corporate bonds).

Another important selection factor is the fund's historical performance. Relatively few funds have outperformed the market as a whole over long periods of time, but some have consistently done better than others. Each fund's prospectus will give some indication of its rate of return during the last five or ten years. Most funds will show what a typical investment would have returned in the form of dividends and capital gains. Various investment sources will also provide comparative information on large numbers of mutual funds. Investors should use this information to select those funds that have regularly been above average in their investment performance.

In analyzing the performance of mutual funds, it is important to note that many funds perform quite differently in bull markets as compared to bear markets. Growth funds, especially those that concentrate in speculative issues, tend to do well when economic conditions are good and the general trend of the stock market is up. However, these same funds have been relatively poor performers when market conditions are weak and the economy is in a decline. In contrast, income funds and some balanced funds tend to do better than growth funds when the market is weak. Few funds have been able to turn in better than average performance under all market conditions.

Investors should concentrate on those funds with low sales charges, management fees, and expense ratios. As noted previously, funds differ considerably as to the cost of purchasing their shares. This should not be the only consideration, but high sales charges can sharply reduce an investor's overall rate of return on investment. Similarly, funds that charge high portfolio management fees have to provide better than average returns to compensate for those charges. Funds also have normal business expenses and these charges, referred to as a fund's "expense ratio," should be a factor in selecting a particular mutual fund for investment.

The range of services offered by the fund is another important consideration in making a selection. Most funds will provide for automatic reinvestment of dividends into additional shares of the fund. Another common feature is automatic payout of a specified amount on a monthly, quarterly, or annual basis. This feature is especially important to older investors who may be using the fund to provide retirement income. In addition, many offer convenient methods for purchasing shares at the day's net asset value, either by telephone, by wire transfer, or by logging onto the Internet.

It is desirable that a fund be a part of a family of funds or discount brokerage fund supermarket that provide the investor with flexibility in terms of diversification and the opportunity to alter his investment objective. As noted previously, few funds have done well under all market conditions, and the investor should be prepared to transfer investments when market conditions change. Also, it is not unusual for one person to have a variety of investment needs, and the opportunity to make investments in a number of funds within the same management group is attractive.

When comparing funds some of the factors that apply to the selection of mutual funds are:

- fund objective
- management style and discipline
- fund size
- performance record
- sales charges
- expense ratio
- special services

Fund objectives should match the investor's personal goals. Each fund states its objectives in its advertising and provides a more detailed explanation in its prospectus. An investor should review a fund's performance record over a period of at least five years.

Load and no-load are terms used to indicate whether or not a fund levies a direct sales charge. Such charges can range from 3 to 8.5 percent of the initial investment. It would appear that investors would always be better off by purchasing no-load funds, but this is not necessarily the case. The overall performance record of a good load fund can offset the absence of a sales charge in a mediocre no-load fund.

While all funds charge an advisory fee, these vary considerably from fund to fund. Investors should search for those funds with good performance records and relatively low advisory fees. These fees are reported in the fund's prospectus or annual report.

Investors should select funds from those organizations that provide a wide range of special services to fund holders. These services include:

- the ability to transfer from one fund to another
- automatic reinvestment of dividends
- automatic payments from the fund (this typically requires a minimum investment)
- service and information provided with respect to Keogh and IRA accounts
- information and service provided by customer service representatives; via telephone or online

4.2 VARIABLE ANNUITIES

Section Overview:

4.2.1 Characteristics of Variable Annuities

4.2.2 Annuities

4.2.3 Advantages of Annuities

4.2.4 Disadvantages of Annuities

4.2.5 Types of Annuities

4.2.6 Tax Implications

4.2.1 CHARACTERISTICS OF VARIABLE ANNUITIES

A variable annuity has many of the characteristics and features of a mutual fund. Typically, these include ownership of a large portfolio of securities and management by professional investment advisers.

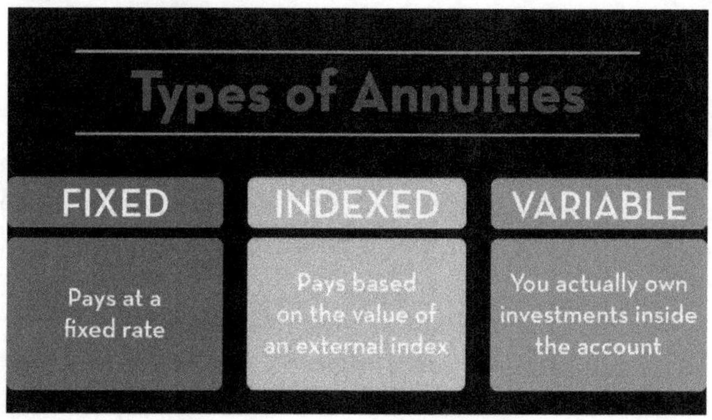

A variable annuity allows the holder of an annuity contract, usually issued by an insurance company, to invest in a family of mutual funds with the purpose of accumulating savings, usually for retirement. The accumulated balance is then disbursed as a series of payments or a lump-sum payment upon retirement (or other planned event). The amount available for distribution is contingent on the performance of the mutual funds selected.

As an alternative to mutual funds, variable annuities offer the advantages of tax-deferral for any dividends or capital gains earned until the income is withdrawn, and a waiver on taxes normally required for fund transfers between mutual funds. Generally, variable annuities also guarantee that a beneficiary will never receive less than the sum of the contributions if the annuity holder dies before the annuity starting date.

On the other hand, money in variable annuities is tied up for long periods of time, which can be a disadvantage if the investment strategy is not long-term in focus. Additionally, to the extent the gain on the funds inside the annuity are from long-term share appreciation, this capital gain is converted to ordinary income at the time of withdrawal and does not receive any favorable tax treatment, as do long-term capital gains from mutual funds. Variable annuities are also illiquid because the IRS imposes a 10 percent penalty tax on premature distributions (generally before age 59½) and insurance companies also impose surrender charges. Expenses, too, are usually high—typically 2 percent of total assets versus a 1 percent charge for mutual funds. Finally, declining back-end surrender charges are frequently imposed over a seven-year period, whereas no-load mutual funds carry no such levy. Load mutual funds, however, impose a sales charge up to

8.5 percent that is paid up-front and does not decline if no withdrawals are made during the first few years.

Overall, variable annuities perform similarly to mutual funds. On the whole, variable annuities present better investment opportunities when:

- the investor's tax rate is higher during the accumulation phase and lower during the payout phase
- the accumulation period is longer
- the rate of return is higher
- the annual expense differential is smaller
- payments will be taken from the annuity contract in the form of one of the annuity options rather than as a lump sum.

Also, a variable annuity is more likely to be the better investment if you are comparing it to a load mutual fund rather than a no-load mutual fund.

Figure 4.1 compares the after-tax accumulation of a variable annuity with a no-load fund over various accumulation periods assuming: a $25,000 initial investment; a 9 percent pre-tax rate of return (after investment management expenses); a 1 percent annual charge in excess of the annual mutual fund expenses for the annuity; a 34 percent combined federal and state income tax rate; annuity payments/withdrawals that commence after age 59½ (no 10 percent penalty); and no surrender charges on the annuity after year five.

Figure 4.1

COMPARISON OF VARIABLE ANNUITY VERSUS MUTUAL FUND					
	No-Load Mutual Fund After-Tax Value		Variable Annuity After-Tax Value		
End of	Total	Total Retirement Payout Over 20 Years	Total	Lump-Sum Surrender	Total Retirement Payout Over 20 Years
5 Years	$33,361	$57,890	$36,733	$32,744	$57,890
10 Years	44,518	44,250	53,973	44,122	81,060
12 Years	49,518	86,700	62,954	50,050	93,140
15 Years	59,407	103,080	79,304	60,841	115,120
20 Years	79,276	137,560	116,524	85,406	165,160

The comparison shows that the variable annuity breaks even with the mutual fund in twelve years and outperforms the mutual fund for every holding period beyond twelve years. The annuity builds to over $85,406, versus the $79,276 an investor would receive from the mutual fund if he were to invest for twenty years before taking a lump-sum withdrawal. The advantage would be even greater if the investor were to take distributions from the annuity over twenty years. In this case, the investor would break even after waiting only five years to begin distributions, receiving a total of over $165,000 after tax, about 20 percent more than if the investor had systematically withdrew funds from the mutual fund during the twenty-year retirement period. If the investor's tax bracket were to drop to 25 percent after retirement (down from 34 percent before retirement), the retirement payout would increase to over $184,000.

The annuity break-even period is quite sensitive to changes in some assumptions, so comparisons should be run using assumptions applicable to each investor's situation. It should be noted that variable annuities are taxable as ordinary income, while mutual funds may be taxable at capital gains or ordinary income rates.

4.2.2. ANNUITIES

Annuities are the only investment vehicles that can guarantee that investors will not outlive their income, and do this in a tax-favored manner. In addition, annuities are available with a host of features to meet a wide variety of investor needs. The taxation of annuities is governed by Internal Revenue Code Section 72.

Technically, annuities are contracts providing for the systematic liquidation of principal and interest in the form of a series of payments over time. However, this really refers to the payout phase of an annuity; in fact, annuities can (and often do) have an accumulation phase that also lasts for a substantial period of time.

An annuity is established when an investor makes a cash payment to an insurance company, which invests the money—this may be a single large cash payment or a series of periodic payments over time. The money remains invested with the insurance company and is periodically credited with some growth factor (the accumulation phase of the annuity). In return for making a deposit into an annuity, the insurance company ultimately agrees to pay the owner (or owners) a specified amount (the annuity payments) periodically, beginning on a specified date (the payout phase of the annuity).

If the specified date for payouts to begin is within one year of the date the contract is established (i.e., a single cash payment is made and the insurance company begins a systematic liquidation of the payment back to the owner within one year), the annuity is called an immediate annuity. If, alternatively, the specified date for payouts to begin is later than one year, the annuity is called a deferred annuity (because deposits are made now, but the payout is deferred). An immediate annuity only has a payout phase; a deferred annuity has both an accumulation and a payout phase.

If the payout phase of the annuity is a life annuity, the company promises that payouts will continue for as long as the annuitant (or annuitants) lives; the annuitant(s) can never outline the income stream. (*Note:* technically, although, the owner of the annuity and the annuitant typically are the same person, occasionally the owner and the annuitant are different individuals.)

If the payout phase is a fixed-period annuity (also called a term-certain annuity), the company promises to pay stipulated amounts for a fixed or guaranteed period of time independent of the survival of the annuitant. An annuity payout can also utilize a combination of the life and fixed-period options, such as "for the greater of ten years or the life of the annuitant(s)."

In addition to differentiating between immediate and deferred annuities and fixed-period and term-certain payouts, insurers also categorize annuities as to whether they are fixed or variable. (Be careful not to confuse a "fixed annuity" with a "fixed-period payout.") Classification as a fixed or variable annuity refers to the underlying investments during the accumulation phase of the annuity: a fixed annuity is invested in the general fixed account of the insurance company, while a variable annuity is invested in separately managed sub-accounts (that function similarly to mutual funds) selected by the annuity owner. Variable annuities often have additional features to help manage the risk of the underlying investments, such as guaranteed death benefits or newer "living benefits" that provide company guaranteed payments for owners (or beneficiaries) even if those payments would be higher than actual investment performance would indicate.

Newer annuities also may offer a variable option during the payout phase (whether for a fixed or term-certain period). A variable annuitization contract provides payments that may fluctuate up or down depending upon the performance of the underlying sub-account investments. A fixed annuitization contract provides payments that remain the same through the payout phase (or occasionally increase by some set rate to keep pace with inflation; however, this rate is (1) predetermined and contractual, (2) still invested in the insurance company's general account, and, (3) thus, still considered a "fixed payout").

Annuities purchased from an insurance company are called "commercial annuities" while those purchased from a person or entity that is not in the business of selling annuities are called "private annuities." Technically, the living proceeds received from a life insurance contract are also considered annuities if they consist of periodic payments of both principal and interest.

Annuities grow tax deferred during the accumulation phase, although withdrawals during this phase are taxed on a Last In First Out (LIFO) basis—meaning that withdrawals during the accumulation phase are considered to be withdrawals of growth first (fully taxable) and principal second. Payouts during the annuitization phase are split: a portion of each payment is considered principal, and a portion is deemed interest/growth. Insurers determine the proportions of each payment that is principal and interest/growth at the annuity's beginning payment date. The proportions are based upon the already accumulated growth, an assumed internal growth factor for the payout period, and the expected length of the payout period. All amounts distributed that are considered interest/growth are taxed as ordinary income, regardless of the phase or timing of the withdrawal. In addition, certain withdrawals before the age of 59½ may be subject to an additional 10 percent tax penalty.

Although investors may find the tax-deferral feature of annuities to be quite advantageous, the primary reason investors should consider purchasing annuities is for the risk management features. Annuities can provide a variety of guarantees, whether protecting against interest rate risk, reinvestment risk, superannuation (living too long, such as outliving one's assets), or certain market volatility risks. Annuities are first and foremost a risk management tool.

The risk and return characteristics of fixed and variable annuities are so fundamentally different that each type is more or less suitable for various purposes. However, some form of annuity would be indicated in the following circumstances:

1. When investors want a retirement income that they can never outlive.
2. When investors (often retired) want a monthly income equal to or higher than could be generated by other conservative investments and are willing to liquidate principal.
3. As a means to avoid probate and pass a large sum of money by contract to heirs in order to reduce the possibility of a will contest.
4. When investors desire a tax deferred accumulation of interest. The interest earned inside an annuity owned by an individual grows income tax-free and is not taxed until it is withdrawn.
5. In order to be free of the responsibility of investing and managing assets (in the case of a fixed annuity or an annuity payout; this is not applicable to a variable deferred annuity, as the owner still retains the burden of making all investment selections).
6. As a supplement to an IRA. With limited opportunity for pre-tax contributions to IRAs, many clients are seeking opportunities of making regular after-tax contributions to an investment vehicle after reaching the IRA contribution limits. The annuity may be a good choice because contributions are not limited.
7. Fixed annuities, in particular, would be indicated: (a) when safety of principal is a paramount consideration (this can be particularly important in some retirement planning scenarios); (b) when investors want a guarantee that a given level of interest will be credited to their investment for a long period of time; or (c) when investors desire a conservative complement to other investment vehicles.
8. Variable annuities, in particular, would be indicated: (a) when investors want more control over their investment and are willing to bear the risk associated with their investment selections; or (b) when investors are looking to increase their potential retirement income.
9. When investors would like to invest their money in the types of vehicles available in variable sub-accounts, but desire some aspect of risk management, such as the guaranteed death benefits or living benefits offered by most insurance companies.

4.2.3 ADVANTAGES OF ANNUITIES

An annuity protects and builds a person's cash reserve. The insurer guarantees principal and interest (in the case of a fixed annuity; a variable annuity is subject to the performance of the underlying selected sub-accounts), and the promise (if purchased) that the annuitant can never outlive the income stream. This makes annuities particularly attractive to those who have retired and desire, or require, fixed monthly income and lifetime guarantees.

An annuity allows a client to invest in the market while moderating risk. The insurer may provide guarantees of death proceeds or a certain annuitization amount (if purchased) within a variable annuity, thus providing clients with guarantees that otherwise would be unavailable to those clients who purchased the underlying investments directly. This makes a variable annuity particularly attractive to those clients who have retired or are nearing retirement and need (or want) to hold riskier investments while trying to moderate risk.

A client can "time" the receipt of income and shift it into lower bracket years. This ability to decide when to be taxed allows the annuitant to compound the advantage of deferral.

Because the interest on an annuity is tax deferred, an annuity paying the same rate of interest (after expenses) as a taxable investment will result in a higher effective after-tax yield.

The risk management factors available, especially in variable annuities, may enable clients to take on greater risk in the underlying investment options (e.g., equities, smaller capitalization equities, high yield bonds, etc.) while still maintaining a reasonable overall risk exposure due to the underlying guarantees.

Adjusted Gross Income (AGI) may be reduced in years where the annuity is held with no withdrawals (thanks to the tax deferral features of the accumulation phase). In addition, annuitants may recognize less taxable income during the payout phase, due to the partial recovery of basis associated with each payment. A reduced AGI can bring tax savings, as many other income tax rules are calculated based upon AGI and, generally, a lower AGI results in lower taxation (and vice versa). A reduced AGI can create tax savings by lowering the amount of Social Security includable in income, reducing the floor threshold for deduction of medical expenses (7.5 percent of AGI) or miscellaneous itemized deductions (2 percent of AGI), and avoiding the threshold for phase out of exemptions and itemized deductions.

4.2.4 DISADVANTAGES OF ANNUITIES

Receipt of a lump sum (either at retirement, or to a beneficiary at death) could result in a significant tax burden because income averaging is not available (however, planning can moderate this if the proceeds are annuitized).

The cash flow stream of a fixed payout may not keep pace with inflation, particularly for longer-term payout phases such as a life annuitization.

Annuity owners generally incur a 10 percent penalty tax on withdrawals of accumulated interest during the accumulation phase prior to age 59½, unless the annuity owner is disabled (this may also apply to the annuitization phase if the annuity was not an immediate annuity and the owner selected certain short payout terms).

With a few limited exceptions, annuity contracts held by corporations or other entities that are not natural persons, are not treated as annuity contracts for federal income tax purposes. This means that income on the contracts for any taxable year are treated as current taxable ordinary income to the owner of the contract regardless of whether or not the owners make any withdrawals.

If the client is forced to liquidate the investment in the early years of an annuity, management and maintenance fees and sales costs could prove expensive. Total management fees and mortality charges can run from 1 to 2½ percent of the value of the contract (occasionally as high as 3 percent in the case of variable annuities with a number of underlying guarantees). Most insurers charge a "back-end" surrender charge if the owners terminate contracts within the first few years after purchase to compensate the insurers for the up-front sales charges that they typically do not levy.

Owners are taxed on investment earnings at the owners' ordinary income tax rates when they receive payments, regardless of the source or nature of the returns. Consequently, investment earnings attributable to long-term capital appreciation (typically in variable annuities) do not enjoy the more favorable long-term capital gain tax rate that otherwise generally would apply. This has become even more disadvantageous in recent years with the reduction of the maximum long-term capital gain rate to 15 percent or even 5 percent or zero percent. Furthermore, investment earnings attributable to dividends on stocks that would qualify for the 15 percent maximum tax rate if the stocks were held outside an annuity also are taxed at the owner's ordinary income tax rate (although owners/annuitants will not be taxed on these dividends until they receive payments). Consequently, variable annuities, where the annuity owners, generally, are more inclined to invest in equities, have been much less attractive under the recent tax regime of lower capital gains and dividend tax rates.

However, the American Taxpayer Relief Act of 2012 (ATRA) increased the tax rate for qualified dividend income and capital gains for certain higher income taxpayers. For tax years beginning after 2012, the maximum rate on qualified dividend income and capital gains is 20 percent for taxpayers in the 39.6 percent income tax bracket. Consequently, for high-income taxpayers these increased tax rates on capital gains and dividend income make annuities relatively more attractive than they were while the maximum tax rate was limited to 15 percent.

For taxpayers in the 25, 28, 33, or 35 percent income tax brackets, the maximum rate on qualified dividend income remains at 15 percent. For taxpayers in the 15 percent and 10 percent income tax brackets, the tax rate on qualified dividend income was reduced to 5 percent in 2003 through 2007, and to 0 percent for tax years beginning after 2007. Also, ATRA eliminated the sunset provision that was included in prior legislation so that these tax rates will apply to qualified dividend income permanently (that is, until newly-enacted legislation changes these provisions of the code).

4.2.5 TYPES OF ANNUITIES

Annuities are classified according to:

- how premiums are paid
- what residual values, if any, are paid upon the death of the annuitant
- when benefit payments begin
- how many lives are covered
- what investment options are available to the owner of the annuity contract
- how benefits are calculated.

It is important to bear in mind that a change in almost any of the above classifications results in an adjustment in the payout the annuity provides to maintain an actuarially equivalent benefit. Figure 4.2 shows how annuities are classified.

Figure 4.2

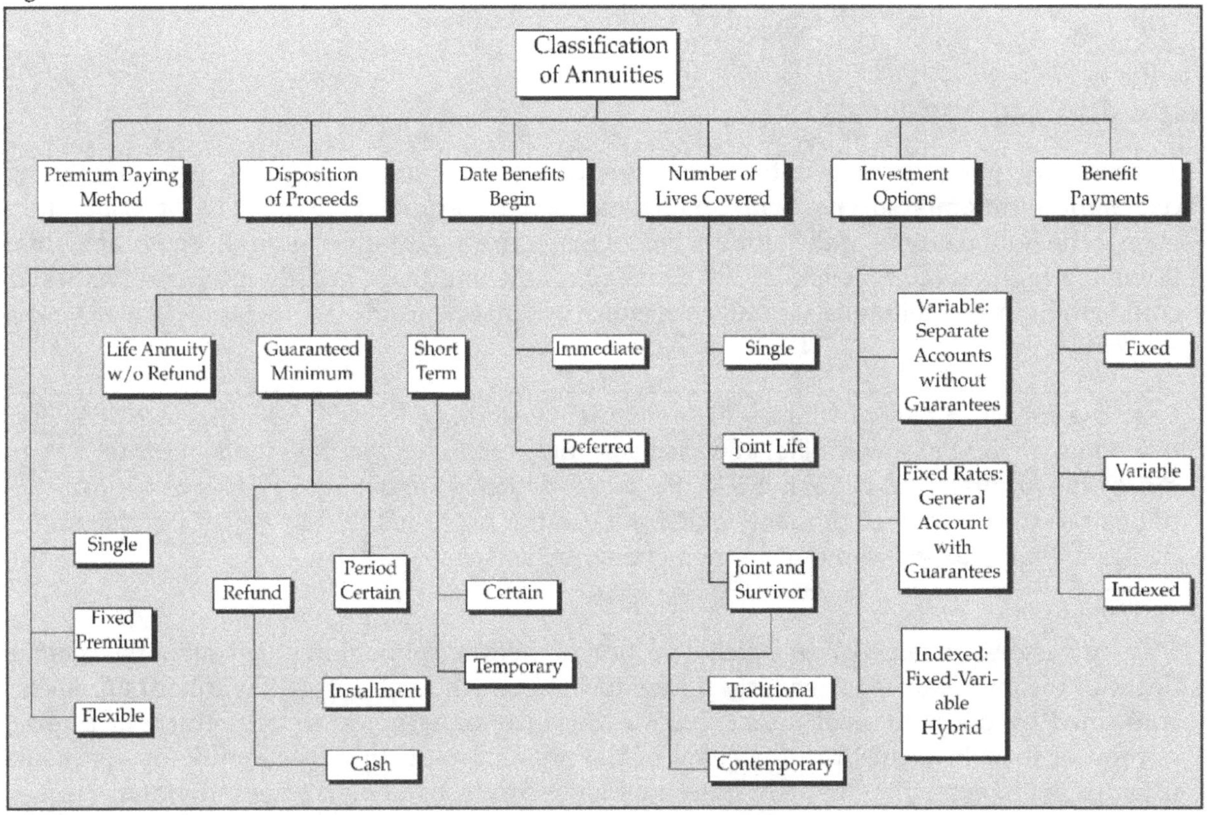

Premium Paying Method

Single premium annuities are often the ideal vehicles for people who have come into large cash sums. A single premium annuity will convert such amounts, for example, from an inheritance, from the sale of a business or a large piece of real estate, or from a qualified pension or profit-sharing plan lump-sum distribution, into a lifetime or certain fixed-period stream of payments. Immediate annuities are virtually always single-premium annuities (clients with subsequent investment amounts would simply purchase another immediate annuity). Single-premium structures also occur sometimes with deferred fixed annuities that provide for guaranteed interest crediting rates for a specified period (to prevent subsequent investments at these guaranteed rates if general interest rates decline in the future). Single-premium structures are relatively rare amongst deferred variable annuities.

Fixed-premium annuities are favored by investors who do not have large cash sums to invest but who desire a regular investment program with a forced saving feature. Typically, these instruments require purchasers to make fixed annual (semiannual, quarterly, monthly or even weekly) premium payments that continue until the desired annuity starting date (the date when payouts begin). Because the periodic premiums are fixed, the total accumulation, and, therefore, the ultimate annuity payout, is very predictable. Fixed-premium annuities today are relatively uncommon, having been replaced instead by flexible-premium annuities.

Flexible-premium annuities allow the contract owner to invest (make premium contributions) at any time and in any amount desired. In rare instances, the insurance company requires certain minimum annual contributions within the first few years, but after this initial period (or from the start in most cases) the insurers generally place no restrictions or requirements on purchasers with regard to the timing or amount of further contributions.

Disposition of Proceeds

A *life annuity* with no refund feature continues annuity payouts only as long as the annuitant (or one of the annuitants) survive, with no final payment or refund at the death of the last annuitant, even if the total paid out of the annuity is less than the amount invested in the contract. This can involve a high amount of risk, as the death of a lone annuitant shortly after contract issuance could result in a forfeiture of virtually the entire original deposit.

Example. If Mr. Smith purchases an immediately annuity for $50,000 that provides for payments of $300/month for life, and dies after only receiving two payments, his total return out of the contract will be only $600. He will forfeit the remaining $49,400 of his original deposit to the insurance company, which will use the proceeds to help offset the payments due to annuity holders who outlive their life expectancies.

Many investors are reluctant to forfeit a portion of their investment in the event of the premature death of the annuitant—particularly if they have heirs who will ultimately inherit all assets not consumed by the individual during his life, Because many investors are reluctant to forfeit a portion of their investment in the event of the premature death of the annuitant—particularly if family members will ultimately inherit all assets not consumed by the individual during his life – insurance companies also offer annuity contracts with minimum payback guarantees. These guarantees take two forms – *refund annuities* and *period-certain annuities.*

Refund annuities promise to pay the difference between the amount invested in the contract (generally the total of the premiums paid) and the annuity payments actually paid out before the death of the annuitant. This refund takes the form either of a lump-sum cash payment or of installment payouts. *Period-certain annuities* promise to make payments for a stipulated period, such as five, ten, or twenty years, or for the annuitant's life, whichever is longer. However, keep in mind that, due to the time value of money, this guarantee still does not make the annuity holder entirely "whole" in comparison to having invested the assets in an alternative to begin with (where their funds would have ostensibly been *growing* during this time period, not merely preserving the original principal amount).

The payout period also may be short-term—that is, for a specified period generally shorter than the expected life (or lives) of the annuitant(s). *Term-certain annuities* operate similarly to the amortization of a loan. Payments continue for a specified term only, regardless of when the annuitant dies. A *temporary annuity* is a variation on the period-certain annuity concept. However, rather than paying a specified amount for the *longer* of the annuitant's life or the specified term, a temporary annuity continues payments only for the *shorter* of the annuitant's life or the specified term.

Date Benefits Begin

An *immediate annuity* begins annuity payments within one year after the purchaser contributes all premiums. People commonly use immediate annuities when they wish to convert a large lump-sum amount, such as a substantial distribution from a qualified pension or profit sharing plan, the settlement proceeds of a lawsuit, or simply a sizeable amount of cash, into an immediate income stream. In contrast, as the name suggests, *deferred annuities* delay or defer payments for a period of time (the accumulation phase) after the purchaser has completed making premiums or contributions. People frequently use deferred annuities when they have cash to invest before retirement and wish to postpone the beginning of the annuity payments until retirement or later.

Number of Lives Covered

The annuity payout period may depend on one or two lives, or, less commonly, more lives. A *single-life annuity* (with no refund feature) makes payments until the single covered life (the sole annuitant) dies. In the case of annuities based on two or more lives, payouts may continue until the last annuitant dies (or, more rarely, only until the first annuitant dies, depending upon the exact terms of the contract). Annuities whose payments continue until the last death of the covered lives are called *joint-and-last-survivor annuities,* or just joint-and-survivor annuities. Those annuities whose payments cease upon the first death are called *joint-life annuities.* Currently, joint-and-survivor annuities are much more common than joint-life annuities.

A joint-and-survivor annuity may pay one amount while both annuitants are alive and the same, or another (lesser) amount, after the first death. The surviving annuitant often receives some specified percentage (called the survivor-benefit ratio) of the amount payable before the first death. Survivor-benefit ratios typically range from 50 to 100 percent, with 50, 66, 75, and 100 percent being the most common ratios.

Example. A joint-and-75 percent-survivor annuity paying a $50,000 annual joint benefit would pay $37,500 per year to the survivor after the first death. The amount of the survivor-benefit ratio generally is selected at the inception of the payout phase (annuitization) of the contract.

The benefit payable to the survivor also may depend on which annuitant dies first. The *traditional joint-and-survivor annuity* has a principal annuitant and a secondary annuitant or beneficiary. The survivor-benefit ratio applies only to the benefit payable to the surviving secondary annuitant after the principal annuitant's death. If the principal annuitant outlives the secondary annuitant, the insurer does not reduce the benefit payments. These types of payment structures are particularly common in joint-and survivor-annuity payments from defined-benefit pension plans (where the former employee is the principal annuitant). In recent years an alternative form of the joint-and-survivor annuity has become popular. This *contemporary joint-and-survivor annuity* pays the reduced benefit to the survivor regardless of which annuitant dies first. These types of payment structures are most common from commercially available joint-and-survivor annuities. For a given total investment, insurance companies can afford to pay relatively higher joint-and-survivor benefits on these annuities than on traditional joint-and-survivor annuities.

Investment Options

Fixed-rate annuities are similar to universal life policies in that amounts credited to cash values are based on the insurer's current declared rate, subject to a minimum guarantee of about 3 to 4.5 percent (varying by annuity contract and insurance company). Insurers may guarantee rates paid on new money (current contributions) for one to five years (or occasionally as long as ten years). The currently declared rate depends on the performance of the insurer's general investment portfolio or general account, which is largely invested in fixed income investments such as bonds and mortgages. Although interest credits to the annuity depend on market rates on these types of fixed income investments, the cash value itself is not market valued. Similar to a savings account, once the insurer credits interest, the cash value will not decline if the market value of the underlying assets in the insurer's general account declines. (However, some insurers levy a market adjustment to the annuity contract value based upon interest rate changes in the event of early surrender). The insurer bears the market risk.

Analogously, variable annuities are similar to variable insurance policies. The annuity owner may choose to invest contributions and cash values in a broad spectrum of investment options or separate accounts, which are similar to mutual funds (although the investor is limited to the selection of investment choices that are offered within the annuity contract). The investment options usually include diversified stock, bond, and money market funds and frequently include specialized stock funds, foreign stock and bond funds, real estate equity and mortgage funds, and even asset allocation funds (a type of balanced fund where the insurer's investment manager allocates investments among the other funds). In contrast with fixed-rate annuities, cash values depend on the market value of the underlying assets in the selected separate accounts. Variable annuity owners bear the market risk of investment and forego minimum interest rate guarantees (although some limited guarantees may be available, subject to additional costs and substantial restrictions). However, they have the flexibility to choose their investment portfolio and the potential to earn far greater total returns than they would earn on fixed-rate annuities.

Indexed annuities (IAs), also called Equity Index Annuities (EIAs) are a hybrid of fixed and variable annuities. The returns on IAs are linked to an equity index, such as the S&P 500 index. However, the annuity is not actually invested in the stocks making up the index. Rather, like with fixed annuities, the insurer pays the returns to IAs from its general account. However, the insurer bases the amount allocated to the IA on some percentage, for example, 85 percent, of the appreciation in the reference index (often subject to annual caps and/or interest spreads). If the index declines in value, the insurer credits the IA with a minimum guaranteed amount (which may be 0 percent, but is generally never negative). In this way, IAs attempt to provide investors with some of the upside potential of the equity markets, with the downside protection of more conservative general-account investments.

Benefit Payments

Annuity benefit payments may be fixed or variable. Fixed-benefit annuities guarantee a minimum annuity benefit payment per dollar of accumulated value, similar to settlement options under life insurance policies. Variable-benefit annuities make no guarantees. Variable benefit payments depend on the market value of the assets in the separate accounts.

4.2.6 TAX IMPLICATIONS

Annuitants' investment in an annuity is returned in equal tax-free (return of capital) amounts during the payout phase. Any additional amount received is taxed at ordinary income rates. This means each payment consists of two parts: the first part is considered return of capital and is, therefore, nontaxable, while the second part of each payment is considered return on capital (income) and is, therefore, taxable at ordinary rates.

The amount of each period's payment that will be considered nontaxable is determined by the following ratio, called the exclusion ratio:

$$\frac{\text{Investment in Contract}}{\text{Expected Return}}$$

The exclusion ratio is expressed as a percentage and applies to each annuity payment equally through the payout phase. For instance, assume a seventy-year-old purchases an annuity. He pays (the investment in the contract is) $12,000 for the annuity. Assume his expected return throughout the payout phase is $19,200.

The exclusion ratio is $12,000/$19,200, or 62.5 percent. If the monthly payment he receives is $100, the portion that he can exclude from gross income is $62.50 (62.5 percent of $100). The $37.50 balance of each $100 monthly payment is ordinary income.

The full amount of each annuity payment received would be tax-free if the investment in the contract exceeds the expected return (i.e., when the exclusion ratio would be greater than or equal to 100 percent).

The excludable portion of any annuity payment may not exceed the unrecovered investment in the contract (unless the annuity started before January 1, 1987). The unrecovered investment in the contract is the policyowner's premium cost, reduced by any dividends received in cash or used to reduce premiums, and by the aggregate amount received under the contract on or after the annuity starting date to the extent it was excludable from income. Thus, the unrecovered investment in the contract is reduced each time an annuity payment is made, by the amount of the payment that is excluded from income by the exclusion ratio. This rule limits the total amount the policyowner can exclude from income to the total amount of his contribution. Once an annuitant has fully recovered his investment in the contract, which generally occurs at the end of the *expected* payout term, 100 percent of each subsequent payment will be taxable. Payments can continue beyond the expected payout term when the annuitant actually lives longer than his or her actuarial (expected) life expectancy.

Some annuities provide a refund if the annuitant dies before recovering his entire cost. The present value of the refund option must be ascertained by government tables and subtracted from the investment in the contract. This would also apply if the annuity payout phase incorporated a combined life expectancy and term certain structure.

The expected return is the total amount that the owner (or owners) should receive given the payments specified (which include an assumed internal growth rate) multiplied by the certain term or life expectancy according to the government's tables (currently Table V for single lives and Table VI for joint and survivor annuities). For instance, under Table V, a seventy-year-old has a life expectancy of seventeen years. If he (or she, because the life expectancy tables are unisex) receives $100 a month, the expected return would be $20,400 ($1,200 a year x seventeen years).

When an annuitant dies before receiving the full amount guaranteed under a refund or period-certain life annuity, the owner or beneficiary receiving the balance of the guaranteed amount will have no taxable income (unless the amount received by the beneficiary plus the amount that had been received tax-free by the annuitant exceeds the investment in the contract).

If the refund or commuted (present) value of the remaining installments is applied by the owner or beneficiary to purchase a new annuity, payments received will be taxed under the annuity rules to the beneficiary. The insurer will consider the refund amount to be the beneficiary's investment in the new contract and the insurer will determine a new exclusion ratio. This option is often selected if the guaranteed refund amount will exceed the unrecovered investment in the contract and would otherwise create a partially taxable lump-sum payment.

If the owner was receiving payments under a joint and survivor annuity, the surviving owner excludes from income the same percentage of each payment that was excludable by the first annuitant (assuming that the joint annuitants were joint owners). An income tax deduction may be available to the survivor owner/annuitant to the extent inclusion of the annuity in the estate of the first to die generated an estate tax (under the rules for income in respect of a decedent).

When an owner makes a partial withdrawal from the contract and takes a reduced annuity for the same term, a portion of the amount withdrawn will be subject to income tax.

When an owner makes a partial withdrawal from the contract (allocable to an investment in the contract made after August 13, 1982) and chooses to take the same payments for a different term, to the extent the cash surrender value of the contract exceeds the investment in the contract, gain will be realized in the form of a taxable withdrawal of interest.

Income earned by a variable annuity is not taxed during the accumulation period. No tax will be payable until the earlier of: (a) the surrender of the contract; (b) a withdrawal from the contract; or (c) the time payments under the annuity begin (annuitization). To obtain annuity treatment, however, the underlying investments of the segregated asset account must be "adequately diversified" according to IRS regulations.

Payments made as an annuity under a variable annuity are not subject to the same exclusion ratio as is a regular fixed annuity. This is because it is impossible to determine the expected return. Instead, the following formula is used:

$$\frac{\text{Investment in Contract}}{\text{Number of Years of Expected Return}}$$

If there is a period certain or refund guarantee, the investment in the contract is adjusted accordingly. If payments are made for a fixed number of years without regard to life expectancy, the divisor is that fixed number of years. If payments are made for a single life, use IRS Table V. If payments are to be made on a joint and survivor basis, use Table VI. As in the case of a fixed annuitization, the exclusion ratio no longer applies once an annuitant reaches his life expectancy and has fully recovered his investment in the contract.

If payments drop below the excludable amount in any given year, the annuitant can elect to redetermine the excludable amount in the next tax year in which he receives an annuity payment. The loss in exclusions is divided by the number of years remaining (in the case of a fixed period annuity). In the case of a life annuity the loss is divided by the annuitant's life expectancy computed as of the first day of the first period for which an amount is received as an annuity.

For instance, assume a sixty-five-year-old taxpayer purchased an annuity for $21,000. The contract provides variable annual payments for life. His life expectancy is twenty-one years so he may exclude $1,000 of each annuity payment from income ($21,000/21). Assume on his seventieth birthday he receives only $150, $850 less than his excludable amount. At age seventy his life expectancy is seventeen years. He may elect to add $50 ($850/17) to his $1,000 exclusion, a total of $1,050 which he may exclude that year and in subsequent years.

If an annuitant dies before payments received equal cost, the owner can take a loss deduction for the amount of the unrecovered investment, provided the annuity starting date was after July 1, 1986. So if a wife purchases a single premium nonrefundable annuity (whether on her own life, or alternatively on the life of her husband), and the annuitant dies before all costs have been recovered, a loss deduction will be allowed.

The deduction for the unrecovered investment in the contract is an itemized deduction, but not a miscellaneous deduction. Therefore, it is not subject to the 2 percent floor. If the decedent/annuitant is the owner, the loss is taken on the decedent's final return, and will be treated as a business loss, eligible to be carried back if the loss exceeds the income shown on the decedent's final return. Otherwise, if the owner is not the decedent/annuitant, the owner takes the loss on his tax return. In addition, these deductions can ultimately be taken by the estate or any other beneficiary that receives post-death payments.

Amounts payable under a deferred annuity contract at the death of an annuitant (prior to the contract's maturity) will be partially taxable as ordinary income to the beneficiary. The taxable amount is equal to the excess of (a) the death benefit (plus aggregate dividends and any other amounts that were received tax free) over (b) total gross premiums.

Beneficiaries can elect to delay reporting of the gain in the year of the annuitant's death if the beneficiary applies the death benefit under a life income or installment option within sixty days of the annuitant's death. The beneficiary will then report income according to an exclusion ratio. The beneficiary's investment in the contract will be the same as the annuitant's investment in the contract. The expected return is based on the income the beneficiary will receive and the beneficiary's life expectancy.

Owners of annuities often take dividends, make cash withdrawals, or take other amounts out of their annuity contracts before the annuity starting dates. Such amounts are taxable as income to the extent that the policy cash value exceeds the investment in the contract—this results in a LIFO (last in, first out) type of treatment where all interest/growth is taxed before any tax-free return of capital payments can occur.

This interest first rule was imposed to discourage the use of annuity contracts as short term investment vehicles. Under this rule, a loan is treated as if it were a cash withdrawal.

Likewise, to the extent the owner uses a contract as collateral for a loan, the owner will be taxed on the amounts borrowed (to the extent that the amount received is less than or equal to the gain inherent in the contract). If the amount received exceeds the built-in gain, the excess of what was borrowed over potential gain is considered a tax-free return of the contract owner's investment. With respect to contracts entered into after October 21, 1988, amounts borrowed increase investment in the contract to the extent they are includible in income under these rules.

In applying the interest first rule, all contracts entered into after October 21, 1988 and issued by the same company to the same policyholder during any twelve-month period are treated as one contract.

Premature distributions (those made before the dates in the following list) are subject not only to the normal tax on ordinary income but also to a penalty tax of 10 percent. The 10 percent penalty applies only to the amount of the distribution that is included in income.

The penalty for premature distributions will not apply to any of the following:

(a) payments that are part of a series of substantially equal periodic payments made for the life (or life expectancy) of the taxpayer or the joint lives (or joint life expectancies) of the taxpayer and his beneficiary (unless the series of payments is modified under certain circumstances);

(b) payments made on or after the time the contract owner reaches age 59½;

(c) payments made on account of the contract owner's disability;

(d) payments made from qualified retirement plans and IRAs (but these are subject to other similar premature distribution requirements);

(e) payments made to a beneficiary (or annuitant's estate) on or after the death of an annuitant;

(f) distributions under an immediate annuity contract;

(g) an annuity contract purchased on the termination of certain qualified employer retirement plans and held until the employee separates from service;

(h) payments allocable to investment in the contract before August 14, 1982.

If an annuity owner dies before the starting date of the annuity payments, the cash value of the contract must either be distributed within five years of death or used within one year of death to provide a life annuity or installment payments payable over a period not longer than the beneficiary's life expectancy. However, if the surviving spouse is the beneficiary, the spouse can elect to become the new owner of the contract instead of selecting one of the above options.

The 10 percent premature distribution penalty tax does not apply to required after-death distributions.

If the annuity contract is transferred by gift, the tax deferral on the inside build up that was allowed to the original contract owner is terminated. The donor of the gift is treated as having received non-annuity income in an amount equal to the excess of the cash surrender value of the contract over the investment in the contract at the time of the transfer. The recipient of the gift will take a new basis in the contract equal to the donor's investment in the contract, plus the amount of gain recognized on the gift (note that the new basis, the sum of the donor's basis and the donor's investment in the contract, generally is equal to the fair market value of the contract).

Tax-free buildup within the contract is allowed only to *natural persons*. If an annuity contract is held by a person who is not a natural person, then the annuity contract is not treated as an annuity and the income on the contract is treated as ordinary income received or accrued by the owner during that taxable year.

Corporations are not natural persons. Neither is the typical trust, although a trust acting as the agent for a natural person would itself be considered a natural person. But if an employer is the agent for its employees, the contract will be considered as if owned by the employer. The employer will therefore be taxed on the inside build up. This means annuities are no longer appropriate tax advantaged investments for nonqualified deferred compensation agreements.

Exceptions from the natural persons rules allow tax-free buildup of the following annuities:

(a) Annuities received by the executor of a decedent at the decedent's death;

(b) Annuities held by a qualified retirement plan or IRA;

(c) Annuities considered qualifying funding assets (used to provide funding for structured settlements and by property and casualty insurance companies to fund periodic payments for damages);

(d) Annuities purchased by an employer on termination of a qualified plan and held until all amounts under the plan are distributed to the employee or his beneficiary;

(e) Annuities which are immediate (i.e., those which have a starting date no more than one year from the date the annuity was purchased and provide for a series of substantially equal periodic payments to be made at least annually over the annuity period).

Chapter 5

INVESTMENT RISK AND RETURN

5.1 INVESTMENT RISK

Section Overview:

5.1.1 Introduction

5.1.2 Variability in Expected Return

5.1.3 Types and Sources of Risk

5.1.4 Investment Risk Management

5.1.1 INTRODUCTION

Most people think of investment risk as the potential for loss. They envision the dollar value of their hard-earned assets shrinking due to forces beyond their control.

Because people purchase investments with the expectation of gain, focusing on the potential for loss alone is insufficient in explaining investment risk.

The notion of investment risk must take into account the possibility that the return may be positive (but greater or less than expected), zero, or negative. There can be wide variations in the magnitude of either positive or negative returns. When one examines all possibilities (positive or negative returns and the variations in the magnitude of each type of return), one can more accurately define investment risk as the variability in the expected return from an investment. The greater the potential variation in the investment's expected return, the greater is the actual risk of owning the investment.

5.1.2 VARIABILITY IN EXPECTED RETURN

Investors must examine each investment separately because the various forces affecting return have a different impact on each type of investment. For example, if interest rates increase, the prices of electric utility stocks may be adversely affected because many investors purchase utility stocks for the income they provide.

Investors, who normally would be in the market for income-producing stocks such as utilities, would be attracted to newly issued bonds offering a higher current return. Some holders of utility stocks will sell and invest the proceeds in bonds offering more attractive returns. The lack of buyers and the increase in the number of sellers will drive down the prices of utility stocks until their current dividend yield is competitive with the newly issued, higher interest bonds.

However, the prices of growth stocks such as those in the tech industry will be influenced much less by rising interest rates. Investors purchase growth stocks for their long-term capital gains potential and show less concern with current dividend yield than do investors who hold more income-oriented stocks with higher dividend yields.

The total investment risk for a particular asset depends on the combined effect of many factors. Before investing in certain products, it is important to understand the various risks that are associated with them. Investments may be exposed to a multitude of different types or sources of risk.

5.1.3 TYPES AND SOURCES OF RISK

Actuarial Risk – Risk an insurance underwriter covers in exchange for premiums, such as the risk of premature death.

Agency Risk – Agency risk is the risk associated when a principal delegates decisions to an agent who may not always act in the principal's best interest. The most common principal-agent conflict in the investment management industry is between the client and the investment advisor. A principal-agent conflict occurs when the objectives of the client and the agent are not perfectly aligned. There is a widespread area of research in economic and financial theory involving the design of agency incentive and compensation systems that better correlate the agent's rewards with the achievement of the client's objectives. Principal-agent conflicts arise in the control, regulatory, legal, and incentive arrangements for government agencies, professional management of firms, professional portfolio and money managers, financial advisers, and many other areas. However, whatever the compensation arrangement, conflicts will inevitably arise.

For instance, basing a money manager's compensation on the rate of return earned by the fund he manages may seem to match investors' objectives for higher returns with the agent's incentive for compensation. However, because money managers rarely have to pay investors if they happen to lose money in a given evaluation period (unless investors can prove malfeasance or fraud), the money manager has an incentive, perhaps, to take on greater risks in the search for exceptional gains than is consistent with the risk level the investors wish to bear. In addition, the investors and the manager may have different time horizons. The manager may be inclined to engage in transactions that enhance measured performance over the current evaluation period, but at the potential loss of future performance.

Asset Class Risk – Stocks, bonds, and cash are the three major asset classes (but certainly not the only ones). If investors allocate a disproportionate amount to any of the three main categories, or totally ignore one or two of them, they are subject to asset class risk. It is generally prudent to diversify across all major asset classes even when investors want to give primary emphasis to, say, stocks.

Bid-Ask Spread Risk – Securities sold over-the-counter by investment banking houses that make a market in the shares are subject to the risk that the bid-ask price spread will change. Dealers charge one price, the ask price, when they sell these securities and another lower price, the bid price, when they buy. The spread, or difference, is the profit the market maker gets for making the market in the security and helps to cover the market makers' costs in maintaining an inventory of the securities. Depending upon supply and demand conditions in the security or the entrance or exit of market makers in a particular security, the spread may change over time. For example, investors buying a security when the spread is narrow may think that they will later be able to sell the security at only a small discount from the ask price. However, if the spread increases, the effective cost of the round-trip transaction will rise.

Business (Company) Risk – Business risk is an economic or operating risk reflected in the variability of a firm's earnings. Changes in earnings or the variability of earnings may result in changes in the investing public's perception of the company and sudden changes in the price of the stock. In worst case scenarios, companies may fail, leaving their stocks or bonds worthless. The best defense against this particular risk is to invest in more than one company and in companies engaged in different lines of business. Business risk is composed largely of four risk subcategories:

Management risk – Financial difficulties can arise from management's inability to handle change or the failure to adapt to changing competitive conditions. Some companies are slow to take advantage of cost-cutting technologies and gradually become high-cost producers who are unable to survive in a highly competitive marketplace.

Product or obsolescence risk – Shifting demand or changes in consumer tastes and preferences can quickly result in companies producing unwanted goods. Sometimes this risk is termed *technological* or *innovative risk*, as new innovations or technologies make a company's products or processes no longer state-of-the-art.

Legislative/regulatory/tax risk – Changes in the law can affect a company's fortunes. For example, if the federal government abandons protectionist policies that artificially raise the price of sugar in the United States to over 43 cents a pound and allow U.S. companies to purchase sugar on world markets at world prices (around twenty-six cents a pound), the makers of corn sweeteners would suddenly find their companies unable to compete. They would be stuck with production facilities they could no longer use. Their earnings would decline, their prospects would deteriorate, and the prices of their stocks would suddenly decline. Other companies such as Coca Cola and Pepsi, who purchase sugar in large quantities, would see a dramatic decrease in the price of a major raw material. The market would immediately recognize their higher earnings potential and bid up their stock prices.

Financial risk – This is the risk related to the mix of debt and equity used by a firm to raise capital. The more debt in a firm's capital structure, the greater its financial risk. Debt financing, as opposed to equity financing, obligates a firm to make periodic interest payments and to repay the amount borrowed at some future date. Before a firm can distribute dividends to its common stockholders, it must meet its fixed-payment obligations. Failure to meet these obligations when they are due will result in insolvency or bankruptcy.

Call (Prepayment, Redemption) Risk – Many bonds and some preferred stocks are issued with what is known as a call feature. The call feature gives the issuer the right to call the bond – to retire it after a certain date or on several dates before maturity. Having the right to call the bond does not mean that the issuer has a duty or obligation to exercise the call. Generally, bonds will be called only when it is profitable for the issuer to do so. This occurs when interest rates have declined since the bonds were issued. The high interest issue is then called and replaced with a new issue that is sold at a much lower interest rate. So call risk inherently includes *reinvestment risk* as well.

Example. Suppose an investor purchases a bond with a 9 percent coupon, and expects it to pay that rate for the next ten years. Suddenly, the bond is called. The investor receives the principal amount of the bond (and perhaps a little more as the call price is generally a little more than the principal value), but when the investor attempts to reinvest the funds in the bond market, the investor finds the interest rate is now 7 percent for similar issues. Suddenly the investor's interest income drops from $90 to $70 on a $1,000 bond – a 22 percent decline. This is what call risk is all about.

Country Risk – This refers to the risk that a country will not be able to honor its financial commitments. When a country defaults, it can harm the performance of all other financial instruments in that country, as well as other countries with which it has relations. Country risk applies to stocks, bonds, mutual funds, options, and futures that are issued within a particular country. In addition, this danger is associated with single-country mutual funds or closed-end funds and ADRs sold or traded in the United States. This type of risk is most often seen in emerging markets or countries that have a severe deficit. Investing globally introduces many potential risks — including currency fluctuation, the potential for diplomatic and political instability, regulatory and liquidity risks, foreign taxation, and differences in auditing or other financial standards. Investing in foreign stocks can deliver great rewards, but investors must be aware of the risks and plan accordingly.

Credit or Default Risk – This is the risk that a government, company, or individual will be unable to pay the contractual interest or principal on its debt obligations. This type of risk is of particular concern to investors who hold bonds within their portfolio. Government bonds, especially those issued by the federal government, have the least amount of default risk and the lowest interest rates among bond issuers, while corporate bonds tend to have the highest amount of default risk, but also the higher interest rates. Bonds with lower chances of default are considered to be investment grade, and bonds with higher chances are considered to be junk bonds. Bond rating services, such as Moody's Investor Services, Standard and Poor's, and Fitch Ratings rate bonds on the basis of their perceived default risk. These ratings determine which bonds are deemed investment grade, and which bonds are junk.

Currency (Foreign Exchange) Risk – Foreign holdings may change in value as the value of currency changes. If the U.S. dollar grows stronger relative to foreign currencies, investors will experience a currency loss on their foreign securities. As an example, assume American investors invest in some Canadian stock in Canadian dollars. Even if the share value appreciates, they may lose money if the Canadian dollar depreciates in relation to the American dollar. Conversely, if the U.S. dollar weakens relative to foreign currencies, investors who invest in the foreign securities will enjoy a bonus.

Fluctuating exchange rates are of particular concern to single-country investors. Currency fluctuations can be devastating for individuals who hold funds for short periods. Some foreign-stock fund managers hedge their portfolios against adverse currency moves with currency futures or forward contracts.

Depth of Market Risk – Depth of market risk is related to bid-ask spread risk and is related to securities that are relatively thinly capitalized. An investor trying to sell a relatively sizeable position in a thinly capitalized stock may find that there are not enough willing buyers at the current price to absorb his entire sale. Consequently, the very act of selling may depress the price and reduce the investor's gain or increase his loss.

Discount or Premium Risk – Closed-end investment companies listed on organized exchanges or sold over the counter typically trade at values different from their Net Asset Values (NAV). The NAV is the value at which the securities underlying a share in the fund would trade if they were purchased directly in the market, rather than through the closed-end fund.

More often than not, closed-end fund shares trade at a discount from NAV, which can be a boon for investors. For instance, assume a closed-end stock fund is trading at a 10 percent discount from NAV and the underlying stocks are paying a 3 percent dividend yield relative to their market values as independently traded stocks. Investors who buy the stocks through the closed-end investment company essentially get to purchase $100 worth of stock for only a $90 investment. Consequently, the dividend yield on their investment is 3.33 percent. In addition, if the underlying stock values increase 20 percent, the closed-end fund investors' share will increase by 20 percent if the discount remains steady at 10 percent.

Discounts and premiums on closed-end funds vary over time. Suppose the discount from NAV increases from 10 percent to, say, 15 percent at the same time the underlying securities increase in value by 20 percent. The closed-end fund investors will earn a respectable 13.33 percent, but that is still about 6.67 percent less than the 20 percent they otherwise would have earned by investing directly in the underlying stocks. But there can be more negative effects as well. If the value of the underlying securities had fallen by 20 percent while the discount also increased by 5 percent, the closed-end fund investors would have lost 24.44 percent as compared with only a 20 percent loss on a direct investment in the underlying stocks.

But suppose the discount from NAV decreases from 10 percent to 5 percent at the same time the underlying securities increase in value by 20 percent. The closed-end fund investors would have gained 26.67 percent as compared with only a 20 percent gain on a direct investment in the underlying stocks. If the value of the underlying securities had fallen by 20 percent while the discount also decreased by 5 percent, the closed-end fund investors would have lost 15.56 percent as compared with a 20 percent loss on a direct investment in the underlying stocks.

Some funds trade at a discount due to high expense ratios or management fees. In these cases discounts will likely persist over time.

Although most closed-end funds usually sell at a discount from NAV, some frequently sell for premiums above NAV, especially among those funds investing in foreign stocks. The reason for this phenomenon is that individual investors often would find it extremely difficult to trade directly in all the underlying foreign securities of the fund, so they are willing to pay a premium to include these assets in their overall portfolio for diversification and asset allocation purposes.

Documentation Risk – The risk of loss due to an inadequacy or other unforeseen aspect involving the legal documentation of the financial contract.

Event Risk – Mergers, acquisitions, and other major restructurings can significantly affect a specific investment asset. For example, when one firm announces its intention to acquire another, the share prices of both companies are affected. This risk applies to bonds to some extent as well, but is not a consideration for other assets such as savings accounts and U.S. Treasury securities.

Financial Risk – This is the risk related to the mix of debt and equity used by a firm to raise capital. The more debt is in a firm's capital structure, the greater is its financial risk. Debt financing as opposed to equity financing obligates a firm to make periodic interest payments and to repay the amount borrowed at some future date. Before a firm can distribute dividends to its common stockholders, it must meet its fixed-payment obligations. Failure to meet these obligations when they are due will result in the company's insolvency or bankruptcy. The market's perceived level of this risk affects not just the company's cost of borrowing for bond issues and the value of its stock, but also the availability of lines of credit and financing for inventories and working capital, its credit terms with suppliers, and, ultimately, much of its cost of doing business.

Geographical or Location Risk – This is the risk associated typically with real estate, where the old saw goes: the three most important elements are location, location, and location! However, it is a broader concept, as well, relating to regional economic factors. In that sense, it is a smaller-scale version of *country risk*. For instance, certain regions of the United States, such as Texas, Oklahoma, and North Dakota are heavily involved in the oil business. If the oil industry has a serious downturn, the regional economies will suffer, affecting other companies and industries within the region such as financial institutions, real estate, and retail sales. Similarly, many companies have their headquarters in Delaware because of its favorable tax and regulatory environment. However, if state government policies would change, these companies could be adversely affected.

Industry or Sector Risk – This risk relates to uncertainties caused by particular features of the industry sector in which a company operates.

These risks can vary dramatically. New technologies, for example, are always going to expose investors to higher uncertainty of future returns than the market average – because of the inherent uncertainty of their new products and new markets – and they will certainly be more uncertain than food retailers. Food will never go out of fashion.

Industry risks can be identified and differentiated on a scale from low to high, relative to the market average. As investors demand rewards for bearing higher risk, investors can expect that overall stocks in the technology sector will offer higher returns than stocks in food retailing. However these returns are less likely to be realized than the lower, less risky returns in foods. Still, a very efficient company in the technology sector may suffer less than an inefficient food retailer.

Inflation (Purchasing Power) Risk – The purchasing power of the dollar declines during periods of inflation. While inflation has been moderate in recent years, it has been quite substantial during many past periods. For example, in the early 1980s, inflation rose to over 14 percent. Assets that are most susceptible to this risk include fixed income securities such as corporate and municipal bonds, and cash assets such as savings accounts and CDs. Generally speaking, real estate and equity investments such as common stocks tend to increase in value and pay higher dividends over time. It is not unusual for these investments to fail to keep up with inflation in the short run, but, over the long run, both the prices of these assets and the income they generate have generally more than kept up with inflation.

The risk associated with inflation is not so much with the level of inflation, because investments tend to be priced in the market to yield returns that account for anticipated inflation and give investors the real returns that are commensurate with their risk levels. The actual risk is with respect to *unanticipated* changes in inflationary expectations. But these changes can sometimes be beneficial as well. For instance, nobody anticipated in the early 1980s the speed with which President Reagan's tax and economic policies brought inflation rates down. Investors in long-term bonds reaped a capital appreciation windfall as interest rates fell in concert with inflation rates.

However, the level of inflation is also important because tax rates are applied to nominal yields, not real yields, so effective real tax rates rise as interest rates rise.

Inflation as Tax – Inflation is effectively a form of tax. It is an indirect tax, but no less real than the income tax investors pay directly to the government. For instance, if investors earn 7 percent on an investment when inflation is progressing at 4 percent, their actual or real return is less than 3 percent. In other words, they can now buy only roughly 3 percent more than they could before they invested, and the result does not yet even reflect the direct income taxes.

The logic of this is straightforward. For each dollar invested today at, say, 5 percent annually, investors will have $1.05 next year. If inflation progresses at, say, 3 percent annually, investors will need $1.03 next year to buy what could be bought for a dollar today. The real inflation-adjusted increase in their wealth per dollar invested is equal to $1.05/$1.03, which is equal to 1.0194. In other words, the real return on investment is 1.94 percent. If 5 percent is the nominal rate and 3 percent is the expected inflation rate, then the real rate of return is equal to 1.94 percent, as this example demonstrates.

In this case, the 3 percent inflation rate is equivalent to a whopping 61.2 percent tax on the 5 percent nominal return (0.612 × 5% = 3.06%; 5% – 3.06% = 1.94%).

Interaction of the Inflation Tax and the Income Tax – Income taxes are paid on nominal returns, not real returns. Consequently, as inflation rates increase, real effective income tax rates also increase.

Example. Assume an investor's marginal income-tax rate is 36 percent and the inflation rate is zero. In this case, the real return on an investment would be equal to the nominal return. An investment earning, say, 3 percent ordinary interest income before tax would provide a real after-tax return of 1.92 percent (3% × 0.36 = 1.08%; 3% – 1.08% = 1.92%).

Now assume that inflation is 3 percent instead of zero percent and that the nominal return on investment is correspondingly higher, say 5 percent. Checking the formula above, the real return is 1.94 percent before tax. Assuming that ordinary interest income comprises the return, the nominal after-tax rate of return is 3.30 percent [5% × (1 – 0.34)]. Applying the formula above once again to this nominal after-tax rate of return of 3.30 percent, a real after-tax rate of return of 0.29 percent is derived, or just slightly more than just a one-quarter-of-one-percent real increase in wealth. As was shown above, in the absence of inflation, the same 3 percent real before-tax rate of return was worth almost 2 percent in real terms after tax.

One must measure the total effective tax rate (combining both the inflation tax and the income tax) relative to the nominal return. In the example above, investors in the 36 percent tax bracket earning nominal returns of 5 percent in a 3 percent inflation environment end up with just slightly more than a half of a percent increase in their real after-tax wealth. The effective tax rate on their nominal returns is 94.2 percent (5% – 0.29% = 4.71% taxed away; 4.71% ÷ 5% = 94.2% effective real tax rate on nominal returns).

If the return on investment is composed of both ordinary and capital elements, the analysis becomes more difficult. The actual real after-tax rate of return will depend not only on the ordinary income tax rate but also on the capital gains tax rate, as well as the timing of recognition of gains and the length of the investment horizon.

Interest Rate Risk – Interest rate risk is really two different risks – called *capital value risk* and *reinvestment risk* – that reflect two different sides to the interest rate risk coin. *Capital value risk* arises from the behavior of bond prices in response to changes in interest rates. Whenever interest rates rise, the prices of previously issued bonds (offering lower interest payments) will fall. This has nothing to do with the creditworthiness of the issuer; it simply reflects the fact that bonds are currently being issued that pay higher rates of interest than paid by the older bonds. In order to sell the older bonds, their prices will have to fall. As the prices of bonds fall, their current yields to investors rise. So the prices of the previously issued bonds will have to fall sufficiently to make them attractive to buyers who could purchase the newly issued bonds paying higher interest rates. If investors expect market interest rates to rise, they might want to avoid purchasing long-term bonds unless they think the current price already reflects the market's anticipation of rising interest rates. Similar to inflation, it is *unanticipated* changes in interest rates that present a risk. Generally, the longer a bond has to maturity, the greater will be the price drop for any increase in interest rates.

The price of a bond in secondary markets is a function of its coupon yield, the time it has to maturity, and the movement of market interest rates since it was first issued. Interest rates and bond prices move in opposite directions. When interest rates drop, bond prices increase; and when interest rates increase, bond prices drop.

Premium Bond – A premium bond is one that sells for a price greater than its par value. Bonds will sell at a premium whenever interest rates fall below the coupon rate on the bond.

Discount Bond – A discount bond sells in secondary markets at less than its par value. This occurs whenever market interest rates exceed the bond's coupon rate.

There are two times when investors can be fairly certain a bond will sell at close to its par value: first, when it is just issued (unless it is a zero-coupon bond) and, second when it is about to mature. What happens between those dates depends not only on the direction of interest rates but also on the magnitude of interest rate changes. The larger the change in interest rates, the larger will be the swing in bond prices.

According to Figure 5.1, if an investor wants to reduce the price volatility of a bond portfolio, the investor should shorten the maturities. For any given increase in interest rates, the price volatility of a five-year bond is much less than the price volatility of a twenty-five-year bond. Generally, longer-term bonds provide higher coupons (interest payments) to compensate investors for this added volatility. For most individual investors, however, the slight increase in interest income is generally not worth the increase in risk due to added price volatility.

Figure 5.1

Years to a bond's maturity	The approximate market prince of a $1,000 par value bond paying $40 annual coupon payment (4% coupon rate) when interest rates increase to:		
	4.50%	5.00%	5.50%
5 years	$978	$957	$936
25 years	$926	$859	$799

Of course, if interest rates fall, the market value of the bond will increase.

Reinvestment risk is the other side of the interest rate risk coin. If interest rates rise, investors in shorter-term notes and bonds can profitably reinvest at higher rates and avoid the capital value loss associated with longer-term investments. However, if interest rates fall, then the shorter-term note and bond owners will have to reinvest at lower rates when they could have locked in higher rates by originally buying longer-term bonds.

Inventory Risk – Inventory risk is the possibility that price changes, obsolescence, or other factors will shrink the value of a company's inventory. For example, oil companies, whose reserves are essentially their inventory, and refiners, who may have substantial amounts of oil in process, can be greatly affected by changes in the price of crude oil or of the retail prices of gasoline or other petroleum derivative products.

Legislative/Regulatory/Tax Risk – Statutes, regulations, and tax laws in effect today may be extinct tomorrow or new regulations or laws may be enacted. For example, the long-term capital gains tax rate has been changed at least seven times in the last thirty years. The introduction of Individual Retirements Accounts (IRAs) in 1974 gave investors a tax-advantaged vehicle to help them save for retirement. Initially, anyone with earned income could open one, contribute up to $2,000 annually, and then take a full deduction on that amount. Years later, the tax code was amended, placing certain limitations on deductibility, thereby detracting from the tax benefits of IRAs. Conversely, in 1997, Congress enhanced the traditional IRA, introduced two new variations – the Roth IRA and the Education IRA – and lowered the tax rate on long-term capital gains. Changes in the banking regulations were certainly partly responsible for the S&L crisis of the 1980s and 1990s and have unquestionably changed the landscape in the financial services industries. The Smoot-Hawley tariff is believed by most economists to be one of the principal factors precipitating the Great Depression of the 1930s. Since then, Congress has passed NAFTA and other free-trade legislation that has had both adverse effects for some industries and positive effects for others. The only thing that remains the same in the area of law and regulation is that it constantly changes.

Liquidity Risk – Liquidity risk is related to bid-ask spread risk and depth of market risk. The possibility of not being able to sell an asset when one wants to at a relatively known value, adds an element of risk to an investment. Generally, savings accounts, money market funds, and other assets that can be quickly converted into cash are considered highly liquid. Many bond issues are less liquid because they may suffer from depth of market risk and they are subject to greater capital value risk, so they cannot be converted to cash at a highly certain value if interest rates change. On the other extreme, collectibles, most real estate, IRAs, and deferred annuities are considerably less liquid, as they either do not have ready markets or restrictions are placed on access to cash values. Listed stocks are readily marketable, but are considered less liquid than, say CDs, in the sense that the value at which they can be sold or converted to cash is much less certain because of market price fluctuations. Of course, a majority of stocks traded over the counter are even less liquid, because they have more bid-ask spread risk and depth of market risk than listed stocks.

Longevity Risk – This is the risk that a person will live longer than the period his income can support. Longevity risk is of paramount concern for individuals planning for retirement.

Management Risk – Management risk is related to agency risk. In the case of companies, the risk is related to the poor judgment or malfeasance of a company's professional management. In the case of professional investment managers, the majority of actively managed funds under-perform broad market benchmarks. Even though a fund has beaten the market in the past, there are no guarantees it will continue to do so. A star manager may leave, lose his touch, or find that his style is out of favor. Individuals who stick with poorly run funds risk substantial under performance, which can compound over time. Investors in index mutual funds avoid management risk.

Market Risk – This is the most familiar of all risks. It is the day-to-day fluctuations in a stock's price. It is also referred to as volatility. Market risk applies mainly to stocks and options. As a whole, stocks tend to perform well during a bull market and poorly during a bear market – volatility is not so much a cause but an effect of certain market forces. Volatility is a measure of risk because it refers to the behavior, or temperament, of an investment rather than the reason for this behavior. Because market movement is one reason why people can make money from stocks, volatility is important for returns, and the more unstable the investment, the more chance its value can move dramatically either way.

More broadly, the term market risk is sometimes used to encompass all the political, economic, geographic, and other forces that can influence the financial markets and affect the return of most assets. Economic risk is the term for the uncertainty of broad economic variables such as economic growth levels, inflation, interest rates, foreign exchange rates, import-export prices, etc. The general market environment, such as periods of bull and bear markets, may exert influence on the performance of individual securities. But some companies will be more vulnerable to market risk than others. A high exchange rate, for example, will hit electronic and electrical equipment manufacturers who target export markets, more than food retailers who target the domestic market, because a high exchange rate will make those electrical goods more expensive in foreign markets.

But it is not conclusive. A really efficient company in the electronics sector may suffer less than an inefficient food retailer. Most investors are familiar with market risk, as the media gives a great deal of attention to the performance of the stock market. It is important to remember that this risk affects virtually every asset class to some extent.

Measurement Risk – Measurement risk is the risk associated with the collection and accuracy of financial data and with the proper use and application of that data for estimating future company or security values.

Political Risk – Political risk includes legislative/regulatory/tax risk that government legislation or action will have an adverse effect on investment. This can be in the form of high taxes, prohibitive licensing, or the appointment of individuals or regulators whose policies interfere with investment growth. Political risks also include wars, changes in government leadership, politically-motivated embargoes, and the like.

Purchasing Power Risk – Purchasing power risk is another name for inflation risk.

Security Risk – Security risk is a broad risk term encompassing all the risk factors associated with a particular stock, bond, option, or other financial security. For instance, for a bond it may include its default risk, liquidity risk, capital value risk, documentation risk, call risk, and the like.

Size Risk – Size risk is the risk associated with a firm's size. Studies have found that risk and return characteristics vary, systematically, by the size of companies.

Style Risk – Style risk is a term generally related to whether stocks are classified as value or growth stocks. Style risk isn't limited to the value and growth dimension, however, as stocks can be classified by their market capitalizations (large and small). Investors may select managers or funds that are described as large-cap value or small-cap growth, for instance. Studies conducted by Fama and French and others have shown that value stocks and growth stocks (as well as large cap and small cap stocks) have systematically different risk and return profiles, which makes them essentially separate asset classes. During certain times in the business cycle, value stocks may outperform growth stocks and, at other times, growth stocks may outperform value stocks. Therefore, style risk arises when investors fail to allocate their portfolio to both classes and, thus, expose themselves to the risk that they are investing in the wrong class at the wrong time.

Systematic Risk – Systematic risk is a widespread or economy-wide risk that influences a large number of assets. Examples of systematic risk are political events, inflation, and the business cycle. It is virtually impossible to protect oneself against this type of risk. However, one can manage exposure to such broad risks by allocating one's portfolio among various asset classes that have differing exposures to widespread risk factors.

Tax (Rate) Risk – Investors have to be cognizant that changes in tax laws could make their holdings more or less valuable.

Timing Risk – Timing risk works two ways. Investors run the risk of investing when security prices hit their peak. They also take the risk that they may need to sell their investments for a loss during a market setback because they need to fund a planned or unplanned expense.

Tracking Risk – Risk associated with failure of managers of indexed funds to accurately, timely, and cost-effectively track and match the underlying index's performance.

Underwriting Risk – Underwriting risk is the risk taken by an investment banker that a new issue of securities purchased outright will not be bought by the public and/or that the market price will drop during the offering period.

Unsystematic (Specific, Diversifiable) Risk – It is risk that does not have wide spread impact, such as the impact an economic recession has on virtually all investment assets. Rather, it is an idiosyncratic risk that affects a particular company or security, or a very small number of assets. An example is news that affects a specific stock, such as a sudden strike by employees. Diversification is the only way to protect oneself from unsystematic risk.

5.1.4 INVESTMENT RISK MANAGEMENT

Unfortunately, there is really no such thing as a risk-free investment. Even United States T-bills have a remote risk of default and are subject to at least some inflation risk. In addition, investors that invest short term, always face reinvestment risk, that is, the risk that they will not be able to reinvest at a rate equal to that which they could have originally locked in long term. Risk can never be completely eliminated. However, there are several strategies that may help manage investment risk.

Diversification – Because each asset class and each specific asset carries its own unique degree of risk, it may be best to diversify capital across a broad range of investments. An appropriate mix of aggressive, moderate, and conservative investments could help balance the overall risk of a portfolio.

Asset Allocation – Before choosing individual investments, it is prudent to determine how much money should be allocated to each asset class – cash, bonds, and stocks (as well as other classes such as real estate, commodities, foreign securities, and the like). By blending one's portfolio, an investor can reduce short term volatility, while maintaining the potential to achieve long term financial goals.

Professional Management – Many investors have turned to professionally managed products such as mutual funds, variable annuities, and variable life insurance. Along with offering diversification, each portfolio is closely monitored by an expert manager who makes investment decisions based on careful analysis and thorough research.

Modern portfolio and capital market theory posits that investors who are willing to bear greater investment risk can expect to earn greater returns over the long run. However, the theory does not say that all risks will be rewarded. Investors are only rewarded for bearing systematic risks, those risks that cannot be diversified away.

Many of the types or sources of risk described above are diversifiable. The diversifiable risks tend to be those more closely related to specific companies or securities, such as management risk and default risk. However, those risks that are more industry, sector, or asset-class related become more difficult to diversify and require investors to balance those risks by investing in a wide array of sectors or asset classes. Those risks that are economy, market wide, and worldwide. These risks cannot be eliminated entirely, but investors can manage their exposure to such risks by applying the principles of modern portfolio and capital market theory.

5.2 MEASURING INVESTMENT RISK

Measuring investment risk is a critical but difficult aspect of investment planning. This chapter describes and explains the principal risk measures, such as variance and standard deviation, semivariance and semideviation, skewness, kurtosis, correlation and covariance, and beta. A brief review of probability distributions is useful before examining these ways of measuring risk.

5.2.1 PROBABILITY DISTRIBUTIONS

Of all the ways to describe risk, the simplest and possibly most accurate is "the uncertainty of a future outcome." The anticipated return for some future period is known as the *expected return*. The actual return over some past period is known as the *realized return*. The simple fact that dominates investing is that the realized return on an asset with any risk attached to it may be different from what was expected.

Financial economists define *volatility* as the range of movement (or price fluctuation) from the expected level of return. The more a stock, for example, goes up and down in price, the more volatile that stock is. Because wide price swings create more uncertainty of an eventual outcome, increased volatility usually is equated with increased risk. Being able to measure and determine the past volatility of a security is important in that it provides some insight into the riskiness of that security as an investment.

Investors and analysts should be at least somewhat familiar with the study of probability distributions. Because investors do not know with certainty the returns they will earn on their investments, they must estimate the return. An investor may expect the total return on a particular security to be 10 percent for the coming year, but in truth this is only a point estimate within a range of possible outcomes.

To deal with the uncertainty of returns, investors need to think explicitly about a security's distribution of probable total returns. Given that investors must deal with the uncertain future, a number of possible returns could occur.

In the case of a Treasury bond paying a fixed rate of interest, there is (almost) 100 percent certainty, barring a financial collapse of the economy, that the bond will pay the interest when due. The probability of this occurrence is close to 1.0, because no other outcome is possible. But nothing is ever really certain. In this instance, the *nominal* return is almost certain, but the *real* return (representing what the investor can actually buy with the current dollars of interest relative to what those dollars could have bought at the time the investor made the investment) is *not*. Although the nominal amount and timing of the interest payment is virtually certain, the inflation rate and, therefore, the purchasing power of the interest payment is still very uncertain.

With the possibility of two or more outcomes, which is the norm for common stocks and virtually all other investments, investors must consider each possible outcome and assess the probability of its occurrence. The result of considering these outcomes and their probabilities together is a probability distribution consisting of the specification of the likely returns that may occur and the probabilities associated with these likely returns.

Probabilities represent the likelihood of various outcomes and typically are expressed as a decimal (they are sometimes expressed as fractions). The sum of the probabilities of all possible outcomes must be 1.0, because they must completely describe all the (perceived) likely occurrences.

How are these probabilities and associated outcomes obtained? In the final analysis, investing for some future period involves uncertainty and, therefore, subjective estimates. Although investors may rely heavily on past occurrences (frequencies) to estimate the probabilities, they must adjust these estimates based on the past for any changes expected in the future.

Probability distributions can be either *discrete* or *continuous*. Discrete probability distributions assign a probability to each of a finite number of possible outcomes. For example, a coin toss involves a discreet probability distribution with two possible and equally likely outcomes (assuming a fair coin). Continuous probability distributions involve an infinite number of possible outcomes over some range (which may itself be limited or infinite) where probabilities of specific outcomes along the continuum are described by what is called a *probability density function*. The most familiar continuous distribution is the *normal distribution* depicted by the well-known bell-shaped curve often used in statistics. It is called a two-parameter distribution because one only needs to know the mean and the variance to fully describe the distribution.

Although not all probability distributions have an expected value, most of those useful in describing events in the real world do. For most risk and return analyses in investment planning the reasonably applicable probability distributions involve discreet or continuous ranges of possible outcomes that are "dense" in the sense that potential outcomes are equally or nearly equally spaced along the potential range of outcomes and the probabilities associated with these outcomes are generally greater towards the middle of the range of possible outcomes and generally smaller towards the ends of the potential range of outcomes. In such cases, the *expected value* of the distribution is a good estimate of the single most likely outcome from the particular probability distribution. The expected value is the simple average of all possible return outcomes, where each outcome is weighted by its respective probability of occurrence.

5.2.2 STANDARD DEVIATION AND VARIANCE

Probability distributions differ with respect to the potential range and probabilities associated with potential outcomes, or, in a single term, the "dispersion" of potential outcomes. One can use a number of measures to describe or characterize the dispersion of a distribution. Investors typically use *variance* or *standard deviation* (two related measures of dispersion), at least as a first approximation, to calculate the total risk associated with the expected return.

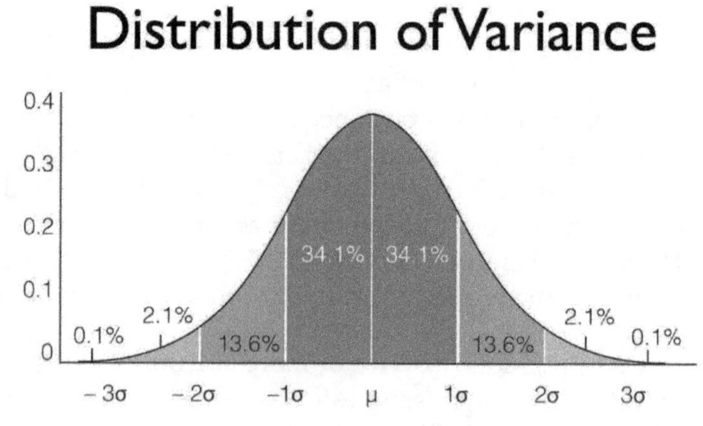

What is the standard deviation and what relevance does it have?

Technically, the *standard deviation* is a statistical measure defined as the square root of the variance of returns. The *variance* of returns is the expected value of the average squared differences from the mean of the distribution. Technicalities aside, it is simply a metric of how much, on average, any particular observation of a randomly distributed variable (in this case, the returns on various asset classes) have differed from the average or mean value of the distribution. Because one can use variance, volatility, and risk in this context synonymously, remember that the larger is the standard deviation, the more uncertain is the outcome.

For example, assume a sack contains balls with numbers ranging from zero to one-hundred. A person picking a ball from the sack is equally likely to draw each ball. By repeatedly picking balls from the sack and replacing each ball after it is selected, this person should expect the average value of the balls selected to be close to fifty, because fifty is the average value. By the law of large numbers, the average of the numbers of the selected balls should get closer and closer to fifty as the number of draws increases. The implication is that if a person had to guess what value will turn up in any particular draw and wanted to minimize the potential error of the guess, the best guess would be fifty, the expected or mean value of the possible outcomes. The greatest possible error a person can make by guessing the mean (fifty) is fifty, because the minimum and maximum possible values that a person could actually draw are zero and one-hundred, respectively. If a person guessed any value other than fifty, the error could exceed fifty. For example, if a person guessed twenty and the ball actually drawn had the number one-hundred, the error would be eighty.

Even though the mean value (fifty) is the best possible guess, it is not necessarily a good guess in the sense of being anywhere near the value that one actually will draw. Even though fifty is the best guess, one would expect most picks to differ substantially from fifty. As explained previously, by guessing fifty, the result could still be wrong by as much as fifty. What the standard deviation substantially attempts to measure is by how much one would expect, on average, any given draw to differ from the best guess of fifty.

Suppose a person knows that the value of a ball drawn from the sack has a value equal to or less than fifty. What then would be this person's best guess? Clearly, the answer is twenty-five because twenty-five is the average of the values from zero through fifty. By guessing twenty-five, this person could never be off by more than twenty-five. The analysis is similar if a person knows the value of the drawn ball is equal to or greater than fifty before making the guess as to its value. In this case, the best guess is seventy-five, because that is the mean value over the range from fifty to one-hundred. By guessing seventy-five, one could never be wrong by more than twenty-five. Therefore, even when a person does not know whether the ball drawn is either above or below fifty, the person does know that if it is above fifty, it will be above fifty by an average of twenty-five; if it is below fifty, it will be below fifty by an average of twenty-five. In other words, the guesser knows that the best guess of the mean value of fifty will differ from the actual number drawn by an average absolute value of twenty-five. For this distribution, twenty-five is the *mean absolute deviation*, the usual or average amount by which the values drawn differ from the mean of the distribution, which is closely related to the standard deviation.

Many very informed investors believe that investments whose distributions of returns have large standard deviations are riskier than those having smaller standard deviations because the future outcomes are much less certain. This idea is not entirely inappropriate, but it is also not entirely correct, because it does not encompass the entire scope of the issue.

For example, assume now that all the balls with values below forty and above sixty are thrown out of the sack. The best guess regarding the value of a ball drawn from the sack is still fifty, because the mean value has not changed. However, the mean absolute deviation is now just five, not twenty-five (standard deviation is 5.77). What does this tell a person about the best guess? It tells one nothing about what the best guess should be. It is still fifty. What it tells a person is the relative goodness of the best guess. In the first case with numbers ranging from zero to one-hundred, fifty is the best guess, but it is not a very good guess, because a person could be wrong by up to fifty. In the second case, with numbers ranging from forty to sixty, the best guess is still fifty, and it is a relatively good guess, because a person could be wrong by at most ten and would expect to be wrong by only five, on average.

Suppose now that as a ball is drawn from either sack, a person will receive or pay an amount based on the outcome. If the value of the drawn ball exceeds fifty, the person will receive the difference between the value on the drawn ball and $50. If the value of the drawn ball is less than fifty, the person will have to pay the amount by which the draw is less than $50. Regardless of from which sack one draws the ball, the expected payoff/payout is $0. However, most people would agree that drawing balls from the sack containing balls numbered from zero to one-hundred (with a mean absolute deviation of twenty-five and a standard deviation of 28.9) is riskier than drawing balls from the sack with balls numbered from forty to sixty (with a mean absolute deviation of five and a standard deviation of 5.77). In this sense, the standard deviation is a good indicator of risk.

However, now suppose the sack containing the balls from forty to sixty is reconstituted to include only the balls numbered from zero to twenty. The expected or mean value is now ten, but the mean absolute deviation is still five. The payoff/payout rules also are now changed to pay the person the amount by which the number on any drawn ball exceeds ten and for the person to pay back the amount by which the number of any drawn ball falls below ten. In this case, should one still consider draws from the sack containing balls numbered from zero to one hundred riskier?

No one would say that drawing from the sack containing balls numbered zero to one-hundred is riskier than drawing from the sack containing balls numbered zero to twenty, even though the mean absolute deviation (or standard deviation) of the number of outcomes for the sack containing balls numbered zero to one-hundred remains twenty-five, or five times greater than the mean absolute deviation of draws from the sack containing balls numbered from zero to twenty. Draws from the zero-to-twenty sack still have an expected payoff of $0; the person has a 50 percent chance of losing money on any particular draw, and could lose as much as $10 [ball zero - ten] if the worst occurs.

In contrast to draws from the zero-to-twenty sack, draws from the zero-to-one-hundred sack have an expected payoff of $40 [fifty average value of a ball minus ten] and the person has only a 10 percent chance of losing money on any particular draw [the chance of losing money is limited to balls zero to nine; ten is breakeven]. In addition, the maximum potential loss on a draw from the zero-to-one-hundred sack is still $10, exactly the same as the maximum potential loss on a draw from the zero-to-twenty sack. Therefore, drawing from the zero-to-one-hundred sack presents one with the possibility of losing, at most, $10 [ball zero - ten] (the same as drawing from the zero-to-twenty sack), only a 10 percent chance of losing any money (as compared to a 50 percent chance from the zero-to-twenty sack), an expected gain of $40 (as compared to $0 from the zero-to-twenty sack), and a maximum potential gain of up to $90 [ball one-hundred - ten] (as compared to only $10 from the zero-to-twenty sack).

Clearly, draws from the zero-to-one-hundred sack are no more risky (in terms of loss) than draws from the zero-to-twenty sack, even though the uncertainty regarding the payoff of draws from the zero-to-one-hundred sack as measured by the mean absolute deviation is five times greater than the uncertainty regarding the payoff from the zero-to-twenty sack (the standard deviation is 5.006 times larger). Therefore, the standard deviation alone is an incomplete and sometimes misleading indicator of risk. In the area of investment analysis, risk assessment must also include differences in expected values and the downside or loss potentials of the alternative investments.

Consequently, the standard deviation can best be described as a measure of the "goodness" or confidence one can place in a best guess estimate (mean value) of the outcome of a random variable. As applied to investment returns, the expected value may be the best guess of future returns, but if the standard deviation of returns is large, the best guess still may not be a very good guess.

Also, the standard deviation is at best only a partial or incomplete and, sometimes misleading, measure of the riskiness of an investment relative to another investment. In order for standard deviations to take on any real meaning when comparing alternative investments, investors must use standard deviations relative to the investments' expected returns. That is, standard deviations are useful in conjunction with expected returns to measure each investment's return per unit of risk—its return bang per risk buck, so to speak. The standard deviation of equity returns (i.e., S&P stocks and small-capitalization stocks) is greater than the standard deviation of fixed-income investment returns (i.e., corporate and government bonds and Treasury bills) for all investment horizons. However, at longer investment horizons, equities dominate fixed income investments. Despite greater standard deviations, equities can and should be viewed as less risky investments than bonds and Treasury bills for longer investment horizons. (Bonds, T-bills, and other fixed-income investments often should be part of the asset-allocation mix for investors' longer-term investment portfolios, but any of these asset allocation classes would rarely if ever be the most suitable asset class for long-term investment if the portfolio were required to restrict investment to just one asset class.)

One of the nice characteristics of the standard deviation is that if returns are normally distributed, investors can predict that actual realized returns will fall within one standard deviation above or below the mean about 68 percent of the time and within two standard deviations above or below the mean about 95 percent of the time.

Calculating a standard deviation using probability distributions involves making subjective estimates of the probabilities and the likely returns. However, investors cannot avoid such estimates because future returns are uncertain. The prices of securities are based on investors' expectations about the future. The relevant standard deviation in this situation is the *ex ante* standard deviation and not the *ex post* standard deviation based on past realized returns.

Although investment analysts use standard deviations based on past realized returns as proxies for *ex ante* standard deviations, investors should remember that one usually cannot extrapolate the past into the future without modifications. *Ex post* standard deviations may be convenient, but they are subject to errors.

One important point about the estimation of standard deviation is the distinction between individual securities and portfolios. Standard deviations for well-diversified portfolios tend to be reasonably steady over time and, therefore, one can fairly reliably use historical calculations in projecting the future. Moving from well-diversified portfolios to individual securities, however, makes historical calculations much less reliable. Fortunately, the primary rules of portfolio management are to allocate the amount invested among various investment classes and to diversify by holding a broad array of securities across the entire portfolio as well as within each asset class. By following these rules the standard deviations of well-diversified portfolios may be more stable than those of individual securities.

One further very important point is that the standard deviation is a measure of the *total* risk of an asset or a portfolio, including, therefore, both systematic and unsystematic risk. It captures the total variability in the asset's or portfolio's return whatever the sources of that variability.

5.2.3 SEMIVARIANCE

Some investment experts have criticized the use of standard deviation as a measure of risk because it considers the possibility of returns above the expected return as well as below the expected return. Investors, however, do not view possible returns above the expected return as an unfavorable outcome. Rather, they see the possibility of upside return deviations as a positive, not a negative, so many investors think that only potential deviations below the expected return really matter in their consideration of risk.

Harry Markowitz, the father of modern portfolio theory, recognized this limitation and suggested a measure of downside risk – the risk of realizing an outcome below the expected return – called the *semivariance*. The semivariance is similar to variance except that this calculation gives no consideration to returns above the expected return.

In some cases, investors may be more concerned with the chance that an investment's return will fall below some benchmark or target return, such as T-bill rates, rather than the expected return of the investment. In such cases, investors may use a measure called the *downside volatility* or *semivolatility*. One computes the semivolatility in exactly the same way as the semivariance, except that one ignores all returns above a benchmark or target return (sometimes called the minimal acceptable rate of return, or *mar*), such as the risk-free rate, rather than the expected return.

The square root of the semivariance is sometimes called the semideviation, although there does not appear to be any universally accepted term for this concept. Semideviation is to semivariance as the standard deviation is to variance. Investment analysts sometimes use the term downside deviation to refer to the square root of the semivariance, but more frequently they seem to use downside deviation to refer to the square root of the downside volatility, which is computed with respect to a minimal acceptable rate of return (mar) or target rate of return that is different from the expected return.

There is some confusion in the financial community surrounding semivariance. This is because the semivariance metric actually comes in two flavors or variants. Essentially, one variant measures downside risk in absolute terms and the other in relative terms. In either case one computes the numerator of the semivariance in the same way: by summing the squares of the negative deviations from the mean (i.e., using only the sample values below the mean of all the observations).

Equation 5.1

$$SSND = \sum_{j=1}^{n^{<\mu}} (r_j - \mu)^2$$

Where: μ = the average of all the return values,

SSND = Sum of Squared Negative Deviations (using all return values below the average, μ),

$n^{<\mu}$ = the number of return values that are less than the average return, μ, and

r_j = the jth of $n^{<\mu}$ return values that are less than the average return, μ.

The difference in the two semivariance variants arises in the values used in the denominator of the calculation. In what we will call here the absolute variant, one divides the sum of the SSND by the number of observed values below the mean minus one. For instance, if there are twenty observations, but only eight are below the mean of the twenty observations, then the sum of the squared deviations of these eight observations are divided by seven (eight observations – one) to derive the absolute semivariance.

To compute what we call the relative semivariance, one divides the SSND by the number of all observations, both below and above the mean, minus one).

Specifically, the formulas for the absolute and relative semivariances are as follows:

Equation 5.2

$$sv_r = \frac{SSND}{n-1}$$

Equation 5.3

$$sv_a = \frac{SSND}{n^{<\mu}-1}$$

Where sv_r and sv_a are the *relative* and *absolute* semivariances, respectively, and the other variables are the same as described previously.

Taking the square root of the absolute or relative semivariance gives one the absolute or relative semideviation, exactly as taking the square root of the variance gives one the standard deviation.

Here's how the absolute and relative concepts of the semivariance or semideviation come into play.

In an absolute sense, many investors feel that only the possible downside outcomes (potential losses) matter with respect to risk assessment. Many investors perceive potential upside outcomes (potential gains) as a bonus, and not important in their assessment of risk. Thus, if the expected returns on two different investments are the same, but one has a greater semivariance, many investors would choose the investment with the smaller semivariance. They perceive the investment with the smaller semivariance as offering the same expected return as the other investment while burdening the investor with less risk of loss.

However, many other investors feel just as strongly that one cannot entirely ignore the upside return potential when assessing risk. These investors therefore prefer to use the relative concept of semivariance in a two-step process. First, they compute the relative semivariance (using the formulas shown earlier). They then take another step and divide the semivariance computed in this way by the regularly computed variance of all observations to derive a ratio that represents the proportion of the total variance of the returns that is explained or attributable to the downside negative or downside deviations.

For example, assume two investors are each evaluating the same two investments. These two investments have equal expected returns. The first investor, a proponent of the absolute approach to calculating and using semivariance for risk assessment computes the absolute semivariance of the two investments and finds that the semivariances, like the expected returns, are equal. This investor announces that he is indifferent between the two investments because he would be getting the same expected return and bearing the same downside risk with each investment.

However, when the second investor, who prefers the relative approach, finishes his calculations for the two investments, he finds that one of the investments has a relative semivariance to variance ratio of ½. What this ratio means is that the downside risk associated with this investment is exactly matched by the upside gain potential. He then follows the same methodology with the second investment and finds that the second investment has a relative semivariance to variance ratio of 1/3. What this ratio says is that only one-third of the overall variability of this investment is attributable to downside deviations from the mean while two-thirds of the overall variability is attributable to upside gains. In this case, then, the absolute semivariance (downside risk) and expected returns are equal for both investments, but the second investment has two times the variability for outcomes above the mean as the first investment. Therefore, the second investment offers what appears to be twice the upside gain potential as the first investment.

Even though many financial professionals argue that semivariance (semideviation) is conceptually superior to variance (standard deviation), in practice, because of some difficult math problems, most researchers and analysts use the variance and standard deviation as the risk measures of choice. As it turns out, when the return distribution is symmetrical (the same shape above and below the mean), then the variance (standard deviation) gives exactly the same answers as the semivariance (semideviation). With notable exceptions, stock return distributions do seem to be reasonably symmetrical, especially for average annual compound returns over longer investment horizons.

However, the distributions of returns on many securities are not normally distributed for shorter-term investment horizons. Even for longer-term horizons, certain types of investments, such as options, futures, and other derivatives, technology stocks, media stocks, telecom stocks, many hedge funds, and other alternative investments, tend to have persistent but diminishing skewness in their return distributions. In these cases, the standard deviation can be an incomplete and misleading measure of risk, even when used in conjunction with expected returns for risk/return analyses.

5.2.4 COVARIANCE AND CORRELATION

The principal conclusion of Harry Markowitz's seminal book, *Portfolio Selection,* which heralded the era of modern portfolio and capital market theory (as well as the era of high-powered quantitative analyses), was that investors could put portfolios of risky stocks together in such a way that the portfolio as a whole actually could be less risky than any one of the individual stocks in it. This conclusion follows in part from the concept of covariance among securities, or lack thereof.

As the term suggests, *covariance* means varying together. Covariance is a measure of the degree to which two variables move in a systematic or predictable way, either positively or negatively. If two variables move in perfect lockstep, up and down, then they are said to exhibit *perfect positive covariance*. For example, the pressure and temperature of a fixed volume of gas at sea level exhibit perfect covariance. Double the pressure of a given volume of gas and the temperature will change proportionally, and vice-versa. Or, halve the temperature of a gas and the pressure also will decline proportionally, and vice versa.

Two variables that move perfectly in lockstep, but in opposite directions, are said to exhibit *perfect negative covariance*. For instance, if one doubles (halves) the pressure on a gas and wants to keep the temperature unchanged, the volume for the gas must increase (decrease) in direct proportion to the change in pressure.

If two variables are completely independent, showing no systematic relationship, their covariance is zero.

Correlation is a normalized version of covariance where values can range from –1 (perfect negative covariance) to +1 (perfect positive covariance). Letting σ_{12} represent the covariance between two variables, σ_1 the standard deviation of variable 1, σ_2 the standard deviation of variable two, and ρ_{12} the correlation of the two variables, the relation between correlation and covariance is as follows:

Equation 5.4

$$\rho_{12} = \frac{\sigma_{12}}{\sigma_1 \cdot \sigma_2} = \frac{\text{Covariance of Variables 1 and 2}}{\text{Std Dev Variable 1 times Std Dev Variable 2}}$$

Expressed as a function of covariance, covariance is equal to the correlation times the standard deviations of the two variables:

Equation 5.5

$$\sigma_{12} = \rho_{12} \cdot \sigma_1 \cdot \sigma_2$$

Markowitz showed that if investors reallocate money within their portfolios to add securities that do not exhibit perfect covariance with their current portfolio, the total risk of the portfolio as measured by variance or standard deviation would decline. For example, assume an investor holds just one stock, S_1, with a standard deviation of σ_1. Thus, the standard deviation of the investor's initial "portfolio" of one security is σ_1. If the investor sells off part of his interest in S_1 and uses the proceeds to buy another stock, S_2, with a standard deviation of σ_2, the variance per dollar of investment in his portfolio, σ_p^2, is given by the following equation:

Equation 5.6

$$\sigma_p^2 = \left(w_1^2 \cdot \sigma_1^2\right) + \left(w_2^2 \cdot \sigma_2^2\right) + \left(2 \cdot w_1 \cdot w_2 \cdot \sigma_{12}\right)$$

Here, σ_{12} is the covariance between S_1 and S_2, and w_i is the proportion of the portfolio invested in stock S_i.

Alternatively, one can express the variance of the portfolio in terms of correlation rather than covariance:

Equation 5.7

$$\sigma_p^2 = \left(w_1^2 \cdot \sigma_1^2\right) + \left(w_2^2 \cdot \sigma_2^2\right) + \left(2 \cdot w_1 \cdot w_2 \cdot \rho_{12} \cdot \sigma_1 \cdot \sigma_2\right)$$

Assume, first, for illustration, that the weight invested in each stock is equal, 50 percent, that the standard deviations of the stocks are equal, $\sigma_1 = \sigma_2$, and that the returns on the two stocks are independent, that is, the covariance and correlation are zero, then, the variance of the portfolio is:

$$\sigma_p^2 = \left(0.5^2 \cdot \sigma_1^2\right) + \left(0.5^2 \cdot \sigma_2^2\right)$$
$$\sigma_p^2 = \left(0.25 \cdot \sigma_1^2\right) + \left(0.25 \cdot \sigma_2^2\right)$$
$$\sigma_p^2 = \left(0.25 \cdot \sigma_1^2\right) + \left(0.25 \cdot \sigma_1^2\right)$$
$$\sigma_p^2 = \left(0.5 \cdot \sigma_1^2\right)$$

By splitting the portfolio equally between two independently distributed stocks, the investor cuts the variance of the portfolio in half. In fact, for each additional independent stock added to the portfolio, the variance declines in proportion to the number of stocks, n, that is:

Equation 5.8

$$\sigma_p^2 = \frac{\sigma_1^2}{n}$$

This equation explains the principle of diversification. By splitting a portfolio into more and more securities, the variance attributable to the nonsystematic (uncorrelated with the market) risks approaches zero as the number of securities increases.

Taking the square root of each side of the equation to derive the standard deviation, one can see that the standard deviation of the portfolio declines by the square root of the number of independently distributed securities in the portfolio:

Equation 5.9

$$\sigma_p = \frac{\sigma_1}{\sqrt{n}}$$

In other words, the standard deviation of a portfolio split into one-hundred identically distributed but independent securities is ten times less than the standard deviation of any one of the securities alone.

Now, assume instead that the investor starts once again with just one stock, S_1, but then splits his portfolio evenly between stock S_1 and stock S_3, which, once again, for illustration, is assumed to have a standard deviation, σ_3, equal to σ_1. However, in this case assume the return on S_3 is perfectly negatively correlated with the return on S_1. Then the variance of the portfolio is:

$$\sigma_p^2 = (0.25 \cdot \sigma_1^2) + (0.25 \cdot \sigma_3^2) + (2 \cdot 0.25 \cdot \rho_{13} \cdot \sigma_1 \cdot \sigma_3) \text{ or, because } \rho_{13} = -1,$$
$$\sigma_p^2 = (0.25 \cdot \sigma_1^2) + (0.25 \cdot \sigma_3^2) - (2 \cdot 0.25 \cdot \sigma_1 \cdot \sigma_3) \text{ and now replacing } \sigma_3 \text{ with } \sigma_1,$$
$$\sigma_p^2 = (0.25 \cdot \sigma_1^2) + (0.25 \cdot \sigma_1^2) - (2 \cdot 0.25 \cdot \sigma_1 \cdot \sigma_1)$$
$$\sigma_p^2 = (0.25 \cdot \sigma_1^2) + (0.25 \cdot \sigma_1^2) - (0.5 \cdot \sigma_1 \cdot \sigma_1)$$
$$\sigma_p^2 = 0$$

Thus, if two securities are perfectly negatively correlated, splitting one's investment equally between the two securities completely eliminates all variability.

Finally, assume instead the investor starts once again with just S_1 in his portfolio, but then puts half his money into security S_4, with a standard deviation equal to that of S_1 and a perfect positive correlation with S_1 of +1. The variance of the portfolio is, substituting immediately for $\sigma_1 = \sigma_4$ and $\rho_{14} = 1$:

$$\sigma_p^2 = (0.25 \cdot \sigma_1^2) + (0.25 \cdot \sigma_1^2) + (2 \cdot 0.25 \cdot 1 \cdot \sigma_1^2)$$
$$\sigma_p^2 = (0.25 \cdot \sigma_1^2) + (0.25 \cdot \sigma_1^2) + (0.5 \cdot 1 \cdot \sigma_1^2)$$
$$\sigma_p^2 = \sigma_1^2$$

The portfolio's variance remains unchanged. There is no risk reduction advantage to adding perfectly positively correlated assets to one's portfolio.

In the real world, instances of either perfectly negatively correlated or perfectly positively correlated securities are extremely rare, if not nonexistent. In fact, instances of correlations between securities that are negative at any level do exist, but are relatively few. However, investors do not need negative correlations between securities for them to benefit by adding securities to their portfolio. As long as a security added to a portfolio is not perfectly positively correlated with the existing portfolio, the addition of the security will reduce the portfolio's risk as measured by variance or standard deviation.

This concept is a central principle of modern portfolio and asset allocation theory. As long as there are any classes of assets whose returns are not perfectly correlated with investors' current portfolios, these investors can further reduce the risk of their portfolios by adding securities from those asset classes.

5.2.5 SYSTEMATIC RISK – BETA

While standard deviation determines the volatility of a security or fund according to the dispersion of its returns over a period of time, beta, another useful statistical measure, determines the volatility, or risk, of a security or fund in relation to that of its index or benchmark. In the single factor *Capital Asset Pricing Model*, the index or benchmark is the "market" portfolio, often measured by the S&P 500 index. When investors use beta to compare funds or to measure an investment manager's performance, the benchmark frequently is the average of the funds in that mutual fund category.

A fund with a beta very close to one means the fund's performance closely matches the index or benchmark – a beta greater than one indicates greater volatility than the overall market or the benchmark portfolio, and a beta less than one indicates less volatility than the market or the benchmark.

Example. If a fund has a beta of 1.05 in relation to the S&P 500, the fund, on average, has been moving 5 percent more than the index. Therefore, if the S&P 500 increased 15 percent, the fund would be expected to increase 15.75 percent. On the other hand, a fund with a beta of 2.4 would be expected to move 2.4 times more than its corresponding index. If the S&P 500 moved 10 percent, the fund would be expected to rise 24 percent, and, if the S&P 500 declined 10 percent, the fund would be expected to lose 24 percent.

Investors expecting the market to be bullish may choose funds exhibiting high betas, which increase investors' chances of earning high returns in up markets. If an investor expects the market to be bearish in the near future, the funds that have betas less than one are likely a good choice because they would be expected to decline less in value than the index. For example, if a fund had a beta of 0.5 and the S&P 500 declined 6 percent, the fund would be expected to, on average, decline only 3 percent. Be aware of the fact that beta by itself is limited and can be skewed due to factors other than the market risk affecting the fund's volatility.

5.2.6 R-SQUARED (R^2)

The R-squared of a fund (also called the coefficient of determination) is a measure of what proportion of a security's or portfolio's total variability is explained by its relationship to a benchmark or index and how much is its independent risk unrelated to the benchmark or index. When used in conjunction with ratings of mutual funds or the performance of professional managers it advises investors if the beta of a mutual fund is measured against an appropriate benchmark. Measuring the correlation of a fund's movements to that of an index, R-squared describes the level of association between the fund's volatility and market risk, or more specifically, the degree to which a fund's volatility is a result of the day-to-day fluctuations experienced by the overall market.

R-squared values range between zero and 1, where zero represents no correlation and one represents 100 percent correlation. If a fund's beta has an R-squared value that is close to one, the beta of the fund should be trusted. On the other hand, an R-squared value that is close to zero indicates that the beta is not particularly useful because the fund is being compared against an inappropriate benchmark.

If, for example, a bond fund were judged against the S&P 500 (an equity index), the R-squared value would be very low. A bond index such as the Lehman Brothers Aggregate Bond Index would be a much more appropriate benchmark for a bond fund, so the resulting R-squared value would be higher. Obviously the risks apparent in the stock market are different than the risks associated with the bond market. Therefore, if the beta for a bond were calculated using a stock index, the beta would not be trustworthy.

An inappropriate benchmark will skew more than just beta. Alpha is calculated using beta, so if the R-squared value of a fund is low, it is also wise not to trust the figure given for alpha.

5.2.7 SKEWNESS

Skewness measures the coefficient of asymmetry of a distribution. In contrast with the normal distribution, or bell curve, where both tails of the distribution are symmetrical mirror images of each other, skewed distributions have one tail of the distribution that is longer than the other. Figure 5.2 shows two distributions with equal means and standard deviations, but one has positive skewness and the other has negative skewness.

Figure 5.2

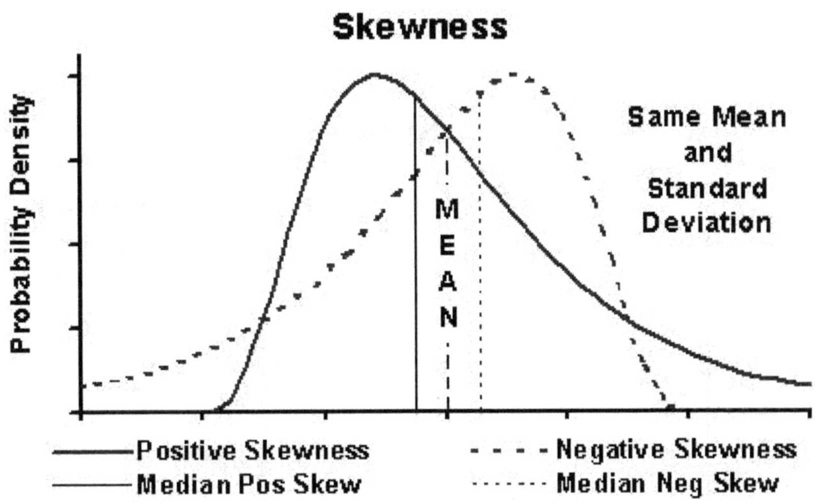

If investors base their investment decisions solely upon means and risk as measured by standard deviations, they should be indifferent between these two distributions because the means and standard deviations are equal. However, a risk-averse investor does not like negative skewness. In this case, the investment with negative skewness has a substantial downside tail exposing the investor to low or negative returns below the worst potential returns on the investment with positive skewness. In addition, the investment with positive skewness offers investors the potential for upside returns far above any they could ever expect from the negatively skewed investment.

It would seem almost inescapable that any risk adverse investor would prefer the positively skewed investment to the negatively skewed investment. Although this is in fact true, it may not be quite as evident as it first appears. Figure 5.2 also shows the medians of the two distributions. In symmetric distributions, such as the normal distribution, the mean and median are equal, but in skewed distributions, they are different.

The median is the point where there is a 50 percent probability that realized returns will fall below (or above) that value. In positively skewed distributions, the median is below the mean. In negatively skewed distributions, the median is above the mean. What this means is that an investor actually has less than a 50 percent chance of earning the mean return in a positively skewed investment, but *more* than a 50 percent chance of earning the mean return on a negatively skewed investment. So although the means and standard deviations of these two investments are identical, an investor actually has a higher chance of earning at least the mean return with the negative skewed investment than with the positively skewed investment. Therefore, although all risk adverse investors will prefer the positively skewed to the negatively skewed investment when their means and standard deviations are identical, it does not mean that they would always prefer a positively skewed investment to a symmetrically distributed investment with the same mean and standard deviation, or other possible combinations of means, standard deviations, and skewness.

5.2.8 KURTOSIS

Kurtosis measures the degree of "fatness" in the tails of a distribution. Figure 5.3 shows an example of a symmetric distribution that has a positive coefficient of excess kurtosis relative to a normal distribution. The distributions have equal means and standard deviations.

Figure 5.3

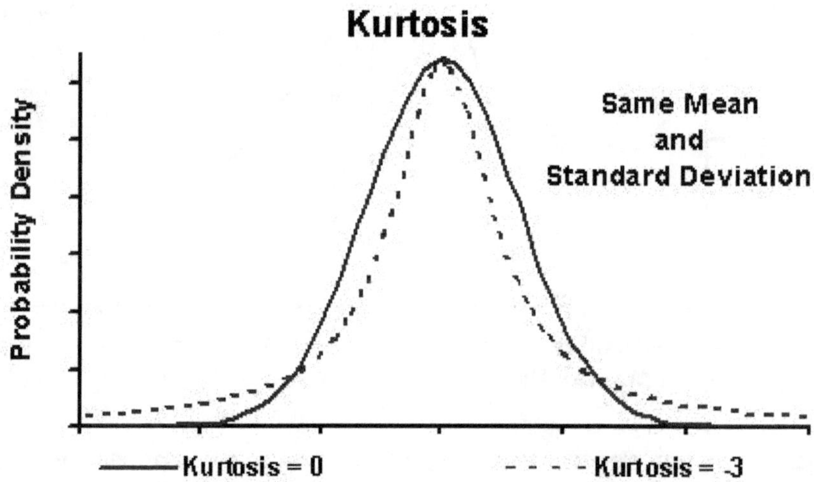

It is easy to see that risk-averse investors prefer a distribution with low kurtosis (that is, where tails are thin and returns are more likely to fall closer to the mean). Although the extra fatness in the downside tail is exactly matched by the excess fatness in the upside tail, risk averse investors will always weight the potential downside returns heavier than the potential upside returns. Consequently, they will always prefer a lower excess kurtosis. If investors use only means and standard deviations to choose among investments and some of those investments have either positive or negative excess kurtosis, they will be ignoring an important factor in making the best choice.

One of the reasons posited for the small-stock premium being higher than it should be in theory under the mean-variance framework of the capital-asset pricing model is that small cap stocks exhibit greater excess kurtosis and negative skewness than larger stocks. For instance, the risk of total failure and bankruptcy is unquestionably greater for most small businesses than it is for most large ones. Negative skewness does not get any greater than –100 percent! Because the mean-variance framework of much of modern portfolio and capital market theory does not account for these factors, it cannot explain this excess return anomaly.

5.2.9 SKEWNESS AND KURTOSIS COMBINED

Distributions can exhibit both skewness and excess kurtosis. Figure 5.4 shows an example of two negatively skewed distributions, but one also has a positive excess kurtosis.

Figure 5.4

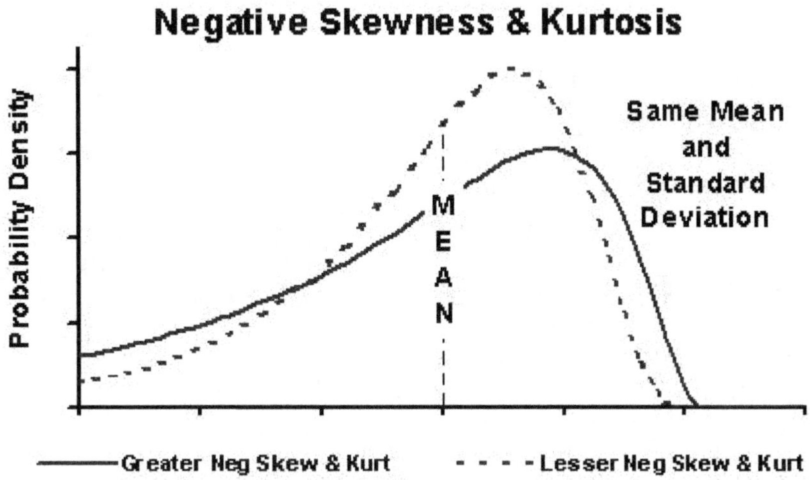

As soon as skewness begins to be negative the impact of a high excess kurtosis is significant for a risk-averse investor. The most interesting situation is when the return distribution has a negative skewness of –1 (or below) and an excess kurtosis higher than one. In this case, the probability of having a huge negative return increases dramatically. For a distribution with a skewness of –1 and an excess kurtosis of –5 (technology stocks, media stocks, telecom stocks or hedge funds may have this kind of excess kurtosis level), a mean-variance approach will conclude that an investor will not lose more than –3.5 percent in the next one day with 99 percent probability. However, an approach that accounts for skewness and kurtosis gives instead a 99 percent probability of not losing more than 7.4 percent in the next one day. The difference is substantial: more than a 100 percent underestimation of the potential one-day loss when using just the mean-variance approach that ignores skewness and kurtosis.

In conclusion, for optimization, simulation, and investment selection, the investor's approach should account not only for volatility, but also for skewness and kurtosis when the return distribution over the relevant period is likely to be significantly different than the normal distribution.

5.3 INVESTMENT RETURN

Section Overview:

5.3.1 Total Return

5.3.2 Holding Period Return

5.3.3 Annualized Returns

5.3.4 Nominal and Real (Inflation-Adjusted) Returns

5.3.5 Internal Rate of Return and Net Present Value

5.3.6 Time-Weighted and Dollar-Weighted Annual Returns

5.3.7 After-Tax Return and Taxable-Equivalent Return

5.3.8 Risk-Adjusted Returns

5.3.1 TOTAL RETURN

An analytical method of comparison is an objective way to assess the relative risks and potential rewards from alternative investments. Although the ultimate decision as to which investments one should make may be subjective, investors' should base their initial assessments on both factual and measurable information.

The techniques this chapter addresses are all based on the time value of money concept. The general principles of present value and future value, may be sufficient in themselves to evaluate the return on a particular investment. But, in many cases, the more sophisticated approaches described below may be more appropriate or necessary.

Rate of return means different things in different contexts, depending upon a host of factors. Consequently, financial economists and investors use a wide variety of terms to describe returns in these different contexts, such as *total return, holding period return, annualized return, simple return, compound return, arithmetic average return, geometric average return, time-weighted return, dollar-weighted return, nominal return, real (inflation-adjusted) return, risk-adjusted return, after-tax return, taxable-equivalent return, internal rate of return,* and various *modified internal rate of return* measures. Although financial professionals do not always define and use these terms in exactly the same way, the following descriptions are commonly accepted definitions for the various measures.

The term total return means the total gain or loss over a specified period relative to an initial dollar investment at the beginning of the period. All investments potentially have some combination of six components or sources of return for which a proper analysis must account:

- Cash inflows from the investment (outflows to the investment)
- Price or capital appreciation (price or capital depreciation)
- Debt amortization (negative amortization)
- Tax shelter (tax payments)
- Other tangible property received (paid)
- Intangible but measurable benefits or services received (paid)

In addition, because the ultimate goal of investing is to enhance real future wealth, investors cannot ignore the potential erosion of their future purchasing power as a result of inflation.

Cash flows in the form of interest payments, dividends, rents, royalties, and the like are the most obvious and ubiquitous source of return. Also, for many investments, changes in the market value of the investment each period, such as a stock's price increase or decrease, are part of the investor's total return for each period. When an investment is leveraged through the use of borrowing, the analysis must account for changes in the debt balance. If an investment generates a net cash flow of $100, but the investor's debt is also reduced (debt amortization) during the period by $10, the investor is in fact $110 wealthier than at the start of the period.

Although investors frequently compute total returns without accounting for taxes, investors can use and spend only the amount they get to keep after paying taxes. Consequently, any income, capital gain, personal property, or other tax payments attributable or allocable to the investment reduce the investor's total return. Conversely, if interest payments on debt used to finance investments are tax-deductible or the investment generates depreciation deductions, real estate tax deductions, or other tax deductions, the tax savings so generated each period increase the investor's return above and beyond the amount measured solely by cash flow, price changes, and debt reduction.

If an investor receives any other tangible property, such as shares of stock in lieu of cash interest payments, the total return includes the market value of the property received. Finally, the total return must include the value of any intangible but measurable benefits received. For example, if an investor purchases a commercial office building and in the transaction receives an easement for a private access road, he should include the market or use value of the easement for each period in the total return.

To compute the rate of return on investment for any period one simply divides the total return by the investor's *equity* in the investment at the beginning of the period.

An investor's equity in an investment at any point in time is the sum of all cash contributions, plus debt amortization, plus price appreciation or less price depreciation. For example, assume an investor purchases a residential rental unit for $100,000 with an initial cash outlay of $20,000 and borrowing of $80,000. The investor's initial equity is $20,000 (the amount of cash paid, not the total purchase price of the property). After one year, the investor's net operating cash flow (after debt-repayment) is $5,000, the debt balance has been reduced by $1,500, and the market value of the property has risen to $102,500. Additional cash flow from net tax savings (on interest and depreciation deductions in excess of taxable rental income) equal $1,000. The investor's total return for the year is $10,000 ($5,000 cash flow + $1,500 debt reduction + $2,500 price appreciation + $1,000 net tax savings), which is a 50 percent return on the initial $20,000 equity investment. At the end of the year, the investor's equity in the investment has increased to $24,000 ($20,000 original equity + $1,500 debt reduction + $2,500 price appreciation). Each year or period of evaluation may generate a different rate of return (as both the return for the time period, and the underlying equity, may change). Consequently, analysts often use different measures of the rate of return to generalize the results or performance of an investment over a number of holding periods.

5.3.2 HOLDING PERIOD RETURN

The holding period return is simply the total return for a specified period over which an investment is held.

Equation 5.10

$$\textit{Holding Period Return} = (\textit{Final Value} - \textit{Initial Value})$$

Equation 5.11

Holding Period Rate of Return = Holding Period Return/Initial Value

---

Example. Suppose a person invested $1,000 in an S&P 500 index ETF (SPY) at the end of 2002 and held the investment for fifteen years until the end of 2017 while reinvesting the cash flows. This investor would have accumulated about $1,902.53 by the end of 2017. The fifteen-year holding period return is $902.53 ($1,902.53 – $1,000) and the fifteen-year holding period rate of return is 90.25 percent ($902.53 / $1,000).

Annualized Returns

Because comparing investment returns over different holding periods is difficult, the standard practice is to express returns in annualized terms. One may express the annualized return in one of two ways – as a *simple* or a *compound* annual return. Which expression is the better measure depends on the context in which one uses it, as is described below. Two closely related terms that are also applicable in these contexts are the *arithmetic average annual return* and the *geometric average annual return.*

Simple (Arithmetic) Average Annual Returns

Investors compute the *simple annual return* by dividing the holding period return by the number of years in the holding period. Essentially, the simple annual return is the rate of return computed by stretching or shrinking the holding period to be equal to just one year and stretching or shrinking the holding period return proportionately. As a result, it computes the annual rate as if the holding period were actually one year without assuming any reinvestment of principal and interest.

Equation 5.12

Simple Annual Return = Holding Period Return/Number of Years

For instance, in the example above, the simple annual return 6.02 percent (90.25 percent / 15).

If the holding period is less than a year, say a month, then the simple annual return of the one-month holding period return is determined by dividing the one-month holding period return by 1/12 – in other words, by multiplying or stretching the period by a factor of twelve.

Example. Suppose an investor pays $9,960 for a T-bill maturing at $10,000 in three months. The three-month (1/4th year) holding period return is $40 and the three-month holding period rate of return is 0.401 percent ($40 / $9,960). Because the holding period is stretched by four times its original length to equal a year, the simple annual rate of return is equal to four times the three-month holding period rate of 0.401 percent, or about 1.60 percent (0.401% × 4).

The *arithmetic average return* corresponds conceptually to the simple return, only applied to a series of holding period returns. If investors want to find the arithmetic average annual return of a series of one-year holding period returns they simply sum the one-year holding period returns and divide by the number of years of returns.

Equation 5.13

$$Arithmetic\ Average\ Return = \sum Annual\ returns\ /\ Number\ of\ Years$$

For example, if an investment earns 10 percent, –5 percent, and 15 percent over three years, the arithmetic average annual rate of return is 6.67 percent [(10% – 5% + 15%) / 3 = 6.67%].

Compound (Geometric) Average Annual Returns

In contrast with the simple annual return, one computes the *compound annual return* by assuming earnings and principal are being reinvested rather than by stretching or contracting the holding period. Investors calculate the compound annual return of an *n*-year holding period rate of return by adding one to the holding period return, taking the nth root of this sum, and subtracting one.

Equation 5.14

$$Compound\ Annual\ Return = (1 + Holding\ Period\ Return)^{1/n} - 1$$

Example. The three-month T-bill described earlier has a three-month holding period rate of return of 0.401 percent. The compound annual rate of return is the annual rate investors would earn if they could continue to reinvest the earnings and principal at a three-month holding period rate of 0.401 percent for each of the next three three-month periods. If this were the case, each initial dollar of investment would grow to $1.0161 [$(1.00401)^4$] by the end of one year. With this assumption, the compound annual rate of return is about 1.61% which is *greater* than the simple annual rate of 1.60 percent, as computed above.

The compound annual rate of return for the S&P 500 index ETF investment with a 90.25 percent fifteen-year holding period rate of return is 4.38 percent [$(1.9025)^{1/15}$ – 1 = 1.0438 – 1 = 4.38%]. In other words, in this case the compound annual rate of return is the annual rate of return that, if principal and cash flows were reinvested each year at this rate, would provide a 90.25 percent holding period return over a fifteen-year period. This 4.38 percent compound annual rate is about 1.64 percent *less* than the simple annual rate of 6.02 percent computed above.

The compound return is known as a *geometric average return.* To calculate the geometric average annual return for a series of one-year holding period returns, add one to each period's return, compute the product of these sums over all periods, extrapolate the nth root of the product, where *n* is the number of years, and subtract one.

Equation 5.15

$$Geometric\ Average\ Return = \left(\prod_{j=1}^{n}\left(1 + r_j\right)\right)^{\frac{1}{n}} - 1$$

Example. The three-year accumulation of $1 invested as described above (earning 10 percent, –5 percent, and 15 percent) with earnings and principal reinvested is 1.20175 [(1 + 10%) x (1 – 5%) × (1 + 15%)]. Taking the third root of 1.20175 and subtracting one, the resulting geometric average annual return is 6.32 percent [$(1.20175)^{1/3}$ – 1 = 1.0632 – 1 = 6.32%)]. This result is *less* than the simple (arithmetic) annual rate of 6.67 percent.

Simple (Arithmetic) Versus Compound (Geometric)

As the examples above demonstrate, simple (arithmetic average) annual rates differ from compound (geometric average) annual rates. Is there a systematic relationship and is one measure better than another?

First, for any investment providing a net positive return over a given holding period, the simple annual rate is always equal to or greater than the compound annual rate if the reference holding period is greater than a year and always equal to or less than the compound annual rate if the holding period is less than a year. Similarly, for any series of (on average, positive) annual holding period returns, the arithmetic average annual return is always equal to or greater than the geometric average annual return. In addition, the greater is the variability of the annual holding period returns, the larger the difference will be.

The logic of these results may not be immediately apparent, but, if one thinks about it, it takes a lower return to achieve the same terminal value if one assumes that cash flows are reinvested and compounded.

Second, whether one measure is better than another depends upon how one intends to use it. If the objective is to measure historical performance as, for example, to compare the past performance of two different mutual funds, then the compound or geometric average returns are the better measures. If one is looking to estimate future returns based upon historical performance, the simple or arithmetic average returns are the better measures for estimating returns in any given future year. This is because, in general, the simple or arithmetic average is an unbiased estimate of expected future returns for a single year.

However, if investors are attempting to estimate the average annual rate at which they could expect their money to grow over a period of years in the future, the compound or geometric average returns are the ideal measures. In general, using the simple or arithmetic average return to estimate expected future average returns over a number of years would lead to significant overestimations of future wealth accumulations (because, as noted above, the arithmetic average tends to be higher than the geometric, and the difference is magnified by increased variability). The reason for this is demonstrated by the example below.

Example. Suppose a person invests $100 and earns a 100 percent return the first year and a negative 50 percent return the second year. This investor has an average annual rate of return of 25 percent, right? [(100% – 50%) / 2 = 25%]. Wrong! The investment grows from $100 to $200 when it earns a 100 percent return the first year and then falls back to $100 when it loses 50 percent of the $200 accumulated investment the second year. The investor starts with $100 and ends with $100 two years later, so the actual average annual return is 0 percent (the geometric average annual return), not 25 percent (the arithmetic average annual return)!

Although this is an extreme example, the effect generally is the same, albeit to a lesser degree, in all other cases.

5.3.4 NOMINAL AND REAL (INFLATION-ADJUSTED) RETURNS

Nominal returns are simply the actual returns earned over a given period computed without accounting for changes in the purchasing power of the dollar (inflation). The inflation-adjusted or real rate of return represents the return adjusted for changes in the general level of the prices of goods and services that investors could purchase if they liquidated their investments. One computes the real rate of return by dividing one plus the nominal rate of return by one plus the inflation rate, and then subtracting one:

Equation 5.16

$$Real\ Rate\ of\ Return = \frac{(1 + Nominal\ Rate\ of\ Return) - 1}{(1 + Inflation\ Rate)} = \frac{(Nominal\ Rate - Inflation\ Rate)}{(1 + Inflation\ Rate)}$$

Example. An investor buys 100 shares of XYZ Corp. for $10,000 and holds the shares for five years. During the five-year period, the stock pays no dividends but grows to a value of $14,000. The nominal five-year holding period rate of return is 40.0 percent ($4,000 / $10,000). Now assume that the general level of prices has increased by 10% percent over the five-year period. The real five-year holding period rate of return is 27.27 percent [(1.40) / (1.10) – 1].

Investors must use care when adjusting real holding period returns to real annualized returns. For instance, the *simple* annual *real* return computed by dividing the 27.27 percent real five-year holding period return by five years is 5.45 percent. However, if, instead, one first computes the *simple* annual *nominal* return by dividing the five-year *nominal* holding period return of 40.0 percent by five years and then computes the *simple* annual inflation rate by dividing the five-year holding period inflation rate of 10.0 percent by five years, the results are 8.0 percent and 2.0 percent, respectively. Computing the *simple* annual *real* rate of return using these rates results in a value of 5.88 percent, not 5.45 percent! So which is the "real" *simple* annual *real* return?

In contrast, if one computes the *compound* annual *real* return from the five-year real holding period rate of return of 27.27 percent, the result is 4.94 percent [$(1.2727)^{1/5}$ – 1]. If, instead, one first finds the *compound* annual *nominal* return from the five-year nominal holding period rate of return of 40.0 percent and then the *compound* annual inflation rate from the 10.0 percent five-year holding period inflation rate, the results are 6.96 percent [$(1.40)^{1/5}$ – 1] and 1.92% [$(1.10)^{1/5}$ – 1], respectively. Now, using these two annual rates to compute the *compound* annual *real* rate of return also gives a result of 4.94 percent (1.0696/ 1.0192 – 1).

Therefore, annualizing real holding period returns using the *compound*-return methodology is consistent, regardless of whether one first computes the real holding period return and then annualizes that real holding period return or first annualizes the nominal holding period return and holding period inflation rate and then computes the real return. In contrast, if one is using the simple-return methodology, one will derive different annualized real returns, depending upon the order of the computations. Although there is no definitive consensus on which order of computations is the correct methodology for computing the simple annual real rate of return, the authors strongly favor first calculating the real holding period rate of return and then deriving the simple annual real rate of return. Computing the simple annual real return in this way has the theoretical advantage of starting the determination with the conceptually correct real holding period return and also the practical advantage of requiring one less step in the calculations.

5.3.5 INTERNAL RATE OF RETURN AND NET PRESENT VALUE

The Internal Rate of Return (IRR) and the Net Present Value (NPV) are essentially two-sides of the same coin. To understand the internal rate of return, one must first understand net present value. Net present value is simply the current value of a stream of cash flows discounted at some appropriate rate of return representing the investor's opportunity cost rate (best alternative rate).

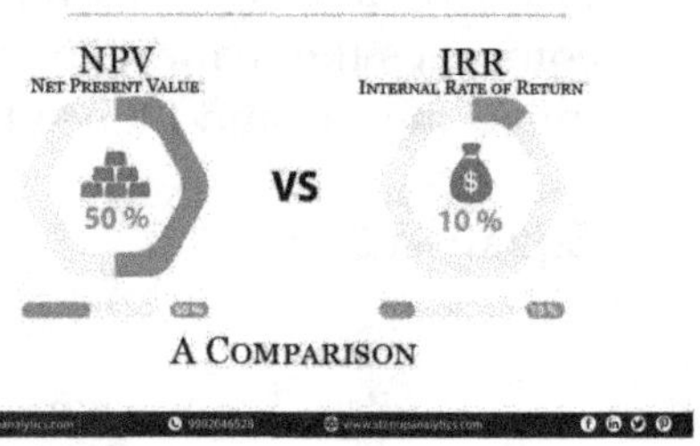

Equation 5.17

$$NPV = \sum_{0}^{n} \frac{c_n}{(1+r)^n}$$

Where:

- C is either a cash outlay to the investment (negative) or a cash withdrawal from the investment (positive);
- r is the investor's required rate of return; and
- n is the period number, starting with 0 for the immediate period.

Example. Assume an investor's opportunity cost rate is 6 percent. Assume also that the investor is contemplating a three-year investment involving a $1,000 cash outlay at the beginning of year one, a $2,000 cash outlay at the beginning of year two, a $1,000 cash withdrawal at the beginning of year three, and a terminal value of $2,236.75 at the end of year three (beginning of year four). What is the net present value of this investment, after the value of each cash flow item is discounted for its appropriate time period?

$$\begin{aligned} NPV &= -\frac{\$1,000}{(1.06)^0} - \frac{\$2,000}{(1.06)^1} + \frac{\$1,000}{(1.06)^2} + \frac{\$2,236.75}{(1.06)^3} \\ &= -\frac{\$1,000}{1} - \frac{\$2,000}{1.06} + \frac{\$1,000}{1.1236} + \frac{\$2,236.75}{1.910} \\ &= -\$1,000 - \$1,886.79 + \$890.00 + \$1,878.02 \\ &= -\$118.77 \end{aligned}$$

The net present value is – $118.77.

A negative net present value means that this investment does not earn the investor's required 6 percent rate of return. However, the key objective of evaluating an investment in terms of NPV is to determine whether it is positive or negative (whether it earns more or less than the investor's required rate of return). The *magnitude* of the NPV is not necessarily a valid way to select between two different investment choices (selecting between multiple investment options is covered in greater detail later in this chapter).

So what annual rate of return does this investment earn? The rate of return that equates the NPV to zero is the annual rate of return earned by the investment. In other words, the internal rate of return is the value of r in Equation 35.8 that makes NPV = 0. The following table shows that 3.823 percent is the internal rate of return.

$$
\begin{aligned}
NPV &= -\frac{\$1{,}000}{(1.03823)^0} - \frac{\$2{,}000}{(1.03823)^1} + \frac{\$1{,}000}{(1.03823)^2} + \frac{\$2{,}236.75}{(1.03823)^3} \\
&= -\frac{\$1{,}000}{1} - \frac{\$2{,}000}{1.03823} + \frac{\$1{,}000}{1.07792} + \frac{\$2{,}236.75}{1.11913} \\
&= -\$1{,}000 - \$1{,}926.36 + \$927.71 + \$1{,}998.65 \\
&= -\$0.00
\end{aligned}
$$

Net present values and internal rates of return are essential tools for measuring investment returns and comparing and analyzing alternative investments. How these tools are used to measure returns and in investment analysis is discussed in considerable detail later in this chapter.

5.3.6 TIME-WEIGHTED AND DOLLAR-WEIGHTED ANNUAL RETURNS

The time-weighted annual return is the geometric (compounded) annual return measured on the basis of periodic market valuations of assets. This is the preferred method for evaluating the performance of investment managers because it eliminates the impact of cash contributions and disbursements (inflows and outflows). However, in principle it requires valuations to be made on the occasion of each cash flow. One can obtain approximations to this measure by prorating cash flows to successive valuation points or by computing internal rates of return between valuation points. If there are no interim cash flows, the time-weighted return, compounded annually, determines the ending value of an investment.

In contrast, the dollar-weighted annual return is the rate of return that discounts an investment's or portfolio's terminal value and interim cash flows back to its initial value. It is equivalent to an internal rate of return. The dollar-weighted return can be misleading for purposes of comparative performance measurement, because it is influenced by the timing and magnitude of contributions and disbursements that are beyond the control of the portfolio manager. However, if investors want to compute the average annual return they actually have earned on an investment over a given period where they have made cash withdrawals and/or contributions during that period, they should use the dollar-weighted return (internal rate of return) method.

A simple example can demonstrate the difference. Earlier, the discussion described a three-year investment that had one-year holding period returns of 10 percent, –5 percent, and 15 percent. The geometric average annual return or time-weighted return is computed by compounding these returns over the three-year period, resulting in a geometric or time-weighted average annual return of 6.32 percent, as shown earlier. However, assume now that a person invests $1 the first year, another $2 the second year, and withdraws $1 the third year. In this case, the dollar-weighted return is equivalent to the internal rate of return (which will be discussed further below) of a \$1 outflow at the beginning of the first year, a \$2 outflow at the start of the second year, a \$1 inflow at the beginning of the third year, and a \$2.24 withdrawal at the end of the third year (the terminal value). This series of cash flows has an internal rate of return (a dollar-weighted annual return) of only 3.87 percent (as compared to the 6.32 percent time-weighted annual return). This makes sense because the greatest amount of money was deposited in the second year (when the one-year return was negative) and less money was invested during the years of positive returns. As a result, the negative returns received a greater dollar-weight than the positive returns (in comparison to equal weightings under the time-weighted return), resulting in a lower dollar-weighted annual return than the time-weighted annual return.

5.3.7 AFTER-TAX RETURN AND TAXABLE-EQUIVALENT RETURN

What investors get to keep after paying taxes is what matters. Virtually all financial planning issues and investment choices involve tax considerations. The real value of any financial planning strategy or tactic or investment choice relates to the real spendable dollars that each option provides relative to the alternatives. For instance, nominal yields on taxable bonds are virtually uniformly higher than returns on tax-free municipals of comparable maturity. However, for some taxpayers in high tax brackets, the tax-free yields of municipal bonds are higher than the after-tax yields from taxable bonds, so the tax-free municipals are the preferable investment.

If one assumes that the investment return is entirely currently taxable, then the after-tax return (also called the *tax-free-equivalent return*) is simply equal to the before-tax return less the taxes on the return. Specifically, if the tax rate is assumed to be t and the before-tax rate of return is r, then the after-tax return, r_{at}, is:

Equation 5.18

$$r_{at} = r \bullet (1 - t).$$

For example, investors earning 6 percent before tax, whose tax rate on that income is 28 percent, will earn 4.32 percent after tax [6% × (1 – 28%) = 4.32%].

The taxable-equivalent return is the reverse of the after-tax return; representing the before-tax return (r) an investor would have to earn to equal, after tax (t), the return on a tax-free investment (r_{at}):

Equation 5.19

$$r = r_{at} \,/\, (1 - t).$$

Although people frequently use these formulas to compute after-tax returns, they are often not an accurate measure. Only a relatively small class of investments, such as money market funds, bank accounts, and the like provide investment returns that are entirely currently taxable. Other investments, such as stocks, real estate, and the like provide some combination of currently taxable income and income, return, or gain on which tax is deferred. In addition, a whole host of vehicles such as qualified retirement plans, commercial annuities, life insurance, Section 529 plans, Coverdell educational savings accounts, and the like provide unique tax incentives that one cannot account for using the simple formulas above.

In many financial planning and investment situations, not only the level of taxation but also the timing of taxation is a critical factor. Between two investments providing identical before-tax returns and identical total tax burdens, the one that defers some or all of the taxation to a later date generally is preferable.

5.3.8 RISK-ADJUSTED RETURNS

Investment analysts developed risk-adjusted return measures to help investors gauge how much return they were getting per unit of risk. They combine both volatility (level of risk) and return in one measure, permitting a rank ordering of investments. Investments ranking high on a risk-adjusted return scale demonstrate a favorable trade-off between risk and reward: either the returns were high enough to compensate for the additional risk taken, or, the returns may not have been extraordinarily high, but the risk taken was much lower than expected.

Various popular methods exist to measure an investment's risk-adjusted return. Some use standard deviation; others use beta. Risk-adjusted returns are most appropriate when used in "apples to apples" comparisons. Measures using standard deviation, for example, should compare funds in the same category or peer group. Beta relates a fund's volatility to a benchmark – usually the S&P 500 Index – so it is important to use an appropriate benchmark for a fair comparison.

Chapter 6

FIXED-INCOME SECURITIES

6.1 UNITED STATES GOVERNMENT SECURITIES

Section Overview:

6.1.1 Direct Issues

United States government securities are issues of the United States Treasury and various government agencies used to finance the activities of the federal government. Government securities include direct issues of the Treasury such as bills, notes, and bonds, as well as bonds of governmental agencies such as the Government National Mortgage Association (GNMA).

6.1.1 DIRECT ISSUES

A Treasury bill (T-bill) is a short-term debt security with an original maturity of four, thirteen, twenty six, or fifty two weeks. Treasury bills are purchased in minimum amounts of $100. These bills are issued on a discount basis (i.e., sold at less than their par or face value) and redeemed at face value without interest on their maturity date. All bills except fifty two-week bills are auctioned every week. The fifty two-week bill is auctioned every fourth week.

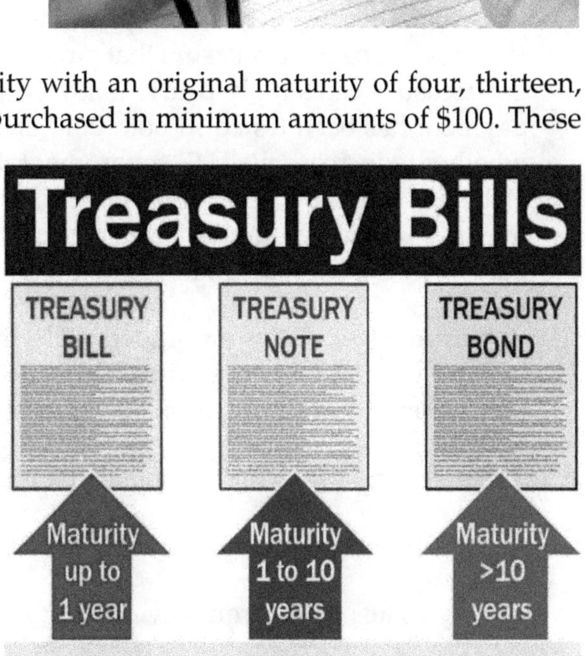

A Treasury note is a medium-term debt security, paying interest semi-annually. Notes have a fixed maturity date greater than one year and can extend for up to ten years from the date of issue. The minimum face value denomination for a Treasury note is $100. Treasury notes are issued with original maturities of two, three, five, seven, and ten years.

A Treasury bond is a long-term debt security, which, like Treasury notes, also pays interest on a semi-annual basis. Treasury bonds are issued with a fixed maturity of thirty years. The minimum denomination for a Treasury bond is $100, and interest is paid semi-annually. The price and yield of a Treasury bond are determined at auction. The Treasury auctions bonds at original issue in February, May, August, and November. The price may be greater than, less than, or equal to the face value of the bond.

Another unique group of securities issued by the United States Treasury are Treasury Inflation-Indexed Securities, often called Treasury Inflation-Protected Securities, or TIPS. Interest payments and the principal value of these bonds are adjusted every six months to reflect changes in inflation as measured by the Consumer Price Index (CPI). The United States Treasury issues five, ten, and thirty-year TIPS notes. The Treasury auctions five-year TIPS in April, August, and December; ten-year TIPS in January, March, May, July, September, and November; and thirty-year TIPS in February, June, and October.

The US government also issues savings bonds in minimum denominations of $25. EE bonds earn a fixed rate of return. I bonds earn a combined rate composed of a fixed rate of return known when the bond is purchased, and an inflation rate that the Treasury calculates twice a year based on the Consumer Price Index for all Urban Consumers (CPI-U). Savings bonds have a unique feature in that the maximum that can be purchased in any one year for one social security number is $10,000. Electronic EE and I bonds come in any amount to the penny for $25 or more. For example, you could buy a $50.26 bond.

Individual investors who desire a high quality investment with very little risk of default often purchase treasury securities. The United States government has never defaulted on even one of its obligations since it first found itself in debt in 1790. To only a slightly lesser degree, the securities of United States government agencies, such as the World Bank and Postal Service offer low risk and high quality.

Since the Treasury can simply print money or raise taxes to pay interest on its obligations, an investor can be relatively sure that payments will be timely made in the amounts promised. While the Treasury can simply print money or taxes can be raised to pay obligations, this certainty of payment has been tested in both 2011 and 2013 when there was substantial political debate on whether to increase the U.S. government debt ceiling. In both instances, the debate went into the 11th hour before the debt ceiling was raised. This caused a great deal of angst in the world financial markets and has led some market participants to conclude that payment on U.S. government debt may indeed have some minimal default risk due to political considerations.

Government securities are traded daily in very large volume by thousands of individuals and institutions and therefore offers a high degree of marketability. This insures a ready market and the availability of information on prices and returns.

The following list includes some of the investment benefits of purchasing government securities:

- United States government securities are virtually free of the risk of default
- The income from government securities is assured
- Government securities are readily accepted by virtually every financial institution as collateral for loans

- The securities of the federal government and its agencies are easily and quickly convertible to cash

- Government issues provide a high degree of security and comfort for risk conscious investors

- Because of the variety of government issues, purchases can be tailored to meet the investor's goals and objectives

- The interest earned on Treasury securities is not subject to state and local taxation. This can be of considerable advantage to an investor in a high tax bracket

- TIPS provide long-term inflation protection through the semi-annual adjustment of interest payments and principal values to reflect changes in the Consumer Price Index (CPI).

On the other hand, there are a number of disadvantages to owning government securities. For example,

- United States government securities provide a rate of return that is generally lower than other fixed income securities

- Long-term government issues, like any long-term, fixed income investment, are subject to a high degree of interest rate risk. Therefore, the prices of United States government and agency bonds fluctuate substantially with changes in interest rates

- With the exception of TIPS, the purchasing power of the fixed amount of dollars paid by these issues will be eroded over time by the effects of inflation. This problem can be particularly acute if the instruments are long term

T-bills are offered according to a regular schedule. Four, thirteen and twenty-six week bills are offered every week by the Treasury. The fifty-two week bill is offered every fourth week. Thirteen and twenty-six week bills are offered on Monday and four-week bills are offered on Tuesday. You can find out the date of the next scheduled offering of notes and bonds by logging onto the Internet (www.treasurydirect.gov).

Federal government securities, including TIPS, can be purchased: (1) by using the Treasury Direct system on the internet; (2) from a commercial bank; or (3) through a brokerage firm.

Individual investors can purchase United States Treasury securities over the Internet through the Treasury Direct system (www.treasurydirect.gov). To open a Treasury Direct account, the individual must first create an account online. Once the Treasury Direct account is opened, the individual can purchase new issues of bills, notes, and bonds by computer in amounts as small as $100. The amount of the purchase will be automatically deducted from the investor's checking account on the day the securities are issued. Similarly, when the security matures, the par value will be deposited to the same checking account. In addition to the convenience of the Internet, purchases made through Treasury Direct are free of commissions or other fees. Upon original issue, investors can purchase T-bills in two ways: (1) with a *noncompetitive bid*, you agree to accept the discount rate determined at auction. With this bid, you are guaranteed to receive the bill you want, and in the full amount you want; and (2) with a *competitive bid*, you specify the discount rate you are willing to accept. With a competitive bid, your bid may be: (1) accepted in the full amount you want if the rate you specify is less than the discount rate set by the auction, (2) accepted in less than the full amount you want if your bid is equal to the high discount rate, or (3) rejected if the rate you specify is higher than the discount rate set at the auction.

Many individual investors prefer the convenience of purchasing United States government securities from their local bank or brokerage firm. They merely call their banker or broker or login to their brokerage account and indicate the amount they desire to invest and the particular security they desire to purchase. The bank will then send the security to the investor, while a broker may offer to hold the security in the customer's account.

When an investor purchases a security directly from the United States Treasury, there are no charges or commissions.

Making a purchase through a bank or broker will typically be more expensive. Banks may charge a commission as well as a premium on purchases under $100,000. Because these charges may vary considerably, it is wise for an investor to compare the fees and premiums charged by a number of banks and brokers.

Aside from commissions, an investor's cost in purchasing government securities from a bank or broker will be different from the cost of a direct purchase from the federal government. First, the bank or broker will either purchase the securities on the open market or will sell the investor issues from their inventory. This means the investor must pay the "asked" market price, which may be higher or lower than the price at which the note or bond was originally issued.

Another consideration is the amount of interest accrued on the note or bond since the last interest payment date. The investor is entitled only to the interest beginning with the date of his purchase. Therefore he must pay the seller of the security the amount of interest accrued since the last payment date in addition to the price of the note or bond itself. Of course, on the next payment date the investor will receive the full amount of interest for the period.

Unlike most other investments, all government securities with similar maturities have the same risk and reward characteristics. Therefore, selecting the "best of its type" will depend on the investor's goals and objectives. Planners should focus on the investor's needs for liquidity, income, and tax deferral in selecting among T-bills, notes, and bonds.

Example. Anne Lewis desires to have a high degree of liquidity since she feels interest rates are likely to increase sharply in the months ahead. Clearly, she should not purchase long-term notes or bonds since they will decline in value as rates increase. Anne should concentrate any investments in short-term issues such as T-bills that mature relatively quickly and that will enable her to reinvest at the higher interest rate.

6.2 CORPORATE BONDS

Section Overview:

6.2.1 Structure of Corporate Bonds

6.2.2 Purchasing Corporate Bonds

6.2.3 Fees and Other Acquisition Costs

6.2.4 Investment Characteristics

6.2.1 STRUCTURE OF CORPORATE BONDS

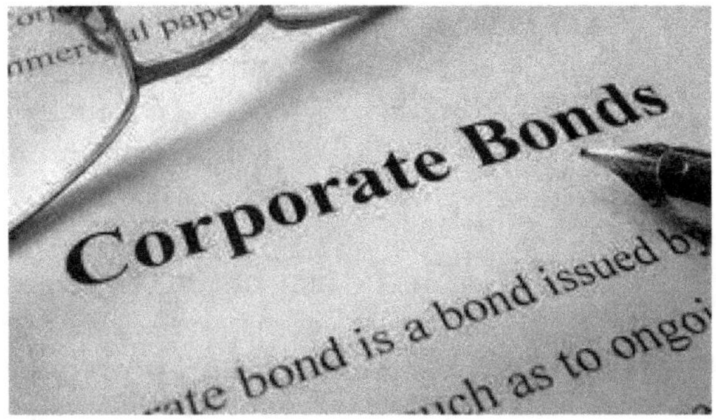

A bond is the legal evidence of a long-term loan made by the bondholder to the corporation that issued the bond. Typically the loan must be repaid as of a specified date, referred to as the "maturity date." Until the bonds are redeemed (i.e., paid off by the corporation), interest at a stated rate is paid, generally every six months, by the corporation to the bondholder. The interest rate paid on the bonds is usually fixed when the bonds are issued and does not change during the life of the bond.

An important subset of corporate bonds consists of so-called high yield issues, those that generally do not qualify for investment grade ratings by the major credit rating agencies. In Wall Street jargon, such issues are sometimes referred to as "junk" bonds.

Income and principal of corporate bonds are often considered relatively safe. Semiannual interest payments and eventual repayment of the principal on an unsecured corporate bond (a debenture) are guaranteed by the general credit of the issuing corporation. Obviously, the security of both interest and principal are in direct proportion to the financial strength of the issuer. Income and principal payments on a secured bond are backed by specified collateral, such as real property owned by the corporation, as well as by the earning power and other assets of the firm.

The payment of both interest and principal to bondholders takes precedence over payment of dividends on either preferred or common stock. In the event of corporate insolvency or bankruptcy, holders of secured bonds generally will receive better treatment than unsecured creditors, general creditors, or stockholders.

Once issued, the amount and timing of bond payments cannot be changed by the issuing corporation regardless of its financial condition (unless it files a petition under the bankruptcy code). Unlike the payment of dividends on stocks, which is made at the discretion of the board of directors, interest payments on bonds are a nondiscretionary legal obligation. Because of this fixed commitment, it is possible for an investor, through careful selection of individual issues, to be assured of a regular income. For example, by selecting six bonds, each with a different semiannual payment date, an investor can receive an interest check every month.

The gain on the sale of a bond held for more than one year is eligible for long-term capital gain treatment. Likewise, if the bond is held to maturity, and the maturity value (par value) exceeds the price paid for a bond purchased on the market, the difference would generally be treated as a long-term capital gain. For example, if an investor had purchased an AT&T bond on the market in 2006 at a price of $900, and the bond matured in 2013 at its par value of $1,000, the difference of $100 would be treated as a long-term capital gain.

In the United States, taxation differs however when certain bonds are purchased at a discount upon original issue. When such a bond is purchased at a price less than the original issue price, the difference between the purchase price and the original issue price must be treated as interest income rather than capital gain. That income is recognized on an annual basis and the owner will receive a Form 1099 showing the taxable amount, when the bond is sold, or when it matures.

Compared to many other investments, corporate bonds provide a high current rate of return on capital. Historically, the current yield on corporate bonds has ranged from 1 percent to 8 percent higher than the dividend yield on common stocks. High yield bonds provide a higher level of current income when compared to investment grade bonds (those issues rated BBB or higher by Standard & Poor's, or Baa by Moody's). They also have the potential for significant capital appreciation if a bond's rating is upgraded at some future point in time. Of course, they have more default risk than higher rated bonds, so have more downside risk.

While the interest payments on bonds are fixed as to the amount and almost certain to be paid, their purchasing power may be eroded by inflation. The longer the period of time to maturity, the more likely that the purchasing power of each fixed dollar payment will decline.

For example, assume that an inflation rate of 3 percent annually exists and that an investor purchases a bond paying $80 each year. His inflation-adjusted interest income would be equivalent to $69.01 after five years and only $59.53 after ten years. Examined another way, the investor's income after five years would have to be $92.74 and after ten years $107.51, to keep pace with a 3 percent annual inflation rate.

Interest payments are fixed when the bonds are issued. The dollar amount of these payments will not change even if the financial condition of the company or the economy improves. Since bondholders are creditors and not owners of the corporation, they do not share in the growth or prosperity of the company. This means that the fixed interest on bonds may be unattractive when compared with potentially increasing payments available from other investments such as equity securities or real estate. For example, dividends from common stocks and rental income from real estate investments can increase substantially over time.

Inflation will also reduce the purchasing power of a bondholder's principal. The longer the period of time the bondholder has to wait for repayment of principal, the more significant that effect may be. Assume that an investor purchases a bond for $1,000 and that the bond will mature in ten years. At a 3 percent rate of inflation, the $1,000 repayment he will receive in ten years would be equivalent to only $744.09 in current dollars.

Bond prices fluctuate with changes in current market interest rates. If interest rates paid on newly issued bonds increase, older bonds paying lower rates of interest will be less attractive to investors. In order to sell older bonds having lower interest rates, their price must be reduced. The effect of this decline in price is to make old bonds competitive with new ones in terms of their "yield to maturity." (Yield to maturity is the average annualized rate of return that an investor will earn if a bond is held until it matures.)

Example. If market interest rates increase from 8 percent to 10 percent, a twenty-year bond paying 8 percent will fall in price from $1,000 to $828. Why? Because, by purchasing new bonds, investors can now earn 10 percent on every $1,000 they invest rather than 8 percent. Therefore, the price of the 8 percent bond must be lowered until it produces a yield to maturity equivalent to the yield on the new 10 percent bond.

Of course, the reverse is also true. If market interest rates fall, the price of previously issued bonds will rise. In this situation bondholders will demand a higher price for their bonds since they are more attractive than new issues with lower interest rates.

If the overall financial condition of the issuing corporation deteriorates, the resale price of their bonds is likely to fall. A decline in the financial strength of the corporation would be reflected in a lower credit standing for the firm and, therefore, a lower quality rating for the bond issue. The lower quality rating results in a perception of increased risk and diminished worth in the minds of investors. In return for this increased risk, potential buyers will demand a higher rate of return. Since interest payments cannot be increased, the only way to satisfy a potential buyer's demand for a higher rate of return is for the seller to lower the price. An improvement in the issuer's financial condition and credit rating will typically result in higher bond prices.

An investor's ability to sell his bonds at a given time may be adversely affected by any one or more of the following factors:

- The smaller is the size of the issue; the less likely are the bonds to be actively traded

- The issue may be owned in large blocks by only a few large institutions, such as banks and pension funds, resulting in low levels of trading activity and a relatively restricted market

- If the quality rating of the issuer has declined since the bond was purchased, there may be fewer interested buyers. This, of course, makes a sale more difficult.

Today, most corporate bonds are issued as general credit obligations (debentures). Although such bonds provide a greater degree of security for investors than an equity (stock) investment, they still involve a greater degree of risk than a secured debt obligation, such as a mortgage. Bonds backed by real assets of the corporation provide an investor with the specific security of the mortgaged property.

Corporate bonds are often issued in the form of subordinated debentures, which generally have security preference over only the equity of the issuing company. Such debentures are subordinated in security to all other creditors, including general creditors. Because of the higher risk associated with subordinated debentures, they usually will pay a higher interest rate than general credit obligations, and to make them more attractive are often are issued with warrants for the purchase of common stock of the issuing company, or are convertible into such stock.

High yield bonds typically involve additional risks, such as: (a) greater price volatility than investment grade bonds with similar maturities; (b) increased risk of default (failure to pay principal and/or interest as stated in the bond indenture); and (c) less liquid markets with higher bid-ask spreads than for investment grade bonds.

6.2.2 PURCHASING CORPORATE BONDS

Corporate bonds can be purchased directly by calling any brokerage firm as well as many banks and other financial institutions. Bond prices are established through dealers on the basis of supply and demand. Most bonds are traded on the Over-The-Counter (OTC) market rather than on an organized stock exchange. The corporate bond market tends to be quite opaque and difficult to navigate for the small investor. However, many of the most active and largest bond issues are traded on the New York Stock Exchange (NYSE). The NYSE launched its NYSE Bonds system in April 2007, replacing the older Automated Bond System with a system that is much friendlier to individual investors. Still, only about 15 percent of the world's bonds are offered in transparent, easily monitored exchanges.

Information on new bond issues will generally appear in the form of "tombstone ads" in the business section of major newspapers. The example shown in Figure 6.1 indicates the issuer of the bond as well as the size of the issue, its maturity date, and interest rate. Also shown are the "underwriters," the brokerage firms who originally purchased the bonds from the issuing corporation. The bonds are available from other brokerage firms, but there is a big advantage in purchasing them from one of the original underwriters—there is no commission payable on the purchase. However, much like "hot equity IPOs, it can be very difficult for small individual investors to access new bond issues.

Figure 6.1

COMPREHENSIVE BOND CALCULATOR	
INPUT: FACE VALUE OF BOND	$1,000.00
INPUT: ORIGINAL PURCHASE PRICE	$ 890.00
INPUT: CURRENT MARKET PRICE	$ 980.00
INPUT: COUPON INTEREST RATE	0.0875
INPUT: YEARS TO MATURITY	7
BOND CALCULATIONS:	
ANNUAL INTEREST PAID	$ 87.50
GAIN (OR LOSS)	$ 90.00
ORIGINAL ACCRETION (OR AMORTIZATION)	$ 110.00
CURRENT YIELD	0.089
APPROXIMATE YIELD TO MATURITY	0.091

Reprinted with permission from *Number Cruncher*, Leimberg & LeClair, Inc.

In periods of changing interest rates, bonds will frequently trade at a premium (i.e., sell above par value) or at a discount (i.e., sell below par value).

The prices of bonds are also influenced by their maturity date. The period of time to maturity can range from a few days to more than thirty years. Price volatility is directly related to the length of time to maturity. Long-term bonds tend to fluctuate more in price than short-term bonds.

The price volatility of bonds is also related to the size of their coupon or stated interest rate. Higher coupon bonds fluctuate less in price that low coupon bonds, as more of their return comes in the form of the coupon payment.

The majority of bonds are held by institutional investors who tend to trade in round lots (i.e., large blocks of securities amounting to $100,000 or more). Individual investors typically make smaller purchases referred to as "odd lots." Since the market is dominated by institutional investors, individual investors must proceed with caution and perform their due diligence when transacting in this sophisticated marketplace. The selection of a particular broker or bond dealer can affect the price an investor pays for the bond for the following reasons:

1. The commission or fees charged by different brokers can vary considerably, as noted below.

2. Some brokers may be willing to sell bonds at a lower price in order to reduce their inventory of a particular issue.

The Financial Industry Regulatory Authority, a non-governmental regulatory agency, offers pricing information on recent bond transactions through its TRACE system. Before a client agrees to buy a bond through a broker, have them look at the recent quotes for the bond in question or a comparable issue. This will allow the client to make an approximate calculation of how much of a spread the broker is charging. Markups on bond purchases can be substantial and are basically hidden from investors as the only required disclosure is the transaction fee.

Some investors prefer to achieve safety of principal and income through the diversification available from a mutual fund of corporate bonds. These bond funds are managed portfolios holding a large variety of corporate bonds of different maturities and issuers. The fund market has expanded to the point that investors can purchase specialized sector bond funds – concentrating investments in corporate bonds in financials, industrials, and utilities, for example. An additional advantage of corporate bond funds is that they are typically more liquid than individual issues.

6.2.3 FEES AND OTHER ACQUISITION COSTS

The investor will pay no commission on the purchase of a new issue; the corporation selling the bonds or the underwriter absorbs the sales costs. In all other cases, buyers and sellers can expect to pay a brokerage fee ranging from $2.50 to $20.00 per bond. Some brokers will charge a minimum fee regardless of the number of bonds being bought or sold.

6.2.4 INVESTMENT CHARACTERISTICS

Investors interested in buying corporate bonds should consider the following:

a) *Quality Rating of the Bond* – as assigned by a professional appraisal service such as Standard & Poor's Bond Guide or Moody's Investors Service. These run from "AAA" (highest rating) to "D" (default), though conservative investors probably should not consider bonds rated lower than BBB. This rating is a current assessment of the creditworthiness of the issuer and is based on information furnished by the company or obtained by the rating service. The ratings take into consideration the nature and provisions of the obligation, likelihood of default, and protection afforded the holder in the case of bankruptcy.

b) *Current Yield* – the rate of return based on the current market price of the bond. This is obtained by dividing the annual interest amount by the current purchase price of the bond.

c) *Yield to Maturity* – the rate of return on a bond held to its maturity date and redeemed by the issuer at its par value. Yield to maturity includes any gain (or loss) if the bond was purchased below (or above) its par value.

d) A maturity date should be consistent with the investor's projected cash flow or capital needs objectives.

It may be desirable to coordinate maturities with potential shifts in tax brackets. In other words, an investor should select maturities that delay the gain until he or she will be in a lower tax bracket or can utilize offsetting deductions.

Preference should be given to the larger issues of strong, well-managed corporations. The bonds of such firms are likely to be actively traded and more liquid. This increased marketability will make the bonds easier and less costly to sell in a short time.

Bonds with shorter maturity dates will generally have greater price stability than longer-term bonds with the same quality rating (although the tradeoff will likely be a lower yield).

For high yield bonds, investors would be wise to: (a) diversify their holdings across issuers and industry sectors—concentrating in only a few issues greatly increases the risk of holding junk bonds; (b) adjust their portfolios over economic cycles—increasing holdings during periods of economic expansion and reducing them as the economy slows or contracts; and (c) monitor the rating agencies, which often put companies on a "credit watch" list prior to downgrading an issue.

6.3 MUNICIPAL BONDS

Section Overview:

6.3.1 Structure of Municipal Bonds

6.3.2 Purchasing Municipal Bonds

6.3.3 Fees and Other Acquisition Costs

6.3.4 Investment Characteristics

6.3.1 STRUCTURE OF MUNICIPAL BONDS

A municipal bond, also known as a tax-exempt bond, is a debt instrument issued by a state, county, city, or other non-federal governmental agency. Like corporate bonds, these issues typically pay a fixed rate of interest. Interest from these bonds generally is exempt from federal income tax and may also be exempt from state, county, and local taxes as well. (Some so-called private purpose or private activity municipal bonds are issued in taxable form.)

The three basic types of municipal bonds are:

1. *General Obligation Bonds* – General obligation bonds are backed by the full faith and credit of the issuer's taxing authority. These bonds are typically issued to finance the general operations, functions, and programs of the issuing authority. These bonds have a strong claim on the tax revenues of the taxing authority and are generally considered the safest form of municipal bonds.

2. *Revenue Bonds* – Revenue bonds are generally issued to finance municipally owned airports, toll roads, toll bridges, hospitals and other public capital projects or public services (such as sewage treatment plants or public transportation systems) where user

fees or specific assessments are intended to repay the debt. Therefore, bondholders must rely upon the adequacy of the fees or assessments received by the municipality to pay interest on the bonds. The issuing municipality frequently may promise to pay interest from general tax revenues if fees and assessments are inadequate. However, revenue bonds are generally junior to the issuer's general obligation bonds, so revenue bondholders bear greater risk of default if the revenues prove insufficient and the municipality's general tax receipts cannot cover the deficit.

3. *Private Purpose Bonds* – Private purpose or private activity bonds are issued to finance certain activities that do not constitute the normal activities or functions of government. These bonds generally are used in the trade or business of persons other than state or local governments. The interest on these bonds is not tax-exempt for federal income tax purposes (although it is usually exempt from the issuing state or local government's income tax). However, within limits, certain private activity bonds used for qualified purposes such as industrial development, student loans, qualified mortgages and veterans' mortgages, and waste disposal facilities may be exempt from federal income tax.

Income from these bonds is exempt from federal income tax. Compared to an alternative investment producing taxable income, municipal bonds may provide a higher after-tax return. For example, a tax-exempt yield of 5.00 percent is equivalent to an 8.28 percent taxable yield assuming the investor is in a 39.6 percent (in 2017) tax bracket. Of course, the higher an investor's tax bracket, the greater the advantage of tax-exempt income.

If the investor were in a lower bracket, the benefit of the tax-free bond would be reduced. For instance, if the investor described above were in a 15 percent rather than a 39.6 percent bracket, a tax-exempt yield of 5.00 percent would be equivalent to only a 5.88 percent taxable return.

To compare tax-free with taxable yields, use the following formula:

$$\frac{\text{Tax Free Return}}{(1 - \text{Tax Rate})} \times 100\% = \text{Taxable Equivalent Yield}$$

For example, if a tax-exempt bond yields 3.5 percent and the investor is in a 28 percent tax bracket, the taxable equivalent yield is:

$$\frac{3.5\%}{1 - 0.28} = \frac{3.5\%}{0.72} = 4.86\%$$

Income from municipal bonds may also be exempt from state, county, and city income taxes. Generally, the income is exempt from taxation only within the state where the bond was issued. The chart in Figure 6.2 shows the tax status of municipal bond income in the various states.

Figure 6.2

STATE	STATE'S OWN BONDS	OTHER STATE'S BONDS
Alabama		X
Alaska (no tax)		
Arizona		X
Arkansas		X

STATE	STATE'S OWN BONDS	OTHER STATE'S BONDS
California Income		X
Colorado		X
Connecticut		X
Delaware		X
District of Columbia		
Florida		
Georgia		X
Hawaii		X
Idaho		X
Illinois	X(2)	X(2)
Indiana		
Iowa	X(2)	X
Kansas		X
Kentucky		X
Louisiana		X
Maine		X
Maryland		X
Massachusetts		X
Michigan		X
Minnesota		X
Mississippi		X
Missouri		X
Montana		X
Nebraska		X
Nevada (no tax)		
New Hampshire		X
New Jersey		X
New Mexico		X
New York		X
North Carolina		X
North Dakota		X(3)
Ohio		X
Oklahoma	X(4)	X(4)
Oregon		X
Pennsylvania		X
Rhode Island		X
South Carolina		X
South Dakota (no tax)		
Tennessee		X
Texas (no tax)		
Utah	X(2)	X(1)(2)
Vermont		X

STATE	STATE'S OWN BONDS	OTHER STATE'S BONDS
Virginia		X
Washington (no tax)		
West Virginia		X
Wisconsin	X(2)	X(2)
Wyoming (no tax)		
Source FMSBonds.Com		

Bonds are designated "X" if taxable. All others are exempt or excluded from tax, or no income taxes are levied by those states. In certain cases, these designations pertain only to general obligation bonds or to bonds in general. For example, a state may not generally exempt bonds, but some bonds may be specifically exempted by the laws authorizing their issuance.

(1) Income earned from a bond issued by another state is taxable only if such other state imposes a tax on Utah bonds.
(2) Interest from some obligations is exempt from tax.
(3) Taxable only if long form is used.
(4) Some bonds may be exempt by state law.

Principal and income are relatively safe. This is because a general obligation municipal bond is a debt obligation that has a strong claim on tax revenues. Payment on most tax-exempt municipal bonds has priority over many other government obligations. However, some bonds, known as revenue bonds, must be paid from specific revenues rather than from general taxes. Examples would be bonds issued for the construction of toll roads or sewage treatment plants. Such bonds are considered riskier than general obligation bonds and generally pay a higher yield.

As with any fixed income investment, municipal bonds provide minimal protection against inflation. For example, the fixed income earned may not keep pace with an increasing cost of living. Similarly, the bond principal may not provide the purchasing power at maturity or sale that would have been available through another investment.

Bond prices will fluctuate with changes in market interest rates. When interest rates rise, bond values decline. Conversely, if interest rates drop, bond prices rise.

There may be a limited market for municipal bonds, particularly those issued in small amounts that are not actively traded. The result is that an investor who wants to sell an issue quickly may have to accept a lower price. This may be advantageous to buyers.

Bid-ask spreads (the difference in the price a broker is willing to pay a seller and the asking price for the same bond) is often quite large and can have a significant effect on the total return to the investor.

According to the Securities Industry and Financial Markets Association, in the United States there are more than 50,000 states, cities counties and other local entities that issue a total of more than 2 million different municipal bonds. Therefore, it is very difficult to track more than a small subset of the market.

The exemption of interest income from federal income and often state and local taxation has been explained above. Note that in calculating the relative advantage of a tax-exempt bond, one should use the tax rate applicable after all allowable deductions and adjustments rather than the rate shown for gross income.

Capital gains (or losses) realized on the sale of these bonds are subject to normal capital gain (or loss) treatment. Special rules apply to municipal bonds having original issue discounts and bonds purchased in the secondary market at a price other than par. While often ignored—even by many practitioners—investors are required to amortize any discount from par that they paid for a bond over its remaining life and include this amount *in their return as ordinary income!*

Although municipal bonds are loosely called tax-exempt, gifts of these bonds generally are subject to federal (and in many cases state) gift taxation. A bequest of municipal bonds is subject to the federal estate tax as well as applicable state death taxes.

Interest paid on certain private purpose bonds (such as industrial development bonds and private activity bonds) and on arbitrage bonds issued by or on behalf of state or local governments is not tax-exempt. For tax purposes, such nonexempt issues are government bonds taxed like Treasury bonds. However, interest on certain categories of private activity bonds is tax-exempt. In general, the interest earned on these qualifying private activity bonds is a tax preference item.

6.3.2 PURCHASING MUNICIPAL BONDS

Municipal bonds can be purchased from bond dealers, banks, brokerage firms, and in a few cases directly from the issuer. The major national online brokerage firms have access to a large pool of municipal bonds and since they do not have any inventory of bonds themselves, they will not try to sell bonds they own. Bonds can also be purchased from local and online dealers. These dealers have expertise in these issues, but will often try to steer customers to bonds in their inventory.

Each dealer in bonds establishes a price based on supply and demand. Larger dealers set prices based on the amount for which similar lots of the same bonds can be sold or acquired. The point is that there is no national auction market for municipal bonds as there is for stocks and the bid-ask spreads can be quite large.

Municipal bond pricing is quite opaque. When comparing bonds, be sure to check the yield to maturity of each bond.

Example. A ten-year, 3.5 percent bond selling at par ($1,000) and paying interest semi-annually will have the same yield as a 6 percent bond selling at $1,209 that also pays interest semi-annually and matures in ten years. Both will yield 3.5 percent if held to maturity.

Rather than purchase bonds on their own, some investors prefer the greater diversification available through municipal bond unit trusts while others utilize municipal bond mutual funds. A unit trust is a fixed portfolio, which means that the underlying bonds do not change and are not managed (i.e., there is no continual buying and selling of positions). Small investors find this approach appealing because of:

- the increased safety through diversification;
- professional selection and management;
- security (the unit trust safeguards the securities themselves); and

- convenience (the unit trust collects the interest and principal and pays it out on a regular basis or automatically reinvests it).

Therefore, unit trusts are best for long-term holdings when a certain fixed income is desired. As the unit trust's holdings mature (or as the bonds are paid off through sinking funds), fund holders are paid on a pro rata basis. Unit trusts are self-liquidating, which means that when assets drop below approximately 20 percent of the original investment, the fund ends and unit holders receive their share of the current price of the portfolio.

A municipal bond mutual fund is similar to a unit trust except that its underlying portfolio is managed (i.e., there is a periodic purchase and sale of bonds to take advantage of changing market conditions). Shares of a municipal bond mutual fund are bought and sold on the open market. The prices fluctuate with the changing value of the underlying securities. If an investor expects to sell in a relatively short period of time (e.g., within three years), a managed tax-exempt fund is a better choice than a unit trust.

6.3.3 FEES AND OTHER ACQUISITION COSTS

When municipal bonds are purchased directly from a broker or a bank there is a sales charge or brokerage commission. These fees will vary depending on the amount invested and the number of bonds purchased. Some institutions charge fees based on the number of bonds while others calculate fees on the total dollars invested. These costs range from $5 to $10 per bond. As with other thinly traded securities, the significant costs involved relate to the dealer markup of the bonds.

When a newly issued municipal bond is purchased directly from the issuer, there are no sales charges or brokerage fees. If municipal bonds are purchased through a unit trust, a load (i.e., sales charge) of 3.5 percent to 5.0 percent is typically added to the value of the purchase.

Example. An investor may pay $40 per unit (units are generally valued at $1,000). This means less money is at work and penalizes an investor who liquidates holdings quickly. Unit trusts often will charge a small annual fee to cover supervision, evaluation expenses and trustee fees. All of these sales charges represent a significant drag on the return on the investment.

Purchasers of municipal bond mutual funds may pay a sales charge (in what is known as a load fund), or may select a fund with no sales charge (in what is known as a no-load fund). Both of these types of funds charge an annual management fee, which will usually range from 0.5 percent to 1.0 percent of net asset value. This annual management fee is deducted from the assets of the fund itself and is not paid directly by individual investors.

6.3.4 INVESTMENT CHARACTERISTICS

Investors contemplating a direct purchase of municipal bonds should compare:

(a) *The quality rating of each bond.* Bond ratings can be found on the Internet or in the local library through services such as Standard & Poor's (www.standardandpoors.com), Moody's (www.moodys.com), and Fitch's (www.fitchratings.com). Ratings of AAA or Aaa indicate the highest quality bonds, while those rated CCC or lower are quite speculative.

(b) *Current yield*. Current yield means the coupon amount divided by the current price of the bond. For example, a bond paying $90 per year in interest that is priced at $850 will have a current yield of 10.59 percent.

(c) *Yield to maturity*. The most popular measure of yield in the bond market is yield to maturity. The yield to maturity is simply the interest rate that will make the present value of the bond's cash flows equal to its current market price plus accrued interest. To find the yield to maturity, determine the expected cash flows and then search for the interest rate that will make the present value of cash flows equal to the market price plus accrued interest. Basic financial calculators will solve for yield to maturity once the appropriate inputs are made. For example, the bond described above, with a 6 percent coupon rate, maturing in ten years, paying interest semiannually and selling for $1209 will have a yield to maturity of 3.5 percent.

Purchasing a bond issued in the investor's state of residence may result in a higher after-tax yield. For example, if the investor lives in Pennsylvania, which has an income tax, the income from Pennsylvania Turnpike Bonds would be exempt. The income would be exempt from both federal and state (and sometimes city) income taxes.

Select a maturity date of ten years or less. For two bonds with the same quality rating, the bond with the shorter maturity date will typically have greater price stability (though perhaps a lower yield as well).

Schedule maturities according to projected cash flow or capital needs. An investor planning to retire in ten years should select a discount bond maturing in a decade.

Search for large issues of general obligation bonds of state governments, and revenue bonds of large, well known authorities. These bonds are more marketable and will be easier and less costly to sell quickly.

6.4 ZERO-COUPON BONDS

Section Overview:

6.4.1 Zero-Coupon Bonds

6.4.2 Stripped Bonds

6.4.3 Target-Maturity Mutual Funds

6.4.4 Deep-Discount, Low-Coupon (Market Discount) Bonds

6.4.1 ZERO-COUPON BONDS

Zero-coupon bonds are sold at a deep original issue discount from their face value. Investors receive the face value at maturity rather than periodic interest payments. Corporations and governmental entities issue zero-coupon bonds. Some zero-coupon bonds issued by state and municipal governments are tax-exempt. For example, a zero-coupon bond issued at $500 and maturing in ten years at $1,000 provides a yield of 7.18 percent.

With zero-coupon bonds, investors know their exact yield to maturity since they do not have to worry about reinvesting cash flows at, perhaps, lower rates of interest than they are receiving on the bond. If the bond is held to maturity and does not default, the return is guaranteed. Consequently, zero-coupon bonds are especially appropriate when investors wish to lock in a rate of return and be assured of a specified accumulation at a given future date (i.e., the maturity date).

Taxable zeros are very attractive conservative investments for retirement plans. The tax shelter feature of the retirement plan allows the unpaid, but otherwise taxable accruing interest to be tax deferred.

Tax-exempt zeros are suitable conservative investments for high-tax-bracket investors who wish to accumulate wealth, have little need for current cash flow, and who do not desire to worry about reinvestment of cash flows.

Zero-coupon securities are frequently used to meet specific financial or investment goals, especially when the date of a future need is known well in advance.

Although investors are assured that they will receive a reinvestment rate equal to the yield to maturity if they hold the bond to maturity, they derive this certainty by foregoing the opportunity to reinvest at higher rates if market interest rates rise.

Prices of zero-coupon bonds are much more sensitive to changes in interest rates than coupon bonds of comparable term and quality. Consequently, if an investor has to sell a zero-coupon bond before maturity, there is no assurance that he will realize the anticipated yield, particularly if interest rates have risen since the bond was issued.

Many zero-coupon bonds are callable at the discretion of the issuer. If a zero-coupon bond is called before maturity—which is more likely to occur when interest rates have fallen—the investor will generally not be able to reinvest the proceeds at the yield to maturity he enjoyed on the zero-coupon bond.

The investor must generally include accruing interest in his taxable income (unless it is a tax-exempt issue) even though no cash is received until the bond matures, is sold, or is called.

6.4.2 STRIPPED BONDS

Stripped bonds are artificially manufactured zero-coupon bonds. These zero-coupon bonds are manufactured when investment bankers buy blocks of coupon-paying bonds and separate them into two components: (1) the coupons (which have been stripped from the bond); and (2) the principal (the stripped bond). Each component is sold separately. The principal is sold at enough of a discount to provide a competitive market yield to maturity.

Prices of stripped bonds are more sensitive to interest rate changes than prices of coupon-paying bonds of the same quality and maturity. Specifically, the market price of stripped bonds will fall (rise) when market interest rates increase (decrease) much more than the market price of comparable coupon-paying bonds. In addition, the size of the move in the market price associated with a given change in market interest rates will be greater the longer is the term until maturity of the bond. Consequently, in periods of historically low interest rates, such as in the early years of the 2010-2020 decade, investors bear considerable risk of sustaining large capital losses in the event market interest rates rise and they are forced to sell the stripped bonds before they mature.

Many stripped bonds are callable at the discretion of the issuer. If a strip is called before maturity—which is more likely to occur when interest rates have fallen substantially—the investor will generally not be able to reinvest the proceeds at the yield to maturity he enjoyed on the stripped bond. However, some strips are issued with call protection to assure investors that the bond will not be called for a specified period or not at all. Corporate and municipal strips are more likely to be callable than United States Treasury-based strips.

Stripped tax-free municipal bonds have one very important advantage over original issue zero-coupon municipals—most of the tax-free strips are not callable while virtually all of the zero-coupon municipals are callable. Consequently, investors who buy tax-free strips have much more certainty about the holding period and their reinvestment yield. Furthermore, some of the new tax-free strips are guaranteed by pre-refunding. In other words, they are backed by United States Treasury bonds that have been purchased to guarantee payment if the municipality goes bankrupt, or is slow in paying investors when the bonds matures.

Unless the bond is a tax-exempt municipal issue, interest is subject to tax as it accrues even though no cash is paid until the bond matures or is called. However, in the case of a tax-exempt bond, a portion of the original issue discount may be treated as if it comes from a taxable obligation.

The Original Issue Discount (OID) rules generally determine the amount of interest that accrues each period for tax purposes. Generally, OID must be accrued at a constant rate, effectively equal to the yield to maturity. The accrued interest each period is added to the investor's basis in the bond. Gain or loss, if any, upon disposition of the bond prior to maturity is equal to the difference between the sale price and the original issue price plus the accrued interest to the date of sale.

If the underlying securities are federal government issues, there is some question as to whether the interest is exempt from state taxation. If the interest is United States government interest, the interest is exempt from state tax. If the interest is from the investment banker who manufactures the strip, the interest would be subject to state taxation.

6.4.3 TARGET-MATURITY MUTUAL FUNDS

Another way to purchase zero-coupon instruments is through a target-maturity mutual fund. These open-end, no-load mutual funds—which typically require $2,500 as a minimum investment—specify a particular termination date. These funds invest in Separate Trading of Registered Interest and Principal of Securities (STRIPS) and coupon-paying Treasury bonds that match the specified termination date, pay little or no interest during the life of the fund, and pay out a lump sum at the fund's termination date.

Some care should be exercised in the selection of target-maturity mutual funds. Some of the funds listed as target-maturity mutual funds are actually hybrid funds that combine STRIPS maturing at specified dates with investments in equities or other assets. The objective of these funds is to assure that investors will receive at least a minimum value at a specified future date together with the earnings and appreciation, if any, on the other assets. Although these hybrid funds may have a place in satisfying investors' objectives, they will not have the same risk, return, and tax features as pure target-maturity mutual funds.

6.4.4 DEEP-DISCOUNT, LOW-COUPON (MARKET DISCOUNT) BONDS

Investors may acquire low-coupon bonds at substantial discounts from their face values, depending on the coupon rate and the remaining time to maturity. Investors are assured that the portion of the interest that is cash deferred until the bond matures will be effectively reinvested at the original yield to maturity, similar to zero-coupon bonds.

6.5 ASSET-BACKED SECURITIES

Section Overview:

6.5.1 Asset-Backed Securities

6.5.2 Mortgage-Backed Securities

6.5.1 ASSET-BACKED SECURITIES

Asset-Backed Securities (ABS) are debt-type securities that are secured by a pool of similar debt obligations or receivables. The market for these securities arose in the early 1980s with the advent of Mortgage-Backed Securities (MBS) also sometimes referred to as Collateralized Debt Obligations (CDO). Now virtually all forms of debt obligations and receivables have been securitized in the United States: residential mortgages; home equity loans; manufactured housing loans; timeshare loans; auto, truck, RV, aircraft and boat loans and leases; credit card receivables; equipment loans and leases; small business loans; student loans; trade receivables (of just about any type – e.g., airline tickets, telecommunications receivables, toll road receipts); and lottery winnings. These investments have a tarnished reputation given their role in the recent financial crisis. Essentially the instruments were structured to receive high credit ratings which hindsight has demonstrated were not deserved.

Investors should be cautioned to carefully understand the risk of these instruments and should be reminded of the importance of a diversified portfolio. For most non-corporate or non-institutional investors, mortgage-backed securities are the most familiar and accessible class of asset-backed securities. Residential mortgage-backed securities are simply ownership of an interest in a pool of residential mortgages. A trustee is assigned to hold the titles to all mortgages in the pool and to see that all mortgages and properties are in acceptable form and that payments are properly made.

Three of the best-known sources of these instruments are the Government National Mortgage Association (GNMA), the Federal National Mortgage Association (FNMA), and the Federal Home Loan Mortgage Corporation (FHLMC). GNMA is a wholly-owned U.S. government corporation within the Department of Housing and Urban Development. FNMA is a government-sponsored corporation currently operating under conservatorship overseen by the Federal Housing Finance Agency due to problems stemming from the financial crisis. FHLMC was created by Congress and is also currently under conservatorship of the Federal Housing Finance Agency. The securities they issue are appropriately nicknamed, "Ginnie Maes," "Fannie Maes," and "Freddie Macs," respectively. State and local government agencies, as well as institutions in the private sector, such as the Bank of America, also issue various types of mortgage-backed securities. These privately-issued securities are known collectively as "Connie Macs."

Although the markets and types of non-mortgage asset-backed securities are growing rapidly, the principal market for non-institutional investors is still mortgage-backed securities. Consequently, this chapter will focus on mortgage-backed securities.

Because interest rates on residential mortgages usually are higher than short-term money market rates or even long-term corporate bond rates, these issues provide one of the highest rates of return available from debt instruments. GNMAs, for example, typically offer the highest yield of any actively traded, federally guaranteed security.

Holders of mortgage-backed securities are usually promised a monthly payment of interest and principal, whether or not the issuer has actually collected these sums. (In the case of straight pass-through certificates, GNMA guarantees only the proper performance of the mortgage servicing and the payment of only that interest and principal actually collected. In the case of modified pass-through certificates, GNMA guarantees the timely payment of principal and interest, whether or not collected by the originating association.)

There is a secondary market for mortgage-backed securities, especially for those issued by federal agencies. In the private sector, the larger is the issuer, the more active is the market for mortgage-backed securities of that issuer. This means that under normal circumstances investors will have little or no difficulty in selling their securities if the need arises. However, liquidity dried up in the mortgage-backed securities market during the financial crisis that began in late 2007.

The selling price of an issue is not guaranteed and is subject to change as the level of mortgage interest rates changes – a fact demonstrated in the recent financial crisis. Additionally, if mortgage rates rise, the price of previously issued securities tends to decline because more attractive rates are available in the marketplace. Likewise, if rates fall, the price of existing issues will tend to increase.

Early repayments of mortgage loans may be subject to prepayment penalties. This operates to the advantage of investors because these amounts are passed through and added to their monthly income.

Like other interest-sensitive assets, the price of mortgage-backed securities will tend to fall when market interest rates rise. This potential for capital depreciation could seriously affect the investor who is forced to sell his investment before it matures.

Mortgage-backed securities are subject to two types of inflation risk: (1) the risk that the purchasing power of their income will erode over time; and (2) the risk that the purchasing power of capital received at maturity will have diminished. This second risk is minimized to a degree by the very nature of the instrument itself – the investor constantly recovers principal that is available for reinvestment or current consumption.

A direct investment in mortgage-backed securities is difficult for many investors because a high minimum investment is required. For instance, a GNMA certificate has a principal value of $25,000 at its inception. (The actual amount an investor pays may be less than $25,000 if the pool of mortgages has been in existence for some time and some of the original principal has been repaid.) However, investors may overcome this disadvantage by investing in mutual funds that specialize in mortgage-backed securities. Later sections of this chapter discuss these funds in more detail.

Mortgage-backed securities carry the risk that the underlying mortgages will be paid off more quickly than anticipated and, thus, the holder will receive the stated interest for a shorter time period than desired.

Mortgages are prepaid for a variety of reasons as homeowners relocate and refinance. The prepayment experiences on mortgage-backed securities vary depending on the underlying mortgages, and there is no way of accurately predicting an individual security's life. However, the general level of interest rates will affect prepayments because refinancing becomes more or less economically advantageous. For example, a new thirty-year mortgage would have an average life of twenty years based on the scheduled amortization included in the monthly payments. When a large group of these mortgages are aggregated, however, about 10 percent of these mortgages on average are pre-paid when interest rates and housing conditions remain constant. If one assumes an annual prepayment rate of 10 percent, a mortgage pool's average life is reduced to about eight years. This average life could be even shorter, though, if market interest rates decline substantially below the existing mortgage rates, leading more homeowners to refinance. Conversely, when interest rates on new issues rise substantially above the existing mortgage rates, fewer homeowners refinance and mortgage-backed securities will tend to be paid off more slowly than otherwise anticipated.

Figure 6.3 shows the cash flow patterns for three mortgage securities in which the underlying mortgages are prepaid at annual rates of 5 percent, 15 percent, and 25 percent. The mortgage securities with prepayments running at about 15 percent provide annual cash flows (both interest and principal) of 20 percent to 25 percent of one's initial investment in the first few years, with declining rates of cash flow as the years pass. In contrast, the mortgage security that is experiencing 5 percent in prepayments has a much steadier cash flow. The security experiencing 25 percent prepayments has even higher cash flows in the initial years. As the figure illustrates, owning a portfolio of mortgage securities is like owning a substantial portion of bonds with a relatively short maturity, a moderate portion of bonds with an intermediate maturity, and a small portion of bonds with a long maturity. This helps explain why mortgage securities generally experience less dramatic interest-rate-related price changes than most ten-year-or-longer maturity bonds.

Figure 6.3

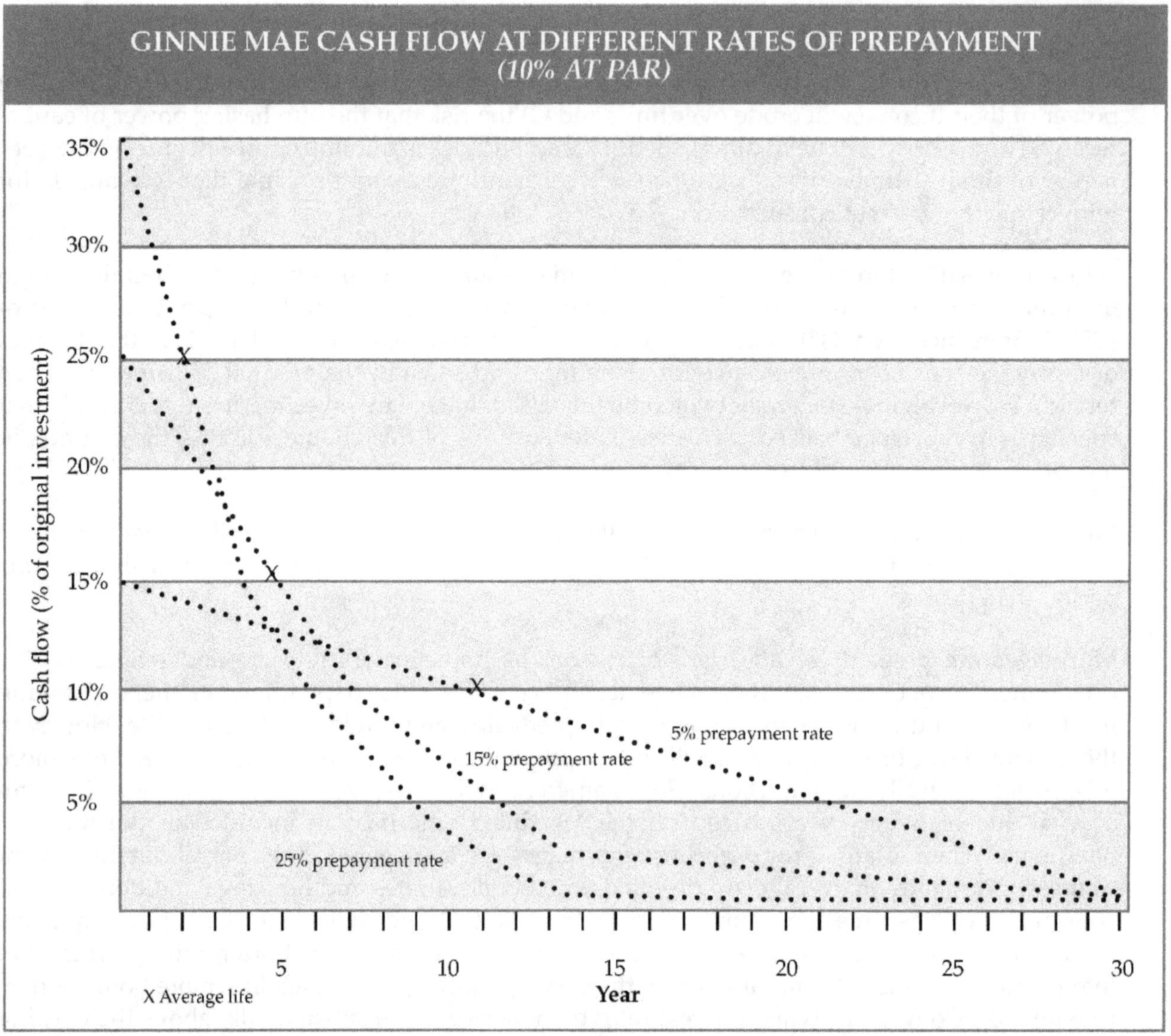

Because the periodic payments from mortgage-backed securities include both interest and a return of principal, mortgage-backed bondholders face greater reinvestment risk than regular bondholders. The periodic payments must be reinvested and if interest rates have fallen, that money will be reinvested at lower rates, thus, lowering future total return. Also, prepayments generally accelerate when it is least desirable from the mortgage-backed security holder's point of view. If market interest rates decline substantially below the existing mortgage rates, more homeowners are likely to refinance, forcing the mortgage-backed security holder to reinvest the payments at lower yields. Conversely, prepayments generally are delayed when it is most desired (i.e., under conditions of higher interest rates).

Investors purchasing mortgage-backed securities at a premium in the secondary market are at especially high risk from early prepayment. Rapid payoffs will reduce their realized yield. This occurs because investors are unlikely to fully amortize (i.e., recover) the premium before the bonds are repaid.

As shown in the financial crisis – the liquidity for these instruments can dry up and result in high volatility of prices and difficulty unloading securities.

6.5.2 MORTGAGE-BACKED SECURITIES

The two general types of mortgage-backed securities are: (1) pass-through certificates, and (2) mortgage-backed bonds. In the pass-through arrangement, investors actually own a share of the pooled mortgages. The stream of income generated by payments of principal and interest on mortgage loans is passed through to the investor. Mortgage-backed bonds are general obligations of issuing institutions and do not constitute a sale of assets as is the case with the pass-through arrangement. This debt is collateralized by a pool of mortgages that is held by a trustee representing the bondholders. Payments of principal and interest on mortgage-backed bonds are made out of the institution's overall asset earnings generated primarily through mortgage loans.

Pass-through Certificates

There are several variations of pass-through certificates. A *straight pass-through* pays principal and interest as they are collected from the mortgage pool. If payments on the underlying mortgages are delayed, payments to holders of pass-through investors are similarly delayed. A *partially modified pass-through* guarantees that monthly principal and interest payments will be made to a certain extent, even if not collected from the mortgage pool. For example, the issuer might guarantee payments up to 5 percent of the original or current principal amount of the certificate. A *modified pass-through* guarantees payment of the scheduled monthly principal and interest payments, irrespective of the amounts that are collected from the mortgage pool.

Mortgage-backed Bonds

There are essentially four types of mortgage-backed bonds:

1. pay-through bonds;
2. straight mortgage-backed bonds;
3. collateralized mortgage obligations (CMOs); and
4. Real Estate Mortgage Investment Conduit (REMIC) bonds.

Pay-throughs (also called cash-flow bonds) are designed so that the required amortization from the pool of mortgages will at all times be at least equal to the payments of both interest, at the coupon rate, and scheduled principal on the bonds. Additional payments of principal are made to bondholders when there are prepayments on the mortgage pool. Therefore, the life of the bonds is determined by the life of the mortgage pool. Although these instruments are treated differently than pass-throughs from the issuer's standpoint (because they are considered the debt of the issuer rather than a sale of claims on the underlying mortgage pool), they are functionally equivalent to pass-throughs from the investor's perspective. (Some pay-throughs are not fully amortizing; some may have balloon payments due at maturity.)

Straight mortgage-backed bonds are similar to conventional corporate bonds, except that a mortgage pool rather than the general assets of a regular corporation secures them. They feature scheduled interest payments on a monthly, quarterly, semi-annual, or annual basis. Principal typically is not scheduled to be repaid until the bonds mature, although interim principal repayments are not uncommon. The issuer often is required to maintain a specified amount of mortgages in the mortgage pool. If a mortgage is prepaid or foreclosed, the issuer usually must substitute similar mortgages into the pool. Many straight mortgage-backed bonds are callable at the discretion of the issuer, similar to most conventional corporate bonds. In many cases these issues have a sinking fund feature that requires the issuer to deposit principal received on the underlying mortgages in an escrow account and to call (i.e., buy back) a specified portion of the outstanding bonds at specified intervals or when the sinking fund reaches certain levels. The bonds generally are called by random lot. In other words, some bondholders, determined at random, periodically are required to redeem their bonds before the maturity date.

Collateralized mortgage obligations (CMOs) and *REMIC bonds* (i.e., regular interests in REMICs) are more complicated hybrid securities combining features of pass-through certificates and conventional corporate bonds. These bond issues typically have several classes of interests (technically called, tranches) with differing rights to interest and principal from the underlying mortgage pool. They are designed to give investors the benefit of the high yields characteristic of other mortgage-backed securities without the same degree of uncertainty as to when principal will be repaid.

Maturity

Most of the residential mortgages that make up the pools behind these issues are thirty-year mortgages. However, homeowners may pay off their mortgages in advance (which typically occurs when a home is sold or when interest rates fall making refinancing attractive), make partial prepayments (which reduce the average life of the pool), or go into default. Taking all of these factors together, the average life of most mortgage-backed securities tends to be about 8½ years in length. However, older pools with lower interest rate mortgages are not likely to be paid off as quickly and will have a longer average life. Mortgage pools of VA and FHA mortgages tend to have longer average lives than other mortgage pools. Mortgage-backed bonds typically are issued with maturities ranging from five to twelve years.

Determining Yield

The yield an investor will actually receive on mortgage-backed securities depends critically on the rate of prepayments on the underlying mortgages. Both the yield quotation and the projected maturity depend on the specific prepayment assumption. Realized prepayment depends on the demographic, financial, and contractual nature of the underlying mortgage assets, as well as on the structure and guarantees of the mortgage-backed security issue itself.

The *quoted yield* on a mortgage-backed security is the Internal Rate of Return (IRR) of all cash inflows (i.e., the interest and principal payments) and cash outflows (i.e., the price paid for the security). Simply stated, the IRR can be viewed as follows: If the investor placed the purchase price of the security in an interest-bearing savings account paying interest equal to the IRR, he could withdraw cash from the account exactly matching the projected cash flows from the security with no balance left over. The quoted yield (IRR) depends critically on when prepayments of principal are assumed to occur. Yields have been quoted in different ways by different dealers, making comparisons based on quoted yields extremely difficult, and often irrelevant.

The Weighted Average Life (WAL) is commonly used in the secondary mortgage market as a measure of the effective maturity of a mortgage pool. The WAL will be longer if the assumed prepayments are slower but shorter if the assumed prepayments occur faster. A number of conventional specifications of assumed prepayment rates have been used.

The first and simplest specification is to assume the standard mortgage yield. This specification assumes there is no prepayments whatsoever until year twelve on thirty-year mortgages, when all the mortgages in the pool are assumed to prepay entirely. Of course, in reality some prepayments are inevitable before year twelve. Therefore, a quoted yield based on these standard prepayments assumptions seriously understate the potential yield on a security trading at a deep discount, and it overstates the potential yield on one selling at a premium.

A second prepayment specification bases assumed prepayments on FHA experience. The FHA compiles historical data on the actual incidence of prepayments on the mortgage loans it insures. The quoted yield is determined by assuming some ratio of FHA experience. For example, if prepayments are expected to be slower than historical FHA experience, a ratio of 75 percent of the FHA experience might be used. The benefit of this method is that it uses historically validated assumptions, including in particular the tendency to have higher prepayments in the first few years of the mortgage pool than in later years. The problem with this method is that it incorporates information on a variety of market conditions and mortgages that may not reflect the attributes of the underlying mortgage pool. Figure 6.4 shows the annual FHA prepayment rates based on 1981 experience. After the recent financial crisis and the fact that much of the crisis was related to mortgage loans, there has been intense scrutiny of FHA loans and both prepayment and default of those loans. The historical prepayment rate given in this figure is simply presented to help in understanding of this method in comparison with the other methods.

A third prepayment specification is the Constant Prepayment Rate (CPR). This specification assumes that the percentage of the principal balance that is prepaid during a given year is a constant, such as 6 percent. Because of its simplicity, the CPR method has often been used to determine quoted yields. Figure 6.4 shows the annual prepayment rates based on a 4 percent constant assumed rate.

Figure 6.4

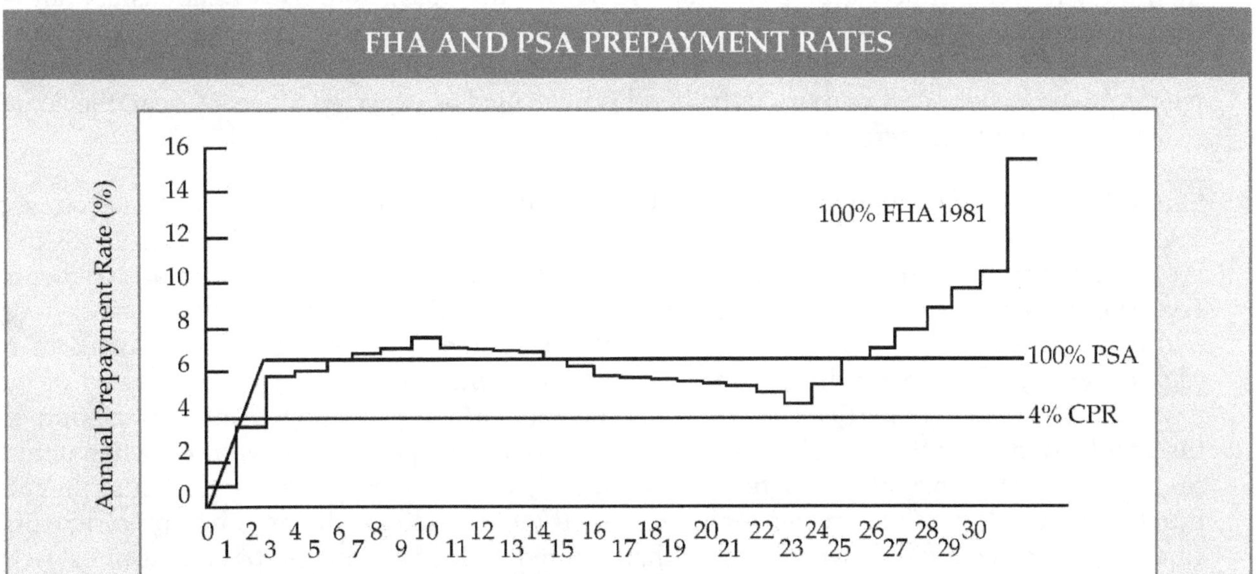

Finally, many quoted yields are now based on the standard prepayment experience offered by the Public Securities Association (PSA), an industry trade group. The PSA's goal is to bring some standardization to the marketplace. Essentially, the PSA standard is a combination of the PSA experience method and the CPR method. The first thirty months of the PSA standard calls for a steadily rising prepayment rate. After that, the rate is assumed constant at 6 percent. Figure 6.4 shows the assumed annual prepayments using the PSA standard method. Similar to the FHA method, the prepayments may be expected to be faster or slower than normal. For example, 150 percent of the PSA standard would project prepayment rates that are, again, half as great as under normal conditions.

The yield an investor actually realizes may vary significantly from the quoted yield if the actual rate of prepayments of principal differs from the assumed rate of prepayments that was used to calculate the quoted yield.

Investors who buy mortgage-backed securities at a premium (i.e., when the coupon rate paid on the security exceeds the current market rate of return for comparable securities) will realize yields that are less than the quoted yields if actual prepayments are faster than assumed when computing the quoted yield. This general principle can be demonstrated with a simple example. A regular bond maturing in two years with a face value of $1,000 and paying an annual coupon of $100 is priced at $1,017.59–a $17.59 premium over the face value. The quoted yield (IRR), assuming the bond is not "called" (i.e., prepaid) before the end of the second year, is therefore 9 percent. In other words, bonds of similar quality selling at their face values of $1,000 carry coupon rates of 9 percent. However, if the bond is called for $1,000 after the first year, the actual yield is 8.1 percent. (The $100 coupon less the $17.59 loss in value on the bond divided by the original investment of $1,017.59 equals 8.1 percent.) Consequently, the realized yield when principal is prepaid after year one (rather than after year two as assumed when computing the quoted yield) is less than the quoted yield of 9 percent. Although assumed and actual principal repayment schedules for mortgage-backed securities are more involved than in this simple example, the same general relationship between quoted and realized yields holds.

Conversely, realized yields on mortgage-backed securities purchased for premiums will be higher than quoted yields if actual prepayments are slower than assumed. This relationship can be demonstrated by simply reversing the example described previously. An investor who purchases the bond for $1,017.59 and anticipates that it will be called after one year for $1,000 expects a yield (quoted yield) of 8.1 percent. If the bond is not called as expected after one year, the actual realized yield will be 9 percent.

Similarly, investors who buy mortgage-backed securities at a discount (i.e., when the promised interest rate is less than current market rates for comparable securities) will realize yields that are greater than the quoted yields if actual prepayments are faster than assumed prepayments. For example, an investor who buys a $1,000 face-value bond with an 8 percent annual coupon and a two-year maturity for $982.41 (a $17.59 discount) has an expected yield to maturity (quoted yield) of 9 percent. If the $1,000 face value of the bond is prepaid at the end of the first year, the realized yield is 9.93 percent. (The $80 coupon plus the $17.59 appreciation on the bond divided by the $982.41 purchase price equals 9.93 percent.) Therefore, when actual prepayments of principal are faster than assumed, the realized yield on debt instruments purchased at a discount is greater than the quoted yield based on the assumed prepayments. Conversely, realized yields will be lower than quoted yields if actual prepayments are slower than assumed prepayments.

In the absence of defaults, investors who buy mortgage-backed securities at par (i.e., when the promised interest rate is equal to current market rates for comparable securities) will realize yields equal to the quoted yield, regardless of when prepayments occur.

In addition, regardless of whether investors purchase their securities at a premium, a discount, or at par, the timing of prepayments will also significantly affect their potential total return, including reinvestment. Specifically, if actual prepayments are faster than assumed, reinvestment return will be lower than expected if interest rates have fallen. If interest rates have risen, reinvestment return will increase. Conversely, if actual prepayments are slower than assumed, reinvestment return will be either higher or lower than expected depending on whether interest rates have risen or fallen, respectively.

The greater is the difference between the assumed prepayments and the actual prepayments, the greater is the difference between the quoted and realized yield. Consequently, to compare potential investments in mortgage-backed securities and to determine a realistic estimate of the potential yield, investors must understand the types of prepayment assumptions that are used to compute quoted yields.

Investors in mortgage-backed securities report the interest income as ordinary income in the year received. Each investor will receive from the issuer a monthly statement indicating what part of the distribution represents (1) scheduled amortization of principal, (2) interest, and (3) unscheduled collection of principal.

The portion of each monthly payment that represents the return of principal is a nontaxable repayment of the original investment. However, in some cases, principal payments may represent a discount on the purchase of the mortgages in the past or, if the bond is acquired in the secondary market, a market discount, and to this extent the investor must include the portion attributable to discount as ordinary income in the year received. The investor must therefore report as ordinary income his ratable share of any discount income realized on the purchase of each of the mortgages in the pool under the "original issue discount" and "market discount" rules.

Prepayment penalties, assumption fees, and late payment charges passed through to the investor are ordinary income reportable in the year received.

Gains on the sale of these issues typically are capital gains. But, if an investor purchased a new issue at a discount, the remaining unrecognized portion of the discount will be taxed as ordinary income. Similarly, any remaining unrecognized market discount will be taxed as ordinary income.

Amounts withheld from the investor by the issuer of the certificate to pay servicing, custodian, and guarantee fees are expenses incurred for the production of income and as such are deductible as miscellaneous itemized deductions. However, these miscellaneous items must be combined with certain miscellaneous items from other sources, and the total is deductible only to the extent it exceeds 2 percent of the investor's adjusted gross income.

Many large mutual fund organizations sponsor funds that specialize in mortgage-backed securities. They invest shareholders' funds in a diversified portfolio of securities issued by GNMA, FNMA, FHLMC, and private issuers such as the Bank of America. These funds are particularly attractive to small investors who may not be able to invest $25,000 directly in mortgage-backed securities. They also offer automatic monthly reinvestment of interest, principal, or both, for investors who do not need additional income. In some cases mutual funds employ financial futures as well as put and call options to hedge against changes in interest rates that affect the rate of prepayments. This provides investors with some additional protection against the prepayment risk and reinvestment risk inherent in direct ownership of mortgage-backed securities.

Real Estate Investment Trusts (REITs) offer some of the same features as mortgage-backed securities even though they are quite different in form. Investors in REITs purchase common shares in the REIT instead of bonds. These funds are then invested by the investment trust in a diversified portfolio of real estate such as apartment buildings, shopping centers, office complexes, and real estate mortgages. In order to qualify as a real estate investment trust under the Internal Revenue Code, the entity must obtain 90percent of its income from rents, dividends, interest, and gains from the sale of securities and real estate properties.

Collateralized mortgage obligations (CMOs) and Real Estate Mortgage Investment Conduits (REMICs) are more sophisticated versions of the conventional mortgage-backed bonds and pass-through participation certificates. They differ largely in that they entail segmenting the cash flows from the underlying mortgages into various classes or tranches with differing principal balances, interest rates, average lives, prepayment characteristics, and final maturities. These more sophisticated designs enable investors with different investment horizons, risk-reward preferences, and asset-management requirements to acquire the classes or tranches of mortgage-backed securities that best meet their objectives.

6.6 FIXED-INCOME VALUATION

Section Overview:

6.6.1 Fixed-Income Terminology

6.6.2 Bond Pricing

6.6.3 Market Interest Rates

6.6.4 Interest Rate Volatility

6.6.5 Special Cases

6.6.1 FIXED-INCOME TERMINOLOGY

Yield measures the annual (or semi-annual, or some other time period) rate of return on an investment in fixed-income securities (securities that offer a stated rate of return). In evaluating fixed-income investments such as corporate or government bonds, the investor is faced with a variety of measures of investment return or yield: current yield; yield-to-maturity; yield-to-call; after-tax yield; taxable equivalent yield; and realized compound yield.

The terminology associated with fixed-income investing provides a foundation for understanding the differences between seemingly similar yields and ultimately for managing fixed-income investments (i.e., bonds).

Bonds represent debt. The *issuer* of the bond is borrowing funds. The original purchaser of the bond is effectively making a loan to the issuer. The *principal* of the bond is the amount the issuer borrows and promises to repay. The principal is also referred to as the face value or par value of the bond. Bonds are usually issued in $1,000 increments and have a specified *maturity date* on which the issuer promises to repay the principal.

The *coupon rate* is the interest rate the issuer promises to pay each period on the borrowed funds. The term "coupon" comes from the fact that bonds were formerly issued in bearer-form (where the interest and principal were payable to the bearer, or holder, regardless of the person it was originally issued to). With the original bearer-form bonds, the individual or agent in possession of the bond would literally clip a coupon off of the bond and send it in to receive each interest payment. The coupon would note the amount of a specific interest payment and date the payment was due. There was generally one coupon for each interest payment due.

The coupon rate is also known as the *stated rate*. Most bonds pay interest semi-annually; a small number of bonds pay interest annually or quarterly. Bonds that do not have/pay a coupon rate of interest are called zero-coupon bonds.

Example. Palmetto Enterprises, Inc. issues bonds with a total face value of $10,000,000 on July 1, 2013. The bonds pay a coupon rate of 3.5 percent semi-annually and mature in five years on June 30, 2018. Purchasers of each $1,000 bond will receive cash interest payments of $35 every six months, on December 31 and June 30. The company will pay each $1,000 bondholder $35 in interest on each of these dates and promises to repay the $1,000 at maturity.

6.6.2 BOND PRICING

While a bond has a specified face value, the bond cannot necessarily be bought or sold at this price. Circumstances change, and investors will demand different interest rates at different times. Only if the bond offers a coupon rate of return equal to the return then required by investors will it sell for exactly face value. The example above presented a bond issued in face value increments of $1,000 and paying interest of 3.5 percent semi-annually. If a bond investor requires a 3.5 percent semi-annual rate of return for an investment at this risk level, then $1,000 is a fair price.

But what if a new investor considering a purchase of the bond requires a semi-annual rate of 4 percent for this bond's level of risk? Because the bond is only paying 3.5 percent semi-annually, the investor would purchase the bond only if it were offered at a discount from face value.

As with practically any other investment, the current value (selling price) of a bond can be determined by taking the present value of the future cash flows expected to be received:

Equation 6.1

$$V_0 = \frac{C_1}{(1+r)^1} + \frac{C_2}{(1+r)^2} + \frac{C_3}{(1+r)^3} + \ldots + \frac{C_n}{(1+r)^n}$$

Here, V_0 is the current value, C is the cash flow for each period (1, 2, 3...), r is the required rate of return, and n is the number of periods. Dividing by $(1 + r)^n$ is the mathematical formula for taking the present value of each cash flow. For example, if an investor expects to receive $1 one year from today and the desired rate of return of 10 percent (r = 0.10), the present value would be $0.9091 ($1.0/1.1). If the investor expects to receive $1 in two years, the present value would be $0.8264 ($1/1.1^2). Rather than using the formula to determine the present value, a present value table for a single sum for each cash flow, a present value table for an ordinary annuity for the series of cash flows, or a financial calculator can be used.

In the case of a bond, the cash flows include interest to be received each semi-annual period and the face value to be received at maturity. This can be expressed as:

Equation 6.2

$$V_0 = \frac{C_1}{(1+r)^1} + \frac{C_2}{(1+r)^2} + \frac{C_3}{(1+r)^3} + \ldots + \frac{C_n}{(1+r)^n} + \frac{Face_n}{(1+r)^n}$$

In this version of the discounted cash flow equation, C represents each periodic coupon payment and Face represents the face or par value of the bond to be received at maturity (n).

For the Palmetto Enterprises bond the cash flows would be as follows:

Semi-annual Period	Cash Flow
1	35.00
2	35.00
3	35.00
4	35.00
5	35.00
6	35.00
7	35.00
8	35.00
9	35.00
10	1,035.00
Total	1,350.00

Note that since the bond matures in five years and there are semi-annual payments, there are ten semi-annual periods. In periods one through nine, the bond investor will receive coupon payments of $35.00 each period. In period ten, the bond investor receives the final interest payment, plus the face value of the bond.

Taking the present value of each cash flow (discounted at the investor's required rate of return, 4 percent semi-annually) and summing them would produce the following:

Semi-annual Period	Cash Flow	Present Value
1	35.00	33.65
2	35.00	32.36
3	35.00	31.11
4	35.00	29.92

Semi-annual Period	Cash Flow	Present Value
5	35.00	28.77
6	35.00	27.66
7	35.00	26.60
8	35.00	25.57
9	35.00	24.59
10	1,035.00	699.21
Total	1,350.00	959.45

While the bondholder will receive nominal cash flows of $1,350, they are worth just $959.45 in today's dollars given a desired semi-annual rate of return of 4 percent. Stated another way, if the bondholder invested $959.45 and achieved a semi-annual rate of return of 4 percent, the bondholder would have an equivalent total return at the end of the time period as the promised cash flow stream shown above. The fair price of this bond that would satisfy the investor's required rate of return is therefore $959.45. Since this bond has a par value of $1,000.00, it is said to sell at a discount, or 95.945 percent of par. So whenever the market's desired or required rate of return exceeds the bond's coupon rate of interest, the bond will sell at a discount.

The reverse is also true: If the investor required a rate of return of only 3 percent semi-annually for a bond of this risk level, an investor would be willing to pay more than the $1,000 par value. The fair price would be determined as above, using a 3 percent discount rate:

Semi-annual Period	Cash Flow	Present Value
1	35.00	33.98
2	35.00	32.99
3	35.00	32.03
4	35.00	31.10
5	35.00	30.19
6	35.00	29.31
7	35.00	28.46
8	35.00	27.63
9	35.00	26.82
10	1,035.00	770.14
Total	1,350.00	1,042.65

The bond would need to sell at a premium, or 104.265 percent of par value. At this price, the bondholder would expect to earn 3 percent semi-annually. Note, however, that the investor receives the coupon rate of interest in cash in all cases.

Let's summarize the present value of the bond given the various desired rates of return:

Desired Semi-annual Rate of Return	Present Value of Bond
4.0%	$ 959.45
3.5%	$1,000.00
3.0%	$1,042.65

This exercise illustrates the important principle that bond prices and returns are inversely related; all else being equal, the higher the desired (or required) rate of return, the lower the value of the bond to the investor. This makes sense, as a rational investor who wishes to achieve a certain rate of return, and will contractually receive precisely the stated rate of interest from the bond, can only achieve the desired return by purchasing the underlying bond at a discount or premium – such that the total return, at the end of the period, will be adjusted by the gain or loss on the face value of the bond to achieve this goal.

In practice, the required rate of return is not that of a single investor, but of all investors in aggregate – the market rate of interest. This is the rate of return that market participants require in order to purchase a particular bond or other offerings that are functionally equivalent. All investors will generally be purchasing a bond based upon the market rate of interest because, in the aggregate, any bond that is over-priced relative to the market rate of interest will not be sold until the seller lowers the price, while any bond that is underpriced will be quickly snatched up by market participants until the seller realizes the price can be raised. The market rate of interest is equivalent to the yield realized if the bond is purchased on the open market and is held to its maturity date – and is generally called the *yield-to-maturity*.

Assume now that the investor purchases the above bond for $1,042.65, which is the price available in the open market. Knowing the semi-annual interest payments, the face value, and the number of payments (as these are all stated quite clearly on the bond), Equation 6.2 can be solved for r, the required rate of return. This tells what rate of interest is required by the market. In this case, the required rate of return is 3 percent semi-annually. This is the expected rate of return from the investment or its yield-to-maturity.

More formally, the yield-to-maturity can be defined as the rate of return that will make the net present value (present value of future cash flows minus the initial investment) of investing in the bond zero – assuming:

1. The bond is held to maturity;
2. All promised interest and principal payments are received when due; and
3. Coupon payments can be reinvested at the same rate of interest (specifically, the yield to maturity).

Equation 6.3

$$\frac{\text{Present Value of Future Cash Flows} - \text{Initial Investment}}{\text{Net Present Value}}$$

The mathematically-inclined reader will note that when the net present value is zero, the yield is equal to, and also known as, the internal rate of return.

Example. If the semi-annual yield or internal rate of return is 4 percent, both the price of a five-year $1,000 bond with a coupon rate of 3.5 percent and the present value of the future cash flows is $959.45, and the net present value is zero ($959.45 – $959.45 = $0). And, if the semi-annual yield or internal rate of return is 3 percent, both the price of a five-year $1,000 bond with a coupon rate of 3.5 percent and the present value of the future cash flows is $1,042.65, and the net present value is zero ($1,042.65 – $1,042.65 = $0).

A much more complex and important question is, "How do investors arrive at the desired or required rate of return?" In the next section, the factors that underlie the market's required rate of return are examined.

6.6.3 MARKET INTEREST RATES

The market rate of return is determined by a variety of factors at any given time. There are two primary components to the required rate of return: the risk-free rate and the risk premium.

A risk-free asset is one whose future return can be predicted with near certainty. The typical example is a three-month Treasury bill, which is virtually risk-free. As a component of the required rate of return, the risk-free rate of return is that return that would be expected if an investment had virtually no risk. The risk-free rate is the amount necessary to properly compensate the lender for the use of his cash before risk is taken into consideration. Expected inflation is a major factor in determining this risk-free rate.

Short of treasury bills though, most investments in bonds (such as corporate bonds) entail at least some degree of risk (such as risk of default). Therefore, a charge must be imposed, in addition to the risk-free rate, to compensate the lender for the risk taken. The additional return that must be paid to compensate investors for such risk is called the risk premium.

The higher the risk the higher the interest rate required by investors – investors demand that bonds pay at least the risk free rate plus a premium for risk. Figure 6.5 shows recent yields on corporate bonds by credit rating and time to maturity. Note that, in general, the higher the risk (lower the credit rating) the higher the interest rate currently required.

Figure 6.5

US CORPORATE BOND YIELDS BY MATURITY AND CREDIT RATING – AUGUST 18, 2013

Rating	2 yr	5 yr	10 yr	30 yr
AAA		1.80%	3.65%	4.91%
AA	0.65%	2.13%	3.63%	3.56%
A	0.86%	2.28%	3.91%	5.13%
BBB		5.82%	6.24%	6.69%

Source: www.bondsonline.com

Bond Yields

Having reviewed the factors that determine the required return on a bond investment, one must then be sure that the price of the bond reflects those factors. While this should be straightforward, an array of interest rates is quoted by market participants to communicate the price of a single bond. This section is designed to clarify the meaning and distinctions among: coupon rate, yield-to-maturity, after-tax yield, taxable equivalent yield, current yield, realized compound yield, and yield-to-call.

The coupon rate of interest determines the periodic cash interest payment that will be made by the issuer to the bondholder(s). The yield-to-maturity is the effective rate that the bondholder expects to receive based upon the actual selling price of the bond (which may not necessarily be the same rate the issuer pays in interest and principal repayments). Only if the bond is currently selling at par value will the coupon rate equal the yield-to-maturity. If the bond is callable (redeemable by the issuer prior to maturity at a predetermined price), then it is also useful for the bondholder to compute the expected *yield-to-call.*

The yield-to-call is the internal rate of return obtained by solving the bond present value equation in Equation 6.2 and using the call price for the principal payment and the number of periods until the first call is possible for the time to maturity.

Equation 6.4

$$V_0 = \frac{C_1}{(1+r)^1} + \frac{C_2}{(1+r)^2} + \frac{C_3}{(1+r)^3} + \ldots + \frac{C_n}{(1+r)^n} + \frac{Call\ Price_n}{(1+r)^n}$$

As before, V_0 is the selling price of the bond. Now n is the number of periods to the call date and Call Price is the price to be received by the bondholder if the bond is called (the call price usually includes a small "call premium," or slight excess above the face value). Call prices are normally expressed as a percentage of face value. For example, a $1,000 par value bond callable at 102 would have a call price of 102 percent of the $1,000 par, or $1,020. Using the example, the bond is initially offered at par value of $1,000.00 and is callable at the end of six periods (three years) at 102. V_0 is $1,000, Call Price is $1,020, each coupon payment is $35 and n is six. Solving for r results in a value of 3.803 percent semi-annually [r is the discount rate at which the present value of the cash flow to the call date equals the bond purchase price of $1,000]. This is the bond's yield-to-call at issue.

Semi-annual Period	Cash Flow	Present Value
1	35.00	33.72
2	35.00	32.48
3	35.00	31.29
4	35.00	30.15
5	35.00	29.04
6	1,055.00	843.32
Total	1,230.00	1,000.00

It was noted earlier that the rate of return actually realized on a bond investment held to maturity could differ from the expected yield-to-maturity (or yield-to-call). This is due to reinvestment risk. Let's reconsider the case of the $1,000 bond from the example above. If it is sold at par value, then the expected yield-to-maturity is 3.5 percent semi-annually. If interest rates subsequently fall to 3 percent before any coupon payments are received, the investor must reinvest those amounts at only 3 percent. The bondholder's wealth at the end of the period is $1,401.24. This is comprised of the accumulated coupon payments reinvested at 3 percent semi-annually and the principal that is received at maturity. The *realized compound yield* can be found by solving an internal rate of return problem. Here, one uses $1,000 as the initial investment (Present Value) $1,401.24 as the wealth at the end of ten periods, and 10 is the number of periods; solving for the rate of return results in a realized compound yield of 3.43 percent. This is lower than the expected yield-to-maturity of 3.5 percent since the interest payments were reinvested at a lower rate than the yield-to-maturity.

Semi-annual Period	Cash Flow	Future Value
1	35.00	45.67
2	35.00	44.34
3	35.00	43.05
4	35.00	41.79
5	35.00	40.57
6	35.00	39.39
7	35.00	38.25
8	35.00	37.13
9	35.00	36.05
10	1,035.00	1,035.00
Total	1,350.00	1,401.24

The future value of each payment is calculated by multiplying the cash flow by $(1 + i)^n$, where n is the remaining number of periods until maturity and i is the reinvestment rate. Thus, the future value for the first period equals \$45.67 [\$35 × $(1 + 3\%)^9$]. The realized compound yield, r, is then calculated as follows: $(FV / PP)^{1/p} - 1$, where FV equals the future value of payments, PP equals the purchase price of the bond, and p equals the number of periods. Thus, r equals 3.43 percent [$(1{,}401.24 / 1{,}000)^{1/10} - 1$].

Since most bonds (other than municipal bonds) are subject to federal income tax, it is also useful to express all of these yields on an after-tax basis:

Equation 6.5

$$\textit{After Tax Yield} = \textit{Before Tax Yield} \times (1 - \textit{Tax Rate})$$

If the expected semi-annual yield-to-maturity is 3.5 percent and the tax rate is 25 percent, the *after-tax yield* would be 2.625 percent on a semi-annual basis. In the case of a nontaxable bond (municipal bond), the process can be reversed to determine the *taxable equivalent yield* of a tax-free bond:

Equation 6.6

$$\textit{Taxable Equivalent Yield} = \frac{\textit{Tax Free Yield}}{(1 - \textit{Tax Rate})}$$

If a municipal bond has a tax-free yield-to-maturity of 3 percent and the tax rate is 25 percent, then the taxable equivalent yield would be 4.0 percent. In other words, a tax-free bond yielding 3 percent is equivalent to a taxable bond yielding 4.0 percent when the investor's tax rate is 25 percent.

Both to minimize confusion and because bond math is customarily performed using semi-annual rates, all yields have been expressed in semi-annual form. However, although the math is done on a semi-annual basis, bonds are frequently discussed in terms of annual rates. The coupon rate can be converted to an annual rate by simply multiplying by two. So, the 3.5 percent semi-annual rate bond pays a coupon of 7.0 percent annually. However, calculating the actual *annualized yield* is slightly more complicated since the interest must be compounded (interest is earned during the second six months on the interest payment received after the first six months). A compound annualized yield can be obtained as follows:

Equation 6.7

$$\textit{Annualized Yield} = ((1 + \textit{Non Annualized Yield})^{n} - 1) * 100$$

In this equation, n is the number of compounding periods and Non-Annualized Yield is the periodic yield (such as semi-annual yield) and is expressed in decimal format. So a 3.5 percent (0.035) semi-annual yield-to-maturity converts to an annualized yield of 7.1225 percent (a little higher than doubling due to the compounding of interest).

The *current yield* is an approximation as to how much the bondholder is earning from his investment on a current basis – the yield based upon the interest payments received relative to the exact current price of the bond. It is measured as the *annual* coupon interest payment divided by the price of the bond. If the $1,000 bond is sold at par, the current yield would be ($35 × 2) / $1000 or 7.0 percent. When a bond is sold at par, the annual coupon rate, expected yield-to-maturity, and current yield are all equal. For the earlier bond example, if the current market rate of interest is 3 percent semi-annually (6.09 percent effective annual rate) and the bond sells at $1,042.65, the current yield would be 6.71 percent ($70/$1,042.65). Note that for a bond sold at a premium, the current yield is less than the coupon rate (7 percent) because the coupon rate essentially assumes the bond is priced at par, and more than the expected yield-to-maturity (6.1 percent) because of the lower rate that will be earned on reinvested funds If the required semi-annual return were 4 percent (8.16 percent effective annual rate), then the bond would sell for $959.45. The current yield would be 7.30 percent. For a discount bond, the current yield is more than the coupon rate (7 percent) but less than the expected yield-to-maturity (8.16 percent) (the bond discount boosts the total return as the bond is purchased for $959.45 but will mature and pay the bondholder $1,000).

Figure 6.8 presents bond prices as presented in the Yahoo Finance.

Figure 6.8

SELECTEDYAHOO FINANCE CORPORATE BOND DATA AS OF AUGUST 18, 2013

Company	Price	Coupon	Maturity	Yield to Maturity	Current Yield	Fitch Rating
Ford Motor Credit	109.00	6.5%	Aug 1, 2018	4.9%	6.0%	BB
Humana Inc.	113.00	6.3%	Aug 1, 2018	4.1%	5.6%	BBB

The Ford Motor Credit Bond is selling at a premium (109 percent to par value. As a result, the yield-to-maturity is lower than the promised coupon payment. This bond matures in five years and offers a yield to maturity of 4.9 percent. The Humana Inc. Bond is has the same maturity but is lower risk (BBB rating versus BB) so it offers a lower yield to maturity of 4.1 percent

6.6.4 INTEREST RATE VOLATILITY

As already seen, there is an inverse relationship between interest rates (required returns) and bond prices; when interest rates rise, bond market prices decline. Interestingly, some bonds are more sensitive to changes in interest rates than others. That is, a given change in interest rates results in a greater change in some bond prices than in others. This section will explore some of the factors that affect a bond's sensitivity to interest rates and thus its price volatility.

Figure 6.7 shows the relationship between the yield-to-maturity and the bond price for the sample bond ($1,000 par value, 3.5 percent semi-annual coupon, and maturing in five years).

Figure 6.7

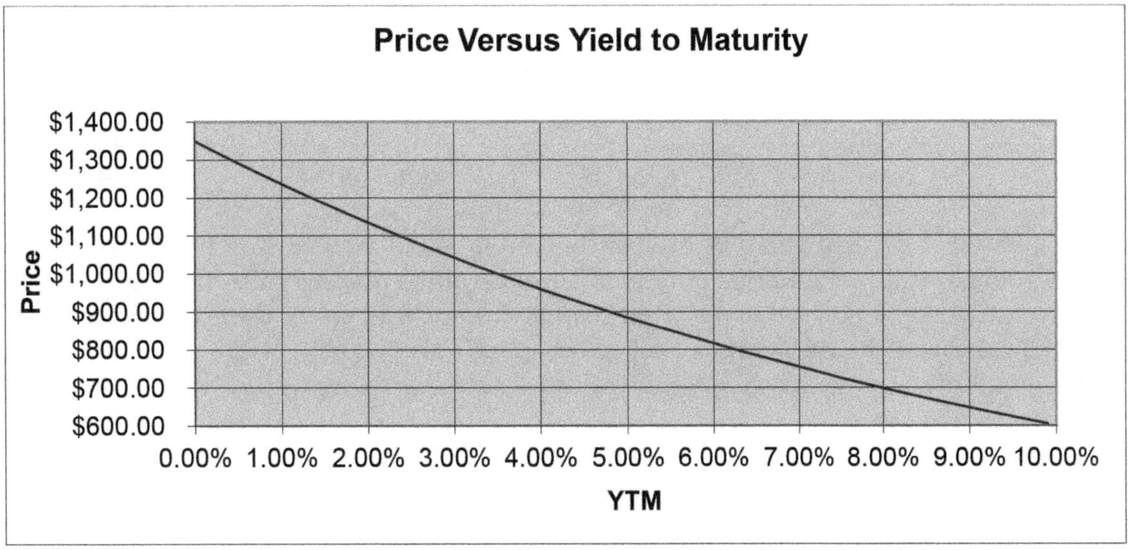

This relationship between bond yields and bond prices shows that a 1 percent (relative) change in interest rates (as measured by YTM) produces some relative change in the price of the bond. From the previous example and the above graph, it is known that if the required market rate of interest is 3.5 percent semi-annually, the bond price should be $1,000.00. If interest rates decline to 3 percent semi-annually, then the bond price will rise to $1,042.65. This is usually referred to as a one-hundred basis point change (fifty basis points semi-annually = one-hundred basis points annually) in interest rates (100 basis points = an absolute 1.00 percent). The price of the bond rose by $42.65, which is 4.265 percent of the original price. So a one-hundred basis point (or 1 percent absolute) decline in annual interest rates (fifty basis points or 0.5 percent semi-annually) caused the price of the bond to change by 4.265 percent and in the opposite direction (interest rate decline caused a price increase). This is a measure of the bond's volatility. By definition, a more volatile bond will show a greater change in price for a given change in interest rates.

As an investor in bonds, it is certainly important to understand the potential change in the price of the investment. This factor will be one major determinant in the selection of bonds in which to invest (as it is a major element of risk given that interest rates do in fact fluctuate). Furthermore, the expected volatility of a bond can potentially be used as part of an investment strategy.

Fortunately, a bond's volatility can be estimated using a concept known as duration. Duration is the weighted average time until receipt of all of a bond's cash flows. For the sample bond, the maturity is five years. However, since cash flows occur throughout the bond's life, the weighted average time is less than five years. The duration can be measured precisely by discounting each expected cash flow by the current market rate of interest (4 percent semi-annually here) and weighting each one by the period in which it occurs:

Semi-annual Period	Cash Flow	Present Value	PV times Period
1	35.00	33.82	33.82
2	35.00	32.67	65.35
3	35.00	31.57	94.70

Semi-annual Period	Cash Flow	Present Value	PV times Period
4	35.00	30.50	122.00
5	35.00	29.47	147.35
6	35.00	28.47	170.84
7	35.00	27.51	192.57
8	35.00	26.58	212.64
9	35.00	25.68	231.13
10	1,035.00	733.73	7337.31
Total	1,350.00	1,000.00	8,607.69

The sum of the present value of each cash flow is $1,000.00 which is the bond's current price given a 3.5 percent required rate of return. The sum of the present value multiplied by the period in which each cash flow occurs is $8,607.69. Dividing this sum by the current price of the bond ($1,000) produces the duration of 8.6 periods ($8,607.69/$1,000), or the weighted average time until receipt of the bond's cash flows. Duration is normally expressed in years rather than periods, 4.3 years in this case.

This process can be expressed by the following formula for duration determined in periods:

Equation 6.8

$$Dur = \frac{\sum_{t=1}^{n} \frac{Ct(t)}{(1+i)^t}}{\sum_{t=1}^{n} \frac{C_t}{(1+i)^t}}$$

Where C is each cash flow for time period t. The numerator represents the sum of the present value of each cash flow multiplied by the time period. The denominator represents the sum of each present value (the price). This value may need to be adjusted if the period is not already expressed in terms of years.

Since duration is calculated based upon the current price and current yield-to-maturity, it will change as the price and yield-to-maturity change. The calculated duration is therefore valid only for the current price and yield. This version of duration is more formally known as Macaulay duration, named for Frederick Macaulay, who derived it in a paper published in 1938. As noted above, Macaulay duration is expressed in years, so the Macaulay duration for the example bond is 4.3 years.

Macaulay duration can also be approximated, avoiding the need to compute all of the present values. The approximation formula is:

Equation 6.9

$$Dur = \frac{1+y}{Y} - \frac{(1+y)+T(c-y)}{c[(1+y)^T - 1]+y}$$

Where y is the yield-to-maturity, c is the coupon rate, and T is the time to maturity. For the sample bond, using y = .035, c = .035, and T = 10 (all in periods) yields an approximation for duration of 8.6 periods or 4.3 years.

Take this one step further to measure the interest rate sensitivity of a bond. Divide Macaulay duration (in periods) by one plus the periodic (semi-annual in this case) yield-to-maturity.

Equation 6.10

$$D = \frac{Macaulay\ Duration}{1 + y}$$

Where D is modified duration and y is the yield-to-maturity per period (the annual yield-to-maturity divided by the number of compounding periods per year). For the previous sample bond, 4.3/1.035 equals 4.15. Modified duration measures the approximate relative change in the bond price for every one-hundred basis point (1 percent) change in *annual* interest rates. Since there is an inverse relationship in bond yields and prices, the change (Δ) in the price of a bond can be expressed as:

Equation 6.11

$$\frac{\Delta P}{P} = -D(\Delta y) \text{ or } \frac{\Delta P}{P} = \frac{Macauley\ Duration(\Delta y)}{1 - y}$$

Where Δy is the change in annual yield in decimal form. So for the bond at hand, a decline in semi-annual interest rates from 3.5 percent to 3 percent is a move of fifty basis points semi-annually or one-hundred basis points annually. In decimal form this is 0.01 (1 percent). A decrease of one-hundred basis points on an annual basis should cause the bond price to change by approximately –4.15*(–.01) = +0.0415 or +4.15 percent. This is close to the observed price increase of the sample bond above, from $1,000.00 to $1,042.65 (which was 4.265 percent).

Note that duration provides only an approximation of the percentage change in price for a given (absolute) change in interest rates. Duration, as formulated here, measures the slope of a straight-line tangent to the curve presented in Figure 6.7 at a semi-annual yield of 3.5 percent and a price of $1,000.00. Note also that, in fact, the relationship shown in Figure 6.7 is *not* a straight line but is a curve. As one moves along any particular tangent line (where the slope of the line represents duration) from the intersection/starting point (i.e., a more substantial interest rate change), the curvilinear relationship 'curves' away and the distance between the tangent line and the actual relationship curve increases. This represents the "error" of the estimate under the duration formula (the tangent line) from the actual effect of an interest rate change (the relationship curve). As a result of the curvature of the relationship, duration is a fairly accurate predictor for very small changes in interest rates, but not for larger changes – even the one-hundred basis point changes presented here partially revealed the inaccuracy.

As a further check of understanding duration, consider the special case of zero-coupon bonds. Investors in "Zeroes" (as this type of bond is often labeled) receive no periodic interest payments. Instead, the interest accrues from the purchase date and is received along with the principal at maturity. Since the desired rate of return is always greater than zero, zero-coupon bonds will always sell at a discount.

Example. TRR Financial Enterprises is raising debt to fund a business acquisition. In order to preserve cash flow while integrating this new business, TRR decides to issue zero-coupon bonds with a total face value of $5,000,000. Each $1,000 bond matures in five years. Given the risk level of TRR and current market conditions, investors desire a 4 percent semi-annual rate of return on their investment.

Pricing a zero-coupon bond is easier than pricing a coupon bond, since there is only one cash flow involved. The investor will receive $1,000 at maturity in five years. The present value of $1,000 over ten semi-annual periods at a 4 percent semi-annual rate is $675.56 – the price that investors would buy this bond when initially issued. This is 67.6 percent of par value and a substantial discount to $1,000.

How would an investor calculate the duration of a zero-coupon bond? In this and only this special case, one can see that the duration is exactly equal to the remaining life of the bond. For a five-year zero-coupon bond that is currently priced at $675.56 and is expected to return $1,000 at maturity, the duration is calculated as follows:

Present value of the (single) cash flow = $675.56

Time to maturity = 5.

So, according to Equation 6.8, duration equals 5 × (675.56) / (675.56) = 5. Therefore, the duration of a zero-coupon bond is identical to its remaining life. This is logical, as duration is the average weighted time to receive the cash flows of a bond – if the only cash flow occurs five years from now, then the average weighted time is the average of one number – the time to maturity, or five years.

Across all bonds, a higher duration equates to higher bond price volatility. Since volatility is directly related to duration, one can infer that zero-coupon bonds are more volatile than other bonds of the same maturity, all else being equal. Further, all else equal, bonds with a longer maturity (hence a longer duration) are more volatile than bonds of shorter maturity.

Because the relationship between interest rates and bond prices is curvilinear, as noted earlier, one can modify the measure of duration to predict bond volatility more precisely. Recall from Figure 6.7 and the discussion above that duration measures the slope of a line tangent to the curve at a particular point. However, the relationship between price and yield itself is curvilinear – this phenomenon is called *convexity*. Convexity is a measure of the curvature of the relationship between bond yields and prices. Specifically, convexity can help explain the movement in bond prices that is not accounted for by duration. Convexity is determined by taking the duration computation one step further and multiplying (PV times t) by (t+1):

Semi-annual Period	Cash Flow	Present Value	PV times Period	(PV times t) times (t+1)
1	35.00	33.82	33.82	67.63
2	35.00	32.67	65.35	196.04
3	35.00	31.57	94.70	378.82
4	35.00	30.50	122.00	610.01
5	35.00	29.47	147.35	884.07
6	35.00	28.47	170.84	1,195.85
7	35.00	27.51	192.57	1,540.54
8	35.00	26.58	212.64	1,913.72
9	35.00	25.68	231.13	2,311.25
10	1,035.00	733.73	7,337.31	80,710.41
Total	1,350.00	1,000.00	8,607.69	89,808.33

The total of the last column is divided by the price of the bond times the number of compounding periods squared times (one plus y) squared.

Convexity for this bond is therefore: 89,808.33 / ((1,000.00 * 4) $(1.035)^2$) or 20.9593.

Incorporating these factors together, the price change in a bond using both duration and convexity can be measured as:

Equation 6.12

$$\frac{\Delta P}{P} = -D(\Delta y) + \frac{1}{2}\,Convexity\,(\Delta y)^2$$

For the bond, the change in price for a one-hundred basis point decline in interest rates can be measured as (–4.15(–.01) + 0.5 × 20.9593 × (0.0001) = 0.0425 or 4.25 percent. Recall that the bond in question actually increased in value 4.265 percent. Although the expected change did not fully anticipate the actual change, it was substantially closer than the initial estimate of 4.15 percent based upon modified duration alone. Note that convexity is always a good thing for the bond investor, regardless of whether interest rates rise or fall. If interest rates fall, convexity augments the increase in the price of the bond. If interest rates rise, convexity dampens the decline in the price. This is evident in the original example: a one-hundred basis point decline in rates caused the bond price to increase to $1,042.65, or 4.265 percent; a one-hundred basis point increase in rates caused the bond price to decline to $959.45, or (only) 4.055 percent. It is important to remember that due to convexity the price change for a rise in interest rates is not equal to the (opposite-direction) price change for an equivalent decline in interest rates. Therefore, when evaluating the potential consequences of interest rate changes, both effects should be evaluated separately – particularly for large interest rate changes, where the impact of the curvilinear nature of the relationship (i.e., convexity) is larger.

The combination of duration and convexity allow us to predict movements in the bond's value for certain expected changes in interest rates.

6.6.5 SPECIAL CASES

U.S. Treasury Bills are short-term securities issued for four, thirteen, twenty-six, and fifty-two week periods. They are issued on a discount basis (non-interest paying zero-coupon bonds); in increments of $1,000 face value. The price quotes for Treasury bills are somewhat unusual compared to other fixed-income investments and warrants some explanation. Consider the following quote from the U.S. Treasury web site (www.publicdebt.treas.gov):

Term:	182-Day (26 week)
Issue Date:	08-15-2013
Maturity Date:	02-13-2014
Discount Rate:	0.075%
Investment Rate:	0.076%
Price Per $100:	99.962
CUSIP:	912796BY4

Treasury bill prices are quoted in terms of the Discount Rate, sometimes called a bank discount rate. The price is derived by computing the discount based upon a 360-day year and the maturity in days of the bill:

$$100 - ((182 / 360) \times (0.00075 \times 100)) = 99.962$$

However, to evaluate the bill compared to other fixed-income investments, examine the annualized yield-to-maturity rather than the discount rate. The Treasury refers to this as the Investment Rate or equivalent coupon yield. To compute the yield-to-maturity on a Treasury bill, calculate the internal rate of return for a single period with a present value of 99.962 and a future value (par) of 100.000. The resulting rate is 0.038 percent, which is the yield-to-maturity for a 182-day period. The annualized rate listed by the Treasury is 0.038% × 365/182 or 0.76%. This is not a compounded rate.

While the size of the U.S. market for convertibles is dwarfed by the markets for equities and nonconvertible bonds, it is a market that continues to grow in size and importance along with the growth in related derivative securities (for example, options).

Why do investors purchase convertible bonds? In short, convertibles offer much of the upside potential of an equity security *and* the downside protection of a bond. The upside portion of this interesting combination stems from the fact that the holder has the right to surrender the bond in exchange for a fixed number of shares of the common stock, which rise in value if the shares appreciate. The downside protection is a result of the combination of two factors. First, the bondholder need not acquire the stock if its price does not rise. Second, provided the issuer remains solvent, the investor can hold the bond to maturity and collect its face value at maturity or sell it to another investor in the interim period.

Convertible bonds pay the coupon rate of interest semi-annually on the face amount of the security. So a convertible bond with a $1,000 face value and a coupon rate of 5.5 percent will pay $27.50 (i.e., ½ × .055 × $1,000) twice each year. In addition, assume this convertible bond can be converted into 16⅔ shares of common stock. In this case the *conversion ratio* is 16.667 and implies a *conversion price* of $60, which is simply the face value ($1,000) divided by the conversion ratio (16.667). To summarize, the convertible investor has the right to acquire 16.667 shares for each $1,000 bond by surrendering the bond for this pre-specified number of shares of the common stock.

In assessing the potential risk of a convertible investment, the prospective investor must break this hybrid investment vehicle into its two components and examine each in turn. Convertibles are called hybrid securities because they have both equity and fixed-income characteristics.

If the current price of the stock of the issuer is $50 and the investor could elect to surrender the bond today in exchange for 16⅔ shares, then clearly the convertible could not be priced less than $833.33 (16⅔ shares × $50 per share) in today's market because investors would simply buy and convert it, thereby reaping an immediate (arbitrage) profit. This amount, $833.33, is known as the convertible's *conversion value*.

One must also consider the fixed-income component alone in the process of assessing the downside risk of this investment. What price would the convertible bond move toward in the event that investors decide today that the common stock has little or no potential to exceed its conversion price? In effect, the convertible bond would then be priced as if it were a straight bond of the issuer. So, if a twenty-year (forty coupon payment) straight $1,000 par value bond of this firm with a 5.5 percent annual coupon rate (payable $27.50 each semiannual period) were priced for a semi-annual yield-to-maturity of 3.5 percent, the convertible bond would then be priced to yield about the same rate of return.

Using the same approach to value bonds as earlier in this chapter, one could compute its expected market price as the present value of the future stream of interest and principal payments discounted at the appropriate rate (3.5 percent semi-annually in this case): $839.84. The value of the convertible as a bond alone is called its *bond value*. This indicates a second possible *floor price* to which the convertible could descend. Clearly, the convertible will not be priced in the market below its price as a straight bond because it also contains the conversion option, which has some non-zero market value.

The conclusion of the preceding two-stage analysis is that the minimum price of a convertible is the *greater* of its Bond Value and its Conversion Value. To complete this assessment of the downside risk of a convertible, its *conversion premium* is defined as the percentage difference between its current market price and its theoretical minimum value. Assuming the bond is currently selling for $1,050 its conversion premium would be $210.16 or 25.02 percent ($210.16/839.84). This is the premium the market is willing to pay for the potential increase in the stock price.

Chapter 7

EQUITY SECURITIES

7.1 COMMON STOCKS

Section Overview:

7.1.1 Characteristics

7.1.2 Common Stock Selection Strategies

7.1.3 Evaluating New Issues of Stock

7.1.4 Short Selling

7.1.1 CHARACTERISTICS

Common stock represents an ownership interest in a corporation. Each shareholder is entitled to a proportionate share of the control, profits, and assets of the corporation. Stockholders exercise control through voting rights and receive a share of corporate profits through dividends. In the event the corporation is sold or liquidated, owners of common stock will share the net proceeds after creditors, bondholders, and preferred stockholders claims have been satisfied.

shutterstock.com • 1356427889

Over the long run, common stocks have provided an average annual rate of return almost twice that of fixed income investments. Returns on stocks have averaged nearly 12 percent over the past eighty-five years while fixed income securities such as corporate bonds and government securities have averaged only around 6 percent. From 1988 through 2012, the Standard & Poor's 500 Stock Index earned a compound annual rate of return of 9.71 percent.

Common stocks are generally very liquid securities. This means that they can quickly and easily be converted to cash if necessary. This liquidity itself enhances their value.

The huge number of common stocks available makes it possible for investors to select securities that are compatible with their own particular investment requirements and risk-taking preferences. For example, public utility stocks have traditionally been selected by investors with a preference for security and stable income while growth stocks may be more attractive to those who are willing to accept greater risk and do not need current income.

Unlike many real estate investments, common stocks do not require personal involvement in the day-to-day management of the enterprise. How much time the investor spends on managing his or her portfolio is another matter and depends on many variables including: personal preference and investment style; availability of time; and the degree of knowledge and skill of the investor.

The market price of stocks can fluctuate widely over time. Day-to-day changes in share prices are inevitable and beyond the investor's control. Most investors remember that the Dow Jones Industrial Average (DJIA) lost nearly 23 percent on Black Monday (September 19, 1987). However, few investors probably recall that there were four separate days in 2008 in which the DJIA lost in excess of 6.98 percent.

Even over fairly long time periods, stock prices can decline substantially. For example, the S&P 500 Stock Index fell by 9.1 percent in 2000, declined another 11.9 percent in 2001, and an additional 22.1 percent in 2002. However, this was the first consecutive three-year decline since the late 1930's. Further evidence of this volatility is that in 2008 the S&P 500 index fell by 37 percent and then gained 26.5 percent in the very next year. This volatility may be unsettling to conservative investors for whom preservation of capital is a high priority.

The prices of individual securities may be adversely affected by factors unrelated to the financial condition of the business itself. These factors may include political events, natural disasters, changes in tax laws or interest rates, and general economic conditions.

It is possible that an investor could lose all or a significant portion of his investment. For instance, if an individual was forced to sell shares during a depressed market, the result might be a permanent and significant loss of capital.

Payment of dividends on common stock is not guaranteed. Although many corporations have traditionally paid regular dividends, the declaration of a dividend, as well as the specific amount, is at the discretion of the corporation's board of directors. Thus, dividends may vary with changes in the general financial condition of a company and the market as a whole. This may pose a potential problem for investors who desire a regular income.

Historically, dividends on common stock have generally been taxed as ordinary income. In some recent years, some dividends were classified as qualified dividends and qualified for the preferred tax rate of zero percent or 15 percent. To be a qualified dividend, the investor must have held the stock for more than sixty days during the 121-day period that begins sixty days before the ex-dividend date. The American Taxpayer Relief Act of 2012 extended these low tax rates on qualified dividends for taxpayers with taxable income below that does not put them in 39.6 percent tax bracket. For taxpayers with income above this level, qualified dividends are taxed at 20 percent.

Capital gains income from the sale of stock held longer than one year is generally taxed at a special long-term capital gains rate. The rate that applies depends on which ordinary income tax bracket a person falls under. The long term capital gains rate is zero if total income (including capital gain income) places a person in the ten or fifteen percent tax brackets. The capital gains rate is 15 percent if total income (including capital gain income) places one in the twenty-five percent tax bracket or higher. Starting with the year 2013, there is a new long-term capital gains rate of 20 percent which applies to taxpayers falling within the 39.6 percent tax bracket. Also beginning in 2013, capital gain income is subject to an additional 3.8 percent Net Investment Income Tax (NIIT) for taxpayers with income at or above a certain threshold. Capital gain income from assets held one year or less is taxed at the ordinary income tax rates in effect for the year.

Losses on the sale of common stock will be short-term or long-term depending on how long the stock was held. Capital losses are deductible dollar-for-dollar against short-term capital gain, long-term capital gain, and finally, to a limited degree, against ordinary income.

Example. Assume Dick Goldman had a capital paper loss of $8,000 and an actual realized short-term gain of $5,000 in the same year. If he sold the depressed shares and recognized the $8,000 loss, $5,000 of the loss would be used to wipe out the entire short-term gain. This would leave a $3,000 loss that could be used to reduce his ordinary income. (The maximum amount of ordinary income that may be offset in one tax year is $3,000; any excess capital loss may be carried over to the succeeding tax year.) Qualified dividend income is *not* eligible to offset capital losses.

Year-to-year appreciation in share prices is not taxable unless and until the investor realizes the gain by selling the stock or otherwise disposing of it in a taxable transaction. This makes it possible to defer the gain until a tax year in which the investor is in a lower tax bracket. For example, Bob Norton might deliberately delay the sale of highly appreciated stock until after retirement when he will be in a lower tax bracket.

It may be possible to avoid taxation on the gain entirely. Generally, if an investor holds appreciated stock until his death, the gain is never taxed. This is because the basis of the stock is stepped-up to its fair market value for federal estate tax purposes.

Example. Bob Norton purchased stock for $30 per share, and it is worth $130 per share at the time of his death. The new basis of the stock in his executor's hands would be stepped-up to $130. If the executor sold the stock the next day for $130 there would be no gain. This is because the amount realized ($130) minus the adjusted basis ($130) would be zero and, therefore, there would be no taxable gain.

Common stocks are typically purchased through a brokerage firm. Once an account is established by providing certain personal and financial information, brokers will transact orders for the purchase or sale of shares. These orders are commonly transacted electronically via the internet or over the telephone. Electronic trading through online brokerage firms is growing rapidly. One factor contributing to this growth is the very low cost of such transactions. Fees paid on these trades are generally lower than $10, which is a fraction of the regular brokerage commission charge. Be advised, however, that full-service brokerage firms offer advice and more personalized service.

Once stock has been bought or sold, the investor is notified by mail (and also electronically if the transaction was done via internet trading) in the form of a written confirmation. The confirmation will show the date of the transaction, the name of the company involved, the number of shares, the transaction price per share, the total value of the transaction, and the commissions or fees charged.

Until recent years, companies issued paper stock certificates to evidence ownership. Now, the ownership of stock is almost exclusively recorded electronically via the Direct Registration System (DRS) built by the Depositor Trust Clearing Corporation (DTCC). In fact, companies are no longer required to provide paper certificates to stockholders, even when requested. For customers who want physical certificates, if available, many brokers charge $500 or more to produce a paper certificate.

Many investors prefer to own common stocks indirectly through mutual funds. These funds provide a number of advantages such as: (1) diversification; (2) professional management; (3) automatic reinvestment of dividends; and (4) ease of record keeping.

When common stocks are purchased through a broker or a bank, there is a sales charge commonly called a brokerage commission or fee. The amount of the fee will be dependent upon the amount invested, the number of shares purchased, and the level of service or advice provided by the broker or bank.

Commission charges will vary widely and investors should compare the rates charged by various sources when buying or selling shares. Substantial transaction cost differences exist between full-service and discount brokerage firms. However, transaction costs are not the only factor to consider in buying or selling shares of stock. The information, advice, and other services provided by a full-service firm may easily justify a higher commission rate for many investors.

7.1.2 COMMON STOCK SELECTION

Professional security analysts rate common stocks according to their (1) overall quality, (2) security, and (3) growth potential. The process involves an analysis of various factors such as product and industry position, corporate resources, and financial policy. Among the rating services that can be found in the local library (or on the Internet) are Standard & Poor's (www.standardandpoors.com), Moody's (www.moodys.com), the Value Line Investment Survey (www.valueline.com), and Morningstar (www.morningstar.com). Standard & Poor's and Moody's issue quality ratings for common stocks. These rankings do not take into account the current price of a stock, which is a critical factor in making a particular purchase or sale. A highly rated stock may be overpriced while a stock with a low rating may be attractively priced and a good buy. Standard & Poor's also publishes research that attempts to evaluate the prospects for a particular stock based on their proprietary research.

The Value Line Investment Survey contains a number of useful ratings. Each stock covered is rated for timeliness, safety, and technical analysis, and is also issued a financial strength rating, price stability score, growth persistence score and earnings predictability score. Conservative investors usually avoid those stocks rated B or lower by Standard & Poor's or Moody's or those with a Value Line safety ranking lower than three.

Extensive information and investment advisory services are offered by most brokerage firms. They can provide recommendations on specific industries or individual companies in the form of research reports by their own analysts. Brokerage firms also make available information that they in turn purchase from one or more professional research firms.

A wealth of information can be obtained at no cost by contacting the company and requesting a copy of its annual report. This report contains information on the company's activities, its financial condition, products and services, general outlook, management personnel, dividend payments, and future prospects. A more detailed version of this report, known as a 10-K report, can also be obtained upon request by contacting the company or from the Securities and Exchange Commission's Electronic Data Gathering, Analysis and Retrieval (EDGAR) database. Investors seeking current income should examine the dividend payment record of the company in question. The services listed above will indicate the current dividend being paid on the stock, if any, and the amounts paid in prior years. Brokerage firms can provide lists of companies that have paid dividends consistently for many years and those firms that have increased their dividends regularly. The Value Line Investment Survey ranks stocks according to their current dividend yield percentage. This ranking would enable an investor to quickly select those stocks providing the highest level of dividend income per dollar of investment.

7.1.3 EVALUATING NEW ISSUES OF STOCK

New issues should be evaluated very much the same as seasoned stocks—very carefully, and according to a standard procedure. That procedure should include studying the prospectus. Specifically, look for positive answers to:

1. What does the firm do?
2. What is its major product?
3. Who are the firm's major competitors? Look for businesses with a unique product that cannot be quickly or easily copied by major competitors.
4. How long has the firm been in business and has it survived major economic downturns?
5. How stable and experienced is the management of the company and what exceptional talent or experience does it possess?
6. What is the magnitude of the company's profit and what is the trend?
7. How large is the company?
8. What is the source of the company's revenues and how dependent is it on any one source?
9. What is unique about the company—not only from the positive side but also from the negative side (e.g., what unusual down side risks or liabilities does it have)?
10. Has the firm been audited by a national accounting firm and, if so, has the firm qualified its endorsement?
11. What is the expected dividend per share for the issue? (Find price/earnings ratio by dividing net earnings for the latest twelve-month period by the number of shares the company intends to issue.) Divide the expected offering price by the company's past earnings per share to estimate the price/earnings for the new issue. Most new growth-oriented companies have P/E ratios higher than the average S&P.
12. What is the reputation of the underwriter bringing the company public? Try to select a company that has a strong underwriter. In general, bigger investment banks with strong reputations bring quality companies public. Be more skeptical of companies being underwritten by smaller investment banks with lesser reputations.

7.1.4 SHORT SELLING

Selling short is a technique used by both aggressive and conservative investors. The aggressive investor who feels the price of the stock will fall can earn money by selling short. The conservative investor can use short selling to defer the tax on gains. Short selling means that you sell shares you "borrow" from a broker with the hope that the stock will decline in price in the near future.

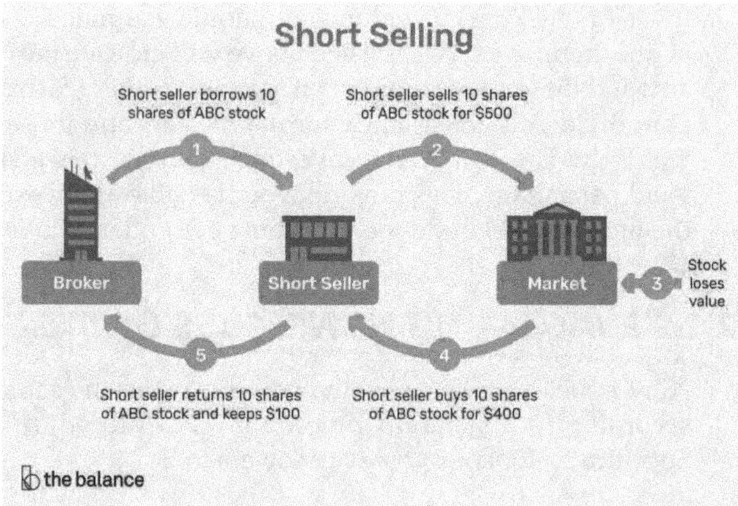

Short selling works like this:

1. The client calls the broker and says, "Sell 10 shares of ABC stock short."

2. The broker tells the client that the stock is currently selling for $50 per share. In a short sale the client must sell on an uptick. That means he can sell only if the last sale was at a price higher than the sale preceding it. The client can specify a target price for the sale (this is called a limit order) or the client can specify that the stock is to be sold at market or on the next uptick.

3. Assume the stock ticks up to the sell price and the trade is executed. The broker will borrow shares from one of its customer's holdings to deliver to the buyer. (When the client signs the new account agreement with his or her broker, the investor is agreeing to let them do this.) The client will be charged the standard commission for selling the stock.

4. The purchaser of the stock pays the broker and in return receives the stock certificates.

5. The client must put up 50 percent of the value of the borrowed stock in cash (or 100 percent of the value of the borrowed stock in securities) since this is a credit transaction. The money or securities are placed in the client's margin account. Interest is typically not charged on the transaction since the broker has the proceeds from the short sale as well as the initial margin.

6. The client must then decide when to close out the short sale by buying the stock back. As long as the stock is falling, the investor can continue to compare the price with the company's prospects to time the buy-back. If the stock begins to rise, however, the investor has to calculate the risk of catastrophic loss. A buyer can only lose his or her investment. If they buy $500 worth of XYZ, they can lose $500 if the stock drops to zero. A short seller who sells short $500 can lose a theoretically infinite amount. If the shorted stock was selling at $50 per share and subsequently goes to $500 per share, it will cost the investor $5,000 to buy it back—ten times their original investment. This is not a silly example. Ask anyone who shorted internet stocks in 1999.

Selling short is highly risky because if the stock goes up instead of down, the client will have to buy back the stock at its higher price. The leverage that increases the client's gain if he is right also increases his loss if he is wrong. If the stock increases rapidly in value, the stock brokerage firm will issue the client a maintenance call or margin call. This is a notice from the firm that the client must put more money into his margin account. This call will typically be issued when the margin account balance (the sum of what the client put into the account plus the proceeds from the short sale) falls below 130 percent of the current market value of the stock. The broker will automatically close out the client's position if the additional call money is not added to the account. (Many experts advise that it is better to take the loss than to put up more margin and lose more money).

Selling short should be considered only if the client has:

- researched the particular stock and the state of its industry group thoroughly
- checked the volume of short sales of that stock (if many others have also shorted the stock, when they begin to buy the stock to cover their positions, it may drive the price of the stock back up)
- considered the tax implications (all gains from short sales will be taxed at ordinary rates regardless of when the short sale is covered)
- has sufficient resources to ride out an adverse environment.

7.2 PREFERRED STOCK

Section Overview:

7.2.1 Characteristics

7.2.2 Preferred Stock Selection

7.2.1 CHARACTERISTICS

A preferred stock is a security that combines some of the features of both bonds and common stocks.

Most preferred stocks do not carry voting rights under normal circumstances. Preferred stocks, as their name implies, have a preferred position with respect to the earnings of a corporation. Dividends on preferred stocks must be paid before any dividends can be paid to holders of common shares. Owners of preferred stock have precedence over common stockholders with respect to the assets of the corporation in the event of a sale or liquidation of the company.

Income from preferred shares is relatively certain, especially when compared to dividends on common stock. Typically, dividends on preferred shares are paid on a quarterly basis. While preferred dividends are not a fixed, legal obligation (in the sense that interest on bonds must be paid to avoid default), they must be paid before any common shareholders can receive dividends. Although preferred stockholders typically cannot vote and demand payment of dividends, pressure from common shareholders who want dividend payments will make preferred dividend payments more likely.

Perhaps even more important than pressure by common shareholders is the generally cumulative nature of preferred dividend payments. This means that any preferred dividends that are passed (not paid quarterly as anticipated) must be accumulated by the corporation and eventually paid before any dividends can be paid to common stockholders. For example, if Wells Fargo skipped payments of a quarterly dividend of 50 cents per share for one year on an issue of preferred stock, it would be required to make up the arrearage of $2.00 before resuming payment of common stock dividends.

The investor's capital is relatively secure. This is because after bondholders and other creditors, preferred shareholders take precedence over common stockholders in the event of a corporate sale or liquidation. If XYZ Corp. were to be liquidated, for example, any assets remaining after creditors had been paid would be first allocated to preferred shareholders in proportion to the value of their interests. In some cases, a corporation may have more than one preferred stock issue outstanding. Each of these issues would be assigned an order of priority in terms of sale or liquidation.

The prices of preferred stocks tend to be more stable than those of common stocks. Common stock prices are affected most directly by changes in corporate earnings, which can be highly erratic. Preferred stock prices are more likely to reflect changes in interest rates, which are generally less volatile than changes in the earnings of a corporation. This is especially true for high quality preferred stocks issued by financially sound companies.

However, when interest rates do decline, the prices of preferred shares tend to increase. Obviously, the opposite result occurs when interest rates rise; the price of preferred stocks will typically decline because investors can obtain higher rates on new issues of preferred stock or newly issued bonds. Moreover, since most preferred stocks do not have a maturity date, they have the characteristics of very long-term bonds and will fluctuate significantly more than a shorter-term, fixed income investment for any given change in rates.

Some preferred stocks are convertible. This means that they may be exchanged at a predetermined rate for common stock of the same corporation at the discretion of the preferred stockholder. This will be advantageous when the price of common shares is increasing due to the fixed rate of exchange. Therefore, the preferred stock investor will be able to participate in the equity growth in a manner similar to common stockholders while retaining the relative security afforded the preferred shareholders.

The purchasing power of future fixed preferred stock dividends may be eroded by inflation. The longer the holding period of the investment, the more likely the purchasing power of each fixed dollar payment will decline. For instance, assume inflation takes place at a 3 percent annual rate. A preferred dividend of $10.00 per year will have the purchasing power equivalent of only $7.37 ten years later.

Dividend payments on preferred stock will not increase even if the financial condition of the company or the economy improves. Preferred shareholders do not participate in the growth and prosperity of their company in the same way as do common stockholders.

Some preferred stocks are participating issues. This means that preferred stockholders may be entitled to payments above the normal level of dividends in certain situations. This would occur once common stockholders had received dividends of a specified amount.

For example, the terms of the preferred stock issue may provide that once common shareholders have received dividends amounting to $5.00 per share, both common and preferred stockholders will share equally in any further dividend payments.

Preferred stocks do not provide much opportunity for capital growth. The fixed nature of the dividend payments and the lack of voting rights limit the market's enthusiasm for these issues. (As noted above, however, the convertibility feature of certain preferred stocks may offset this disadvantage and provide the opportunity for significant capital appreciation.)

Dividends received by individuals on preferred stocks are generally taxable at ordinary income rates. Historically, dividends on preferred stock have generally been taxed as ordinary income. In some recent years, some dividends were classified as qualified dividends and qualified for the preferred tax rate of zero percent or 15 percent. To be a qualified dividend, the investor must have held the stock for more than sixty days during the 121-day period that begins sixty days before the ex-dividend date. The American Taxpayer Relief Act of 2012 extended these low tax rates on qualified dividends for taxpayers with taxable income below $400,000 ($450,000 if married filing jointly). For taxpayers with income above this level, qualified dividends are taxed at 20 percent.

It is important to note that qualified dividend income does *not* include certain preferred stock dividends where the dividend paid on the preferred stock is structured and treated as debt by the company.

Profits on the sale of preferred shares are long-term or short-term capital gains depending on how long the stock has been held by an investor. Capital gains income from the sale of stock held longer than one year is generally taxed at a special long-term capital gains rate. The rate that applies depends on which ordinary income tax bracket an investor falls under. The long term capital gains rate is zero if total income (including capital gain income) places the investor in the ten or fifteen percent tax brackets. The capital gains rate is 15 percent if total income (including capital gain income) places the investor in the twenty-five percent tax bracket or higher. Starting with the year 2013, there is a new long-term capital gains rate of 20 percent which applies to taxpayers falling within the new 39.6 percent tax bracket. Also beginning in 2013, capital gain income will be subject to an additional 3.8 percent Net Investment Income Tax (NIIT) for taxpayers with income at or above a certain threshold. Capital gain income from assets held one year or less is taxed at the ordinary income tax rates in effect for the year.

Losses on the sale of preferred stock are subject to capital loss rules. Certain limits are imposed on the utility of capital losses in offsetting ordinary income. Unused capital losses may be carried forward by individuals and applied against future income.

If a share of preferred stock is sold at a loss and then repurchased within a given time period, the investor will be subject to the so-called wash sale rules.

Dividends received on preferred stocks of domestic corporations are subject to the dividends received deduction if the dividends are received by a corporate investor. Up to 30 percent of the dividend will be subject to corporate tax rates.

Preferred stocks held at death in the sole name of the investor will be subject to both federal and state death taxes. Fifty percent of preferred stocks held jointly between spouses will be includable in the gross estate of the first joint owner to die but will generate no federal estate tax because of the unlimited marital deduction.

Preferred stocks may be purchased directly through brokerage firms – both full-service and discount brokerage firms – much like common stock, bonds, or other investments. They may also be purchased through banks which offer brokerage services.

Quite a few preferred stocks are listed on the New York Stock Exchange. These listings are shown immediately below the listings for the same company's common stock. However, the majority of preferred issues are unlisted and trade on the over-the-counter market.

The trading in preferred stocks is dominated by corporations and other institutional investors. This is due to the dividends received deduction (discussed previously) and tends to work against individual investors. Also, the market for preferred stocks is not as active as the market for common shares and trading volume is relatively low compared with that of common stocks.

Individuals may also invest in preferred stocks indirectly through the purchase of shares in a mutual fund or an Exchange Traded Fund (ETF). Income funds, which emphasize a high rate of current return on investment, frequently purchase large blocks of preferred stock. The mutual fund and ETF approach offer the added attractions of diversification and professional management in addition to high yield and relative price stability.

When preferred stocks are purchased through a broker, a regular sales commission is added to the price of the preferred shares. If shares are purchased indirectly through a mutual fund, the fund's regular sales fee will apply in the case of a load fund. If a no-load fund is used, there will be no sales charge added to the purchase price of the shares. Both types of funds will normally charge a management fee and an account maintenance fee in addition to any sales fees.

7.2.2 PREFERRED STOCK SELECTION

Because preferred stockholders are mainly interested in security and a high yield, the financial condition of the issuer is of primary concern. Investors should evaluate the soundness of the company or rely on the published ratings of firms such as Standard & Poor's or Moody's Investors Services. The following factors will be important in evaluating the company's financial condition:

(a) The company's earnings record, particularly the growth of earnings or at least a pattern of stable earnings during the past ten years.

(b) Earnings available to pay preferred dividends should be several times the amount actually required. Preferred stockholders do not have first claim on a company's earnings. Earnings are first used to pay any interest due to bondholders. Then, preferred dividends are paid before any payments are made to common stockholders. The company should have enough earnings to pay interest and dividends even if earnings should decline for a year or two.

This concept of a "margin of safety" is important due to the limitations placed on the dividends from preferred issues. One prominent investment text states preferred stocks should be selected "on a recession or depression basis." Since preferred dividends will not be increased no matter how prosperous the firm may be, the investor must be more concerned with the payment of those dividends under the worst of circumstances.

(c) Because preferred dividends are paid from cash, investors should review the liquidity of the company before investing. An attractive company will have a substantial cash position as well as large amounts of short-term assets.

(d) The preferred stock issue should be relatively small compared with the other capital of the firm. This means that the amount of preferred dividends will be a small obligation compared with bond interest or even common dividends. This relatively small size generally adds to the overall security of the issue.

Investors should compare the dividend yield available from a preferred stock with other issues of apparent similar quality. If one issue offers a rate of return substantially higher than other similar issues, it may be an indication of excessive risk and more due diligence may be warranted.

Depending on their own risk preferences, investors may want to compare the yields available from bonds as an alternative to a preferred stock. Bonds do provide a greater degree of security than preferred stocks because the interest payments on bonds must be made in order for the firm to avoid bankruptcy. Preferred dividends can be passed, or deferred, even if they are cumulative. This may be difficult for some investors, particularly those who are dependent on a regular flow of investment income.

7.3 SECURITY VALUATION

Section Overview:

7.3.1 Discounted Cash Flow Methods

7.3.2 Discounted Dividend Models

7.3.3 Discounted Free Cash Flow Models

7.3.4 Capitalized Earnings

7.3.5 Market Based Methods

7.3.6 Asset Based Methods

7.3.1 DISCOUNTED CASH FLOW METHODS

Security valuation is the use of analytical methods to estimate the intrinsic value (as opposed to the observed market price) of a security. The intrinsic value is then compared to the market price to determine whether the security appears attractively priced.

There are several classes of valuation methods for assessing a security's intrinsic value, including:

- Discounted Cash Flow Methods
- Market Based Methods
- Asset Based Methods

The focus of this chapter is valuing equity securities (stock). Equities are most commonly valued using the first two categories: discounted cash flow methods and market based methods. Less often used are asset based methods that entail valuing a company based upon its underlying net assets (assets less liabilities, or book value). Asset based methods are more likely to be used when the company is expected to be liquidated.

As with any investment, the intrinsic value of a stock can be estimated by calculating the present value of the future cash flows expected to be received:

Equation 7.1

$$V_0 = \frac{C_1}{(1+r)^1} + \frac{C_2}{(1+r)^2} + \frac{C_3}{(1+r)^3} + \ldots + \frac{C_n}{(1+r)^n}$$

Here, V_0 is the current value, C is the cash flow for each period (one, two, three...), r is the required rate of return, and n is the number of periods. Dividing by $(1 + r)^n$ is the mathematical formula for taking the present value of each cash flow. For example, if an investor expects to receive $1 one year from today and has a desired rate of return of 10 percent (r = 0.10), the present value would be $0.9091 ($1.0/1.1). If the investor expects to receive $1 in two years, the present value would be $0.8265 ($\$1/1.1^2$). Rather than using the formula to determine the present value, a present value table can be used to determine the present value of each cash flow or a financial calculator can be used.

Example. Assume an investor is considering investing in an entity that promises a return of $1 per year for three years. At the end of the three years the entity is expected to liquidate and pay the investor an additional $10. If the investor requires a 10 percent rate of return for this investment, how much is it worth today? The present value would be:

$$V_0 = \frac{\$1}{(1.1)^1} + \frac{\$1}{(1.1)^2} + \frac{\$11}{(1.1)^3} = \$0.9091 + \$0.8265 + \$8.2644 = \$10$$

So a fair price for this investment would be $10.00. If the market price were $9, the investment would be undervalued given the investor's expectations and required return. If the investment is purchased for $9, the expected return would be greater than the required return of 10 percent. If the market price was above $10, the investment would be considered overvalued and the expected return would be less than 10 percent.

In practice, valuing the cash flows from a stock is not as easy as in this stylized example. Future cash flows must first be estimated. There are several cash flows that can be used in a discounted cash flow approach. Two of the most common are dividends and free cash flow to equity. Dividends are cash flows that are actually distributed by the firm to shareholders. Free cash flow to equity is the cash flow the company generates from its operations after deducting any needed investments in the new assets. Free cash flow to equity may be distributed to shareholders as dividends or kept by the firm for future use. The next section presents discounted dividend valuation and the subsequent section presents discounted free cash flow valuation. Finally, this chapter addresses the use of earnings in place of cash flow in valuation models (termed capitalization of earnings).

It is also important to understand the role of the discount rate (desired or required rate of return) in the present value equations used throughout this chapter. It is the rate at which an investor is indifferent between receiving a smaller amount of money today or a larger amount in the future. In the investment world, this number is highly dependent on both the general level of interest rates and the investor's degree of risk aversion.

7.3.2 DISCOUNTED DIVIDEND MODELS

As the actual cash flows an investor will receive from stock holdings, dividends are an appropriate cash flow to value. Modifying the general cash flow model to consider the present value of dividends (D):

Equation 7.2

$$V_0 = \frac{D_1}{(1+r)^1} + \frac{D_2}{(1+r)^2} + \frac{D_3}{(1+r)^3} + \ldots + \frac{D_n}{(1+r)^n}$$

A share of stock's current value can be determined by forecasting future dividends per share and discounting them back to the current value at the required rate of return, r. Absent evidence to the contrary, a company is generally considered to be a going concern with dividend streams that continue into perpetuity.

That a company will continue paying dividends forever may seem an aggressive assumption. However, the further out in time a dividend occurs, the less it is worth in today's dollars. Consider a stock that is expected to pay a dividend of $1 at the end of each of the next thirty years and assume that an investor requires a 10 percent rate of return. The present value of each dividend is:

Year	Dividend	Present Value
1	1.00	0.9091
2	1.00	0.8264
3	1.00	0.7513
4	1.00	0.6830
5	1.00	0.6209
6	1.00	0.5645
7	1.00	0.5132
8	1.00	0.4665
9	1.00	0.4241
10	1.00	0.3855
11	1.00	0.3505
12	1.00	0.3186
13	1.00	0.2897
14	1.00	0.2633
15	1.00	0.2394
16	1.00	0.2176
17	1.00	0.1978
18	1.00	0.1799
19	1.00	0.1635
20	1.00	0.1486

Year	Dividend	Present Value
21	1.00	0.1351
22	1.00	0.1228
23	1.00	0.1117
24	1.00	0.1015
25	1.00	0.0923
26	1.00	0.0839
27	1.00	0.0763
28	1.00	0.0693
29	1.00	0.0630
30	1.00	0.0573
Total	30.00	9.4269

In present value terms, each subsequent dividend in the table above is worth incrementally less than the previous dividend. By year thirty, the $1 dividend is worth less than six cents in today's dollars.

Only thirty years of dividends were presented in this example; forecasting dividends in perpetuity would be inconvenient, to say the least. Fortunately, the process can be simplified for value estimation. If it is assumed that the dividends are constant forever (as they were for thirty years in the table above), the present value of future dividends can be tersely stated as:

Equation 7.3

$$V_0 = \frac{D}{r}$$

This is the formula for a no-growth dividend discount model. It is based on the formula for a perpetual annuity (or perpetuity) where the dividend does not increase over time. So, if a company is expected to pay a constant $1 dividend forever and an investor requires a 10percent return, the company's intrinsic value is $10 ($1 / 0.10). This is a little higher than the table above, where the dividend was only expected for thirty years.

Will the expected intrinsic value of this security be higher next year? Note that since dividends do not change, the expected price next year will remain $10 unless the required rate of return changes. In this case the expected return is based solely on the dividend to be received each year. The dividend yield (dividend divided by price) would be 10 percent ($1 / $10), the same as the required rate of return.

Example: Mark Mitchell is considering an investment in a regional utility that has paid the same annual dividend for the past 10 years of $1.25 per share. Mark views this investment as relatively low risk, but lacking in growth. Mark determines that he would be happy to receive a return of 8 percent per year on such investments. Using the no-growth dividend discount model Mark computes an intrinsic value of $15.62 ($1.25 / 0.08). Mark observes that the current market price is $17.50 and concludes that this is not a satisfactory investment since the market price exceeds his computed intrinsic value.

There are few cases (some utilities and preferred stock issues) in which one can expect a constant, eternal stream of dividends. However, the formula's assumptions can be relaxed to permit a dividend that grows at a constant rate, g:

Equation 7.4

$$V_0 = \frac{D_1}{r - g}$$

This is the formula for a constant growth dividend discount model (also known as the Gordon Growth Model), where D_1 is next year's expected dividend, r is the investor's required rate of return, and g is the rate at which dividends are expected to grow. Another version of this formula starts with this year's dividend rather than next year's expected dividend:

Equation 7.5

$$V_0 = \frac{D_0(1 + g)}{r - g}$$

This formula is mathematically equivalent to the prior formula since next year's dividend is the same as this year's dividend plus one year of growth.

Assume that a company paid a dividend this past year of $1.00 and that the dividend is expected to grow at a constant rate of 5 percent per year. The required rate of return is 10 percent. The intrinsic value of this security would be:

$$V_0 = \frac{D_0(1 + g)}{r - g} = \frac{1.00(1.05)}{(0.10 - 0.05)} = \$21$$

Note that adding a growth rate of 5 percent increased the value of the security from $10 in the no-growth case to $21 in the growth case. This is due to the fact that, not only is next year's dividend expected to grow at 5 percent, but so are all future dividends. By year thirty, the expected dividend will be $4.32.

In this case, the expected price of the security will change next year – assuming the required rate of return and expected growth rate do not change. The value at time one (V_1) would be:

$$V_1 = \frac{D_2}{r - g} = \frac{1.1025}{(0.10 - 0.05)} = \$22.05$$

Why is the price expected to increase from $21.00 to $22.05, an increase of 5 percent? This is a result of the expected growth rate of 5 percent. Investors in stocks derive two sources of returns—the dividend yield and the expected growth in share price (appreciation). Rewriting the dividend discount model and using the observed market price, rather than intrinsic value, results in:

Equation 7.6

$$r = \frac{D_1}{P} + g$$

Here r is the expected return, D_1 is next year's expected dividend, P is the current observed market price, and g is the expected growth rate. So, if a security is expected to pay a dividend next year of $2.00, dividends are expected to grow at 6 percent per year, and the current price is $40, the expected return would be 11 percent (5 percent dividend yield plus 6 percent growth).

Example. Evelyn Garcia is considering an investment in a large manufacturing company that paid dividends last year of $1.95. Evelyn believes that dividends will grow at 4 percent per year. Evelyn would like to earn an 11 percent return on this investment. Using the constant growth dividend discount model, Evelyn computes an intrinsic value of $28.97 [($1.95 × (1 + 0.04)) / (0.11 – 0.04)]. Evelyn observes that the current market price is $26 and concludes that this investment meets her criteria. Based on the current market price, Evelyn expects a return of 11.80 percent [(($1.95 × (1 + 0.04)) / $26) + 0.04].

What if growth is not expected to be constant? The dividend discount model can be extended to permit two (or more) separate growth rates.

Example. Salazar Ventures, Inc. (SVI) paid a dividend last year of $1.00. An investor who requires a return of 10 percent expects SVI's dividend to grow 10 percent a year for the next three years. Subsequently, the growth rate is expected to fall to 5 percent in perpetuity. To apply a two-stage model, first estimate the dividends for the next three years, and compute their present value:

Year	Dividend	Present Value
1	1.10	1.0000
2	1.21	1.0000
3	1.33	1.0000

The total present value of the first three years (stage one) of dividends is $3.00. The second stage applies the constant growth dividend discount model to estimate the value of the stock at the end of year three:

$$V_3 = \frac{D_3(1+g)}{r-g} = \frac{1.33(1.05)}{(0.10-0.05)} = \$27.93$$

The intrinsic value of SVI's stock at the end of year three is expected to be $27.93.

To determine the value today, discount the $27.93 back to the present for three years at the required return of 10 percent. This results in a present value of $20.98. Adding the second stage result to the $3.00 (present value of dividends) from stage one results in a total value today of $23.98.

7.3.3 DISCOUNTED FREE CASH FLOW MODELS

What if a company does not pay dividends? Other discounted cash flow models are available, and are often preferred over dividend-based models even when the company pays dividends.

One of the most frequently used discounted cash flow models is based on *free cash flow to equity* rather than dividends. Free Cash Flow to Equity (FCFE) is the company's operating cash flow, less capital investments and net debt repayments (repayments net of borrowing). While this cash flow is available for distribution as dividends, many companies choose to retain it for future use.

FCFE can be viewed as the cash flow that would be available to an entity that acquired control of the subject company. Even shareholders who buy only a few shares of stock have an interest in the value of a firm on a FCFE basis since the potential exists for some other entity to acquire control of the subject company or for the subject company to begin paying dividends at some future date.

A FCFE model is simply a dividend discount model where the dividend is replaced by FCFE per share:

Equation 7.7

$$V_0 = \frac{FCFE_1}{r - g}$$

The intrinsic value is denoted by V_0, as before. $FCFE_1$ represents next year's forecast of free cash flow to equity. The required rate of return for an equity investment is r and the estimated growth in FCFE is g.

If a company has estimated FCFE of $3.50 per share next year, is expected to grow its FCFE 3 percent annually, and requires a return of 12 percent, the intrinsic value using this model would be $38.89. As with the dividend discount model, the FCFE model can be expanded for multiple growth stages as in the example above, by replacing dividends with FCFE per share. This method is frequently used to value acquisitions including closely held businesses.

Free Cash Flow to the Firm (FCFF) is another alternative that is often used in valuing firms in leveraged buyouts or where the new owner plans to change the capital structure of the acquired firm. Free cash flow to the firm is the cash flow available to all capital providers, including debt and equity holders. It is therefore a broader concept. When valuing equity using free cash flow to the firm, the value obtained is that of the overall enterprise (debt plus equity), not just the value of the equity (stock).

Companies that are able to generate free cash flow (whether FCFE or FCFF) are often viewed as attractive takeover candidates. Free cash flow is also often discussed in company press releases as one metric to evaluate how well the company is doing.

7.3.4 CAPITALIZED EARNINGS

The previous two sections presented models based on discounting some measure of future cash flows. Another approach is to discount earnings rather than cash flows. This method is related to the market multiple (Price/Earnings) approach that is discussed later and is very often used for public companies. The capitalized earnings method is frequently used to evaluate real estate investments (including real estate investment trusts). In a capitalized earnings approach, some measure of historic earnings is divided by a capitalization rate (encompassing both the required rate of return for risk and expected growth) to obtain intrinsic value:

Equation 7.8

$$V_0 = \frac{Earnings}{Capitalization\ Rate}$$

The capitalization rate can be determined by subtracting the expected growth rate from a required rate of return that compensates for risk, as in the previous discounted cash flow models. The required rate of return, however, is not the same as that used in discounted cash flow models. Cash flows such as dividends and free cash flow are available to be spent currently, whereas investors may be unable to access earnings (for example, the company may reinvest them in inventory or other assets). Another approach, used frequently in real estate, is to develop a capitalization rate by looking at similar real estate companies/projects and determining their implied capitalization rate.

Example. Bill Grant wants to value a real estate project that had net operating earnings of $100,000 last year. Net operating earnings are defined as revenues minus all operating expenses. Operating expenses exclude income taxes and interest expense. Bill identifies several other real estate projects that sold recently and are similar in size, expected growth and amenities to the subject property:

Property	(1) Net Operating Income	(2) Sales Price	Effective Capitalization Rate (1)/(2)
A	$150,000	$1,875,000	0.080
B	$200,000	$2,350,000	0.085
C	$180,000	$2,000,000	0.090

On average, the subject companies have a capitalization rate of 0.085 or 8.5 percent. Bill uses this rate to estimate the intrinsic value of his subject property:

$$V_0 = \frac{Earnings}{Capitalization\ Rate} = \frac{\$100{,}000}{0.085} = \$1{,}176{,}471$$

Care must be taken when using a capitalization of earnings approach since earnings are subject to a great deal of management discretion regarding accounting conventions. Earnings may be overstated (or even understated) and result in an inappropriate estimate of value.

7.3.5 MARKET BASED METHODS

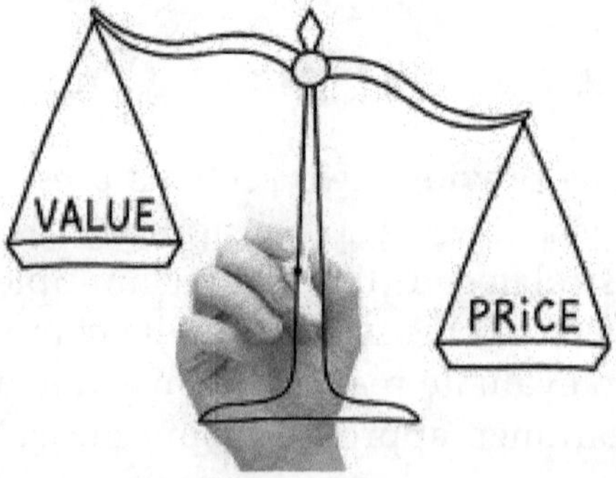

A market-based approach to valuation involves estimating the intrinsic value of a security with reference to the value of other similar securities. This is done by comparing the market price, divided by some fundamental value such as earnings for the subject company, to that of similar peer companies. This method is sometimes referred to as a market multiple, price multiple, or guideline company method. Several market multiples are commonly used for this comparison:

- Price/Earnings
- Price/Free Cash Flow
- Price/Sales
- Dividend/Price (Dividend Yield)

Note that the last one listed is evaluated inversely to the others. Customarily, investors like to think in terms of dividend yields rather than price as a multiple of dividends.

Price/Earnings Approach

A price/earnings ratio (P/E) is a stock's price per share divided by earnings per share. It is a measure of relative value. A P/E ratio of fifteen indicates that the price is fifteen times the earnings per share of the company. A high P/E ratio relative to other companies indicates that the company is expensive relative to earnings.

What is the appropriate P/E for a company? The P/E ratio is directly related to the dividend discount model presented earlier. Let's revisit Equation 7.3, the no-growth dividend discount model from earlier:

$$V_0 = \frac{D}{r}$$

First, let's replace intrinsic value, V_0, with the current observed market price, P:

$$P = \frac{D}{r}$$

A no-growth company is one in which earnings are paid out as dividends to shareholders rather than being reinvested in the company (either because the company simply chooses to or has no opportunities for growth). Therefore, for a no-growth company, earnings are equal to dividends and:

$$P = \frac{E}{r}$$

Where P is the price per share, E is the earnings per share and r is the required rate of return. Now dividing both sides by E results in:

$$\frac{P}{E} = \frac{1}{r}$$

In this modification of the dividend discount model, it can be seen that the P/E ratio for a no-growth company should be equal to one divided by the required rate of return. So, a no-growth company having a required rate of return of 10 percent (r = 0.10) would have a theoretical P/E ratio of 10 (1 / 0.10). This is also known as a justified or warranted P/E. The intrinsic value of a no-growth company can be assessed by multiplying the justified P/E times the earnings per share:

Equation 7.9

$$V = Justified\ P\ /\ E \times Earnings\ Per\ Share$$

Say that the no-growth company with a justified P/E of ten has earnings per share of $1.20. Its intrinsic value would be $12.00 (10 × $1.20).

Now let's take a look at a theoretical or justified P/E for a growth company. The formula derived from the dividend discount model is:

Equation 7.10

$$\frac{P}{E} = \frac{Payout\ Ratio\,(1 + g)}{r - g}$$

Where P/E is the current price divided by last year's earnings per share, Payout Ratio is the proportion of earnings paid out as dividends (in decimal form), r is the required rate of return based on risk, and g is the expected growth rate.

A company that pays out 40 percent (0.40) of its earnings as dividends, is expected to grow at 7 percent (0.07), and has a required return of 10 percent (0.10), would have a justified P/E of 14.27 [(0.40 × (1 + 0.07)) / (0.10 – 0.07)]. If last year's earnings were $1.50, the intrinsic value would be $21.40 (14.27 × $1.50).

Since the theoretical P/E formulas are derived directly from the dividend discount model, they will provide the same estimate of intrinsic value as the dividend discount model. Nonetheless, the distinct models are useful in understanding which factors influence P/E ratios.

Two critical factors are risk (which impacts r) and expected growth. A company with higher risk than other companies will have a higher required rate of return and therefore should trade at a lower P/E ratio. On the other hand, a company with a higher growth rate should trade at a higher P/E ratio.

A market multiple or guideline valuation approach uses these concepts to assess the relative value of a subject company. Assume an investor is comparing a company to three similar peer companies (same industry, similar size, etc.). They have the following P/E ratios:

Company	Price	Earnings Per Share	P/E Ratio
Subject	$20.00	$1.00	20
Company X	$26.00	$2.00	18
Company Y	$24.00	$1.50	16
Company Z	$25.20	$1.80	14

Absent any additional information, it appears that the subject company is overvalued since its price relative to earnings is higher than those of the three peer companies. How much overvalued? If it is assumed that the subject company deserves a P/E multiple equal to the median (i.e., middle, which in this case is the same as the average) multiple of the peers (16), then the intrinsic value would be $16.00 ($1.00 × 16) and the stock could be considered overvalued by $4.00 ($20 – $16).

However, perhaps the subject company does not deserve the same multiple as the peer companies. Why could this be true? Even similar companies have different exposure to risk and growth. If the subject company has a higher growth rate than its peers (or lower risk), it might deserve its higher multiple. A commonly used method of assessing P/E ratios relative to growth is to compute a PEG ratio:

Equation 7.11

$$PEG = \frac{P}{E} \div g$$

Here, expected growth is in percentage form (e.g., g = 100 × 10% = 10). Adding expected growth to the subject and peer companies yields:

Company	P/E Ratio	Expected Growth	PEG Ratio
Subject	20	10%	2.00
Company X	18	9%	2.00
Company Y	16	8%	2.00
Company Z	14	8%	1.75

Adjusting for growth, it can be seen that the subject company has the same P/E relative to growth as companies X and Y. It would appear that its higher P/E is justified by its higher growth expectations. Company Z appears to be the best value in terms of price relative to earnings and growth.

Care must be taken when using the PEG ratio for several reasons. Expected growth is normally only available for short periods of time (e.g., five years). Companies that have a lower but more persistent growth rate may be penalized by the model. Also the PEG formula assumes a linear relationship between growth and P/E ratios, which is not strictly correct. Lastly, the PEG ratio does not consider differences in risk between the companies, which is another major factor in justified P/E ratios.

P/E ratios in general are further limited in that earnings can be subject to differences between companies due to accounting methods and other non-operating reasons that can make companies difficult to compare. Ideally, peer companies should be in the same industry, of similar size, and use similar accounting methods. Above all, it is imperative to remember that any estimate of future growth is just that—an estimate. No one, even experienced Wall Street analysts can predict the future with certainty.

P/E ratios are not only useful in evaluating companies, but are useful in evaluating the holdings of mutual funds. One metric used to evaluate equity mutual funds is the average (or median) P/E ratio of the underlying stocks.

P/E ratios can also be viewed in an inverse format as E/P. E/P is known as the earnings yield. A company with a P/E of twenty would have an earnings yield of 5percent. This is an alternative view of value. Companies with high P/E ratios have low earnings yields and companies with low P/E ratios have high earnings yields.

Price/Free Cash Flow Approach

Another market multiple that can be used to assess intrinsic value is the Price/Free Cash Flow or P/FCFE ratio. A theoretical P/FCFE model can be derived as:

Equation 7.12

$$\frac{P}{FCFE} = \frac{1 + g}{r - g}$$

Where FCFE is free cash flow to equity for the last year. A company with a required return of 10 percent and growth rate of 5 percent would have a justified P/FCFE ratio of twenty-one. Practically speaking, a P/FCFE approach involves comparison of a subject company's ratio to those of similar companies to determine if it appears properly valued. As with the P/E ratios, differences may be justified by differences in risk and growth.

Price/Sales Approach

Price to Sales (P/S) is yet another multiple that can be used for a relative valuation. A theoretical P/S ratio is:

Equation 7.13

$$\frac{P}{S} = \frac{\text{Profit Margin} \times \text{Payout Ratio} \times (1 + g)}{r - g}$$

Profit margin is a company's earnings divided by sales, payout ratio is the portion of earnings paid out as dividends, g is the expected growth rate, and r is the required rate of return. The practical application is the same as with the P/E ratio where the P/S ratio is compared to those of peer companies.

Dividend Yield Approach

Another valuation metric utilizes price per share and dividends. While a Dividend Multiple (P/D) could be computed, it is more traditional to express relative dividend valuation in terms of Dividend Yield (D/P). Companies with high dividend yields would indicate a good value (low price relative to dividends). Some investors have a preference for investing in stocks with high dividend yields, especially in light of favorable tax treatment in recent years. Companies with low dividend yields (or zero) are likely to be growth oriented companies that choose to reinvest cash flow in the business. Other investors often favor growth stocks and prefer to defer receipt (and taxation) of income.

7.3.6 ASSET BASED METHODS

A less frequently used approach is to assess the value of a company based on the book value of its assets. Book value is the amount reported on the company's financial statements. A balance sheet shows the assets a company owns and the claims against those assets.

Alpha Beta, Inc.
Balance Sheet
As of December 31, 2013

Cash			$ 500,000
Equipment			2,000,000
Total Assets		$2,500,000	
Liabilities		$1,000,000	
Stockholders Equity	1,500,000		
Total Liabilities And Equity			$2,500,000

Book value (assets minus liabilities) for this firm is $1,500,000. This is also known as stockholders equity – the amount that stockholders have invested over time in the company. If the company has 50,000 total shares outstanding (owned by stockholders), book value per share is $30 ($1,500,000 / 50,000). Most companies sell for more than their book value for a couple of reasons; many of the assets are reported on the balance sheet based at what the company paid for them, which may not reflect their current value. Additionally, most companies are more valuable as a going concern than the sum of their assets minus liabilities. If the value of assets can be determined, the book value can be adjusted. Alternatively, the book value per share can be used to compute a Price to Book Value ratio (P/B) and a relative valuation can be performed as in the market approach presented in the previous section.

Chapter 8

OPTIONS AND OPTION STRATEGIES

8.1 STOCK OPTIONS

Section Overview:

8.1.1 Call Options

8.1.2 Put Options

8.1.3 Stock Warrants and Rights

8.1.4 Purchasing Options

8.1.5 Fee Structure

8.1.6 Options Selection Strategy

8.1.1 CALL OPTIONS

An option is a contract that is bought and sold—it gives the buyer and holder a right (but not a requirement) to force the seller of the contract to complete a certain transaction. The transaction is generally for a certain amount of goods (i.e., shares of an underlying stock) at a specified price at a certain point in time when the contract is set to expire (or for some contracts, anytime in the specified period of time before the contract expires). Options are a form of derivative instruments—so named because their value is a derivative of the price of the underlying stock (or other property) with which they are associated.

A call option is a contract that gives the holder the right to purchase a specified number of shares of common stock (or other investment) at a fixed price for a stated period of time. For example, an investor who anticipated an increase in the price of ABC stock could purchase a call option for one-hundred shares instead of the stock itself. The call option might have a term of nine months and would have a fixed exercise price. At any time during the period of the contract, the holder could exercise his option and purchase one-hundred shares of the stock at the stated price regardless of how high the actual price of ABC had risen.

8.1.2 PUT OPTIONS

A put option is a contract that gives the holder the right to sell a specified number of shares of common stock at a set price for a given period of time. For example, if an individual owned one-hundred shares of ABC and expected the price of the stock to decline, he could purchase a put option giving him the right to sell his shares at a stated price any time during the term of the option contract regardless of the actual market price of ABC stock (the benefit being that, if the market price in fact rose instead of declining, the individual would still own the stock).

Most investors typically think of either buying or selling the stock itself. But, because both puts and calls are property, they may be bought or sold independently of the underlying stock. Investors may buy or sell either (or both) of these contracts depending upon their own investment strategies.

Example. Charlee Leimberg expects ABC to increase in value and therefore buys a call that gives her the right to purchase one-hundred shares of the stock at a fixed price, say $65, for the next six months. Assume that the current market price of ABC is $62 per share. The cost of her call option might be $2 per share, or $200 for the contract ($2/share x 100 share bundle).

If the market price of ABC stock were to jump to $70 per share, the value of her call would also increase. The minimum value of the contract would be $500 (the difference between the market price of $70 and her exercise price of $65 times the one-hundred shares associated with the contract). The value of her contract could actually be higher than $500 if the contract still had a significant amount of time until the expiration date. That is because investors might anticipate further appreciation in the value of the stock, which in turn would be reflected in the price of the call option.

Charlee's sister, Lara, might have an entirely different opinion about the price of ABC stock. If she expects the price to decline, she may decide to sell a call on one-hundred shares of the stock. This means that Lara would be on the other side of her sister's transaction—she would receive $200 in return for agreeing to sell one-hundred shares of the stock at a price of $65 per share any time during the next six months. If the price of ABC remains below $65 per share, Charlee will let her option to buy the stock expire (because it would not make sense for her to utilize the option to purchase the stock at $65/share from Lara when she could purchase it outright in the market for less), and the right that she never used will have cost her $200 (a $200 loss). Lara, on the other hand, will have a profit of $200 from the transaction and will not have to deliver the stock.

Put options work as a natural opposite to call options. An investor would buy a put if he expected a stock's price to decline. The put would give him the right to sell at a fixed price potentially higher than the actual market price of the stock. The seller of a put contract expects the market price of the stock to remain stable or to increase.

Example. If John Mullen expects ABC to decline from its current price of $62 per share, he could purchase a put option that would give him the right to sell the stock at a price of $60. If the share price were to fall to $58, he could exercise his option and receive $60 per share instead of the lower market price.

Example. John's associate, Mike Dunleavy, feels that the price of ABC will not go below $60 per share and offers to sell a put at that price for $1 per share. If he is correct, then the option will not be exercised, he will not have to purchase the stock, and he will have a profit of $100. If the stock's price does decline, the option will be exercised, and Mike will have to purchase the stock for $60 per share even though the actual market price may be significantly less—he might pay $60/share (as required by the put option) for a stock that might only be valued in purchase price above the current market value) will be somewhat offset by the $100 premium he received for selling (also called writing) the contract.

Options are often used by investors:

1. When investors wish to speculate on a movement in securities—either up, down, to stay within a certain range, or to move outside a certain range—without actually buying or selling the underlying securities themselves.

2. When an investor wishes to create a leveraged situation in his investment portfolio. In this case the leverage comes about due to the fixed price at which either a put or a call contract is exercised. This price referred to as the exercise price or strike price, does not change during the life of the contract regardless of the movements in the price of the underlying stock.

Example. Assume a stock is currently selling for $60 per share. A call option is available on that same stock and has an exercise price of $55 per share. The option alone will sell for at least the $5 per share difference between the stock price and the exercise price (and possibly for more). If the price of the underlying stock were to double to $120 per share, the investor who merely purchased the stock would have a gain of 100 percent [($120 – $60) / $60 = 100 percent]. If the stock did increase to $120 per share, the value of the option would increase to at least $65 per share ($120 – $55 = $65)—however, the original purchase price of the option was only $5! This is an increase of 1,300 percent [($65 / $5 = 1,300 percent], a return that is 1,200 percent higher than that earned with the purchase of the stock.

---

3. When an investor has limited funds but still wishes to speculate with some of his investments. Puts and calls are generally traded at small fractions of the price of their underlying stocks. For example, if IBM Corp. stock were selling at $190 per share, a call option to purchase one-hundred IBM shares at an exercise price of $190 might trade for $1,000, whereas the purchase of one-hundred IBM shares at $70 per share would be $19,000.

4. When an investor wishes to generate additional income from a stock portfolio without initially selling any of the positions. By selling call options on shares in his portfolio to speculators, the writer of these options can receive a fee or premium for taking part in the contract. For instance, Lara Leimberg, in the example above, received $200 for selling a call contract, and if the call option wasn't exercised, she would still be able to

keep her underlying stock as well. Note, however, that if the stock price does rise such that the call option is exercised, the call writer will be required to provide stock to the option buyer at the specified strike price.

5. When an investor desires to hedge a stock or his entire portfolio against unexpected declines or other unfavorable moves in the price of the stock. John Mullen, in the previous example, was protecting himself against a substantial decline in the value of his ABC shares by buying a put contract. The option guaranteed him a right to sell his stock at a minimum price of $60 per share, which might turn out to be much higher than the actual stock price in the event of a decline (thus hedging and preserving his account against the decline).

The fixed exercise price of these option contracts creates a leverage factor that may be advantageous to the investor. For example, if a common stock were to double in value, a 100 percent increase, the value of a call option on the same stock might increase as much as 500 percent or more.

Option trading requires a relatively small investment on the part of the investor.

Income earned from the sale of either put or call contracts is paid to the investor immediately no matter what the term of the contract may be.

An investor can substantially hedge the risk of most or all of her potential portfolio losses without actually selling the underlying stock positions until desired.

Leverage operates in both directions, and a decline (rise) in the price of a stock will typically result in a much larger percentage loss for the buyer of a call (put) option.

Example. If stock purchased at $60 per share were to drop to $30, the result is a 50 percent decline in market value. If an investor purchased an option to buy the stock at $55 per share when the market price was $60 per share, the call would have been worth at least $5 per share. But, when the stock drops to $30 per share, the value of the option will become almost nil—a 100 percent loss!

Most puts and calls have a relatively short life span—typically not more than nine months. However, another form of options is available called Long-term Equity AnticiPation Securities (LEAPS)—these long-term options generally have terms extending as far as two years and nine months from issue. In either case, options are sometimes referred to as wasting assets because they will be of no value after a particular point in time, the expiration date—unless the stock price does in fact move (or not move) as desired.

Call options, though they enable the holder to purchase shares of common stock, have neither voting rights nor are they entitled to receive any dividends declared and paid during the term of the option. Even though the life of an option is relatively short (no more than nine months) this lack of income can be an important (and/or costly) disadvantage.

Options generally are classified as capital assets for tax purposes, though they are subject to some special rules because of their unique nature.

Investors who buy call options will have a capital gain or loss if the option is sold in a closing transaction. Gain or loss is calculated by subtracting the sale price of the option from the purchase price (including any brokerage fees included in either transaction). Because exchange-traded call options are issued for a term of only nine months, any capital gain or loss will be short-term.

No gain or loss is realized upon the exercise of a call option. A capital gain or loss is realized only when the stock acquired through exercise of the call is sold. The cost of the call is added to the purchase price of the stock in computing the gain or loss for tax purposes. The holding period is measured from the day after the call option is exercised, not from the date the call was purchased.

Investors who write calls or purchase put options and then close out their positions by repurchasing them will recognize any capital gain upon the closing. However, because dispositions involving options are subject to the wash sale rule, loss on the sale of a call option within thirty days before or after the date of purchase of substantially identical stocks or securities may not be recognized. Instead, such a loss will generally increase the basis of the replacement stock or securities. It is important to note that an option to acquire or sell an underlying stock, and the underlying stock itself, are considered substantially identical property for the purposes of the wash sale rules. If the option expires unexercised, the investor will realize a short-term capital gain.

An investor who writes a call option that is exercised will realize a capital gain or loss upon exercise. The capital gain or loss is actually realized on the underlying stock that must be sold/delivered to the call option buyer—the premium the investor received for writing the call is added to the selling price of the stock in calculating the amount of capital gain or loss.

Exercising a put option constitutes a sale of the stock and is a taxable event. The cost of the put is subtracted from the selling price of the stock in computing capital gain or loss for tax purposes. The date of exercise of the put option is treated as the sale date of the stock.

Investors who write puts and repurchase their put obligations will realize a short-term capital gain or loss on the closing. If the option expires unexercised, the investor will realize a short-term capital gain, because exchange-traded call options are issued for a term of only nine months.

When a put option is exercised, the writer is required to purchase the stock put to him. However, this is not treated as a taxable event for the writer of the put contract. Instead, the put writer deducts the premium received for writing the put from the purchase price of the stock. The holding period for the stock is measured from the date of exercise of the put.

The tax consequences of many options structures become more complicated when multiple options are held at once, and/or including positions in the underlying stock.

8.1.3 STOCK WARRANTS AND RIGHTS

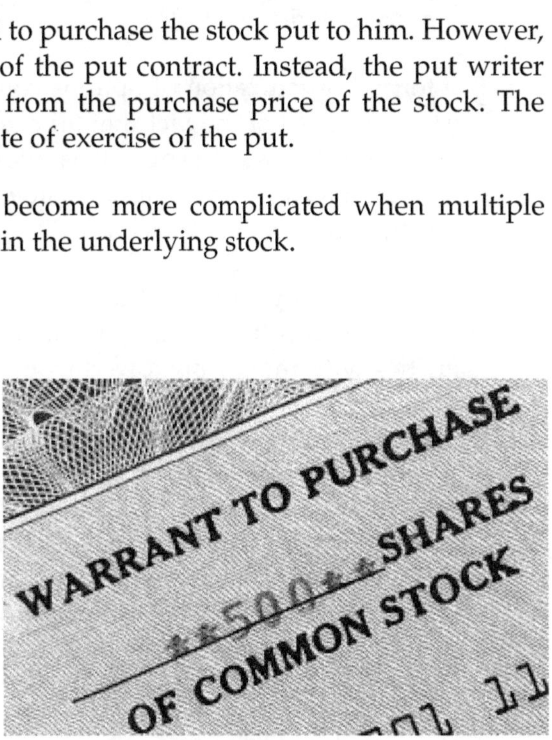

Stock purchase warrants have many of the same features as call options. They enable the owner of the warrant to purchase a certain number of shares of stock at a fixed price for a given period of time. The original term of the warrant is generally much longer than a put or call option, frequently lasting for several years. However, warrants are offered by corporations and are frequently issued in connection with the sale of other securities such as bonds or preferred stock. Some warrants are listed on the organized securities exchanges, but the majority are traded in the over-the-counter market. The fixed exercise price of warrants creates the same type of leverage provided by options.

Stock rights are another form of option that enables existing shareholders to purchase new stock being issued by a corporation. Generally one right is issued for each share of stock an investor owns, and the rights entitle the stockholder to purchase additional shares at a stated price (or often fractional shares—sometimes it will take multiple rights to purchase a single share of stock). Rights have an extremely short life span and generally must be exercised within a month or so of the new stock offering.

8.1.4 PURCHASING OPTIONS

Put and call stock options are traded on several organized exchanges, most of which are related to stock exchanges. The first exchange to be organized especially for trading of options was the Chicago Board Options Exchange (CBOE), which began operating in April, 1973. The CBOE was an extension of the Chicago Board of Trade that had a long history of trading options on agricultural commodities. Since 1973, trading in puts and calls has extended to the American Stock Exchange, the Pacific Coast Stock Exchange, the Philadelphia Stock Exchange, and the New York Stock Exchange. Several firms operate as market-makers at the various exchanges to help maintain liquidity and fair pricing for all traded options. Options traded through all of these exchanges are ultimately issued and maintained by the Options Clearing Corporation (OCC). Today these options may be traded on more than 3,000 different underlying stocks. Recently the CBOE began offering mini options on some securities. Mini options have a contract size of ten underlying shares rather than one-hundred.

Options are also now available on market indices, exchanged traded funds, credit events and volatility indices. As a result individual and institutional investors can speculate on the direction of markets, the volatility of markets and engage in options strategies such as covered calls on the Standard & Poors 500 Index.

The formal organization of options contracts has brought tremendous popularity to the options markets because of the fact that all exchange-traded options contracts are standardized (i.e., all based upon the same terms). This allows all buyers and sellers to know exactly what they are receiving in the options contract (aside from their possibly differing beliefs about the underlying security), which makes the contracts easier to evaluate, and far more liquid.

Buying or selling puts and calls is very similar to buying or selling the underlying security. However, option trades must be made through a margin account that allows a customer to buy securities with money borrowed from a broker. Transactions are made through brokerage firms that relay the orders they receive to the trading floors of the options exchanges. Orders are carried out by the exchange and the results of the trade are reported back to the brokerage firm, which in turn notifies its customer.

To execute a transaction an investor can merely call his broker and state, "Please purchase five ABC April-sixty call option contracts for my account." A written record of the trade automatically will be sent to the buyer or seller of the option contract confirming the transaction. This is the only evidence of the purchase or sale that the investor will receive. This is due to the fact that the option is a contract to buy or sell rather than an actual security.

Once a trade has been made, the position of the buyer or seller remains open until one of three events occurs:

1. *The option may expire without being exercised.* Expiration of an option series will close out all positions open at that time. This is the result frequently desired by sellers of call options who hope to keep the premium they received and to keep their shares of stock as well.

2. *The option may be exercised and the underlying shares of stock will have to be transferred.* For example, if a call option is exercised, the seller will have to deliver shares of stock at the exercise price to be paid by the buyer of the call.

3. *The buyer or seller of the option may close out his original position.* This is done simply by entering an order opposite to the first order.

Example. Assume Greg Murphy had purchased a put option allowing him to sell DEF stock at a price of $70 per share. Greg now wishes to close out his position and may do so by selling the exact same option contract. The two option contracts offset each other and, at that point, Greg has neither an option to buy or sell. He may have had a profit or loss on his original position. The amount of the gain or loss will depend upon the change in price of the initial option contract from the date of purchase or sale until the position is closed. For example, Greg may have paid $5 per share, or $500 in total, for the original put option. If the contract were selling for $300 when he closed out his position, he would have a loss of $200 on the transaction.

8.1.5 FEE STRUCTURE

Commissions on the purchase or sale of option contracts are similar to those paid on other security transactions. Brokerage firms typically charge a percentage of the value of the transaction with a minimum commission of $25 or $30. For example, a single contract trade amounting to $250 may involve a commission of $25. Ten contracts amounting to $2,500 may result in a commission of $150. Commissions can be much lower at deep discount brokers.

8.1.6 OPTIONS SELECTION STRATEGY

Because investors can buy or sell puts or calls (while buying, selling, or holding the underlying security) there are a great many different option strategies available at any given time. Perhaps the first decision that must be made is an estimate of whether the stock market as a whole, or any one stock, is likely to advance or decline. If the market is moving upward, investors are more likely to want to buy calls or sell put options. If the market or a stock is weak, then a strategy of buying puts or selling calls may be in order.

The volatility of the underlying stock has a lot to do with the movement of both put and call options. The more active a particular issue, the more likely the option will have a wide swing in price. Speculators should look for stocks that experience fairly rapid movements, either up or down, over a relatively short period of time. More conservative investors may want to concentrate on options where the underlying stock is relatively stable in price.

The period of time to expiration of the option should be considered before any purchase or sale is made. The longer the term of the option, the more likely the price of the stock to change significantly, and the greater the volatility of the option. Again, investors who wish to speculate will tend to prefer longer-term options, while conservative investors will prefer shorter maturities.

The dividends paid on the underlying stock have a significant impact on the value of an option. Option holders do not receive any dividends, which are paid only to holders of actual stock. Therefore, options on high dividend-paying stocks will tend to be less valuable than those on issues with low dividends, or none at all.

8.2 OPTION SPANNING AND SYNTHETICS

Section Overview:

8.2.1 Spanning

8.2.2 Option Profiles

8.2.3 Option Premiums

8.2.1 SPANNING

The concept of spanning is important to understanding hedging and is related to the concept of creating synthetic securities. A market or security is spanned if investors can combine derivatives in that market or on that security to reproduce the risk and return characteristics of the underlying market or security. In other words, investors can create or exactly reproduce the returns on that market or security by creating synthetic markets or securities. When this is possible, investors can also create synthetic derivatives of each of the derivatives of that market or security by combining positions in the market or security together with some combination of the other derivatives in that market or on the security.

The benefit of spanning is that it makes markets more efficient, because investors will exploit price differentials in the synthetics relative to the underlying market or security through arbitrage and force all the instruments into price conformity. Consequently, the derivative instruments become even better and more reliable instruments for hedging.

8.2.2 OPTION PROFILES

To see how this works, consider the following profit profiles for two option contracts. Figures 8.1 and 8.2 show the profit profiles for call options and put options, respectively.

A profit profile shows the gain or loss an investor would realize on the option position for different prices of the underlying stock at *expiration* of the option. In Figures 8.1 and 8.2, the price of the stock at the initiation of the option is assumed to be $50. The exercise price of the option is also $50, or at the money. For ease of illustration, the option premium is assumed to be $10 for both the call and the put (which usually would not be the case in actuality).

Figure 8.1

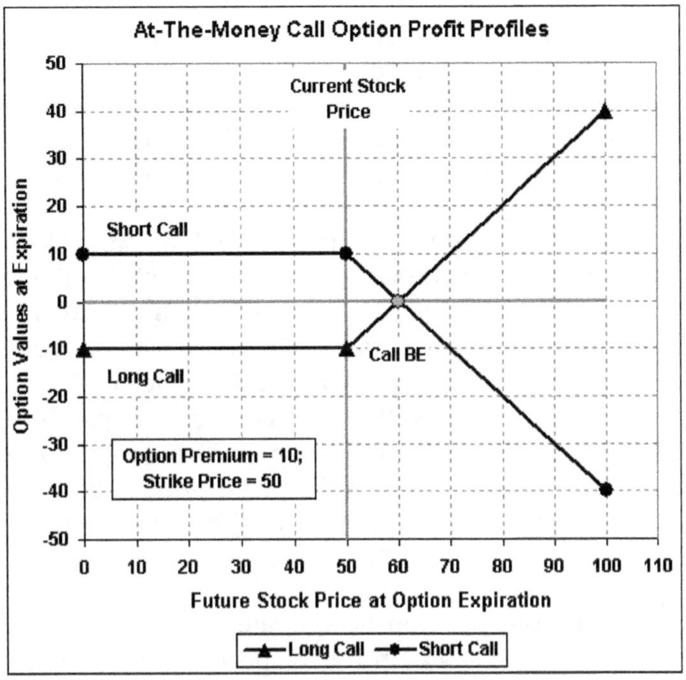

Figure 8.2

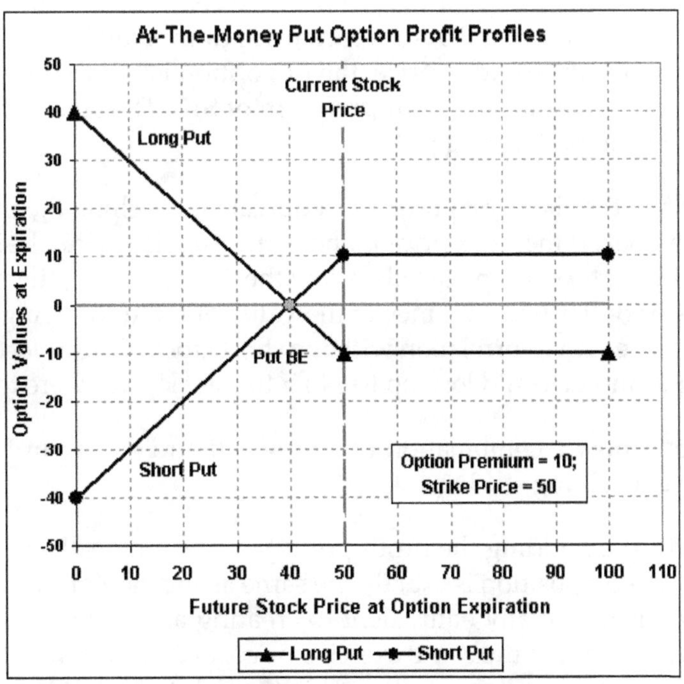

If an investor *buys* a call option giving him the right to buy the stock, he is *long* in the call. If the investor *writes* a call, collects the premium, and is obligated to sell the stock if the buyer exercises the option, he is *short* in the call. Analogously, if the investor buys a put giving him the right to sell the stock, he is long in the put. If he writes a put, collects the premium, and is obligated to buy the stock if the buyer exercises the put, he is short in the put.

The long call position is equivalent to buying just the upside potential of the stock above the exercise price. For each dollar that the stock price exceeds the exercise price, the long call will increase by one dollar at expiration—perfect positive correlation. Therefore, the long call's profit profile is potentially unlimited. For each dollar the stock price falls below the exercise price, the option is worth the same amount—zero—so the investor can lose no more than the $10 premium he paid for the call. In this case, the investor will break even if the stock price rises to $60 (when the stock appreciates enough for the investor to recover the initial premium cost of the option).

If the long call is equivalent to buying the upside potential of the stock, the short call position must be equivalent to selling the upside potential of the stock. So the profit profile of the short call position shows the investor making $10 (the call premium) if the price of the stock remains at or below the exercise price of $50. As the price of the stock rises above $50, the short call's profit declines on a dollar-for-dollar basis with increases in the price of the underlying stock—perfect negative correlation. At $60 for the stock, the short call position just breaks even (the loss on the price appreciation perfectly matches the original premium earned when the call was written). At prices above $60 for the stock, the short call's profit profile shows ever-increasing losses. In contrast with the long call, the loss on a short call position is potentially unlimited. The gain on the short call is limited to the premium of the call option when it is written.

The profit profile of the long put position is equivalent to buying the upside gain potential of a short position in the underlying stock. In this respect it is analogous to the long call position with respect to a long position in the stock. As the price of the stock falls below the exercise price, the profit profile of the long put increases dollar-for-dollar with decreases in the price of the stock—perfect negative correlation (or perfect positive correlation with a short stock). The profit potential is limited only by the fact that the stock price cannot fall below zero. For each dollar the stock price ends up above the exercise price, the put option is worth the same amount—zero—so the investor can lose no more than his put premium of $10. The stock price has to fall to $40 for the investor to break even on the long put.

Similar to the short call, the short put position is equivalent to selling the upside gain potential of a short position in the stock. If the stock price is above the exercise price, the investor pockets the $10 premium as profit. But if the stock price falls below the exercise price, the profit profile of the short put declines dollar-for-dollar with declines in the value of the underlying stock—perfect positive correlation (or perfect negative correlation with the short stock). The investor will break even if the stock price falls to $40 and he could lose up to $40 if the stock price were to fall all the way to zero.

Figure 8.3 now shows how a combination of a long call and short put has essentially the same profit profile as the underlying stock.

Line LC + SP is derived by adding the profit profiles of the long call and short put together. The gain or loss on the LC + SP position is exactly the same as the gain or loss on the stock. So holding the LC + SP position is essentially equivalent to creating a "synthetic" stock. Any combination of a long call and a short put at the same exercise price, even if different than the current market price, together with a corresponding investment in the risk-free asset to keep the total investment amount equivalent, will be technically equivalent to owning the stock outright. Similarly, a combination of a short call and a long put, together with the corresponding investment in the risk-free asset, will be equivalent to a short sale of the underlying stock. This is evidenced in Figure 8.3 by the fact that the two lines (Long Stock and LC+SP) have equivalent slopes—that is, for any particular change in the price of the stock, there is an equivalent change in the value of the investor's position, regardless of whether he holds the stock or the options.

Figure 8.3

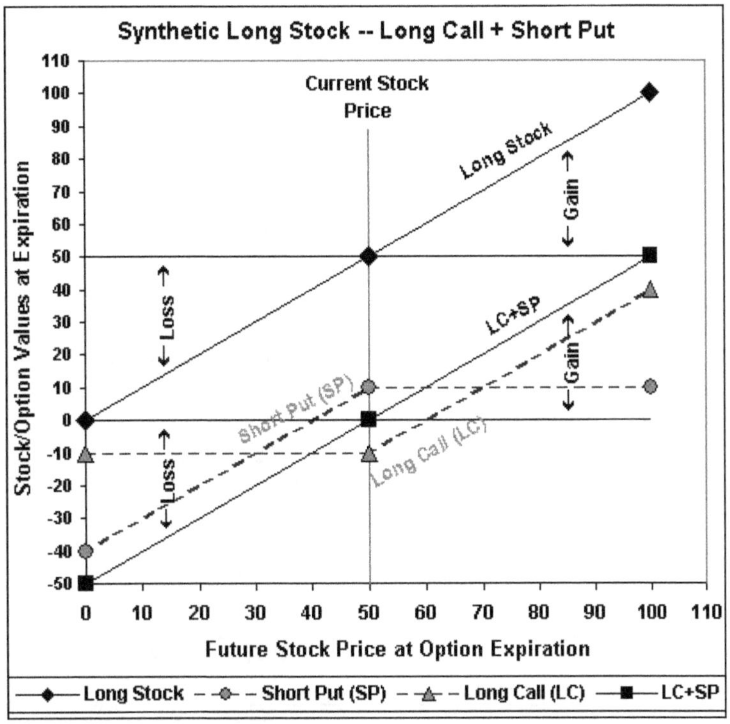

Figures 8.4 and 8.5 now show the profit profiles of combinations of the options and holdings of the underlying stock.

Figure 8.4

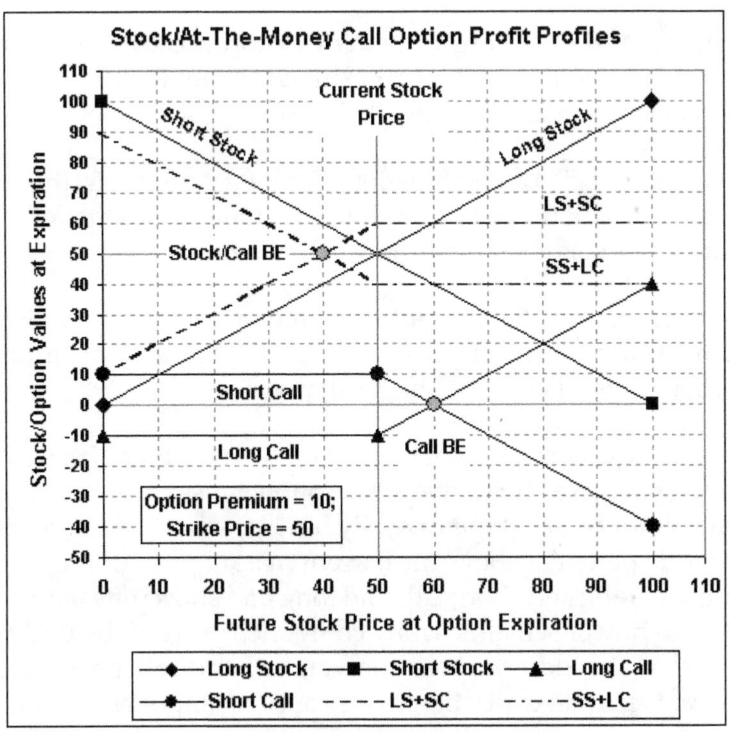

Figure 8.5

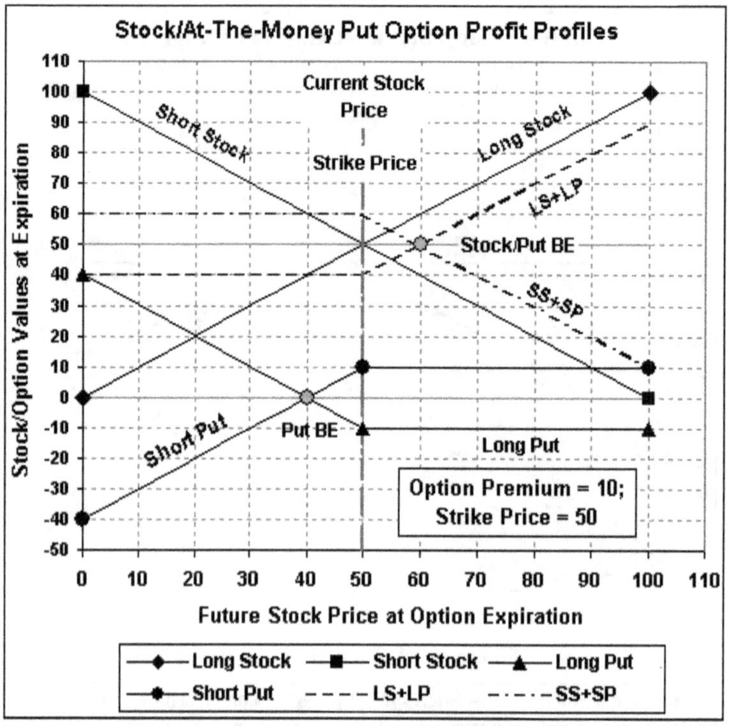

For reference, the profit profiles of the naked options are shown at the bottom of the graphs. Line LS + SC in Figure 8.4 shows the profit profile of a long position in the stock combined with a short position in the call—called a "covered call" position. Notice, that the profit profile of the long stock + short call position is exactly the same as the profit profile of the short put position shown in Figure 8.2. The LS + SC or covered call position is a synthetic short put.

The SS + LC line of Figure 8.4 is a combination of a short position in the underlying stock and a long call. The profit profile of this combined position is equivalent to the profit profile of the long put position shown in Figure 8.2, so the SS + LC position is a synthetic long put.

The LS + LP line of Figure 8.5 is a combination of a long position in the underlying stock and a long put position on the stock that has a profit profile identical to that of the long call position in Figure 8.1. This combination is a synthetic long call position.

Finally, line SS + SP of Figure 8.5 is a combination of a short position in the stock and a short put position which has a profit profile identical to the short call position shown in Figure 8.1. The SS + SP combination is a synthetic short call position.

Obviously, these are not the only combinations of these instruments that investors can create. For instance, instead of buying an at-the-money call option, investors can buy long calls with exercise prices that are either in- or out-of-the-money. By buying an out-of-the-money call, they purchase only some of the upside potential above the current market price of the stock, rather than all of it. Various combinations of long and short calls and long and short puts with different exercise prices can permit investors to buy or sell almost any component part of the underlying security's profit profile over a given term. In addition, investors can buy and sell long and short positions in puts and calls with different terms to expiration to buy or sell components of the underlying security's profit profile that essentially begin and end at different times in the future. The possible strategies and hedging opportunities are nearly endless. The Option Strategies section will discuss some of the more commonly used combinations.

8.2.3 OPTION PREMIUMS

The amount one pays for an option is called the option premium. The premium is composed of two elements: the intrinsic value and the speculative value. Each of these values can fluctuate over time based on many factors.

The intrinsic value of an option is simply the amount by which the option's strike price is in-the-money. For example, if an investor owns a call option with a strike price of $45 when the market price of the underlying security is $50, the intrinsic value is $5. In the case of a put option on the same stock, the intrinsic value of the put option is $5 if the strike price is $55 and the market price of the underlying security is $50. Essentially, the intrinsic value of the option is the profit that could be realized if the option was exercised immediately, and the underlying stock was sold at fair market value (disregarding the cost of the option). If the option's strike price is at- or out-of-the-money, the intrinsic value is $0. Of course, the intrinsic value change throughout the term until the option expires, as the market price of the underlying security fluctuates. At, or just before, expiration of the option, the intrinsic value and the premium become one and the same, because the speculative value of the premium disappears as time erodes.

The speculative value of the premium is a function of several variables: the volatility of the price of the underlying security; (2) the length of the remaining term until the option expires; (3) the dividend payout rate and the timing of dividend payments, if any; (4) the level of the risk-free rate appropriate to the remaining term until the option expires; and (5) how far in- or out-of-the-money the strike price is.

The underlying security's price volatility is a factor because the prices of more volatile securities are more likely to move into a range where the option is in (or further in) -the-money. All else being equal, the speculative value for more volatile securities will be greater than that for less volatile securities. In addition, if the underlying security's volatility increases (decreases) during the term until the option expires, the speculative premium will also increase (decrease).

The longer the term until the option expires, the greater the likelihood that the option will move into (or deeper into) the money. Consequently, all else being equal, speculative value diminishes as the option approaches its expiration date.

The prices of stocks paying dividends tend to decrease by the amount of dividends paid per share when the stock goes ex-dividend. Consequently, the stock's intrinsic value will decrease by the amount of the dividend, yet the option-holder does not receive the dividend. Therefore, the speculative value for call options on stocks paying higher dividends tends to be lower than that on stocks paying low or no dividends, if all else is equal. Specifically, the speculative value is less because a call option will repeatedly lose intrinsic value due to the payment of dividends, reducing the upside potential for the investor. For put options, on the other hand, the effect is just the opposite.

If the risk-free (opportunity cost) rate is lower, the present value of future potential benefits is higher. Therefore, the speculative value will be greater when interest rates are lower. Conversely, a higher risk-free rate means that the investor may have attractive gains available from risk-free options and will demand a greater return (i.e., spend less for the option via a reduced speculative premium) to compensate for the risk of the option.

Finally, the deeper an option is in- or out-of-the-money, the less likely it is that its status will change substantially (i.e., from out-of-the-money to in-the-money, or vice-versa), so the speculative value tends to diminish as the stock price moves further away from the strike price. The speculative premium approaches a value of zero asymptomatically as the stock price moves further and further from the strike price.

Generally, there are two kinds of options available for most investors: American options and European options. The difference between the two is that holders can exercise American options before the expiration date, whereas they must wait until the expiration date to exercise European options. Because option premiums always include at least some speculative value until just before they expire, investors holding American options will almost always be better off if they sell the options rather than exercise them if they wish to close out the position before the expiration date. But the investor does need to factor in the transaction cost of selling the option in the open market, including the implications of the bid/ask spread.

8.3 OPTION STRATEGIES

Section Overview:

8.3.1 Long Call

8.3.2 Short Call

8.3.3 Long Put

8.3.4 Short Put

8.3.5 Covered Call

8.3.6 Protective Put

8.3.7 Bull Spread

8.3.8 Bear Spread

8.3.9 Collar

8.3.10 Straddles

8.3.11 Strangle

8.3.12 Butterfly

8.3.13 Calendar Spread

The previous discussion described the profit profiles for long call; short call; long put; and short put positions but did not elaborate on the strategic reasons for taking these positions. The following discussion will briefly explain the strategic opportunities these positions present alone before addressing how to use them in various combinations to achieve various objectives. Keep in mind

that options can be written or bought on individual securities and futures contracts, sector, industry, or asset class indexes or futures contracts, or broad-based market indexes or futures contracts—so investors can use them for speculative or risk hedging purposes at each of those levels within their portfolios. Also, listed options generally expire in less than a year, but long-term options, called LEAPS, have terms of up to two years and eight months from issue (and warrants may have expiration dates of five to seven years or longer). Also, options written and traded over the counter can have terms of almost any duration to which the parties to the transaction agree.

8.3.1 LONG CALL

In general, the purchase of a naked call option is a bullish strategy employed when an investor thinks the market will rise significantly in the relative short term (before expiration of the option). Generally, the more bullish the investor's perspective, the higher the exercise or strike price he may want for the call. Premiums decline as the strike price rises, so bullish investors potentially can still gain considerably while putting less money at risk—or can create greater leverage by purchasing a greater quantity of lower-premium options. The profit potential is theoretically unlimited and rises as the market rises. The break-even point at expiration is the strike price plus the premium. The downside risk is limited to the premium paid and generally no margin is required.

An investor also can use long calls as an effective and flexible defensive strategy when the asset allocation mix of a portfolio diverges from a preferred position. An investor can use long calls to quickly and relatively inexpensively increase the effective portfolio weights in those asset classes that are underweighted until the investor can rebalance the portfolio with sales or purchases of the securities in the portfolio. Figure 8.1 (shown earlier) illustrates the profit profile of a long call.

8.3.2 SHORT CALL

Shorting calls (i.e., writing calls) is appropriate if an investor's strategic view is relative certainty that the market will not rise and he is unsure or unconcerned about whether it will fall. Investors who are quite confident in their view should write at-the-money calls or even in-the-money calls. If they are less certain of their view, they should write out-of-the-money calls. The upside gain on the position is limited to the premium received if the market price of the underlying stock is at or below the strike price. The downside risk is unlimited (unless the short call is covered). Losses on the position worsen as the market price of the stock rises. An investor, who likes the idea of the strategy, but not the potentially unlimited downside risk, might be interested in a bear spread (described later). Because this is a short position, margin is always required to assure performance in the event the option is exercised. Figure 8.1 (shown earlier) illustrates the profit profile of a short call.

8.3.3 LONG PUT

Investors with a bearish perspective on market conditions for the underlying asset and who expect the market value of the underlying asset to fall significantly over the term of the option should consider buying puts. In general, investors with more bearish perspectives should look for lower exercise prices to minimize their outlay (or increase their leverage) while still expecting sufficient price movement to make a profit on the put (in a similar manner to the bullish investor in a long call). The maximum profit potential of a long put is equal to the entire strike price of the stock less the premium paid (which would apply if the value of the stock went to $0). The break-even point at expiration is equal to the original stock price minus the premium paid. Maximum losses are limited to the premium paid (which the investor will incur if the market price of the underlying asset is equal to or above the strike price at expiration). Investing in a long put requires no margin. Figure 8.2 (shown earlier) illustrates the profit profile of a long put.

8.3.4 SHORT PUT

Selling a put is a moderately bullish strategy when investors are virtually certain that the market will not go down (much, if at all), but are unsure or unconcerned about whether it will rise. If investors are very bullish, then they could consider selling puts with strike prices that are more in-the-money to get the larger premiums. The profit potential is limited to the premium received. The breakeven point at expiration is the strike price less the premium. Margin is always required to help secure the investor's obligation to sell under the contract. The potential loss is almost unlimited (almost, because the underlying price cannot fall below zero)—the maximum loss is the strike price of the contract minus the premium received. If this basic strategy is appealing, but the potential downside risk is unacceptable, investors may prefer a bull spread Figure 8.2 (shown earlier) illustrates the profit profile of a short put.

8.3.5 COVERED CALL

A covered call is a long position in the stock combined with a short call. It has the same profit profile and characteristics as a short put. Figure 8.4 (shown earlier) illustrates the profit profile for a covered call—line LS + SC.

For most investors, this relatively neutral position is employed to increase income when they expect the market price of the underlying stock to fluctuate within a fairly narrow range over the term of the option. It tends to work best when the investor expects short-term price weakness due to company-specific factors, or industry or sector or even overall factors, but has a generally optimistic forecast in the longer term. The upside potential at expiration of the option is limited to the strike price minus the market price of the stock (when the option is purchased) plus the premium received on the sale of the call. Essentially, upside appreciation potential on the stock is sold for immediate cash. The downside potential is large—the investor is still long on the underlying stock, which can experience a decline limited only by the fact that it cannot drop below $0. But the investor will retain the premium of the written call to slightly mitigate such a loss. But the most serious potential loss could be the opportunity lost if the market price of the stock rises sharply. Margin is always required.

8.3.6 PROTECTIVE PUT

A protective put is a long position in a stock combined with a long position in a put. If the stock and put are acquired at the same time, it is called a married put. The protective put position has the same profit profile and characteristics of a long call. Figure 8.5 (shown earlier) illustrates the profit profile at expiration of a protective call—line LS + LP.

The protective put is a strategy employed when investors hold a stock long, generally with gains, and are bearish regarding the relatively short-term prospects for the market price of the stock. The put protects the value of the stock, while not preventing the position from benefiting in the event of a market rise. The profit potential is unlimited, being the ordinary return on the stock minus the fixed premium paid for the put option. The downside risk is limited to the premium paid for the put if the stock position is entirely hedged by puts, because the gains on the puts will offset the stock losses as the market falls. No margin is required.

8.3.7 BULL SPREAD

The bull spread is a moderately bullish strategy investors may employ when they are fairly certain that the market will not fall but want to cap the risk of loss. To reduce the cost of limiting the downside risk, investors sell an offsetting position that also limits their upside potential. It is a conservative strategy for investors who think that the market is more likely to rise than to fall.

Investors may implement the bull spread in two different ways:

1. *Bull Spread–Call* – Investor buys an in-the-money call (typically) and sells an out-of-the-money call (typically) with strike prices roughly equally spaced below and above the current market price of the stock. More aggressive or confident investors can set the strike prices higher.

2. *Bull Spread–Put* – Investor buys an out-of-the-money put (typically) and sells an in-the-money put option (typically) with strike prices roughly equally spaced below and above the market price of the stock. More aggressive or confident investors can set the strike prices higher.

In these examples, the current stock price is assumed to be $50, the lower strike price is $45, and the higher strike price is $55. The profit profiles for the call-based bull spread and the put-based bull spread are nearly identical, but the initial outlay for the two positions differs considerably. The initial net premium for the call-based bull spread is $4.44; the put-based bull spread generates a net premium of –$5.27. The upside potential is limited in each case. For the call-based bull spread, it is limited to the difference in the strike prices, $10, less the net initial payout for the options, $4.44, or $5.46; for the put-based bull spread, it is limited to the net initial pay-in, or $5.27. The downside risk is also limited in both cases. For the call-based bull spread, the maximum potential loss is the net initial payout, or $4.44; for the put-based bull spread, the maximum potential loss is the difference between the strike prices, $10, less the net initial pay-in, $5.27, or $4.73. In this case, the break-even stock price is approximately equal to the current stock price.

The higher the investor sets the strike price relative to the current market price, the greater is the investor's upside potential and the lesser is the investor's maximum possible loss. But the break-even point also moves higher. For example, using the same parameters as for Figures 8.6 and 8.7, except that the strike prices are set at $55 and $65, instead of $45 and $55, the call-based bull spread and put-based bull spread profit profiles are as shown in Figures 8.8 and 8.9, respectively.

Figure 8.6

Bull Spread – Call

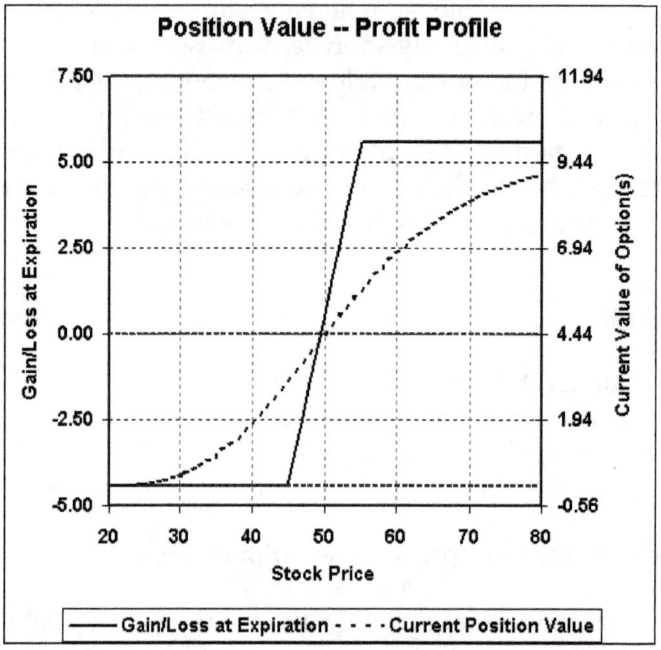

Figure 8.7

Bull Spread – Put

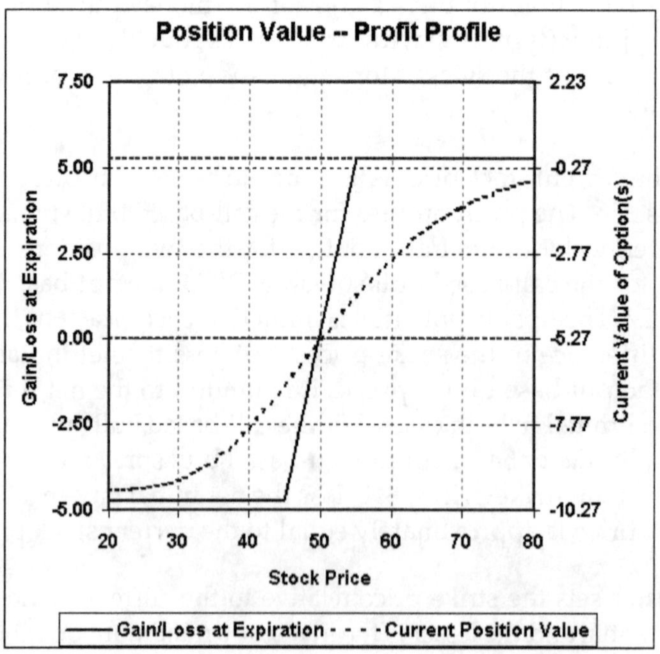

Figure 8.8

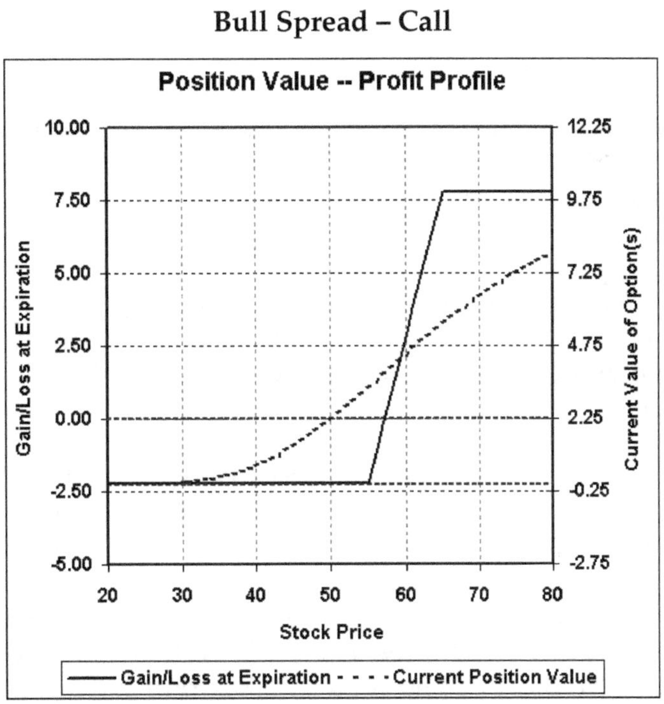

Figure 8.9

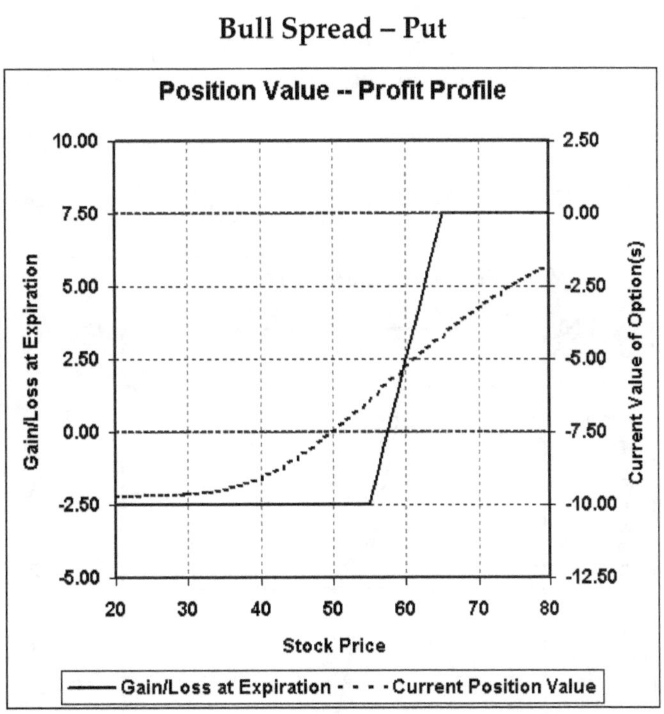

8.3.8 BEAR SPREAD

The bear spread is the moderately bearish analog to the vertical bull spread. Investors may employ this strategy when they think that the market will not rise, but they want to limit their risk of loss. To reduce the cost of limiting the risk of loss, investors sell an offsetting position that also limits their potential gain. It is a conservative strategy for investors who think that the market is more likely to fall than rise.

Investors may implement the bear spread in two different ways:

1. *Bear Spread–Call* – Investor sells an in-the-money call (typically) and buys an out-of-the-money call (typically) with strike prices roughly equally spaced below and above the current market price of the stock. More aggressive or confident investors can set the strike prices lower.

2. *Bear Spread–Put* – Investor sells an out-of-the-money put (typically) and buys an in-the-money put option (typically) with strike prices roughly equally spaced below and above the market price of the stock. More aggressive or confident investors can set the strike prices lower.

In Figure 8.10 and Figure 8.11, the current stock price is assumed to be $50, the lower strike price is $40, and the higher strike price is $50 (i.e., an aggressive bear spread). The profit profiles for the call-based bear spread and the put-based bear spread are nearly identical, but the initial outlay for the two positions differs considerably. The initial net premium for the call-based bear spread is –$5.83 (net amount investor receives); the put-based bear spread generates a net premium of $3.87 (net amount investors pays). The upside potential is limited in each case. For the put-based bear spread, it is limited to the difference in the strike prices, $10, less the net initial payout for the options, $3.87, or $6.13; for the call-based bear spread, it is limited to the net initial pay-in, or $5.83. The downside risk is also limited in both cases. For the put-based bear spread, the maximum potential loss is the net initial payout, or $3.87; for the call-based bear spread, the maximum potential loss is the difference between the strike prices, $10, less the net initial pay-in, $5.83, or $4.17. In this case, the break-even stock price is approximately equal to $46.

Figure 8.10

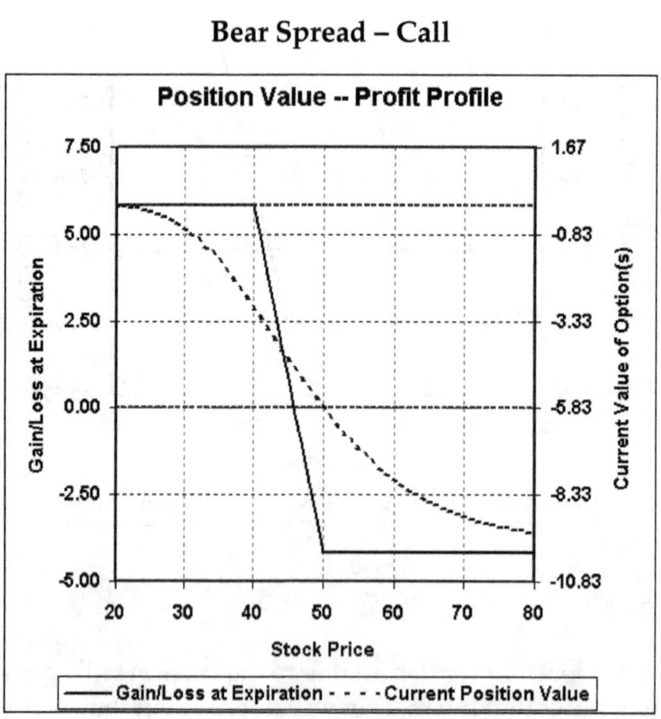

Figure 8.11

Bear Spread – Put

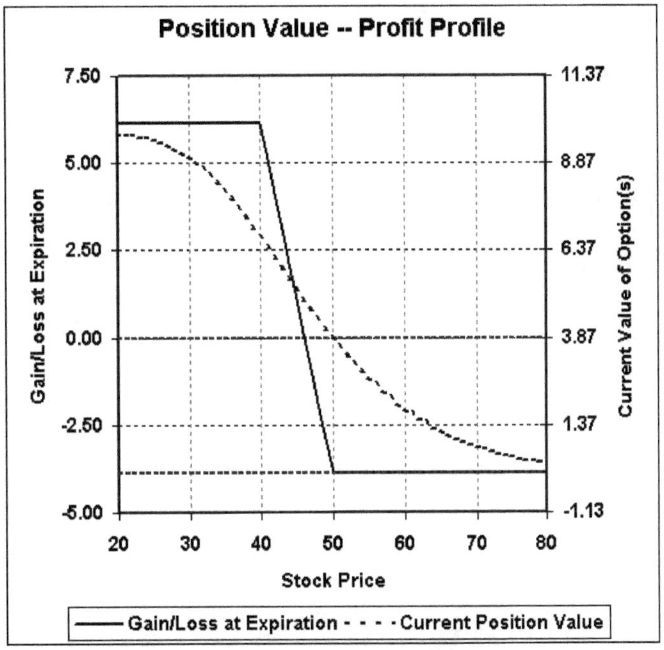

8.3.9 COLLAR

A collar is a hedging strategy whereby an investor who wishes to minimize potential loss in the value of a long equity position sells an out-of-the-money covered call option and uses the premium received to reduce or offset the cost of an out-of-the-money put option, thus limiting the investor's downside risk. But the downside protection comes at the expense of foregoing some potential upside gains. The maturity of a collar can range from several months to several years, and both options may (or may not) mature simultaneously. If the call option is written in the OTC market, the investor can negotiate the strike price and premium so that the investor's out-of-pocket cost for the put and call options is reduced to zero—a zero-premium collar. In many cases, investors can pick out-of-the-money puts and calls on listed options exchanges whose premiums also come close to zeroing out. Investors who have legal restrictions or practical limitations on selling their stock (e.g., restricted or unregistered stock, or stock with a low cost basis) may find collars especially useful. The collar has a profit profile very similar to the vertical bull spread.

Figure 8.12 shows the profit profile of a collar where the current stock price is $50, and the strike prices on the short call and long put are $60 and $45, respectively.

Although infrequently used, investors could also create a short collar to hedge against adverse price movements when they are short in an equity position. To create a short collar that is analogous to the long collar shown in Figure 8.12, sell a call with a strike price of $45 and buy a put with a strike price of $60. The profit profile will be similar to that of a bear spread.

Figure 8.12

Collar

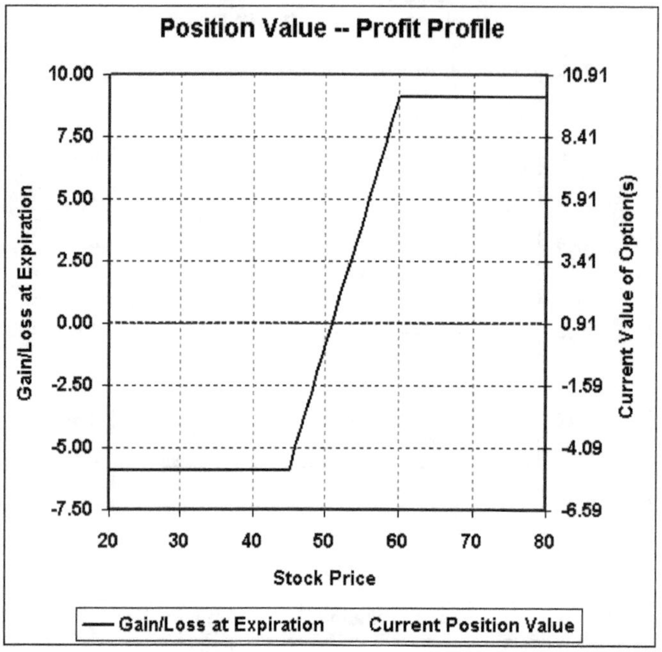

8.3.10 STRADDLES

If investors think that the market will be very volatile in the short-term or a company is facing a situation that could greatly impact the stock price, either up or down, such as a ruling in a major lawsuit or the awarding of a major government contract, they can buy a straddle. The long straddle position will reward them if the price moves substantially either up or down. In contrast, if investors think that the market will be less volatile, they can sell a straddle and profit if the price does not move outside of a given range.

The long straddle is created by buying a call option and a put option with the same strike price; usually, at the money. The upside potential of the long straddle is unlimited. The largest possible loss is equal to the two premiums paid for the long call and long put. The breakeven point is equal to the strike price plus or minus the sum of the long call and long put premiums (because a movement in either direction brings either the call, or the put, into the money, a straddle investor can profit with a move price in *either* direction beyond the boundaries of the breakeven points).

The short straddle is created by selling a call and a put for the same strike price; usually, at the money. The upside potential is limited to the sum of the two premiums received on the short call and short put. The downside risk is unlimited. The breakeven point is the strike price plus or minus the sum of the short call and short put premiums (where the investor profits as long as the stock price stays *within* the boundaries of the breakeven points).

Figures 8.13 and 8.14 show the profit profile of a long straddle and a short straddle, respectively, where the current stock price and both strike prices are equal to $50.

Figure 8.13

Long Straddle

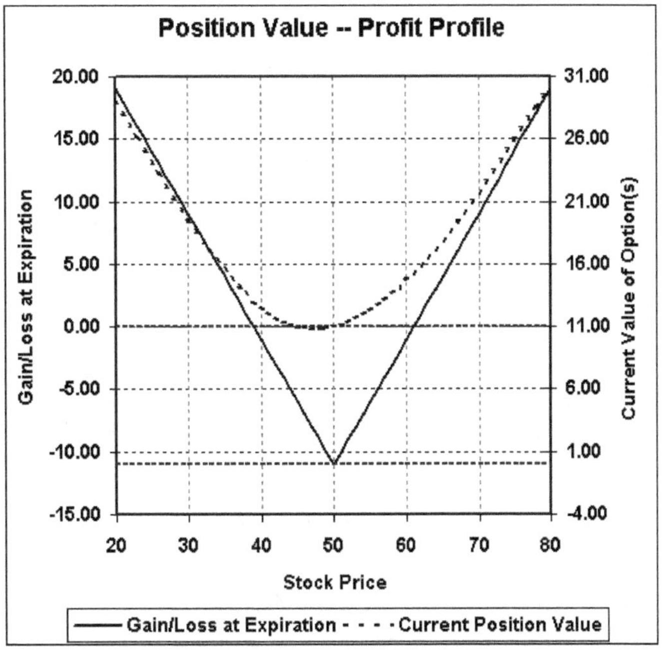

Figure 8.14

Short Straddle

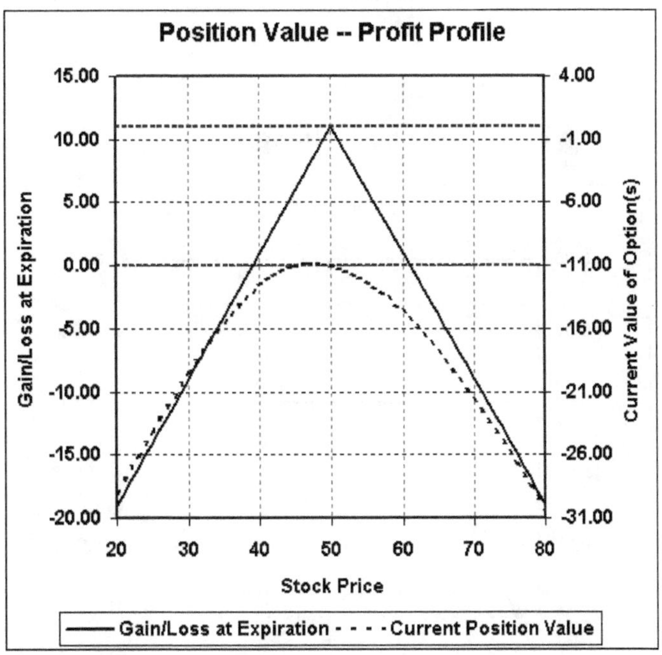

8.3.11 STRANGLE

Strangles are variations on straddles. Investors use them for the same purposes. But instead of buying or selling an at-the-money call and a put, the investor buys or sells an out-of-the-money call and put. This reduces the premium cost for the long strangle as well as the maximum possible loss (which is equal to the sum of the premiums on the long call and the long put). But it also requires the stock price to move further before the investor breaks even. Similar to the straddle, the upside potential is unlimited.

Figure 8.15

Long Strangle

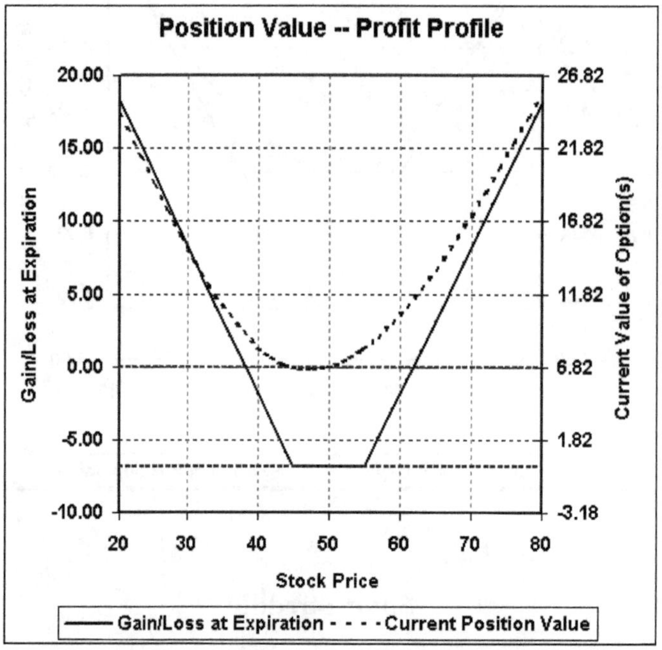

Figure 8.16

Short Strangle

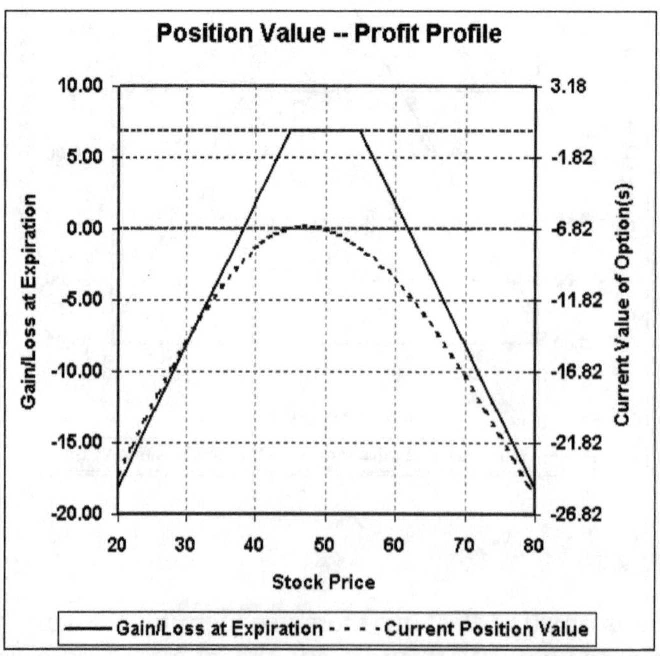

For the short strangle, the lower premiums reduce the investor's maximum potential gain, which is equal to the sum of the premiums on the short call and the short put. But the range in which the stock price can fluctuate until expiration is wider, so the investor is more likely to make some profit on the position.

Figures 8.15 and 8.16 show the profit profile for a long strangle and a short strangle when the current stock price is $50 and the strike prices on the put and call are $45 and $55, respectively.

8.3.12 BUTTERFLY

Butterflies are another variation on straddles with essentially the same objectives; however, they employ two additional out-of-the-money options. When investors create a long butterfly, they add an out-of-the-money short call and an out-of-the-money short put to the at-the-money long call and at-the-money long put of the long straddle to reduce the net premium paid for the position. The tradeoff is that the butterfly has a limited upside potential.

In the case of the short butterfly, investors add an out-of-the-money long call and an out-of-the-money long put to the at-the-money short call and the at-the-money short put of the short straddle to limit the downside risk. The tradeoff is that the net premium the investor receives is less and, consequently, the maximum upside is less than it would be with a straddle.

Figures 8.17 and 8.18 show the profit profiles of a long butterfly and short butterfly, respectively. In this case, the current price of the stock and the strike price on the two in-the-money options are $50. The strike prices for the out-of-the money short call and short put are $60 and $40, respectively.

Figure 8.17

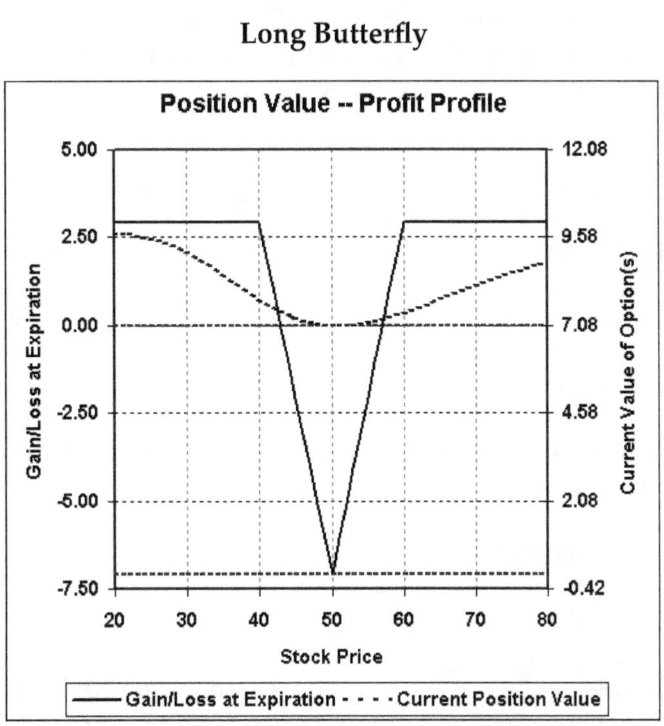

Figure 8.18

Short Butterfly

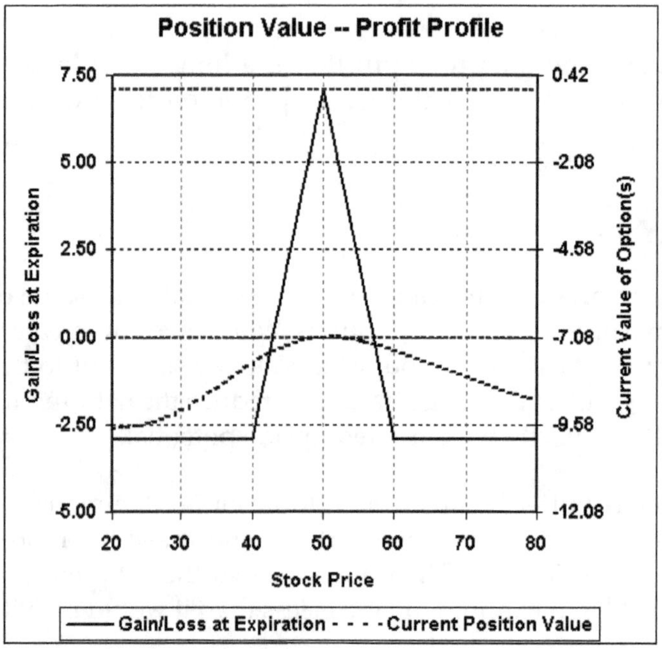

8.3.13 CALENDAR SPREAD

Calendar spreads are also known as time spreads. The most common type of calendar spread consists of opposing positions in two options of the same type (either both puts or both calls) that have the same exercise price, but expire at different times. Investors can create a long (short) time spread position by selling (buying) a short-term call option and buying (selling) a longer-term call option. The investor of the long position would profit when the price of the underlying asset is close to the strike price of the short call at its expiration.

8.4 TAX IMPLICATIONS

Section Overview:

8.4.1 Constructive Sale Rules

8.4.2 Straddle Rules

Taxes are a key factor in evaluating how to most efficiently minimize risk in taxable portfolios. For hedging strategies, two primary rules govern taxation:

1. the constructive sale rules, and

2. the straddle rules.

The constructive sale rules govern when investors initiating a hedge position have to treat the transaction as a sale of the hedged security (i.e., as a taxable event), even though no actual sale has taken place.

The straddle rules govern the tax aspects of closing a hedge position, including such issues as tolling or freezing capital gain holding periods and capitalizing the carrying costs (interest expense, commissions, and the like) of the hedge strategy.

For most hedging situations, a primary objective is to avoid constructive sale treatment and the requirement to recognize the gain (if an actual sale has not occurred). If investors can also avoid the negative aspects of the straddle rules, then the hedging strategy can be a much more tax-efficient strategy.

8.4.1 CONSTRUCTIVE SALE RULES

Certain transactions attempting to neutralize future gain and/or loss in a current appreciated stock holding are treated as constructive sales, which cause recognition of gain. A constructive sale is a transaction in which the owner of an appreciated security enters into one of the following three transactions:

- A short sale of the same or substantially identical property;
- An offsetting notional principal contract with respect to the same or substantially identical property; or
- A futures or forward contract to deliver the same or substantially identical property.

The term "substantially identical" is normally considered to be securities issued by the same issuer, which are commercially identical in all major aspects including dividend provisions. Normally, securities issued by two different issuers are not considered substantially identical unless, for example, the companies are merging, are days away from a merged close, and the common stock of each company is trading for all practical intents and purposes as the same security. Correlated pricing (meaning that the prices move virtually in lock-step) in the market is the key test for securities being considered substantially identical.

Initiating a put option purchase is not a constructive sale.

An investor who purchases a put option should not have the transaction treated as a constructive sale, even if the put option is for a stock the put holder already owns. Limited guidance exists on what is a constructive sale. What guidance does exist suggests that strategies that trigger constructive sale treatment are those that eliminate *nearly all potential gain and loss.* Out-of-the-money put options only reduce some, but not all, of the potential loss and none of the gain. Thus, purchasing a put option on stock already owned should not trigger the constructive sale rules with respect to the stock. But, in theory, if the put option is "deep-in-the-money" when the investor initiates the hedge and, therefore, it is a close proxy for the stock itself, a purchase could trigger a constructive sale or taxable event.

A short sale on stocks or indexes not otherwise owned is not a constructive sale.

A short sale of a stock or stock index that is not otherwise owned by an investor is not a constructive sale because the shorted stock is not substantially identical to securities held long in the investor's portfolio. For example, selling short Ford Motor Company (which is not otherwise owned by the investor) to hedge against a potential decline in a highly appreciated position in GM Motors is not a constructive sale resulting in tax, even though the stocks are in the same industry and their stock prices are correlated (albeit imperfectly). This technique of shorting a different, but price-correlated, stock in the same industry is beneficial for avoiding the constructive sale rules while hedging against market-wide and industry-specific risks. But it is still a considerably less effective hedge (because of the imperfect correlation) than shorting against the box, which is a perfect hedge (because of the perfect correlation), because the investor is still bearing substantial company-specific risk. GM's stock could still decline while Ford's stock remained level or rose due to business factors or circumstances unique to GM (e.g., labor problems, problems with a key component parts supplier, lawsuits, liability, a recall associated with a critical design flaw in a major product line, etc.).

Selling short a stock or stock index already owned is a constructive sale (except for a few limited exceptions for short-term short sales) that triggers tax. Therefore, selling short against the box is a wise hedging strategy generally only if the reasons for hedging the position and keeping the long stock position, rather than just selling the stocks held long; outweigh the cost of accelerating the tax. This may also be beneficial if the investor seeks to hedge away the risk of a stock that otherwise cannot be sold because of restrictions on the particular account or shares held.

Initiating a non-abusive collar should not be a constructive sale or taxable event.

Creating collars that do not essentially freeze the value of the stock within a relatively tight range (abusive collars) should not trigger a constructive sale of the underlying stock. Generally, collars are unlikely to be considered abusive if the term of the transaction is three years or less and the difference between the floor and ceiling price of the collar is at least 20 percent

There are other exemptions from the constructive sale rule, such as short-term hedges relating to shorting the same stock, but for most situations the put option, the short sale against a similar but different stock or index, and the collar are the most often used hedging techniques that can avoid the constructive sale rules.

Avoiding Constructive Sale Treatment

Investors are required to ignore the constructive sale rules if they close the offsetting position prior to January 30th of the following tax year and retain their original position for at least sixty days after closing the offsetting position. But investors must "go bare" for that sixty days—that is, without entering into another offsetting position for that sixty-day period. If they enter into an offsetting position during that sixty-day period, the original constructive sale in the prior year is reinstated.

Example. On May 1 last year, an investor bought one-hundred shares of ABC Corporation stock for $1,000. On September 3 last year, she sold short one-hundred shares of ABC stock for $1,600, triggering the constructive sale rules. The investor held both of these positions until January 10 of this year. On that date, she closed the offsetting short position for $1,800 and kept the long position open until at least March 11 (at least sixty days). During that sixty-day period, the investor did not enter into any other offsetting positions that would reduce risk of loss on the original position. Because the investor met the exceptions to the constructive sale rules, she has no constructive sale for last year. When she closes her short position on January 10, she recognizes a short-term capital loss of $200 for this tax year. Her cost basis for the long position remains at $1,000, but her holding period is now deemed to have started on January 10 of this year.

Example, On May 1 last year, an investor bought one-hundred shares of ABC Corporation stock for $1,000. On September 3 last year, she sold short one-hundred shares of ABC stock for $1,600, triggering the constructive sale rules. The investor held both of these positions until January 10 of this year. On that date, she closed her offsetting short position for $1,800. But because of fluctuations in the stock, the investor sells the long position on March 1 (well before the sixty-day required holding period ending March 11) for $1,500. The investor has now violated the exceptions to the constructive sale rules and she must recognize the constructive sale of the original position last year (when the constructive sale actually took place), and not in the current year, when she actually sold the stock.

8.4.2 STRADDLE RULES

Avoiding the constructive sale rules is usually a paramount tax issue when hedging. A second tax issue is whether the hedge is a straddle. While the constructive sale rules apply to transactions that attempt to lock in value within a certain range, eliminating the chance for both gain and loss, the straddle rules are broader and include most situations where a taxpayer is attempting to limit losses on an appreciated security by owning another security. If a hedge is a straddle, numerous tax implications arise with respect to closing out the hedge. The tax impact of a straddle is usually much less onerous than a constructive sale, but the straddle rules are nonetheless a very important tax factor with hedges.

Straddle Defined

The Internal Revenue Code defines a straddle as "offsetting positions with respect to personal property." A taxpayer holds offsetting positions "if there is a substantial diminution of the taxpayer's risk of loss from holding any position with respect to personal property by reason of his holding 1 or more other positions… (whether or not of the same kind)." Therefore, if an investor shorts a stock or buys a put option on a stock held long, that position creates a straddle.

In evaluating if the offsetting positions meet the facts and circumstances test of "intent to substantially limit risk of loss," the Internal Revenue Code provides several tests, which, if met, result in a rebuttable presumption that a straddle exists. These rebuttable presumptions assume a position is a straddle if the hedge involves the same security as the protected security, even if in substantially different form. These tests also presume a straddle exists if the hedge is sold or marketed as an offsetting position (regardless of the name used). But these tests require that there be an inverse relationship in valuation changes between the offsetting positions. The bottom line is that straddle rules will apply to nearly any hedge that reduces the investor's potential for loss on an existing position within his portfolio.

To summarize the basic straddle rules:

1. A straddle occurs when an investor owns stock (or a call option on the stock) and then enters into an offsetting position such as:

   a. an option on such stock or substantially identical stock; or

   b. a position with respect to substantially similar or related property (not including stock).

2. Property is substantially similar or related to stock when the fair market value of the offsetting position primarily reflects the performance of:

   a. a single firm;

   b. the same industry; or

   c. the same economic factors (such as interest rates, commodity prices, a stock market index, or foreign currency rates as well as other economic factors).

3. In addition, changes in the fair market value of the offsetting positions must be reasonably expected to move inversely to the market value of the position held. The price relationship does not have to be one-to-one. The prices may move as a fraction or multiple of each other. In other words, if appreciated stock is on one side of the position, then a put option on the same stock or substantially similar stock on the other side of the position is a straddle.

4. Absent final regulations, a straddle does not appear to exist with an offsetting position in substantially similar stock.

Stock acquired before January 1, 1984, is not subject to the straddle rules. For these stocks, investors can purchase puts against stock positions with identical correlation and protection, yet without adverse tax implications under either the constructive sale or straddle rules.

Many other hedge strategies have straddle implications, including selling short or buying puts on an index fund (either broad based or by sector). These strategies can offer higher correlation than hedge strategies employing short sales or puts on a different stock in the same industry as the appreciated stock.

Position	Example	Straddle/Constructive Sale?
Sell Short a Substantially Similar Stock Not Otherwise Owned	Sell Short Ford to Hedge a Position in GM	No/No
Sell Short a Stock Already Owned	Sell Short GM to Hedge a Position in GM	Yes/Yes
Purchase of Put Option on Substantially Similar Stock to a Position Owned	Purchase a Put Option on Ford to Hedge a Position in GM	Yes/No
Purchase of Put Option on Stock Already Owned	Purchase a Put Option on GM to Hedge a Position in GM	Yes/No
Non-Abusive Collar on Stock Already Owned	Purchase Put Option & Sell Call Option on GM to Limit Values to a Range	Yes/No

Straddle Rule Tax Implications on Closing the Straddle

If an investor is in a straddle position:

- The capital gain holding periods are suspended during the time of the offsets. The holding period of the hedged security remains long-term if it was long-term at the time the investor initiated the hedge; non-long-term hedged securities have their holding periods started anew when the offsetting position (i.e., straddle) is closed. The holding periods for put options or other similar offsetting positions acquired to initiate the hedge remain short-term because they are prevented from becoming long-term by the suspension effect of the straddle.

- Investors may take no current deduction for losses to the extent of any unrealized gain in the offsetting positions. Therefore, losses on a straddle are deferred until unrealized gains on the offsetting position are eliminated or realized. But losses on a straddle in excess of any unrealized gains may still be taken. Any deferred losses are carried forward into the subsequent tax year.

- Investors must capitalize all carrying charges and interest expense (including margin) during the offset period (net of dividends) and add them to the basis of the long stock position. This has the effect of reducing the amount of capital gain when the investor sells the long stock position.

One of the major concerns of the straddle rules are that they may convert what otherwise would have been long-term capital gain into short-term capital gain for tax purposes. For example, assume an investor owns one-hundred shares of XYZ corp. that he purchased three years ago for $50 per share. The stock is now worth $100 per share, so he has a substantial unrealized long-term capital gain. He thinks the company's prospects are good in the long run, but the stock price and the stock's P/E are at their historical highs. Consequently, he fears that the price may decline in the relative short run. If he sells the shares now, he must realize and pay tax on the long-term gain of $5,000. If instead the investor purchases a put option on the stock with an exercise price per share equal to the stock's current market price of $100, he can protect himself from any loss resulting from a downward price adjustment during the term of the hedge.

Suppose the investor purchases the option to create the hedge. The hedge is not treated as a constructive sale, but it is subject to the straddle rules. Now suppose for illustration purposes that the price of the stock falls all the way to the investor's original $50 purchase price by the time the option expires. The investor will have lost the entire $5,000 long-term gain on the stock in his portfolio, but gained $5,000 on the put (less the cost of the put, of course). Now if he closes out the put by either selling the put or buying new shares in the market at $50 to deliver on the put contract for $100 per share, the $5,000 gain (less the cost of the put) will be short-term. Consequently, as a result of the transaction, he would have hedged his economic position (less the cost of the put), but converted what otherwise would have been a long-term gain taxable at the lower capital gains rate into a short-term capital gain taxable at his ordinary income tax rate (assuming he has realized no other offsetting losses in his portfolio).

Of course, he could and generally should avoid this short-term capital gain treatment by delivering the stock he held in his portfolio to satisfy the put. Because the stock delivered in this case would have a long-term holding period, the gain would be taxed as long-term gain. As a result, he would end up having exactly the same amount of money after tax as he otherwise would have had if he had originally sold the stock rather than create the hedge, but less the cost of creating the hedge.

Actually, had he originally sold the stock and then reinvested the after-tax proceeds elsewhere, for instance, at worst in a risk-free asset like T-bills, he would also have the additional after-tax interest income from the T-bills. So the hedge has cost the investor, at a minimum, the amount he paid to buy the put and create the hedge (plus commissions and other transaction costs) plus the after-tax income he could have earned by investing in a risk-free asset.

This example demonstrates two important points. First, investors must carefully assess the tax consequences of hedges that are treated as straddles and how they close out their straddle positions in light of their overall tax situation and objectives. Second, hedges are not free lunches. Hedges have both direct costs and indirect (opportunity) costs that investors must weigh relative to the benefits or objectives they hope to achieve by entering into the hedge transaction.

Chapter 9

HEDGING AND DERIVATIVE SECURITIES

9.1 HEDGING

Section Overview:

9.1.1 Hedging Strategies

9.1.2 Fundamental Investment Principles

9.1.1 HEDGING STRATEGIES

The Chicago Board Options Exchange (CBOE) defines hedging as "a conservative strategy used to limit investment loss by effecting a transaction that offsets an existing position." In essence, hedging is a form of investment insurance, which, like traditional life, property, and casualty, or liability insurance, transfers risk from one person or entity to another. And, just like traditional insurance, hedging involves tradeoffs. Hedgers likely must pay a premium or be otherwise willing to forego potential investment returns to shift risk.

Quite frankly, as many possible hedging strategies exist as the creative mind can structure. In addition, what one investor may perceive as a risky strategy, another may perceive as representing a hedge, depending on each investor's circumstances, other investment holdings, view, forecast of future events, and/or perception of market conditions.

Investors may employ hedging strategies and tools to reduce risk, or even "immunize" their investment holdings in stocks, bonds and other debt instruments, commodities, futures, and other investments against almost any conceivable risk, including market risk, sector or industry risk, company or business-specific risk, purchasing power risk, currency risk, interest rate risk, country-specific risk, reinvestment risk, liquidity risk, callability risk, default or credit risk, selection risk, management or agency risk, etc.

The scope of these hedging strategies and tools ranges from those employed at the portfolio level to the asset-class, sector, or industry level, to the individual security or investment instrument level. The time frame for employing hedging strategies may range from same-day or overnight to years.

Hedging strategies are sometimes employed for special or unusual circumstances, such as to protect the current value of stock subject to restrictions on sale, from a decrease in value before the restriction expires. Some institutional investors adopt computer-aided hedging strategies, called portfolio insurance techniques, as part of an ongoing portfolio policy and objective to assure at least a minimum portfolio return in both up and down markets and from year to year. The same tools and strategies used for conservative hedging purposes are also employed—many argue aggressively, or even speculatively, rather than defensively—by hedge funds that attempt to capitalize on what their managers see as market imperfections or as opportunities to beat the market using market timing or business cycle sector-rotation techniques. But, don't let the name fool you.

Hedging involves tools (certain investment instruments) and techniques (strategies). In the techniques or strategies area, first and foremost are the fundamental principles of sound investing—diversification and asset allocation. Investors can usually eliminate nearly all of the company-specific risk of stocks, the security-specific risk of individual investment instruments, selection risk, and country-specific risk by diversifying and investing in a large number of securities within a given asset class, sector, or industry, and across a large number of countries. This reduces the amount invested in any particular aspect of the portfolio, and, accordingly, minimizes the potential loss that might be experienced in proportion to the total portfolio.

Similarly, investors can further reduce their exposure to loss within a given asset class, sector, or industry by allocating portions of their portfolio among different assets or asset classes whose returns are not highly positively correlated (or are even negatively correlated) with each other. This reduces the odds that several aspects of the portfolio might experience declines at once (and in fact may increase the odds that one element is increasing while another is experiencing losses). In general, investors should consider allocating their investments among domestic and foreign stocks, short-, intermediate-, and long-term bonds and other debt instruments, real estate, commodities, etc. and the subclasses within each larger asset class to minimize these types of risks

Many of the tools involved in hedging are "derivative" securities, such as options contracts, forward and futures contracts, and other derivatives that are essentially just variations or combinations of regular options and forward or futures contracts. How investors use these tools to accomplish hedging objectives is discussed in more detail in the How It Is Done section.

Because hedging tools and techniques are virtually unlimited in choice and flexibility, the situations in which hedging might be involved also become nearly limitless. Some of the more popular or frequent situations where hedging tools and techniques might be indicated include:

1. Investors want to protect current security values from price decline when they must make quick decisions with limited information. In many situations, investors can protect portfolio appreciation by using measured and well-reasoned strategies and fundamental portfolio and investment management techniques after a thorough examination of all relevant facts. Yet, large declines in value too often occur when investors do not have adequate time to fully digest the reliable information and to sort through the rumors and untruths, while waiting for the release of the true facts. While non-taxable accounts can sell without concern over taxes, hedging strategies may provide investors holding

highly appreciated positions with security against loss until they have the requisite time to properly evaluate all relevant information and then later decide whether to hold the security (with no taxable sale), or to sell (and incur the applicable taxes).

2. Situations when an investor is uncomfortable with a large percentage of value in a single stock—that is, a concentrated portfolio—but does not wish to sell and trigger capital gains taxes at the present time.

3. An investor has a large holding that is facing an almost certain dramatic movement up or down, but the question remains in which direction the stock will move? For instance, the stock of a company facing a major litigation will almost certainly decline dramatically if the company loses the suit and increase significantly if it wins the suit. Investors can set up hedges that will protect them from serious loss (or even protect gains) regardless of the outcome of the suit.

4. An investor may own a large position in a stock that has trading restrictions due to Initial Public Offering (IPO) lock-up provisions, or trading restrictions imposed by the government or the company due to insider status or other factors. Hedging may allow this investor to control the risk of loss in a position that may have substantial value now, but may not when he is ultimately allowed to sell.

5. An individual with a short life expectancy due to advanced age or illness (or as spousal beneficiary of a marital trust) may wish to protect against a decrease in equity portfolio value (to protect the value of the assets for heirs), but may not wish to sell because the appreciated positions would receive a step-up in basis at death (and would incur substantial capital gains taxes if sold before death).

6. An individual may be in need of liquidity for a new home purchase, payments to creditors, or other cash flow needs, but does not wish to trigger capital gains taxes. By entering into a hedge strategy, the minimum value of the appreciated position can be fixed, providing an asset that can serve as collateral for loans.

7. Investment advisers, trust officers, investment managers, or other fiduciaries responsible for other people's money want to meet their fiduciary duty to protect the value of the total portfolio—they can achieve this by diversifying and hedging against declines in the value of their clients' investments. The duty to diversify and hedge appreciated or concentrated holdings (and the duty to recommend diversification and hedging) is not the focus of this chapter. But, specific cases provide an excellent fact pattern for an overview of the claims that can arise in the area of the financial adviser's duty to diversify or recommend hedging strategies.

9.1.2 FUNDAMENTAL INVESTMENT PRINCIPLES

Although not traditionally considered a hedging strategy, per se, simply employing the sound investment fundamentals of diversification and asset allocation, whenever possible, is the best way for investors to reduce the risk of their investments. While any individual company's stock value and price volatility is related to both industry and overall market factors, the single biggest contributor to an individual stock's price volatility is its individual business risk. A company's business risk is *unsystematic* risk that investors can eliminate by diversifying into many companies rather than just one or a few. On the average, the losses sustained on the stocks of companies that (unexpectedly) perform poorly for their own peculiar reasons will be offset by comparable gains on the stocks of other companies that (unexpectedly) perform well for their own unique reasons. By diversifying into a number of companies, investors will earn the average return for the group, but with considerably less average return volatility than that associated with any single company within the group. In fact, the greater is the extent that these assets are less than perfectly positively correlated (or inversely correlated), the better are the odds that multiple positions will not experience declines simultaneously. The same basic ideas and rules apply to bonds, commodities, futures, real estate, and other investment assets and asset classes.

Even broad diversification within a sector, industry, or asset class still exposes investors to sector, industry, or asset-class risk factors as well as market-wide risk factors—what are called systematic risk factors. Investors can manage the level of their exposure to *systematic* risk factors by diversifying across sector, industry, or asset classes—the process of asset allocation and portfolio management. Different sectors, industries, and asset classes tend to respond differently to changing economic conditions, periods in the business cycle, and various economic, social, political, and other major events. In other words, the values of investments associated with different asset classes are less than perfectly positively correlated. Using the principles of asset allocation and portfolio management, investors can diversify across asset classes to minimize the risk in their portfolios from individual sector, industry, and asset class risks and to derive an overall portfolio exposure to market-wide risk and volatility that is consistent with their risk tolerance and risk and return objectives. When investors fully embrace these fundamental investment principles, the need to hedge investments in any particular security, group of securities, industry, or asset class is lessened.

In some cases investors cannot or do not wish to fully exploit these fundamental investment principles. At any given time, for whatever reasons, investors might have a concentrated portfolio (a portfolio that has a large position in a particular security or asset class and, therefore, is greatly exposed to risks associated with that investment) that they cannot (e.g., trading restrictions) or choose not to (e.g., expectations about positive future performance) fix using the fundamental principles of investment and portfolio management – these investors should consider hedging strategies.

For instance, the principal investment of an owner of a small closely held import-export business dealing principally with just two foreign countries is his business. Generally, such people will be grossly under-diversified and therefore exposed to business, industry, foreign currency, and country-specific risk factors that they cannot easily mitigate through diversification and asset allocation. However, such a person may be able to engage in hedging operations both outside and inside of his business to hedge his business, industry, currency, and country risks.

Example: Some institutional portfolios, trust funds, college endowment funds, charitable foundation funds, and others employ hedging strategies called "portfolio insurance" techniques to set floors or minimums on the amount the funds earn over any given period. These funds typically have reasonably predictable required outlays and want to assure that they can meet these obligations without eroding the principal of the funds. They are willing to forego some upside earnings potential in order to prevent losses below some specified level. Although they generally employ the fundamentals of modern investment, asset allocation, and portfolio theory to structure their base portfolios, they will use options and futures contracts and options contracts on futures contracts on broad-based market and asset-class indexes and other strategies to hedge against declines in value below their designated limit.

In less volatile markets, investors generally can rebalance their portfolios periodically and incrementally with an eye towards minimizing the tax consequences and transactions costs of rebalancing by matching recognition of gains and losses while not deviating too substantially from their preferred risk/return profile. But in more volatile markets, investors' portfolios may quickly deviate from their preferred mix among asset classes and expose them to market and asset-class risk levels that they deem unacceptable. Making adjustments all at once to move back to their preferred asset mix and risk/return profile may be difficult and expensive as well as disadvantageous for tax purposes. Sales of assets in those asset classes that have appreciated substantially and where the investor is overweighted may result in large realizations of gains (and a subsequent large tax bill) that the investor may not be able to easily offset with sales of loss assets without also incurring substantial transactions costs. In such cases, the investors can enter into temporary hedging positions in options and/or financial futures that are long positions in those asset classes that are underweighted in their portfolios and short positions in those asset classes that are overweighted in their portfolios and buy time to make tax-and-cost-efficient transactions in the underlying securities to rebalance to their preferred asset mix.

So even when investors employ the fundamentals of modern investment and portfolio theory to construct a risk/return profile that meets their objectives, at times, they may still wish or need to engage in tactical hedging operations.

9.2 DERIVATIVES

Section Overview:

9.2.1 Derivatives Markets

9.2.2 Selling a Forward Contract or Futures Contract

9.2.3 Offsetting Notional Principal Contract or Equity Swap

9.2.4 Pre-Paid Forward Sale

9.2.1 DERIVATIVES MARKETS

Given the limitations, risks, and adverse tax consequences (under the constructive sale rules) of stop-loss orders, short sales, and other essentially short-sale equivalents, many investors have turned to options, futures, and other derivative instruments to achieve their hedging objectives. To understand why, one must understand derivative instruments and markets.

Derivatives are so named because they "derive" their value in reference to the value of some other security or property. These instruments do not represent an ownership interest in the security or property. Rather, they provide investors with the *right* or *obligation* to buy or sell securities or property or to receive payments based upon the performance of some underlying security or property sometime in the future. The number of new derivative instruments being introduced into the markets and the growth in the volume of trading in these markets has been tremendous. This rapid expansion of derivative instruments provides investors with an ever-increasing arsenal for hedging an ever-expanding list of risks. The prevalence and usefulness of these instruments in hedging operations, as well as the risks associated with the misuse or misapplication of these instruments makes it imperative that financial advisers and investors understand the fundamental nature of these instruments and their relation to markets. This is vital for anyone who seeks to successfully employ these tools in hedging strategies.

In contrast with the stock market or other markets trading ownership interests or claims on real or personal property, the derivatives markets are "*zero-sum*" games. A zero-sum game is one in which the average gain and loss of all participants in the game is zero. For example, since 1926, the average investor (i.e., the average result amongst all investors) in the S&P 500 index of stocks has earned about 10 percent (compounded) annually, ignoring transactions costs. But the average investor in every options, futures, or other derivatives market, for however long all of these the markets have existed, *by design*, has earned exactly 0 percent, ignoring transactions costs.

The reason for the difference between the derivatives and the stock markets is that the market for stocks is, on average, a long market. That is, it represents ownership in the productive capacity of the economy, which has a positive value. So, although some investors may sell short shares of the market, the average position must represent a long position in the productive capacity of the economy. As knowledge grows, technology advances, and labor productivity improves, the entire economy grows (i.e., experiences *real* growth after inflation), providing more, on average, for everyone. Therefore, it is a positive-sum game.

In contrast, derivative securities do not represent, on balance, any ownership interest in anything. They are essentially side bets on economic values and, as such, have a total economic value of zero. For example, suppose two farmers disagree about what the price of a bushel of wheat will be in nine months. One thinks it will be less than $6.50, while the other thinks it will be more than $6.50. The one who thinks it will be less than $6.50 says he is willing to put his money where his mouth is and bet that it will be less than $6.50. He proposes that they agree today that he must sell, and the other farmer must buy, 5,000 bushels of his wheat in nine months for $6.50 per bushel (which would be higher than he expects the price to actually be, producing a profit for him). The other farmer takes him up on his bet. If the farmer proposing the bet is right and the price of wheat is less than $6.50 per bushel in nine months, he wins the bet and pockets the difference between the market price (less than $6.50) and the $6.50 target price of the bet.

Their bet neither creates nor destroys any wheat. It does not have any effect on the price of wheat whatsoever. If the price of wheat rises above $6.50 per bushel, say to $7.00, the farmer who wins the bet and buys the 5,000 bushels for $6.50 will realize a quick $2,500 gain ($0.50 per bushel times 5,000 bushels) when he turns around and sells the wheat for $7.00. The farmer losing the bet will forfeit exactly $2,500 by selling the 5,000 bushels of wheat for $6.50 per bushel, when he could otherwise have sold it for $7.00 per bushel. Of course, they could just settle up by having the farmer losing the bet pay the winner $2,500 in cash. So, one farmer's gain is the other farmer's loss—the bet is a zero-sum game.

The bet between the two farmers is essentially a forward contract. All of the forward and futures contracts on the various commodities and financial instruments are just variations on this simple example. For every long position where someone agrees to buy a given amount of some commodity or financial instrument for a given price at a specified time in the future there must be an equal and offsetting short position where someone agrees to sell under the same terms.

Although described as zero-sum games, the derivatives markets are actually *negative-sum* games, because each side of every transaction pays commissions and/or other transactions costs.

If investing in these derivative instruments is a losing proposition on average, the question naturally arises as to why such markets exist and why anyone would invest in them. A good question!

The answer is risk asymmetry—different risk tolerances and capacities. Two parties can enter opposite sides of a transaction with each having the perception that the position reduces his risk. For instance, assume following up from our farmers' bet example that the bet is instead between the farmer and the local baker. The farmer is willing to agree to sell the wheat in nine months for $6.50 per bushel because he knows that amount will be sufficient for him to recoup his costs and still make an acceptable profit. He can rest assured that he can continue his farming the next year. Sure, he would like to sell at $7.00 if the price is that high, but he would gladly give up the additional $0.50 per bushel to insure that he still gets the $6.50 even if the price falls to $6.00. Conversely, the baker would love to buy the wheat at $6.00 per bushel if the price is that low, but he also would gladly pay the extra $0.50 to insure that he can buy the wheat at $6.50 per bushel even if the price rises to $7.00. For the farmer, the risk is that prices will fall; for the baker, that prices will rise; so they are both better off agreeing to set the price in advance to eliminate their risk. Both are willing to give up potential gains to reduce their risk.

The derivatives markets would not be nearly as immense and diverse if it were not for differences in investors' risk tolerances, capacities to bear risk, and differing expectations about future prices. Just as some people like to bet the horses or play blackjack in Vegas, some investors are willing to speculate on the values of derivative securities, even though they are neither producers nor users of the products. In fact, the vast majority of the positions in the futures markets are closed out prior to the expiration of the contracts by buying or selling offsetting positions. These investors provide both liquidity and depth to the markets, making them more efficient at pricing or valuing the underlying assets. Derivatives markets also allow the transfer of risk from those who want to eliminate (or minimize) risk to those who want to bear risk.

Therefore, basically the derivatives markets are risk transfer mechanisms. As such, they add to overall economic efficiency by reducing and transferring risks and promoting more efficient planning and production throughout the economy. Although investing in derivatives is in aggregate a zero-sum game (or negative-sum game, after transactions costs), the derivatives markets as a whole add value to the economy.

Options markets, like futures markets, are also a zero-sum game (or negative-sum game after transactions costs). Similar to futures contracts, options contracts deal with the delivery of a specified amount of some financial instrument, commodity, or other property at a specified price (called the strike or exercise price) on (or before, depending on the type of contract) some specified future date. Also similar to the futures markets, for each "long" position there is an equal and opposite "short" position. The principal distinction is that options give one side of the position the *right, but not the obligation*, to buy or sell and the other side the *obligation* to sell or buy if the other side exercises his right. In futures markets, both sides of the transaction have the obligation to either buy or sell depending on whether they are "long" or "short" in the transaction (but only if the position is still "open" at the time of exercise—as mentioned earlier, the vast majority of futures contracts are closed out before this).

Derivatives are highly leveraged instruments. For example, on September 22, 2013, the underlying notional value of an S&P 500 index option (SPX) was $1,709.70. The premium for an October 2013 call with a strike price of $1,700 was $30.00 ($9.70 intrinsic value and $20.30 speculative premium). If the price of the underlying index had risen to $1,750 say, at expiration in October 2013, the call option would have been worth $50. This represents a $20.00 gain on the option above the initial $30.00 investment, or a 67 percent return for the one month period until expiration. If an investor had paid $1,709.7 to buy the underlying index directly, the gain would have been $40.30. This represents just a 2.4 percent return for the same period and based upon the movement of the same underlying investment.

Leverage is one feature that makes options and other derivatives such good hedging vehicles (and also such appealing speculative instruments, for those that are so inclined). The markets generally are rather liquid and investors can take offsetting positions with just pennies on the dollar relative to the securities held long. Consequently, they provide investors with a great deal of flexibility. But the leverage is inherently risky and investors may lose all of their initial investment, or more, depending upon the type of hedge and the instruments they use. Therefore, misuse of these instruments for hedging purposes can lead to severe losses, far in excess of the original risk that was meant to be hedged. A discussion of all the features and characteristics of derivatives is beyond the scope of this chapter.

Finally, the proliferation of derivative instruments stems from a desire to span the market and to provide vehicles capable of hedging many different types of risk in addition to potential losses in appreciated positions. For instance, one particular type of financial futures contract, the interest-rate swap, permits investors with variable interest rates on their assets and fixed interest on their obligations to exchange the variable interest for fixed interest. Equity swaps trade returns on an equity index for returns on another equity index or a bond or interest rate index or security. By entering into an equity swap, investors who are long on the index (or close substitutes) can essentially replace part or all of their exposure to loss on the equity position by exchanging the returns on a specified amount of the equity index for, say, interest payments tied to the twenty-year Treasury bond index. Effectively, they change the composition of their portfolio and their risk/return profile without actually having to sell part or all of their position in the index. Currency futures permit investors to hedge currency risks; new swap derivatives permit investors to replace variable or fixed rate payments with inflation-adjusted payments; and the list goes on and on.

9.2.2 SELLING A FORWARD CONTRACT OR FUTURES CONTRACT

A forward contract is a contract negotiated privately or traded over-the-counter to deliver a security at a specific time in the future, at a specific price. Also, with the recent advent of single-stock listed futures contracts on an ever-increasing number of companies, investors can now sell standardized futures contracts on many companies. Because these futures and forward contracts are substantially identical property, the use of this hedging strategy will trigger the constructive sale rules.

Example: Adams owns 1,000 shares of Z stock, currently valued at $100 per share. He contracts with Burrows to deliver 1,000 shares of Z stock, at $101 per share in three months.

9.2.3 OFFSETTING NOTIONAL PRINCIPAL CONTRACT OR EQUITY SWAP

An offsetting notional principal contract is one where the holder of a security or bundle of securities agrees to pay substantially all of the investment yield (interest, dividends, etc.) and appreciation from the security or the bundle of securities for a specified period. Generally, in return, the investor receives interest based upon an interest rate index, such as the LIBOR rate, or a bond index, such as the twenty-year U.S. Treasury bond index. In addition, the investor generally is also reimbursed for substantially any loss of value in the security or bundle of securities. This arrangement should run afoul of the constructive sale rules, because it is essentially equivalent to the sale of the stock at its current price and the purchase of the bond index.

Example: Johnson owns 1,000 shares of XYZ stock, valued at $100 per share. She contracts with Masters as follows: Any dividends on the stock and any appreciation in value will be delivered to Masters. In return, Masters will pay Johnson interest on $100,000 based upon the LIBOR rate and will reimburse Johnson for any drop in the value of XYZ stock value below $100 per share.

9.2.4 PRE-PAID FORWARD SALE

A pre-paid forward sale is a risk management strategy suitable for investors whose primary goal is to monetize a concentrated equity position without incurring an immediate tax liability. The pre-paid forward sale may be appropriate for investors who have legal restrictions or practical limitations on selling their stock (e.g., restricted or unregistered stock, or stock with a low cost basis).

Investors may receive an up-front payment of 75 percent to 95 percent of the value of their stock rather than the traditional payment for the full contract amount at the time the contract matures. Generally, the investor making the forward sale has no obligations to the counterparty until the expiration of the transaction. The amount of the up-front payment may be affected by several factors, including the term of the transaction (generally, more discount of the upfront payment with longer terms), the level of an investment's upside potential (less discount or even a premium if the upside potential is substantial), prevailing interest rates (more discount with higher interest rates), and other market conditions. Essentially, this is a variation of the equity swap, because the investor selling the stock in the forward sale effectively transfers all potential appreciation or loss on the stock (payable at the end of the contract term when the stock is transferred) for the interest or other investment income or returns he will earn by investing the up-front payment.

What these hedging techniques have in common is that the owner of the securities continues to hold the securities. All, or most, risk of loss—and opportunity for gain—on the securities is transferred from the owner to someone else. The owner has effectively disposed of the securities, while retaining nominal ownership. They also have the unfortunate consequence (generally) of triggering the constructive sale rules.

9.3 FINANCIAL FUTURES

Section Overview:

9.3.1 Futures Markets

9.3.2 Futures Contracts

9.3.1 FUTURES MARKETS

The previous chapter discussed options which allow the purchaser to speculate on the future direction of the price of an underlying asset such as a security. Another instrument that allows the investor to speculate on the future direction of an asset's price is a futures contract. The difference between the two is that an option is a right but not an obligation whereas a futures contract comes with an obligation to complete the contract (or enter into an offsetting contract before expiration). Futures are standardized contracts calling for future delivery of a specified number or notional value of a specified asset, for a specified price, at a designated future date. The price at which delivery will be made is determined at the present time, but delivery is scheduled for some future date.

Example: An investor may trade through the CME Group on June 15 to purchase a futures contract in US Treasury Bond certificates for actual delivery on the last trading day of November. The price and the number of contracts to be traded are set at the time of purchase or sale (June 15), and not at the time of delivery (the last trading day of November).

Underlying assets in future contracts can be financial in nature, such as currencies, or can involve other assets such as commodities or real estate. Today they are also available on events such as weather futures.

The financial futures market includes:

1. *Currency Futures* – contracts on foreign currencies;

2. *Interest-Rate Futures* – contracts on U. S. Treasury bonds, notes, bills, GNMA bonds, foreign government bonds, and other interest-related notional instruments, or benchmarks based upon such things as the Federal Funds Rate, or the LIBOR (London Inter-Bank Offered Rate) or differences in interest rates between sovereign nations;

3. *Index Futures* – contracts on broad-based domestic or foreign stock indexes (e.g., the S&P 500 Index or the EAFE Index), or contracts on indexes of interest-related instruments (e.g., Treasury bonds);

4. *Narrow-Based Index (NBI) Futures* – contracts based on a small basket of stocks from a narrow sector of the market (e.g., airlines or chemicals);

5. *Single Stock Futures* – contracts on individual stocks; and

6. *Real Estate Futures* – contracts on residential and commercial real estate in a composite index or in select metropolitan areas. These are relatively new products based on the S&P Case/Shiller price indices.

In addition, the futures markets are introducing creative new contracts all the time, and some of these contracts do not fit easily within the six financial futures categories listed above or within the traditional commodity futures categories. For instance, the CME Group (which now includes the Chicago Mercantile Exchange, Chicago Board of Trade, and New York Mercantile Exchange) has several futures contracts that are based not on the performance of the S&P 500 Index or the Dow Jones Industrial Average, per se, but rather just on the volatility or variance of these indices over various investment horizons. The Chicago Mercantile Exchange (CME) also lists futures contracts based not directly on financial instruments or commodities, as such, but rather on broad economic factors such as U.S. gross domestic product and the U.S. international trade balance. Futures are also now available on Exchange Traded Funds (ETF) which typically mirror broad or narrow indices. Further, investors may now trade futures based upon a home price index.

Two distinct trading arenas comprise the financial futures market – exchange-traded futures and over-the-counter futures. Exchange-traded futures are contracts listed on organized exchanges, such as the CME Group, OneChicago (single stock futures), and other exchanges. These contracts have standardized features with respect to the amount of the product involved in each contract, the margin requirement, the settlement dates, etc. In addition, these contracts are subject to the "mark-to-market rule" that essentially settles differences in the long and short positions daily to assure that parties to the contracts maintain adequate margin.

The inter-bank, Over-The-Counter (OTC) futures market is essentially a negotiated private placement market, generally involving contracts on millions of dollars of financial instruments. In this market, contracts are much less standardized than in the exchange-traded futures market; terms and amounts can vary depending upon the desires of each party, and the contracts generally are not marked-to-market every day. Whereas virtually any investor who has the financial wherewithal to qualify for margin trading can invest in exchange-traded futures, the principal participants in the OTC futures market are large financial institutions and international corporations, professional traders and arbitrageurs, and governments. Because the vast majority of individual investors do not participate in the OTC futures market, the principal focus of this chapter will be on exchange-traded futures.

Most investors in the financial futures market do not plan to take delivery of the item purchased (or make delivery in the case of a sale). Less than 3 percent of contracts traded are settled by the buyer's receiving, or the seller's making delivery of the actual instrument on which the contract is based. The real purpose of the transaction is to transfer the risk (and potential reward) of price fluctuations from the hedger to the speculator, not to take actual possession of the asset.

Most investors close out their sale or purchase positions by entering into an offsetting transaction instead of taking or making delivery. This is accomplished by simply reversing their original position. For example, if an investor buys a futures contract on Treasury bills, he can close out the position by selling the identical contract prior to expiration.

Like all markets in derivatives (i.e., instruments that derive their value based upon some other financial instrument), the futures market is a zero-sum market. What this means is that for each investor who gains one dollar in this market, another investor must lose one dollar; for each long position in the futures market there is an equal, but opposite, short position. In contrast with the stock market, where most investors are long in the market and the average investor gains if the market rises or loses if the market falls, the average investor in the futures market must always earn zero. In fact, the average investor actually does worse than earn zero, because commissions and transaction costs reduce the average net return to below zero—and that's before taxes!

Why would anyone invest in a market where the average net return is negative? Financial futures can be employed in ways that range from highly speculative to ways intended to manage and limit price risks. In general, investors have one of three objectives when investing in financial futures: (1) speculating, (2) hedging, or (3) arbitraging (described in number five in the following list). Therefore, these tools are indicated when investors want to:

1. Speculate on anticipated increases or decreases in the price of the underlying financial instrument, or to speculate on a particular stock, bond, currency, or other financial instrument's performance relative to another's performance. Such individuals can take large risks (which hopefully will result in similarly large returns) by purchasing financial futures contracts at a fraction of the price of actually owning the underlying securities or currencies.

2. Hedge current holdings of a particular position in a financial instrument against the risk of an adverse price change. For example, large financial institutions (e.g., banks and life insurance companies) typically hold large portfolios of mortgages and long-term securities that can fluctuate significantly in price as market conditions change. Such investors can use long or short positions in financial futures to better match the duration of their assets and future liabilities as market conditions or the nature of their liabilities change.

3. Establish, in advance, a definite purchase or selling price for a financial instrument that actually will not be bought or sold until sometime in the future. For instance, a person who has contracted to purchase an expensive foreign product (say a Rolls Royce) with a specified payment due in the foreign currency (pounds) at a future date (say 3 months) faces the risk that the dollar may fall in value relative to the foreign currency (pounds or Euros) in the intervening time. In that case, although the contract price is fixed in the foreign currency, the dollar cost of the product would increase. But this person can buy a currency future today to lock in the future price of the foreign currency without having to put up the entire purchase price in dollars to purchase the foreign currency today.

4. Temporarily alter a stock portfolio's composition—as, for example, between different industry sectors—without having to acquire or liquidate shares of stock. This strategy may be employed for speculative and hedging purposes. For instance, speculators who are trying to time the business cycle through sector-rotation techniques can own a core portfolio that essentially matches the overall stock market. But as they anticipate changes in the business cycle, they can use broad-based equity index futures and narrow-based index futures to increase their effective investment in those sectors they expect to do better, and reduce their effective investment in those sectors they expect to do worse. In contrast, an investor may be bullish on the market for the long term, but is fearful that the current political, economic, or international environment is such that the market may react badly in the relative short run. This investor could take the sell side of broad-based equity futures and reduce the risk associated with a market downturn without the hassle and expense of liquidating or rebalancing a large portion of his stock portfolio.

5. Create investment portfolios with specific risk and reward characteristics by combining stock futures with exchange-traded equity options (i.e., puts and calls). Such strategies can be used for speculative, hedging, or arbitraging purposes. One of the theoretical purposes of the derivatives markets is to make the markets for the underlying securities more efficient. Various combinations of derivatives have risk and return characteristics that are theoretically equivalent to owning the underlying security directly. Consequently, arbitrageurs watch the derivative markets and the underlying security's market to quickly take advantage of any differential between the price of the underlying security itself and the price of the combination of derivatives that is its theoretical equivalent.

9.3.2 FUTURES CONTRACTS

The terms of futures contracts are standardized by the various exchanges where they are traded. The coupon rate, maturity, issuer, and other terms are the same for each contract of a particular type. For example, a contract for 2-Year Treasury Notes will state the value of the underlying bills (typically $200,000), the maturity date of the contract, and the exchange where it is traded. These terms are identical for all similar contracts, and they remain fixed for the life of the contract. The only item that varies is the price of the contract, making for ease of quotation and trading.

Financial futures offer investors a high degree of leverage on their investments because of the low margin requirements involved. For example, the initial margin for the CME Group contract on $200,000 of 2-Year Treasury Notes is less than $1,000. This leverage offers speculators the opportunity for large returns on the relatively small investment they want to make. Low margins also make it possible for institutions to hedge their portfolios at a reasonable cost.

The financial futures market is highly liquid. On any given day billions of dollars of futures contracts will be traded on the various organized exchanges. New positions can be created and old ones closed out with little difficulty, and at relatively low cost in terms of commissions and fees.

All futures contracts are guaranteed by the clearinghouse that processes the transactions. In actuality, the clearinghouse becomes the other side of every trade—the buyer from every seller and the seller to every buyer. This arrangement improves market performance by eliminating concern over the creditworthiness of the opposing parties, assuring delivery of the underlying securities, and adding to flexibility in closing out positions.

Financial futures are an extremely volatile investment area where substantial price changes can take place in a very short period of time. Investors must have both the financial and emotional capacity to operate in this area where gains and losses are settled on a daily basis.

Because all accounts are settled on a daily basis, investors are subject to frequent margin calls, and must be prepared to invest additional funds or risk having their futures positions closed out by the brokerage firm.

Trading strategies in financial futures tend to be complex arrangements compared to many other kinds of investments, such as the simple purchase of a stock or a bond. This is due to the fact that a futures transaction generally accompanies some other investment rather than being carried out in isolation. For example, an investor in a large portfolio of individual stocks may hedge that investment with a broad index futures contract. Keeping track of these multi-part investments requires much more time and energy than most other investments.

Financial futures generally are considered to be "executory contracts" (i.e., contracts that require performance at some future date). Gains and losses on regulated futures contracts are capital gains and losses, regardless of the nature of the underlying property.

Any gain or loss required to be reported by an investor on a futures contract is treated as if 40 percent of the gain or loss is short-term and 60 percent is long-term gain or loss. Net capital gains (i.e., the excess of long-term capital gains over short-term capital losses) are generally taxable at a maximum rate of 20 percent.

Under the "marked-to-market" tax rules, gains and losses on futures contracts owned by an investor at the end of the tax year, or at any time during the year, must be reported annually, even if the investor has not realized such gains or losses. A contract that is still in existence at the end of the year is, therefore, treated as if it were sold for its fair market value on the last business day of that year.

Investors can use put and call stock options to accomplish some of the same purposes as financial futures. Investors with large portfolios of common stocks can use options to hedge their stock positions while increasing the income from those portfolios. Similarly, speculators can purchase calls (puts) in anticipation of an increase (decrease) in stock prices, and invest a relatively small sum compared with the cost of actually buying (or selling) the underlying stock.

Stock purchase warrants also offer some of the same advantages in terms of leverage and relatively low investment that make financial futures attractive. Warrants are particularly attractive to speculators who hope to profit from a much larger percentage increase in the value of a warrant if the underlying stock increases in value.

Another alternative method of participating in futures is through a managed financial futures account, which is similar in concept to a common stock mutual fund. It is the only method of participation in which the investors do not have their own individual trading accounts. Instead, the investor's money is combined with that of other pool participants and, in effect, traded as a single account. Gains or losses are shared in proportion to each participant's investment in the pool. The advantages of this arrangement are that it offers potentially greater diversification of risks, participants' losses are generally limited to their investment in the pool (because most pools are formed as limited partnerships), and the individual participants are not generally subject to margin calls. The disadvantages include the risk of bad management and the additional management fees and organizational or administrative expenses that may reduce the amount available for investment in futures contracts.

9.3.3 PURCHASING FUTURES CONTRACTS

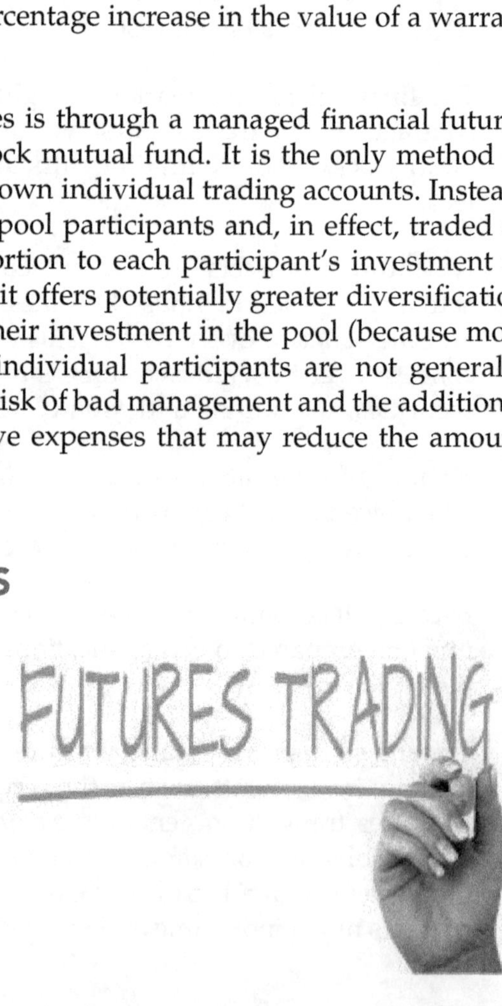

Financial futures are traded on several organized exchanges, most of which are located in either Chicago or New York and most fall under the new CME Group (www.cmegroup.com). Buying or selling financial futures is quite similar in many ways to buying or selling stocks or bonds. Transactions must be carried out through a "margin account" with a brokerage firm that sends orders to the trading floors of the various futures exchanges. Orders are executed on the exchange floor, and the results of the trade are reported back to the brokerage firm, and in turn to the customer.

To execute a transaction an investor can call his broker and state, "Buy a 2-year Treasury note futures contract for my account at 105." This represents a contract for $200,000 face value of U.S. Treasury Notes. The price paid by the investor is 105, or $210,000. But only a relatively small margin position ($1,000) will typically have to be deposited by the investor. A written record of the transaction will be sent to the buyer confirming the transaction. This is the only evidence of the purchase that the investor will receive. This is due to the fact that the futures transaction involves a contract to buy or sell, rather than an actual security.

Once an investor initiates the trade the position of the buyer or seller remains open until one of two events occurs. One possibility is that the buyer will accept delivery of the underlying instruments on the settlement date. The seller of the contract is obligated to make delivery to the buyer. As noted in the Introduction, less than 3 percent of futures contracts are settled in this fashion.

Much more common will be a closing out of the buyer's or seller's position by executing another trade that is the opposite of the first transaction. The buyer sells or the seller buys, and the original positions are offset and eliminated. Continuing our example of the buyer of a Treasury note contract, he may decide to close out his position when the price of the contract reaches 110, or $220,000. At that point he would sell the identical contract and recognize a profit of $10,000, the difference between the purchase price of $210,000 and the sale price of $220,000. (This example does not include commission costs and is intended for illustration purposes only.)

9.3.4 FEES AND OTHER ACQUISITION COSTS

Commissions on the purchase or sale of financial futures contracts are similar to those paid on other security transactions. Brokerage firms typically charge a percentage of the value of the transaction with a minimum commission of $25 or $30. Brokerage charges are relatively high on single unit trades, and most active investors will trade in multiples of five or ten contracts at a time.

9.3.5 SELECTION STRATEGIES

An accurate forecast of interest rates is an essential part of an effective financial futures strategy. Estimating the direction of interest rate changes and the amount of change is critical to establishing profitable contract positions. For example, buyers of financial futures contracts will generally benefit if interest rates fall. When this happens the value of securities such as Treasury bonds will increase, and so will the value of contracts to take delivery on these issues in the future. Sellers of futures contracts will tend to lose money under these circumstances. Conversely, when interest rates rise, buyers of futures contracts will see the value of their contracts decline while sellers will benefit from the fall in value of the underlying securities.

Individuals and institutions seeking to hedge their portfolios should determine the appropriate maturity structure of those portfolios in selecting the best financial futures contract. The portfolio hedged by the futures contract should be of approximately the same maturity as the securities underlying the futures contract. For example, an investor with a long-term bond portfolio would hedge that portfolio by using a futures contract on Treasury bonds rather than one based on short-term Treasury bills.

The period of time until settlement of the futures contract should be considered before any purchase or sale is made. The longer the term of the contract, the more risk is generally involved for sellers and the more advantage for buyers. These conditions are reflected in the price of the contract along with the volatility of the underlying securities.

9.3.6 MINI STOCK INDEX FUTURES

Mini stock index futures contracts are legally binding agreements to buy or sell the cash value of the underlying index at a specific future date. Each of the mini stock index products has a different value. To determine a contract's value, an investor must know its multiplier and the current index futures level.

Example. The CME's E-mini S&P 500 multiplier is $50. If the S&P 500 futures index level is 1,600, multiply that by $50 (1,600 × $50 = $80,000). If an investor purchases one E-mini S&P 500 contract at 1,600, his is trading an instrument with an underlying value of $80,000. Futures contracts move in minimal increments called "ticks," and the value of the tick is different for each product. For example, the E-mini S&P 500 futures tick value is 0.25 futures index point, or $12.50 per contract. Thus, a move of one tick, from 1,600.00 to 1,600.25, equals $12.50. With this move, a long (buying) position would be credited $12.50, and a short (selling) position would be debited $12.50. A move of one entire E-mini S&P 500 futures index point—the equivalent of four ticks—would equal $50, and so on.

Trading mini stock index futures offers investors many advantages, including:

- *Exposure to the Leading U.S. and Foreign Stocks* – Investors now can have exposure to the S&P 500, S&P 400 Midcap, S&P Asia 50, NASDAQ Composite, NASDAQ-100, NASDAQ Biotechnology, Russell 1000, Russell 2000, NYSE Composite, MSCI EAFE, and Value Line Indexes with just one futures trade.

- *Affordability* – Mini stock index futures (generally) require one-fifth the margin of the standard futures contracts, enabling investors to control a large basket of stocks for a fraction of the cost.

- *Opportunity* – These futures contracts provide a variety of investment opportunities, including: the choice of taking a bullish or bearish position; the ability to increase or hedge portfolio exposure; and the ability to spread against other index products.

- *Accessibility* – Mini stock index futures provide investors with online opportunities to take advantage of market moves virtually twenty-four hours a day.

- *Integrity* – CME customers and members are protected from default on futures and options contracts by the exchange's sophisticated risk management and surveillance processes. The CME Clearing House acts as guarantor to each of its clearing members, thus ensuring the integrity of all trades. CME's system has proven to be outstandingly effective, even under the most stressful market conditions. The other exchanges have similar measures to insure the integrity of the transactions on their exchanges.

Stock index futures are cash settled, just like their standard contract counterparts; thus, there is no delivery of the individual stocks. Likewise, mini stock index futures' daily settlements and quarterly expirations use the same price as the standard index futures. Identical daily settlement prices allow mini contracts to benefit from the liquidity of the larger contracts. Like the standard index futures contracts, all mini stock index futures positions are settled in cash to the respective standard contract on the third Friday of the quarterly contract month. The final settlement price for S&P 500 futures is based on the opening prices of the component stocks in the index, or on the last sale price of a stock that does not open for trading on the regular scheduled day of the final settlement.

9.4 COMMODITY FUTURES

Section Overview:

9.4.1 Commodity Futures Contracts

9.4.2 Characteristics

9.4.3 Purchasing Commodities Futures Contracts

9.4.4 Selection Strategies

9.4.1 COMMODITY FUTURES CONTRACTS

A commodity purchase represents ownership of a definite physical item such as oil, natural gas, sugar, wheat, corn, lumber, or pork bellies. Other commodities include orange juice, cotton, cocoa, coffee, and eggs. The purchaser is buying—not a paper ownership right—but the actual item itself. The units of purchase are measured by given weights, sizes, or shapes. For example, a wheat contract may be described as "No. 2, soft red winter wheat" and each contract represents a 5,000 bushel purchase.

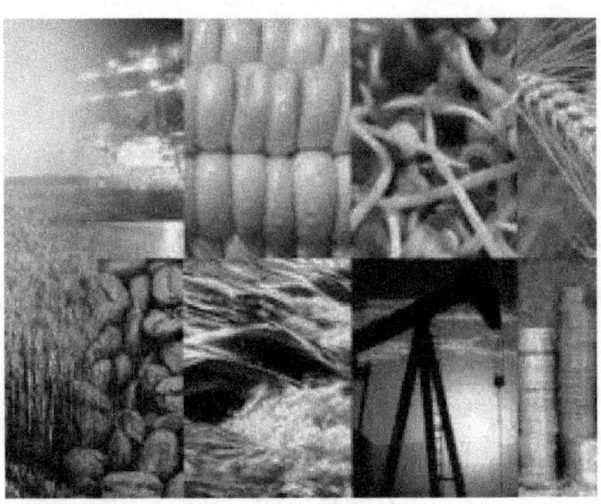

Most investors purchasing commodities buy a contract to either make or accept a delivery of a specified commodity on a given future date—thus the term "futures contract." As noted in the previous chapter, futures are standardized contracts calling for future delivery of a specified number or notional value of a specified asset, for a specified price, at a designated future date. If the contract runs to its termination, the investor must complete the contract by either making a delivery of the commodity or paying cash in acceptance of the commodity. Despite stories of carloads of wheat or corn being dumped on someone's lawn, the vast majority (over 96 percent) of commodity futures contracts are closed out before they mature.

Weather can have a large impact on the price of commodities. Additionally it can impact other industries such as the insurance industry. As a result of the need to hedge against changes in temperature and major storms a market has developed for weather derivatives – both futures and options.

Commodities contracts are most frequently used:

1. When the investor is willing to take very high risks. Although the potential rewards of commodities trading are extremely high (it is possible for an investor to double his money in only a few days), over 70 percent of commodities speculators will lose money, and aggregate losses are typically five to six times greater than gains.

2. When the investor is able to risk substantial amounts of capital to meet the minimum necessary to enter a contract, allow reasonable diversification of positions, and to respond to margin calls. Margin is an amount of money deposited by both buyers and sellers of futures contracts to ensure performance of the terms of the contract. A brokerage firm may "call" for additional margin to bring the funds in a customer's account up to the required level.

3. When the investor desires a very high degree of leverage in his investments. This leverage comes from the low margin requirements on commodities investments. Compared to margins of 50 percent when investing in common stocks, margins on commodity investments are extremely low. An investor can finance 90 to 95 percent of the value of the contract at the time of purchase. (The actual cash required will vary according to the commodity and the standards of the broker handling the transaction.) The margin for commodities is considered a security deposit. Therefore, unlike margins for securities that are interest bearing, the investor pays no interest on the unpaid balance in a commodities contract.

4. When the investor has the emotional stability to accept frequent and possibly significant losses. Clearly, commodities trading is not for the fainthearted.

5. When the producer of a particular commodity would like to hedge one risk by taking an offsetting one. For example, assume a farmer plants winter wheat. He has calculated that he must receive a price of $ X.XX per bushel to break even. Yet, he has no assurance of what the price will be when he is ready to bring the wheat to market. To assure himself of at least a minimum price he enters into a futures contract guaranteeing a price of $ Y.YY per bushel upon delivery of the wheat. If the cash market price is below the price guaranteed in the futures contract, the farmer will exercise the contract, deliver the wheat, and obtain his expected profit. Conversely, if the cash price is above the contract price, the farmer will likely sell his wheat in the cash market, buy back his futures contract, and presumably increase his profit.

6. When a seller or buyer of commodities, for which price can vary based on weather changes, or a company which could be impacted by the occurrence or non-occurrence of a significant weather event such as a hurricane or record snowfall desire to hedge their exposure.

In essence, the futures exchange serves the function of finding someone to complete the opposite side of the contract. That someone is the investor (speculator). This individual assumes the risk because he feels he can profit from price movements before the delivery date of the contract. For example, the speculator may feel that wheat prices will rise sharply in the next few months, and that there will be a corresponding increase in the value of his contract (because the contract gives him the right to buy wheat at a fixed price below the expected market price).

9.4.2 CHARACTERISTICS

A speculator in commodities has the potential of making enormous profits in a relatively short period of time. Assume corn is selling at $5.00 per bushel and an investor purchases one 5,000 bushel contract. Instead of putting up $25,000, he is allowed to deposit only $2,700. If the price of corn rises to $5.50 (a price change of only 10 percent), he will have made a profit of $2,500 ($0.50 × 5,000 bushels), less commissions. But, comparing his profit of $2,500 to his outlay of $2,700, the percentage return is 93 percent (lowered slightly by commissions).

For a given investment budget, the extremely low margin requirements for commodities permit more diversification than would be possible in the stock and bond markets.

Producers of various commodities can transfer the risk of price changes to speculators and lock in a particular price when they bring their commodity to market.

An investor's position can be completely wiped out by a relatively small change in the price of the commodity. This is due to the very low margin requirements of the contract, and the inherent volatility of the commodity markets. In the example above, the investor purchased a 5,000-bushel contract for corn selling at $5.00 per bushel. Instead of putting up $25,000, his broker allows him to deposit only $2,700. If the price of corn were to drop by $0.55 per bushel, the value of the contract would have declined by $2,700 and his margin would have been eliminated. This would result in a call from his broker for additional margin in order to maintain his position.

It is very likely that an investor who puts up small amounts of margin will often have that margin eliminated. Unless the investor is willing to put up additional margin, his position will be closed out and the contract terminated. This may occur a number of times before the investor will be able to discern and follow a trend in the market.

Unlike other securities markets, positions in commodities are marked-to-the-market on a daily basis. This means that at the close of trading each day, the clearinghouse for the exchange calculates the gains and losses on all open positions and transfers those gains or losses into or out of all margin accounts. Profits may be withdrawn by an investor, but losses are deducted immediately from the investor's account. If the remaining margin declines below the level of the required maintenance margin, a margin call will be issued asking that additional funds be added to the account to bring it back to the minimum margin level. Should the investor fail to do so, his position will be closed by the firm handling his account. In other words, the brokerage firm will terminate the investor's interest in the contract. It does this by either buying or selling an offsetting contract.

Each commodity has a daily price limit, and once that limit is reached trading stops for the day. For example, the maximum daily price movement for soybeans, one of the most active commodity markets, is seventy cents per bushel. This represents a value of $3,500 per contract on a 5,000 bushel contract. The purpose of this limit is to protect the commodity markets from severe price fluctuations that could result from news of crop damage, weather reports, and other natural or market occurrences. This restriction on trading can cause the investor to be locked in to a position when the market is unavailable to buy or sell the commodity.

For instance, Mary Satin owns a futures contract for wheat. A newly issued crop report indicates a tremendous surplus that causes a panic in the market. Prices fall sharply, and before Mary can act, the drop in price has reached the maximum daily limit. That causes all trading in wheat to stop and Mary is forced to hold her contract until trading resumes. By that time it may be even more difficult to close out her position.

Net gains on all speculative commodity futures contracts are taxed at a maximum effective rate of 23 percent. This is due to the fact that net gains on all speculative transactions are treated as though they are 40 percent short-term capital gains and 60 percent long-term capital gains. The usual holding period rule for determining whether a gain or loss is short-term or long-term is ignored.

All open positions (those that have not been closed out, exercised, or that have expired) at the end of the tax year are treated as if they had been closed on the last day of the year. In other words, any gain or loss inherent in a futures contract at the end of the year (or at any time during the year) must be reported annually, even if the investor has not actually realized those gains or losses. Therefore, if a contract has not been terminated or transferred before the end of the tax year, it is artificially treated as though the investor had sold it for its fair market value on the last business day of the year. Profits or losses from these open positions are combined with those positions that were actually closed during the rest of the year.

Net futures trading losses may be applied against the investor's other capital gains. If a net loss on futures transactions still exists, these may be carried back three years. If any loss still remains it may be carried forward into succeeding years.

Rather than buying commodities directly, an investor may purchase shares in a mutual fund that specializes in these investments. This alternative is especially attractive for the individual who does not have the expertise or time necessary to watch his investments on a day-to-day basis. Such attention is absolutely essential in the commodities area due to the rapid price movements and low margin positions. Commodity funds offer professional management and the constant attention demanded by this volatile market.

A commodity pool is an alternative to mutual funds, but has many of the same characteristics. For instance, in order to participate in a diversified portfolio of commodity futures with professional management, individuals will purchase units in the pool. Their money is combined and invested in a number of active commodities. In many cases the pool will be closed out when 50 percent of the original capital is lost. These are normally structured as limited partnerships requiring a minimum investment of $5,000 or more. In addition to a minimum investment, these pools typically require that investors have a minimum income and wealth position.

9.4.3 PURCHASING COMMODITIES FUTURES CONTRACTS

Investors may trade contracts on commodities through their brokerage firms in much the same way as they buy and sell securities. A separate margin account is required and settlement on this account will be made on a daily basis as described above.

An investor may also take part in a so-called managed account program with a particular commodities broker or trading firm. Under this arrangement, the commodities broker has the discretionary power to trade for the investor's account. An added characteristic of these managed accounts is that the broker may participate in the profits earned on the account in addition to any commissions that may be generated by the trading activity.

Investors may also invest in commodities through mutual funds that may be purchased through a broker or, in the case of some funds, directly from the fund itself. Minimum investments generally range from $1,000 up to $10,000. An advantage of these funds is that they enable individuals to participate in a portfolio of commodity contracts that provides a degree of diversification that the small investor may not be able to achieve otherwise.

A commission or service charge is applied to a commodities trade in much the same fashion as the buying or selling of stocks and bonds.

9.4.4 SELECTION STRATEGIES

Investors should concentrate their attention on a few commodities rather than spread their investment over a large number of different contracts. More time and effort will be needed to follow commodity positions than similar investments in stocks and bonds, and the average investor will generally be less knowledgeable about commodity markets.

Select markets that are active and that have a large open interest (i.e., the number of contracts in a commodity that have not been closed out, exercised, or allowed to expire). The level of open interest is reported daily in newspaper commodity pages and on websites such as that of the CME Group (www.cmegroup.com). Conversely, beginning investors should avoid "thin" markets that are especially prone to volatile price swings because of the relatively low number of contracts and the small number of active traders. Some of the more active commodities are soybeans, wheat, cocoa, and copper.

Inexperienced traders should begin with a conservative position of one or two contracts that mature in a distant month. This will require a relatively small investment and give the investor time to study the market and get better acquainted with its characteristics before making greater commitments. Also, buying contracts in distant months will reduce the amount of trading and the amount of commissions charged.

It is generally a good idea to put in a stop-loss order 5 percent below the market price when buying a commodity, and 5 percent above the market for a short sale. This approach will limit the investor's losses while allowing for continued gains if the market moves in the anticipated direction.

Be careful of putting up additional margin to maintain a contract. If asked to do so it means that the market is moving against the investor and will likely continue to do so. It is better to liquidate this position and take a small loss rather than continue to increase the investment and risk a major loss of capital.

This is an area where an experienced adviser is invaluable. Investors should look for a firm with a strong background in commodities, and deal with a broker who is a specialist in the field. It is not likely that a broker whose area of expertise is stocks and bonds will also be knowledgeable in the area of commodities. Diversified investors may want to maintain a separate brokerage account for their commodities trading activity.

Chapter 10

ALTERNATIVE INVESTMENTS

10.1 REAL ESTATE

Section Overview:

10.1.1 TYPES OF REAL ESTATE INVESTMENTS

Real estate is land and the buildings and improvements on land. Real estate, by definition, includes natural assets, such as minerals, under the land. Because of the obvious limited supply of land, especially in desirable locations, real estate has long been viewed as an attractive investment alternative.

Real estate typically is classified into four major categories:

1. Land
2. Residential
3. Commercial
4. Industrial

Land – can be subdivided into five subcategories: (a) unimproved; (b) farm land; (c) recreational; (d) ranches; and (e) subdivided lots.

Residential – can be subdivided into three subcategories: (a) single family dwellings; (b) multiple family dwellings (such as apartments and condominiums); and (c) hotels and motels (transient dwellings).

Commercial – can be subdivided into five subcategories: (a) residential rental; (b) office buildings; (c) retail stores; (d) shopping centers; and (e) specialty buildings (such as banks, movie theaters, stadiums, and bowling alleys).

Industrial – can be subdivided into four subcategories: (a) factories; (b) warehouses; (c) industrial parks; and (d) utility facilities (such as power plants).

An investor should select the type of real estate that will best meet the specific objectives of the investment plan. For example, unimproved land can provide substantial, long-term appreciation, but usually will not generate any significant current flow of income.

Investors should consider real estate investments when they:

1. Desire an investment with tax shelter potential;
2. Need a long-term hedge against inflation;
3. Require a relatively constant cash flow;
4. Are looking for long-term appreciation;
5. Prefer a tangible investment (many investors – for psychological reasons – are more comfortable with an asset that they can see, touch, and physically possess); and
6. Want to make maximum use of leverage (lenders are willing to advance large sums of money on the security of real estate for long periods of time at relatively low interest, because real estate is not only tangible and stationary, but is also reasonably stable in value).

10.1.2 ADVANTAGES OF REAL ESTATE INVESTING

Real estate has numerous different tax related advantages:

a) Owners may deduct:

i. Expenditures that are considered ordinary and necessary in the production or collection of income or in the preservation of the real estate's value as an investment;

ii. The costs of supplies, labor, and other components necessary to keep the property in good repair;

iii. Real estate property taxes;

iv. Interest on the unpaid balance of the mortgage (subject to limitations imposed by the tax law); and

v. Losses incurred on the sale of real estate (subject to limitations discussed later).

b) A tenant leasing business property may deduct reasonable rental costs;

c) The full cost of buildings and real estate improvements (i.e., cost excluding land) is depreciable.

d) Sellers may report gain on the sale of real estate over more than one taxable year. This may allow the investor to defer the payment of tax until they receive cash proceeds from an "installment sale" of the property (although interest payments may be due on certain deferred tax liabilities).

e) One parcel of real estate can be exchanged for another without the immediate recognition of taxable income. Tax on appreciation can be postponed an indefinite number of times (and for an indefinite period of time) if each trade meets the strict requirements of the tax-free exchange rule of the Internal Revenue Code (Code section 1031).

f) Upon the involuntary conversion of real estate (such as through fire or condemnation), the investor does not have to pay any tax upon the receipt of cash from insurance or condemnation award, so long as the cash is reinvested in qualified property (essentially property of similar use) having equal or greater value.

g) Liquidity (cash) can be obtained from real estate, including any appreciation, without paying taxes, through a mortgage on the property. (Of course, upon sale of the property, the investor is taxed upon the entire appreciation.)

h) The cost of rehabilitating certain buildings or structures may qualify for a special investment tax credit.

However, real estate is also subject to special passive activity tax rules that may limit the ability to use real estate losses to offset income from other sources.

Real estate is tangible. As mentioned earlier, many investors prefer an asset that can be seen, touched, fenced in, and built upon. It feels more "real" than intangible investments, such as life insurance or common stocks, which do not exist in a physical sense.

Real estate has historically proven itself as an excellent hedge against inflation. Real estate tends to increase in value while prices are rising and the value of the dollar is declining.

Each parcel of real estate is unique. Because no two parcels can share the same location, no two can be exactly alike. The monopoly each real estate owner has on each individual location is itself of value.

Because of its great value as security for a loan, real estate enables an investor to obtain maximum potential leverage.

10.1.3 DISADVANTAGES OF REAL ESTATE INVESTING

Real estate is almost always relatively illiquid. Because there is no organized market on the national or local level for real estate comparable to the stock or commodity exchanges, real estate is difficult to convert to cash quickly.

Other reasons that real estate is not as liquid as other investments include: (a) the usual difficulty in finding a willing buyer at the desired selling price (because the property must suit the buyer with respect to a multiplicity of factors, including location, financing, timing, potential income, etc.); (b) the length of time involved in the closing process (typically thirty to ninety days); and (c) the need for the purchaser to obtain financing in most cases.

Some degree of management is necessary with all real estate investments. For example, a properly managed real estate investment requires that someone maintain the physical premises, collect rents, and pay bills. If investors do not possess the requisite expertise (or do not have the time or inclination to obtain or exercise that expertise) they must hire a professional manager. This makes many small real estate investments impractical.

Typically, the investment in real estate is large in amount and will require the commitment of investable funds for a long period of time. Compared to stocks, which investors can purchase for as low as pennies per share and can sell nearly instantaneously, real estate requires many thousands of dollars (not all of which need be put up by the investor, but can be leveraged) that may remain locked in for many years.

Costs related to the purchase or sale of real estate reduce its value as an investment that can produce a short-term gain. Such costs, which include transfer taxes, title insurance, appraisals, financing fees and "points," title recording and notary fees, and sales commissions, may run as high as 10 percent to 15 percent of the cost of the real estate itself.

Real estate, by definition, cannot be moved. This immobility can become a distinct disadvantage when the investor moves to a new location and can no longer properly manage the investment personally.

Once land has been improved with a building, this improvement is often difficult and expensive to modify or remove. For instance, a building designed as a warehouse can be converted to an apartment house to meet a shift in market demand, but only at great expense and considerable trouble. This disadvantage is often referred to as "fixity" of investment.

It is often difficult or impossible to assess the economic risks and projected return on a real estate investment with any degree of exactness. This is because factors that are difficult to forecast – such as changes in consumer demand, levels of maintenance and repair expenses, and changes in tax laws – are involved in the analysis.

Because the investment return on real estate is significantly affected by the available tax benefits, such investments are most susceptible to the risk of challenge by the IRS.

10.1.4 TAX IMPLICATIONS

All the ordinary and necessary expenses, paid or incurred by a real estate investor during the taxable year in carrying on a trade or business, are deductible. Deductible expenses include costs incurred in the production or the collection of investment income. Expenditures for the management, conservation, or maintenance of real estate property held either to produce income or for appreciation are also deductible.

Typical deductible expenses that a real estate investor might incur include utilities such as electric and gas, rental commissions, trash removal, and insurance.

Routine repair and maintenance expenses – those that do not appreciably add to the value of the property or significantly add to its life span but merely keep it in efficient running order – are deductible in the year the outlay is incurred.

The cost of most improvements must be capitalized. This means that the owner cannot currently deduct the cost of an item that increases the longevity or the value or alters the use for which the property is suitable. However, investors can add such expenditures to their basis in the property. They then recover such capitalized costs through depreciation deductions in future years.

Amounts paid for real property taxes (subject to a limitation for certain taxes incurred during construction) are deductible when paid. The tax permits investors to deduct real estate taxes paid in the year the property is acquired. However, the buyer and the seller must allocate those taxes on a day-by-day basis between themselves according to the number of days, during the year, that each owns the property.

Certain taxes are in fact improvement assessments that add to the value of the property. Owners, therefore, must capitalize these assessments rather than currently deduct them. Examples of such taxes include assessments for sidewalks and sewers. The owners may deduct the cost of these items over a period of years according to a cost recovery schedule provided in the Internal Revenue Code.

Owners must also capitalize construction period taxes and then amortize them as part of the basis of the constructed property. Therefore, owners must depreciate such capitalized taxes only over the applicable depreciable life of the property.

Lessees may currently deduct rental expenses for the use of business property. This deduction by the lessee of property enables the owner/investor of the property to charge a higher rental, thus increasing the value of the property.

Owners who pay interest on amounts borrowed to finance the purchase of investment real estate may deduct the interest currently. However, investors must consider certain special rules, which may limit the deductibility of:

a) construction period interest;

b) investment interest;

c) prepaid interest;

d) "points;" and

e) passive losses.

Owners must capitalize construction period interest and add it to the basis of the property being constructed. For example, if an investor incurred $10,000 of interest expense during a one-year construction period, the investor could not deduct any of the interest paid in that year's return.

Instead, the investor could depreciate the interest as part of the cost of the constructed property over the applicable depreciable life of the property once the property is placed in service.

Financing through debt is almost universal in real estate investment. This makes it critical that the adviser and the client be aware that there are limitations on the deduction of interest expense.

Real estate investments are subject to the at risk rules, which may limit the deductibility of losses from real estate that is leveraged.

Land is not depreciable. But improvements upon the land are eligible for depreciation deductions. In fact, in most cases the tax losses generated by depreciation deductions are the most important part of the tax shelter afforded by real estate. However, such tax losses are subject to the passive activity rules.

The key to the tax shelter value of real estate lies in the fact that depreciation is a non-cash charge against income. Depreciation creates an artificial loss enabling an investor to recover the cost of the asset over a specified period of time. In many cases, this tax benefit precedes any actual cost (resulting from reduction in the value of the property due to wear and tear or obsolescence). In addition, by financing (i.e., using leverage), the investor may depreciate the full cost of the building and improvements even though the investor (a) borrowed most of the costs from the mortgagee, (b) may have no personal liability on the mortgage debt (nonrecourse debt), and (c) may not make the actual cash outlays to repay the debt for many years.

Sellers can defer the tax on the gain upon the sale of real estate. Subject to certain limitations, the installment sale rules of Code section 453 permit investors to delay reporting any gains or paying any taxes until they receive money. For example, an individual in a high tax bracket this year could agree to sell the property before year-end but defer receipt of any sales proceeds until next year. In fact, installment sales rules are so flexible that a seller does not need to accept any cash proceeds for five, or ten, or even fifteen years. The law does not set a limit as to how long the parties can agree to extend the payment period. As long as the seller will receive at least one payment after the close of the taxable year in which the disposition occurs, the seller may apply the installment sale rules to defer tax.

Parties to sales often use installment sales as a vehicle for financing the sale, in lieu of (or in addition to) third party financing, such as from a bank. However, just as a bank requires the payment of interest for the use of the unpaid balance of the loan, the tax law "expects" that the parties will provide for interest on the loan inherent in an installment sale. Tax law cannot dictate the stated interest rate agreed to by the parties or even that there be interest actually charged. But, if an interest obligation is not stated in the installment sale agreement, or if the stated rate is insufficient under the law, IRC Section 483 will treat a portion of the sales price as built-in interest.

This imputation of interest on the unpaid balance of the sales proceeds has the effect of reducing the potential capital gain on the sale of the property, and increasing the ordinary income to the seller.

Example. Alex Benjamin sells a parcel of unimproved land to Sara Gail for $500,000. Alex paid $100,000 for the land five years ago. Alex agrees to accept $200,000 in cash at closing, with the balance in installments of $100,000 on January 1 of each of the next three years.

It appears the sales price is $500,000. But when interest is imputed on the $300,000 unpaid balance, it becomes obvious that if part of that $300,000 is treated as interest, then the real sales price must be significantly less than $500,000. In this example, if the Internal Revenue Service were to impute a 10 percent interest rate on the $300,000 unpaid balance, the effect would be to treat approximately $51,314 of the total installment payment as interest (taxable to the seller and deductible by the buyer) and only $248,686 of the installment payments as principal. For tax purposes, the total sales price would be only $448,686 ($200,000 received at settlement plus the $248,686 principal payments on the installments). The adjusted capital gain would be $348,686 ($448,686 adjusted sales proceeds less $100,000 basis).

The benefits of installment sales of real estate may be limited if the seller pledged the installment receivable as security for a loan. This limitation, as well as other restrictions on the use of the installment method.

In addition, the purchaser of real estate that is financed by seller-provided installment sale debt will be subject to the at risk rules, which may limit the deductibility of certain losses. Investors who incur losses on the sale of real estate held for investment or used in a trade or business generally may deduct the losses in the year incurred. Such losses are measured by the excess of (a) the investor's adjusted basis (generally cost less accumulated depreciation) in the property over (b) the proceeds from the sale of the property.

Losses incurred upon the sale of personal use realty, such as an individual's residence, are not deductible (even if the owner expected the property to appreciate).

The tax treatment for losses incurred on the sale of real property held purely for investment (such as unimproved land) will be different from the treatment of losses from the sale of real property used in a trade or business (such as a manufacturing plant).

Real estate held purely for investment is treated as a capital asset. If all capital losses exceed all capital gains, they offset ordinary income dollar-for-dollar up to a maximum of $3,000 per year. Any unused losses may be carried forward.

Real property used in a trade or business is not a capital asset. Such property, if held for the long-term holding period before being sold, is called "Section 1231 Property." A loss from the sale of real estate that is Section 1231 property is totaled with all other losses and gains from the sale of Section 1231 property recognized during the year. If the net of all Section 1231 gains and losses is a gain, the net gain will be treated as a capital gain. If the net of all Section 1231 gains and losses is a loss, the total loss will be treated as an ordinary loss.

It is possible, under certain circumstances, for an investor to trade (exchange) properties with another party and postpone all or a portion of the gain that would normally have to be recognized on a sale. This postponement or partial avoidance of taxation is known as a "like-kind" exchange. (Although this is sometimes referred to as a tax-free exchange because no tax is payable at the time of the transaction, it is more proper to refer to it as a tax deferred exchange; the tax on the exchange is usually paid when the property received in the transaction is subsequently sold.)

Owners also may often defer tax upon what is known as an involuntary conversion. Involuntary conversion is the destruction of property by fire or other casualty. Involuntary conversions may also arise when a governmental body condemns a property using its right to take private property and convert it to a public use.

When the investor receives payment through insurance or governmental compensation for property involuntarily converted, tax law treats that money as if it were the proceeds from a sale. Fortunately, the owners of the condemned property can usually defer any realized gain on that "sale" if the investor reinvests the full proceeds in similar (like kind) property within three years from the end of the year in which they receive the proceeds. If dispossessed owners reinvest less than their entire proceeds, they can defer only a proportionate amount of the gain.

Investors can convert part of the appreciated value of property into cash without either selling it or otherwise triggering a tax on any gain. They can accomplish this by using the property as security for a loan. However, there may be limitations on the deductibility of the loan interest.

The cost of constructing or rehabilitating certain buildings or structures may qualify for a special investment tax credit. The properties eligible for this credit include: (a) qualified low-income housing; (b) certified historic structures; and (c) buildings that were first placed in service before 1936.

Few investments are comparable to real estate because of its unique characteristics, location, and potential for significant tax shelter benefits, relatively constant cash flow, and psychological comfort. Other investments, such as stocks, do provide a long-term hedge against inflation, the possibility of substantial appreciation, and the potential to maximize the use of leverage. However, no other investments possess all these characteristics to the extent of real estate.

10.1.5 PURCHASING REAL ESTATE INVESTMENTS

An individual typically will purchase real estate in his own name directly from the seller or through a real estate broker or agent. However, most investors acquiring real estate for tax shelter investment purposes purchase an interest in a partnership or other investment entity.

Investors may hold real estate in any of the following forms:

a) outright ownership;

b) general partnership or joint venture;

c) limited partnership;

d) corporate (C corporation);

e) S corporation;

f) Limited Liability Company (LLC); or

g) Real Estate Investment Trust (REIT).

Each of these forms of ownership has advantages and disadvantages with respect to the liability incurred, management efforts required, income tax implications, transferability, and continuity of the entity upon the death of the investor.

Outright ownership of real estate does not protect the individual investor from full personal liability relating to the ownership and operation of the property. For example, an investor can be held financially accountable for negligent acts resulting in injury to a visitor on the property. Debts incurred with respect to the investment typically require the personal guarantees of the outright owner and therefore subject all his other assets to the claims of creditors.

An outright owner has full management responsibility. Owners can hire agents, however, to assume such tasks as maintenance, rental collection, and paying the bills.

All the tax benefits and costs of outright ownership are personal to the investor. The investor's individual tax return will reflect the taxable income and deductible expenses of the property.

An outright owner can convey the title to all or a portion of the property at any time without restriction.

The death of an individual owner results in the termination of the individual ownership form. The property will then pass through the investor's estate to his heirs or by operation of law to his joint owners.

General Partnership

A general partnership is one in which two or more individuals join together for investment purposes. Usually, a general partner is jointly and individually liable for all the debts and any obligations incurred by the partnership.

If a partner cannot pay his part of the obligations of a partnership, the remaining partners are liable to the total extent of their financial resources. Suppose Howard and Jonathan form a partnership and each invested $30,000 in cash that is used to buy real estate. A visitor slips on the doorstep and successfully sues the partnership for $80,000. Howard has no assets other than his investment in the partnership. Jonathan has other investments totaling $500,000. Assuming there is no insurance; the injured party would first take over the partnership property (worth $60,000) and then look to Jonathan for the remaining $20,000.

By law, all the general partners may be held responsible for the management of the property. However, usually only one or a few partners are actively involved in operations. Subject to specific exceptions included in the partnership agreement, each general partner has the authority to bind the partnership (and therefore the other partners) to any contracts or commitments.

The tax code does not tax partnerships as separate entities. In general (absent any special allocation provisions), income, deductions, and credits flow through to the partners according to their proportionate ownership. Each partner reports his share of partnership income, deductions, and credits as if each owned that percentage of the property individually. A partner's share of partnership losses is deductible only to the extent of his basis (investment) in the partnership.

The terms of the partnership agreement generally spell out the partners' rights to transfer their interests in the property. Such agreements generally preclude the sale or gift of an individual's partnership interest without approval of the other partners or without first offering that interest to the other partners.

The death of an individual partner may cause the termination of the partnership unless the terms of the partnership agreement provide otherwise. In most cases, the partnership agreement provides for the purchase of the deceased partner's interest by the remaining partners.

Limited Partnership

A limited partnership permits certain partners (so-called, limited partners) the benefit of limited liability. (Such partnerships must have at least one general partner with full liability.) For this reason, limited partnerships are quite popular as a means of owning real estate. In fact, most tax shelter real estate investments are syndicated in this form.

Many limited partnership investments are heavily leveraged. Where the limited partners are not at risk to pay a proportionate amount of the debt in the event the partnership activities cannot generate enough cash to pay off the loans, the limited partners generally cannot fully deduct partnership losses.

Limited partners are passive investors and cannot actively participate in daily management without risking full personal liability. (However, limited partners may participate in general policy decisions concerning the long-term goals of the venture.) Management authority in a limited partnership is vested solely in the general partner.

As in the case of a general partnership (absent some kind of special allocation arrangement), income, deductions, and credits of a limited partnership flow through to the partners according to their proportionate ownership. Each partner, whether general or limited, reports his share of partnership income, deductions, and credits as if each owned that percentage of the property individually. A limited partner's share of partnership losses is deductible only to the extent of the partner's basis (investment) in the partnership.

Also similar to general partnerships, the terms of the partnership agreement typically restrict a limited partner's rights to transfer his interest in the property. However, limited partnership agreements generally are more restrictive than general partnership agreements in precluding the transferability of an individual's partnership interest.

The death of an individual limited partner generally will not cause the termination of the partnership. In most cases, the partnership agreement provides for the deceased partner's heirs to succeed to his interest. However, the death of the sole general partner who is an individual may cause the dissolution of the partnership, unless the partnership agreement provides for a successor general partner. This is one reason why many general partners are corporations.

The most common form of tax shelter-oriented real estate investment ownership is a limited partnership. Interests in such a partnership are generally sold by real estate syndicators.

A syndicated partnership consists of two types of owners, the syndicator-promoters (sometimes referred to as developers) and the investors. A promoter typically will acquire a property (sometimes the promoter will merely obtain an option to buy the property) and then attempt to sell it to a group of investors. In addition to fees, the promoter will retain an ownership interest as a portion of the compensation for its efforts. Alternatively, promoters may form an investment group, raise cash, and then seek to obtain suitable property on behalf of the investors.

Investors with an interest in a syndication can obtain information through a representative of a registered broker-dealer. An offering brochure (usually called an offering memorandum) is provided to potential investors and describes the objectives, benefits, and risks of the venture.

Corporation

A major benefit of investing in corporate form is the limited liability it provides. This applies whether the corporation is being taxed as a regular (C) corporation or has elected to be taxed as an S corporation. Specifically, the investor is not personally liable for negligent acts of the corporation and its employees and officers. Unless the investor has been personally negligent (outside his role as a corporate employee), full liability stops with the corporation.

Limited liability also applies to corporate borrowing; technically, a creditor can look only to the corporation for payment of a debt and may not reach through to the assets of the individual shareholders. But, as a matter of practice, many lenders will not make loans to closely-held corporations unless the individual shareholders personally cosign or guarantee payment of the debt. Once a shareholder does sign as an individual, the lender can look to that person for payment if the corporation defaults on its obligations.

Centralized management is another feature of the corporate form. The responsibility to manage and authority to run a corporation rests with the board of directors elected by the shareholders. These directors, who typically in closely-held corporations are the controlling shareholders, select officers to handle the day-to-day operations. (Often these officers are also shareholders and members of the board of directors. But it is also common for shareholders to be purely passive investors who do not participate in any way in the operation or management of the company.)

Continuity of life is another feature of the corporate form. A corporation does not terminate at the death of one or more of its owners. Legally, the corporation has an indefinite life. This continuity enhances the corporation's ability to raise large amounts of capital for long-term investment.

Finally, enhanced transferability of interests is another feature of the corporate form. A shareholder in a regular corporation (unless restricted by corporate bylaws or a shareholders' agreement) can transfer any number of shares to any party at any time. A shareholder in an S corporation has similar freedom of transferability. However, the transfer of shares to certain restricted parties (see next section) will terminate S corporation status.

A regular (C) corporation is treated for tax purposes as a tax entity entirely separate from its owners. A C corporation must file its own tax return and its income is subject to a special corporate income tax rate schedule. Because the corporation is considered a separate tax entity, once it earns and pays tax on the income, the net remaining after taxes belongs to the corporation itself, and not its shareholders. Those net corporate earnings generally can be distributed to the shareholders only as a dividend, which is then taxable to them upon receipt.

Note that corporate earnings paid to shareholders typically will be taxed twice, once to the corporation and then again to the shareholders when paid out to them. This means that the real estate investor operating in corporate form suffers two disadvantages: first, the earnings of the investment are taxed twice and, second, if the corporation operates at a loss, that loss can be utilized only by the corporate entity and cannot be passed through to the investor.

S Corporation

An S corporation is treated essentially the same as a C corporation except for taxation. However, S corporations also are subject to certain shareholder limitations designed to insure that income is still taxed at the shareholder level. The S corporation may not have more than 100 shareholders, all of whom are individuals or certain trusts, none of whom are nonresident aliens, and may not have more than one class of stock. An S corporation in many respects is taxed similarly to a partnership. Although it provides the corporate benefits of limited liability, centralized management, continuity of life, and free transferability of interests, its profits, losses, deductions, and credits are passed through the entity to the tax returns of the individual shareholders.

Essentially, the corporation pays no federal income tax. The shareholders are taxed on the net income of the S corporation, whether or not it is distributed to them.

The obvious advantage of an S corporation to investors is this ability to enjoy the benefits of partnership-like flow-through taxation. The total of the deductions for interest, depreciation, and other expenses of operating and maintaining the investment property is netted against the corporation's operating income. A shareholder's share of losses is deductible only to the extent of the shareholder's (a) basis in the stock, plus (b) the amount of any loans which may have been made by the shareholder to the corporation. A shareholder can carry forward to future years any losses disallowed in a given year as a result of this limitation.

Limited Liability Company (LLC)

Limited Liability Companies (LLCs) combine the limited liability protection of corporations for all owners with the pass-through of tax items (such as income, deductions, and credits) of partnerships. Before 1990, only Wyoming and Florida had enabling statutes for LLCs. However, with the explosion of LLC laws in the mid-1990s, this business entity form is used for many purposes including professional service firms, family businesses, and numerous others, including holding and managing real estate.

Briefly, LLCs are noncorporate entities under which neither the owners (known as members) nor those managing the business are personally liable for the LLC's obligations. As a result of the temporal nature of LLCs, the limitations on the transfer of ownership interests, and the possibility of direct management by the owners, a properly structured LLC will be treated as a partnership or, in the case of a single-member LLC, a proprietorship (if the member is an individual), or as a division of the member (if the member is a business entity). Pass-through entities, such as partnerships and S corporations, are not subject to federal income tax at the entity level.

The key advantage that the LLC affords its members is the insulation of each member from liability for the entity's debts and liabilities, regardless of the extent to which any member participates in the conduct of the LLC's business and affairs. Generally, prior to the enactment of LLC legislation, the only way to combine the limited liability afforded by a corporation and the pass-through taxation of partnerships was by forming a limited partnership to own and operate the business with a corporation to serve as the general partner. However, the use of a limited partnership with a thinly capitalized corporate general partner presented a significant risk of being taxed as an "association" taxable as a corporation.

Another advantage is that most state LLC statutes provide for management directly by the members, although they do permit the parties to provide, by agreement, for managers. LLC members do not lose their limited liability by participating in LLC management, unlike limited partners in a limited partnership who do lose that protection by participating in management.

The elements of liability protection and partnership tax treatment coupled with the ability of limited partners to be involved are, in themselves, sufficient to cause LLCs to replace joint ventures and to replace general and limited partnerships in real estate ventures. The ability of the entity to hold and pass title tends to simplify multijurisdictional problems.

One problem with LLCs is that state laws regarding the organization and operation of LLCs are not uniform. Each statute provides a set of statutory default rules that govern the LLC and its members unless the members agree to opt out of a particular provision. Thus, one of the first planning choices in using an LLC is to select a place of organization. For most local and regional business organizations, the organization's home-state enabling statute will likely be the best choice due to convenience and local law familiarity. However, the statutory default rules and the ability to tailor certain special business arrangements sometimes may be major considerations in deciding on a state of organization.

Despite the complexity associated with differing state law rules, LLCs have become extremely popular entities for real estate investments for several reasons in addition to their offering an attractive combination of limited liability for all owners, whether actively participating in management or not, and flow through of tax benefits.

First, owners can design LLCs to hold and manage many properties or to hold and manage just one property. Those LLCs that involve a broader number of owners, especially owners who are unrelated and mostly unknown to each other, can be designed to hold many properties, similar to limited partnerships or REITs. (However, many banks and lenders are reluctant to lend to multi-property LLCs because they do not want a problem at a separate property to compromise their security interest in the property on which they are lending. Therefore, the multi-property format often is limited to only the larger and proven syndicators who the lenders trust to repay their debts.)

For smaller syndicates of more close-knit joint ventures, family syndicates, or for single owners, the ownership group can create a separate LLC for each property. The advantage here is that liabilities that may arise from one-property LLC are isolated to that one one-property LLC. In general, claimants or creditors making claims upon the one property in a particular LLC of the ownership group's many LLCs cannot make claims upon the assets of the ownership group's other LLCs. In contrast, in the multi-property LLCs claimants can attach any and all properties in the LLC.

Second, owners can use multiple LLCs for one property to isolate various functions of ownership and management. For example, one LLC could hold title to the property while a second LLC is set up to manage the property and, perhaps, a third LLC is created to provide various services. Using LLCs in this way creates many advantages, such as ways to reallocate cash flows and expenses and the like, as well as to limit liabilities to the assets associated with each LLC. However, these arrangements can become complex, for both tax and liability purposes, and, therefore, may require close scrutiny in design by tax and accounting professionals to avoid potential pitfalls.

10.1.6 FEES AND OTHER ACQUISITION COSTS

Investors purchasing real estate on their own can expect to pay a number of acquisition costs. These include broker's commissions, legal fees, title examination and registration fees, title insurance, and state and/or local transfer taxes.

The costs of investing in a syndicated real estate venture will be higher than an investment where the owner finds, develops, and manages the property because these responsibilities are assumed by the developer/promoter. An investor can expect to pay more when investing through a public offering than a private placement (one that is not required to meet certain state and/or federal securities commission disclosure standards). This is because a private placement does not involve all the costs associated with full SEC registration.

Total fees and commissions in a public syndication will typically range from 16 percent to 26 percent of the amount invested. In the case of a private offering, total costs generally range from 13 percent to 25 percent. Obviously, the actual total costs will vary considerably with each investment. It is therefore critical that the investor thoroughly review the offering materials and factor the estimated costs into any investment analysis.

Historically, most real estate purchases have been financed by use of long-term (fifteen- to thirty-year) fixed rate mortgages. For example, an investor could finance 80 percent of the cost of purchasing a $1,000,000 building by obtaining a thirty-year bank loan of $800,000, bearing a fixed rate of interest on the unpaid balance. However, because of uncertainties in interest rates and the effects of inflation, other techniques of structuring the financing of real estate, at various times, have become more popular. These techniques include:

1. *Adjustable Rate Mortgages (ARMs)* – The applicable interest rate payable is adjusted periodically (usually annually) as the "money market" dictates.

2. *Equity Participation Loans* – The lender agrees to a fixed or only moderately adjustable interest rate on the condition that upon the sale of the property he will share in the gain realized.

3. *Lease with Purchase Option* – Typically, a third party purchases the property and leases it to the user. The user is given an option to purchase the property at the end of the lease period. The option price is either predetermined or established by the fair market value at the date of the sale. This technique is employed when the user does not have either the immediate ability to purchase the property from the seller or a high enough tax bracket to utilize the tax benefits of ownership.

4. *Installment Sales* – In these cases, the seller agrees to finance the purchase by taking an installment note from the buyer who makes periodic payments at agreed-upon intervals (usually monthly or quarterly), based upon a specified fixed interest rate or variable interest rate linked to some specified interest rate index, and with a specified term, such as ten, twenty, or thirty years. In some cases, these installment sales may determine the installment payments based, say, upon a thirty-year amortization, but call for a balloon payment of the balance of the loan in five or ten years. These types of arrangements are more commonly used when parents sell properties to children whose current income and credit rating might not permit them to qualify for other financing, but who are likely to be able to qualify for traditional financing in five to ten years.

10.1.7 SELECTION STRATEGIES

Because of the unique nature of real estate, best is a relative term. An investor should study each of the following major criteria:

1. Location of the property. This is the most important single factor and will determine present and future market demand.

2. Soundness of construction and appropriateness of design for intended use. Maintenance costs will be higher with poor construction and rental income may be lower than anticipated if the project is not suited for its intended use.

3. Cost of capital. The interest rate that must be paid on the purchase debt will significantly affect the ultimate profitability of the venture.

4. Financing fees. Requiring payment of "points" has become a prevalent practice. These are paid to the lender on both the construction financing and the permanent mortgage. Each point is 1 percent of the borrowed amount.

5. The cost of operating and maintaining the property. A review of the track record of the promoter/manager in similar projects is particularly helpful.

6. Organization and offering expenses.

7. Sales commissions.

8. Construction costs. (Check to see if the general partner's fee will be reduced if costs of construction are higher than projected.)

9. Fees paid to the general partner for managing the partnership and the underlying investment property.

10. Projected cash flow and tax results from operations.

10.2 REITS REAL ESTATE INVESTMENT TRUSTS

Section Overview:

10.2.1 Types of REITs

10.2.2 Advantages of REITs

10.2.3 Disadvantages of REITs

10.2.4 Tax Implications of REITs

10.2.5 Alternative Strategies

10.2.6 Purchasing REITs

10.2.7 Selection Strategies

10.2.1 TYPES OF REITS

A Real Estate Investment Trust (REIT) is essentially a publicly-traded closed-end investment company that invests in a managed, diversified portfolio of real estate or real estate mortgages and construction loans rather than in financial securities such as stocks and bonds. Although REITs are corporations or trusts, they are not subject to tax at the corporate level if they distribute at least 90 percent of their net annual earnings to shareholders and meet certain other requirements (discussed in later sections). Investors must pay the tax on the REIT's earnings as the earnings are distributed. Therefore, REITs allow investors to share, with limited liability, the financial and tax benefits of real estate while avoiding the double taxation inherent in corporate ownership.

Investors have three types of REITs to choose from:

(1) *Equity REITs* – acquire ownership interests in commercial, industrial, or residential properties. Income is primarily received from the rentals of these properties.

(2) *Mortgage REITs* – invest in real estate indirectly by lending funds for construction and/or permanent mortgages. In some cases mortgage REITs invest in mortgage-backed securities such as "Ginnie Maes" or other mortgage-backed obligations.

(3) *Hybrid REITs* – combine the features of both equity and mortgage REITs.

10.2.2 ADVANTAGES OF REITS

Limited Liability – REIT shareholders are treated like holders of common stock in a regular corporation. Thus, the liability of REIT shareholders is limited to the amount of their investment.

No Corporate-Level Tax – If the REIT distributes 90 percent of its income to shareholders (and meets certain other requirements described in Tax Implications), there is no corporate-level tax. Therefore, REIT shareholders enjoy limited liability while avoiding the double tax of corporate ownership.

Pooling of Resources. – REITs pool individual investors' funds to acquire real estate interests and provide small investors with access to real estate investment opportunities not normally available to them through direct investment in real estate.

Knowledgeable Professionals. – REITs use the services of knowledgeable professionals who provide expert management and have a proven track record. Management compensation represents only a small portion of the overall expenses of these trusts. Thus, the major portion of the REITs' profits flows directly to the investors.

Record-Keeping – The REIT keeps detailed records of transactions, income and losses, distributions, expenses, and reports such information regularly to investors, sparing them the responsibility and inconvenience of record-keeping.

Small Denominations – Most REITs sell for less than $50 a share and, as with other stock investments, there is no minimum number of shares an investor must buy. However, because of the transaction costs involved, it is generally best to purchase shares in multiples of one-hundred.

Ability to Leverage Investments – Many REITs use both short-term and long-term debt to finance their asset purchases. If the returns on the REIT's investments exceed the interest paid on the debt, the investor's returns are enhanced. However, the use of debt increases the investor's risk because actual returns may not be adequate to pay the interest on the debt.

Utility as Collateral –Investors may use their shares in a REIT as collateral for loans from their bank or broker, subject to limits set by the Federal Reserve.

Liquidity – REITs are easily marketable and are widely traded on the various exchanges. In contrast, direct investments in real estate are generally extremely illiquid. In addition, when investors sell a direct investment in real estate, they must typically sell the entire asset. On the other hand, the REIT investor may sell as few shares as the situation requires and continue holding the balance.

Discounts from Book Value – REITs generally have sold at discounts ranging from 5 percent to 20 percent of their book values. In other words, the price paid for a share has typically been less than an investor would have to pay to buy a pro rata share of the assets in the REIT portfolio directly. This discount in effect creates positive leverage for the investor.

Example. Assume a mortgage REIT is selling at a 10 percent discount from book value and the mortgages are yielding 10 percent inside the REIT. Since the REIT investor is in essence acquiring interests in the mortgage pool at ninety cents on the dollar, his pro-rata share of interest is ten cents for every ninety cents invested. This translates into a yield of 11.1 percent.

High Dividend Payouts – This is based on the requirement that REITs distribute 90 percent of their income.

Automatic Dividend Reinvestment – Most REITs allow investors to automatically reinvest dividends (similar to the reinvestment option allowed by mutual funds).

Diversification in a Real Estate Portfolio – REITs can provide investors with a high degree of risk reduction through diversification because the investment policy of many trusts requires them to spread their investments over wide geographical regions as well as among various property types.

Inflation Hedge – Real estate has historically proven itself as an excellent hedge against inflation. Equity REITs should provide the same inflation-hedging potential as direct real estate investments. In contrast, mortgage REITs, because they invest in mortgages and other loans where interest rates and principal balances are fixed, will tend to be poor inflation hedges. However, mortgage REITs that invest in variable-rate mortgages and loans will provide some inflation-hedging potential because interest rates will tend to move in concert with inflation.

Diversification Beyond Stocks and Bonds – By including real estate investments in their portfolios, investors can reduce their risks and enhance their expected returns beyond what they would enjoy with a portfolio containing only stocks and bonds, or only real estate. In some years when stocks and bonds perform poorly, real estate performs well; in other years, the opposite is often true. Consequently, the returns on a portfolio that includes stocks, bonds, and real estate will tend to fluctuate less severely than returns on portfolios containing only one of these asset categories.

10.2.3 DISADVANTAGES OF REITS

Loss of Control – Professional management makes the investment easier for the investor, but it also reduces the investor's control and flexibility in the management of the investment. With direct investments, the investor can choose to buy and sell specific assets when it is advantageous for tax or other reasons to do so. With an investment in a REIT, the REIT management buys and sells assets at its discretion. Because the REIT must distribute to investors at least 90 percent of the income from both rents or interest and gains on sales of assets, the timing of such transactions may be disadvantageous to the investor.

Lower Potential Returns – Although diversification reduces risk, it also reduces the potential for substantial gains. Investors who can afford to invest directly in real estate, and who are knowledgeable enough to manage their own real estate portfolios, may be able to do better by investing directly than they could with REIT investments.

Management Fees and Administrative Charges – Although management fees are small relative to the overall amount of money involved (typically 0.5 percent to 1.5 percent of the value of the investment), they are still an additional expense that investors may not incur if they manage their own investments. However, these fees are at least partially offset by economies of scale that reduce other transaction costs (e.g., legal fees, loan origination charges) that typically would be higher for an individual investor.

No Flow-Through of Tax Benefits – The REIT may pass only tax-sheltered income through to the investors; they may not pass losses through. In contrast, losses flows through to investors with direct investments in real estate or with interests in limited partnerships (other than those taxed as corporations).

Discounts from Book Values – As described earlier in the discussion of advantages, REIT shares generally have sold at a discount from their book values. Purchase at a discount enhances an investor's yield; however, because these discounts vary over time an investor might be faced with the additional risk that share values may decline because of an increase in the discount. If the discount increases after investors have acquired shares in a REIT, they may suffer a capital loss or a reduction in their gain when they sell their shares.

Considerable Risk – REIT share prices can be just as volatile as stock prices. The amount and sources of risk vary considerably depending on: (a) the type of REIT; (b) the management philosophy; and (c) its actual asset/liability makeup.

Poor Inflation Hedge – Mortgage REITs that invest in fixed rate mortgages, which have investment characteristics similar to bonds, are not likely to be good inflation hedges. If inflation rises and causes interest rates to rise, the value of the underlying mortgages and loans typically will fall. Consequently, in inflationary times, share values in mortgage REITs are likely to decline. However, mortgage REITs that invest in variable-rate mortgages and loans will provide some inflation-hedging potential because interest rates will tend to move in concert with inflation.

10.2.4 TAX IMPLICATIONS OF REITS

REITs are not subject to federal income tax if they satisfy several Internal Revenue Code provisions requiring that the REIT:

a) distribute at least 90 percent of net annual earnings to shareholders;

b) derive at least 75 percent of gross income from real estate – usually rents, mortgage interest, and gains for selling real estate;

c) invest at least 75 percent of the REIT's portfolio in real estate, loans secured by real property or mortgages on real estate, shares in other REITs, cash or cash items, or government securities;

d) have at least one-hundred shareholders and makes sure that no more than half the outstanding shares are owned by five or fewer individuals at any time during the second half of each taxable year; and

e) is managed by one or more trustees or directors.

Although REITs invest in real estate (which is generally subject to the passive activity rules), distributions are treated as investment income, like dividends on stock, and not as passive activity income.

Shareholders pay taxes on distributions (i.e., dividends paid) from the REIT's earnings. Unlike a real estate limited partnership (which is not taxed as a corporation), REITs cannot offer flow-through tax benefits; however, some trustees pass on cash flow in excess of income as a nontaxable return of capital. Consequently, distributions may include portions that are treated as ordinary income, capital gains or losses, and nontaxable return of capital.

Distributed income *generally* is taxed as ordinary income to shareholders. However, under JGTRRA 2003 "qualified dividend income" (generally, dividends paid by domestic corporations and certain foreign corporations to shareholders) is treated as net capital gain and is therefore eligible for the lower 0 percent, 15 percent or 20 percent tax rates (the latter for high-income taxpayers with income taxed in the 39.6 percent tax bracket), instead of the higher ordinary income tax rates). Because REITS generally do not pay corporate income taxes, *most* ordinary income dividends paid by REITS do *not* constitute qualified dividend income, and, consequently, are not eligible for the 0 percent, 15 percent or 20 percent rates. However, a small portion of dividends paid by REITS may constitute qualified dividend income – for example, if the: (a) dividend is attributable to dividends received by the REIT from non-REIT corporations, such as taxable REIT subsidiaries; or (b) income was subject to tax by the REIT at the corporate level, such as built-in gains, or when a REIT distributes less than 100 percent of its taxable income. Unless designated by the REIT as qualified dividend income, all distributions are ordinary income dividends.

Capital gains and losses on the sale of assets in the REIT's portfolio retain their character and are taxed as gains or losses to the investors when distributed. For tax purposes, depreciation (which is a noncash expense) is subtracted from net operating income to derive the REIT's taxable income. Therefore, cash distributions may exceed net income. The tax code treats distributions in excess of net income as a nontaxable return of capital. Shareholders must reduce the basis in their shares by any such excess distributions.

The tax code also treats gains or losses realized when investors sell their shares in a REIT as capital gains or losses. The cost basis for determining gain or loss on sale is the original cost of the shares less cash distributions received in excess of the REIT's net income.

REITs are exempt from the requirement that certain pass-through entities report to shareholders, as income, their shares of expenses of the fund, which would be miscellaneous itemized deductions if incurred by the shareholders individually.

10.2.5 ALTERNATIVE STRATEGIES

REITs allow investors to enjoy many of the benefits of direct investments in real estate; however, by investing through a REIT, investors give up many of the potential advantages of direct real estate investments. One of the major distinctions is that the tax code treats distributions as investment income, and not passive activity income as they would be treated if the real estate were held directly. Furthermore, taxable losses on REIT properties do not flow through to shareholders as they would if the properties were held directly. Consequently, REIT shareholders cannot use taxable losses (income) on REIT properties to offset taxable income (losses) from other real estate investments or other passive activities.

Many Real Estate Limited Partnerships (RELPs) offer investors a pooled real estate investment similar to an equity REIT. However, similar to direct real estate investments, real estate limited partnerships (other than those taxed as corporations) have the flow-through characteristic that is lacking in a REIT.

Mutual funds that invest in mortgages or mortgage-backed securities offer an investment opportunity that is very similar to a mortgage REIT. One important distinction is the leveraging potential. Most mutual funds that invest in real estate mortgages or mortgage-backed securities limit the amount of borrowing the fund may employ to leverage its investments. Although the amount of borrowing allowed varies from one mortgage REIT to another, many mortgage REITs employ substantial borrowing to finance their asset acquisitions. This feature has both pros and cons, because such leverage can either enhance or depress returns to investors, depending on whether the returns generated by the assets acquired with the debt exceed the interest that the REIT must pay on the debt. Other advantages associated with real estate mutual funds include a high level of diversification, professional management, and ease of ownership.

Mortgage-backed pass-through certificates, mortgage-backed bonds, and Collateralized Mortgage Obligations (CMOs) are all investments in pools of mortgages that are similar to mortgage REITs.

Except for pass-through certificates (such as Ginnie Maes), the tax code typically treats mortgage-backed securities as debt for tax purposes whereas the tax code treats shares in mortgage REITs like common stock. From the investor's perspective, in many cases this may be a distinction without a difference. However, certain items are treated differently for tax purposes at the investor level such as original issue discounts and market discounts on the underlying mortgages, as well as the timing of recognition of principal repayments. In these respects mortgage REITs are much less complicated investments for investors.

Also, most mortgage-backed securities are backed by a fixed pool of mortgages; the pool is liquidated as the mortgages are repaid. In contrast, most mortgage REITs have indeterminate lives. They continue to acquire additional mortgages as the older mortgages in the pool are paid off. However, some REITs, called "finite-life REITs," or "FREITs," liquidate their holdings by a given date and distribute the proceeds to investors. FREITs are also unincorporated trusts, while REITs are incorporated.

Some mortgage REITs invest in mortgage-backed securities. Investors who buy shares in these REITs are essentially buying a pool of mortgages.

10.2.6 PURCHASING REITS

Many REITs are listed on the national and regional exchanges. Others are traded in the over-the-counter market. Like common stocks, investors looking for shares acquire them from stock brokerage firms, discount brokers, and through many banks and other financial institutions.

Brokers typically charge a commission when investors purchase or sell shares. The fee will depend on (1) the amount invested, (2) the number of shares purchased, (3) whether the shares are purchased through a full-service broker or a discount broker, and (4) the market in which the shares are traded.

Like common stocks, REIT shares trade in round lots of one-hundred shares, with odd-lot transactions (less than one-hundred shares) involving higher commissions. Discount brokerage fees vary widely and can be as little as less than $10 per transaction. Regular full service commissions can be many multiples of the discount brokerage fees.

The fee paid to acquire shares that are traded over-the-counter is essentially the "bid-ask spread." Market makers in the Over The Counter (OTC) market maintain a bid price at which they will purchase shares and an ask price at which they will sell shares. The bid price is always lower than the ask price. The difference, or spread, is the market maker's profit for making a market in the shares. The size of the spread depends on how many shares are outstanding and the volume of trading in the shares. The spread is smaller for very actively traded shares with a large number of shares outstanding.

10.2.7 SELECTION STRATEGIES

There are over 150 publicly traded REITs available to investors in U.S. markets. These REITs have a wide variety of investment objectives and vary considerably in terms of (1) size, (2) fees, (3) management performance, (4) investment philosophy, (5) capital structure, and (6) asset characteristics. The selection process for REITs is at least as involved as that for stocks or mutual funds because REITs share many of the characteristics of each. Investors should consider many factors when making their selections. When selecting a REIT:

> *Ascertain the type of REIT that best meets the investor's objectives with regard to income versus growth and tolerance for risk.* Equity REITs generally provide moderate income and opportunities for increasing cash flows and capital appreciation. Mortgage REITs generally provide higher income, but less opportunity for growth. Hybrid REITs provide a combination of both types of REITs. As a group, equity REITs are considered riskier than mortgage REITs, but in individual cases the opposite is often the case. Risk factors are discussed later.
>
> *Determine whether the management's investment philosophy is consistent with the investor's.* The prospectus that accompanies an initial public offering always includes a section describing the proposed activities of the trust. Read that section to see if the fund's objective and methods are consistent with the client's. Investors who buy REIT shares in the market after the original offering should obtain a copy of the original prospectus from their broker, if possible. They should also look at the annual reports for the most recent several years to confirm that the REIT management is maintaining a consistent investment philosophy. Among the items that should be considered are:
>
> a) *The types of assets that the REIT will invest in* – The type of assets the REIT acquires is critical in determining the risk and return characteristics of the REIT and the relative emphasis on income versus capital growth. For example, mortgage REITs that provide construction and development loans will be significantly riskier, and potentially much more profitable, than REITs that invest in government-insured mortgage-backed securities. However, because the default experience on construction and development loans is much higher than on other types of mortgage financing, cash flows from REITs that invest in these loans may fluctuate year to year much more than cash flows from REITs that invest in more secure mortgages.
>
> Investors seeking stable income should avoid REITs that direct their investments to construction and development loans. In contrast, these types of REITs may be more suitable for investors who are looking for high yields and are less concerned with yearly fluctuations.

Some equity REITs focus on new construction and recently completed properties that have not yet been fully rented. Others invest only in "proven" properties that have a well-established rental history. The REITs that focus on new properties typically provide low cash flows from rents, but considerable growth potential and substantial capital gains when properties are sold. REITs that invest in proven properties generally provide higher and more predictable cash flows from rents, but less potential for growth and only moderate capital gains when properties are sold. Investors should seek out those REITs whose investment focus will provide the income and growth characteristics they desire.

b) *Whether the REIT will employ leverage and, if so, whether it places limits on the amount of debt it can employ* – Leverage can increase investors' returns, but only with a corresponding increase in risk and potentially greater fluctuations in annual returns. In the early 1970s, many REITs had dismal performances, in large part because they were over-leveraged and managed their debt poorly. Since then, REITs generally have been more conservative in the use of debt to finance their asset acquisitions. However, many REITs still employ debt to leverage their investments. Investors should look at what limits, if any, the REIT places on the use of leverage. In general, only the most aggressive and risk tolerant investors should consider REITs that use debt extensively.

c) *Whether the trust will provide broad diversification or concentrate its investments in a particular type of real property (such as motels, health care facilities, or apartments)* – some REITs restrict their investments to specific segments of the market, such as health care facilities or motels or residential construction loans. The advantage of such segmentation is that the managers typically know the chosen market segment better than other market segments and can use their expertise to select the better opportunities within that market segment.

The disadvantage is that the REIT is less diversified and, therefore, is exposed to additional economic risk. For example, if a REIT specializes in motels, a general downturn in travel and tourism or overbuilding may adversely affect its returns. However, at the same time, demand for health care facilities, or new office space may be booming.

Economic and business factors that are detrimental to any one segment of the market will have less effect on REITs that invest across many market segments. Unless investors feel that one particular market segment offers exceptional opportunities, they often will be better off from a risk standpoint by selecting a REIT that invests in many market segments.

d) *Whether the trust will diversify geographically* – Some REITs also limit their diversification by investing within one geographical region. The advantage of regional specialization is that managers are closer to their market. Successful real estate investing requires a great deal of hands-on management and local knowledge. REIT managers that invest within a region they know well are less likely to make poor investments. Consequently, many of the smaller REITs limit their geographical scope. However, such regional specialization exposes the REIT to the same kind of risk as market segmentation. One geographical region may be suffering adverse business conditions while other regions are booming. Investors who invest in REITs that are geographically diversified reduce their exposure to this kind of risk.

e) *Whether the trust will limit the placement of assets in any one project* – Investors should not ignore one last, but critical, aspect of diversification. REITs may limit the proportion of their total assets that they may invest in one project. Clearly, if a major portion of a REIT's total investment is in one or two projects, the REIT essentially lives or dies by those projects. Investors who do not hold considerable real assets elsewhere and, thus, are unable to provide their own diversification, generally should look for REITs that limit the proportion of their total investment that they may place in any given project.

f) *Whether the trust will emphasize income or capital appreciation when selecting its investments* – To a great extent, the type of assets the REIT acquires will dictate its policy regarding income and capital appreciation. Clearly, mortgage REITs will typically emphasize income, while equity REITs will typically seek at least some capital appreciation. However, how the management directs the portfolio and, in particular, its policy regarding when it sells properties will affect cash flows and growth potential.

   Equity REITs that pursue essentially a "buy-and-hold" philosophy will often provide relatively stable, but increasing, cash flows. As the values of the properties in the REIT's portfolio increase, the REIT's share value should also appreciate. Equity REITs that specialize in new construction often will hold properties until they are rented to capacity, and then sell those properties (presumably for substantial gains). Because REITs must distribute 90 percent of their net income (including gains on sales), investors have to recognize and pay taxes on the gains to the extent the REITs distribute cash. Consequently, such REITs may earn substantial gains on their properties, but the net effect to investors is higher (and more volatile) cash flows, and less potential appreciation in their share value. Therefore, the management's philosophy and policy regarding how they direct their portfolio will greatly affect the manner in which they realize returns (i.e., as cash flows or as appreciation in share value).

Evaluate the historical performance of those REITs that match the investor's investment objectives and philosophy – The S&P U.S. REIT Index defines and measures the investable universe of publicly traded REITS domiciled in the U.S. At the time of the writing of this book, the index contained 128 REITs. The Morgan Stanley Capital International (MSCI) Index represents approximately 85 percent of the US REIT universe and is designed to ensure that the index is investable and replicable.

a) The single most important factor in selecting a REIT is the quality of management. Some of the personal data about management personnel can be found in *Who's Who in Business, Who's Who in America,* or *Dun's Reference Book of Corporate Managements.* Investors should also try to evaluate the management's experience by looking at the performance of previous real estate ventures managed by the team. Success in the past does not guarantee success in the future, but a history of poor performance does suggest less than average prospects for future success.

b) The critical factors that reflect on the quality of management and the potential performance of a REIT are as follows: (i) dividend payout record; (ii) expense ratios; (iii) vacancy rates; (iv) length of time the REIT management has been in business; (v) the quality or value of the properties in which the REIT invests; and (vi) the percentage of ownership held by the managers of the company.

   Historical information regarding earnings, dividends, assets, liabilities, expense ratios and the like can be obtained for many REITs from reports issued by investment advisory services such as Value Line, Moody's, and Standard & Poor's. The REITs' annual reports also present additional information. Furthermore, advisory services give REITs ratings. Conservative investors generally should avoid REITs that are rated "B" or lower by Moody's or Standard & Poor's, as well as those with a Value Line rating lower than "3."

Project future performance – This, of course, is the most difficult step in the selection process. Growth will depend on the future income from the REIT's holdings. Income will depend on the rent and, sometimes, the sales level of the REIT's properties. Potential investors may place some reliance on professional appraisals of the REIT's properties to estimate future income growth and appreciation potential. But appraisals do not always reflect the same standards and each rater may derive their ratings using different assumptions regarding rent multipliers or capitalization rates (which are techniques used to value the projected rental stream from a property). In addition, vacancy rates, poor regional economic growth, and overbuilding in the geographic region or the particular market segment favored by the REIT can all affect REIT income. High levels of debt may also cause shareholder dividends to be low.

Given the complexity of selecting the "best" REIT of its type, investors should consider buying shares in several REITs that have the basic investment characteristics and investment philosophy the investor is seeking. By diversifying among several REIT holdings rather than buying just one REIT, investors can expect about average performance, but they will also minimize downside exposure.

10.3 GOLD AND OTHER PRECIOUS METALS

Section Overview:

10.3.1 Advantages of Investing in Precious Metals

10.3.2 Disadvantages of Investing in Precious Metals

10.3.3 Tax Implications

10.3.4 Purchasing Precious Metals

10.3.5 Fees and Other Acquisition

10.3.6 Selection Strategies

10.3.1 ADVANTAGES OF INVESTING IN PRECIOUS METALS

Gold, silver, and platinum are the most common of the precious metal investments. They are valued primarily for their scarcity and, to a lesser extent, for their utility for scientific and industrial purposes.

Because precious metals are tangible or physically possessable assets, they provide a degree of psychological security matched by few other investments.

Precious metals can be purchased in relatively small quantities and in a variety of forms. For instance, an investor can purchase gold by the bar or purchase an ounce (or even less) at a time by buying a coin such as the Canadian Maple Leaf. Such coins are available in amounts as low as one-half or one-quarter ounce.

Because all of the precious metals have some utility for scientific and industrial purposes, there is an underlying demand for them as a commodity in addition to their speculative or investment value. Silver is used extensively for jewelry and photographic purposes. Gold is used extensively for jewelry, dental, medical, and industrial purposes. Platinum is used in catalytic converters, laboratory equipment, dental equipment and jewelry.

Historically, precious metals held over a very long period have proven to be a relatively safe and stable form of investment. Many investors have purchased gold, for example, as a long-term hedge against inflation.

10.3.2 DISADVANTAGES OF INVESTING IN PRECIOUS METALS

Precious metals are a highly speculative form of investment. For example, the price of gold is determined more by international, political, and psychological factors than by normal economic factors of supply and demand.

Historically, the prices of precious metals have been highly volatile and the investor is subject to a high risk of significant loss of capital in a short period of time. Panic buying of gold could quickly reverse itself. For instance, the price of gold fell by over 25 percent during a three-month period in the first half of 2013.

Precious metals have frequently been controlled by various governments. For instance, the United States government hoarded gold in its vaults for many years and forbade U.S. citizens from owning and selling gold privately for investment or speculation until 1975.

Direct investments in precious metals typically yield no current income. This makes gold relatively "expensive" when other investments are yielding high rates of return in the form of dividends or interest.

Investment in physical precious metals involve storage costs, either directly or indirectly. There may also be shipping and insurance charges.

Sales tax may accrues and be payable as well as there may be assay (assessment) costs involved in the purchase.

10.3.3 TAX IMPLICATIONS

Taxable gain is realized and must be recognized (i.e., reported) to the extent an investor receives more upon disposition than he paid. Therefore, to the extent that the selling price exceeds the investor's tax basis, he must realize a gain.

No gain is reportable until the investment is disposed of in a taxable transaction. Therefore, the appreciation on a precious metals investment will remain untaxed until the asset is sold. This can be particularly advantageous to high tax bracket investors.

A loss from a precious metals transaction is allowable to the extent an investor paid more for the asset than he received from the sale. To the extent that the investor's basis exceeds his selling price, he has a deductible loss.

Gain or loss on a precious metals transaction is a capital gain or capital loss assuming the metal is held as an investment, rather than by a dealer for trading purposes. The length of time the metal was held prior to disposition will determine whether the capital gain or loss will be long-term or short-term. Unlike other capital assets, net long term capital gains from the sale of metals are treated like collectibles and subject to a maximum tax rate of 28 percent (rather than a maximum of 20 percent for other capital assets).

No gain or loss must be reported if one precious metal is exchanged solely for another. This favorable rule applies only if the metal received is of the same nature and the same character as the metal given up in the exchange. Therefore, if an investor exchanges gold coins for gold bullion, or trades gold bullion for certificates of gold, no gain or loss is recognized on the transaction. Likewise, if bullion-type coins of one country are exchanged for bullion-type coins of another country, no taxable income or loss would be generated.

Note that the tax-free exchange rules are strictly construed. A gain or loss would be triggered by the exchange of a "numismatic" coin for a "bullion-type" coin. (A numismatic coin such as the $20 U.S. gold piece is valued for its rarity and condition; its metal content is only one of many factors contributing to its value. Conversely, a bullion-type coin, such as the Canadian Maple Leaf, is valued solely for its metal content and the type of metal, purity, and weight are the primary value determinants.)

An exchange of any two different types of metals will trigger the recognition of gain or loss. For instance, gain or loss would be triggered by the exchange of a silver bullion-type coin for a gold bullion-type coin.

The exchange of a precious metal for property other than a similar type of precious metal will result in a reportable gain or loss.

Coins acquired in a taxable transaction must be valued for tax purposes at their fair market value rather than at their face value. For instance, a Fifty Peso Mexican coin with a gold content of 1.2057 ounces will be worth much more than fifty pesos.

10.3.4 PURCHASING PRECIOUS METALS

There are a number of ways to invest depending on the type of metal. Gold or silver can be purchased as:

- coins of the bullion-type, such as the U.S. Gold Eagle, the Canadian Maple Leaf, or the Mexican Peso
- bars (i.e., ingots of one or more ounces)
- certificates, which certify that a specific warehouse is holding a given amount of that metal for the investor
- Exchange-Traded Products (ETPs) such as Exchange-Traded Funds (ETFs), Exchange-Traded Notes (ETNs), and Closed-End Funds (CEFs)

Investors who wish to buy small quantities of gold should consider coins. They are easy to purchase, store, and resell. The most popular bullion-type coins – including the South African Krugerrand and the Canadian Maple Leaf – have a fine gold content of exactly one troy ounce. These coins generally have no numismatic value. This means that the value of an investor's holding can be figured by multiplying the price of gold for immediate delivery (the so-called "spot" or cash price) by the number of ounces held. It is important that investors only transact with reputable coin dealers. Fake gold coins are not uncommon, and are usually made of gold-plated lead.

Many investors prefer to purchase gold in the form of small wafers called ingots. Ingots are sold in standard weights ranging from as little as one gram (0.0322 oz.) to as much as 400 troy ounces. The typical investor will purchase ingots in one-ounce quantities.

Gold should be purchased only from a recognized dealer. Its fineness (the maximum is 0.999) should be stamped on the ingot. Investors should not purchase a bar with a lesser fineness. The ingot should be stamped with the name of a recognized refiner and should be accompanied by an assay certificate. This assures the purchaser of its purity and authenticity, and will typically save the cost of another assay when sold.

There are dealers, such as International Precious Metals (www.preciousmetals.com), who specialize in precious metals. Investors can establish accounts and obtain a firm, binding quote over the telephone or the Internet. Payment may be made by cashier's check or wired funds typically postmarked by noon of the day after purchase.

10.3.5 FEES AND OTHER ACQUISITION COSTS

Gold, silver, and platinum are purchased at the market value plus a premium. That premium can range from as little as 0.5 percent to as much as 2 to 3 percent or more. This premium covers the dealer's profit and the cost of fabricating the metal. Premiums decline with the quantity of the metal purchased and may be less than 0.5 percent for a one-hundred-ounce bar.

An investor who desires to take physical possession of a precious metal must pay insurance and shipping costs in addition to possible sales taxes. A representative shipping and insurance charge for an ounce of gold is $10.

Many investors prefer not to accept the risk and the expense involved in taking physical possession of a precious metal. Gold certificates programs offered by a number of large dealers, banks and brokerage firms allow investors to invest in gold without taking physical possession. The investor receives a certificate stating that he owns a specified number of troy ounces in an independent bank depository. The investor can sell his holding at any time or take delivery of the bullion. The Perth Mint Certificate Program is an example of an entity that issues gold certificates and it is the only government backed precious metal certificate program in the world.

The obvious advantage of storage certificate programs is the savings in delivery costs. The investor also may save sales taxes and fabrication charges by using an independent bank depository. There are minimum investments required. For instance, The Perth Mint Program has a minimum initial investment of $5,000, while other dealers' minimums are substantially less. Some dealers may allow additional investments of amounts as small as $100. Purchase commissions widely vary, for instance the Perth Mint has a 1.75 percent fee on all purchases plus a $10 certificate charge. Some programs charge annual storage fees – typically 0.5 percent of the value of the investor's holdings and a commission (0.75 to 1 percent) is paid upon the sale of the metal. It pays the investor to comparison shop for a storage certificate program.

10.3.6 SELECTION STRATEGIES

In making a selection among the various types of precious metals, an investor should consider the following factors:

a) *The price of one metal compared with another*. For instance, if silver were trading at $20 per ounce and gold were trading at $1,335 per ounce, and if other factors were equal, the small investor might opt for an investment in silver because it is more affordable.

b) *The position of the price relative to recent highs and lows of the metal*. An optimistic investor might choose silver at $20 per ounce if its recent high was $49.75 per ounce over gold selling at $1,327 per ounce with a recent high of $1,924 per ounce.

c) *The potential downside risk*. One metal may be used for many more scientific and industrial purposes than another and, therefore, may have a higher "floor" than the other. Silver and platinum generally have more industrial uses than gold.

d) *Other value determinants such as sensitivity to political changes and supply and demand influences*. For instance, an individual anticipating a major gold mining strike might prefer to invest in gold rather than silver or platinum.

Compare the premium charge imposed by a number of dealers. Premiums can vary significantly from one dealer to another. Other ancillary costs can also vary significantly from one dealer to another.

Deal only with reputable dealers who are willing to ship within 48 hours of payment, if delivery is requested, and who are willing to exchange gold for cash.

When storing gold, deal only with a firm that has been in business for a minimum of five years and that is periodically audited by an independent certified public accountant. Gold should be stored in a segregated account and should not be subjected to the claims of the dealer's or the custodian's creditors. If an investor's bullion is mingled with that of other registered holders, his holdings should be clearly identified and available for delivery after the payment of any appropriate charges.

Chapter 11

PORTFOLIO MANAGEMENT, CONSTRUCTION, AND INVESTMENT STRATEGY

11.1 THE INVESTMENT PROCESS

Section Overview:

11.1.1 The Investment Process

11.1.2 Client Life Cycle Analysis

11.1.3 Client Risk Tolerance

11.1.4 The Investment Policy Statement

11.1.1 THE INVESTMENT PROCESS

Previous chapters presented tools and techniques to evaluate specific types of investments such as common stocks, corporate bonds, and government bonds. Next up is the overall investment planning process. This process begins with analyzing an investor's objectives and constraints and ends with evaluating the results of investment decisions. This chapter shows how to develop an investment policy statement to guide the investment process. It also presents return measures useful for evaluating portfolio performance and choosing appropriate asset allocations (the proportion of different asset classes in an investor's portfolio). The final section demonstrates the importance of allocating assets appropriately to meet a client's objectives and constraints. The next chapter presents more advanced topics in asset allocation using modern portfolio theory.

Planning for investments is related to the overall financial planning process. The general steps in the financial planning process are adapted here for the investment planning process:

1. Establishing client-advisor relationships.

2. Gathering client data and determining objectives and expectations.

3. Analyzing the client's financial status, current investments, and special needs.

4. Developing and presenting the Investment Policy Statement.

5. Implementing the investment policy.

6. Monitoring the portfolio.

Note that the first four steps in the process involve gaining an understanding of the client and developing an appropriate investment policy to assist the client in meeting his objectives. The actual decision as to what investments to purchase comes much later. A planner must know the client before implementing an investment strategy.

11.1.2 CLIENT LIFECYCLE ANALYSIS

While each client is unique, there are common themes that impact the creation of an investment policy. One of these themes is that people's needs and resources change over time, and an investment policy must first identify these needs and then reflect these changes.

For example, consider Mary. A twenty-five-year old beginning her career, she has no savings and barely earns enough to pay the bills. At this stage, she is probably mostly concerned with building an emergency fund and reducing risks such as the possibility of disability.

When Mary is thirty-five, she is married with children, and earning more. Her husband also works, and they have more disposable income. They can afford to save some of this income for their future needs, which include a college education for the children and their own retirement.

At sixty-five, Mary and her husband retire and their earned income levels decline dramatically. At this point, they rely on their investments, including retirement plans, to maintain their newfound leisure. Eventually, they will probably want any of their wealth remaining at the time of their death to be passed to their children or charities.

This scenario is familiar to everyone, and is often called the investor life cycle. The investor life cycle is considered to run through three phases:

1. Accumulation phase.

2. Consolidation phase.

3. Spending phase.

During the accumulation phase, the client is accumulating assets — saving and investing for the future. As this is the earliest stage during which investing will occur, there is typically a long time horizon. Clients in this phase are often able to accept more risk since they have time to accumulate wealth. They may therefore prefer a higher risk and return policy, although they have a low level of net worth to be invested. In other cases, clients in the accumulation phase may have more pressing needs. If the client is saving to purchase a home or to build an emergency fund, their time horizon is shorter and risk tolerance may be low despite their long life expectancy.

The consolidation phase occurs when the client's income outpaces expenses and wealth accumulates more rapidly. The client has greater wealth to invest and still has a relatively long time horizon. However, the time horizon shortens over this period to arrive at the spending phase. During this phase, the client typically can tolerate moderate to higher risk in order to achieve higher returns.

The spending phase is when earned income (such as wages) ends and investment income is needed from accumulated retirement and non-retirement funds to meet living expenses. The client typically has a desire for lower risk and higher investment income during this period. Since life expectancies can be long, the time horizon is shorter, but not necessarily short, during this phase.

11.1.3 CLIENT RISK TOLERANCE

A client's willingness to accept investment risk is a function of a number of factors. While most individuals have some degree of risk aversion, some individuals are more tolerant of risk than others. This can be a function of their willingness to undertake risk (for example, based on past experiences) or their ability to take risk (for example, alternative sources of income and/or wealth such as a potential inheritance). A client's time horizon is also relevant. Generally, the longer the investment time horizon, the greater the ability to incur risk.

A useful framework for considering risk tolerance is the economic concept of utility. Utility is the satisfaction that an individual gets from consuming goods and services and, in terms of wealth, the satisfaction conferred by a given level of wealth. Consider Figure 11.1, which shows one possible relationship between wealth and utility. This utility function indicates that as investor wealth increases, the investor's utility increases. Further, there is a linear relationship so that starting at any point such as A, an increase in wealth of \$X will increase utility by the same amount as a decrease in wealth of \$X will decrease utility. An investor with such a utility function is said to be risk-neutral; neither avoiding nor seeking risk.

Figure 11.1

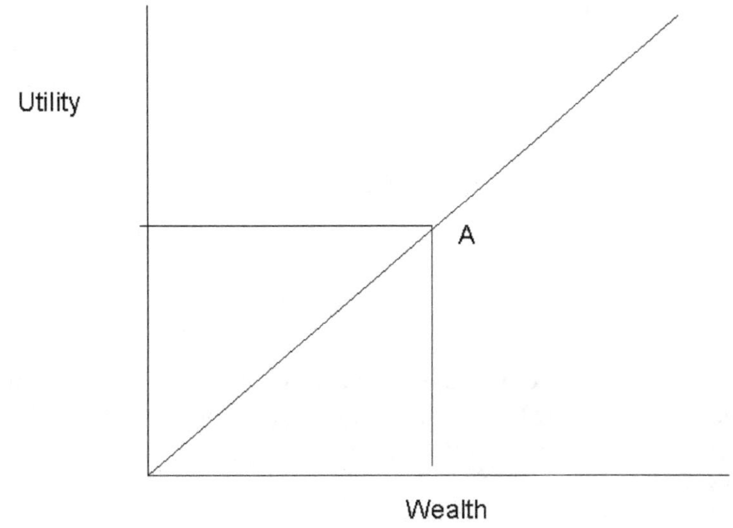

Another possible utility function is presented in Figure 11.2. This function shows a convex utility curve, where utility increases at a faster rate as wealth increases. An investor with wealth at point B would be risk seeking, since he would gain more utility for an $X increase in wealth than he would lose utility for an $X decrease in wealth.

Figure 11.2

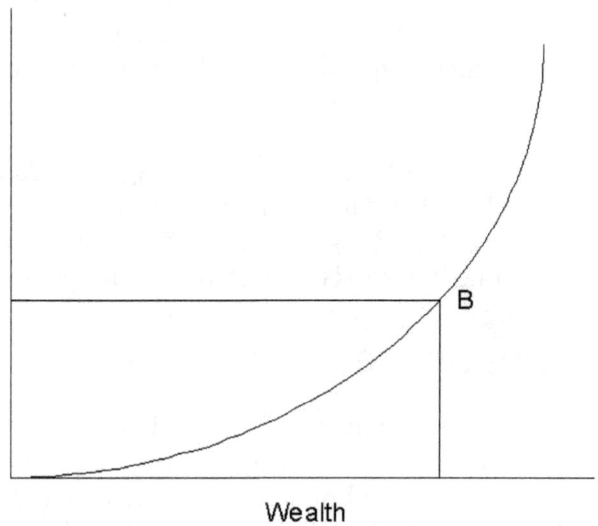

Lastly, Figure 11.3 shows a concave utility function, where utility increases at a slower rate as wealth increases. An investor with wealth at point C will be risk-averse, because as wealth decreases by $X the investor's utility decreases by more than it increases when wealth increases by $X.

Figure 11.3

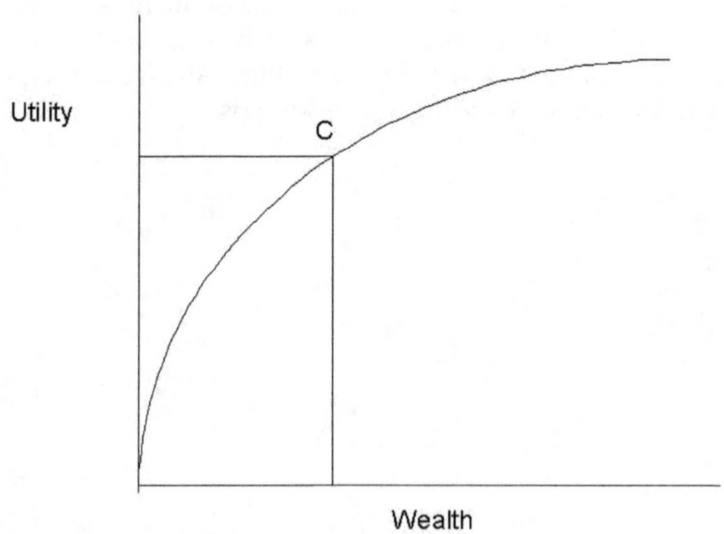

For most goods and services, economists assume diminishing marginal utility – the more a person has of a good, the less satisfaction he gets from each additional unit. If investors have diminishing marginal utility for wealth, they would exhibit the risk-averse utility function presented in Figure 11.3.

One problem with utility is that it cannot be measured, so it is not easy to assess an individual's risk preferences. Additionally, research on the behavior of individuals indicates that these utility functions do not capture the subtlety of human utility functions. In their well-known work on Prospect Theory, Kahneman and Tversky found that investors do not exhibit the same behavior for gains and losses. Kahneman and Tversky performed experiments where individuals were faced with choices such as:

> Choice A: Participate in a gamble where there is a 50 percent chance of winning $1,000 and a 50 percent chance of winning nothing.
>
> Choice B: Receive $450 with certainty.

They found that individuals exhibit risk aversion behavior when faced with choices involving a sure gain (they tended to take Choice B), but when faced with choices involving a sure loss or a possibility of a loss they exhibit risk seeking behavior. They conclude that individuals' utility functions appear to be concave for gains and convex for losses.

While an investor's risk tolerance cannot be measured precisely, questionnaires have been developed which provide a good starting point to understanding a client's risk tolerance relative to other investors. Professor William Droms has been a leader in developing risk tolerance questionnaires with his Global Portfolio Allocation Scoring System (PASS), which is designed to categorize investors into risk tolerance categories. Recently Droms and Stauss presented a modified version of this scoring system that considers the interaction of risk tolerance and time horizon. Figure 11.4 presents the questionnaire proposed by Droms and Strauss. The minimum score on this questionnaire is six and the maximum thirty. Clients with a higher score and longer time horizon will have a higher tolerance for and ability to take risk.

Droms and Stauss stress that the risk tolerance questionnaire is only a starting point in understanding the client in order to develop an appropriate investment policy statement.

Figure 11.4

	Strongly Agree	Agree	Neutral	Disagree	Strongly Disagree
Earning a high long-term total return that will allow my capital to grow faster than the inflation rate is one of my most important objectives.	5	4	3	2	1
I would like an investment that provides me with an opportunity to defer taxation of capital gains to future years.	5	4	3	2	1
I do not require a high level of current income from my investments.	5	4	3	2	1
I am willing to tolerate some sharp down swings in the return on my investments in order to seek a potentially higher return than would normally be expected from more stable investments.	5	4	3	2	1

	Strongly Agree	Agree	Neutral	Disagree	Strongly Disagree
I am willing to risk a short term loss in return for a potentially higher long-term rate of return.	5	4	3	2	1
I am financially able to accept a low level of liquidity in my investment portfolio.	5	4	3	2	1
Over what period of time to you expect to remain invested in this portfolio?	Short-term (3 years or less)	Intermediate (4 to 7 years)		Long-term (over 7 years)	

*Global Portfolio Allocation Scoring System (PASS) chart used with permission of Dr. William G. Droms, CFA.

11.1.4 THE INVESTMENT POLICY STATEMENT

A client's Investment Policy Statement should be developed in accordance with the client's objectives and constraints. Objectives include the desired return and level of risk that the client is willing and able to take. Constraints are limitations that must be considered in the investment process, such as liquidity, time horizon, taxes, and legal or regulatory restrictions. Lastly, constraints can include unique client circumstances and other self-imposed client preferences.

Determining the objectives for risk and return must be done simultaneously due to their interrelatedness. Generally, the higher the risk, the higher the return required by investors. A starting point is to determine the return necessary to meet the investor's objectives. For example, if the investor wants to accumulate $1,000,000 over the next twenty years and can deposit $20,000 at the end of each year, an 8.8 percent return is necessary.

The next issue is whether that return can be achieved at a risk level appropriate for the investor. Risk is often measured as the standard deviation of returns (a measure of total risk). However, individual investors may perceive potential losses to be more important than potential gains. Standard deviation includes both upside and downside deviations. Consider the historical return data for 1928 through 2012 provided in Figure 11.5:

Figure 11.5

Asset Class	Average Return	Standard Deviation	Proportion of years with a loss
Large Stocks (S&P 500)	11.3%	19.9%	28.2%
Government Bonds (10 year)	5.4%	7.7%	17.6%
Treasury Bills (3 month)	3.6%	3.2%	0.0%
Consumer Price Index	3.2%	4.1%	8.2%

Source: Based on data from 1928 to 2012 obtained from Aswath Damodoran and the Bureau of Labor Statistics

The data exhibit the expected positive relationship of risk and returns. Investments with the highest return had the highest risk measured based on both standard deviation and proportion of years with a loss. Treasury bills represent a risk-free rate of return. The consumer price index represents a level of inflation.

The investor's desired rate of return should be obtainable and consistent with risk tolerance. Financial advisers often present long term historical risk and return data to clients to demonstrate potential returns and risk. Historical returns do not necessarily predict future returns, but they do provide guidance as to what is possible. If an investor desires a long-term compound return of 15 percent with a standard deviation of 5 percent and no negative returns, this is not likely achievable given the historical data. The return exceeds that exhibited by any of the asset classes in the past and the risk is certainly much lower than could likely be achieved for that level of return.

Historical index returns are not achievable because they do not include fees and expenses. Use of index fund return data does consider some fees and expenses. Care must also be taken when using nominal historic returns. Some historical periods had high returns, but also high inflation. If current or expected inflation differ at the time the investment policy is being developed, consideration should be given to using real (inflation-adjusted) returns. Further historical returns do not reflect the current economic environment. For example, while on average long term government bonds returned 5.4 percent per year from 1928 to 2012 they are currently priced to provide a much lower return going forward.

The ability to achieve a desired return is also a function of certain constraints. The liquidity constraint is the client's desire to maintain a certain level of liquid assets (such as cash). The time horizon constraint relates to the timing of expected withdrawals. A long time horizon generally allows the investor to accept more risk. If the investor has particular needs (or desires) for cash at particular dates (such as for a second home purchase), this must be factored into the investment policy. Because taxes have a significant impact on net investment returns, any tax constraints must be considered. If the account is tax-deferred, there is more investment flexibility (except that municipal bonds would not be appropriate). If the account is taxable, tax favored investment returns such as long-term gains and dividends should be considered. Any legal or regulatory constraints should be examined. For example, if the client has a trust, the trust document must be examined. Further, the need to adhere to state law "prudent man/prudent investor" provisions must be considered. Some clients have unique circumstances or preferences that can lead to constraints on the investment policy. For example, the investor may wish to avoid tobacco or military-industrial stocks or may prefer mutual funds to individual securities.

Once the client's objectives and constraints are determined, they should be put in writing as an Investment Policy Statement to guide asset allocation and security selection for the client's accounts.

11.2 RETURN MEASURES FOR PORTFOLIO EVALUATION

Section Overview:

11.2.1 Risk-Adjusted Performance Measures

11.2.2 Risk-Adjusted Measures and Investment Policy

11.2.1 RISK-ADJUSTED PERFORMANCE MEASURES

Previous chapters have shown a variety of return measures such as holding-period returns and internal rates of return. Which of these is appropriate when evaluating portfolio performance? Further, should the performance be compared to the risk-free rate or some other benchmark such as a market index?

Let's look at a hypothetical example. Assume an investor deposits $100,000 in a professionally managed account. One year later, the account has grown in value to $110,000 and the investor withdraws $30,000 (remaining value $80,000). At the end of the second year, the account value is $84,000. No other additions or withdrawals were made. During the same two years, the risk-free rate remained constant at 2 percent and a relevant benchmark earned 9 percent the first year and 6 percent the second.

The investor's return could be measured as the holding-period return over the two years:

Equation 11.1

$$R_H = \frac{MV_E - MV_0 + D}{MV_0}$$

Where R_H is the holding-period return

MVE is the market value of the account at the end

MV0 is the market value at the beginning and

D is the net distributions during the time period (contributions minus withdrawals)

For this investor the holding-period return is:

$$R_H = \frac{MV_E - MV_0 + D}{MV_0} = \frac{84{,}000 - 100{,}000 + 30{,}000}{100{,}000} = 0.14 \text{ or } 14\%$$

This return measure informs the investor that they have earned 14 percent over the holding period, but since the holding period is two years, it is not that useful in comparing to benchmarks or prior periods. Return measures are usually expressed on an annual basis.

The holding-period return could be computed for each year individually. The holding period return for year one is:

$$R_H = \frac{MV_E - MV_0 + D}{MV_0} = \frac{80{,}000 - 100{,}000 + 30{,}000}{100{,}000} = 0.10 \text{ or } 10\%$$

The holding-period return in year two is:

$$R_H = \frac{MV_E - MV_0 + D}{MV_0} = \frac{84{,}000 - 80{,}000}{80{,}000} = 0.05 \text{ or } 5\%$$

So the investor earned 10 percent in the first year and 5 percent in the second. These annual returns can be compared to the benchmark since there were no withdrawals or deposits during the year, only at the beginning or end of the year. Year one returns of 10 percent beat the benchmark by 1 percent and returns in year two trailed the benchmark by the same 1 percent. Note that, had there been interim withdrawals or deposits, holding-period returns for sub-periods would need to be calculated.

Having beaten the index one year and trailed it the next by a similar amount, how should the manager's performance be evaluated? The simple average of the holding period returns is 7.5 percent for both the manager and the benchmark. However, the simple average does not adequately capture the performance during the two-year period.

To measure the geometric average performance of the account over the period, the internal rate of return for the portfolio can be computed over the two-year time period. Using a financial calculator with the following inputs:

Cash Flow Time Zero	(100,000)
Cash Flow Time One	30,000
Cash Flow Time Two (Value)	84,000

Solving for the internal rate of return yields 7.9 percent. The internal rate of return is also known as a dollar-weighted return. The investor earned more than the simple average of 7.5 percent in this instance due to the timing of the withdrawal. By withdrawing funds after the 10 percent return and before the lower 5 percent return, the investor earned a higher average return. Note, however, that since the dollar-weighted return is an internal rate of return, it implicitly assumes that cash flows are re-invested at the same rate.

While the dollar-weighted return may measure the return to the investor, it does not measure the performance of the portfolio manager. The decision to withdraw funds was made by the investor and should not be included in the manager's evaluation.

Instead, a time-weighted return is used. The time-weighted return is measured as:

Equation 11.2

$$R_P = [(1 + R_1)(1 + R_2)(1 + R_3)\dots(1 + R_N)]^{1/N} - 1$$

It measures the geometric return, excluding the impact of contributions and withdrawals, over the period. As such, it is an appropriate measure of the portfolio manager's performance. For this example, the time-weighted return would be:

$$R_P = [(1 + R_1)(1 + R_2)(1 + R_3)\dots(1 + R_N)]^{1/N} - 1 = [(1.10)(1.05)]^{1/2} - 1 = 7.47\%$$

In this case, the portfolio manager's performance was an average annual return of 7.47 percent over the two years. This is slightly less than the simple average and quite a bit less than the dollar-weighted average that included the impact of the investor's withdrawal. It can also be compared to the benchmark index by calculating the time-weighted benchmark return of [(1.09)(1.06)]1/2 – 1 = 7.48. Doing so, it is discovered that although the magnitudes of the outperformance in year one and underperformance in year two were equal; the manager's annual returns over the entire period fell very slightly behind those of the benchmark. Fortunately, the difference turned out to be minimal.

The return earned is only one component of portfolio performance. Another important component is the amount of risk taken to achieve the return. Portfolio performance can and should (assuming risk-averse investors) be evaluated on a risk-adjusted basis. In risk-adjusted measures, return is compared to the portfolio's riskiness. A high return relative to risk is desirable. In this section, four types of risk-adjusted returns are examined: the Sharpe ratio, the Treynor ratio, the information ratio, and Jensen's alpha.

The Sharpe ratio measures the excess return of a portfolio relative to risk and is computed as:

Equation 11.3

$$\text{Sharpe Ratio} = \frac{R_P - R_f}{\sigma_P}$$

The numerator represents a portfolio's excess return over the risk-free rate. The denominator measures the portfolio's risk as the standard deviation of portfolio returns (total risk). If the Sharpe Ratio is negative, the portfolio's return was lower than the risk-free rate. The higher the Sharpe Ratio, the better the performance.

For this extended example, the following is used: a risk-free rate of 3 percent, a portfolio's ten year time-weighted return of 7.5 percent annually and standard deviation of 10.00 percent, and the benchmark return and standard deviation of 7.5 percent and 8.0 percent, respectively. Plugging in these numbers gives the portfolio a Sharpe ratio of 0.45 [(7.5 – 3.0) / 10.0]. By comparison, the benchmark index has a Sharpe ratio of 0.56 [(7.5 – 3.0) / 8.0]. The benchmark's much higher Sharpe ratio indicates that it was much less risky than the portfolio given their similar returns.

The Treynor ratio also measures the excess return relative to risk but measures risk as Beta:

Equation 11.4

$$\text{Treynor Ratio} = \frac{R_P - R_f}{\beta_P}$$

As with the Sharpe ratio, a positive number indicates greater returns than the risk-free rate and a higher ratio is preferred. If it is assumed the portfolio had a Beta of 1.2, a Treynor ratio is derived of 3.75 [(7.5 – 3.0) / 1.2]. Typically, the portfolio Beta is measured against the benchmark, so the benchmark should have a Beta of 1.0 and a resulting Treynor ratio of 4.5 [(7.5 – 3.0) / 1.00]. This measure also shows the manager produced worse risk-adjusted returns than the benchmark. Note, however, that if the Beta of a portfolio differs significantly from that of the benchmark it could signal that the chosen benchmark is inappropriate because it does not reflect the manager's style (or that the manager is inappropriate because he does not follow the investment guidelines).

Using the risk-free rate as the hurdle rate for determining the excess return may not be a high enough hurdle for some. An alternative is to calculate an information ratio, which measures excess return relative to the benchmark portfolio:

Equation 11.5

$$\text{Information Ratio} = \frac{R_P - R_B}{\sigma_{Excess}}$$

The risk measure is the standard deviation of the excess return. For this portfolio, excess return is zero because its long term return equaled that of the benchmark and it had a higher standard deviation so the information ratio need not be computed.

Jensen's alpha is another risk-adjusted performance measure. However, it is measured quite differently:

Equation 11.6

$$\alpha = R_p - [R_f + \beta_p (R_m - R_f)]$$

Alpha is measured as the portfolio's return in excess of that predicted by the capital asset pricing model. An alpha of zero indicates that the portfolio earned its expected rate of return given its risk (measured as Beta). A positive alpha indicates that the portfolio manager has added value. Given this example, alpha equals –0.90 [7.5 – {3.0 + 1.2 × (7.5 – 3.0)}]. The negative alpha indicates this portfolio manager has not performed as well as predicted by the capital asset pricing model.

Note that for risk-adjusted measures using Beta, a diversified portfolio is assumed. Standard deviation measures total risk and does not assume a diversified portfolio. The Sharpe and Treynor ratios will provide similar rankings for well diversified portfolios.

Selecting an Appropriate Benchmark

As has been previously described, understanding how to measure portfolio results compared to a benchmark is an important consideration. An equally important consideration is which benchmark to use. The most frequently cited benchmark is the S&P 500 index, but this may not be appropriate for every investor as it consists only of large-cap U.S. stocks, which may not be similar to the investor's portfolio.

Appropriate benchmark selection should follow naturally from the investment planning process. Once the client's preferences, constraints, risk tolerance, and return requirements are established and a mix of assets is selected to accomplish these goals, a benchmark should be chosen that reflects the same goals. For example, if the client's asset allocation is 50 percent large-cap stocks and 50 percent intermediate-term bonds, the benchmark should have a similar construction. A single benchmark containing the same proportions of each asset would be acceptable, as would a combination of two separate single-asset class benchmarks. In some cases, the choice may depend on whether the investor has chosen separate equity and fixed income managers or whether a single investment manager is responsible for the entire account. Complex allocations may even require construction of a custom benchmark.

While the terms "benchmark" and "index" are often substituted for each other, an appropriate benchmark could be a published index, a custom composite of assets or indexes, or a peer group of similar funds or managers. Regardless of which type of benchmark is chosen, the CFA Institute and other global investment bodies generally agree that it should meet the following criteria:

1. *Representative of the asset class or mandate* – An investor in small-cap stocks should not choose a manager who invests in S&P 500 names, nor should they compare their small-cap manager to that index.

2. *The benchmark should be investable* – This means that the investor should be able to invest in the benchmark as an alternative to hiring an active manager. There is no sense in comparing performance to a benchmark that could not be reasonably matched (such as a market-weighted portfolio of all the real estate in the world.)

3. *Should be constructed in a disciplined and objective manner* – Some managers believe the benchmark should be easy to beat so their performance looks better. The investor may prefer a tougher standard. The benchmark should have neither bias.

4. *Formulated from publicly available information.*

5. *Acceptable by the manager as the neutral position* – The manager should be comfortable with comparisons to the benchmark.

6. *Consistent with the investor's status* – The benchmark should be consistent with investor's status regarding taxes, time horizon, etc.

In short, the benchmark should reflect both the client's needs and the manager's style. Otherwise, either the manager or the benchmark was not selected well.

11.2.2 RISK-ADJUSTED MEASURES AND INVESTMENT POLICY

Risk-adjusted measures can be useful in setting investment policy for a client and in explaining the importance of asset allocation to the client. Based on the historical data presented earlier, the return versus risk data provided in Figure 11.6 can be computed. Sharpe ratios were computed using average returns relative to Treasury bills and the standard deviation of returns for the asset class. Note that although large stocks have a high level of risk, they have the highest risk-adjusted return. Government bonds have the next highest risk-adjusted return.

Figure 11.6

Asset Class	Average Return	Sharpe Ratio	Proportion of years with a loss
Large Stocks (S&P 500)	11.3%	0.39	28.2%
Government Bonds (10 year)	5.4%	0.23	17.6%
Treasury Bills (3 month)	3.6%	0.00	0.0%
Consumer Price Index	3.2%	-0.10	8.2%

To demonstrate the importance of diversification among asset classes, five portfolios are formed as presented in Figure 11.7 and the same measures computed. The equity portion of the portfolio consists of large stocks. The fixed income portion of the portfolio consists of equal weights of government bonds and Treasury bills. By creating portfolios with asset classes that are not perfectly correlated, the overall risk has been reduced and the risk-adjusted returns are higher than could be obtained with any single asset class. Note that several of these portfolios have Sharpe ratios higher than that for stocks alone. The investor can select the portfolio that matches their risk tolerance and provide a decent return relative to risk.

Figure 11.7

Asset Allocation	Average Return	Sharpe Ratio	Proportion of years with a loss
90% Equity 10% Fixed Income	10.6%	0.39	28.2%
75% Equity 25% Fixed Income	9.6%	0.40	27.1%
50% Equity 50% Fixed Income	7.9%	0.42	22.4%
25% Equity 75% Fixed Income	6.2%	0.43	11.8%
10% Equity 90% Fixed Income	5.2%	0.35	7.1%

This example is based on a simple portfolio formation that did not consider the correlations of the asset classes or the appropriateness of the individual asset classes.

11.3 ASSET ALLOCATION AND PORTFOLIO CONSTRUCTION

Section Overview:

11.3.1 Asset Allocation

11.3.2 Controlling Volatility

11.3.3 Monte-Carlo Simulation

11.3.4 Individual Security Selection

11.3.1 ASSET ALLOCATION

Asset allocation involves selecting the proportions of various types of assets to include in a portfolio. Proper asset allocation improves a portfolio's risk-adjusted return. The asset allocation decision is a prelude to selecting individual securities or funds for portfolio inclusion.

The relationship of return and risk is an important investment planning concept. Generally, riskier investments must offer a higher potential return to compensate for the added risk. However, combining two or more risky assets can actually reduce the risk of the overall portfolio, as long as the assets are not highly correlated. Highly correlated assets tend to move in the same direction and at a similar magnitude, while assets that are not highly correlated do not. Investors can use non-highly correlated assets to build portfolios with more favorable risk/return relationships.

Consider four potential investments that have the following expected returns for next year depending on three possible economic environments, each of which is equally likely to occur:

Economic Environment	Expected Returns			
	Asset A	**Asset B**	**Asset C**	**Asset D**
Strong	6%	15%	20%	5%
Normal	6%	10%	10%	10%
Weak	6%	5%	0%	15%
Expected Return	6%	10%	10%	10%
Variability	+/– 0%	+/– 5%	+/– 10%	+/– 5%

Expected return is the asset's average return under all three business conditions. Variability (risk) is simply the range of potential outcomes relative to the expected return. Note that Asset A is a risk free asset, with an expected return of 6 percent and no variability. Assets B, C, and D all offer an expected return of 10 percent but at different levels of risk. Assets B and D are equally risky, while Asset C is riskiest. For a risk-averse investor, Assets B and D appear preferable to C because they offer lower variability for the same expected return. The choice between A, B, and D depends on whether the higher return of B or D is sufficiently enticing for the investor to take on the risk relative to A.

However, the investor doesn't have to choose only one asset. Instead, let's take a look at three potential portfolios where an equal amount of two assets (50 percent of each) is purchased. Note that all three portfolios offer the same 10 percent expected return as the individual assets.

Economic Environment	Expected Returns		
	Portfolio BC	**Portfolio CD**	**Portfolio BD**
Strong	17.5%	12.5%	10.0%
Normal	10.0%	10%	10.0%
Weak	2.5%	7.5%	10.0%
Expected Return	10.0%	10.0%	10.0%
Variability	+/– 7.5%	+/– 2.5%	+/– 0%

The variability of Portfolio BC is the average variability of assets B and C. This portfolio does not achieve any reduction in risk because Assets B and C are perfectly positively correlated (a correlation coefficient of 1.0). They both do well in strong business conditions and poorly in weak conditions.

The expected variability of Portfolio CD is less than the variability for each of the individual assets. This portfolio would be preferred to individual assets B, C, and D because it offers the same expected return but with lower risk. This is because assets C and D are negatively correlated. One asset is always up when the other is down.

Similarly, the Portfolio BD offers the same expected return as assets B, C, and D, but no variability. Again, this is due to the fact that B and D are perfectly negatively correlated. In fact, this portfolio offers a higher return for the same expected risk as Asset A, making it the most preferable portfolio for a risk-averse investor.

By combining assets that are not highly correlated together in portfolios, the investor can achieve a more favorable risk/return relationship. It is not necessary for assets to be negatively correlated to achieve this benefit. Small positive correlations (assets that occasionally, but not always, move in the same direction) also reduce risk. In fact, combining assets that are less than perfectly positively correlated reduces risk.

Modern Portfolio Theory and Asset Allocation

The ability to reduce risk for a given level of return is a fundamental principal of Modern Portfolio Theory (MPT). Properly constructed portfolios of assets that are not highly correlated achieve the highest possible return for a given level of risk. MPT measures risk as standard deviation of returns. The standard deviation for a portfolio of assets can be determined as:

Equation 11.7

$$\sigma_p = \sqrt{\sum_{i=1}^{N} \omega_i^2 \sigma_i^2 + \sum_{i=1}^{N} \sum_{j=1}^{N} \omega_i \omega_j \sigma_i \sigma_j Corr_{ij}}$$

The standard deviation for the portfolio, p, is based upon the weights, w, and standard deviation of each asset, σ, in the portfolio and the correlation between all pairs of assets, i and j. For a two-asset portfolio, this can be expressed more simply as:

Equation 11.8

$$\sigma_p = \sqrt{\omega_1^2 \sigma_1^2 + \omega_2^2 \sigma_2^2 + 2\omega_1 \omega_2 \sigma_1 \sigma_2 Corr_{1,2}}$$

Now consider two assets with the following expected returns, standard deviations, and correlation:

	Asset	
	A	**B**
Expected Return	10.00%	6.00%
Standard Deviation	20.00%	5.00%
Correlation	0.2	

The low correlation between A and B indicates that there should be a benefit from combining these assets in a portfolio. Consider the following potential portfolios, with varying weights of A and B in the portfolio:

Portfolio	Asset A	Asset B	Expected Return	Standard Deviation
1	0	100.00%	6.000%	5.00%
2	10.00%	90.00%	6.400%	5.28%
3	20.00%	80.00%	6.800%	6.20%
4	30.00%	70.00%	7.200%	7.53%
5	40.00%	60.00%	7.600%	9.09%
6	50.00%	50.00%	8.000%	10.78%
7	60.00%	40.00%	8.400%	12.55%
8	70.00%	30.00%	8.800%	14.38%

Portfolio	Asset A	Asset B	Expected Return	Standard Deviation
9	80.00%	20.00%	9.200%	16.23%
10	90.00%	10.00%	9.600%	18.11%
11	100.00%	0.00%	10.000%	20.00%

The expected return is always the weighted average return of the underlying assets. For example, for portfolio six the expected return is 8 percent [(0.5 × 10%) + (0.5 × 6%)]. The standard deviation of each portfolio is based upon the standard deviation formula for the two-asset portfolio in the exhibit.

Note that portfolios one and eleven represent the individual assets. For a risk averse investor, note that relative to portfolio one, portfolio two offers a 6.7 percent higher return [(6.4% / 6%) – 1] but has only a 5.6 percent [(5.28% / 5%) – 1] increase in standard deviation. The return/risk can also be computed, which is 1.20 [6% / 5%] for portfolio one and 1.212 [6.4% / 5.28%] for portfolio two. Portfolio two offers a greater return relative to risk compared to portfolio one. Similarly at the other end of the spectrum, moving from portfolio eleven to portfolio ten, there is a reduction in return of 4 percent (1 – (9.6% / 10%)], but a 9.4 percent reduction [1 – (18.11% / 20%)] in standard deviation. The relationship between risk and return for these portfolios is demonstrated in Figure 11.8. An investor could choose the combination of assets A and B which provides them with their desired return while maintaining an acceptable level of risk.

Figure 11.8

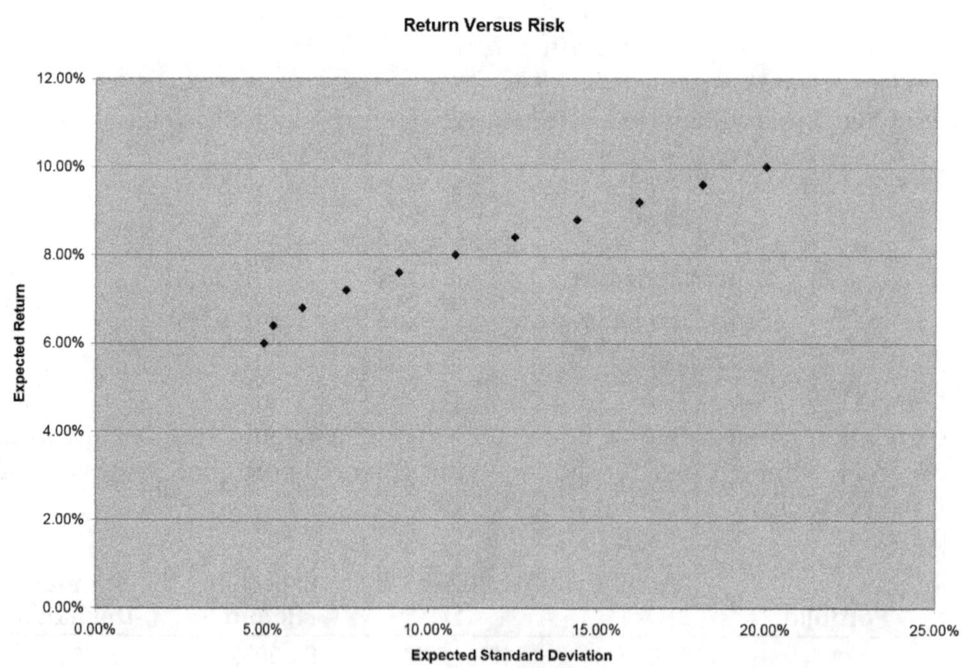

Portfolios of more than two assets make the math more complex, but the basic concepts are the same. Adding assets with low or negative correlations to the rest of the portfolio improves the return/risk relationship.

Overall portfolio asset allocation decisions are made using the expected returns, standard deviation, and correlations between asset classes, rather than individual assets. An asset class is a group of securities with similar characteristics. Broadly speaking, the major asset classes include stocks, bonds, real estate, cash, commodities, and international investments. Within each asset class, however, there can be various gradations that sometimes constitute their own asset class. For example, an investor may consider growth stocks and value stocks to be separate asset classes. Likewise, Treasury Bonds can differ greatly from high-yield bonds in terms of their risk and return. It makes sense to consider these subsets of broad asset classes when forming a portfolio. Commercial asset allocation software packages have varying numbers of asset classes available.

Asset allocation strategies must also consider the appropriateness of each asset class for the particular investor or account. For example, municipal bonds would likely be excluded as an asset class for non-taxable or tax deferred accounts.

Using asset allocation software and the expected returns, standard deviations, and correlations of the asset classes, the advisor should attempt to generate an "efficient frontier" of potential portfolios. The efficient frontier represents those portfolios with the highest expected return for a given level of expected risk as depicted in Figure 11.9.

Figure 11.9

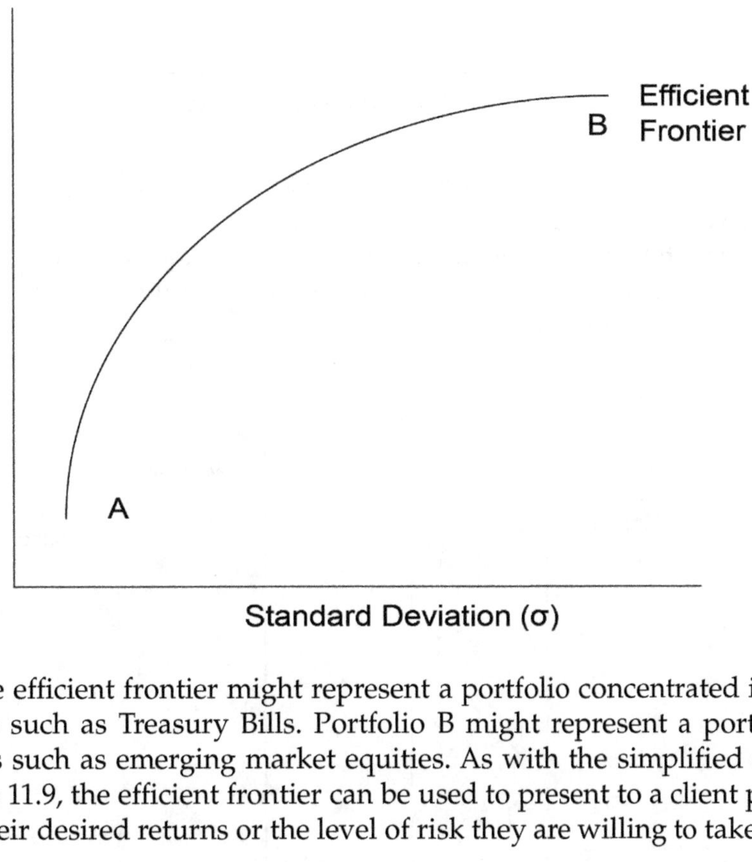

Portfolio A on the efficient frontier might represent a portfolio concentrated in short-term fixed income securities such as Treasury Bills. Portfolio B might represent a portfolio concentrated in risky securities such as emerging market equities. As with the simplified example for assets A and B in Figure 11.9, the efficient frontier can be used to present to a client potential portfolios based on upon their desired returns or the level of risk they are willing to take.

Efficient frontiers can easily be generated based upon historical relationships between asset classes or based upon expected relationships. The challenge is determining which point on the efficient frontier should be selected for a particular client. Theoretically, if the utility (satisfaction) that an investor obtains from different levels of returns relative to risk could be measured, a set of indifference curves for each investor could be drawn. Indifference curves represent the different combinations of risk and return to which an investor is indifferent. Optimally an investor would select the investor's highest indifference curve that touches the efficient frontier as depicted in Figure 11.10. This represents the point of highest utility for the investor.

Figure 11.10

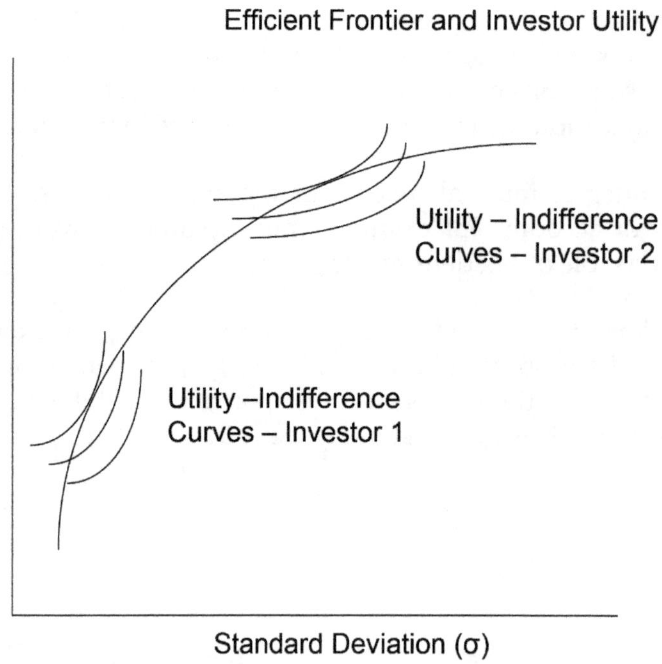

Lacking a precise measure of an individual's risk/return preferences, advisors typically use judgment to select an appropriate point on the efficient frontier based on some measure of the investor's risk tolerance. One approach involves classifying investors as conservative, intermediate, or aggressive. The investor is then placed in the relevant section of the efficient frontier as shown in Figure 11.11.

Figure 11.11

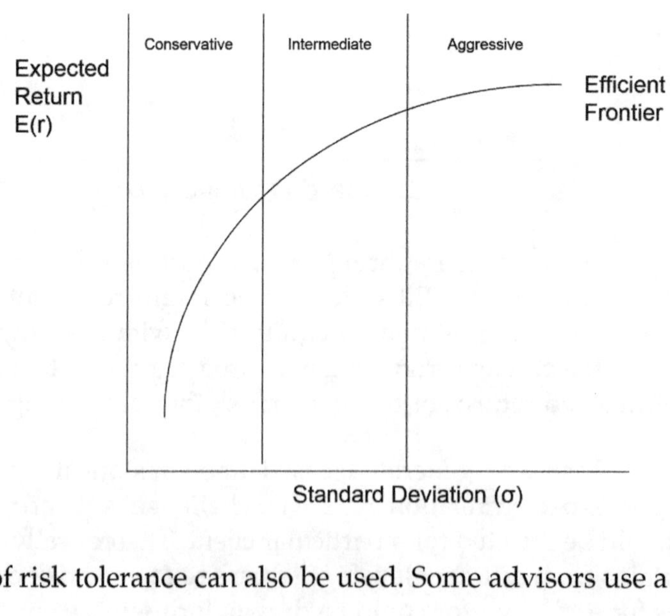

Additional degrees of risk tolerance can also be used. Some advisors use a scale such as:

- Aggressive Growth
- Growth

- Growth and Income
- Income
- Safety

The categories including growth are typically concentrated in equities, with a large portion of the expected return derived from appreciation. Income, by contrast, typically includes investments such as bonds where the current yield is an important component of return. Note that when constructing a portfolio based on a client's investment policy statement, the advisor should include the constraints and preferences in determining an appropriate allocation.

Strategic Asset Allocation

A strategic asset allocation can be thought of as the long-range plan for a portfolio. Taking into consideration the long-range return requirements and risk tolerance, allocations to various asset classes are developed as described earlier. The strategic allocation typically is not altered to take into account short-term issues such as current market conditions (perceived current relative value of different asset classes). Instead, assets are periodically rebalanced to conform to the original allocation.

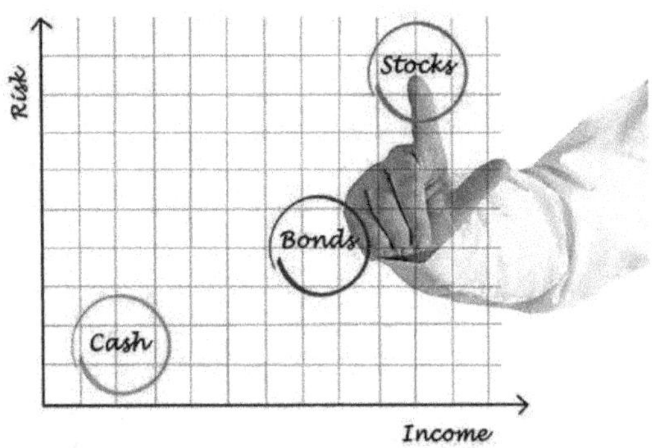

This rebalancing is necessary because the asset classes will have different returns. For example, over the long term equities usually have a higher return than bonds. If the strategic allocation is 50 percent stocks and 50 percent bonds and stocks have a higher return, over time, the portfolio will have a greater than 50 percent position in stocks. To bring the allocation back to the overall strategic allocation, enough stocks would have to be sold and bonds purchased to get back to the 50/50 allocation. Note that if dividends and interest are reinvested in the same asset class or held in cash, this will also impact the rebalancing. An advantage to rebalancing within a strategic asset allocation is that it enforces a discipline to sell the best performing asset classes and buy the lowest performing (buy low, sell high). Alternatively, a momentum investing strategy would suggest no rebalancing – letting the winners run.

Example. Consider an investor who has created a strategic asset allocation of 30 percent bonds, 30 percent commodities, and 40 percent stocks, and who has set a guideline that the portfolio will be rebalanced when any asset class varies from the strategic allocation by more than 500 basis points (5 percent). Over the next five years, the assets exhibit the following return pattern:

Year	Bonds	Commodities	Stocks
1	2.43%	13.54%	4.91%
2	4.34%	20.25%	10.88%
3	4.10%	38.59%	28.68%
4	10.25%	–15.94%	–22.10%
5	8.44%	–21.44%	–11.89%

How frequently will the portfolio be rebalanced? How will strategic rebalancing affect the ending value of the portfolio relative to letting the winners run?

First, let's consider an initial portfolio of $1 million that is allowed to run:

Year-end	Bonds	Commodities	Stocks	Total
0	300,000	300,000	400,000	1,000,000
1	307,290	340,620	419,640	1,067,550
2	320,626	409,596	465,297	1,195,519
3	333,772	567,658	598,744	1,500,175
4	367,984	477,174	466,422	1,311,579
5	399,042	374,868	410,964	1,184,873

The ending value of the portfolio is $1,184,873.

Now let's consider the percentage of the portfolio in each asset for the period:

Year-end	Bonds	Commodities	Stocks	Total
0	30%	30%	40%	100%
1	29%	32%	39%	100%
2	27%	34%	39%	100%
3	22%	38%	40%	100%
4	28%	36%	36%	100%
5	34%	32%	35%	100%

At the end of year one, the allocations are 29 percent bonds, 32 percent commodities, and 39 percent stocks. No allocation has drifted by more than 500 basis points from the strategic goal, so no rebalance is necessary. The same applies at the end of year two.

At the end of year three, however, the allocation to bonds has fallen by 800 basis points relative to the strategic allocation, and the allocation to commodities has risen by 800 basis points. According to the guidelines, the portfolio needs to be rebalanced. Doing so results in the following adjustments:

Year-end	Bonds	Commodities	Stocks	Total
3	450,052	450,052	600,070	1,500,175
4	496,183	378,314	467,454	1,341,951
5	538,061	297,203	411,874	1,247,138

Note that by letting this newly rebalanced portfolio run, the ending value of $1,247,138 is $62,265 higher than the original ending value. However, going forward, the percentage of assets changes as follows:

Year-end	Bonds	Commodities	Stocks	Total
3	30%	30%	40%	100%
4	37%	28%	35%	100%
5	43%	24%	33%	100%

Once again, at the end of year four there is an imbalance of more than 500 basis points – this time there is too high an allocation to bonds. The portfolio must be rebalanced a second time at the end of year four, to the following allocations:

Year-end	Bonds	Commodities	Stocks	Total
4	402,585	402,585	536,780	1,341,951
5	436,564	316,271	472,957	1,225,792

After the new rebalancing is completed and the final year elapses, the ending value of the portfolio is still $40,919 better than would have been achieved from letting the assets run from year one on. However, it is $21,346 *lower* than it would have been if the second rebalancing had not been done. This is because in year five bonds continued to do well, while stocks and commodities continued to fall.

Because there is no way of knowing in advance whether the trends will continue or reverse in a given year, it is generally best to decide in advance how frequently to rebalance in order to retain the desired level of risk for the client's portfolio.

Tactical Asset Allocation

In contrast to strategic allocation, tactical asset allocation attempts to capitalize on changing market conditions. In a tactical asset allocation, the overall asset allocation is frequently adjusted to take advantage of perceived opportunities in the current market. For example, in a high interest rate environment, the advisor may shift the asset allocation to favor long-term bonds. If U.S. equities are perceived to be undervalued, the advisor may overweight them. The rewards of tactical asset allocation depend on the advisor's ability to predict which asset classes will perform best in the near term. Strategic asset allocation is generally a low turnover investment strategy, while tactical asset allocation generally results in high turnover.

Example. The investor starts with the same $1 million portfolio and strategic allocation guidelines as in the previous example. However, the advisor is given discretion to shift the allocation tactically once per year as long as the starting allocations are within 500 basis points of each asset's strategic goal. The advisor decides to follow a momentum strategy that overweighs the previous year's top-performing asset by 500 basis points and underweights the worst-performing asset by 500 basis points. The resulting performance is as follows:

	Bonds	Commodities	Stocks	Total
Beginning of year 1	300,000	300,000	400,000	1,000,000
Performance	2.43%	13.54%	4.91%	
End of year 1	307,290	340,620	419,640	1,067,550
New allocation	25%	35%	40%	
Beginning of year 2	266,888	373,643	427,020	1,067,550
Performance	4.34%	20.25%	10.88%	
End of year 2	278,470	449,305	473,480	1,201,255

	Bonds	Commodities	Stocks	Total
New allocation	25%	35%	40%	
Beginning of year 3	300,314	420,439	480,502	1,201,255
Performance	4.10%	38.59%	28.68%	
End of year 3	312,627	582,687	618,310	1,513,624
New allocation	25%	35%	40%	
Beginning of year 4	378,406	529,768	605,449	1,513,624
Performance	10.25%	–15.94%	–22.10%	
End of year 4	417,193	445,323	471,645	1,334,161
New allocation	35%	30%	35%	
Beginning of year 5	466,956	400,248	466,956	1,334,161
Performance	8.44%	–21.44%	–11.89%	
End of year 5	506,367	314,435	411,435	1,232,238

The manager's tactical rebalancing results in a higher ending value than either the untouched portfolio or the one that was strategically rebalanced. However, the $6,446 improvement over strategic rebalancing may not have justified the higher trading costs from larger and more frequent allocation adjustments.

11.3.2 CONTROLLING VOLATILITY

Asset allocation is a means of controlling the volatility that is inherent in investment returns. Some investors may have a high degree of risk tolerance and desire to achieve the maximum possible return regardless of risk. Other investors may not sleep well at night with volatile portfolio values. Even investors who think they can tolerate risk may have circumstances where volatility can impair their ability to maintain a certain standard of living. Take for example a long-term historical return on large stocks of 10 percent and a long term inflation rate of 3 percent. An investor has $1,000,000 at retirement and desires to withdraw the maximum amount possible each year while maintaining the purchasing power of the portfolio each year and not running out of money during any foreseeable life expectancy. One might naively assume that the investor could withdraw 7 percent each year starting with $70,000 the first year (and increasing the dollar amount by inflation in each subsequent year). Unfortunately, it turns out that is not possible unless there is no volatility in returns. If the stock market achieved 10 percent returns each and every year it would be possible, but with volatility the maximum safe withdrawal rate is much lower. In fact, studies have shown that the maximum safe withdrawal rate given historic volatility of returns for a stock is less than 4 percent.

As noted in previous sections, creating a diversified portfolio with assets that are not highly correlated can reduce the volatility of an investment portfolio. Time also moderates volatility. If an investor has a long time horizon before investment withdrawals are to begin, the impact of volatility is dampened over time. Additionally, volatility can be managed using hedging strategies and options strategies such as a covered call (selling a call option on a currently held investment). A covered call sells some of the upside and reduces the potential downside (from the collection of the option premium), reducing the standard deviation of the portfolio. Downside risk can also be reduced through the purchase of put options.

11.3.3 MONTE-CARLO SIMULATION

Expected returns and standard deviation are not necessarily constant over time. Nor is the return in an individual period predictable. Returns in each asset class are probabilistic. Investors may also make periodic deposits and withdrawals, further increasing the difficulty of predicting long-term returns and risk. If an investor desires a particular level of retirement income, what is the assurance that this level of income is likely to be obtained?

Monte-Carlo simulation assesses the likelihood of an expected outcome. In a Monte-Carlo simulation, a computer program randomly chooses returns from an expected distribution of returns for each period (perhaps rebalancing the asset allocation if required under the strategy). Each run results in an ending expected portfolio value. The process is run many times (generally more than 1,000), to achieve a distribution of ending values. This process can help assess the probability of achieving a certain value or income in the future (including the possibility that an individual will outlive his retirement assets).

Example. As noted in the prior section, volatility has a significant impact on the ability of a client to make desired withdrawals during retirement. The impact of volatility on the sustainability of retirement distributions can be demonstrated using Monte-Carlo simulation. Assume that an investment adviser has the following market expectations:

	Expected Long-Term Arithmetic Average Return	**Expected Long-Term Standard Deviation of Returns**
Stocks	9.0%	20.0%
Bonds	4.0%	8.0%

Expected long-term correlation of stocks and bonds 0.20

Consider a retired client who has a $1,000,000 portfolio. The client would like to withdraw as much as possible each year with that amount increasing for inflation. Ideally the client would like to withdraw about $40,000 (4 percent of the initial portfolio amount) adjusted for inflation each year. Using one Monte-Carlo simulation software (MCRetire – www.effisols.com) using a 9 percent expected return for stocks, 20 percent expected standard deviation for stocks, and 3 percent inflation, the probability of success (the ability to withdraw $40,000 each year adjusted for inflation over the next thirty years without running out of money) can be computed.

Running one million iterations, the Monte-Carlo simulation reveals that there is about a 73 percent probability of success with a 100 percent stock portfolio. In other words, in 27 percent of the thirty-year time periods the client would run out of money within thirty years, not an attractive scenario for most clients. The software can also be run to output the maximum safe initial withdrawal given a certain desired probability of success. Let's say a client wants to be 95 percent certain not to run out of money. Monte-Carlo simulation reveals that the maximum safe withdrawal amount is about 2.2 percent ($22,000 rather than $40,000). Running the Monte-Carlo simulation with a 100 percent bond portfolio reveals that there is a 36 percent probability of success at withdrawing $40,000. Conversely, to achieve a 95 percent probability of success with bonds, the maximum safe initial withdrawal rate is about 2.4 percent. While the expected return on stocks was higher than that of bonds, bonds had a lower volatility. The probability of success was lower than for a stock only portfolio, but the sustainable withdrawal was higher. However, neither the stock only nor the bond only portfolios are very attractive.

By creating a portfolio of these two asset classes that are not highly correlated, the sustainability of withdrawals can be improved. Take a portfolio of 50 percent stocks and 50 percent bonds. From the given data, the expected return on the portfolio would be 6.5 percent with a standard deviation of 11.5 percent. Running Monte-Carlo simulation reveals that the combined portfolio would have a 73 percent probability of succeeding with a 4 percent withdrawal rate. To achieve a 95 percent probability of success the maximum safe withdrawal rate would be about 2.9 percent. The diversified portfolio outperforms both the stock only and bond only portfolios in terms of a higher sustainable withdrawal amount, once again demonstrating the advantages of asset allocation in controlling volatility.

Note, however, that the diversified portfolio has a lower expected return than the stock only portfolio and the average expected wealth accumulation would be lower than a stock only portfolio. In other words while the probability of obtaining a $40,000 withdrawal is about the same for an all stock portfolio as with a diversified portfolio, the all stock portfolio will result in a higher ending wealth in years in which it is successful. Unfortunately clients only get one observation for their retirement years – no do-overs allowed! This is consistent with using a higher equity allocation during the pre-retirement years and switching to a more diversified portfolio during retirement years for risk adverse clients.

The preceding example was for illustrative purposes only. Each Monte Carlo software is presumably unique. Calculated results may vary.

11.3.4 INDIVIDUAL SECURITY SELECTION

Once the asset allocation decision has been made, the next step is to select individual securities (stocks, bonds, etc.) or mutual funds within each asset class. As with the overall asset allocation strategy, this can be either passive or active. In a passive approach, the advisor selects broad diversified portfolios (such as index mutual funds or exchange-traded index funds) representing each asset class.

In an active approach, the advisor selects individual securities or traditional, actively managed mutual funds within each asset class that are expected to outperform their peers. The active approach requires more frequent monitoring, security selection, and buy/sell decisions. The choice between the active and passive approaches depends upon an advisor's beliefs about market efficiency and the advisor's ability to select, in advance, better performing securities or funds. Efficient markets generally assume rational behavior by market participants, but a number of anomalies have been shown to occur. A study of behavioral finance can help the advisor understand investor behavior both in selecting investment strategies and educating clients to avoid some common pitfalls.

11.4 MARKET EFFICIENCY

Section Overview:

11.4.1 Efficient Market Theory (EMT)

11.4.2 Strong Form EMT

11.4.3 Semi-Strong Form EMT

11.4.4 Weak Form EMT

11.4.5 EMT Anomalies

11.4.1 EFFICIENT MARKET HYPOTHESIS (EMT)

The Efficient Market Theory (EMT) hypothesizes that securities markets process information efficiently. This implies that new information about a security is quickly (almost instantaneously) reflected in its price.

In order for a market to be efficient, certain conditions must be met. These include a large number of profit maximizing investors competing in the market and a free, random flow of information. When these conditions are present, the market is assumed to be efficient.

Beginning with the first point, a large number of profit-seeking market participants ensures that no trader is able to manipulate the market. If a participant tries to drive the price of a security too high or too low, other investors will recognize the mispricing and sell or buy to offset the rogue trader. Note that this does not imply that prices will always adjust immediately to the "correct" price. Rather, the efficient market theory requires only an equal likelihood that prices are either too high or too low (no bias that would allow investors to earn excess returns).

An efficient market requires that news flow be random and freely available. If positive or negative announcements can be consistently predicted, a trader can take advantage of them. As long as the timing is uncertain, all traders have an equal opportunity to profit or loss from a given speculation.

Given a market with many traders, a quick reaction to information is generally a given. Still, there could be other factors limiting an investor's ability to trade. For example, exchange rules put in place after the 1987 market crash include "circuit breakers" that halt trading when the market is up or down more than a certain amount. It has been argued that these rules reduce efficiency, as investors are prevented from fully responding to important events.

11.4.2 STRONG FORM EMT

In its strong form, efficient market theory posits that all information, whether public or not, is reflected in security prices. In other words, this is a perfect market assumption. In a strong-form efficient market, no participants – even company executives or other insiders – would be able to consistently perform better than the market other than by random luck.

11.4.3 SEMI-STRONG FORM EMT

The semi-strong form of efficient market theory states that all public information is reflected in stock prices. This includes prices of securities, security volume data, financial reports, press releases, statements of company officers, newspaper articles, and the work of sell-side securities analysts, as well as many other types of information.

11.4.4 WEAK FORM EMT

To be weak form efficient, security prices need reflect only market data, such as historical trade prices, volume, and order size. In a weak form efficient market, an investor could use fundamental analysis tools such as financial statement analysis and other fundamental information to glean information that has not been efficiently priced. This information could then be used to outperform the market. However, technical analysis (charting of security price and volume data) would still fail to provide consistent out-performance, because it relies on market data.

11.4.5 EMT ANOMALIES

There are a number of research studies that show that some basic fundamental strategies can result in an investor out-performing the market. These are known as EMT anomalies.

Stocks paying high dividend yields have been shown to perform better over time than low dividend yield stocks. Similarly, stocks with low price/book, price/sales, and price/earnings ratios have been found to outperform those stocks with higher price multiples. Likewise, low-beta stocks have been found to outperform high beta stocks.

The market appears to over and under react to news. Sometimes it takes several quarters for news to be fully reflected in stock prices and, in other cases, news causes an overreaction that is later corrected. Studies have been done showing that the market overreacts, and others indicate that there is persistent under-reaction. Note that unless an investor can predict whether the market reaction to news will be too much or not enough, the efficient market hypothesis would hold.

Some research has demonstrated a "January effect" under which the market tends to perform better in January. Some of this effect may be explained by the timing of tax selling. Late in the year, investors who want to minimize taxes will sell stocks that have gone down in order to incur a capital loss. Under the tax rules, if the investor desires to repurchase the security, he must wait thirty days, which can cause buying in January.

Shares of firms with small market capitalization (the size effect) or few dedicated analysts (the neglect effect) tend to perform better than others. In some ways, this is not so much an anomaly as a validation of the efficient market theory. Few analysts or a small market cap could reduce buyers' willingness to take a chance on such names. As a result, the first requirement of an efficient market – that there be many participants – is violated.

The Value Line effect is a finding that stocks ranked highest by Value Line have been found to outperform the market in certain periods. This is considered to be an efficient market anomaly, because this consistent outperformance should be recognized by the market and reflected in the stock price as soon as the ranking is published.

The existence of the various anomalies calls into question the relative efficiency of the markets. The research studies that uncovered these anomalies relate to particular time periods and, of course, do not guarantee they will work in future periods. In addition, identifying anomalies should cause traders to act on them, which in turn helps to achieve a greater level of market efficiency.

11.5 BEHAVIORAL FINANCE

Section Overview:

11.5.1 Mental Accounting

11.5.2 Confirmation Bias

11.5.3 Optimism/Overconfidence

11.5.4 Loss Aversion/Framing

11.5.5 Herding

11.5.6 Use of Heuristics

Behavioral finance involves the study of how investors make decisions. Investors often use mental shortcuts or demonstrate consistent biases in their decision making. Understanding these concepts can assist the advisor in understanding market behavior and anomalies and helping clients make better decisions. Some investment managers and mutual funds attempt to exploit these behavioral issues in making securities investments. This section explores some common behavioral finance issues.

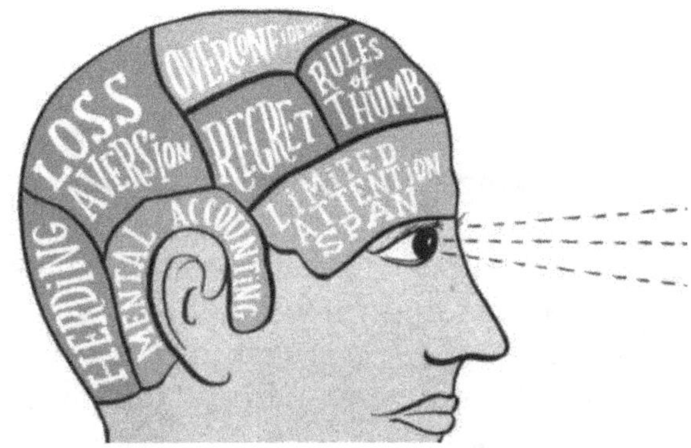

11.5.1 MENTAL ACCOUNTING

Investors (and consumers) have been shown to have "categories of money" such that all dollars are not equivalent. They categorize money into buckets. Imagine that a ticket to a hockey game is purchased for $100. When the individual arrives for the game, he discovers that he has lost his ticket. Question 1 – Does he spend another $100 to purchase another ticket? Consider another example where the individual has not yet purchased a ticket. When he arrives for the game, he discovers that he has lost $100 in the parking lot. Question 2 – Does he spend another $100 to purchase a ticket? Belsky and Gilovich (1999) find that most people answer no to Question 1 but yes to question 2 because in the first situation $200 would be charged to the entertainment "mental account." In the investment arena, clients may be inclined to mentally view money differently depending upon the source, such as an inheritance versus earned money, or principal versus capital gains.

11.5.2 CONFIRMATION BIAS

People tend to search for and select information which confirms their beliefs. This is a dangerous bias that can lead to bad investment decisions. For example, in evaluating an individual security for investment, the advisor or client may examine a half dozen analysts' reports and select the one that confirms his prior beliefs (buy, sell, or hold). Of course, the analyst writing the report may have used confirmation bias in evaluating data for purposes of reaching his recommendation based on other relationships the analyst may have with the company. Advisors need to be aware of the potential existence of this bias in evaluating reports of others and in making their own evaluations. An independent, objective frame of mind should be strived for.

11.5.3 OPTIMISM/OVERCONFIDENCE

People tend to believe that they are better than average (while everyone wants to be – by definition, they cannot all be above average). For example, in a survey of British drivers, 95 percent of them felt they were above average. Analysts, investors, and advisors may be overconfident in their abilities to forecast company earnings, future growth rates, investment returns, and similar future events. Overconfidence can be reduced by considering many different possibilities or alternatives.

11.5.4 LOSS AVERSION/FRAMING

Individuals are generally willing to take more risk to avoid a certain loss, but are conservative in locking in gains and avoiding risk. Aversion to losses also results in a reluctance of investors to sell losing investments. They may feel they can "avoid" the loss by not selling the investment, even though the investment has declined in value. This kind of behavior can result in an investor holding a portfolio of "losers" as they sell their winners. This behavior is also very inefficient from a tax perspective as the investor realizes gains – and pays taxes on them – and, at the same time avoids taking loses and realizing the tax benefits from a loss.

11.5.5 HERDING

Individuals may engage in herding behavior. This can be demonstrated with financial analysts who forecast earnings for a company. Analysts may want to stay with the herd by having a forecast that is similar to the forecast of other analysts. Having a forecast that is much higher or lower than the "herd" can result in being out on a limb if the analyst is wrong. If an individual is wrong, but in with the herd there is no loss in reputation.

11.5.6 USE OF HEURISTICS

Individuals often use heuristics (shortcuts) in making decisions. These include representativeness, availability, and anchoring. In representativeness, individuals make judgments based on similar past events. Availability involves making decisions based on how recent or vivid information is. For example, they may view the market more positively if recent returns have been positive even though market returns may actually exhibit some reversion to the mean. Similarly, they may become increasingly pessimistic if the market has declined recently. Anchoring involves individuals anchoring on a current number such as a stock price or returns and make adjustments from that number, rather than making an independent assessment of potential outcomes. These simple shortcuts ease decision making but can result in bad investment decision, such as buying investments that have recently increased in value rather than buying those that have recently declined.

11.6 INVESTMENT STRATEGIES

Section Overview:

11.6.1 Fundamental Analysis

11.6.2 Technical Analysis

11.6.3 Timing of Investment Purchases and Sales

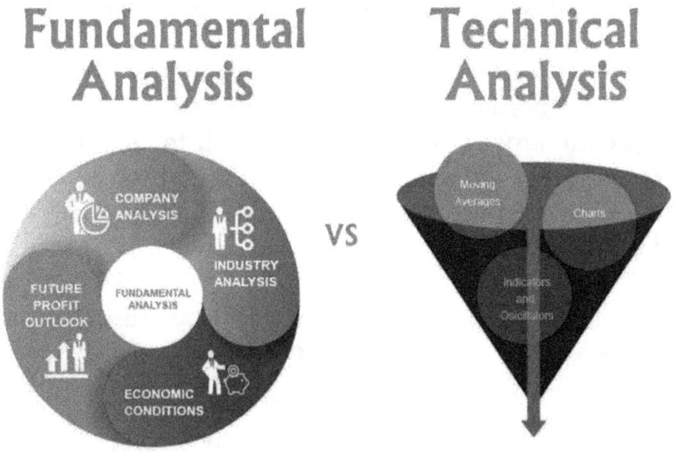

Passive investment strategies implicitly assume markets are efficient, and that, therefore, reducing investment trading and research costs is more important than pursuing "market out-performance." A passive approach typically involves purchasing a basket of securities that represents a market index and holding them for the long term (perhaps with periodic rebalancing). A passive approach typically does not focus on individual security selection.

By contrast, active management strategies either assume the market is inefficient or that inefficiencies within the market can be profitably exploited. A great deal of time and effort is expended in security selection and the timing of purchases and sales.

Active security selection usually involves fundamental analysis, technical analysis, or both. Fundamental analysis examines company-specific factors such as profitability, risk, relative valuation, and growth prospects. Technical analysis studies market information such as price and volume to identify important trends and opportunities.

11.6.1 FUNDAMENTAL ANALYSIS

Many managers use fundamental analysis techniques to identify securities they believe are mispriced. Fundamental analysis can be employed using either a top-down or a bottom-up philosophy.

Top-down managers begin with an overview of the entire economy and market. The idea behind such research is that one must first understand where the overall economy is headed in order to identify the asset classes, economic sectors, and, ultimately, securities that are likely to outperform. In a top down approach, the final step is typically to examine the fundamentals of a particular company whose securities are of interest.

Bottom-up analysts often call themselves stock-pickers. They attempt to identify the best securities and the price at which to buy them, regardless of sector or industry considerations. Bottom-up analysts typically begin by examining company fundamentals, often by screening large databases of securities for information the analyst finds interesting. Only after they have identified securities of interest do they consider the prospects for the industry, sector, and economy.

Some investors blend both top-down and bottom-up approaches in an attempt to add value across the spectrum.

Company Fundamentals

In order to understand some of the fundamental factors analysts look for, first some basic company financial information is presented. There are three important financial statements on which analysts focus: (1) the balance sheet; (2) the income statement; and (3) the statement of cash flows. There are other financial statements (such as a statement of owners' equity), schedules, and footnotes that are also useful in understanding the three primary statements.

The *balance sheet* reflects the company's financial position as of a particular date. Figure 11.12 presents a basic balance sheet for a hypothetical electronics retailer. The balance sheet presents the company's resources (assets) and the claims against those resources (liabilities and equity). The resources must always equal the claims (hence the term balance sheet).

Figure 11.12

Howard's Electronic Retailers, Inc.
Balance Sheet As Of December 31 (in millions of dollars)

	2012	**2013**
Cash	$ 10	$ 15
Accounts Receivable	50	60
Inventory	100	120
Current Assets	160	195
Property, Plant and Equipment	640	730
Accumulated Depreciation	(300)	(330)
Total Assets	$ 500	$ 595
Accounts Payable	$ 40	$ 45
Accrued Expenses	30	38
Current Liabilities	70	83
Long Term Debt	200	240
Total Liabilities	270	323
Common Stock	100	115
Retained Earnings	130	157
Total Equity	230	272
Total Liabilities and Equity	$ 500	$ 595

The balance sheet heading indicates that the company has a calendar year end and that all numbers are denominated in millions. The balance sheets as of year-end 2012 and 2013 are both presented. The company's assets are classified either as current or long-term. Current assets are expected to be used up in a single operating cycle, typically one year. Non-current assets have a lifetime that spans multiple operating cycles.

United States accounting conventions list assets in order of how quickly they can be converted into cash. Not surprisingly, therefore, cash is normally the first asset presented. The balance sheet cash account includes cash on hand, in banks, and other short-term deposits (such as certificates of deposits).

Accounts receivable represents money the company is owed by its customers for goods or services that have been provided. For example, when a doctor provides services and bills the patient at a later date, an accounts receivable balance is created from the time the service is performed until the bill is paid.

Inventory is the unsold merchandise and materials on hand at the end of the year.

Property, plant, and equipment are long-term fixed assets of the company such as buildings, equipment, vehicles, and furniture. These assets are not used up in a single year, but rather benefit the company over time. Generally Accepted Accounting Principles (GAAP) require that companies report the costs associated with money earned in the same period the money is earned, a concept known as the matching principle. For example, because a factory helps a company earn money for many years; GAAP requires that the cost of the factory be spread out over many years. When the company earns money later, the relevant factory costs are recognized at the same time.

The cost a company recognizes for a fixed asset in the future period is called depreciation. Essentially, depreciation is an estimation of the economic wear and tear on the fixed assets over time.

Total assets are the sum of current and noncurrent assets. For Howard's Electronic Retailers, Inc. (HERI), there were total assets of $500 million at the end of 2012 and $595 million at the end of 2013.

Liabilities are also classified as current or noncurrent. Just as assets are listed in order of how quickly they are likely to be turned into cash or used up, liabilities are listed in the order they are expected to be paid.

Accounts payable represent the amounts owed to suppliers. Accrued expenses represent additional expenses payable to others such as employees, the government, or landlords.

Long-term debt represents amounts due to creditors such as banks. For example, when a company buys vehicles, it may choose to finance the purchase. In a way, financing long-lasting assets with liabilities that are paid off over time is the economic (as opposed to accounting) version of the matching principle.

Equity represents the amount owners have invested in a business, either initially or by reinvesting the company's earnings. Common stock represents the amounts paid into the company when the stock was first sold to shareholders. Retained earnings are the earnings accumulated in the company (not paid out to shareholders as dividends) since inception.

The *income statement* shows how profitable a company was during a particular time period. Figure 11.13 presents income statements for HERI. Typically three years of the income statement are presented in a company's annual report. For HERI, income statements for December 31, 2011, 2012, and 2013 are provided.

The top line of the income statement, revenues, is the total amount received (or due) from customers for goods and services provided during the period. Cost of goods sold represents the cost of those goods (or services), such as materials and labor used directly in delivering the goods (or services). The difference between revenues and cost of goods sold is called gross profit. Gross profit is a basic measure of how the company is doing. The higher the gross profit, the better.

Operating expenses are other expenses incurred in the operation of a business, such as overhead. Operating income is the subtotal reflecting gross profit minus operating expenses.

Figure 11.13

Howard's Electronic Retailers, Inc.
Income Statement For the year ended December 31 (in millions of dollars)

	2015	2016	2017
Revenues	$ 750	$ 800	$ 900
Cost of Goods Sold	560	600	713
Gross Profit	190	200	187
Operating Expenses	100	120	130
Operating Income	90	80	57
Interest Expense	18	18	18
Pre-Tax Income	72	62	39
Income Tax Expense	21	19	12
Net Income	$ 51	$ 43	$ 27
Shares Outstanding (millions)	100	100	102
Earnings Per Share	$ 0.51	$ 0.43	$ 0.26

Interest expense is the interest paid to creditors for the use of their money during the period. Pre-tax income is the subtotal that includes operating and non-operating (financing) results. Income tax is the amount owed on the reported income. Net income, commonly termed "the bottom line," is the overall net profit during the period. When net income is divided by the number of shares of stock outstanding, the result is known as "Earnings Per Share" (EPS). EPS allows each investor to determine his share of net income.

As discussed earlier, the matching principle requires that revenues be reported when earned and expenses when incurred. This does not necessarily coincide with when the cash is received or paid. As a result, the third important financial statement, the cash flow statement, presents the cash received and paid out during the period. Figure 11.14 presents the cash flow statement for HERI.

Figure 11.14

Howard's Electronic Retailers, Inc.
Statement of Cash Flows For the year ended December 31 (in millions of dollars)

	2015	**2016**	**2017**
Operating			
Net Income			
Plus Depreciation	$ 51	$ 43	$ 27
Change in Working	25	25	30
Capital	(20)	10	(17)
Operating Cash Flow	56	78	40
Investing			
Capital Expenditures	(60)	(70)	(90)
Investing Cash Flow	(60)	(70)	(90)
Financing			
Borrowing	0	0	40
Issuance of Stock	0	0	15
Financing Cash Flow	0	0	55
Total Cash Flow	(4)	8	5
Beginning Cash	6	2	10
Ending Cash	$ 2	$ 10	$ 15

Cash flow is important because it is necessary to pay employees, suppliers, creditors, and, ultimately, owners. The cash flow statement is divided into three sections: operating cash flows, investing cash flows, and financing cash flows. Operating cash flows relate to operating the business. Investing cash flows relate to investments in long-term assets. Financing cash flows relate to financing the company, such as issuing/repaying debt, issuing/repurchasing shares, and paying dividends.

Generally, it is preferable to have strong, positive operating cash flows that can be used to invest in long-term assets and repay capital providers (debt and equity).

Recent accounting scandals have highlighted the importance of paying attention to the cash flow statement. Some companies abuse and pervert accounting guidelines to overstate net income. If a company has rising net income but declining operating cash flow, this is a warning sign and the company should be scrutinized carefully.

Company Ratios

In order to evaluate how a company is doing over time and relative to other companies in the industry, financial performance and position must be compared. Because comparisons between companies of different sizes or growth rates can be difficult, analysts often create ratios to remove the impact of size differences. Ratios can be categorized as: liquidity and solvency, efficiency, profitability, and price multiples. Some common ratios in each of these categories are presented in Figure 11.15.

Figure 11.15

Category	Ratio	Formula
Liquidity & Solvency	Current Ratio	Current Assets / Current Liabilities
	Debt Ratio	Total Liabilities / Total Assets
	Times Interest Earned	Earnings Before Interest and Taxes / Interest Expense
Efficiency	Accounts Receivable Turnover	Sales / Average Accounts Receivable
	Inventory Turnover	Cost of Goods Sold / Average Inventory
	Total Asset Turnover	Sales / Average Total Assets
Profitability	Net profit margin	Net Income / Sales
	Return on assets	Net Income / Average Total Assets
	Return on equity	Net Income / Average Total Equity
Price Multiples	Price/Earnings	Price Per Share / Earnings Per Share
	Price/Book Value	Price Per Share / Book Value Per Share
	Price/Operating Cash Flow	Price Per Share / Operating Cash Flow Per Share

Liquidity and solvency ratios show the ability of a company to pay short- and long-term obligations, respectively. HERI has a current ratio of 2.35 ($195/$83) indicating that it has $2.35 of current assets for every $1.00 of current liabilities. When the current ratio is greater than one, current assets are sufficient to satisfy current liabilities. A company with a higher current ratio is less likely to default on its payments, but an extremely high current ratio may indicate the company is not using its resources efficiently.

HERI's debt ratio is 54.29 percent (323/595), indicating that a little more than half of its assets are financed with liabilities. In terms of solvency, a lower number would indicate lower financial risk.

However, debt can be beneficial if the company can use the debt-financed assets to earn more than it pays in interest.

Times interest earned measures whether the company earns enough operating income to make its interest payments. HERI has a times interest earned ratio of 3.17 ($57/$18), meaning it can cover its interest slightly more than 3 times over.

Efficiency ratios provide insight into how well the company is managing various activities. Accounts receivable turnover indicates how quickly the company collects money owed by its customers. A high number means the company collects its receivables quickly. HERI has an accounts receivable turnover ratio of 16.36 [$900 / (($50 + $60) / 2)]. On average, this means it takes 22.31 days (365/16.36) on average to collect receivables. Similarly, inventory turnover measures how often the company turns over its inventory. HERI turned over its inventory 6.48 times per year [$713 / (($100 + $120) / 2)] (equivalent to 56.33 days of inventory on hand [365 / 6.48]). Total asset turnover indicates the company's overall efficiency. HERI has a total asset turnover ratio of 1.64 times. This indicates that HERI generates $1.64 in sales for every $1.00 invested in assets.

Profitability ratios indicate the company's relative profitability. HERI's net profit margin of 3.0 percent ($271/$900) indicates that it earns $3.00 for every $100.00 in revenue. HERI has a return on assets ratio of 4.93 percent [$27 / (($500 + $595) / 2)] indicating that it earns $4.93 of profits for every $100.00 invested in assets. Lastly, HERI's return on equity is 10.76 percent [$27 / (($230 + $272) / 2)], indicating that it earned $10.76 in profits for every $100.00 invested by the owners.

The price multiples indicate the relative valuation of the company by the market. A low ratio indicates a low valuation relative to some fundamental measure, and could indicate that the company is a bargain or that investors expect it to do poorly. A high ratio could indicate overvaluation or high expected future growth. The price earnings (P/E) ratio is the price per share relative to earnings per share. The price to book (P/B) ratio is the price share divided by book value (stockholders' equity) per share. Price to operating cash flow is the price per share relative to operating cash flow per share. Assuming a price of $4.00 per share for HERI, its price multiples are:

P/E	15.38 [4 / .26]
P/B	1.50 [4 / (272 / 102)]
P/OCF	10.20 [4 / (40 / 102)]

The company is selling for 15.38 times earnings, 1.5 times book value (accounting basis for equity), and 10.20 times operating cash flow. These measures can be compared to peer companies and the overall market to assess the company's relative valuation.

Example. Landstar System, Inc. provides transportation services, mainly truckload transportation over medium distances. The company does not own its own vehicles, but instead uses technology to match loads sourced by commissioned agents with drivers who provide their own vehicles. As a result, Landstar's fixed asset base is relatively small.

An investor looking at Landstar in early 2006 would have found the following information in the company's annual report (most companies show the most recent year first in the annual report - the treatment used in this example):

Year ended December 31, in thousands of dollars	2005	2004	2003
Total revenue	2,520,523	2,021,282	1,597,791
Net income	119,956	71,872	50,700
Cash flow from operating activities	6,529	49,744	53,396

At first glance, the investor at that time would have been pleased with the company's rapid revenue growth rate (24.7 percent in 2005 and 26.5 percent in 2004). In addition, net profit margins (net income divided by total revenue) had risen from 3.2 percent in 2003 to 3.6 percent in 2004 and 4.8 percent in 2005. However, each year the cash flow had fallen even though the company reported higher income. An investor looking at the cash flow statement would determine that rising receivables were the culprit.

A look at the footnotes to the financial statements provides this explanation:

> Included in revenue at the global logistics segment for the 2005 and 2004 fiscal years was $275,929,000 and $63,790,000, respectively, of revenue related to disaster relief efforts for the storms that impacted the United States during these years. These emergency transportation services were provided primarily under a contract between Landstar Express America, Inc. and the United States Department of Transportation/Federal Aviation Administration (FAA)....
>
> Included in accounts receivable at December 31, 2005 was trade accounts receivable due from various departments of the United States Government of $226,057,000, which includes $215,250,000 in trade receivables from disaster relief services provided under the contract with the FAA. The decrease in cash provided by operating activities was primarily due to an increase in trade receivables resulting in large part from revenue related to the emergency transportation services provided under the FAA contract. The financing of a portion of this $215,250,000 receivable from the FAA with borrowings under the Company's revolving credit agreement is the primary reason for the increase in long term debt....
>
> The FAA contract expired December 31, 2006.

So, the investor could use ratios and fundamental analysis to spot a potential problem, which could then be tracked to its source using other information. If the 10K had not disclosed this information, the investor could have tried calling management to ask for an explanation.

However, as is often the case, the answer leads to more questions. The investor can feel more confident about the company's ability to collect the receivables (the United States Government is a reliable customer) and can easily explain the falling cash flow in spite of rising income. In fact, the March quarter 10Q shows $97 million in cash flow against $24 million net income, as a good portion of the disaster relief receivables were collected. However, the information also reveals that a large portion of the growth depended on severe weather that may not affect the company in the same way again since the contract with the U.S. Government expired in 2006. Looking back today we have the benefit of hindsight but as might be expected from the above analysis revenue dropped slightly in 2007. Revenue recovered a bit in 2008 but then dropped again with the onset of the financial crisis that hit the United States and world economies.

Fundamental Screening

Because there are more than 10,000 potential public company investments to consider, advisors are unable to examine the financial statements and ratios in detail for each company. Therefore, the process often begins by screening a large database of securities to identify a small number that have desirable attributes. For example, a value manager may look for companies with relatively low price multiples but strong profitability and growing cash flows. The database could be screened to select companies that meet these criteria. The smaller sample of companies that is produced can then be analyzed in more detail.

11.6.2 TECHNICAL ANALYSIS

Technical analysis assumes that fundamental information is reflected in market data such as price and trading volume and, therefore, the analyst can focus on charts of such data to make investment decisions. This does not necessarily mean that markets are perfectly efficient. For example, if markets react slowly to new information, this can be found by looking at the trend in a price chart and making an investment decision based on this trend. Technical analysis includes a study of charts depicting trends in price and volume indicators as to when a trend is expected to continue or reverse. While many view technical analysis as the antithesis of fundamental analysis, some analysts view them as complementary tools. Technical analysts can benefit the investor by understanding how fundamentals may be driving trends and fundamental analysts can benefit from using trend information to time buy and sell decisions.

Charting

In its simplest form, technical analysis involves preparing a chart of past price and volume data. Figure 11.16 presents a typical bar chart for CF Industries.

Figure 11.16

Source: Stockcharts.com

The top portion of the chart depicts price information. Each bar on the graph summarizes a day's trading activity: showing the open, high, low and closing prices. In this case each daily bar is filled in to look like a candlestick. The candlestick body represents the open and close for the day (clear depicts the close was higher than the open while solid depicts the close lower that the open). The wicks depict the high and low for the day. Another format you may see is a bar format shown in Figure 11.17, where the bar depicts the opening price with a horizontal line to the left, the closing price with a horizontal line to the right. The vertical bar depicts the range of prices for the day from the low (bottom) to the high (top).

Figure 11.17

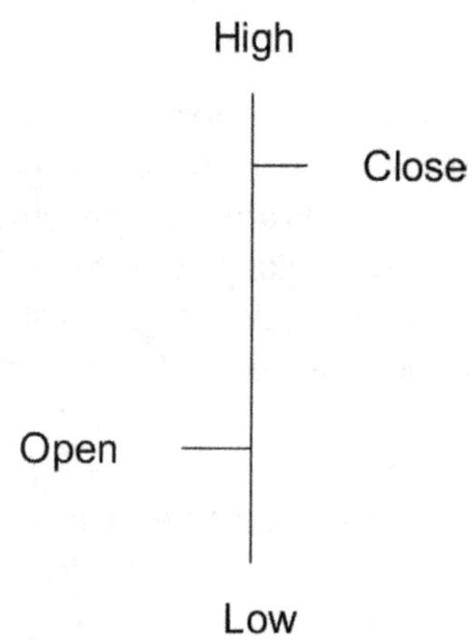

The price trend for the last several days appears to be down. In technical analysis, a trend is generally considered to continue until a reversal signal or pattern emerges in the chart. One such signal compares the price to a moving average of price over some period. The solid lines in the price area within Figure 11.16 represent a moving average of the last seventeen, thirty-four and 200 days of prices. A reversal of the short-term trend is signaled when the price crosses the moving average line or when a shorter moving average crosses over a longer moving average. When the price falls below the moving average (or a shorter moving average falls below a longer moving average) it is considered a sell signal. When the price rises above the moving average (or a shorter moving average rises above a longer moving average) it generates a buy signal.

Some technical analysts believe that certain patterns in prices signal a trend reversal. One such pattern is a head and shoulders top, depicted in Figure 11.18.

Figure 11.18

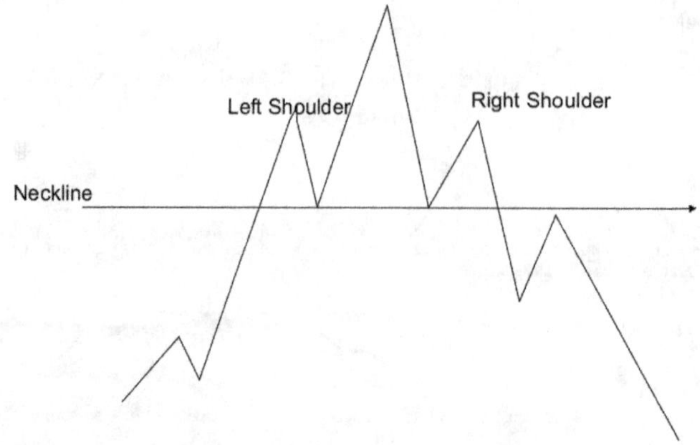

The jagged line in Figure 11.18 represents a summary of the price action. The line with an arrow is added to show the point at which a sell signal would be generated. This is termed the neckline. When a price chart forms a head and shoulders pattern, the analyst watches as the right shoulder is formed to see if the price falls below the neckline, which would be a sell signal.

Figure 11.16 also shows vertical bars superimposed below the daily price data depicting daily volume information. In technical analysis, trading volume is used to confirm signals generated by price data. For example, a decreasing volume pattern with each subsequent peak (left shoulder, head, and right shoulder) accompanying the head and shoulders pattern confirms the strength of the sell signal. It indicates that fewer people are willing to buy as the pattern develops.

Support and resistance are two important concepts in technical analysis. Consider the price pattern in Figure 11.19. The arrow indicates a support line. Each time the price falls to this line, it rebounds indicating that buyers are coming into the market and purchasing the security at that price.

Figure 11.19

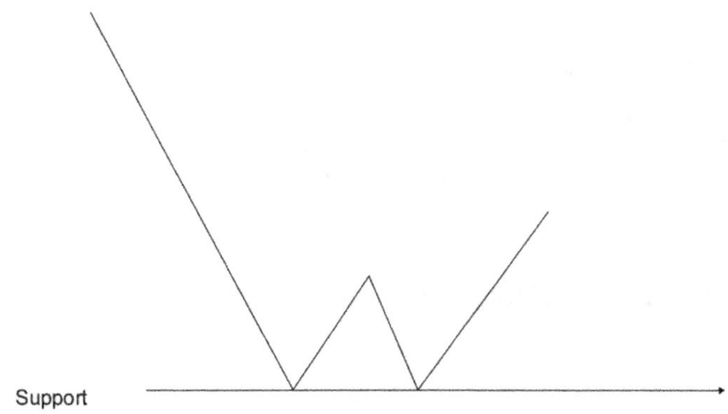

Figure 11.20 presents a resistance level pattern. Resistance levels indicate a point at which sellers step in to sell at a particular price, driving the price down.

Figure 11.20

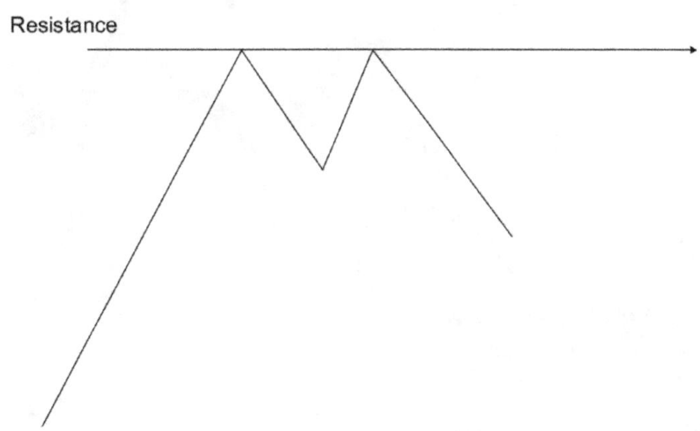

Support (resistance) levels may be useful in indicating target purchase (sale) prices. Care must be taken when using support and resistance levels because the support and resistance lines can be broken (for example due to new fundamental news). Breaking a support or resistance line can indicate that a new trend is forming.

Overall Market Analysis

In addition to charting individual securities, technical analysis involves the evaluation of overall security markets. Technical indicators can be used to determine the trend in the overall market and evaluate when it is desirable to make an investment in a particular asset class or alter asset allocations. Technical analysis of security markets can include the use of sentiment indicators, flow of funds indicators, and market structure indicators.

Sentiment indicators are used to evaluate the overall bullishness or bearishness of the market. Commonly used sentiment indicators include the volatility index, put/call ratio, short-interest ratio, and insider trading activity.

Volatility Index. The Chicago Board Options Exchange (CBOE) Volatility Index® (VIX®) is a measure of market expectations of near-term volatility derived from S&P 500® stock index option prices (www.cboe.com). According to the Chicago Board Options Exchange (CBOE):

> "VIX is based on real-time option prices, which reflect investors' consensus view of future expected stock market volatility. During periods of financial stress, which are often accompanied by steep market declines, option prices – and VIX – tend to rise. The greater the fear, the higher the VIX level. As investor fear subsides, option prices tend to decline, which in turn causes VIX to decline. It is important to note, however, that past performance does not necessarily indicate future results." (www.cboe.com, Frequently Asked Questions, as of September 20, 2013).

Figure 11.21 demonstrates the relationship of the VIX® and the S&P 500® index in recent periods.

Figure 11.21

Source: CBOE.com as of September 20, 2013.

Put/Call Ratio. The CBOE also presents daily data on the ratio of put options to call options for equities, indices, and their total (equity plus indices). The ratio is the daily volume of put options divided by the daily volume of call options. The lower the ratio the more bullish market participants are and the higher the ratio the more bearish market participants are. However, sentiment indicators such as this are contrary indicators, bullishness of market participants gives a bearish signal for the market and bearishness of market participants gives a bullish signal for the market. This accounts for overconfidence of market participants at market tops and pessimism at market bottoms. Figure 11.22 presents CBOE Total Put/Call ratio data as of August 7, 2013.

Figure 11.22

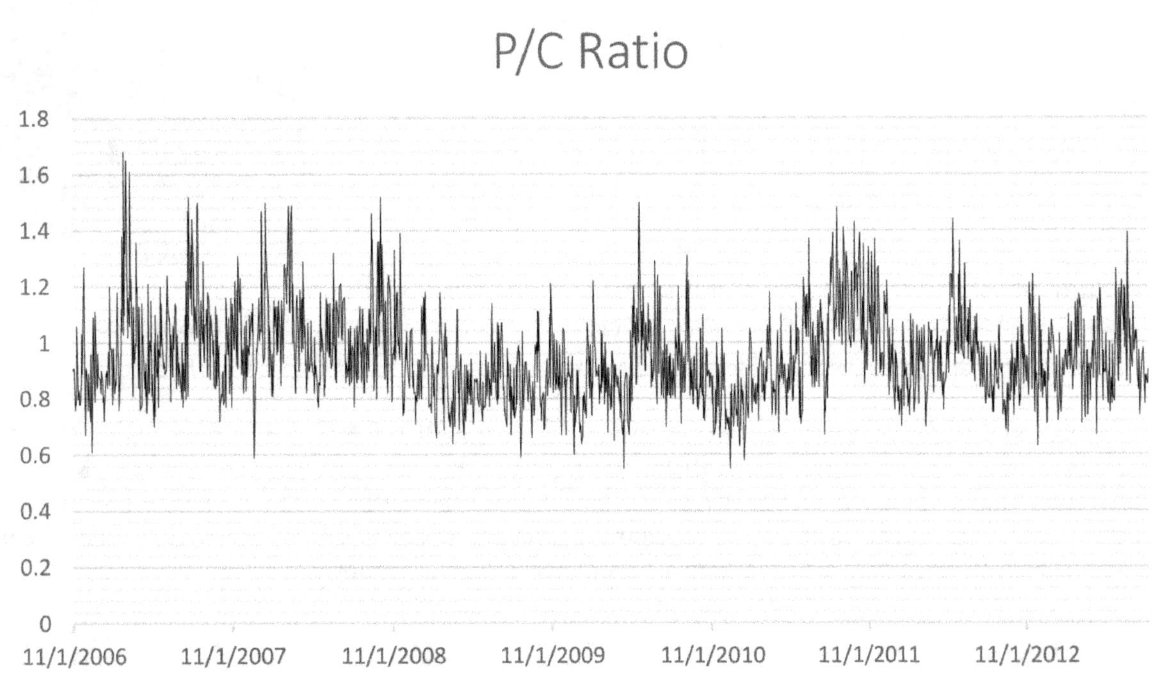

Source: CBOE.com

Short Interest Ratio. The short interest ratio measures the volume of short sales for an index or security relative to average volume. This is a contrary sentiment ratio, because a high ratio indicates a high level of short activity and is considered bullish, whereas a low ratio is considered bearish.

Insider Trading. While the overall market is often wrong at market tops and bottoms, insiders have been found to generally be right at tops and bottoms. High insider buying relative to insider selling is therefore a bullish sentiment indicator. Low insider buying relative to selling is bearish.

Flow of funds indicators are used to assess the prospects for inflows or outflows of cash into the market or sectors. Flow of funds analysis involves examining trends of sources of cash, such as the cash positions of large investors like mutual funds and pension funds. For example, mutual fund data can be obtained from the Investment Company Institute. Flow of funds analysis also involves examining potential demands for cash, such as new public offerings, and overall liquidity in the economy.

Market structure indicators examine charts of market indices for patterns and trends in both prices and volume (as with individual stocks discussed earlier). Market indices that are subject to analysis include the Dow Jones Industrial Average, S&P 500 Composite, Dow Jones Transportation Average, Dow Jones Utility Average, the NASDAQ, and Russell indices. Other market structure indicators include those that examine market breadth. Market breadth measures the extent to which issues underlying the indices are participating in the market trend. A market trend is stronger when more issues are participating. A popular measure of market breadth is the Advance/Decline line, which measures the number of issues advancing in excess of those declining. An increasing advance/decline line is positive for the overall market.

11.6.3 TIMING OF INVESTMENT PURCHASES AND SALES

In addition to selecting the right individual securities for purchase, the advisor must decide on the right price and the timing of the purchase and subsequent sale. This section explores purchase and sale strategies.

Market Timing

Market timing attempts to anticipate the market's broad direction and individual security prices, but the focus is usually on the broader market. Investors who believe stocks are too expensive will favor other asset classes. Those who believe stocks are undervalued will sell other asset classes to buy more stocks.

The timing can be based on economic trends, stock prices, or valuation levels. For example, when stocks are above their normal P/E multiple range, this may be an indicator to reduce stock holdings. Similarly, when an individual security is at the high (low) end of its normal valuation range, this may be a sell (buy) indicator. Technical charts of market indices and individual securities can be useful in generating buy and sell signals in a market timing strategy.

Buy and Hold

In contrast to market timing, a buy and hold strategy does not attempt to anticipate moves in the market or even moves in individual security prices. Rather, such a strategy relies on the notion that a well-planned investment policy will result in a portfolio that best meets an investor's risk and return profile. Buy and hold strategies tend to be long-term oriented, whereas market timing strategies are generally short-term in nature.

One advantage of a buy and hold strategy is that it reduces transaction costs. Another is its simplicity. A disadvantage of a buy and hold strategy is that it can distort an investor's asset allocations. Consider an investor who decided in January 2009 that her appropriate asset allocation was 50 percent stocks and 50 percent bonds. She makes a single decision to buy the assets in those proportions and promptly forgets about it. By year-end 2012, stocks have vastly outperformed bonds. Because of this relative difference in performance, stocks now comprise two thirds of her portfolio. She has unintentionally changed her asset allocations to favor stocks – just before the stock market crashes and bonds enjoy several years of superior performance.

A buy and hold strategy implies that only one investment decision is made (to buy). Occasionally, however, passive market timing strategies such as rebalancing will be described as buy and hold. It could be argued that one decision is made to "buy" the chosen allocation, and the later adjustments simply conform to the original strategy. It is important to understand which definition of buy and hold a particular pundit may espouse.

Passive Investing or Indexing

Passive investment strategies seek to mimic the returns on a benchmark index, such as the Standard & Poor's 500. The goal of a passive investment manager is not to beat the benchmark index, but rather to match it as closely as possible. But if no attempt is made to provide returns superior to the benchmark, why should an investor choose a passive strategy?

The main advantage of passive investing is reduced cost. Because benchmark index constituents change only occasionally, trading costs are lower than with most actively managed strategies. Also, active strategies require skilled analysts and managers. There is no need for active security selection in a passive indexing strategy.

One way to construct a passive portfolio is to simply buy and hold the securities in the index at the appropriate weightings. This method is known as replication, and its main advantage is low tracking error with the index. However, replication can be difficult to accomplish for many reasons. For one thing, in small portfolios replication is likely to require owning partial shares. Furthermore, investment flows, such as new investment, withdrawals, or dividends, would require the proceeds to be distributed to buy or sell tiny amounts of each stock in the index. An alternative is the use of index mutual funds or exchange-traded index funds.

A second means of constructing an indexed portfolio is sampling. Under this strategy, several securities are chosen in such a way as to be representative of the overall index. Doing so reduces trading costs and minimizes the need to buy small quantities of many stocks. However, it increases specific security risk and is unlikely to track the benchmark well.

11.7 FORMULA INVESTING

Section Overview:

11.7.1 DOLLAR COST AVERAGING

Formula investing is a strategy that seeks to limit the role of emotions in investing by adhering to a strict set of rules. Typically, formula investment strategies involve making fixed periodic investments through dollar cost averaging or dividend reinvestment plans. These two strategies can effectively lower the average cost of both equity and fixed-income securities in fluctuating markets. Other formula investing techniques, such as bond laddering and bond barbell strategies, are designed to minimize risk of interest rate fluctuations.

Dollar cost averaging is a simple strategy practiced by many investors. The strategy is to simply make regular, periodic investments in a security without regard to price. 401(k) investors automatically investing a certain amount each paycheck are practicing dollar cost averaging. The premise behind dollar cost averaging is to take advantage of market fluctuations to buy more shares when prices are low and fewer when prices are high.

Contrast an investment strategy where an investor purchases the same number of shares of a mutual fund each month with a dollar cost averaging strategy where an investor purchases the same dollar amount of a mutual fund each month. An investor has approximately $1,000 of discretionary income each month and would like to purchase shares of a mutual fund that is currently selling for $10 per share. Consider the following two strategies:

- Strategy A - Purchase 100 shares per month; and
- Strategy B - Purchase $1,000 per month.

The price for each month of the year and the results of each strategy are presented in Figure 11.23:

- Under Strategy A, the investor has 1,200 shares at the end of the year with an average cost of $10.583 ($12,700 cost / 1,200 shares). The value of the 1,200 shares is $13,200.00 at the final price of $11.00/share ($11 × 1,200 shares), and there is an unrealized gain of $500.00 ($13,200 value – $12,700 cost).
- Under Strategy B, the investor has 1,141.914 shares with an average cost of $10.509 ($12,000 cost / 1,141.914 shares). The value of the shares is $12,561.05 ($11 × 1,141.914 shares) and there is an unrealized gain of $561.05 ($12,561.05 value – $12,000 cost).

By purchasing more shares when the price is low and fewer shares when the price is high, the investor lowered his average cost basis with Strategy B. Consequently, the investor finished with greater investment gains (as measured by the unrealized gains of $561.05 vs. $500.00) on the amounts actually invested. Furthermore, the investor maintained a predictable investment outlay – he was not struck with the need to find additional funds for investment in months when the share price was higher. Dollar cost averaging worked well in this example because prices were fluctuating up and down. What if prices were always trending up?

Figure 11.23

Month	Mutual Fund Share Price	Strategy A – Shares Purchased	Strategy A – Total Cost	Strategy B – Shares Purchased	Strategy B – Total Cost
1	$10.00	100	$1,000.00	100.000	$1,000.00
2	$11.00	100	$1,100.00	90.909	$1,000.00
3	$11.00	100	$1,100.00	90.909	$1,000.00
4	$10.50	100	$1,050.00	95.238	$1,000.00
5	$10.00	100	$1,000.00	100.000	$1,000.00
6	$9.50	100	$ 950.00	105.263	$1,000.00
7	$9.00	100	$ 900.00	111.111	$1,000.00
8	$10.00	100	$1,000.00	100.000	$1,000.00
9	$11.00	100	$1,100.00	90.909	$1,000.00
10	$12.00	100	$1,200.00	83.333	$1,000.00
11	$12.00	100	$1,200.00	83.333	$1,000.00
12	$11.00	100	$1,100.00	90.909	$1,000.00
Total		**1,200**	**$12,700**	**1,141.914**	**$12,000**

Figure 11.24 shows the impact of the two strategies in a continuous uptrend:

- Strategy A has an average cost of $10.55 ($12,660 cost / 1,200 shares), a value of $13,320 ($11 × 1,200 shares), and an unrealized gain of $660 ($13,320 value – $12,660 cost).

- Strategy B has an average cost of $10.54 ($12,000 / 1,138.661 shares), a value of $12.639.14 ($11 × 1,138.661 shares), and an unrealized gain of 639.14 ($12.639.14 value – $12,000 cost).

Note that the dollar cost averaging Strategy B resulted in the lower average cost, but not the maximum gain in this case.

Figure 11.24

Month	Mutual Fund Share Price	Strategy A – Shares Purchased	Strategy A – Total Cost	Strategy B – Shares Purchased	Strategy B – Total Cost
1	$10.00	100	$1,000.00	100.000	$1,000.00
2	$10.10	100	$1,010.00	99.010	$1,000.00
3	$10.20	100	$1,020.00	98.039	$1,000.00
4	$10.30	100	$1,030.00	97.087	$1,000.00
5	$10.40	100	$1,040.00	96.154	$1,000.00
6	$10.50	100	$1,050.00	95.238	$1,000.00
7	$10.60	100	$1,060.00	94.340	$1,000.00
8	$10.70	100	$1,070.00	93.458	$1,000.00
9	$10.80	100	$1,080.00	92.593	$1,000.00
10	$10.90	100	$1,090.00	91.743	$1,000.00
11	$11.00	100	$1,100.00	90.909	$1,000.00
12	$11.10	100	$1,110.00	90.090	$1,000.00
Total		**1,200**	**$12,660**	**1,138.661**	**$12,000**

The dollar cost averaging strategy can also be compared to an initial lump sum purchase. For example, assume that Andrea, a thirty-year old with limited investments, earns a $12,000 bonus received at the end of January. She has a choice of investing the entire amount in an S&P 500 index fund at one time or spreading the investment evenly over the next twelve months. Each share in the fund currently sells for $9.12. If she invests the entire lump sum at once, she can purchase just over 1,315.8 shares. She is not sure whether the market will rise or fall over the next twelve months and decides to spread the investment over the course of the year.

Here are the month-end values for the fund purchases Andrea makes:

Month	Fund	Shares
January	$9.12	109.6
February	$9.16	109.2
March	$8.15	122.7
April	$8.86	112.9
May	$9.36	106.8

Month	Fund	Shares
June	$8.80	113.6
July	$8.56	116.8
August	$8.41	118.9
September	$8.48	117.9
October	$9.16	109.2
November	$9.64	103.7
December	$9.75	102.6
Total:		**1,343.9**

At the end of the year, she has about 1,344 shares, twenty-eight more than she would have purchased had she bought them all up front (1,344 – 1,316). At the final price of $9.75/share, her investment has grown to $13,103 ($9.75 × 1,344 shares) instead of $12,829 ($9.75 × 1,316 shares) – an additional $274. The reason is that, as the market fell early in the year, she was able to buy a larger number of shares each month (at a lower cost). For example, when the market was at 815 in March she bought nearly 123 shares in the fund. When the market briefly rallied to 936 in May, she purchased only 107 shares at the higher price. Because she was able to take advantage of market fluctuations, she ended the year with more than 2 percent of additional value than she would have had by investing as a lump sum up-front.

Dollar cost averaging works best when markets are declining or fluctuating, as the investor is able to buy more shares when prices fall (and purchases fewer shares when prices are higher). In this sense, it is a contrarian strategy. Dollar cost averaging does not work in a steadily rising market, as the investor would be better off buying as much as possible at the lower initial price than to pay more each month for a smaller number of shares. Because markets do tend to rise over the long term, it would usually not make sense for Andrea to spread her investment over years rather than months. However, over a span of months, it is quite possible that Andrea will have the opportunity to make purchases at lower prices.

Even though Andrea has a long time horizon and should buy as much in the early years as possible, she must currently make a decision about investing a specific amount of available cash. By spreading the investment over twelve months, she is able to benefit from market fluctuations (because the market did occasionally decline) and at least ensure that she does not (accidentally) invest all of her money at a market peak. It also allows her to establish an investing discipline.

The consequences of investing at a market peak instead of dollar cost averaging can be quite substantial. For example, assume the returns from the Andrea's example occurred in reverse order, such that the market started at 9.75 and finished at 9.12. The results of this scenario are as follows:

Month	Fund	Shares
January	$9.75	102.6
February	$9.64	103.7
March	$9.16	109.2
April	$8.48	117.9
May	$8.41	118.9
June	$8.56	116.8

Month	Fund	Shares
July	$8.80	113.6
August	$9.36	106.8
September	$8.86	112.9
October	$8.15	122.7
November	$9.16	109.2
December	$9.12	109.6
Total:		**1,343.9**

At the end of the year, Andrea still has about 1,344 shares through a dollar cost averaging program. However, in this case the total shares in the end are worth only $12,256 (1,343.9 shares × $9.12/share). But if Andrea had made a lump-sum investment of her $12,000, she would have only been able to purchase about 1,231 shares at the high price of $9.75/share – at the end of the term, this would have only been worth $11,225 (1,230.8 shares × $9.12/share)! In the first case of a fluctuating but rising market, Andrea's dollar cost averaging strategy allowed her to end the year with an extra 2 percent of additional value – in the latter case, she enjoys an extra $1,031, or over 9 percent of additional value!

For many investors, dollar cost averaging is as much a matter of necessity as of choice. For those that do not have a lump sum available to invest, dollar cost averaging becomes the de facto strategy simply because they make purchases as cash becomes available to invest.

11.7.2 DIVIDEND REINVESTMENT

Dividend Reinvestment Plans (DRIPs) allow shareholders to take dividends in the form of additional shares rather than cash. Many companies with dividend reinvestment plans allow shareholders to purchase shares commission-free (or with a minimal transaction fee) through their dividend reinvestment plan, and others offer shareholders discounted share prices in return for reinvesting dividends. Mutual funds and mutual fund supermarkets at discount brokerage firms also often offer dividend reinvestment plans for mutual funds (generally with no commissions).

In the simplest form, dividend reinvestment plans are a type of dollar cost averaging. Instead of accepting a cash dividend, the dividend is reinvested at the then-prevailing price. For the investor, the most basic advantage relates to cash planning. Why should an investor accept dividends if he doesn't need the income for many years? By reducing costly transaction fees and commissions, the investor is able to put more of his investment dollars to work over the long run and earn more. For plans that allow discounted purchases or other perquisites for shareholders, the advantages can be even greater.

11.7.3 FIXED-INCOME STRATEGIES

Just as with equity investments, bonds are subject to risk. Likewise, bond investors share the desire to maximize their return for a given level of risk.

For risk adverse investors, there are ways to reduce the risk of investing in bonds. For example, an investor who does not want to face any default risk could limit investments to U.S. government bonds. If a somewhat greater return is sought, investing in a diversified portfolio of corporate bonds might be appropriate.

Diversification reduces the negative impact of any single bond defaulting by reducing the amount invested in any particular bond. Risk can also be reduced (although not eliminated) when investing in individual bonds through strategies such as immunization (see Immunization below).

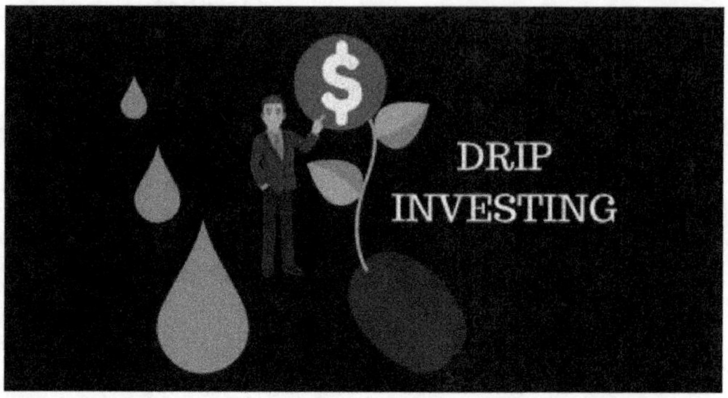

As with any investment, bond investments can be actively managed or left alone. A passive approach usually entails selecting a portfolio of bonds to match an investor's preferences toward factors such as time horizon, tax status, and risk, and simply holding the portfolio until maturity. A passive approach often assumes that markets are relatively efficient and that superior returns cannot be obtained by timing the market or continuously looking for mispriced assets. However, care should still be taken in selecting the bonds to include in the portfolio. As with all investments, individual assets and the portfolio as a whole should be examined for appropriateness. The passive approach can also involve techniques such as immunization (see Immunization below) and laddering (see Ladder Portfolio below) to reduce portfolio risk over time.

An active approach, on the other hand, generally assumes that markets are less than efficient and that superior (to the passive approach) returns can be generated through market timing and asset selection. Active management can involve analyzing particular bonds and sectors or forecasting anything from interest rates to inflation to economic outlook – looking for mispriced securities and seeking to avoid areas that (in the investor's opinion) may decline in value. This will usually result in more active trading or swapping of bonds within the portfolio, and may require substantial additional investments of time for research and analysis. Such strategies also entail significantly higher transactions costs than a passive approach. Passive and active strategies are not always mutually exclusive; some techniques have elements of both and can be useful to all investors.

Immunization

One fixed-income risk reducing strategy is known as immunization. Immunization involves selecting a bond or portfolio of bonds such that interest rate movements result in bond price fluctuations (interest rate risk) and cash flows for reinvestment (reinvestment risk) that offset one another. It was noted in earlier chapters that these two risks move in opposite directions. If interest rates rise, interest rate risk causes the value of the bond to drop, but the investor earns more on any coupon payments that are reinvested. On the other hand, if rates decline, the value of the bond rises, but less is earned from reinvestment.

Macaulay duration measures the point in time when these two risks precisely offset each other. If an investor purchases a bond and sells it when it reaches its duration (as calculated upon purchase), any loss in bond value caused by an increase in interest rates should be offset by the increase in the reinvestment earnings of interest payments. Similarly, if interest rates decline, the loss in reinvested earnings should be offset by an increase in the value of the bonds. By matching the duration of the bond to the investment horizon, interest rate and reinvestment risk can be offset.

Immunization can be accomplished easily using zero coupon bonds, because their maturity is their duration. No computations are necessary. Additionally, zero coupon bonds naturally have no reinvestment risk related to interest payments, because there are no interest payments. If an investor purchases a zero coupon bond and holds it to maturity, the investor will receive his expected yield to maturity (provided there is no default).

Ladder Portfolio

As noted earlier, reinvestment risk is a concern when receiving periodic payments such as interest. Reinvestment risk related to interest payments can be eliminated or reduced by using zero coupon bonds or an immunization strategy (see Immunization above). Reinvestment risk also occurs when bonds mature earlier than the investor needs the proceeds – for example, when no bonds are available that match the investment horizon, or when other bonds seem to present a better investment opportunity based upon other factors (e.g., various forecasts or a discovery based upon analysis and research).

One option might be to purchase very long-term bonds (using immunization or duration) to secure the long-term expected return. The danger in this strategy is that long-term bonds are more sensitive to changes in interest rates than shorter-term bonds. If it turns out that the investor must use the money for an emergency or chooses to retire early, the investor may be stuck at an inopportune time with depressed bond prices in the face of a rising interest rate environment.

Another option is to create a laddered portfolio. In a laddered portfolio, an investor invests in an assortment of bonds with staggered maturities. For example, the investor can structure a portfolio where 10 percent of the bonds mature each year. The bonds would not all mature in the same interest rate environment. If rates rise, the value of the portfolio may fall, but the investor does not need to sell bonds that haven't matured. If cash is needed, the maturing bonds offer a ready source. If cash is not needed, the investor can reinvest the proceeds of the maturing bonds at the new (higher) interest rate.

If interest rates fall, the investor will reinvest the proceeds at a lower rate, but only for 10 percent of the portfolio (and the longer maturity bonds would rise in value.) With a laddered portfolio, the proceeds of maturing bonds would be reinvested in new bonds with a maturity later than those currently in the portfolio.

A bond ladder reduces interest rate risk by staggering maturities among several bonds (each of which represents a rung on the ladder). For a long-term investor, this ends up being similar to a dollar cost averaging strategy. Shorter maturities cushion interest rate (i.e., bond price) risks, while the fact that only a portion of the bonds mature in a given period reduces reinvestment risk. If rates should rise, the maturing bonds can be used to buy bonds offering a higher yield.

Perhaps a greater reason for using a bond ladder is that it enables the investor to match cash flows with planned expenditures. If the investor knows tuition payments will be due each semester for four years, beginning in fifteen years, he can buy bonds maturing at exactly the right times to make the tuition payments. Alternatively, a retired investor can plan a laddered bond portfolio to include regularly maturing bonds that provide the cash necessary for annual living expenses.

Bond ladders also work for unplanned expenses. For example, if the investor loses his job, maturing bonds can be used to supplement lost income. Figure 11.25 presents an example of a bond ladder using treasury bonds of various maturities.

Figure 11.25

Maturity	Yield	Amount Invested	Purpose
3 month	0.250%	$10,000	Emergency fund
2 year	1.0%	$10,000	Hedge against rising rates
3 year	1.5%	$10,000	Higher yield hedge
5 year	2.0%	$10,000	Yield
10 year	3.0%	$10,000	Yield
15 year	3.1%	$20,000	Planned tuition payment
16 year	3.2%	$22,000	Planned tuition payment
17 year	3.3%	$24,000	Planned tuition payment
18 year	3.4%	$26,000	Planned tuition payment
20 year	3.5%	$10,000	Yield
25 year	3.7%	$20,000	Yield, hedge against falling rates
30 year	4.0%	$30,000	Yield, retirement and hedge against falling rates

Barbell Strategy

A barbell strategy offers another means of balancing the risks in a bond portfolio. While a ladder portfolio may stagger holdings across all maturities, the barbell places heavy weights on very long and very short maturities, with no position in intermediate-term securities. Because it requires only long and short maturities, one advantage of the barbell is that it can be established with fewer bonds, reducing complexity and transaction costs. A disadvantage is that the investor may be unable to match maturities with cash needs as effectively.

A barbell allows the investor to create a fairly effective hedge against both interest rate and reinvestment risk, simply and at low cost. If rates go up, the short portion of the barbell can be reinvested at the higher rate and help offset losses in the longer maturity. If rates decline, the long maturity gains make up for the lower interest rate available for reinvestment of the short maturity portion. Figure 11.26 provides an example of a barbell.

Figure 11.26

Maturity	Yield	Amount Invested	Purpose
3 month	0.250%	$50,000	Emergency fund and hedge against rising rates
30 year	4.0%	$50,000	Long-term needs and profit from falling rates

A barbell strategy can also be appropriate based upon the current shape of the yield curve and expected changes in interest rates. A barbell strategy can also result in a portfolio with the same duration as a bullet strategy (a single bond maturity), but with higher convexity. Convexity measures the curvature of the relationship between bond yields and prices. Positive convexity is always a good thing for the bond investor, regardless of whether interest rates rise or fall. If interest rates fall, then convexity will augment the rise in the price of the bond. Interestingly, if interest rates rise, convexity will dampen the decline in the price.

Appendix A

PRESENT VALUE OF LUMP SUM

YEARS	3.0%	3.5%	4.0%	4.5%	5.0%	5.5%	6.0%
1	0.9709	0.9662	0.9615	0.9569	0.9524	0.9479	0.9434
2	0.9426	0.9335	0.9246	0.9157	0.9070	0.8985	0.8900
3	0.9151	0.9019	0.8890	0.8763	0.8638	0.8516	0.8396
4	0.8885	0.8714	0.8548	0.8386	0.8227	0.8072	0.7921
5	0.8626	0.8420	0.8219	0.8025	0.7835	0.7651	0.7473
6	0.8375	0.8135	0.7903	0.7679	0.7462	0.7252	0.7050
7	0.8131	0.7860	0.7599	0.7348	0.7107	0.6874	0.6651
8	0.7894	0.7594	0.7307	0.7032	0.6768	0.6516	0.6274
9	0.7664	0.7337	0.7026	0.6729	0.6446	0.6176	0.5919
10	0.7441	0.7089	0.6756	0.6439	0.6139	0.5854	0.5584
11	0.7224	0.6849	0.6496	0.6162	0.5847	0.5549	0.5268
12	0.7014	0.6618	0.6246	0.5897	0.5568	0.5260	0.4970
13	0.6810	0.6394	0.6006	0.5643	0.5303	0.4986	0.4688
14	0.6611	0.6178	0.5775	0.5400	0.5051	0.4726	0.4423
15	0.6419	0.5969	0.5553	0.5167	0.4810	0.4479	0.4173
16	0.6232	0.5767	0.5339	0.4945	0.4581	0.4246	0.3936
17	0.6050	0.5572	0.5134	0.4732	0.4363	0.4024	0.3714
18	0.5874	0.5384	0.4936	0.4528	0.4155	0.3815	0.3503
19	0.5703	0.5202	0.4746	0.4333	0.3957	0.3616	0.3305
20	0.5537	0.5026	0.4564	0.4146	0.3769	0.3427	0.3118
21	0.5375	0.4856	0.4388	0.3968	0.3589	0.3249	0.2942
22	0.5219	0.4692	0.4220	0.3797	0.3418	0.3079	0.2775
23	0.5067	0.4533	0.4057	0.3634	0.3256	0.2919	0.2618
24	0.4919	0.4380	0.3901	0.3477	0.3101	0.2767	0.2470
25	0.4776	0.4231	0.3751	0.3327	0.2953	0.2622	0.2330
26	0.4637	0.4088	0.3607	0.3184	0.2812	0.2486	0.2198
27	0.4502	0.3950	0.3468	0.3047	0.2678	0.2356	0.2074
28	0.4371	0.3817	0.3335	0.2916	0.2551	0.2233	0.1956
29	0.4243	0.3687	0.3207	0.2790	0.2429	0.2117	0.1846
30	0.4120	0.3563	0.3083	0.2670	0.2314	0.2006	0.1741

YEARS	3.0%	3.5%	4.0%	4.5%	5.0%	5.5%	6.0%
31	0.4000	0.3442	0.2965	0.2555	0.2204	0.1902	0.1643
32	0.3883	0.3326	0.2851	0.2445	0.2099	0.1803	0.1550
33	0.3770	0.3213	0.2741	0.2340	0.1999	0.1709	0.1462
34	0.3660	0.3105	0.2636	0.2239	0.1904	0.1620	0.1379
35	0.3554	0.3000	0.2534	0.2143	0.1813	0.1535	0.1301
36	0.3450	0.2898	0.2437	0.2050	0.1727	0.1455	0.1227
37	0.3350	0.2800	0.2343	0.1962	0.1644	0.1379	0.1158
38	0.3252	0.2706	0.2253	0.1878	0.1566	0.1307	0.1092
39	0.3158	0.2614	0.2166	0.1797	0.1491	0.1239	0.1031
40	0.3066	0.2526	0.2083	0.1719	0.1420	0.1175	0.0972
41	0.2976	0.2440	0.2003	0.1645	0.1353	0.1113	0.0917
42	0.2890	0.2358	0.1926	0.1574	0.1288	0.1055	0.0865
43	0.2805	0.2278	0.1852	0.1507	0.1227	0.1000	0.0816
44	0.2724	0.2201	0.1780	0.1442	0.1169	0.0948	0.0770
45	0.2644	0.2127	0.1712	0.1380	0.1113	0.0899	0.0727
46	0.2567	0.2055	0.1646	0.1320	0.1060	0.0852	0.0685
47	0.2493	0.1985	0.1583	0.1263	0.1009	0.0807	0.0647
48	0.2420	0.1918	0.1522	0.1209	0.0961	0.0765	0.0610
49	0.2350	0.1853	0.1463	0.1157	0.0916	0.0725	0.0575
50	0.2281	0.1791	0.1407	0.1107	0.0872	0.0688	0.0543

PRESENT VALUE OF LUMP SUM (continued)

YEARS	6.5%	7.0%	7.5%	8.0%	8.5%	9.0%	9.5%
1	0.9390	0.9346	0.9302	0.9259	0.9217	0.9174	0.9132
2	0.8817	0.8734	0.8653	0.8573	0.8495	0.8417	0.8340
3	0.8278	0.8163	0.8050	0.7938	0.7829	0.7722	0.7617
4	0.7773	0.7629	0.7488	0.7350	0.7216	0.7084	0.6956
5	0.7299	0.7130	0.6966	0.6806	0.6650	0.6499	0.6352
6	0.6853	0.6663	0.6480	0.6302	0.6129	0.5963	0.5801
7	0.6435	0.6227	0.6028	0.5835	0.5649	0.5470	0.5298
8	0.6042	0.5820	0.5607	0.5403	0.5207	0.5019	0.4838
9	0.5674	0.5439	0.5216	0.5002	0.4799	0.4604	0.4418
10	0.5327	0.5083	0.4852	0.4632	0.4423	0.4224	0.4035
11	0.5002	0.4751	0.4513	0.4289	0.4076	0.3875	0.3685
12	0.4697	0.4440	0.4199	0.3971	0.3757	0.3555	0.3365
13	0.4410	0.4150	0.3906	0.3677	0.3463	0.3262	0.3073
14	0.4141	0.3878	0.3633	0.3405	0.3191	0.2992	0.2807
15	0.3888	0.3624	0.3380	0.3152	0.2941	0.2745	0.2563
16	0.3651	0.3387	0.3144	0.2919	0.2711	0.2519	0.2341
17	0.3428	0.3166	0.2925	0.2703	0.2499	0.2311	0.2138
18	0.3219	0.2959	0.2720	0.2502	0.2303	0.2120	0.1952
19	0.3022	0.2765	0.2531	0.2317	0.2122	0.1945	0.1783
20	0.2838	0.2584	0.2354	0.2145	0.1956	0.1784	0.1628
21	0.2665	0.2415	0.2190	0.1987	0.1803	0.1637	0.1487
22	0.2502	0.2257	0.2037	0.1839	0.1662	0.1502	0.1358
23	0.2349	0.2109	0.1895	0.1703	0.1531	0.1378	0.1240
24	0.2206	0.1971	0.1763	0.1577	0.1412	0.1264	0.1133
25	0.2071	0.1842	0.1640	0.1460	0.1301	0.1160	0.1034
26	0.1945	0.1722	0.1525	0.1352	0.1199	0.1064	0.0945
27	0.1826	0.1609	0.1419	0.1252	0.1105	0.0976	0.0863
28	0.1715	0.1504	0.1320	0.1159	0.1019	0.0895	0.0788
29	0.1610	0.1406	0.1228	0.1073	0.0939	0.0822	0.0719
30	0.1512	0.1314	0.1142	0.0994	0.0865	0.0754	0.0657
31	0.1420	0.1228	0.1063	0.0920	0.0797	0.0691	0.0600
32	0.1333	0.1147	0.0988	0.0852	0.0735	0.0634	0.0548
33	0.1252	0.1072	0.0919	0.0789	0.0677	0.0582	0.0500
34	0.1175	0.1002	0.0855	0.0730	0.0624	0.0534	0.0457
35	0.1103	0.0937	0.0796	0.0676	0.0575	0.0490	0.0417

YEARS	6.5%	7.0%	7.5%	8.0%	8.5%	9.0%	9.5%
36	0.1036	0.0875	0.0740	0.0626	0.0530	0.0449	0.0381
37	0.0973	0.0818	0.0688	0.0580	0.0489	0.0412	0.0348
38	0.0914	0.0765	0.0640	0.0537	0.0450	0.0378	0.0318
39	0.0858	0.0715	0.0596	0.0497	0.0415	0.0347	0.0290
40	0.0805	0.0668	0.0554	0.0460	0.0383	0.0318	0.0265
41	0.0756	0.0624	0.0516	0.0426	0.0353	0.0292	0.0242
42	0.0710	0.0583	0.0480	0.0395	0.0325	0.0268	0.0221
43	0.0667	0.0545	0.0446	0.0365	0.0300	0.0246	0.0202
44	0.0626	0.0509	0.0415	0.0338	0.0276	0.0226	0.0184
45	0.0588	0.0476	0.0386	0.0313	0.0254	0.0207	0.0168
46	0.0552	0.0445	0.0359	0.0290	0.0235	0.0190	0.0154
47	0.0518	0.0416	0.0334	0.0269	0.0216	0.0174	0.0140
48	0.0487	0.0389	0.0311	0.0249	0.0199	0.0160	0.0128
49	0.0457	0.0363	0.0289	0.0230	0.0184	0.0147	0.0117
50	0.0429	0.0339	0.0269	0.0213	0.0169	0.0134	0.0107

PRESENT VALUE OF LUMP SUM (continued)

YEARS	10.0%	10.5%	11.0%	11.5%	12.0%	12.5%	13.0%
1	0.9091	0.9050	0.9009	0.8969	0.8929	0.8889	0.8850
2	0.8264	0.8190	0.8116	0.8044	0.7972	0.7901	0.7831
3	0.7513	0.7412	0.7312	0.7214	0.7118	0.7023	0.6931
4	0.6830	0.6707	0.6587	0.6470	0.6355	0.6243	0.6133
5	0.6209	0.6070	0.5935	0.5803	0.5674	0.5549	0.5428
6	0.5645	0.5493	0.5346	0.5204	0.5066	0.4933	0.4803
7	0.5132	0.4971	0.4817	0.4667	0.4523	0.4385	0.4251
8	0.4665	0.4499	0.4339	0.4186	0.4039	0.3897	0.3762
9	0.4241	0.4071	0.3909	0.3754	0.3606	0.3464	0.3329
10	0.3855	0.3684	0.3522	0.3367	0.3220	0.3079	0.2946
11	0.3505	0.3334	0.3173	0.3020	0.2875	0.2737	0.2607
12	0.3186	0.3018	0.2858	0.2708	0.2567	0.2433	0.2307
13	0.2897	0.2731	0.2575	0.2429	0.2292	0.2163	0.2042
14	0.2633	0.2471	0.2320	0.2178	0.2046	0.1922	0.1807
15	0.2394	0.2236	0.2090	0.1954	0.1827	0.1709	0.1599
16	0.2176	0.2024	0.1883	0.1752	0.1631	0.1519	0.1415
17	0.1978	0.1832	0.1696	0.1572	0.1456	0.1350	0.1252
18	0.1799	0.1658	0.1528	0.1409	0.1300	0.1200	0.1108
19	0.1635	0.1500	0.1377	0.1264	0.1161	0.1067	0.0981
20	0.1486	0.1358	0.1240	0.1134	0.1037	0.0948	0.0868
21	0.1351	0.1229	0.1117	0.1017	0.0926	0.0843	0.0768
22	0.1228	0.1112	0.1007	0.0912	0.0826	0.0749	0.0680
23	0.1117	0.1006	0.0907	0.0818	0.0738	0.0666	0.0601
24	0.1015	0.0911	0.0817	0.0734	0.0659	0.0592	0.0532
25	0.0923	0.0824	0.0736	0.0658	0.0588	0.0526	0.0471
26	0.0839	0.0746	0.0663	0.0590	0.0525	0.0468	0.0417
27	0.0763	0.0675	0.0597	0.0529	0.0469	0.0416	0.0369
28	0.0693	0.0611	0.0538	0.0475	0.0419	0.0370	0.0326
29	0.0630	0.0553	0.0485	0.0426	0.0374	0.0329	0.0289
30	0.0573	0.0500	0.0437	0.0382	0.0334	0.0292	0.0256
31	0.0521	0.0453	0.0394	0.0342	0.0298	0.0260	0.0226
32	0.0474	0.0410	0.0355	0.0307	0.0266	0.0231	0.0200
33	0.0431	0.0371	0.0319	0.0275	0.0238	0.0205	0.0177
34	0.0391	0.0335	0.0288	0.0247	0.0212	0.0182	0.0157
35	0.0356	0.0304	0.0259	0.0222	0.0189	0.0162	0.0139

YEARS	10.0%	10.5%	11.0%	11.5%	12.0%	12.5%	13.0%
36	0.0323	0.0275	0.0234	0.0199	0.0169	0.0144	0.0123
37	0.0294	0.0249	0.0210	0.0178	0.0151	0.0128	0.0109
38	0.0267	0.0225	0.0190	0.0160	0.0135	0.0114	0.0096
39	0.0243	0.0204	0.0171	0.0143	0.0120	0.0101	0.0085
40	0.0221	0.0184	0.0154	0.0129	0.0107	0.0090	0.0075
41	0.0201	0.0167	0.0139	0.0115	0.0096	0.0080	0.0067
42	0.0183	0.0151	0.0125	0.0103	0.0086	0.0071	0.0059
43	0.0166	0.0137	0.0112	0.0093	0.0076	0.0063	0.0052
44	0.0151	0.0124	0.0101	0.0083	0.0068	0.0056	0.0046
45	0.0137	0.0112	0.0091	0.0075	0.0061	0.0050	0.0041
46	0.0125	0.0101	0.0082	0.0067	0.0054	0.0044	0.0036
47	0.0113	0.0092	0.0074	0.0060	0.0049	0.0039	0.0032
48	0.0103	0.0083	0.0067	0.0054	0.0043	0.0035	0.0028
49	0.0094	0.0075	0.0060	0.0048	0.0039	0.0031	0.0025
50	0.0085	0.0068	0.0054	0.0043	0.0035	0.0028	0.0022

PRESENT VALUE OF LUMP SUM (continued)

YEARS	14.0%	15.0%	16.0%	17.0%	18.0%	19.0%	20.0%
1	0.8772	0.8696	0.8621	0.8547	0.8475	0.8403	0.8333
2	0.7695	0.7561	0.7432	0.7305	0.7182	0.7062	0.6944
3	0.6750	0.6575	0.6407	0.6244	0.6086	0.5934	0.5787
4	0.5921	0.5718	0.5523	0.5337	0.5158	0.4987	0.4823
5	0.5194	0.4972	0.4761	0.4561	0.4371	0.4190	0.4019
6	0.4556	0.4323	0.4104	0.3898	0.3704	0.3521	0.3349
7	0.3996	0.3759	0.3538	0.3332	0.3139	0.2959	0.2791
8	0.3506	0.3269	0.3050	0.2848	0.2660	0.2487	0.2326
9	0.3075	0.2843	0.2630	0.2434	0.2255	0.2090	0.1938
10	0.2697	0.2472	0.2267	0.2080	0.1911	0.1756	0.1615
11	0.2366	0.2149	0.1954	0.1778	0.1619	0.1476	0.1346
12	0.2076	0.1869	0.1685	0.1520	0.1372	0.1240	0.1122
13	0.1821	0.1625	0.1452	0.1299	0.1163	0.1042	0.0935
14	0.1597	0.1413	0.1252	0.1110	0.0985	0.0876	0.0779
15	0.1401	0.1229	0.1079	0.0949	0.0835	0.0736	0.0649
16	0.1229	0.1069	0.0930	0.0811	0.0708	0.0618	0.0541
17	0.1078	0.0929	0.0802	0.0693	0.0600	0.0520	0.0451
18	0.0946	0.0808	0.0691	0.0592	0.0508	0.0437	0.0376
19	0.0829	0.0703	0.0596	0.0506	0.0431	0.0367	0.0313
20	0.0728	0.0611	0.0514	0.0433	0.0365	0.0308	0.0261
21	0.0638	0.0531	0.0443	0.0370	0.0309	0.0259	0.0217
22	0.0560	0.0462	0.0382	0.0316	0.0262	0.0218	0.0181
23	0.0491	0.0402	0.0329	0.0270	0.0222	0.0183	0.0151
24	0.0431	0.0349	0.0284	0.0231	0.0188	0.0154	0.0126
25	0.0378	0.0304	0.0245	0.0197	0.0160	0.0129	0.0105
26	0.0331	0.0264	0.0211	0.0169	0.0135	0.0109	0.0087
27	0.0291	0.0230	0.0182	0.0144	0.0115	0.0091	0.0073
28	0.0255	0.0200	0.0157	0.0123	0.0097	0.0077	0.0061
29	0.0224	0.0174	0.0135	0.0105	0.0082	0.0064	0.0051
30	0.0196	0.0151	0.0116	0.0090	0.0070	0.0054	0.0042
31	0.0172	0.0131	0.0100	0.0077	0.0059	0.0046	0.0035
32	0.0151	0.0114	0.0087	0.0066	0.0050	0.0038	0.0029
33	0.0132	0.0099	0.0075	0.0056	0.0042	0.0032	0.0024
34	0.0116	0.0086	0.0064	0.0048	0.0036	0.0027	0.0020
35	0.0102	0.0075	0.0055	0.0041	0.0030	0.0023	0.0017

YEARS	14.0%	15.0%	16.0%	17.0%	18.0%	19.0%	20.0%
36	0.0089	0.0065	0.0048	0.0035	0.0026	0.0019	0.0014
37	0.0078	0.0057	0.0041	0.0030	0.0022	0.0016	0.0012
38	0.0069	0.0049	0.0036	0.0026	0.0019	0.0013	0.0010
39	0.0060	0.0043	0.0031	0.0022	0.0016	0.0011	0.0008
40	0.0053	0.0037	0.0026	0.0019	0.0013	0.0010	0.0007
41	0.0046	0.0032	0.0023	0.0016	0.0011	0.0008	0.0006
42	0.0041	0.0028	0.0020	0.0014	0.0010	0.0007	0.0005
43	0.0036	0.0025	0.0017	0.0012	0.0008	0.0006	0.0004
44	0.0031	0.0021	0.0015	0.0010	0.0007	0.0005	0.0003
45	0.0027	0.0019	0.0013	0.0009	0.0006	0.0004	0.0003
46	0.0024	0.0016	0.0011	0.0007	0.0005	0.0003	0.0002
47	0.0021	0.0014	0.0009	0.0006	0.0004	0.0003	0.0002
48	0.0019	0.0012	0.0008	0.0005	0.0004	0.0002	0.0002
49	0.0016	0.0011	0.0007	0.0005	0.0003	0.0002	0.0001
50	0.0014	0.0009	0.0006	0.0004	0.0003	0.0002	0.0001

Appendix B

PRESENT VALUE OF ANNUITY DUE

YEARS	3.0%	3.5%	4.0%	4.5%	5.0%	5.5%	6.0%
1	1.0000	1.0000	1.0000	1.0000	1.0000	1.0000	1.0000
2	1.9709	1.9662	1.9615	1.9569	1.9524	1.9479	1.9434
3	2.9135	2.8997	2.8861	2.8727	2.8594	2.8463	2.8334
4	3.8286	3.8016	3.7751	3.7490	3.7232	3.6979	3.6730
5	4.7171	4.6731	4.6299	4.5875	4.5459	4.5052	4.4651
6	5.5797	5.5151	5.4518	5.3900	5.3295	5.2703	5.2124
7	6.4172	6.3286	6.2421	6.1579	6.0757	5.9955	5.9173
8	7.2303	7.1145	7.0021	6.8927	6.7864	6.6830	6.5824
9	8.0197	7.8740	7.7327	7.5959	7.4632	7.3346	7.2098
10	8.7861	8.6077	8.4353	8.2688	8.1078	7.9522	7.8017
11	9.5302	9.3166	9.1109	8.9127	8.7217	8.5376	8.3601
12	10.2526	10.0016	9.7605	9.5289	9.3064	9.0925	8.8869
13	10.9540	10.6633	10.3851	10.1186	9.8633	9.6185	9.3838
14	11.6350	11.3027	10.9856	10.6829	10.3936	10.1171	9.8527
15	12.2961	11.9205	11.5631	11.2228	10.8986	10.5896	10.2950
16	12.9379	12.5174	12.1184	11.7395	11.3797	11.0376	10.7122
17	13.5611	13.0941	12.6523	12.2340	11.8378	11.4622	11.1059
18	14.1661	13.6513	13.1657	12.7072	12.2741	11.8646	11.4773
19	14.7535	14.1897	13.6593	13.1600	12.6896	12.2461	11.8276
20	15.3238	14.7098	14.1339	13.5933	13.0853	12.6077	12.1581
21	15.8775	15.2124	14.5903	14.0079	13.4622	12.9504	12.4699
22	16.4150	15.6980	15.0292	14.4047	13.8212	13.2752	12.7641
23	16.9369	16.1671	15.4511	14.7844	14.1630	13.5832	13.0416
24	17.4436	16.6204	15.8568	15.1478	14.4886	13.8750	13.3034
25	17.9355	17.0584	16.2470	15.4955	14.7986	14.1517	13.5504
26	18.4131	17.4815	16.6221	15.8282	15.0939	14.4139	13.7834
27	18.8768	17.8904	16.9828	16.1466	15.3752	14.6625	14.0032
28	19.3270	18.2854	17.3296	16.4513	15.6430	14.8981	14.2105

YEARS	3.0%	3.5%	4.0%	4.5%	5.0%	5.5%	6.0%
29	19.7641	18.6670	17.6631	16.7429	15.8981	15.1214	14.4062
30	20.1885	19.0358	17.9837	17.0219	16.1411	15.3331	14.5907
31	20.6004	19.3920	18.2920	17.2889	16.3724	15.5337	14.7648
32	21.0004	19.7363	18.5885	17.5444	16.5928	15.7239	14.9291
33	21.3888	20.0689	18.8735	17.7889	16.8027	15.9042	15.0840
34	21.7658	20.3902	19.1476	18.0229	17.0025	16.0751	15.2302
35	22.1318	20.7007	19.4112	18.2468	17.1929	16.2370	15.3681
36	22.4872	21.0007	19.6646	18.4610	17.3742	16.3906	15.4982
37	22.8323	21.2905	19.9083	18.6660	17.5469	16.5361	15.6210
38	23.1672	21.5705	20.1426	18.8622	17.7113	16.6740	15.7368
39	23.4925	21.8411	20.3679	19.0500	17.8679	16.8047	15.8460
40	23.8082	22.1025	20.5845	19.2297	18.0170	16.9287	15.9491
41	24.1148	22.3551	20.7928	19.4016	18.1591	17.0461	16.0463
42	24.4124	22.5991	20.9931	19.5661	18.2944	17.1575	16.1380
43	24.7014	22.8349	21.1856	19.7235	18.4232	17.2630	16.2245
44	24.9819	23.0627	21.3708	19.8742	18.5459	17.3630	16.3062
45	25.2543	23.2828	21.5488	20.0184	18.6628	17.4578	16.3832
46	25.5187	23.4954	21.7200	20.1563	18.7741	17.5477	16.4558
47	25.7754	23.7009	21.8847	20.2884	18.8801	17.6329	16.5244
48	26.0247	23.8994	22.0429	20.4147	18.9810	17.7137	16.5890
49	26.2667	24.0912	22.1951	20.5356	19.0772	17.7902	16.6500
50	26.5017	24.2766	22.3415	20.6513	19.1687	17.8628	16.7076

PRESENT VALUE OF ANNUITY DUE (continued)

YEARS	6.5%	7.0%	7.5%	8.0%	8.5%	9.0%	9.5%
1	1.0000	1.0000	1.0000	1.0000	1.0000	1.0000	1.0000
2	1.9390	1.9346	1.9302	1.9259	1.9217	1.9174	1.9132
3	2.8206	2.8080	2.7956	2.7833	2.7711	2.7591	2.7473
4	3.6485	3.6243	3.6005	3.5771	3.5540	3.5313	3.5089
5	4.4258	4.3872	4.3493	4.3121	4.2756	4.2397	4.2045
6	5.1557	5.1002	5.0459	4.9927	4.9406	4.8897	4.8397
7	5.8410	5.7665	5.6938	5.6229	5.5536	5.4859	5.4198
8	6.4845	6.3893	6.2966	6.2064	6.1185	6.0330	5.9496
9	7.0888	6.9713	6.8573	6.7466	6.6392	6.5348	6.4334
10	7.6561	7.5152	7.3789	7.2469	7.1191	6.9952	6.8753
11	8.1888	8.0236	7.8641	7.7101	7.5613	7.4177	7.2788
12	8.6890	8.4987	8.3154	8.1390	7.9690	7.8052	7.6473
13	9.1587	8.9427	8.7353	8.5361	8.3447	8.1607	7.9838
14	9.5997	9.3577	9.1258	8.9038	8.6910	8.4869	8.2912
15	10.0138	9.7455	9.4892	9.2442	9.0101	8.7861	8.5719
16	10.4027	10.1079	9.8271	9.5595	9.3042	9.0607	8.8282
17	10.7678	10.4466	10.1415	9.8514	9.5753	9.3126	9.0623
18	11.1106	10.7632	10.4340	10.1216	9.8252	9.5436	9.2760
19	11.4325	11.0591	10.7060	10.3719	10.0555	9.7556	9.4713
20	11.7347	11.3356	10.9591	10.6036	10.2677	9.9501	9.6496
21	12.0185	11.5940	11.1945	10.8181	10.4633	10.1285	9.8124
22	12.2850	11.8355	11.4135	11.0168	10.6436	10.2922	9.9611
23	12.5352	12.0612	11.6172	11.2007	10.8098	10.4424	10.0969
24	12.7701	12.2722	11.8067	11.3711	10.9629	10.5802	10.2209
25	12.9907	12.4693	11.9830	11.5288	11.1041	10.7066	10.3341
26	13.1979	12.6536	12.1469	11.6748	11.2342	10.8226	10.4376
27	13.3924	12.8258	12.2995	11.8100	11.3541	10.9290	10.5320
28	13.5750	12.9867	12.4414	11.9352	11.4646	11.0266	10.6183
29	13.7465	13.1371	12.5734	12.0511	11.5665	11.1161	10.6971
30	13.9075	13.2777	12.6962	12.1584	11.6603	11.1983	10.7690
31	14.0587	13.4090	12.8104	12.2578	11.7468	11.2737	10.8347
32	14.2006	13.5318	12.9166	12.3498	11.8266	11.3428	10.8947
33	14.3339	13.6466	13.0155	12.4350	11.9001	11.4062	10.9495
34	14.4591	13.7538	13.1074	12.5139	11.9678	11.4644	10.9996
35	14.5766	13.8540	13.1929	12.5869	12.0302	11.5178	11.0453

YEARS	6.5%	7.0%	7.5%	8.0%	8.5%	9.0%	9.5%
36	14.6870	13.9477	13.2725	12.6546	12.0878	11.5668	11.0870
37	14.7906	14.0352	13.3465	12.7172	12.1408	11.6118	11.1251
38	14.8879	14.1170	13.4154	12.7752	12.1897	11.6530	11.1599
39	14.9792	14.1935	13.4794	12.8289	12.2347	11.6908	11.1917
40	15.0650	14.2649	13.5390	12.8786	12.2763	11.7255	11.2207
41	15.1455	14.3317	13.5944	12.9246	12.3145	11.7574	11.2472
42	15.2212	14.3941	13.6460	12.9672	12.3498	11.7866	11.2715
43	15.2922	14.4524	13.6939	13.0067	12.3823	11.8134	11.2936
44	15.3588	14.5070	13.7385	13.0432	12.4123	11.8380	11.3138
45	15.4214	14.5579	13.7800	13.0771	12.4399	11.8605	11.3322
46	15.4802	14.6055	13.8186	13.1084	12.4653	11.8812	11.3490
47	15.5354	14.6500	13.8545	13.1374	12.4888	11.9002	11.3644
48	15.5873	14.6916	13.8879	13.1643	12.5104	11.9176	11.3785
49	15.6359	14.7305	13.9190	13.1891	12.5303	11.9336	11.3913
50	15.6816	14.7668	13.9479	13.2122	12.5487	11.9482	11.4030

PRESENT VALUE OF ANNUITY DUE (continued)

YEARS	10.0%	10.5%	11.0%	11.5%	12.0%	12.5%	13.0%
1	1.0000	1.0000	1.0000	1.0000	1.0000	1.0000	1.0000
2	1.9091	1.9050	1.9009	1.8969	1.8929	1.8889	1.8850
3	2.7355	2.7240	2.7125	2.7012	2.6901	2.6790	2.6681
4	3.4869	3.4651	3.4437	3.4226	3.4018	3.3813	3.3612
5	4.1699	4.1359	4.1024	4.0696	4.0373	4.0056	3.9745
6	4.7908	4.7429	4.6959	4.6499	4.6048	4.5606	4.5172
7	5.3553	5.2922	5.2305	5.1703	5.1114	5.0538	4.9976
8	5.8684	5.7893	5.7122	5.6370	5.5638	5.4923	5.4226
9	6.3349	6.2392	6.1461	6.0556	5.9676	5.8820	5.7988
10	6.7590	6.6463	6.5370	6.4311	6.3282	6.2285	6.1317
11	7.1446	7.0148	6.8892	6.7678	6.6502	6.5364	6.4262
12	7.4951	7.3482	7.2065	7.0697	6.9377	6.8102	6.6869
13	7.8137	7.6500	7.4924	7.3406	7.1944	7.0535	6.9176
14	8.1034	7.9230	7.7499	7.5835	7.4235	7.2698	7.1218
15	8.3667	8.1702	7.9819	7.8013	7.6282	7.4620	7.3025
16	8.6061	8.3938	8.1909	7.9967	7.8109	7.6329	7.4624
17	8.8237	8.5962	8.3792	8.1719	7.9740	7.7848	7.6039
18	9.0216	8.7794	8.5488	8.3291	8.1196	7.9198	7.7291
19	9.2014	8.9451	8.7016	8.4700	8.2497	8.0398	7.8399
20	9.3649	9.0952	8.8393	8.5964	8.3658	8.1465	7.9380
21	9.5136	9.2309	8.9633	8.7098	8.4694	8.2414	8.0248
22	9.6487	9.3538	9.0751	8.8115	8.5620	8.3256	8.1016
23	9.7715	9.4649	9.1757	8.9027	8.6446	8.4006	8.1695
24	9.8832	9.5656	9.2664	8.9845	8.7184	8.4672	8.2297
25	9.9847	9.6566	9.3481	9.0578	8.7843	8.5264	8.2829
26	10.0770	9.7390	9.4217	9.1236	8.8431	8.5790	8.3300
27	10.1609	9.8136	9.4881	9.1826	8.8957	8.6258	8.3717
28	10.2372	9.8811	9.5478	9.2355	8.9426	8.6674	8.4086
29	10.3066	9.9422	9.6016	9.2830	8.9844	8.7043	8.4412
30	10.3696	9.9974	9.6501	9.3255	9.0218	8.7372	8.4701
31	10.4269	10.0474	9.6938	9.3637	9.0552	8.7664	8.4957
32	10.4790	10.0927	9.7331	9.3980	9.0850	8.7923	8.5183
33	10.5264	10.1337	9.7686	9.4287	9.1116	8.8154	8.5383
34	10.5694	10.1707	9.8005	9.4562	9.1354	8.8359	8.5560
35	10.6086	10.2043	9.8293	9.4809	9.1566	8.8542	8.5717
36	10.6442	10.2347	9.8552	9.5030	9.1755	8.8704	8.5856

YEARS	10.0%	10.5%	11.0%	11.5%	12.0%	12.5%	13.0%
37	10.6765	10.2621	9.8786	9.5229	9.1924	8.8848	8.5979
38	10.7059	10.2870	9.8996	9.5407	9.2075	8.8976	8.6087
39	10.7327	10.3095	9.9186	9.5567	9.2210	8.9089	8.6183
40	10.7570	10.3299	9.9357	9.5710	9.2330	8.9191	8.6268
41	10.7791	10.3483	9.9511	9.5839	9.2438	8.9281	8.6344
42	10.7991	10.3650	9.9649	9.5954	9.2534	8.9361	8.6410
43	10.8174	10.3801	9.9774	9.6058	9.2619	8.9432	8.6469
44	10.8340	10.3937	9.9886	9.6150	9.2696	8.9495	8.6522
45	10.8491	10.4061	9.9988	9.6233	9.2764	8.9551	8.6568
46	10.8628	10.4173	10.0079	9.6308	9.2825	8.9601	8.6609
47	10.8753	10.4274	10.0161	9.6375	9.2880	8.9645	8.6645
48	10.8866	10.4366	10.0235	9.6435	9.2928	8.9685	8.6677
49	10.8969	10.4448	10.0302	9.6489	9.2972	8.9720	8.6705
50	10.9063	10.4524	10.0362	9.6537	9.3010	8.9751	8.6730

PRESENT VALUE OF ANNUITY DUE (continued)

YEARS	14.0%	15.0%	16.0%	17.0%	18.0%	19.0%	20.0%
1	1.0000	1.0000	1.0000	1.0000	1.0000	1.0000	1.0000
2	1.8772	1.8696	1.8621	1.8547	1.8475	1.8403	1.8333
3	2.6467	2.6257	2.6052	2.5852	2.5656	2.5465	2.5278
4	3.3216	3.2832	3.2459	3.2096	3.1743	3.1399	3.1065
5	3.9137	3.8550	3.7982	3.7432	3.6901	3.6386	3.5887
6	4.4331	4.3522	4.2743	4.1993	4.1272	4.0576	3.9906
7	4.8887	4.7845	4.6847	4.5892	4.4976	4.4098	4.3255
8	5.2883	5.1604	5.0386	4.9224	4.8115	4.7057	4.6046
9	5.6389	5.4873	5.3436	5.2072	5.0776	4.9544	4.8372
10	5.9464	5.7716	5.6065	5.4506	5.3030	5.1633	5.0310
11	6.2161	6.0188	5.8332	5.6586	5.4941	5.3389	5.1925
12	6.4527	6.2337	6.0286	5.8364	5.6560	5.4865	5.3271
13	6.6603	6.4206	6.1971	5.9884	5.7932	5.6105	5.4392
14	6.8424	6.5831	6.3423	6.1183	5.9095	5.7147	5.5327
15	7.0021	6.7245	6.4675	6.2293	6.0081	5.8023	5.6106
16	7.1422	6.8474	6.5755	6.3242	6.0916	5.8759	5.6755
17	7.2651	6.9542	6.6685	6.4053	6.1624	5.9377	5.7296
18	7.3729	7.0472	6.7487	6.4746	6.2223	5.9897	5.7746
19	7.4674	7.1280	6.8178	6.5339	6.2732	6.0333	5.8122
20	7.5504	7.1982	6.8775	6.5845	6.3162	6.0700	5.8435
21	7.6231	7.2593	6.9288	6.6278	6.3527	6.1009	5.8696
22	7.6870	7.3125	6.9731	6.6648	6.3837	6.1268	5.8913
23	7.7429	7.3587	7.0113	6.6964	6.4099	6.1486	5.9094
24	7.7921	7.3988	7.0442	6.7234	6.4321	6.1668	5.9245
25	7.8351	7.4338	7.0726	6.7465	6.4509	6.1822	5.9371
26	7.8729	7.4641	7.0971	6.7662	6.4669	6.1951	5.9476
27	7.9061	7.4906	7.1182	6.7831	6.4804	6.2060	5.9563
28	7.9352	7.5135	7.1364	6.7975	6.4919	6.2151	5.9636
29	7.9607	7.5335	7.1520	6.8099	6.5016	6.2228	5.9697
30	7.9830	7.5509	7.1656	6.8204	6.5098	6.2292	5.9747
31	8.0027	7.5660	7.1772	6.8294	6.5168	6.2347	5.9789
32	8.0199	7.5791	7.1872	6.8371	6.5227	6.2392	5.9824
33	8.0350	7.5905	7.1959	6.8437	6.5277	6.2430	5.9854
34	8.0482	7.6005	7.2034	6.8493	6.5320	6.2462	5.9878
35	8.0599	7.6091	7.2098	6.8541	6.5356	6.2489	5.9898

YEARS	14.0%	15.0%	16.0%	17.0%	18.0%	19.0%	20.0%
36	8.0700	7.6166	7.2153	6.8582	6.5386	6.2512	5.9915
37	8.0790	7.6231	7.2201	6.8617	6.5412	6.2531	5.9929
38	8.0868	7.6288	7.2242	6.8647	6.5434	6.2547	5.9941
39	8.0937	7.6338	7.2278	6.8673	6.5452	6.2561	5.9951
40	8.0997	7.6380	7.2309	6.8695	6.5468	6.2572	5.9959
41	8.1050	7.6418	7.2335	6.8713	6.5482	6.2582	5.9966
42	8.1097	7.6450	7.2358	6.8729	6.5493	6.2590	5.9972
43	8.1138	7.6478	7.2377	6.8743	6.5502	6.2596	5.9976
44	8.1173	7.6503	7.2394	6.8755	6.5510	6.2602	5.9980
45	8.1205	7.6524	7.2409	6.8765	6.5517	6.2607	5.9984
46	8.1232	7.6543	7.2421	6.8773	6.5523	6.2611	5.9986
47	8.1256	7.6559	7.2432	6.8781	6.5528	6.2614	5.9989
48	8.1277	7.6573	7.2442	6.8787	6.5532	6.2617	5.9991
49	8.1296	7.6585	7.2450	6.8792	6.5536	6.2619	5.9992
50	8.1312	7.6596	7.2457	6.8797	6.5539	6.2621	5.9993

Appendix C

PRESENT VALUE OF ORDINARY ANNUITY

YEARS	3.0%	3.5%	4.0%	4.5%	5.0%	5.5%	6.0%
1	0.9709	0.9662	0.9615	0.9569	0.9524	0.9479	0.9434
2	1.9135	1.8997	1.8861	1.8727	1.8594	1.8463	1.8334
3	2.8286	2.8016	2.7751	2.7490	2.7232	2.6979	2.6730
4	3.7171	3.6731	3.6299	3.5875	3.5460	3.5051	3.4651
5	4.5797	4.5151	4.4518	4.3900	4.3295	4.2703	4.2124
6	5.4172	5.3286	5.2421	5.1579	5.0757	4.9955	4.9173
7	6.2303	6.1145	6.0021	5.8927	5.7864	5.6830	5.5824
8	7.0197	6.8740	6.7327	6.5959	6.4632	6.3346	6.2098
9	7.7861	7.6077	7.4353	7.2688	7.1078	6.9522	6.8017
10	8.5302	8.3166	8.1109	7.9127	7.7217	7.5376	7.3601
11	9.2526	9.0016	8.7605	8.5289	8.3064	8.0925	7.8869
12	9.9540	9.6633	9.3851	9.1186	8.8633	8.6185	8.3838
13	10.6350	10.3027	9.9856	9.6829	9.3936	9.1171	8.8527
14	11.2961	10.9205	10.5631	10.2228	9.8986	9.5896	9.2950
15	11.9379	11.5174	11.1184	10.7395	10.3797	10.0376	9.7122
16	12.5611	12.0941	11.6523	11.2340	10.8378	10.4622	10.1059
17	13.1661	12.6513	12.1657	11.7072	11.2741	10.8646	10.4773
18	13.7535	13.1897	12.6593	12.1600	11.6896	11.2461	10.8276
19	14.3238	13.7098	13.1339	12.5933	12.0853	11.6077	11.1581
20	14.8775	14.2124	13.5903	13.0079	12.4622	11.9504	11.4699
21	15.4150	14.6980	14.0292	13.4047	12.8212	12.2752	11.7641
22	15.9369	15.1671	14.4511	13.7844	13.1630	12.5832	12.0416
23	16.4436	15.6204	14.8568	14.1478	13.4886	12.8750	12.3034
24	16.9355	16.0584	15.2470	14.4955	13.7986	13.1517	12.5504
25	17.4131	16.4815	15.6221	14.8282	14.0939	13.4139	12.7834
26	17.8768	16.8904	15.9828	15.1466	14.3752	13.6625	13.0032
27	18.3270	17.2854	16.3296	15.4513	14.6430	13.8981	13.2105
28	18.7641	17.6670	16.6631	15.7429	14.8981	14.1214	13.4062

YEARS	3.0%	3.5%	4.0%	4.5%	5.0%	5.5%	6.0%
29	19.1885	18.0358	16.9837	16.0219	15.1411	14.3331	13.5907
30	19.6004	18.3920	17.2920	16.2889	15.3725	14.5337	13.7648
31	20.0004	18.7363	17.5885	16.5444	15.5928	14.7239	13.9291
32	20.3888	19.0689	17.8736	16.7889	15.8027	14.9042	14.0840
33	20.7658	19.3902	18.1476	17.0229	16.0025	15.0751	14.2302
34	21.1318	19.7007	18.4112	17.2468	16.1929	15.2370	14.3681
35	21.4872	20.0007	18.6646	17.4610	16.3742	15.3906	14.4982
36	21.8323	20.2905	18.9083	17.6660	16.5469	15.5361	14.6210
37	22.1672	20.5705	19.1426	17.8622	16.7113	15.6740	14.7368
38	22.4925	20.8411	19.3679	18.0500	16.8679	15.8047	14.8460
39	22.8082	21.1025	19.5845	18.2297	17.0170	15.9287	14.9491
40	23.1148	21.3551	19.7928	18.4016	17.1591	16.0461	15.0463
41	23.4124	21.5991	19.9931	18.5661	17.2944	16.1575	15.1380
42	23.7014	21.8349	20.1856	18.7235	17.4232	16.2630	15.2245
43	23.9819	22.0627	20.3708	18.8742	17.5459	16.3630	15.3062
44	24.2543	22.2828	20.5488	19.0184	17.6628	16.4578	15.3832
45	24.5187	22.4955	20.7200	19.1563	17.7741	16.5477	15.4558
46	24.7754	22.7009	20.8847	19.2884	17.8801	16.6329	15.5244
47	25.0247	22.8994	21.0429	19.4147	17.9810	16.7137	15.5890
48	25.2667	23.0912	21.1951	19.5356	18.0772	16.7902	15.6500
49	25.5017	23.2766	21.3415	19.6513	18.1687	16.8628	15.7076
50	25.7298	23.4556	21.4822	19.7620	18.2559	16.9315	15.7619

PRESENT VALUE OF ORDINARY ANNUITY (continued)

YEARS	6.5%	7.0%	7.5%	8.0%	8.5%	9.0%	9.5%
1	0.9390	0.9346	0.9302	0.9259	0.9217	0.9174	0.9132
2	1.8206	1.8080	1.7956	1.7833	1.7711	1.7591	1.7473
3	2.6485	2.6243	2.6005	2.5771	2.5540	2.5313	2.5089
4	3.4258	3.3872	3.3493	3.3121	3.2756	3.2397	3.2045
5	4.1557	4.1002	4.0459	3.9927	3.9406	3.8897	3.8397
6	4.8410	4.7665	4.6938	4.6229	4.5536	4.4859	4.4198
7	5.4845	5.3893	5.2966	5.2064	5.1185	5.0330	4.9496
8	6.0888	5.9713	5.8573	5.7466	5.6392	5.5348	5.4334
9	6.6561	6.5152	6.3789	6.2469	6.1191	5.9952	5.8753
10	7.1888	7.0236	6.8641	6.7101	6.5613	6.4177	6.2788
11	7.6890	7.4987	7.3154	7.1390	6.9690	6.8052	6.6473
12	8.1587	7.9427	7.7353	7.5361	7.3447	7.1607	6.9838
13	8.5997	8.3577	8.1258	7.9038	7.6910	7.4869	7.2912
14	9.0138	8.7455	8.4892	8.2442	8.0101	7.7862	7.5719
15	9.4027	9.1079	8.8271	8.5595	8.3042	8.0607	7.8282
16	9.7678	9.4466	9.1415	8.8514	8.5753	8.3126	8.0623
17	10.1106	9.7632	9.4340	9.1216	8.8252	8.5436	8.2760
18	10.4325	10.0591	9.7060	9.3719	9.0555	8.7556	8.4713
19	10.7347	10.3356	9.9591	9.6036	9.2677	8.9501	8.6496
20	11.0185	10.5940	10.1945	9.8181	9.4633	9.1285	8.8124
21	11.2850	10.8355	10.4135	10.0168	9.6436	9.2922	8.9611
22	11.5352	11.0612	10.6172	10.2007	9.8098	9.4424	9.0969
23	11.7701	11.2722	10.8067	10.3711	9.9629	9.5802	9.2209
24	11.9907	11.4693	10.9830	10.5288	10.1041	9.7066	9.3341
25	12.1979	11.6536	11.1469	10.6748	10.2342	9.8226	9.4376
26	12.3924	11.8258	11.2995	10.8100	10.3541	9.9290	9.5320
27	12.5750	11.9867	11.4414	10.9352	10.4646	10.0266	9.6183
28	12.7465	12.1371	11.5734	11.0511	10.5665	10.1161	9.6971
29	12.9075	12.2777	11.6962	11.1584	10.6603	10.1983	9.7690
30	13.0587	12.4090	11.8104	11.2578	10.7468	10.2737	9.8347
31	13.2006	12.5318	11.9166	11.3498	10.8266	10.3428	9.8947
32	13.3339	12.6466	12.0155	11.4350	10.9001	10.4062	9.9495
33	13.4591	12.7538	12.1074	11.5139	10.9678	10.4644	9.9996
34	13.5766	12.8540	12.1929	11.5869	11.0302	10.5178	10.0453
35	13.6870	12.9477	12.2725	11.6546	11.0878	10.5668	10.0870

YEARS	6.5%	7.0%	7.5%	8.0%	8.5%	9.0%	9.5%
36	13.7906	13.0352	12.3465	11.7172	11.1408	10.6118	10.1251
37	13.8879	13.1170	12.4154	11.7752	11.1897	10.6530	10.1599
38	13.9792	13.1935	12.4794	11.8289	11.2347	10.6908	10.1917
39	14.0650	13.2649	12.5390	11.8786	11.2763	10.7255	10.2207
40	14.1455	13.3317	12.5944	11.9246	11.3145	10.7574	10.2472
41	14.2212	13.3941	12.6460	11.9672	11.3498	10.7866	10.2715
42	14.2922	13.4524	12.6939	12.0067	11.3823	10.8134	10.2936
43	14.3588	13.5070	12.7385	12.0432	11.4123	10.8379	10.3138
44	14.4214	13.5579	12.7800	12.0771	11.4399	10.8605	10.3322
45	14.4802	13.6055	12.8186	12.1084	11.4653	10.8812	10.3490
46	14.5354	13.6500	12.8545	12.1374	11.4888	10.9002	10.3644
47	14.5873	13.6916	12.8879	12.1643	11.5104	10.9176	10.3785
48	14.6359	13.7305	12.9190	12.1891	11.5303	10.9336	10.3913
49	14.6816	13.7668	12.9479	12.2122	11.5487	10.9482	10.4030
50	14.7245	13.8007	12.9748	12.2335	11.5656	10.9617	10.4137

PRESENT VALUE OF ORDINARY ANNUITY (continued)

YEARS	10.0%	10.5%	11.0%	11.5%	12.0%	12.5%	13.0%
1	0.9091	0.9050	0.9009	0.8969	0.8929	0.8889	0.8850
2	1.7355	1.7240	1.7125	1.7012	1.6901	1.6790	1.6681
3	2.4869	2.4651	2.4437	2.4226	2.4018	2.3813	2.3612
4	3.1699	3.1359	3.1024	3.0696	3.0373	3.0056	2.9745
5	3.7908	3.7429	3.6959	3.6499	3.6048	3.5606	3.5172
6	4.3553	4.2922	4.2305	4.1703	4.1114	4.0538	3.9975
7	4.8684	4.7893	4.7122	4.6370	4.5638	4.4923	4.4226
8	5.3349	5.2392	5.1461	5.0556	4.9676	4.8820	4.7988
9	5.7590	5.6463	5.5370	5.4311	5.3282	5.2285	5.1317
10	6.1446	6.0148	5.8892	5.7678	5.6502	5.5364	5.4262
11	6.4951	6.3482	6.2065	6.0697	5.9377	5.8102	5.6869
12	6.8137	6.6500	6.4924	6.3406	6.1944	6.0535	5.9176
13	7.1034	6.9230	6.7499	6.5835	6.4235	6.2698	6.1218
14	7.3667	7.1702	6.9819	6.8013	6.6282	6.4620	6.3025
15	7.6061	7.3938	7.1909	6.9967	6.8109	6.6329	6.4624
16	7.8237	7.5962	7.3792	7.1719	6.9740	6.7848	6.6039
17	8.0216	7.7794	7.5488	7.3291	7.1196	6.9198	6.7291
18	8.2014	7.9451	7.7016	7.4700	7.2497	7.0398	6.8399
19	8.3649	8.0952	7.8393	7.5964	7.3658	7.1465	6.9380
20	8.5136	8.2309	7.9633	7.7098	7.4694	7.2414	7.0248
21	8.6487	8.3538	8.0751	7.8115	7.5620	7.3256	7.1016
22	8.7715	8.4649	8.1757	7.9027	7.6446	7.4006	7.1695
23	8.8832	8.5656	8.2664	7.9845	7.7184	7.4672	7.2297
24	8.9847	8.6566	8.3481	8.0578	7.7843	7.5264	7.2829
25	9.0770	8.7390	8.4217	8.1236	7.8431	7.5790	7.3300
26	9.1609	8.8136	8.4881	8.1826	7.8957	7.6258	7.3717
27	9.2372	8.8811	8.5478	8.2355	7.9426	7.6674	7.4086
28	9.3066	8.9422	8.6016	8.2830	7.9844	7.7043	7.4412
29	9.3696	8.9974	8.6501	8.3255	8.0218	7.7372	7.4701
30	9.4269	9.0474	8.6938	8.3637	8.0552	7.7664	7.4957
31	9.4790	9.0927	8.7331	8.3980	8.0850	7.7923	7.5183
32	9.5264	9.1337	8.7686	8.4287	8.1116	7.8154	7.5383
33	9.5694	9.1707	8.8005	8.4562	8.1354	7.8359	7.5560
34	9.6086	9.2043	8.8293	8.4809	8.1566	7.8542	7.5717
35	9.6442	9.2347	8.8552	8.5030	8.1755	7.8704	7.5856
36	9.6765	9.2621	8.8786	8.5229	8.1924	7.8848	7.5979

YEARS	10.0%	10.5%	11.0%	11.5%	12.0%	12.5%	13.0%
37	9.7059	9.2870	8.8996	8.5407	8.2075	7.8976	7.6087
38	9.7327	9.3095	8.9186	8.5567	8.2210	7.9089	7.6183
39	9.7570	9.3299	8.9357	8.5710	8.2330	7.9191	7.6268
40	9.7791	9.3483	8.9511	8.5839	8.2438	7.9281	7.6344
41	9.7991	9.3650	8.9649	8.5954	8.2534	7.9361	7.6410
42	9.8174	9.3801	8.9774	8.6058	8.2619	7.9432	7.6469
43	9.8340	9.3937	8.9886	8.6150	8.2696	7.9495	7.6522
44	9.8491	9.4061	8.9988	8.6233	8.2764	7.9551	7.6568
45	9.8628	9.4173	9.0079	8.6308	8.2825	7.9601	7.6609
46	9.8753	9.4274	9.0161	8.6375	8.2880	7.9645	7.6645
47	9.8866	9.4366	9.0235	8.6435	8.2928	7.9685	7.6677
48	9.8969	9.4448	9.0302	8.6489	8.2972	7.9720	7.6705
49	9.9063	9.4524	9.0362	8.6537	8.3010	7.9751	7.6730
50	9.9148	9.4591	9.0417	8.6580	8.3045	7.9778	7.6752

PRESENT VALUE OF ORDINARY ANNUITY (continued)

YEARS	14.0%	15.0%	16.0%	17.0%	18.0%	19.0%	20.0%
1	0.8772	0.8696	0.8621	0.8547	0.8475	0.8403	0.8333
2	1.6467	1.6257	1.6052	1.5852	1.5656	1.5465	1.5278
3	2.3216	2.2832	2.2459	2.2096	2.1743	2.1399	2.1065
4	2.9137	2.8550	2.7982	2.7432	2.6901	2.6386	2.5887
5	3.4331	3.3522	3.2743	3.1993	3.1272	3.0576	2.9906
6	3.8887	3.7845	3.6847	3.5892	3.4976	3.4098	3.3255
7	4.2883	4.1604	4.0386	3.9224	3.8115	3.7057	3.6046
8	4.6389	4.4873	4.3436	4.2072	4.0776	3.9544	3.8372
9	4.9464	4.7716	4.6065	4.4506	4.3030	4.1633	4.0310
10	5.2161	5.0188	4.8332	4.6586	4.4941	4.3389	4.1925
11	5.4527	5.2337	5.0286	4.8364	4.6560	4.4865	4.3271
12	5.6603	5.4206	5.1971	4.9884	4.7932	4.6105	4.4392
13	5.8424	5.5831	5.3423	5.1183	4.9095	4.7147	4.5327
14	6.0021	5.7245	5.4675	5.2293	5.0081	4.8023	4.6106
15	6.1422	5.8474	5.5755	5.3242	5.0916	4.8759	4.6755
16	6.2651	5.9542	5.6685	5.4053	5.1624	4.9377	4.7296
17	6.3729	6.0472	5.7487	5.4746	5.2223	4.9897	4.7746
18	6.4674	6.1280	5.8178	5.5339	5.2732	5.0333	4.8122
19	6.5504	6.1982	5.8775	5.5845	5.3162	5.0700	4.8435
20	6.6231	6.2593	5.9288	5.6278	5.3527	5.1009	4.8696
21	6.6870	6.3125	5.9731	5.6648	5.3837	5.1268	4.8913
22	6.7429	6.3587	6.0113	5.6964	5.4099	5.1486	4.9094
23	6.7921	6.3988	6.0442	5.7234	5.4321	5.1668	4.9245
24	6.8351	6.4338	6.0726	5.7465	5.4509	5.1822	4.9371
25	6.8729	6.4641	6.0971	5.7662	5.4669	5.1951	4.9476
26	6.9061	6.4906	6.1182	5.7831	5.4804	5.2060	4.9563
27	6.9352	6.5135	6.1364	5.7975	5.4919	5.2151	4.9636
28	6.9607	6.5335	6.1520	5.8099	5.5016	5.2228	4.9697
29	6.9830	6.5509	6.1656	5.8204	5.5098	5.2292	4.9747
30	7.0027	6.5660	6.1772	5.8294	5.5168	5.2347	4.9789
31	7.0199	6.5791	6.1872	5.8371	5.5227	5.2392	4.9824
32	7.0350	6.5905	6.1959	5.8437	5.5277	5.2430	4.9854
33	7.0482	6.6005	6.2034	5.8493	5.5320	5.2462	4.9878
34	7.0599	6.6091	6.2098	5.8541	5.5356	5.2489	4.9898
35	7.0700	6.6166	6.2153	5.8582	5.5386	5.2512	4.9915

YEARS	14.0%	15.0%	16.0%	17.0%	18.0%	19.0%	20.0%
36	7.0790	6.6231	6.2201	5.8617	5.5412	5.2531	4.9929
37	7.0868	6.6288	6.2242	5.8647	5.5434	5.2547	4.9941
38	7.0937	6.6338	6.2278	5.8673	5.5452	5.2561	4.9951
39	7.0997	6.6380	6.2309	5.8695	5.5468	5.2572	4.9959
40	7.1050	6.6418	6.2335	5.8713	5.5482	5.2582	4.9966
41	7.1097	6.6450	6.2358	5.8729	5.5493	5.2590	4.9972
42	7.1138	6.6478	6.2377	5.8743	5.5502	5.2596	4.9976
43	7.1173	6.6503	6.2394	5.8755	5.5510	5.2602	4.9980
44	7.1205	6.6524	6.2409	5.8765	5.5517	5.2607	4.9984
45	7.1232	6.6543	6.2421	5.8773	5.5523	5.2611	4.9986
46	7.1256	6.6559	6.2432	5.8781	5.5528	5.2614	4.9989
47	7.1277	6.6573	6.2442	5.8787	5.5532	5.2617	4.9991
48	7.1296	6.6585	6.2450	5.8792	5.5536	5.2619	4.9992
49	7.1312	6.6596	6.2457	5.8797	5.5539	5.2621	4.9993
50	7.1327	6.6605	6.2463	5.8801	5.5541	5.2623	4.9995

Appendix D

FUTURE VALUE OF LUMP SUM

YEARS	3.0%	3.5%	4.0%	4.5%	5.0%	5.5%
1	1.0300	1.0350	1.0400	1.0450	1.0500	1.0550
2	1.0609	1.0712	1.0816	1.0920	1.1025	1.1130
3	1.0927	1.1087	1.1249	1.1412	1.1576	1.1742
4	1.1255	1.1475	1.1699	1.1925	1.2155	1.2388
5	1.1593	1.1877	1.2167	1.2462	1.2763	1.3070
6	1.1941	1.2293	1.2653	1.3023	1.3401	1.3788
7	1.2299	1.2723	1.3159	1.3609	1.4071	1.4547
8	1.2668	1.3168	1.3686	1.4221	1.4775	1.5347
9	1.3048	1.3629	1.4233	1.4861	1.5513	1.6191
10	1.3439	1.4106	1.4802	1.5530	1.6289	1.7081
11	1.3842	1.4600	1.5395	1.6229	1.7103	1.8021
12	1.4258	1.5111	1.6010	1.6959	1.7959	1.9012
13	1.4685	1.5640	1.6651	1.7722	1.8856	2.0058
14	1.5126	1.6187	1.7317	1.8519	1.9799	2.1161
15	1.5580	1.6753	1.8009	1.9353	2.0789	2.2325
16	1.6047	1.7340	1.8730	2.0224	2.1829	2.3553
17	1.6528	1.7947	1.9479	2.1134	2.2920	2.4848
18	1.7024	1.8575	2.0258	2.2085	2.4066	2.6215
19	1.7535	1.9225	2.1068	2.3079	2.5270	2.7656
20	1.8061	1.9898	2.1911	2.4117	2.6533	2.9178
21	1.8603	2.0594	2.2788	2.5202	2.7860	3.0782
22	1.9161	2.1315	2.3699	2.6337	2.9253	3.2475
23	1.9736	2.2061	2.4647	2.7522	3.0715	3.4262
24	2.0328	2.2833	2.5633	2.8760	3.2251	3.6146
25	2.0938	2.3632	2.6658	3.0054	3.3864	3.8134
26	2.1566	2.4460	2.7725	3.1407	3.5557	4.0231
27	2.2213	2.5316	2.8834	3.2820	3.7335	4.2444
28	2.2879	2.6202	2.9987	3.4297	3.9201	4.4778
29	2.3566	2.7119	3.1187	3.5840	4.1161	4.7241
30	2.4273	2.8068	3.2434	3.7453	4.3219	4.9840

YEARS	3.0%	3.5%	4.0%	4.5%	5.0%	5.5%
31	2.5001	2.9050	3.3731	3.9139	4.5380	5.2581
32	2.5751	3.0067	3.5081	4.0900	4.7649	5.5473
33	2.6523	3.1119	3.6484	4.2740	5.0032	5.8524
34	2.7319	3.2209	3.7943	4.4664	5.2533	6.1742
35	2.8139	3.3336	3.9461	4.6673	5.5160	6.5138
36	2.8983	3.4503	4.1039	4.8774	5.7918	6.8721
37	2.9852	3.5710	4.2681	5.0969	6.0814	7.2501
38	3.0748	3.6960	4.4388	5.3262	6.3855	7.6488
39	3.1670	3.8254	4.6164	5.5659	6.7048	8.0695
40	3.2620	3.9593	4.8010	5.8164	7.0400	8.5133
41	3.3599	4.0978	4.9931	6.0781	7.3920	8.9815
42	3.4607	4.2413	5.1928	6.3516	7.7616	9.4755
43	3.5645	4.3897	5.4005	6.6374	8.1497	9.9967
44	3.6715	4.5433	5.6165	6.9361	8.5572	10.5465
45	3.7816	4.7024	5.8412	7.2482	8.9850	11.1266
46	3.8950	4.8669	6.0748	7.5744	9.4343	11.7385
47	4.0119	5.0373	6.3178	7.9153	9.9060	12.3841
48	4.1323	5.2136	6.5705	8.2715	10.4013	13.0653
49	4.2562	5.3961	6.8333	8.6437	10.9213	13.7838
50	4.3839	5.5849	7.1067	9.0326	11.4674	14.5420

FUTURE VALUE OF LUMP SUM (continued)

YEAR	6.0%	6.5%	7.0%	7.5%	8.0%	8.5%
1	1.0600	1.0650	1.0700	1.0750	1.0800	1.0850
2	1.1236	1.1342	1.1449	1.1556	1.1664	1.1772
3	1.1910	1.2079	1.2250	1.2423	1.2597	1.2773
4	1.2625	1.2865	1.3108	1.3355	1.3605	1.3859
5	1.3382	1.3701	1.4026	1.4356	1.4693	1.5037
6	1.4185	1.4591	1.5007	1.5433	1.5869	1.6315
7	1.5036	1.5540	1.6058	1.6590	1.7138	1.7701
8	1.5938	1.6550	1.7182	1.7835	1.8509	1.9206
9	1.6895	1.7626	1.8385	1.9172	1.9990	2.0839
10	1.7908	1.8771	1.9672	2.0610	2.1589	2.2610
11	1.8983	1.9992	2.1049	2.2156	2.3316	2.4532
12	2.0122	2.1291	2.2522	2.3818	2.5182	2.6617
13	2.1329	2.2675	2.4098	2.5604	2.7196	2.8879
14	2.2609	2.4149	2.5785	2.7524	2.9372	3.1334
15	2.3966	2.5718	2.7590	2.9589	3.1722	3.3997
16	2.5404	2.7390	2.9522	3.1808	3.4259	3.6887
17	2.6928	2.9170	3.1588	3.4194	3.7000	4.0023
18	2.8543	3.1067	3.3799	3.6758	3.9960	4.3425
19	3.0256	3.3086	3.6165	3.9515	4.3157	4.7116
20	3.2071	3.5236	3.8697	4.2479	4.6610	5.1120
21	3.3996	3.7527	4.1406	4.5664	5.0338	5.5466
22	3.6035	3.9966	4.4304	4.9089	5.4365	6.0180
23	3.8197	4.2564	4.7405	5.2771	5.8715	6.5296
24	4.0489	4.5331	5.0724	5.6729	6.3412	7.0846
25	4.2919	4.8277	5.4274	6.0983	6.8485	7.6868
26	4.5494	5.1415	5.8074	6.5557	7.3964	8.3401
27	4.8223	5.4757	6.2139	7.0474	7.9881	9.0490
28	5.1117	5.8316	6.6488	7.5759	8.6271	9.8182
29	5.4184	6.2107	7.1143	8.1441	9.3173	10.6528
30	5.7435	6.6144	7.6123	8.7550	10.0627	11.5583
31	6.0881	7.0443	8.1451	9.4116	10.8677	12.5407
32	6.4534	7.5022	8.7153	10.1174	11.7371	13.6067
33	6.8406	7.9898	9.3253	10.8763	12.6760	14.7632
34	7.2510	8.5092	9.9781	11.6920	13.6901	16.0181
35	7.6861	9.0623	10.6766	12.5689	14.7853	17.3796

YEAR	6.0%	6.5%	7.0%	7.5%	8.0%	8.5%
36	8.1473	9.6513	11.4239	13.5115	15.9682	18.8569
37	8.6361	10.2786	12.2236	14.5249	17.2456	20.4598
38	9.1543	10.9467	13.0793	15.6143	18.6253	22.1988
39	9.7035	11.6583	13.9948	16.7853	20.1153	24.0857
40	10.2857	12.4161	14.9745	18.0442	21.7245	26.1330
41	10.9029	13.2231	16.0227	19.3976	23.4625	28.3543
42	11.5570	14.0826	17.1443	20.8524	25.3395	30.7644
43	12.2505	14.9980	18.3444	22.4163	27.3666	33.3794
44	12.9855	15.9729	19.6285	24.0975	29.5560	36.2167
45	13.7646	17.0111	21.0025	25.9048	31.9204	39.2951
46	14.5905	18.1168	22.4726	27.8477	34.4741	42.6352
47	15.4659	19.2944	24.0457	29.9363	37.2320	46.2592
48	16.3939	20.5485	25.7289	32.1815	40.2106	50.1912
49	17.3775	21.8842	27.5299	34.5951	43.4274	54.4574
50	18.4202	23.3067	29.4570	37.1898	46.9016	59.0863

FUTURE VALUE OF LUMP SUM (continued)

YEARS	9.0%	9.5%	10.0%	10.5%	11.0%	11.5%
1	1.0900	1.0950	1.1000	1.1050	1.1100	1.1150
2	1.1881	1.1990	1.2100	1.2210	1.2321	1.2432
3	1.2950	1.3129	1.3310	1.3492	1.3676	1.3862
4	1.4116	1.4377	1.4641	1.4909	1.5181	1.5456
5	1.5386	1.5742	1.6105	1.6474	1.6851	1.7234
6	1.6771	1.7238	1.7716	1.8204	1.8704	1.9215
7	1.8280	1.8876	1.9487	2.0116	2.0762	2.1425
8	1.9926	2.0669	2.1436	2.2228	2.3045	2.3889
9	2.1719	2.2632	2.3579	2.4562	2.5580	2.6636
10	2.3674	2.4782	2.5937	2.7141	2.8394	2.9699
11	2.5804	2.7137	2.8531	2.9991	3.1518	3.3115
12	2.8127	2.9715	3.1384	3.3140	3.4985	3.6923
13	3.0658	3.2537	3.4523	3.6619	3.8833	4.1169
14	3.3417	3.5629	3.7975	4.0464	4.3104	4.5904
15	3.6425	3.9013	4.1772	4.4713	4.7846	5.1183
16	3.9703	4.2719	4.5950	4.9408	5.3109	5.7069
17	4.3276	4.6778	5.0545	5.4596	5.8951	6.3632
18	4.7171	5.1222	5.5599	6.0328	6.5436	7.0949
19	5.1417	5.6088	6.1159	6.6663	7.2633	7.9108
20	5.6044	6.1416	6.7275	7.3662	8.0623	8.8206
21	6.1088	6.7251	7.4003	8.1397	8.9492	9.8350
22	6.6586	7.3639	8.1403	8.9944	9.9336	10.9660
23	7.2579	8.0635	8.9543	9.9388	11.0263	12.2271
24	7.9111	8.8296	9.8497	10.9823	12.2392	13.6332
25	8.6231	9.6684	10.8347	12.1355	13.5855	15.2010
26	9.3992	10.5869	11.9182	13.4097	15.0799	16.9491
27	10.2451	11.5926	13.1100	14.8177	16.7386	18.8982
28	11.1671	12.6939	14.4210	16.3736	18.5799	21.0715
29	12.1722	13.8998	15.8631	18.0928	20.6237	23.4948
30	13.2677	15.2203	17.4494	19.9926	22.8923	26.1967
31	14.4618	16.6662	19.1943	22.0918	25.4104	29.2093
32	15.7633	18.2495	21.1138	24.4114	28.2056	32.5684
33	17.1820	19.9832	23.2252	26.9746	31.3082	36.3137
34	18.7284	21.8816	25.5477	29.8069	34.7521	40.4898
35	20.4140	23.9604	28.1024	32.9367	38.5749	45.1461

YEARS	9.0%	9.5%	10.0%	10.5%	11.0%	11.5%
36	22.2512	26.2366	30.9127	36.3950	42.8181	50.3379
37	24.2538	28.7291	34.0040	40.2165	47.5281	56.1268
38	26.4367	31.4584	37.4043	44.4392	52.7562	62.5814
39	28.8160	34.4469	41.1448	49.1053	58.5593	69.7782
40	31.4094	37.7194	45.2593	54.2614	65.0009	77.8027
41	34.2363	41.3027	49.7852	59.9589	72.1510	86.7500
42	37.3175	45.2265	54.7637	66.2545	80.0876	96.7263
43	40.6761	49.5230	60.2401	73.2113	88.8972	107.8498
44	44.3370	54.2277	66.2641	80.8984	98.6759	120.2525
45	48.3273	59.3793	72.8905	89.3928	109.5302	134.0816
46	52.6767	65.0204	80.1795	98.7790	121.5786	149.5009
47	57.4177	71.1973	88.1975	109.1508	134.9522	166.6936
48	62.5852	77.9611	97.0172	120.6117	149.7969	185.8633
49	68.2179	85.3674	106.7190	133.2759	166.2746	207.2376
50	74.3575	93.4773	117.3909	147.2698	184.5648	231.0699

FUTURE VALUE OF LUMP SUM (continued)

YEARS	12.0%	12.5%	13.0%	13.5%	14.0%	14.5%
1	1.1200	1.1250	1.1300	1.1350	1.1400	1.1450
2	1.2544	1.2656	1.2769	1.2882	1.2996	1.3110
3	1.4049	1.4238	1.4429	1.4621	1.4815	1.5011
4	1.5735	1.6018	1.6305	1.6595	1.6890	1.7188
5	1.7623	1.8020	1.8424	1.8836	1.9254	1.9680
6	1.9738	2.0273	2.0820	2.1378	2.1950	2.2534
7	2.2107	2.2807	2.3526	2.4264	2.5023	2.5801
8	2.4760	2.5658	2.6584	2.7540	2.8526	2.9542
9	2.7731	2.8865	3.0040	3.1258	3.2519	3.3826
10	3.1058	3.2473	3.3946	3.5478	3.7072	3.8731
11	3.4785	3.6532	3.8359	4.0267	4.2262	4.4347
12	3.8960	4.1099	4.3345	4.5704	4.8179	5.0777
13	4.3635	4.6236	4.8980	5.1874	5.4924	5.8140
14	4.8871	5.2016	5.5348	5.8877	6.2613	6.6570
15	5.4736	5.8518	6.2543	6.6825	7.1379	7.6222
16	6.1304	6.5833	7.0673	7.5846	8.1372	8.7275
17	6.8660	7.4062	7.9861	8.6085	9.2765	9.9929
18	7.6900	8.3319	9.0243	9.7707	10.5752	11.4419
19	8.6128	9.3734	10.1974	11.0897	12.0557	13.1010
20	9.6463	10.5451	11.5231	12.5869	13.7435	15.0006
21	10.8038	11.8632	13.0211	14.2861	15.6676	17.1757
22	12.1003	13.3461	14.7138	16.2147	17.8610	19.6662
23	13.5523	15.0144	16.6266	18.4037	20.3616	22.5178
24	15.1786	16.8912	18.7881	20.8882	23.2122	25.7829
25	17.0001	19.0026	21.2305	23.7081	26.4619	29.5214
26	19.0401	21.3779	23.9905	26.9087	30.1666	33.8020
27	21.3249	24.0502	27.1093	30.5414	34.3899	38.7033
28	23.8839	27.0564	30.6335	34.6644	39.2045	44.3153
29	26.7499	30.4385	34.6158	39.3441	44.6931	50.7410
30	29.9599	34.2433	39.1159	44.6556	50.9502	58.0985
31	33.5551	38.5237	44.2010	50.6841	58.0832	66.5227
32	37.5817	43.3392	49.9471	57.5265	66.2148	76.1685
33	42.0915	48.7566	56.4402	65.2925	75.4849	87.2130
34	47.1425	54.8512	63.7774	74.1070	86.0528	99.8588
35	52.7996	61.7075	72.0685	84.1115	98.1002	114.3384

YEARS	12.0%	12.5%	13.0%	13.5%	14.0%	14.5%
36	59.1356	69.4210	81.4374	95.4665	111.8342	130.9174
37	66.2318	78.0986	92.0243	108.3545	127.4910	149.9005
38	74.1797	87.8609	103.9874	122.9824	145.3397	171.6360
39	83.0812	98.8436	117.5058	139.5850	165.6873	196.5232
40	93.0510	111.1990	132.7815	158.4289	188.8835	225.0191
41	104.2171	125.0989	150.0431	179.8169	215.3272	257.6469
42	116.7231	140.7362	169.5487	204.0921	245.4730	295.0057
43	130.7299	158.3283	191.5901	231.6446	279.8392	337.7815
44	146.4175	178.1193	216.4968	262.9166	319.0167	386.7598
45	163.9876	200.3842	244.6414	298.4103	363.6791	442.8400
46	183.6661	225.4322	276.4447	338.6957	414.5942	507.0518
47	205.7060	253.6113	312.3825	384.4197	472.6373	580.5743
48	230.3907	285.3127	352.9923	436.3163	538.8066	664.7576
49	258.0376	320.9768	398.8813	495.2190	614.2395	761.1474
50	289.0022	361.0989	450.7358	562.0736	700.2330	871.5138

FUTURE VALUE OF LUMP SUM (continued)

YEARS	15.0%	16.0%	17.0%	18.0%	19.0%	20.0%
1	1.1200	1.1250	1.1300	1.1350	1.1400	1.1450
1	1.1500	1.1600	1.1700	1.1800	1.1900	1.2000
2	1.3225	1.3456	1.3689	1.3924	1.4161	1.4400
3	1.5209	1.5609	1.6016	1.6430	1.6852	1.7280
4	1.7490	1.8106	1.8739	1.9388	2.0053	2.0736
5	2.0114	2.1003	2.1924	2.2878	2.3864	2.4883
6	2.3131	2.4364	2.5652	2.6996	2.8398	2.9860
7	2.6600	2.8262	3.0012	3.1855	3.3793	3.5832
8	3.0590	3.2784	3.5115	3.7589	4.0214	4.2998
9	3.5179	3.8030	4.1084	4.4355	4.7854	5.1598
10	4.0456	4.4114	4.8068	5.2338	5.6947	6.1917
11	4.6524	5.1173	5.6240	6.1759	6.7767	7.4301
12	5.3503	5.9360	6.5801	7.2876	8.0642	8.9161
13	6.1528	6.8858	7.6987	8.5994	9.5964	10.6993
14	7.0757	7.9875	9.0075	10.1472	11.4198	12.8392
15	8.1371	9.2655	10.5387	11.9737	13.5895	15.4070
16	9.3576	10.7480	12.3303	14.1290	16.1715	18.4884
17	10.7613	12.4677	14.4265	16.6722	19.2441	22.1861
18	12.3755	14.4625	16.8790	19.6733	22.9005	26.6233
19	14.2318	16.7765	19.7484	23.2144	27.2516	31.9480
20	16.3665	19.4608	23.1056	27.3930	32.4294	38.3376
21	18.8215	22.5745	27.0336	32.3238	38.5910	46.0051
22	21.6447	26.1864	31.6293	38.1421	45.9233	55.2061
23	24.8915	30.3762	37.0062	45.0076	54.6487	66.2474
24	28.6252	35.2364	43.2973	53.1090	65.0320	79.4969
25	32.9190	40.8742	50.6578	62.6686	77.3881	95.3962
26	37.8568	47.4141	59.2697	73.9490	92.0918	114.4755
27	43.5353	55.0004	69.3455	87.2598	109.5892	137.3706
28	50.0656	63.8004	81.1342	102.9666	130.4112	164.8447
29	57.5755	74.0085	94.9271	121.5006	155.1893	197.8136
30	66.2118	85.8499	111.0647	143.3707	184.6753	237.3763
31	76.1435	99.5858	129.9456	169.1774	219.7636	284.8516
32	87.5651	115.5196	152.0364	199.6293	261.5187	341.8219
33	100.6998	134.0027	177.8826	235.5626	311.2072	410.1863
34	115.8048	155.4431	208.1226	277.9639	370.3366	492.2236

YEARS	15.0%	16.0%	17.0%	18.0%	19.0%	20.0%
35	133.1755	180.3141	243.5035	327.9974	440.7006	590.6683
36	153.1519	209.1643	284.8991	387.0369	524.4337	708.8019
37	176.1247	242.6306	333.3319	456.7035	624.0761	850.5623
38	202.5434	281.4515	389.9984	538.9102	742.6505	1020.6748
39	232.9249	326.4837	456.2981	635.9140	883.7541	1224.8098
40	267.8636	378.7211	533.8687	750.3785	1051.6674	1469.7717
41	308.0431	439.3165	624.6264	885.4467	1251.4842	1763.7261
42	354.2496	509.6071	730.8129	1044.8271	1489.2662	2116.4713
43	407.3871	591.1443	855.0511	1232.8960	1772.2268	2539.7655
44	468.4951	685.7273	1000.4098	1454.8172	2108.9499	3047.7187
45	538.7694	795.4437	1170.4795	1716.6843	2509.6504	3657.2624
46	619.5848	922.7147	1369.4610	2025.6875	2986.4839	4388.7149
47	712.5225	1070.3491	1602.2694	2390.3113	3553.9159	5266.4579
48	819.4009	1241.6049	1874.6552	2820.5674	4229.1599	6319.7495
49	942.3111	1440.2617	2193.3466	3328.2695	5032.7003	7583.6994
50	1083.6577	1670.7035	2566.2155	3927.3581	5988.9133	9100.4393

Appendix E

FUTURE VALUE OF ANNUITY DUE

YEARS	3.0%	3.5%	4.0%	4.5%	5.0%	5.5%
1	1.0300	1.0350	1.0400	1.0450	1.0500	1.0550
2	2.0909	2.1062	2.1216	2.1370	2.1525	2.1680
3	3.1836	3.2149	3.2465	3.2782	3.3101	3.3423
4	4.3091	4.3625	4.4163	4.4707	4.5256	4.5811
5	5.4684	5.5502	5.6330	5.7169	5.8019	5.8881
6	6.6625	6.7794	6.8983	7.0192	7.1420	7.2669
7	7.8923	8.0517	8.2142	8.3800	8.5491	8.7216
8	9.1591	9.3685	9.5828	9.8021	10.0266	10.2563
9	10.4639	10.7314	11.0061	11.2882	11.5779	11.8754
10	11.8078	12.1420	12.4864	12.8412	13.2068	13.5835
11	13.1920	13.6020	14.0258	14.4640	14.9171	15.3856
12	14.6178	15.1130	15.6268	16.1599	16.7130	17.2868
13	16.0863	16.6770	17.2919	17.9321	18.5986	19.2926
14	17.5989	18.2957	19.0236	19.7841	20.5786	21.4087
15	19.1569	19.9710	20.8245	21.7193	22.6575	23.6411
16	20.7616	21.7050	22.6975	23.7417	24.8404	25.9964
17	22.4144	23.4997	24.6454	25.8551	27.1324	28.4812
18	24.1169	25.3572	26.6712	28.0636	29.5390	31.1027
19	25.8704	27.2797	28.7781	30.3714	32.0660	33.8683
20	27.6765	29.2695	30.9692	32.7831	34.7193	36.7861
21	29.5368	31.3289	33.2480	35.3034	37.5052	39.8643
22	31.4529	33.4604	35.6179	37.9370	40.4305	43.1118
23	33.4265	35.6665	38.0826	40.6892	43.5020	46.5380
24	35.4593	37.9499	40.6459	43.5652	46.7271	50.1526
25	37.5530	40.3131	43.3117	46.5706	50.1135	53.9660
26	39.7096	42.7591	46.0842	49.7113	53.6691	57.9891
27	41.9309	45.2906	48.9676	52.9933	57.4026	62.2335
28	44.2188	47.9108	51.9663	56.4230	61.3227	66.7114
29	46.5754	50.6227	55.0849	60.0071	65.4388	71.4355
30	49.0027	53.4295	58.3283	63.7524	69.7608	76.4194

YEARS	3.0%	3.5%	4.0%	4.5%	5.0%	5.5%
31	51.5028	56.3345	61.7015	67.6662	74.2988	81.6775
32	54.0778	59.3412	65.2095	71.7562	79.0638	87.2248
33	56.7302	62.4532	68.8579	76.0303	84.0670	93.0771
34	59.4621	65.6740	72.6522	80.4966	89.3203	99.2514
35	62.2759	69.0076	76.5983	85.1640	94.8363	105.7652
36	65.1742	72.4579	80.7022	90.0413	100.6281	112.6373
37	68.1594	76.0289	84.9703	95.1382	106.7095	119.8873
38	71.2342	79.7249	89.4091	100.4644	113.0950	127.5361
39	74.4013	83.5503	94.0255	106.0303	119.7998	135.6056
40	77.6633	87.5095	98.8265	111.8467	126.8398	144.1189
41	81.0232	91.6074	103.8196	117.9248	134.2318	153.1005
42	84.4839	95.8486	109.0124	124.2764	141.9933	162.5760
43	88.0484	100.2383	114.4129	130.9138	150.1430	172.5727
44	91.7199	104.7817	120.0294	137.8500	158.7002	183.1192
45	95.5015	109.4840	125.8706	145.0982	167.6852	194.2457
46	99.3965	114.3510	131.9454	152.6726	177.1194	205.9842
47	103.4084	119.3883	138.2632	160.5879	187.0254	218.3684
48	107.5406	124.6018	144.8337	168.8594	197.4267	231.4336
49	111.7969	129.9979	151.6671	177.5030	208.3480	245.2175
50	116.1808	135.5828	158.7738	186.5357	219.8154	259.7594

FUTURE VALUE OF ANNUITY DUE (continued)

YEARS	6.0%	6.5%	7.0%	7.5%	8.0%	8.5%
1	1.0600	1.0650	1.0700	1.0750	1.0800	1.0850
2	2.1836	2.1992	2.2149	2.2306	2.2464	2.2622
3	3.3746	3.4072	3.4399	3.4729	3.5061	3.5395
4	4.6371	4.6936	4.7507	4.8084	4.8666	4.9254
5	5.9753	6.0637	6.1533	6.2440	6.3359	6.4290
6	7.3938	7.5229	7.6540	7.7873	7.9228	8.0605
7	8.8975	9.0769	9.2598	9.4464	9.6366	9.8306
8	10.4913	10.7319	10.9780	11.2298	11.4876	11.7512
9	12.1808	12.4944	12.8164	13.1471	13.4866	13.8351
10	13.9716	14.3716	14.7836	15.2081	15.6455	16.0961
11	15.8699	16.3707	16.8885	17.4237	17.9771	18.5492
12	17.8821	18.4998	19.1406	19.8055	20.4953	21.2109
13	20.0151	20.7673	21.5505	22.3659	23.2149	24.0989
14	22.2760	23.1822	24.1290	25.1184	26.1521	27.2323
15	24.6725	25.7540	26.8881	28.0772	29.3243	30.6320
16	27.2129	28.4930	29.8402	31.2580	32.7502	34.3207
17	29.9057	31.4101	32.9990	34.6774	36.4502	38.3230
18	32.7600	34.5167	36.3790	38.3532	40.4463	42.6655
19	35.7856	37.8253	39.9955	42.3047	44.7620	47.3770
20	38.9927	41.3490	43.8652	46.5525	49.4229	52.4891
21	42.3923	45.1016	48.0057	51.1190	54.4568	58.0356
22	45.9958	49.0982	52.4361	56.0279	59.8933	64.0537
23	49.8156	53.3546	57.1767	61.3050	65.7648	70.5832
24	53.8645	57.8877	62.2490	66.9779	72.1059	77.6678
25	58.1564	62.7154	67.6765	73.0762	78.9544	85.3546
26	62.7058	67.8569	73.4838	79.6319	86.3508	93.6947
27	67.5281	73.3326	79.6977	86.6793	94.3388	102.7437
28	72.6398	79.1642	86.3465	94.2553	102.9659	112.5620
29	78.0582	85.3749	93.4608	102.3994	112.2832	123.2147
30	83.8017	91.9892	101.0730	111.1544	122.3459	134.7730
31	89.8898	99.0335	109.2182	120.5659	133.2135	147.3137
32	96.3432	106.5357	117.9334	130.6834	144.9506	160.9203
33	103.1838	114.5255	127.2588	141.5596	157.6267	175.6836
34	110.4348	123.0347	137.2369	153.2516	171.3168	191.7017
35	118.1209	132.0969	147.9135	165.8205	186.1021	209.0813

YEARS	6.0%	6.5%	7.0%	7.5%	8.0%	8.5%
36	126.2681	141.7482	159.3374	179.3320	202.0703	227.9382
37	134.9042	152.0269	171.5610	193.8569	219.3159	248.3980
38	144.0585	162.9736	184.6403	209.4712	237.9412	270.5968
39	153.7620	174.6319	198.6351	226.2565	258.0565	294.6825
40	164.0477	187.0480	213.6096	244.3008	279.7810	320.8156
41	174.9505	200.2711	229.6322	263.6983	303.2435	349.1699
42	186.5076	214.3537	246.7765	284.5507	328.5830	379.9343
43	198.7580	229.3517	265.1209	306.9670	355.9496	413.3137
44	211.7435	245.3246	284.7493	331.0645	385.5056	449.5304
45	225.5081	262.3357	305.7518	356.9694	417.4260	488.8255
46	240.0986	280.4525	328.2244	384.8171	451.9001	531.4607
47	255.5645	299.7469	352.2701	414.7534	489.1321	577.7198
48	271.9584	320.2954	377.9990	446.9349	529.3427	627.9110
49	289.3359	342.1796	405.5289	481.5300	572.7701	682.3684
50	307.7560	365.4863	434.9860	518.7197	619.6717	741.4548

FUTURE VALUE OF ANNUITY DUE (continued)

YEARS	9.0%	9.5%	10.0%	10.5%	11.0%	11.5%
1	1.0900	1.0950	1.1000	1.1050	1.1100	1.1150
2	2.2781	2.2940	2.3100	2.3260	2.3421	2.3582
3	3.5731	3.6070	3.6410	3.6753	3.7097	3.7444
4	4.9847	5.0446	5.1051	5.1662	5.2278	5.2900
5	6.5233	6.6189	6.7156	6.8136	6.9129	7.0134
6	8.2004	8.3426	8.4872	8.6340	8.7833	8.9349
7	10.0285	10.2302	10.4359	10.6456	10.8594	11.0774
8	12.0210	12.2971	12.5795	12.8684	13.1640	13.4663
9	14.1929	14.5603	14.9374	15.3246	15.7220	16.1300
10	16.5603	17.0385	17.5312	18.0387	18.5614	19.0999
11	19.1407	19.7522	20.3843	21.0377	21.7132	22.4114
12	21.9534	22.7236	23.5227	24.3517	25.2116	26.1037
13	25.0192	25.9774	26.9750	28.0136	29.0949	30.2207
14	28.3609	29.5402	30.7725	32.0600	33.4054	34.8110
15	32.0034	33.4416	34.9497	36.5313	38.1899	39.9293
16	35.9737	37.7135	39.5447	41.4721	43.5008	45.6362
17	40.3013	42.3913	44.5992	46.9317	49.3959	51.9993
18	45.0185	47.5135	50.1591	52.9645	55.9395	59.0942
19	50.1601	53.1222	56.2750	59.6308	63.2028	67.0051
20	55.7645	59.2638	63.0025	66.9970	71.2651	75.8257
21	61.8733	65.9889	70.4028	75.1367	80.2143	85.6606
22	68.5319	73.3529	78.5430	84.1311	90.1479	96.6266
23	75.7898	81.4164	87.4973	94.0698	101.1741	108.8536
24	83.7009	90.2459	97.3471	105.0522	113.4133	122.4868
25	92.3240	99.9143	108.1818	117.1877	126.9988	137.6878
26	101.7231	110.5012	120.0999	130.5974	142.0786	154.6369
27	111.9682	122.0938	133.2099	145.4151	158.8173	173.5351
28	123.1354	134.7877	147.6309	161.7887	177.3972	194.6067
29	135.3075	148.6875	163.4940	179.8815	198.0209	218.1015
30	148.5752	163.9078	180.9434	199.8740	220.9132	244.2981
31	163.0370	180.5741	200.1378	221.9658	246.3236	273.5074
32	178.8003	198.8236	221.2516	246.3772	274.5292	306.0758
33	195.9824	218.8068	244.4767	273.3518	305.8374	342.3895
34	214.7108	240.6885	270.0244	303.1588	340.5896	382.8793
35	235.1247	264.6489	298.1268	336.0954	379.1644	428.0254

YEARS	9.0%	9.5%	10.0%	10.5%	11.0%	11.5%
36	257.3760	290.8855	329.0395	372.4905	421.9825	478.3633
37	281.6298	319.6146	363.0434	412.7070	469.5106	534.4901
38	308.0665	351.0730	400.4478	457.1462	522.2667	597.0714
39	336.8825	385.5200	441.5926	506.2515	580.8261	666.8496
40	368.2919	423.2394	486.8518	560.5129	645.8269	744.6524
41	402.5282	464.5421	536.6370	620.4718	717.9779	831.4024
42	439.8457	509.7686	591.4007	686.7263	798.0655	928.1287
43	480.5218	559.2916	651.6408	759.9376	886.9626	1035.9785
44	524.8588	613.5193	717.9049	840.8360	985.6385	1156.2310
45	573.1861	672.8987	790.7954	930.2288	1095.1688	1290.3125
46	625.8628	737.9191	870.9749	1029.0079	1216.7473	1439.8135
47	683.2805	809.1164	959.1724	1138.1587	1351.6996	1606.5070
48	745.8657	887.0774	1056.1896	1258.7703	1501.4965	1792.3704
49	814.0837	972.4448	1162.9086	1392.0462	1667.7711	1999.6079
50	888.4412	1065.9220	1280.2995	1539.3161	1852.3359	2230.6779

FUTURE VALUE OF ANNUITY DUE (continued)

YEARS	12.0%	12.5%	13.0%	13.5%	14.0%	14.5%
1	1.1200	1.1250	1.1300	1.1350	1.1400	1.1450
2	2.3744	2.3906	2.4069	2.4232	2.4396	2.4560
3	3.7793	3.8145	3.8498	3.8854	3.9211	3.9571
4	5.3528	5.4163	5.4803	5.5449	5.6101	5.6759
5	7.1152	7.2183	7.3227	7.4284	7.5355	7.6439
6	9.0890	9.2456	9.4047	9.5663	9.7305	9.8973
7	11.2997	11.5263	11.7573	11.9927	12.2328	12.4774
8	13.7757	14.0921	14.4157	14.7468	15.0853	15.4317
9	16.5487	16.9786	17.4197	17.8726	18.3373	18.8142
10	19.6546	20.2259	20.8143	21.4204	22.0445	22.6873
11	23.1331	23.8791	24.6502	25.4471	26.2707	27.1220
12	27.0291	27.9890	28.9847	30.0175	31.0887	32.1997
13	31.3926	32.6126	33.8827	35.2048	36.5811	38.0136
14	36.2797	37.8142	39.4175	41.0925	42.8424	44.6706
15	41.7533	43.6660	45.6717	47.7750	49.9804	52.2928
16	47.8837	50.2493	52.7391	55.3596	58.1176	61.0203
17	54.7497	57.6554	60.7251	63.9681	67.3941	71.0132
18	62.4397	65.9873	69.7494	73.7388	77.9692	82.4551
19	71.0524	75.3608	79.9468	84.8286	90.0249	95.5561
20	80.6987	85.9058	91.4699	97.4154	103.7684	110.5568
21	91.5026	97.7691	104.4910	111.7015	119.4360	127.7325
22	103.6029	111.1152	119.2048	127.9162	137.2970	147.3987
23	117.1552	126.1296	135.8315	146.3199	157.6586	169.9165
24	132.3339	143.0208	154.6195	167.2081	180.8708	195.6994
25	149.3339	162.0234	175.8501	190.9162	207.3327	225.2208
26	168.3740	183.4013	199.8406	217.8249	237.4993	259.0228
27	189.6989	207.4515	226.9499	248.3662	271.8892	297.7261
28	213.5827	234.5079	257.5834	283.0306	311.0937	342.0414
29	240.3327	264.9464	292.1992	322.3748	355.7869	392.7824
30	270.2926	299.1897	331.3151	367.0304	406.7370	450.8809
31	303.8477	337.7135	375.5160	417.7145	464.8202	517.4036
32	341.4294	381.0526	425.4631	475.2409	531.0350	593.5721
33	383.5210	429.8092	481.9033	540.5335	606.5199	680.7851
34	430.6635	484.6604	545.6808	614.6405	692.5727	780.6439
35	483.4631	546.3679	617.7493	698.7520	790.6729	894.9823

YEARS	12.0%	12.5%	13.0%	13.5%	14.0%	14.5%
36	542.5987	615.7889	699.1867	794.2185	902.5071	1025.8997
37	608.8305	693.8875	791.2109	902.5730	1029.9981	1175.8002
38	683.0101	781.7485	895.1983	1025.5553	1175.3378	1347.4362
39	766.0914	880.5920	1012.7041	1165.1403	1341.0251	1543.9594
40	859.1423	991.7910	1145.4856	1323.5693	1529.9086	1768.9785
41	963.3594	1116.8899	1295.5288	1503.3861	1745.2358	2026.6254
42	1080.0825	1257.6262	1465.0775	1707.4783	1990.7089	2321.6311
43	1210.8124	1415.9544	1656.6676	1939.1228	2270.5481	2659.4126
44	1357.2299	1594.0737	1873.1643	2202.0394	2589.5648	3046.1724
45	1521.2175	1794.4579	2117.8057	2500.4498	2953.2439	3489.0124
46	1704.8836	2019.8902	2394.2504	2839.1455	3367.8381	3996.0642
47	1910.5896	2273.5015	2706.6330	3223.5652	3840.4754	4576.6385
48	2140.9804	2558.8141	3059.6252	3659.8815	4379.2820	5241.3960
49	2399.0180	2879.7909	3458.5065	4155.1005	4993.5215	6002.5434
50	2688.0202	3240.8898	3909.2423	4717.1741	5693.7545	6874.0572

FUTURE VALUE OF ANNUITY DUE (continued)

YEARS	15.0%	16.0%	17.0%	18.0%	19.0%	20.0%
1	1.1500	1.1600	1.1700	1.1800	1.1900	1.2000
2	2.4725	2.5056	2.5389	2.5724	2.6061	2.6400
3	3.9934	4.0665	4.1405	4.2154	4.2913	4.3680
4	5.7424	5.8771	6.0144	6.1542	6.2966	6.4416
5	7.7537	7.9775	8.2068	8.4420	8.6830	8.9299
6	10.0668	10.4139	10.7720	11.1415	11.5227	11.9159
7	12.7268	13.2401	13.7733	14.3270	14.9020	15.4991
8	15.7858	16.5185	17.2847	18.0859	18.9234	19.7989
9	19.3037	20.3215	21.3931	22.5213	23.7089	24.9587
10	23.3493	24.7329	26.1999	27.7551	29.4035	31.1504
11	28.0017	29.8502	31.8239	33.9311	36.1802	38.5805
12	33.3519	35.7862	38.4040	41.2187	44.2445	47.4966
13	39.5047	42.6720	46.1027	49.8180	53.8409	58.1959
14	46.5804	50.6595	55.1101	59.9653	65.2607	71.0351
15	54.7175	59.9250	65.6488	71.9390	78.8502	86.4421
16	64.0751	70.6730	77.9792	86.0680	95.0217	104.9306
17	74.8364	83.1407	92.4056	102.7403	114.2659	127.1167
18	87.2118	97.6032	109.2846	122.4135	137.1664	153.7400
19	101.4436	114.3797	129.0329	145.6280	164.4180	185.6880
20	117.8101	133.8405	152.1385	173.0210	196.8474	224.0256
21	136.6316	156.4150	179.1721	205.3448	235.4384	270.0307
22	158.2764	182.6014	210.8013	243.4869	281.3618	325.2369
23	183.1679	212.9776	247.8076	288.4945	336.0105	391.4843
24	211.7930	248.2140	291.1049	341.6035	401.0425	470.9811
25	244.7120	289.0883	341.7627	404.2722	478.4305	566.3773
26	282.5688	336.5024	401.0323	478.2212	570.5223	680.8528
27	326.1041	391.5027	470.3779	565.4810	680.1116	818.2234
28	376.1697	455.3032	551.5121	668.4475	810.5228	983.0680
29	433.7452	529.3117	646.4391	789.9481	965.7121	1180.8816
30	499.9570	615.1616	757.5038	933.3188	1150.3874	1418.2580
31	576.1005	714.7474	887.4494	1102.4962	1370.1510	1703.1096
32	663.6656	830.2670	1039.4858	1302.1255	1631.6697	2044.9315
33	764.3655	964.2697	1217.3684	1537.6881	1942.8770	2455.1178
34	880.1703	1119.7129	1425.4911	1815.6519	2313.2136	2947.3414
35	1013.3458	1300.0269	1668.9946	2143.6493	2753.9142	3538.0096

YEARS	15.0%	16.0%	17.0%	18.0%	19.0%	20.0%
36	1166.4977	1509.1912	1953.8937	2530.6862	3278.3478	4246.8116
37	1342.6224	1751.8218	2287.2256	2987.3897	3902.4239	5097.3739
38	1545.1657	2033.2733	2677.2239	3526.2999	4645.0745	6118.0487
39	1778.0906	2359.7570	3133.5220	4162.2139	5528.8286	7342.8585
40	2045.9542	2738.4781	3667.3907	4912.5924	6580.4960	8812.6302
41	2353.9974	3177.7946	4292.0172	5798.0391	7831.9803	10576.3562
42	2708.2470	3687.4017	5022.8301	6842.8661	9321.2465	12692.8275
43	3115.6340	4278.5460	5877.8812	8075.7621	11093.4733	15232.5931
44	3584.1292	4964.2733	6878.2911	9530.5793	13202.4232	18280.3117
45	4122.8985	5759.7170	8048.7705	11247.2637	15712.0736	21937.5741
46	4742.4834	6682.4318	9418.2315	13272.9512	18698.5575	26326.2890
47	5455.0059	7752.7808	11020.5009	15663.2625	22252.4734	31592.7469
48	6274.4068	8994.3857	12895.1561	18483.8299	26481.6333	37912.4963
49	7216.7179	10434.6474	15088.5027	21812.0994	31514.3336	45496.1957
50	8300.3756	12105.3509	17654.7181	25739.4575	37503.2469	54596.6350

Appendix F

FUTURE VALUE OF ORDINARY ANNUITY

YEARS	3.0%	3.5%	4.0%	4.5%	5.0%	5.5%
1	1.0000	1.0000	1.0000	1.0000	1.0000	1.0000
2	2.0300	2.0350	2.0400	2.0450	2.0500	2.0550
3	3.0909	3.1062	3.1216	3.1370	3.1525	3.1680
4	4.1836	4.2149	4.2465	4.2782	4.3101	4.3423
5	5.3091	5.3625	5.4163	5.4707	5.5256	5.5811
6	6.4684	6.5502	6.6330	6.7169	6.8019	6.8881
7	7.6625	7.7794	7.8983	8.0192	8.1420	8.2669
8	8.8923	9.0517	9.2142	9.3800	9.5491	9.7216
9	10.1591	10.3685	10.5828	10.8021	11.0266	11.2563
10	11.4639	11.7314	12.0061	12.2882	12.5779	12.8754
11	12.8078	13.1420	13.4864	13.8412	14.2068	14.5835
12	14.1920	14.6020	15.0258	15.4640	15.9171	16.3856
13	15.6178	16.1130	16.6268	17.1599	17.7130	18.2868
14	17.0863	17.6770	18.2919	18.9321	19.5986	20.2926
15	18.5989	19.2957	20.0236	20.7841	21.5786	22.4087
16	20.1569	20.9710	21.8245	22.7193	23.6575	24.6411
17	21.7616	22.7050	23.6975	24.7417	25.8404	26.9964
18	23.4144	24.4997	25.6454	26.8551	28.1324	29.4812
19	25.1169	26.3572	27.6712	29.0636	30.5390	32.1027
20	26.8704	28.2797	29.7781	31.3714	33.0660	34.8683
21	28.6765	30.2695	31.9692	33.7831	35.7193	37.7861
22	30.5368	32.3289	34.2480	36.3034	38.5052	40.8643
23	32.4529	34.4604	36.6179	38.9370	41.4305	44.1118
24	34.4265	36.6665	39.0826	41.6892	44.5020	47.5380
25	36.4593	38.9499	41.6459	44.5652	47.7271	51.1526
26	38.5530	41.3131	44.3117	47.5706	51.1135	54.9660
27	40.7096	43.7591	47.0842	50.7113	54.6691	58.9891
28	42.9309	46.2906	49.9676	53.9933	58.4026	63.2335

YEARS	3.0%	3.5%	4.0%	4.5%	5.0%	5.5%
29	45.2188	48.9108	52.9663	57.4230	62.3227	67.7114
30	47.5754	51.6227	56.0849	61.0071	66.4388	72.4355
31	50.0027	54.4295	59.3283	64.7524	70.7608	77.4194
32	52.5028	57.3345	62.7015	68.6662	75.2988	82.6775
33	55.0778	60.3412	66.2095	72.7562	80.0638	88.2248
34	57.7302	63.4532	69.8579	77.0303	85.0670	94.0771
35	60.4621	66.6740	73.6522	81.4966	90.3203	100.2514
36	63.2759	70.0076	77.5983	86.1640	95.8363	106.7652
37	66.1742	73.4579	81.7022	91.0413	101.6281	113.6373
38	69.1594	77.0289	85.9703	96.1382	107.7095	120.8873
39	72.2342	80.7249	90.4091	101.4644	114.0950	128.5361
40	75.4013	84.5503	95.0255	107.0303	120.7998	136.6056
41	78.6633	88.5095	99.8265	112.8467	127.8398	145.1189
42	82.0232	92.6074	104.8196	118.9248	135.2318	154.1005
43	85.4839	96.8486	110.0124	125.2764	142.9933	163.5760
44	89.0484	101.2383	115.4129	131.9138	151.1430	173.5727
45	92.7199	105.7817	121.0294	138.8500	159.7002	184.1192
46	96.5015	110.4840	126.8706	146.0982	168.6852	195.2457
47	100.3965	115.3510	132.9454	153.6726	178.1194	206.9842
48	104.4084	120.3883	139.2632	161.5879	188.0254	219.3684
49	108.5406	125.6018	145.8337	169.8594	198.4267	232.4336
50	112.7969	130.9979	152.6671	178.5030	209.3480	246.2175

FUTURE VALUE OF ORDINARY ANNUITY (continued)

YEARS	6.0%	6.5%	7.0%	7.5%	8.0%	8.5%
1	1.0000	1.0000	1.0000	1.0000	1.0000	1.0000
2	2.0600	2.0650	2.0700	2.0750	2.0800	2.0850
3	3.1836	3.1992	3.2149	3.2306	3.2464	3.2622
4	4.3746	4.4072	4.4399	4.4729	4.5061	4.5395
5	5.6371	5.6936	5.7507	5.8084	5.8666	5.9254
6	6.9753	7.0637	7.1533	7.2440	7.3359	7.4290
7	8.3938	8.5229	8.6540	8.7873	8.9228	9.0605
8	9.8975	10.0769	10.2598	10.4464	10.6366	10.8306
9	11.4913	11.7319	11.9780	12.2298	12.4876	12.7512
10	13.1808	13.4944	13.8164	14.1471	14.4866	14.8351
11	14.9716	15.3716	15.7836	16.2081	16.6455	17.0961
12	16.8699	17.3707	17.8885	18.4237	18.9771	19.5492
13	18.8821	19.4998	20.1406	20.8055	21.4953	22.2109
14	21.0151	21.7673	22.5505	23.3659	24.2149	25.0989
15	23.2760	24.1822	25.1290	26.1184	27.1521	28.2323
16	25.6725	26.7540	27.8881	29.0772	30.3243	31.6320
17	28.2129	29.4930	30.8402	32.2580	33.7502	35.3207
18	30.9057	32.4101	33.9990	35.6774	37.4502	39.3230
19	33.7600	35.5167	37.3790	39.3532	41.4463	43.6655
20	36.7856	38.8253	40.9955	43.3047	45.7620	48.3770
21	39.9927	42.3490	44.8652	47.5525	50.4229	53.4891
22	43.3923	46.1016	49.0057	52.1190	55.4568	59.0356
23	46.9958	50.0982	53.4361	57.0279	60.8933	65.0537
24	50.8156	54.3546	58.1767	62.3050	66.7648	71.5832
25	54.8645	58.8877	63.2490	67.9779	73.1059	78.6678
26	59.1564	63.7154	68.6765	74.0762	79.9544	86.3546
27	63.7058	68.8569	74.4838	80.6319	87.3508	94.6947
28	68.5281	74.3326	80.6977	87.6793	95.3388	103.7437
29	73.6398	80.1642	87.3465	95.2553	103.9659	113.5620
30	79.0582	86.3749	94.4608	103.3994	113.2832	124.2147
31	84.8017	92.9892	102.0730	112.1544	123.3459	135.7730
32	90.8898	100.0335	110.2182	121.5659	134.2135	148.3137
33	97.3432	107.5357	118.9334	131.6834	145.9506	161.9203
34	104.1838	115.5255	128.2588	142.5596	158.6267	176.6836
35	111.4348	124.0347	138.2369	154.2516	172.3168	192.7017

YEARS	6.0%	6.5%	7.0%	7.5%	8.0%	8.5%
36	119.1209	133.0969	148.9135	166.8205	187.1021	210.0813
37	127.2681	142.7482	160.3374	180.3320	203.0703	228.9382
38	135.9042	153.0269	172.5610	194.8569	220.3159	249.3980
39	145.0585	163.9736	185.6403	210.4712	238.9412	271.5968
40	154.7620	175.6319	199.6351	227.2565	259.0565	295.6825
41	165.0477	188.0480	214.6096	245.3008	280.7810	321.8156
42	175.9505	201.2711	230.6322	264.6983	304.2435	350.1699
43	187.5076	215.3537	247.7765	285.5507	329.5830	380.9343
44	199.7580	230.3517	266.1209	307.9670	356.9496	414.3137
45	212.7435	246.3246	285.7493	332.0645	386.5056	450.5304
46	226.5081	263.3357	306.7518	357.9694	418.4260	489.8255
47	241.0986	281.4525	329.2244	385.8171	452.9001	532.4607
48	256.5645	300.7469	353.2701	415.7534	490.1321	578.7198
49	272.9584	321.2954	378.9990	447.9349	530.3427	628.9110
50	290.3359	343.1796	406.5289	482.5300	573.7701	683.3684

FUTURE VALUE OF ORDINARY ANNUITY (continued)

YEARS	9.0%	9.5%	10.0%	10.5%	11.0%	11.5%
1	1.0000	1.0000	1.0000	1.0000	1.0000	1.0000
2	2.0900	2.0950	2.1000	2.1050	2.1100	2.1150
3	3.2781	3.2940	3.3100	3.3260	3.3421	3.3582
4	4.5731	4.6070	4.6410	4.6753	4.7097	4.7444
5	5.9847	6.0446	6.1051	6.1662	6.2278	6.2900
6	7.5233	7.6189	7.7156	7.8136	7.9129	8.0134
7	9.2004	9.3426	9.4872	9.6340	9.7833	9.9349
8	11.0285	11.2302	11.4359	11.6456	11.8594	12.0774
9	13.0210	13.2971	13.5795	13.8684	14.1640	14.4663
10	15.1929	15.5603	15.9374	16.3246	16.7220	17.1300
11	17.5603	18.0385	18.5312	19.0387	19.5614	20.0999
12	20.1407	20.7522	21.3843	22.0377	22.7132	23.4114
13	22.9534	23.7236	24.5227	25.3517	26.2116	27.1037
14	26.0192	26.9774	27.9750	29.0136	30.0949	31.2207
15	29.3609	30.5402	31.7725	33.0600	34.4054	35.8110
16	33.0034	34.4416	35.9497	37.5313	39.1899	40.9293
17	36.9737	38.7135	40.5447	42.4721	44.5008	46.6362
18	41.3013	43.3913	45.5992	47.9317	50.3959	52.9993
19	46.0185	48.5135	51.1591	53.9645	56.9395	60.0942
20	51.1601	54.1222	57.2750	60.6308	64.2028	68.0051
21	56.7645	60.2638	64.0025	67.9970	72.2651	76.8257
22	62.8733	66.9889	71.4028	76.1367	81.2143	86.6606
23	69.5319	74.3529	79.5430	85.1311	91.1479	97.6266
24	76.7898	82.4164	88.4973	95.0698	102.1741	109.8536
25	84.7009	91.2459	98.3471	106.0522	114.4133	123.4868
26	93.3240	100.9143	109.1818	118.1877	127.9988	138.6878
27	102.7231	111.5012	121.0999	131.5974	143.0786	155.6369
28	112.9682	123.0938	134.2099	146.4151	159.8173	174.5351
29	124.1354	135.7877	148.6309	162.7887	178.3972	195.6067
30	136.3075	149.6875	164.4940	180.8815	199.0209	219.1015
31	149.5752	164.9078	181.9434	200.8740	221.9132	245.2981
32	164.0370	181.5741	201.1378	222.9658	247.3236	274.5074
33	179.8003	199.8236	222.2516	247.3772	275.5292	307.0758
34	196.9824	219.8068	245.4767	274.3518	306.8374	343.3895
35	215.7108	241.6885	271.0244	304.1588	341.5896	383.8793
36	236.1247	265.6489	299.1268	337.0954	380.1644	429.0254

YEARS	9.0%	9.5%	10.0%	10.5%	11.0%	11.5%
37	258.3760	291.8855	330.0395	373.4905	422.9825	479.3633
38	282.6298	320.6146	364.0434	413.7070	470.5106	535.4901
39	309.0665	352.0730	401.4478	458.1462	523.2667	598.0714
40	337.8825	386.5200	442.5926	507.2515	581.8261	667.8496
41	369.2919	424.2394	487.8518	561.5129	646.8269	745.6524
42	403.5282	465.5421	537.6370	621.4718	718.9779	832.4024
43	440.8457	510.7686	592.4007	687.7263	799.0655	929.1287
44	481.5218	560.2916	652.6408	760.9376	887.9626	1036.9785
45	525.8588	614.5193	718.9049	841.8360	986.6385	1157.2310
46	574.1861	673.8987	791.7954	931.2288	1096.1688	1291.3125
47	626.8628	738.9191	871.9749	1030.0079	1217.7473	1440.8135
48	684.2805	810.1164	960.1724	1139.1587	1352.6996	1607.5070
49	746.8657	888.0774	1057.1896	1259.7703	1502.4965	1793.3704
50	815.0837	973.4448	1163.9086	1393.0462	1668.7711	2000.6079

FUTURE VALUE OF ORDINARY ANNUITY (continued)

YEARS	12.0%	12.5%	13.0%	13.5%	14.0%	14.5%
1	1.0000	1.0000	1.0000	1.0000	1.0000	1.0000
2	2.1200	2.1250	2.1300	2.1350	2.1400	2.1450
3	3.3744	3.3906	3.4069	3.4232	3.4396	3.4560
4	4.7793	4.8145	4.8498	4.8854	4.9211	4.9571
5	6.3528	6.4163	6.4803	6.5449	6.6101	6.6759
6	8.1152	8.2183	8.3227	8.4284	8.5355	8.6439
7	10.0890	10.2456	10.4047	10.5663	10.7305	10.8973
8	12.2997	12.5263	12.7573	12.9927	13.2328	13.4774
9	14.7757	15.0921	15.4157	15.7468	16.0853	16.4317
10	17.5487	17.9786	18.4197	18.8726	19.3373	19.8142
11	20.6546	21.2259	21.8143	22.4204	23.0445	23.6873
12	24.1331	24.8791	25.6502	26.4471	27.2707	28.1220
13	28.0291	28.9890	29.9847	31.0175	32.0887	33.1997
14	32.3926	33.6126	34.8827	36.2048	37.5811	39.0136
15	37.2797	38.8142	40.4175	42.0925	43.8424	45.6706
16	42.7533	44.6660	46.6717	48.7750	50.9804	53.2928
17	48.8837	51.2493	53.7391	56.3596	59.1176	62.0203
18	55.7497	58.6554	61.7251	64.9681	68.3941	72.0132
19	63.4397	66.9873	70.7494	74.7388	78.9692	83.4551
20	72.0524	76.3608	80.9468	85.8286	91.0249	96.5561
21	81.6987	86.9058	92.4699	98.4154	104.7684	111.5568
22	92.5026	98.7691	105.4910	112.7015	120.4360	128.7325
23	104.6029	112.1152	120.2048	128.9162	138.2970	148.3987
24	118.1552	127.1296	136.8315	147.3199	158.6586	170.9165
25	133.3339	144.0208	155.6195	168.2081	181.8708	196.6994
26	150.3339	163.0234	176.8501	191.9162	208.3327	226.2208
27	169.3740	184.4013	200.8406	218.8249	238.4993	260.0228
28	190.6989	208.4515	227.9499	249.3662	272.8892	298.7261
29	214.5827	235.5079	258.5834	284.0306	312.0937	343.0414
30	241.3327	265.9464	293.1992	323.3748	356.7869	393.7824
31	271.2926	300.1897	332.3151	368.0304	407.7370	451.8809
32	304.8477	338.7135	376.5160	418.7145	465.8202	518.4036
33	342.4294	382.0526	426.4631	476.2409	532.0350	594.5721
34	384.5210	430.8092	482.9033	541.5335	607.5199	681.7851
35	431.6635	485.6604	546.6808	615.6405	693.5727	781.6439

YEARS	12.0%	12.5%	13.0%	13.5%	14.0%	14.5%
36	484.4631	547.3679	618.7493	699.7520	791.6729	895.9823
37	543.5987	616.7889	700.1867	795.2185	903.5071	1026.8997
38	609.8305	694.8875	792.2109	903.5730	1030.9981	1176.8002
39	684.0101	782.7485	896.1983	1026.5553	1176.3378	1348.4362
40	767.0914	881.5920	1013.7041	1166.1403	1342.0251	1544.9594
41	860.1423	992.7910	1146.4856	1324.5693	1530.9086	1769.9785
42	964.3594	1117.8899	1296.5288	1504.3861	1746.2358	2027.6254
43	1081.0825	1258.6262	1466.0775	1708.4783	1991.7089	2322.6311
44	1211.8124	1416.9544	1657.6676	1940.1228	2271.5481	2660.4126
45	1358.2299	1595.0737	1874.1643	2203.0394	2590.5648	3047.1724
46	1522.2175	1795.4579	2118.8057	2501.4498	2954.2439	3490.0124
47	1705.8836	2020.8902	2395.2504	2840.1455	3368.8381	3997.0642
48	1911.5896	2274.5015	2707.6330	3224.5652	3841.4754	4577.6385
49	2141.9804	2559.8141	3060.6252	3660.8815	4380.2820	5242.3960
50	2400.0180	2880.7909	3459.5065	4156.1005	4994.5215	6003.5434

FUTURE VALUE OF ORDINARY ANNUITY (continued)

YEARS	15.0%	16.0%	17.0%	18.0%	19.0%	20.0%
1	1.0000	1.0000	1.0000	1.0000	1.0000	1.0000
2	2.1500	2.1600	2.1700	2.1800	2.1900	2.2000
3	3.4725	3.5056	3.5389	3.5724	3.6061	3.6400
4	4.9934	5.0665	5.1405	5.2154	5.2913	5.3680
5	6.7424	6.8771	7.0144	7.1542	7.2966	7.4416
6	8.7537	8.9775	9.2068	9.4420	9.6830	9.9299
7	11.0668	11.4139	11.7720	12.1415	12.5227	12.9159
8	13.7268	14.2401	14.7733	15.3270	15.9020	16.4991
9	16.7858	17.5185	18.2847	19.0859	19.9234	20.7989
10	20.3037	21.3215	22.3931	23.5213	24.7089	25.9587
11	24.3493	25.7329	27.1999	28.7551	30.4035	32.1504
12	29.0017	30.8502	32.8239	34.9311	37.1802	39.5805
13	34.3519	36.7862	39.4040	42.2187	45.2445	48.4966
14	40.5047	43.6720	47.1027	50.8180	54.8409	59.1959
15	47.5804	51.6595	56.1101	60.9653	66.2607	72.0351
16	55.7175	60.9250	66.6488	72.9390	79.8502	87.4421
17	65.0751	71.6730	78.9792	87.0680	96.0217	105.9306
18	75.8364	84.1407	93.4056	103.7403	115.2659	128.1167
19	88.2118	98.6032	110.2846	123.4135	138.1664	154.7400
20	102.4436	115.3797	130.0329	146.6280	165.4180	186.6880
21	118.8101	134.8405	153.1385	174.0210	197.8474	225.0256
22	137.6316	157.4150	180.1721	206.3448	236.4384	271.0307
23	159.2764	183.6014	211.8013	244.4869	282.3618	326.2369
24	184.1679	213.9776	248.8076	289.4945	337.0105	392.4843
25	212.7930	249.2140	292.1049	342.6035	402.0425	471.9811
26	245.7120	290.0883	342.7627	405.2722	479.4305	567.3773
27	283.5688	337.5024	402.0323	479.2212	571.5223	681.8528
28	327.1041	392.5027	471.3779	566.4810	681.1116	819.2234
29	377.1697	456.3032	552.5121	669.4475	811.5228	984.0680
30	434.7452	530.3117	647.4391	790.9481	966.7121	1181.8816
31	500.9570	616.1616	758.5038	934.3188	1151.3874	1419.2580
32	577.1005	715.7474	888.4494	1103.4962	1371.1510	1704.1096
33	664.6656	831.2670	1040.4858	1303.1255	1632.6697	2045.9315
34	765.3655	965.2697	1218.3684	1538.6881	1943.8770	2456.1178
35	881.1703	1120.7129	1426.4911	1816.6519	2314.2136	2948.3414

YEARS	15.0%	16.0%	17.0%	18.0%	19.0%	20.0%
36	1014.3458	1301.0269	1669.9946	2144.6493	2754.9142	3539.0096
37	1167.4977	1510.1912	1954.8937	2531.6862	3279.3478	4247.8116
38	1343.6224	1752.8218	2288.2256	2988.3897	3903.4239	5098.3739
39	1546.1657	2034.2733	2678.2239	3527.2999	4646.0745	6119.0487
40	1779.0906	2360.7570	3134.5220	4163.2139	5529.8286	7343.8585
41	2046.9542	2739.4781	3668.3907	4913.5924	6581.4960	8813.6302
42	2354.9974	3178.7946	4293.0172	5799.0391	7832.9803	10577.3562
43	2709.2470	3688.4017	5023.8301	6843.8661	9322.2465	12693.8275
44	3116.6340	4279.5460	5878.8812	8076.7621	11094.4733	15233.5931
45	3585.1292	4965.2733	6879.2911	9531.5793	13203.4232	18281.3117
46	4123.8985	5760.7170	8049.7705	11248.2637	15713.0736	21938.5741
47	4743.4834	6683.4318	9419.2315	13273.9512	18699.5575	26327.2890
48	5456.0059	7753.7808	11021.5009	15664.2625	22253.4734	31593.7469
49	6275.4068	8995.3857	12896.1561	18484.8299	26482.6333	37913.4963
50	7217.7179	10435.6474	15089.5027	21813.0994	31515.3336	45497.1957

Appendix G

TAX EXEMPT EQUIVALENTS

TAX EXEMPT YIELDS	15%	16%	17%	18%	19%	20%	21%	22%	23%
3.00	3.53	3.57	3.61	3.66	3.70	3.75	3.80	3.85	3.90
3.25	3.82	3.87	3.92	3.96	4.01	4.06	4.11	4.17	4.22
3.50	4.12	4.17	4.22	4.27	4.32	4.38	4.43	4.49	4.55
3.75	4.41	4.46	4.52	4.57	4.63	4.69	4.75	4.81	4.87
4.00	4.71	4.76	4.82	4.88	4.94	5.00	5.06	5.13	5.19
4.25	5.00	5.06	5.12	5.18	5.25	5.31	5.38	5.45	5.52
4.50	5.29	5.36	5.42	5.49	5.56	5.63	5.70	5.77	5.84
4.75	5.59	5.65	5.72	5.79	5.86	5.94	6.01	6.09	6.17
5.00	5.88	5.95	6.02	6.10	6.17	6.25	6.33	6.41	6.49
5.25	6.18	6.25	6.33	6.40	6.48	6.56	6.65	6.73	6.82
5.50	6.47	6.55	6.63	6.71	6.79	6.88	6.96	7.05	7.14
5.75	6.76	6.85	6.93	7.01	7.10	7.19	7.28	7.37	7.47
6.00	7.06	7.14	7.23	7.32	7.41	7.50	7.59	7.69	7.79
6.25	7.35	7.44	7.53	7.62	7.72	7.81	7.91	8.01	8.12
6.50	7.65	7.74	7.83	7.93	8.02	8.13	8.23	8.33	8.44
6.75	7.94	8.04	8.13	8.23	8.33	8.44	8.54	8.65	8.77
7.00	8.24	8.33	8.43	8.54	8.64	8.75	8.86	8.97	9.09
7.25	8.53	8.63	8.73	8.84	8.95	9.06	9.18	9.29	9.42
7.50	8.82	8.93	9.04	9.15	9.26	9.38	9.49	9.62	9.74
7.75	9.12	9.23	9.34	9.45	9.57	9.69	9.81	9.94	10.06
8.00	9.41	9.52	9.64	9.76	9.88	10.00	10.13	10.26	10.39
8.25	9.71	9.82	9.94	10.06	10.19	10.31	10.44	10.58	10.71
8.50	10.00	10.12	10.24	10.37	10.49	10.63	10.76	10.90	11.04
8.75	10.29	10.42	10.54	10.67	10.80	10.94	11.08	11.22	11.36
9.00	10.59	10.71	10.84	10.98	11.11	11.25	11.39	11.54	11.69
9.25	10.88	11.01	11.14	11.28	11.42	11.56	11.71	11.86	12.01
9.50	11.18	11.31	11.45	11.59	11.73	11.88	12.03	12.18	12.34
9.75	11.47	11.61	11.75	11.89	12.04	12.19	12.34	12.50	12.66
10.00	11.76	11.90	12.05	12.20	12.35	12.50	12.66	12.82	12.99

TAX EXEMPT YIELDS	15%	16%	17%	18%	19%	20%	21%	22%	23%
10.25	12.06	12.20	12.35	12.50	12.65	12.81	12.97	13.14	13.31
10.50	12.35	12.50	12.65	12.80	12.96	13.13	13.29	13.46	13.64
10.75	12.65	12.80	12.95	13.11	13.27	13.44	13.61	13.78	13.96
11.00	12.94	13.10	13.25	13.41	13.58	13.75	13.92	14.10	14.29
11.25	13.24	13.39	13.55	13.72	13.89	14.06	14.24	14.42	14.61
11.50	13.53	13.69	13.86	14.02	14.20	14.38	14.56	14.74	14.94
11.75	13.82	13.99	14.16	14.33	14.51	14.69	14.87	15.06	15.26
12.00	14.12	14.29	14.46	14.63	14.81	15.00	15.19	15.38	15.58
12.25	14.41	14.58	14.76	14.94	15.12	15.31	15.51	15.71	15.91
12.50	14.71	14.88	15.06	15.24	15.43	15.63	15.82	16.03	16.23
12.75	15.00	15.18	15.36	15.55	15.74	15.94	16.14	16.35	16.56
13.00	15.29	15.48	15.66	15.85	16.05	16.25	16.46	16.67	16.88
13.25	15.59	15.77	15.96	16.16	16.36	16.56	16.77	16.99	17.21
13.50	15.88	16.07	16.27	16.46	16.67	16.88	17.09	17.31	17.53
13.75	16.18	16.37	16.57	16.77	16.98	17.19	17.41	17.63	17.86
14.00	16.47	16.67	16.87	17.07	17.28	17.50	17.72	17.95	18.18
14.25	16.76	16.96	17.17	17.38	17.59	17.81	18.04	18.27	18.51
14.50	17.06	17.26	17.47	17.68	17.90	18.13	18.35	18.59	18.83
14.75	17.35	17.56	17.77	17.99	18.21	18.44	18.67	18.91	19.16
15.00	17.65	17.86	18.07	18.29	18.52	18.75	18.99	19.23	19.48

TAX EXEMPT EQUIVALENTS (continued)

TAX EXEMPT YIELDS	24%	25%	26%	27%	28%	29%	30%	31%	32%
3.00	3.95	4.00	4.05	4.11	4.17	4.23	4.29	4.35	4.41
3.25	4.28	4.33	4.39	4.45	4.51	4.58	4.64	4.71	4.78
3.50	4.61	4.67	4.73	4.79	4.86	4.93	5.00	5.07	5.15
3.75	4.93	5.00	5.07	5.14	5.21	5.28	5.36	5.43	5.51
4.00	5.26	5.33	5.41	5.48	5.56	5.63	5.71	5.80	5.88
4.25	5.59	5.67	5.74	5.82	5.90	5.99	6.07	6.16	6.25
4.50	5.92	6.00	6.08	6.16	6.25	6.34	6.43	6.52	6.62
4.75	6.25	6.33	6.42	6.51	6.60	6.69	6.79	6.88	6.99
5.00	6.58	6.67	6.76	6.85	6.94	7.04	7.14	7.25	7.35
5.25	6.91	7.00	7.09	7.19	7.29	7.39	7.50	7.61	7.72
5.50	7.24	7.33	7.43	7.53	7.64	7.75	7.86	7.97	8.09
5.75	7.57	7.67	7.77	7.88	7.99	8.10	8.21	8.33	8.46
6.00	7.89	8.00	8.11	8.22	8.33	8.45	8.57	8.70	8.82
6.25	8.22	8.33	8.45	8.56	8.68	8.80	8.93	9.06	9.19
6.50	8.55	8.67	8.78	8.90	9.03	9.15	9.29	9.42	9.56
6.75	8.88	9.00	9.12	9.25	9.38	9.51	9.64	9.78	9.93
7.00	9.21	9.33	9.46	9.59	9.72	9.86	10.00	10.14	10.29
7.25	9.54	9.67	9.80	9.93	10.07	10.21	10.36	10.51	10.66
7.50	9.87	10.00	10.14	10.27	10.42	10.56	10.71	10.87	11.03
7.75	10.20	10.33	10.47	10.62	10.76	10.92	11.07	11.23	11.40
8.00	10.53	10.67	10.81	10.96	11.11	11.27	11.43	11.59	11.76
8.25	10.86	11.00	11.15	11.30	11.46	11.62	11.79	11.96	12.13
8.50	11.18	11.33	11.49	11.64	11.81	11.97	12.14	12.32	12.50
8.75	11.51	11.67	11.82	11.99	12.15	12.32	12.50	12.68	12.87
9.00	11.84	12.00	12.16	12.33	12.50	12.68	12.86	13.04	13.24
9.25	12.17	12.33	12.50	12.67	12.85	13.03	13.21	13.41	13.60
9.50	12.50	12.67	12.84	13.01	13.19	13.38	13.57	13.77	13.97
9.75	12.83	13.00	13.18	13.36	13.54	13.73	13.93	14.13	14.34
10.00	13.16	13.33	13.51	13.70	13.89	14.08	14.29	14.49	14.71
10.25	13.49	13.67	13.85	14.04	14.24	14.44	14.64	14.86	15.07
10.50	13.82	14.00	14.19	14.38	14.58	14.79	15.00	15.22	15.44
10.75	14.14	14.33	14.53	14.73	14.93	15.14	15.36	15.58	15.81
11.00	14.47	14.67	14.86	15.07	15.28	15.49	15.71	15.94	16.18
11.25	14.80	15.00	15.20	15.41	15.63	15.85	16.07	16.30	16.54

TAX EXEMPT YIELDS	24%	25%	26%	27%	28%	29%	30%	31%	32%
11.50	15.13	15.33	15.54	15.75	15.97	16.20	16.43	16.67	16.91
11.75	15.46	15.67	15.88	16.10	16.32	16.55	16.79	17.03	17.28
12.00	15.79	16.00	16.22	16.44	16.67	16.90	17.14	17.39	17.65
12.25	16.12	16.33	16.55	16.78	17.01	17.25	17.50	17.75	18.01
12.50	16.45	16.67	16.89	17.12	17.36	17.61	17.86	18.12	18.38
12.75	16.78	17.00	17.23	17.47	17.71	17.96	18.21	18.48	18.75
13.00	17.11	17.33	17.57	17.81	18.06	18.31	18.57	18.84	19.12
13.25	17.43	17.67	17.91	18.15	18.40	18.66	18.93	19.20	19.49
13.50	17.76	18.00	18.24	18.49	18.75	19.01	19.29	19.57	19.85
13.75	18.09	18.33	18.58	18.84	19.10	19.37	19.64	19.93	20.22
14.00	18.42	18.67	18.92	19.18	19.44	19.72	20.00	20.29	20.59
14.25	18.75	19.00	19.26	19.52	19.79	20.07	20.36	20.65	20.96
14.50	19.08	19.33	19.59	19.86	20.14	20.42	20.71	21.01	21.32
14.75	19.41	19.67	19.93	20.21	20.49	20.77	21.07	21.38	21.69
15.00	19.74	20.00	20.27	20.55	20.83	21.13	21.43	21.74	22.06

TAX EXEMPT EQUIVALENTS (continued)

TAX EXEMPT YIELDS	33%	34%	35%	36%	37%	38%	39%	40%	41%
3.00	4.48	4.55	4.62	4.69	4.76	4.84	4.92	5.00	5.08
3.25	4.85	4.92	5.00	5.08	5.16	5.24	5.33	5.42	5.51
3.50	5.22	5.30	5.38	5.47	5.56	5.65	5.74	5.83	5.93
3.75	5.60	5.68	5.77	5.86	5.95	6.05	6.15	6.25	6.36
4.00	5.97	6.06	6.15	6.25	6.35	6.45	6.56	6.67	6.78
4.25	6.34	6.44	6.54	6.64	6.75	6.85	6.97	7.08	7.20
4.50	6.72	6.82	6.92	7.03	7.14	7.26	7.38	7.50	7.63
4.75	7.09	7.20	7.31	7.42	7.54	7.66	7.79	7.92	8.05
5.00	7.46	7.58	7.69	7.81	7.94	8.06	8.20	8.33	8.47
5.25	7.84	7.95	8.08	8.20	8.33	8.47	8.61	8.75	8.90
5.50	8.21	8.33	8.46	8.59	8.73	8.87	9.02	9.17	9.32
5.75	8.58	8.71	8.85	8.98	9.13	9.27	9.43	9.58	9.75
6.00	8.96	9.09	9.23	9.38	9.52	9.68	9.84	10.00	10.17
6.25	9.33	9.47	9.62	9.77	9.92	10.08	10.25	10.42	10.59
6.50	9.70	9.85	10.00	10.16	10.32	10.48	10.66	10.83	11.02
6.75	10.07	10.23	10.38	10.55	10.71	10.89	11.07	11.25	11.44
7.00	10.45	10.61	10.77	10.94	11.11	11.29	11.48	11.67	11.86
7.25	10.82	10.98	11.15	11.33	11.51	11.69	11.89	12.08	12.29
7.50	11.19	11.36	11.54	11.72	11.90	12.10	12.30	12.50	12.71
7.75	11.57	11.74	11.92	12.11	12.30	12.50	12.70	12.92	13.14
8.00	11.94	12.12	12.31	12.50	12.70	12.90	13.11	13.33	13.56
8.25	12.31	12.50	12.69	12.89	13.10	13.31	13.52	13.75	13.98
8.50	12.69	12.88	13.08	13.28	13.49	13.71	13.93	14.17	14.41
8.75	13.06	13.26	13.46	13.67	13.89	14.11	14.34	14.58	14.83
9.00	13.43	13.64	13.85	14.06	14.29	14.52	14.75	15.00	15.25
9.25	13.81	14.02	14.23	14.45	14.68	14.92	15.16	15.42	15.68
9.50	14.18	14.39	14.62	14.84	15.08	15.32	15.57	15.83	16.10
9.75	14.55	14.77	15.00	15.23	15.48	15.73	15.98	16.25	16.53
10.00	14.93	15.15	15.38	15.63	15.87	16.13	16.39	16.67	16.95
10.25	15.30	15.53	15.77	16.02	16.27	16.53	16.80	17.08	17.37
10.50	15.67	15.91	16.15	16.41	16.67	16.94	17.21	17.50	17.80
10.75	16.04	16.29	16.54	16.80	17.06	17.34	17.62	17.92	18.22
11.00	16.42	16.67	16.92	17.19	17.46	17.74	18.03	18.33	18.64
11.25	16.79	17.05	17.31	17.58	17.86	18.15	18.44	18.75	19.07

TAX EXEMPT YIELDS	33%	34%	35%	36%	37%	38%	39%	40%	41%
11.50	17.16	17.42	17.69	17.97	18.25	18.55	18.85	19.17	19.49
11.75	17.54	17.80	18.08	18.36	18.65	18.95	19.26	19.58	19.92
12.00	17.91	18.18	18.46	18.75	19.05	19.35	19.67	20.00	20.34
12.25	18.28	18.56	18.85	19.14	19.44	19.76	20.08	20.42	20.76
12.50	18.66	18.94	19.23	19.53	19.84	20.16	20.49	20.83	21.19
12.75	19.03	19.32	19.62	19.92	20.24	20.56	20.90	21.25	21.61
13.00	19.40	19.70	20.00	20.31	20.63	20.97	21.31	21.67	22.03
13.25	19.78	20.08	20.38	20.70	21.03	21.37	21.72	22.08	22.46
13.50	20.15	20.45	20.77	21.09	21.43	21.77	22.13	22.50	22.88
13.75	20.52	20.83	21.15	21.48	21.83	22.18	22.54	22.92	23.31
14.00	20.90	21.21	21.54	21.88	22.22	22.58	22.95	23.33	23.73
14.25	21.27	21.59	21.92	22.27	22.62	22.98	23.36	23.75	24.15
14.50	21.64	21.97	22.31	22.66	23.02	23.39	23.77	24.17	24.58
14.75	22.01	22.35	22.69	23.05	23.41	23.79	24.18	24.58	25.00
15.00	22.39	22.73	23.08	23.44	23.81	24.19	24.59	25.00	25.42

TAX EXEMPT EQUIVALENTS (continued)

TAX EXEMPT YIELDS	42%	43%	44%	45%	46%	47%	48%	49%	50%
3.00	4.48	4.55	4.62	4.69	4.76	4.84	4.92	5.00	5.08
3.00	5.17	5.26	5.36	5.45	5.56	5.66	5.77	5.88	6.00
3.25	5.60	5.70	5.80	5.91	6.02	6.13	6.25	6.37	6.50
3.50	6.03	6.14	6.25	6.36	6.48	6.60	6.73	6.86	7.00
3.75	6.47	6.58	6.70	6.82	6.94	7.08	7.21	7.35	7.50
4.00	6.90	7.02	7.14	7.27	7.41	7.55	7.69	7.84	8.00
4.25	7.33	7.46	7.59	7.73	7.87	8.02	8.17	8.33	8.50
4.50	7.76	7.89	8.04	8.18	8.33	8.49	8.65	8.82	9.00
4.75	8.19	8.33	8.48	8.64	8.80	8.96	9.13	9.31	9.50
5.00	8.62	8.77	8.93	9.09	9.26	9.43	9.62	9.80	10.00
5.25	9.05	9.21	9.38	9.55	9.72	9.91	10.10	10.29	10.50
5.50	9.48	9.65	9.82	10.00	10.19	10.38	10.58	10.78	11.00
5.75	9.91	10.09	10.27	10.45	10.65	10.85	11.06	11.27	11.50
6.00	10.34	10.53	10.71	10.91	11.11	11.32	11.54	11.76	12.00
6.25	10.78	10.96	11.16	11.36	11.57	11.79	12.02	12.25	12.50
6.50	11.21	11.40	11.61	11.82	12.04	12.26	12.50	12.75	13.00
6.75	11.64	11.84	12.05	12.27	12.50	12.74	12.98	13.24	13.50
7.00	12.07	12.28	12.50	12.73	12.96	13.21	13.46	13.73	14.00
7.25	12.50	12.72	12.95	13.18	13.43	13.68	13.94	14.22	14.50
7.50	12.93	13.16	13.39	13.64	13.89	14.15	14.42	14.71	15.00
7.75	13.36	13.60	13.84	14.09	14.35	14.62	14.90	15.20	15.50
8.00	13.79	14.04	14.29	14.55	14.81	15.09	15.38	15.69	16.00
8.25	14.22	14.47	14.73	15.00	15.28	15.57	15.87	16.18	16.50
8.50	14.66	14.91	15.18	15.45	15.74	16.04	16.35	16.67	17.00
8.75	15.09	15.35	15.63	15.91	16.20	16.51	16.83	17.16	17.50
9.00	15.52	15.79	16.07	16.36	16.67	16.98	17.31	17.65	18.00
9.25	15.95	16.23	16.52	16.82	17.13	17.45	17.79	18.14	18.50
9.50	16.38	16.67	16.96	17.27	17.59	17.92	18.27	18.63	19.00
9.75	16.81	17.11	17.41	17.73	18.06	18.40	18.75	19.12	19.50
10.00	17.24	17.54	17.86	18.18	18.52	18.87	19.23	19.61	20.00
10.25	17.67	17.98	18.30	18.64	18.98	19.34	19.71	20.10	20.50
10.50	18.10	18.42	18.75	19.09	19.44	19.81	20.19	20.59	21.00
10.75	18.53	18.86	19.20	19.55	19.91	20.28	20.67	21.08	21.50
11.00	18.97	19.30	19.64	20.00	20.37	20.75	21.15	21.57	22.00

TAX EXEMPT YIELDS	42%	43%	44%	45%	46%	47%	48%	49%	50%
11.25	19.40	19.74	20.09	20.45	20.83	21.23	21.63	22.06	22.50
11.50	19.83	20.18	20.54	20.91	21.30	21.70	22.12	22.55	23.00
11.75	20.26	20.61	20.98	21.36	21.76	22.17	22.60	23.04	23.50
12.00	20.69	21.05	21.43	21.82	22.22	22.64	23.08	23.53	24.00
12.25	21.12	21.49	21.88	22.27	22.69	23.11	23.56	24.02	24.50
12.50	21.55	21.93	22.32	22.73	23.15	23.58	24.04	24.51	25.00
12.75	21.98	22.37	22.77	23.18	23.61	24.06	24.52	25.00	25.50
13.00	22.41	22.81	23.21	23.64	24.07	24.53	25.00	25.49	26.00
13.25	22.84	23.25	23.66	24.09	24.54	25.00	25.48	25.98	26.50
13.50	23.28	23.68	24.11	24.55	25.00	25.47	25.96	26.47	27.00
13.75	23.71	24.12	24.55	25.00	25.46	25.94	26.44	26.96	27.50
14.00	24.14	24.56	25.00	25.45	25.93	26.42	26.92	27.45	28.00
14.25	24.57	25.00	25.45	25.91	26.39	26.89	27.40	27.94	28.50
14.50	25.00	25.44	25.89	26.36	26.85	27.36	27.88	28.43	29.00
14.75	25.43	25.88	26.34	26.82	27.31	27.83	28.37	28.92	29.50
15.00	25.86	26.32	26.79	27.27	27.78	28.30	28.85	29.41	30.00

Appendix H

TAX RATES AND CREDITS

Income Tax Rate Schedules

	Taxable Years Beginning in 2020
STANDARD DEDUCTION:	
Married, filing jointly	$24,800
Married, filing separately	12,400
Head of Household	18,650
Single	12,400
PERSONAL EXEMPTION:	$4,300*
* Eliminated in a provision in the Tax Cuts and Jobs Act, except for Qualified Disability Trusts.	

SINGLE INDIVIDUALS					JOINT RETURNS AND SURVIVING SPOUSES				
Taxable Income			*Tax on Lower Amount*	*Tax Rate on Excess*	*Taxable Income*			*Tax on Lower Amount*	*Tax Rate on Excess*
$ -0-	to	$9,875	$ -0-	10%	$ -0-	to	$19,750	$ -0-	10%
9,875	to	40,125	987.50	12%	19,750	to	80,250	1,975.00	12%
40,125	to	85,525	4,617.50	22%	80,250	to	171,050	9,235.00	22%
85,525	to	163,300	14,605.50	24%	171,050	to	326,600	29,211.00	24%
163,300	to	207,350	33,271.50	32%	326,600	to	414,700	66,543.00	32%
207,350	to	518,400	47,367.50	35%	414,700	to	622,050	94,735.00	35%
518,400	to	......	156,235.00	37%	622,050	to	......	167,307.50	37%

MARRIED FILING SEPARATELY				
Taxable Income			*Tax on Lower Amount*	*Tax Rate on Excess*
$0	to	$9,875	$ -0-	10%
9,875	to	40,125	987.50	12%
40,125	to	85,525	4,617.50	22%
85,525	to	163,300	14,605.50	24%
163,300	to	207,350	33,271.50	32%
207,350	to	311,025	47,367.50	35%
311,025		......	83,653.75	37%

HEAD OF HOUSEHOLD				
Taxable Income			*Tax on Lower Amount*	*Tax Rate on Excess*
$ -0-	to	$14,100	$ -0-	10%
14,100	to	53,700	1,410.00	12%
53,700	to	85,500	6,162.00	22%
85,500	to	163,300	13,158.00	24%
163,300	to	207,350	31,830.00	32%
207,350	to	518,400	45,926.00	35%
518,400	to	......	154,793.50	37%

TAX RATE SCHEDULE FOR ESTATES AND TRUST				
Taxable Income			*Tax on Lower Amount*	*Tax Rate on Excess*
$ -0-	to	$2,600	$ -0-	10%
2,600	to	9,450	260.00	24%
9,450	to	12,950	1,904.00	35%
12,950	to	......	3,129.00	37%

LUMP SUM DISTRIBUTIONS 10 Yr. Averaging*		
Net Lump Sum Taxable Amount	*Tax*	*Effective Tax Rate*
$10,000	$550	.06
20,000	1,100	.06
30,000	2,521	.08
40,000	4,187	.10
50,000	5,874	.12
75,000	10,305	.14
100,000	14,471	.14
150,000	24,570	.16
200,000	36,922	.18
250,000	50,770	.20
300,000	66,330	.22
500,000	143,682	.29
1,000,000	382,210	.38
2,000,000	882,210	.44
3,000,000	1,382,210	.46
4,000,000	1,882,210	.47
5,000,000	2,382,210	.48

* Amount of tax and effective tax rates rounded.
Income averaging for lump sum distributions is discussed in more detail in Chapter 52.

Glossary

ACCELERATION CLAUSE. The clause in a note, bond, or mortgage giving the creditor (mortgagee) the right to demand, upon default of the debtor (mortgagor), the immediate payment of the unpaid balance of the loan or mortgage.

ACCREDITED INVESTOR. An individual whose net worth exceeds $1 million or whose income exceeds $200,000 for the past two years.

ACCRUED INTEREST. Interest accrued on a bond or other debt obligation since the last interest payment was made. The buyer of a bond pays the market price plus accrued interest. Exceptions include bonds that are in default and income bonds.

ACCUMULATION PHASE. Lifecycle stage in which the client is saving and investing for the future.

ACTIVE INVESTING. An investment strategy that assumes the market is inefficient or that inefficiencies within the market can be profitably exploited. A great deal of time and effort is expended in security selection and the timing of purchases and sales.

ACTUARIAL RISK. Risk an insurance underwriter covers in exchange for premiums, such as the risk of premature death.

ADJUSTABLE-RATE MORTGAGE. A mortgage in which the applicable interest rate payable is adjusted periodically (usually annually) as the "money market" dictates.

AGENCY RISK. The risk associated when a principal delegates decisions to an agent who may not always act in the principal's best interest.

ALPHA. The excess rate of return on a security or portfolio over and above what would be anticipated by a pricing model like the capital asset pricing model.

AMERICAN DEPOSITORY RECEIPTS. Securities issued by a U.S. bank on foreign securities purchased by the bank through a foreign correspondent bank and held in trust for the benefit of the ADR holder.

AMERICAN STYLE OPTIONS. Options that may be exercised any time on or before the expiration date.

AMORTIZE. To pay off a debt by periodic payments set aside for the purpose, or to allocate the cost of an asset over its life.

ANOMALY. Evidence that a certain investment strategy can systematically outperform on a risk adjusted basis. Examples of anomalies include the January effect and the size effect.

ANNUAL EXCLUSION. A federal gift tax exclusion of $10,000 (as indexed; $11,000 in 2004) allowed to the donor each year for each donee, provided the gift is one of a present interest (that is, the donee must be given an immediate right to possession or enjoyment of the property interest).

ANNUAL REPORT. The formal financial statement issued yearly by a corporation.

ANNUITANT. A person who receives the benefits on an annuity.

ANNUITY. A series of payments of a fixed amount for a specified number of years.

ARBITRAGE. The simultaneous purchase and sale of an asset in order to profit on a difference in price.

ARBITRAGE PRICING THEORY. A theoretical model that posits that the expected return on any asset is a result of that security's exposure to multiple risk factors.

ASKED PRICE. The price at which securities are offered to potential buyers; or the price sellers offer to take.

ASSESSED VALUE. Value assigned to property by a public body for property tax purposes.

ASSET ALLOCATION. Is the process of determining the proportions of various types of assets to include in a portfolio.

ASSET-BACKED SECURITIES. Debt-type securities that are secured by a pool of similar debt obligations or receivables.

ASSIGNMENT. The act of transferring any interest in property to another party. The one who transfers the right is the "assignor;" the receiver of the right is the "assignee."

BALANCE SHEET. A statement of the financial position of a business entity at a given time, disclosing the assets, liabilities, and invested capital.

BALLOON PAYMENT. The balance due on a debt instrument at maturity that is in excess of a regular principal payment.

BANKERS ACCEPTANCES. Short-term (thirty to 360 days) drafts drawn on a major bank that are typically used to finance international import/export transactions.

BANKRUPTCY. The condition of a business or individual that has been declared insolvent (unable to pay debts) by a court proceeding and whose financial matters are being administered by the court through a receiver or trustee.

BARBELL STRATEGY. A bond portfolio which is invested in long and short term maturity bonds with none of intermediate term.

BASIS. The original cost of an investment including commissions.

BASIS POINT. Equal to 1/100 of 1 percent.

BEAR. Someone who believes that the stock market will decline. See Bull.

BEAR MARKET. A declining market. See Bull Market.

BEARER BOND. A bond that does not have the owner's name registered on the books of the issuing company and that is payable to the holder. See Coupon Bond, Registered Bond.

BEHAVIORAL FINANCE. The study of how investors actually make decisions.

BENCHMARK. A standard by which the performance of a manager or portfolio can be compared.

BENEFICIARY. The recipient of funds, property, or other benefits from an insurance policy, will, or other settlement. The individual or entity entitled to the beneficial interest of a trust.

BETA. A risk measure that quantifies an asset's relative volatility against an index such as the S&P 500. The index selected has a beta of 1. If the fund tends to rise (or fall) twice as high (or low) as the selected index, then the fund would have a beta of 2.

BID PRICE. The price buyers offer to pay for securities; the price at which sellers may dispose of them.

BIG BOARD. A popular term for the New York Stock Exchange.

BLACK-SCHOLES OPTION PRICING MODEL. A model developed to estimate the price of call option. The call option value is a function of the current stock price, time to expiration, volatility of the stock, strike price of the option, and the risk-free rate of interest.

BLUE CHIP. A company known nationally for the quality and wide acceptance of its products or services, and for its ability to earn income and pay dividends.

BLUE LIST. The trade offering sheets of bond dealers, which list dealers' offerings of municipal bonds for sale all over the country.

BOND. An IOU or promissory note of a corporation or governmental body, usually issued in multiples of $1,000 or $5,000. A bond is evidence of a debt on which the issuer usually promises to pay the bondholders a specified amount of interest for a specified length of time, and to repay the loan on the expiration date.

BOOK VALUE. The net amount (i.e., cost minus accumulated depreciation) at which an asset appears on the books of a company.

BROKER. An agent who handles the public's orders to buy and sell securities, commodities, or other property. For this service a commission is charged.

BULL. A person who believes that the stock market will rise. See Bear.

BULL MARKET. An advancing market. See Bear Market.

BUSINESS-DEVELOPMENT COMPANY. An investment vehicle created to help finance small companies in the initial stages of their development. They are very similar to venture capital funds and are structured like closed-end investment funds.

BUSINESS RISK. Economic or operating risk reflected in the variability of a firm's earnings.

CALENDAR SPREAD. A kind of option strategy. The most common type of calendar spread consists of opposing positions in two options of the same type (either both puts or both calls) that have the same exercise price, but expire at different times. Also known as time spread.

CALL. The process of redeeming a bond or preferred stock issue before its scheduled maturity. Sometimes used to refer to a "call option" (see below).

CALL OPTION. An option to buy (or "call") shares of stock at a specified price for a set period of time.

CALL RISK. The risk borne by the holder of a callable bond that a bond issuer will take advantage of the callable bond feature and redeem the security prior to maturity.

CAPITAL ASSET PRICING MODEL. An asset valuation model that posits that the expected return on an individual asset should be the risk-free rate plus a premium for the systematic or undiversifiable risk of that asset. Risk relative to the market is the measure of risk in this model.

CAPITAL GAIN or CAPITAL LOSS. Profit or loss from the sale of a capital asset. A capital gain is either short-term or long-term. Capital gain is short-term if the asset was held for one year or less; the gain is long-term if the asset was held for more than 1 year. This more-than-one-year period necessary to qualify a capital gain as long-term is often referred to as the "long-term capital gain holding period." *Net* long-term capital gain (i.e., the excess of long-term capital gains over short-term capital losses) is taxed at special 5 percent and 15 percent tax rates. (See Chapter 46, Taxation of Investment Vehicles")

CAPITAL STOCK. All shares representing ownership of a business, including preferred and common. See Common Stock, Preferred Stock.

CAPITALIZATION. The total amount of all the securities issued by a corporation.

CASH FLOW. The amount of cash generated over time from an investment, usually after any tax effects.

CERTIFICATE. The actual piece of paper that is evidence of ownership of stock in a corporation, or of other intangible property.

CERTIFICATE OF DEPOSIT. A debt instrument issued by a commercial bank, savings and loan, credit union, or other thrift institution in exchange for a deposit made by an investor.

CHARITABLE DEDUCTION. A deduction allowed for a reportable gift to a charitable organization.

CLOSED END FUND. Similar to mutual funds in that they use the proceeds from the sale of its shares in order to invest in the securities of other companies, but unlike mutual funds they have a fixed number of shares. Their shares are traded on the open market much like the shares of publicly traded companies.

CLOSING. The conclusion or consummation of a real estate transaction where all documents are signed and a deed or land contract, etc., is transferred.

COLLAR. An options strategy where an investor sells an out of the money call option and used the premium received to purchase an out of the money put option both on a security they currently hold.

COLLATERALIZED MORTGAGE OBLIGATION. A type of mortgage-backed security that creates separate pools of holdings (called tranches) for different classes of debt holders.

COLLECTIBLE. From an investment standpoint, a collectible is any item of property that meets three criteria: rarity; popularity; and ready marketability.

COMMERCIAL PAPER. Unsecured, short-term promissory notes of large firms, usually issued in denominations of $1 million or more.

COMMODITY. A purchase that represents ownership of a definite physical item such as oil, natural gas, sugar, wheat, corn, lumber, or pork bellies.

COMMODITY POOL. A diversified portfolio of commodity futures with professional management, Individuals' money is combined and invested in a number of active commodities.

COMMON STOCK. Securities that represent an ownership interest in a corporation.

CONCENTRATED ACCOUNT. When one position accounts for a significant proportion of the entire balance in the account. Brokerage firms typically require higher margins for greater concentrations or larger balances of concentrated accounts.

CONGLOMERATE. A corporation that has diversified its operations usually by acquiring enterprises in widely varied industries.

CONSOLIDATION PHASE. Lifecycle stage in which the client's income outpaces expenses and wealth accumulates rapidly.

CONSTRUCTIVE SALE. Tax treatment where the authorities treat a transaction (typically options related) as if the underlying security had been sold.

CONVERSION PREMIUM. Of a convertible bond is defined as the percentage difference between its current market price and its theoretical minimum value absent the conversion option.

CONVERTIBLE. A bond, debenture, or preferred share that may be exchanged by the owner for common stock or another security, usually of the same company, in accordance with the terms of the issue.

CONVEXITY. Measures the curvature of the relationship between bond yields and prices. Positive convexity is always a good thing for the bond investor.

CORPORATION. A legal unit organized under state laws that has a continuous life span independent from its ownership. In the event of dissolution, its owners are not responsible for its debt (beyond the amount of their original investment). Corporations can raise capital by issuing securities.

CORRELATION. Is a normalized version of covariance where values can range from –1 (perfect negative covariance) to +1 (perfect positive covariance).

COUNTRY RISK. The risk that a country will not be able to honor its financial commitments.

COUPON. Evidence of interest due on a bond, usually every six months. With a bearer bond, the coupon is detached from the bond and presented for payment of interest to the issuer's agent or the bondholder's bank. In the case of a registered bond, the issuing corporation will mail a check for the semiannual interest to the owner of record on each interest payment date.

COUPON BOND. A bond with interest coupons attached. The coupons are removed ("clipped") as they come due and are presented by the holder for payment of interest. See Bearer Bond, Registered Bond.

COUPON RATE. The stated rate of interest on a bond.

COVARIANCE. A measure of the degree to which two variables move in a systematic or predictable way, either positively or negatively.

COVERED OPTION. An option on stock is covered if the individual who, on exercise of the option, would be required to sell the stock owns the subject stock. Thus, a call option is "covered" if the writer of the call owns the subject stock; a put is "covered" if the purchaser of the put option (who by exercising the put elects to sell his stock) owns the subject stock.

CREDIT RISK. The risk of loss resulting from the failure of a borrower to satisfy the terms on a loan.

CUMULATIVE PREFERRED. A preferred stock having a provision that if one or more dividends are omitted, the omitted dividends must be paid in full before dividends may be paid on the company's common stock.

CURRENCY RISK. The potential gain (or loss) on an investment denominated in a foreign currency due to fluctuations in exchange rates.

CURRENT YIELD. The percentage relation of the annual interest received to the current price of a bond, or other debt obligation.

DEALER. A person or firm acting as a principal in buying and selling securities.

DEBENTURE. A promissory note backed by the general credit of a company and usually not secured by a mortgage or lien on any specific property. See Bond.

DEBT SERVICE. The amount of cash needed to cover periodic mortgage payments or bond interest, including interest and principal.

DEFAULT. Failure to pay principal or interest promptly when due.

DERIVATIVE. A financial asset whose value is derived or dependent upon the value of one or more other assets. Derivatives generally are very highly leveraged instruments.

DISCOUNT. The amount by which a preferred stock or bond may sell below its par value. Also used as a verb to mean "takes into account" (e.g., "the price of the stock has discounted the expected dividend cut"). See Premium.

DIVIDEND. A payment made from earnings to the stockholders of a corporation. It is authorized by the board of directors and paid among the shares outstanding. In the case of common shares, payment is made on a pro rata basis; however, preferred shares may be entitled to a specific dividend rate that is different from that paid common shareholders.

DIVIDEND REINVESTMENT PLAN. A plan whereby a shareholder may have his dividends used to purchase additional shares automatically.

DIVIDEND YIELD. The ratio of the current dividend to the current price of a share of stock.

DOCUMENTATION RISK. The risk of loss due to an inadequacy or other unforeseen aspect involving the legal documentation of the financial contract.

DOLLAR COST AVERAGING. A system of buying securities at regular intervals with a fixed dollar amount of capital.

DOLLAR-WEIGHTED ANNUAL RETURN. The rate of return that discounts an investment's or portfolio's terminal value and interim cash flows back to its initial value.

DOMICILE. A location legally regarded as the main place of residence of an individual or business entity.

DONEE. The recipient of a gift. The term also is used to refer to the recipient of a power of appointment.

DONOR. The person who makes a gift. The term also refers to the person who grants a power of appointment to another.

DUE DILIGENCE. The careful investigation of a potential investment or investment manager.

DURATION. The weighted average time until receipt of all of a bond's cash flows.

EARNINGS PER SHARE (EPS). The earnings available to common stockholders divided by the number of common shares outstanding. It is considered to be a measure of how well a company is doing by its common shareholders.

EFFICIENT-MARKET HYPOTHESIS. The theory that securities markets immediately impound new information. This implies that new information about a security is quickly (almost instantaneously) reflected in its price.

ENHANCED-INCOME NOTES. Debt instruments that promise to pay a coupon or yield higher than the underlying asset which can be a single stock, a basket of stocks or an index. The total return is typically capped below the potential return on the underlying asset to compensate for the higher yield.

EQUITY-INDEX ANNUITY. Annuities with a crediting rate (return) that is tied to an index such as the S&P 500 stock index.

EQUITY LONG/SHORT. A category of investment style in which managers purchase the securities of common stocks they expect to appreciate in value while short-selling common stocks they expect to fall in value.

EQUITY-PARTICIPATION LOAN. A type of real estate financing in which the lender agrees to a fixed or only moderately adjustable interest rate on the condition that upon the sale of the property he will share in the gain realized.

EQUITY REIT. A type of Real Estate Investment Trust that acquires ownership interests in commercial, industrial, or residential properties. Income is primarily received from the rentals of these properties.

ESTATE. An interest in real property. All assets owned by an individual.

ESTATE TAX. A tax imposed upon the right of a person to transfer property at death. This type of tax is imposed not only by the federal government, but also by a number of states.

EURODOLLAR INVESTMENTS. Time deposits denominated in U.S. dollars, but held in banks headquartered outside the United States or in foreign branches of U.S. banks.

EUROPEAN OPTION. Options that may only be exercised on the expiration date.

EVENT-DRIVEN FUNDS. A type of hedge fund that invests in securities of corporations involved in special situations such as bankruptcy, spinoffs, mergers and acquisitions and other restructuring events.

EXCHANGE-TRADED FUND. A security representing a basket of stocks or bonds, like a mutual fund. However, like individual stocks, exchange traded funds are traded on a stock exchange.

EXCHANGE-TRADED NOTE. An unsecured debt security issued by an underwriting bank that promises to pay based on the performance of some underlying index.

EXPIRATION DATE. The last day on which an option (call or put) can be exercised.

EXTRA DIVIDEND. A dividend in the form of stock or cash in addition to the regular or usual dividend a company has been paying.

FIDUCIARY. A person occupying a position of trust, (e.g., an executor, administrator, or trustee).

FINANCIAL RISK. Risk related to the mix of debt and equity used by a firm to raise capital. The more debt in a firm's capital structure, the greater is its financial risk.

FIXED-PERIOD ANNUITY. An annuity contract in which the company promises to pay stipulated amounts for a fixed or guaranteed period of time independent of the survival of the annuitant.

FLOATING-RATE BOND. A bond on which the interest rate is adjusted, usually every six months, for the subsequent six months, according to a formula based on the then prevailing interest rates. The prime rate, federal funds rate, commercial paper rate, and Treasury bill rates are frequently used indices.

FORMULA INVESTING. A strategy that seeks to limit the role of emotions in investing by adhering to a strict set of rules.

FORWARD CONTRACT. A customized contract calling for future delivery of a specified number or notional value of a specified asset, for a specified price, at a designated future date.

FOREIGN EXCHANGE RISK. The risk that foreign holdings may change in value as the value of currency changes.

FREE CASH FLOW TO EQUITY. A company's operating cash flow, less capital investments and net debt repayments (repayments net of borrowing).

FREE CASH FLOW TO THE FIRM. The cash flow available to all capital providers, including debt and equity holders. A concept that is often used in valuing firms in leveraged buyouts or where the new owner plans to change the capital structure of the acquired firm.

FUND OF FUNDS. A hedge fund that takes positions across several hedge fund managers.

FUNDAMENTAL ANALYSIS. The security selection process that examines company-specific factors such as profitability, risk, relative valuation, and growth prospects.

FUTURES CONTRACT. A standardized contract calling for future delivery of a specified number or notional value of a specified asset, for a specified price, at a designated future date.

GENERAL OBLIGATION BOND. A municipal bond backed by the general taxing power of its issuer.

GENERAL PARTNERSHIP. A general partnership is one in which two or more individuals join together for investment purposes. Usually, a general partner is jointly and severally liable for all the debts and any obligations incurred by the partnership.

GIFT. Property or property rights or an interest gratuitously passed on or transferred for less than an adequate and full consideration in money or money's worth to another – whether the transfer is in trust or otherwise, direct or indirect.

GLOBAL MACRO. The broadest investment style in the hedge fund universe. These funds invest based upon macroeconomic factors and have virtually no limitations on the asset classes, security types of geographical locations of investments.

GOVERNMENT BONDS. Obligations of the United States Government; regarded as the highest grade issues in existence.

GROWTH STOCK. Stock of a company with a record of rapid growth in earnings.

GUARANTEED INVESTMENT CONTRACT. A contract issued by an insurance company that guarantees the owner both principal repayment and a fixed or floating rate of interest for a set period of time.

HEALTH SAVINGS ACCOUNT (HSA). A tax-advantaged savings/investment account used in conjunction with high-deductible medical plans to accumulate funds to pay unreimbursed medical expenses.

HEDGE FUND. A professionally managed pool of capital that is largely unregulated and available only to sophisticated (accredited) investors.

HEDGING. The act of balancing the risk of a position with an offsetting position in another security. For example, an investor who owns long-term debt, and who is concerned that interest rates may rise may sell financial futures to hedge that risk.

HIGH-DEDUCTIBLE MEDICAL PLAN. A medical insurance plan that meets certain IRS guidelines regarding the minimum deductible for its plan participants that, if met, permit participants to use a tax-advantage health savings account to accumulate funds to pay future unreimbursed medical expenses.

HOLDING-PERIOD RETURN. The total return for a specified period over which an investment is held.

HYBRID REIT. A type of Real Estate Investment Trust that combines the features of both equity and mortgage REITs

IMMUNIZATION. Selecting a portfolio of bonds such that interest rate risk is offset by reinvestment risk.

INCOME STATEMENT. A statement that summarizes the revenues and expenses of a business for a specified period of time.

INDENTURE. A written agreement under which bonds and debentures are issued, setting forth maturity date, interest rate, and other terms.

INDEX FUNDS. Mutual funds that try to match the performance of some market index by creating a portfolio that replicates the index.

INDUSTRY RISK. The risk related to uncertainties caused by particular features of the industry sector in which a company operates.

INFORMATION RATIO. A risk-adjusted return measure that in the numerator has the return on the asset or portfolio minus the return on its benchmark, and in the denominator has the standard deviation of the excess returns of the numerator.

INITIAL PUBLIC OFFERING. The first time the stock of a private company is sold to the public.

IN-THE-MONEY. Description of a *call* option when the stock price is above the striking price of the call. Description of a *put* option when the stock price is below the striking price of the put.

INTERVIVOS TRUST. A trust created during the settlor's lifetime. It becomes operative during one's lifetime as opposed to a trust under a will, which does not become operative until the settlor dies.

INTEREST. Payments a borrower pays a lender for the use of money. A corporation pays interest on its bonds to its bondholders. See Bond.

INTEREST RATE RISK. The risk associated with the fluctuation in bond prices as interest rates change.

INTERNAL RATE OF RETURN. The discount rate at which the present value of all the future benefits an investor will receive from an investment exactly equals the present value of all the capital contributions the investor will be required to make.

INVESTMENT. The use of money for the purpose of making more money in order to gain income, increase capital, or both.

INVESTMENT COMPANY. See Mutual Fund.

INVESTMENT POLICY STATEMENT. A document used to guide overall investment decisions. It should be developed in accordance with the client's objectives and constraints.

JENSEN'S ALPHA. A risk-adjusted return measure that is measured as the portfolio's return in excess of that predicted by the capital asset pricing model.

JOINT SURVIVORSHIP. A type of life insurance policy that covers two individuals and is not payable until the death of the second (or last) of the insureds.

JOINT TENANCY. The holding of property by two or more persons in such a manner that, upon the death of one, the survivor or survivors take the entire property.

JUNK BONDS. Bonds that do not qualify for "investment grade" ratings by the major credit rating agencies. They generally pay a higher rate of interest than investment grade or higher-rated bonds due to their greater risk of default on interest and principal payments.

KURTOSIS. Measures the degree of "fatness" in the tails of a distribution.

LADDER PORTFOLIO. An investment in a portfolio of bonds with staggered maturities.

LESSEE. The party to whom a lease is granted.

LESSOR. The party who grants a lease.

LETTER STOCK. A stock or bond that is not registered with the Securities and Exchange Commission (SEC) and, therefore, cannot be sold in the public market.

LEVERAGE. The use of funds borrowed at a fixed rate in an attempt to reinvest them at a higher rate. Borrowing against the established equity. The term is also used with investments that offer enhanced return without increased investment, such as options and warrants, even without borrowing.

LEVERAGED LEASE. One in which the lessor finances a portion of the purchase price of the leased property with debt.

LEVERAGED PARTICIPATION NOTES. Debt instruments that pay a multiple of the return on the underlying asset. Examples include leveraged ETFs or ETNs that pay off with a levered or inverse relationship to an index.

LIEN. A claim against property that has been pledged or mortgaged to secure the performance of an obligation. A bond may be secured by a lien against specific property owned by the company issuing the bonds.

LIFE ANNUITY. A type of annuity that the company promises that payouts will continue for as long as the annuitant (or annuitants) lives.

LIFECYCLE FUND. A mutual fund that automatically shifts towards a more conservative mix of investments as it approaches a particular year in the future, known as its target date.

LIMIT ORDER. An order to purchase or sell securities at a set price determined by the customer.

LIMITED LIABILITY CORPORATION. Noncorporate entities under which neither the owners (known as members) nor those managing the business are personally liable for the Limited Liability Corporation's obligations.

LIMITED PARTNERSHIP. A specialized form of business organization in which one general partner manages and operates the business, while the limited partners contribute capital and share in the profits.

LISTED STOCK. The stock of a company that is traded on an organized securities exchange.

LIQUID ASSETS. Cash or assets that can readily be converted into cash without a serious loss of capital.

LOAD. The portion of the offering price of shares of a mutual fund that covers sales commissions and all other costs of distribution. A load incurred on purchase is a "front-end" load. See No-Load Fund. For "back-end" load and "level" load, see Chapter 17 (Mutual Funds).

LONG TERM EQUITY ANTICIPATION SECURITIES. Options with original expiration terms as long as thirty-nine months.

LONGEVITY RISK. The risk that a person will live longer than the period his income can support.

MAINTENANCE MARGIN. The minimum level of equity relative to the market value of the investment. The maintenance margin requirement generally is lower than the initial margin requirement.

MARGIN. The buying of stocks or bonds on credit (known as "buying on margin").

MARKETABILITY. The ease or difficulty with which a security or other asset can be sold in the secondary market.

MARKET NEUTRAL STRATEGY. One in which the fund manager balances long and short positions to ensure a zero (or minimal market exposure).

MARKET ORDER. An order by a customer to buy or sell securities at the best obtainable price.

MARKET PRICE. In the case of a security, the market price is usually considered the last reported price at which a stock or bond has been sold.

MARKET TIMING. An investment strategy that attempts to anticipate the market's broad direction and individual security prices, but the focus is usually on the broader market.

MARK TO MARKET. The process of settling an account each day to reflect changes in the value of the assets.

MASTER LIMITED PARTNERSHIP. An investment that combines the tax benefits of a limited partnership with the liquidity of publicly traded securities

MATURITY. The date on which a loan, bond, or debenture comes due and is to be paid off.

MEASURMENT RISK. The risk associated with the collection and accuracy of financial data and with the proper use and application of that data for estimating future company or security values.

MEDIAN. The point in a probability distribution where there is a 50 percent chance that realized returns will fall below (or above) that value.

MEZZANINE FINANCING. An intermediate stage of the venture capital process. It comes after the initial stage of venture capital funding, and generally just prior to the firm going public.

MODERN PORTFOLIO THEORY. A theory on how investors can construct portfolios to optimize or maximize expected return based on a level of risk, it rests on the assumption that risk is best measured in a portfolio context.

MODIFIED DURATION. Measures the approximate relative change in the bond price for every one-hundred basis point (1 percent) change in annual interest rates.

MODIFIED ENDOWMENT CONTRACT (MEC). A life insurance policy that has failed the seven-pay test of Code section 7702A. Distributions (including loans) from a MEC are taxed less favorably than distributions from a life insurance policy that has met the requirements of the seven-pay test.

MODIFIED INTERNAL RATE OF RETURN. Internal rate of return methods that adjust cash flows for realistic assumptions regarding reinvestment rates, borrowing rates, and the like.

MONEY MARKET. Financial markets in which funds are borrowed or loaned for short periods, typically less than one year.

MONEY-MARKET FUND. A type of mutual fund that invests in short-term government securities, commercial paper, and repurchase agreements.

MONTE CARLO SIMULATION. A method used to assess the likelihood of an expected outcome. A computer program randomly chooses returns from an expected distribution of returns for each period. Each run results in an ending expected portfolio value. The process is run many times to achieve a distribution of ending values.

MORTGAGE. A pledge of property designated as security for a loan.

MORTGAGE BOND. A bond backed by a lien on a specific property.

MORTGAGEE. One who lends funds on the security of specific property (mortgage).

MORTGAGE REIT. A type of Real Estate Investment Trust that invests in real estate indirectly by lending funds for construction and/or permanent mortgages.

MORTGAGOR. The borrower who uses specific property as collateral for a loan.

MUNICIPAL BOND. A bond issued by a state or a political subdivision, such as a county, city, town, or village. The interest paid on many municipal bonds is exempt from federal income taxes and state and local income taxes within the state of issue.

MUNICIPAL PAPER. Short-term debt issued by state, county, or local governments or agencies, where the interest is exempt from federal income taxes and state and local income taxes depending on the investor's residency.

MUTUAL FUND. An investment company that uses the proceeds from the sale of its shares in order to invest in the securities of other companies.

NET ASSET VALUE. A term used in connection with mutual funds, meaning "net asset value per share" – i.e., the total market value of all securities owned by the fund minus liabilities, divided by the number of fund shares outstanding.

NET PRESENT VALUE. The difference between the present value of all future benefits of an investment and the present value of all capital contributions.

NEW ISSUE. Securities offered to the public for the first time.

NO-LOAD FUND. A mutual fund on which no sales commission is paid.

NOMINAL RETURN. The actual returns earned over a given period computed without accounting for changes in the purchasing power of the dollar.

NOMINAL YIELD. The interest rate stated on the bond.

NORMAL DISTRIBUTION. A distribution of outcomes in which both sides of the distribution are mirror images of each other. Also known as a bell curve.

ODD LOT. An amount of a security less than the established "round lot." See Round Lot.

OFFSHORE FUND. A hedge fund structured under foreign law or located outside the U.S.

OPEN INTEREST. The number of futures contracts of a particular type at a point in time that have not been closed out, exercised, or allowed to expire.

OVER THE COUNTER. Unlisted securities; those not traded on a major exchange.

PAR VALUE. The nominal or face value of a bond (or a stock).

PARTNERSHIP. An association of two or more individuals to carry on a business for profit. The life span of the partnership is directly linked to that of the owners. Technically, if a partner dies, the partnership has ended. A partnership raises money based on the personal credit available to the owners.

PASS-THROUGH CERTIFICATES. A type of mortgage-backed security in which investors own a share of the pooled mortgages. The stream of income generated by payments of principal and interest on mortgage loans is passed through to the investor.

PASSIVE INVESTING. A strategy that seeks to mimic the returns on a benchmark index, such as the Standard & Poor's 500. The goal of a passive investment manager is not to beat the benchmark index, but rather to match it as closely as possible.

PAY-BACK PERIOD. Measures the relative periods of time investors needed to recover their investor's invested capital (income benefits received after the pay-back period will be considered gain).

PAY-OUT RATIO. The percentage of earnings paid out in the form of dividends.

PERFORMANCE-PARTICIPATION NOTES. Debt instruments in which the returns are tied to an underlying asset and are designed to track that underlying asset. Also referred to as tracker certificates, they can be based on any underlying asset such as a stock, stock index, bond index, or other nontraditional assets.

POLITICAL RISK. Risk that government legislation or action will have an adverse effect on investment.

PORTFOLIO. Securities held by an individual or institution. A portfolio may consist of bonds, stocks, or other securities of various types of institutions.

PREFERRED STOCK. A class of stock with a claim on the company's earnings before payment may be made on the common stock, and that is usually entitled to priority over common stock if the company liquidates.

PREMIUM. The amount by which a bond (or preferred stock) may sell above its par value.

PREPAYMENT ASSUMPTION. Necessary to value mortgage backed securities, as mortgagees are able to prepay mortgages prior to maturity.

PRICE-EARNINGS RATIO. The price of a share of stock divided by earnings per share for a twelve-month period. For example, a stock selling for $20 with earnings per share of $2 is said to be selling for a price-earnings ratio of ten to one.

PRIMARY MARKET. The market for new issues of stocks or bonds.

PRINCIPAL. The property comprising the estate or fund that has been set aside in trust, or from which income is expected to accrue (corpus).

PRINCIPAL-PROTECTED NOTES. Debt instruments issued by a financial firm that promise to pay a return based on the performance of an underlying stock index such as an S&P, Nasdaq, Russell or Nikkei index.

PRIVATE EQUITY. Any type of equity investment made in a firm that is not listed on an organized exchange.

PRIVATE LIMITED PARTNERSHIP. Limited partnerships having no more than thirty-five limited partners, which allows them to avoid registration with the U. S. Securities and Exchange Commission.

PRIVATE PLACEMENT. Occurs when new securities (stocks or bonds) are sold directly to a single buyer, or a small group of buyers, without going through the process of a public offering.

PRIVATE-PURPOSE BONDS. A type of municipal bond issued to finance certain activities that do not constitute the normal activities or functions of government.

PROBABILITY DISTRIBUTION. Assigns a probability to each of all possible outcomes. Probability distributions can be either discrete or continuous.

PROMISSORY NOTE. A simple legal document that can be used in a wide range of lender-borrower relationships. Signed by both parties, it acknowledges that a loan has been made and sets out the terms under which it is to be repaid.

PROPRIETORSHIP. A type of business owned by one person (also known as a "sole proprietorship"). It raises money based on the owner's personal credit.

PROSPECTUS. A document issued for the purpose of describing a new security issue.

PROTECTIVE PUT. A long position in a stock along with a long position in a put which enables the investor to sell the stock at a specified price.

PROXY. Written authorization given by a shareholder to someone else to represent him and vote his shares at a stockholders' meeting.

PUBLIC LIMITED PARTNERSHIP. A limited partnership that is registered with the SEC and which is offered to the general public through broker/dealers.

PUT OPTION. An option to sell (or "put") a particular security at a specified price within a designated period of time.

R-SQUARED. The R-squared of a fund is a measure of what proportion of a security's or portfolio's total variability is explained by its relationship to a benchmark or index and how much is its independent risk unrelated to the benchmark or index.

RATING. A formal opinion by an outside professional service on the credit reputation of an issuer and the investment quality of its securities.

REAL ESTATE. Land and the buildings and improvements on land. Real estate includes natural assets, such as minerals, under the land.

REAL ESTATE INVESTMENT TRUST (REIT). An organization similar to a mutual fund in which investors pool funds that are invested in real estate or used to make construction or mortgage loans.

REAL RATE OF RETURN. Represents the return adjusted for changes in the general level of the prices of goods and services that investors could purchase if they liquidated their investments.

REBALANCING. The process of selling positions in an asset class that has outperformed and adding to positions asset classes that have underperformed to get back to the target strategic asset allocation.

REFUND ANNUITY. An annuity that promises to pay the difference between the amount invested in the contract (generally the total of the premiums paid) and the annuity payments actually paid out before the death of the annuitant.

REFUNDING. Redeeming an existing bond issue by selling a new bond issue, usually at terms more favorable to the issuer.

REGISTERED BOND. A bond that is registered on the books of the issuing company in the name of the owner. It can be transferred only when endorsed by the registered owner. See Bearer Bond, Coupon Bond.

REINVESTMENT RISK. The risk that interest payments from a bond cannot be reinvested at as high an interest rate as when the bond was purchased.

REIT. See Real Estate Investment Trust.

RELATIVE VALUE FUNDS. Attempt to identify securities and positions that have the same risk and return characteristics and purchase the underpriced securities and sell the overpriced securities. Also known as arbitrage funds.

REVENUE BOND. A municipal bond backed by revenues produced from a particular project, such as a turnpike. See General Obligation Bond.

REVERSE LEVERAGE. When the cost of servicing the debt (both interest and principal) exceeds the total return (both cash flow and appreciation).

REVOCABLE TRUST. A trust that can be changed or terminated during the grantor's lifetime and the property recovered.

RIGHTS. Issued when a corporation plans to raise funds by selling additional shares of common stock to the public. Every current stockholder is typically given one right for each one share of stock they own.

RISK-ADJUSTED RETURN MEASURES. Measures developed to help investors gauge how much return they were getting per unit of risk. Four popular measures include the Sharpe measure, Treynor measure, information ratio, and Jensen's alpha.

RISK-FREE ASSET. An asset whose future return can be predicted with near certainty. The typical example is a 3-month Treasury bill, which is virtually free of default risk.

RISK TOLERANCE. The volatility in investment returns that an individual is willing to bear. A function of both an individual's ability and willingness to accept risk, as well as time horizon.

ROUND LOT. A unit of trading or multiple thereof. On the NYSE the unit of trading is generally 100 shares in stocks and $10,000 par value in the case of bonds.

SECONDARY MARKET. Where existing issues are bought and sold. It may be either an over-the-counter market or through an organized exchange.

SECURITY VALUATION. The use of analytical methods to estimate the intrinsic value (as opposed to the observed market price) of a security. The intrinsic value is then compared to the market price to determine whether the security appears attractively priced.

SEMIVARIANCE. A measure of downside risk – the risk of realizing an outcome below the expected return. Semivariance is similar to variance except that in making this calculation, no consideration is given to returns above the expected return.

SENSITIVITY ANALYSIS. A technique used to determine how different inputs will impact an output under a given set of assumptions.

SEPARATELY-MANAGED ACCOUNT. An individual investment account that is managed by a professional money manager.

SERIAL BOND. A part of an issue that matures in relatively small amounts at periodic stated intervals. See Term Bond.

SETTLEMENT DATE. The date on which money and securities are exchanged (usually three business days after the trade was executed, or one day for government securities and listed options).

SHARPE RATIO. A risk-adjusted return measure that in the numerator has an asset (or portfolio) return in excess of the risk-free rate, and in the denominator has the standard deviation of returns over time from that asset or portfolio.

SHORT SALE. The act of selling securities that are not currently owned with the intention of subsequently repurchasing them in the future at a lower price.

SHORT SALE AGAINST THE BOX. A short sale of securities that are also held long by the investor.

SINKING FUND. Money set aside by the issuer to be used to retire a bond issue.

SKEWNESS. Measures the coefficient of asymmetry of a distribution. In contrast with the normal distribution, or bell curve, where both tails of the distribution are symmetrical mirror images of each other, skewed distributions have one tail of the distribution that is longer than the other.

SPECIALIST. A member of a stock exchange whose function is to maintain an orderly market in certain stocks. Each specialist is responsible for specific issues and must make a market in those issues.

SPENDING PHASE. Lifecycle stage in which earned income (such as wages) ends and investment income is needed from accumulated retirement and non-retirement funds to meet living expenses.

SPREAD. The difference between what a dealer pays for a security and the price at which he offers to sell it.

STANDARD DEDUCTION. The amount set forth in the Internal Revenue Code that may be deducted (along with personal exemptions) by a taxpayer who does *not* itemize.

STANDARD DEVIATION. A statistical measure defined as the square root of the variance of returns.

STOCK DIVIDEND. A dividend paid in shares of stock rather than cash.

STOCK EXCHANGE. A central market place where securities are traded.

STOCK SPLIT. A corporate action in which an existing share of stock is divided into multiple shares. The main reason for stock splits is to lower the stock's price per share in order to make it more affordable.

STOP-LOSS ORDER. An order to sell a security when it reaches a certain price. The intent of a stop loss order is to limit an investor's loss to a set amount.

STRADDLE. A purchase of a call and a put option with the same strike price (long straddle) or a sale of a call and a put option with the same strike price (short straddle).

STRANGLE. A variation of a straddle. Instead of buying or selling an at-the-money call and a put, the investor buys or sells an out-of-the-money call and put.

STRATEGIC ASSET ALLOCATION. The process of determining which assets classes to include in a client's portfolio and in what proportion.

STRIKING PRICE. The price at which an option can be exercised.

STRUCTURED PRODUCTS. Financial assets that consist of various components combined to generate a risk-return profile that is specific to an investor's needs.

SYNDICATE. A group of investment bankers and/or banks that underwrite a bond or stock issue and offer it for public sale.

SYNTHETIC SECURITY. Created by combining positions in securities in order to mimic the properties of another security.

SYSTEMATIC RISK. A widespread or economy-wide risk that influences a large number of assets. Examples of systematic risk are political events, inflation, and the business cycle.

SYSTEMATIC WITHDRAWAL. An arrangement where a mutual fund automatically liquidates sufficient shares to pay an investor a predetermined amount of money at regular intervals.

TACTICAL ASSET ALLOCATION. A short term adjustment (or tilt) to the long-term strategic asset allocation based on expected relative short-term performance of different asset classes.

TAX CREDIT. A direct reduction of income tax liability based on items such as investments, child care, energy conservation, and foreign taxes.

TAX SHELTER. A tax avoidance transaction as classified by the IRS (i.e., a "listed transaction").

TAXABLE YEAR. A twelve-month period (usually the calendar year in the case of individuals) that is used in the calculation of taxable income.

TECHNICAL ANALYSIS. The security selection process that studies market information such as price and volume to identify important trends and opportunities.

TEMPORARY LIFE ANNUITY. One which provides for fixed payments until the earlier of the death of the annuitant(s) or the end of a specified number of years.

TERM BOND. Part of a bond issue that has a single maturity. See Serial Bond.

TERM LIFE INSURANCE. Insurance that can be maintained for a specified period of time such as one year, five years, ten years, or to a specified age such as age seventy. At the end of the specified period, the contract typically expires.

TIME-WEIGHTED ANNUAL RETURN. The geometric (compounded) annual return measured on the basis of periodic market valuations of assets.

TIMING RISK. Investors run the risk of investing when security prices hit their peak. They also take the risk that they may need to sell their investments for a loss during a market setback because they need to fund a planned or unplanned expense.

TRACKING RISK. The risk associated with failure of managers of indexed funds to accurately, timely, and cost-effectively track and match the underlying index's performance.

TRANCHE. A class or pool of holdings that collateralized mortgage obligations are divided into. Tranche is the French word for slice.

TRANSFER AGENT. A professional agency (typically a bank) employed by a corporation to handle the issuance and transfer of securities, payment of dividends, and maintenance of books of the corporation.

TREASURY BILL. Short-term certificate issued by the U.S. federal government that typically mature in three months to one year.

TREASURY BOND. A long-term debt security issued by the U.S. federal government. They are issued with a fixed maturity of thirty years.

TREASURY INFLATION-PROTECTED SECURITIES. A type of bond issued by the U.S. federal government in which interest payments and the principal value are adjusted every six months to reflect changes in inflation as measured by the Consumer Price Index (CPI).

TREASURY NOTES. A medium-term debt security issued by the U.S. federal government. They have a fixed maturity date greater than one year and can extend for up to 10 years from the date of issue.

TREYNOR RATIO. A risk adjusted return measure that in the numerator has an asset (or portfolio) return in excess of the risk-free rate and in the denominator has the beta of that asset or portfolio.

UNDERWRITER. The investment banker (or bankers) who buys the entire issue of securities from the issuer and then sell the securities to individual and institutional investors.

UNDERWRITING RISK. The risk taken by an investment banker that a new issue of securities purchased outright will not be bought by the public and/or that the market price will drop during the offering period.

UNIFORMED MANAGED ACCOUNT. An extension of a separately managed account that holds subaccounts with multiple managers.

UNSYSTEMATIC RISK. An idiosyncratic risk that affects a particular company or security, or a very small number of assets.

VARIABLE ANNUITY. An annuity contract under which the annuity holder has the ability to allocate the annuity premiums among several available investment choices. The annuity holder, not the company issuing the contract, assumes the investment risk associated with the investment decisions.

VARIABLE LIFE INSURANCE. Is like a traditional whole life insurance contract in that it has fixed premiums and a minimum guaranteed death benefit. The difference is that the investment risk and return is shifted to the policyowner.

VARIABLE UNIVERSAL LIFE INSURANCE. A variation of a permanent life insurance policy is a hybrid of universal life and variable life insurance.

VENTURE CAPITAL. A source of financing typically made available to startup firms and small businesses with strong growth potential. It is in generally in the form of an equity investment provided by venture capital funds.

VENTURE-CAPITAL LIMITED PARTNERSHIP. A limited partnership that is formed to invest in small startup businesses.

VOLATILITY INDEX. The CBOE Volatility Index® (VIX®) is a measure of market expectations of near-term volatility derived from S&P 500 stock index option prices

WARRANT. A right or option to buy a stated number of shares of stock at a specified price over a given period of time. It is usually of longer duration than a call option.

WARRANTY DEED. A deed by which a grantor conveys and guarantees good title to real property; the safest form of deed for the buyer.

WASH SALE. Occurs when investors sell or trade stock or securities at a loss and within 30 days before or after the sale investors: (1) buy substantially identical stock or securities; (2) acquire substantially identical stock or securities in a fully taxable trade, or (3) acquire a contract or option to buy substantially identical stock or securities.

WEIGHTED AVERAGE LIFE. A prepayment assumption commonly used in the secondary mortgage market as a measure of the effective maturity of a mortgage pool.

WHOLE LIFE INSURANCE. Traditional permanent life insurance policy, with level premium payments designed to remain in force over the entire lifetime of the insured individual.

YIELD. Also known as return. The dividends or interest paid by a company expressed as a percentage of the current price. A stock with a current market value of $25 per share paying dividends at a rate of $2.50 is said to return 10 percent ($2.50 ÷ $25.00).

YIELD TO CALL. The internal rate of return from holding a bond assuming the bond is called at the earliest time possible.

YIELD TO MATURITY. The average annualized rate of return that an investor will receive if a bond is held until its maturity date. It differs from "yield" or "current yield" in that it takes into consideration the increase to par of a bond bought at a discount, and the decrease to par of a bond bought at a premium.

ZERO-COUPON BOND. A bond that pays no interest during the life of the bond and that is normally issued at a substantial discount from par. The face amount of the bond, when it is paid at maturity, includes the payment of interest.

Index

D

E

F

L

M

N

O